Dover New Hampshire Death Records 1887-1937

Richard P. Roberts

HERITAGE BOOKS
2008

HERITAGE BOOKS
AN IMPRINT OF HERITAGE BOOKS, INC.

Books, CDs, and more—Worldwide

For our listing of thousands of titles see our website at
www.HeritageBooks.com

Published 2008 by
HERITAGE BOOKS, INC.
Publishing Division
100 Railroad Ave. #104
Westminster, Maryland 21157

Copyright © 2002 Richard P. Roberts

All rights reserved. No part of this book may be reproduced or transmitted in any form or by any means, electronic or mechanical, including photocopying, recording or by any information storage and retrieval system without written permission from the author, except for the inclusion of brief quotations in a review.

International Standard Book Numbers
Paperbound: 978-0-7884-2054-2
Clothbound: 978-0-7884-7244-2

CONTENTS

Introduction..1
Death Records 4

INTRODUCTION

Early vital records of many New Hampshire towns can be located either through the State's Vital Records Department or on microfilms made available through LDS Family History Centers. Some, however, have been lost or are inaccessible for various reasons. A valuable, but time-consuming, source of information for events occurring after 1886 is the vital statistics which are provided in a section of the Annual Town Reports of many New Hampshire towns. Many of these town reports have been collected at the New Hampshire State Library in Concord, as well as more local repositories.

The amount of information published in these Annual Town Reports varies tremendously over time. Early records are far more detailed and comprehensive. More recent records are rather cursory, but issues of confidentiality and sensitivity to the privacy of those residents still living offsets the lack of information of genealogical value.

While the information provided is often very helpful, one must remember that it is not fool-proof or universally accurate, nor is it the primary source or the actual vital record itself. The fact that some of the data is self-reported suggests that it is reliable. Errors in transcription, spelling (particularly with respect to French-Canadian and European families), and printing often are obvious but it is sometimes difficult to determine with certainty whether the individuals are from the same families. An attempt has been made to cross-reference those family groups which may have been connected where the similarity is not readily apparent.

Despite these shortcomings, the information contained in the Annual Town Reports can be a valuable tool for the genealogist. Many of the death records from the late 1800's identify individuals born during the 1700's or whose parents were married prior to 1800.

Dover's annual city reports contained the vital records for the years between 1887 and 1937, at which point the information was no longer published. Because of Dover's relatively large population, the births, marriages and deaths for this period would each fill a volume. Since the death records are likely to provide the most useful information for genealogical purposes, those records are being published first.

The information that is contained in the annual reports varies during the time period covered by this book. In summary, the following table lists those pieces of information which were published during various years. Not all of the information is available in every instance.

1887-1889   Name, date of death, age at death, place of death (Dover, unless otherwise indicated), marital status, occupation, color (white, unless otherwise indicated), and name and birthplace of father and mother.

1890-1891   Name, date of death, age at death, place of death (Dover, unless otherwise indicated), marital status, and name and birthplace of mother and father

1892-1893   Name, date of death, age at death, cause of death, place of birth, and birthplace of mother and father

1894-1898   Name, date of death, age at death, place of death (Dover, unless otherwise indicated), cause of death, place of birth, and place of burial (PH = Pine Hill; SM = St. Mary's)

1899-1906   Name, date of death, age at death, place of death (Dover, unless otherwise indicated), cause of death, and place of burial (PH = Pine Hill; SM = St. Mary's)

1907-1930   Name, date of death, age at death, place of death (Dover, unless otherwise indicated), cause of death, and parents' names.

1931-1935   Name, date of death, age at death, place of death (Dover, unless otherwise indicated), and cause of death.

1936-1937   Name, date of death, age at death, place of death (Dover, unless otherwise indicated), and cause of death. * indicates that the individual was brought to Dover for burial and several of these entries contain that person's place of birth.

There are additional resources which are certain to be useful in conjunction with the material contained in this book. Primary among these are Robert Sayward Canney's Early Marriages of Strafford County, published histories of the City of Dover by Scales, Quint and Wadleigh, among others, and the voluminous materials held by the Dover Public Library. The information available there includes city directories for the period covered by this book and earlier and later years, cemetery inscriptions for Dover and surrounding towns, and microfilmed newspaper records which may contain obituaries providing a fuller picture of the lives and families of the individuals listed here.

ABBOTT,
Annie M., d. 5/26/1925 at 68/10/6; paralysis agitans; Ichabod Abbott and Rosetta Wentworth
Caroline A., d. 6/17/1913 at 69/0/28 in Springvale, ME; apoplexy
Charles A., d. 1/7/1918 at 72/1/25 in Lewiston, ME; double lobar pneumonia; Elisha Abbott and Harriet Tate
Charles C., d. 7/10/1922 at 75/11/17; angina pectoris; Walter A. Abbott and Esther Pierce
Charles F., d. 8/15/1897 at 54; heart clot; b. Orange, MA; buried in Sterling Centre
Clara B., d. 11/30/1926 at 72/2/20; angina pectoris; Joseph Leighton and Clarinda Varney
Delia A., d. 3/22/1903 at 67/4/1; rheumatism; PH
Elisha, d. 4/23/1898 at 93; old age; b. Tuftonboro; PH
Emily B., d. 3/29/1888 at 59/7/27; married; b. Newmarket; Thomas Cheswell (Newmarket) and Emily Burleigh (Wolfeboro)
Emma F., d. 12/13/1918 at 71/3/15 in Lewiston, ME; broncho pneumonia
Emma K., d. 12/27/1936 at 83/5/9 in Brentwood; mitral insufficiency
Esther, d. 3/19/1887 at 76/10/19; widow; b. Lebanon, ME; Stephen Pier (US) and Sally (US)
Everett J., d. 12/15/1924 at 62/6/17; carcinoma of face; Charles F. Abbott and Martha D. -----
Francis A., d. 10/27/1896 at 72; malaria; b. Tuftonboro; PH
George Edward, d. 1/9/1915 at 47/6/8; Hodgkins disease; Thomas Abbott and Loraine Proctor
George H., d. 12/25/1903 at 63/3/1; inanition; buried in Rollinsford
Grace, d. 10/29/1892 at 29; heart disease; b. Dover; (Saccarappa, ME; Berwick, ME)
Helen A., d. 10/3/1920 at 68/1/17; embolism; Josiah F. Whitney and Mary Moore
Isaac F., d. 1/14/1895 at 52; suicide - pistol shot; b. Dover; PH
Jennie L., d. 8/12/1899 at 56; gangrene of foot; buried in Rollinsford
John M., d. 4/11/1902 at 31/4/18; fell from R. R. train; PH
John W., d. 4/2/1931 at 99/6/3; cancer of bowel
Joseph S., d. 2/12/1901 at 70/11/1; nephritis; PH
Josephine M., d. 5/5/1894 at 16; consumption; b. Dover; PH
Lizzie J., d. 3/18/1892 at 48; heart disease; b. Berwick, ME; (-----; Berwick, ME)
Lorraine, d. 2/6/1931 at 85/9/22; chronic endocarditis
Mabel G., d. 10/15/1931 at 43/5/1; carcinoma of stomach
Mary A., d. 8/26/1932 at 63/5/27; cerebral hemorrhage
Mary S. J., d. 7/19/1904 at 73/0/21; old age; PH
Mildred E., d. 4/30/1918 at 27/9/3; multiple abscess; Herbert L. Abbott and Henrietta Plaisted

Nancy D., d. 9/22/1890 at 75/8/6; widow; David Campbell (NH) and
 Deborah Goss (NH)
Samuel B., d. 9/8/1912 at 52/0/23; cancer of lower lip; Joseph S. Abbott
 and Delia A. Brownell
Tate, d. 10/28/1891 at 10/5/23; Isaac F. Abbott (Dover) and Lizzie J.
 Cushman (Brunswick, ME)
Thomas, d. 5/24/1921 at 80/0/14; acute bronchitis; Joseph Abbott and
 Isabel -----

ABDELLA,
Faris, d. 1/25/1909 at 35; suicide by hanging

ABOO-ARAB,
Shickory, d. 3/13/1920 at 50; Aboo-Arab and Tacla Hamrah

ABRAHAM,
Jeanette, d. 10/21/1919 at 16; typhoid fever; P. H. Harris and Lola Arlin

ABRAMS,
Barka, d. 11/16/1929 at 74; chr. intest. nephritis
Ella F., d. 6/10/1908 at 54/8/7; cancer; Israel Runnels and Sarah Love
John L., d. 6/9/1935 at 83/9/28; cancer prostate

ACKLEY,
Ann, d. 3/22/1889 at 51/10; housewife; single; b. Ireland; Charles Ackley
 (Ireland) and Ann Mulligan (Ireland)
Bridget, d. 4/28/1906 at 68; influenza
David, d. 9/16/1897 at 60; summer complaint; b. Ireland; SM
John, d. 2/17/1913 at 65; atheronia; Charles Ackley and Ann Mulligan
Margaret, d. 11/14/1920 at 87; cerebral hemorrhage

ACKROYD,
J. Frank, d. 7/27/1905 at 22/6/6 in Tuftonboro; PH
John J., d. 3/7/1906 at 48/8 in Worcester, MA; pneumonia; PH

ADAMOPOULOS,
child, d. 1/26/1919 at -; premature birth; Antonios Adamopoulos and
 Stavroula Goulamos
Stavroulou, d. 1/27/1919 at 25; broncho pneumonia

ADAMS,
child, d. 8/18/1916 at -; premature; Walter Adams and Nellie C. Schuster
Arthur, d. 10/22/1925 at 65; chronic endocarditis
Charles, d. 11/17/1936 at 85/0/1; chr. myocarditis

Charles W., d. 2/2/1891 at 77/6/5; married; Winthrop Adams (Newington) and Dorothy Dame (Rochester)
Ella J., d. 11/24/1903 at 51 in Boston, MA; heart disease; PH
Euganel, d. 10/19/1929 at 38; inter. nephritis
Ezra L., d. 12/15/1930 at 24/3/21; lobar pneumonia; Aldrick L. Adams and Violetta Smith
Florence M., d. 11/3/1893 at 5; catarrhal pneumonia
Fred F., d. 11/22/1931 at 72 in S. Berwick, ME; cerebral hemorrhage
George, d. 8/21/1905 at 1/3/16; diarrhea; PH
George E., d. 12/29/1915 at 52/7/28 in Boston, MA; heart disease
George W., d. 4/13/1921 at 71/5/26; apoplexy; Isaac Adams and Mary A. Lord
Katherine M., d. 11/11/1914 at 80/0/15; intestinal indigestion; John O. Adams and Mary Hilliard
Linwood G., d. 11/28/1909 at 50; tuberculosis
Lizzie V., d. 10/11/1892 at 47; cerebral hemorrhage
Marantha L., d. 12/9/1895 at 43 in Haverhill, MA; PH
Mary A., d. 1/16/1902 at 79/10/14; cerebral hemorrhage; PH
Mary Elizabeth, d. 10/24/1909 at 72/8/17; malignant dis. of bowels; James Libbey and Elizabeth Quimby
Raymond William, d. 8/25/1926 at 0/0/15; premature birth; Walter W. Adams and Margery A. -----
Robert V., d. 10/5/1919 at –; premature birth
Ruth, d. 2/6/1897 at 76; pneumonia; b. Shapleigh, ME; PH
Sarah A., d. 2/8/1916 at 72; val. heart disease; Joseph P. Adams and Dorothy A. Young
Stephen S., d. 6/5/1907 at 73/1/20; heart failure; Daniel Adams and Naomi Stewart
Susan, d. 1/4/1907 at 60; valvular heart disease; Asa Davis and Mercy Cater

ADAMSON,
Jane, d. 5/11/1919 at 88/2/24 in Grafton, MA; senile apoplexy
William J., d. 8/14/1887 at 33/0/12; comb-setter; single; b. Ireland; James Adamson (Ireland) and Jane (Ireland)

ADJUTANT,
Marion A., d. 10/4/1936 at 72; frac. of pelvis

ADLINGTON,
Charles H., d. 3/25/1928 at 79/7/17; cancer rectum; Thomas Adlington and Mary Oxford

ADNOFF,
Benjamin, d. 6/3/1936 at 51/7/21; ac. pulmonary oedema

AGNEW,
child, d. 4/4/1926 at –; stillborn; Joseph E. Agnew and Madeline Adams
Annie, d. 2/14/1927 at 74; arterio sclerosis
Annie M., d. 10/19/1901 at 20/3; tuberculosis; SM
Bridget, d. 6/24/1898 at 58; cerebral softening; b. Ireland; SM
Bridget, d. 6/1/1905 at –; chronic nephritis; SM
Catherine, d. 11/15/1898 at –; paralysis; b. Ireland; SM
Charles, d. 5/16/1929 at 76; arterio sclerosis
Clarence, d. 8/18/1899 at 20; consumption; SM
Eliza, d. 12/26/1906 at 68; exhaustion
Ellen M., d. 12/29/1916 at 71/1/29; broncho pneumonia; Owen Caton and Elizabeth McCabe
Francis, d. 3/31/1892 at 48; phthisis; b. Dover; (Ireland; Ireland)
Frank, d. 8/23/1927 at 77/6/19 in Manchester; arterio sclerosis
Henry, d. 4/26/1893 at 50; acute Bright's disease - grippe; b. Ireland; (Ireland; Ireland)
John, d. 12/13/1888 at 25/7; shoemaker; single; b. Dover; Henry Agnew (Ireland) and Eliza Nugent (Ireland)
John M., d. 8/20/1889 at 0/0/28; b. Dover; Thomas Agnew (Dover) and Margaret McArdle (Scotland)
Julia, d. 9/30/1889 at 3/6; b. Dover; Charles Agnew (Dover) and Kate O'Brien (Ireland)
Michael, d. 1/23/1895 at 48; thoracic aneurism; b. Ireland; SM
Rose, d. 2/2/1892 at 35; phthisis; b. Dover; (Ireland; Ireland)
Stephen, d. 2/22/1907 at 23; pulmonary tuberculosis; Charles Agnew and --- O'Brien
Thomas, d. 10/12/1896 at 64; consumption; b. Ireland; SM
Thomas, d. 11/19/1904 at 34/3/10; pulmonary tuberculosis; SM
Walter T., d. 9/15/1899 at 25; aortic stenosis; SM

AINSWORTH,
child, d. 5/5/1912 at –; miscarriage; William Ainsworth and Mary Cunningham
Joseph G., d. 1/5/1902 at 36/7/7; coma; PH
Joseph G., d. 12/9/1923 at 28/2/11; auricular fibrillosis; Joseph Ainsworth and Elizabeth Owens
Marguerite, d. 2/25/1904 at 3/7/8; consumption; PH

AKERMAN,
Elizabeth N., d. 2/4/1911 at 72/7/19; gastric cancer; Josiah B. Tilton and Nancy Adams
Nellie L., d. 7/16/1905 at 50/5/21; acute gastritis; PH
Will H., d. 10/8/1900 at 22 in Portsmouth; typhoid fever; PH

ALBEE,
Alfarata, d. 11/22/1925 at 75/4/18; arthritis deformans; Jeremiah Kennison and Jane Welch
Fred, d. 6/10/1916 at 48/2/1 in S. Berwick, ME; pulmonary tuberculosis
Sarah, d. 5/16/1916 at 83/0/4; fracture of femur; David Antoine and Sarah

----

ALBERT,
child, d. 11/7/1932 at –; stillborn
Archie, d. 9/23/1904 at 2/8; malnutrition; SM
Jenney, d. 3/30/1936 at 38; cancer uterus

ALDRICH,
Florence C., d. 7/31/1921 at 4-/8/16; diabetes mellitus; Cyrus Pattee and Mary A. Drestal
Frank E., d. 9/12/1917 at 55/11/11; gastro enteritis; James P. Aldrich and Mary J. Stevens
Mary A., d. 2/17/1929 at 71/8/5 in Providence, RI; John Delaney and Ann

ALEXANDER,
Abbie L., d. 4/30/1901 at 41/5/19 in Pittsfield; hepatic cirrhosis; PH
Raymond, d. 4/17/1914 at 0/0/6; icterus neonatorum; Elias Alexander and Jennie Chdied

ALFORD,
Samuel, d. 7/14/1906 at 28; accidental drowning; SM

ALLAIRE,
Cecile, d. 12/18/1901 at 61; cerebral hemorrhage
Emelia, d. 2/10/1907 at 0/0/27; pneumonia; Eugene Allaire and Rose Huneau
Eugene I., d. 12/11/1901 at 0/0/2; unknown
Fernande, d. 11/6/1937 at 26/10/27 in Benton; pul. tuberculosis
Louise, d. 6/25/1897 at 32; tuberculosis of lungs; b. Canada; SM
Rebecca, d. 2/27/1887 at 11; b. Canada; John Allaire (Canada) and Cecile Rouel (Canada)

ALLARD,
Anna B., d. 5/10/1907 at 53/5/30; paresis; John A. Corson and Lizzie Young
Catherine, d. 11/25/1924 at 64; lobar pneumonia; John Harkins and Ellen McGill
Charles M., d. 10/1/1929 at 29 in Boston, MA; aortitis endocarditis; Charles C. Allard and Catherine Harkins

Eliza, d. 12/17/1906 at 86/2/10; senility; buried in Conway
Henry, d. 8/17/1908 at 81; tuberculosis pul.
John W., d. 1/3/1905 at 73/6 in Tuftonboro; organic heart disease; PH
Maurice J., d. 1/10/1907 at 24/9/14; overdose of morphine; John M. Allard
and Annie Seavey

ALLEN,
A. Virginia, d. 7/10/1917 at 49/5/25; pulm. tuberculosis; Samuel Eaton and
Abbie Hatch
Annie N., d. 11/17/1936 at 86/10/13*
Curtis N., d. 8/27/1887 at 64 in Boston, MA
Dorothy Louise, d. 4/28/1927 at – in Portsmouth; atelectosis
Etta Blanche, d. 2/17/1930 at 20/11/7 in Portsmouth; scarlet fever
Florence D., d. 7/10/1920 at 60/4; cancer of breast; Lemuel Bibber and
Jemima Blake
Gertrude B., d. 8/24/1905 at 0/10/29; cholera infantum; buried in So.
Berwick, ME
Harry, d. 6/17/1889 at 1; Mary Brennan
Herschel L., d. 10/18/1937 at 33/5; acute heart failure
Ida C., d. 9/30/1929 at 78; coronary sclerosis; George Allen and Mary J.
Brewster
James J., d. 9/8/1930 at 80/10/3; chronic endocarditis; Nathaniel Allen
James L., d. 6/12/1901 at 61/8/27; paralysis; PH
John, d. 10/4/1911 at 70; nephritis; John Allen and Amelia Valgreen
John, d. 1/23/1914 at 44/9/22; intestinal hemorrhage; John Allen and
Cecelia Ruel
John L., d. 7/21/1895 at 0; cholera infantum; SM
Lucille M., d. 11/22/1912 at 1/1/3 in Laconia; meningitis
Lydia H., d. 3/20/1893 at 64; pneumonia
Margaret M., d. 10/19/1915 at 92/1/19 in Boston, MA; myocarditis
Peter G., Jr., d. 3/5/1915 at 0/10/5; acute pneumonia; Peter Allen and
Rose Belger
Ralph W., Jr., d. 2/14/1930 at 0/0/19 in Portsmouth; scarlet fever
Sarah L., d. 12/25/1925 at 80/8/21; myocarditis; George W. Ransom and
Sophia Bunker
Susan H., d. 3/13/1909 at 62/5/18; heart disease; Sylvestre H. Hebard and
Tryphosa Pratt
Walter H., d. 9/2/1908 at 0/3/12; malnutrition; John M. Allen and Louise A.
Smith
William H., d. 5/10/1914 at 74/5/22; mitral regurgitation; Edward Allen and
Matilda Perkins
Willie, d. 11/5/1909 at 41; endocarditis

ALLEY,
Alice C., d. 3/8/1903 at 66/3/15; cardiac hypertrophy; PH

John M., d. 9/21/1901 at 61/7/29; chronic nephritis; PH
Sarah C., d. 3/12/1907 at 90/2/12 in Haverhill, MA; pneumonia

ALLIS,
Fred, d. 7/1/1930 at 8/1/27; ac. lobar pneumonia; Aid Allis and Basma Shtaid

ALLISON,
Frances, d. 5/22/1916 at 66/8 in Lowell, MA; embolism

ALSOP,
Ada, d. 11/29/1933 at 52/0/5; acute myocarditis

ALTON,
Fred, d. 7/29/1923 at 65; chronic endocarditis

AMADON,
Charles H., d. 10/14/1907 at 58/7/11; chronic bronchitis; John Amadon and Betsy Putney

AMAGNO,
Nichols, d. 8/22/1936 at 65; frac. cer. vertebra

AMAZEEN [see Amerzeen],
George H., d. 7/3/1929 at 76/3/18; valv. heart disease; William H. Amazeen and Eurania J. Richards

AMEDES,
Lutazi, d. 6/23/1913 at 23/7/12; electrocution

AMEIGH,
William, d. 7/2/1894 at 60; diabetes; b. NY; buried in Somersworth

AMERZEEN [see Amazeen],
Eva, d. 7/31/1913 at 51; carcinoma of uterus

AMES,
Abbie L., d. 12/6/1899 at 59; uraemia; buried in Gardiner, ME
Charles E., d. 3/2/1937 at 85/8/5; pros. hypertrophy
Herbert L., d. 10/22/1890 at 14/0/16 in Haverhill
Nancy A., d. 10/5/1900 at 63 in Haverhill, MA; cerebral hemorrhage; PH

AMSDEN,
James L., d. 2/11/1922 at 43/11/29 in Haverstraw, NY; broncho pneumonia

AMUNDSEN,
Helene M., d. 11/8/1907 at 41/10/13; hemoptysis; ----- Andreasen and Helene -----
Otto I., d. 7/11/1915 at 52/1/19; nephritis; Andreas Amundsen and Mathea

ANDEGEE,
Jno., d. 1/14/1890 at 79; black; widower

ANDERSON,
child, d. 2/17/1905 at –; stillborn; PH
Fannie E., d. 10/1/1923 at 50 in Pawtucket, RI; pneumonia
John, d. 2/17/1912 at 49; chronic nephritis
Joseph, d. 1/21/1901 at 37; machinery accident; buried in Adams, MA
Madeline D., d. 3/12/1920 at 13/1/15 in Lynn, MA; lobar pneumonia
Margaret A., d. 3/23/1923 at 47/9/16; Addison's disease; Richard Toas and Ann E. Brown
Petro D., d. 7/12/1888 at 67/10/6 in Providence; widow; b. Norway; Peter Peterson (Europe) and Martha (Europe)

ANDERTON,
Isabelle Richardson, d. 2/7/1937 at 83/3/6*; b. Dover

ANDRENOPOULOS,
Vasilos, d. 8/16/1925 at 58; mult. carci. abdomen; Andrew Andrenopoulos and Christina Parlos

ANDREWS,
child, d. 7/26/1908 at –; stillborn; Fred W. Andrews and Josie M. Kimball
Abbie L., d. 7/10/1920 at 66/0/19 in New Salem, MA; cancer of liver
Annie E., d. 3/12/1900 at 47 in Durham; pneumonia; PH
Ariella S., d. 1/4/1898 at 41; cerebral paralysis; b. Brookfield; buried in Berwick, ME
Emma L., d. 1/16/1898 at 47 in Concord; multiple sclerosis; PH
Frank E., d. 7/21/1932 at 71/3/10; mitral insufficiency
George W., d. 1/1/1905 at 80/10/18; heart disease; buried in Berwick, ME
Jessie W., d. 2/7/1891 at 3/7/23; Frederick Andrews and Ariella S. Tibbetts
Lavina D., d. 2/13/1914 at 75/6/7; acute bronchitis; John Bell and Eunice Davis
Sara, d. 1/13/1919 at 54; broncho pneumonia

ANDRIANOPOULOS,
child, d. 8/2/1921 at –; stillborn; A. Andrianopoulos and Vasilo Pereharo

ANDROS,
Vasileke, d. 6/5/1937 at 63; coronary occlusion

ANESTO,
Hercules, d. 7/21/1933 at 50; chronic bronchitis

ANGUISH,
Margaret M., d. 1/1/1921 at 58; chr. p'r'y'n's nephritis; Samuel Montgomery and Mary -----

ANNABLE,
Jane M., d. 3/10/1900 at 76; pneumonia; PH

ANNIS,
Betsey W., d. 10/6/1889 at 55/4/4; housewife; widow; b. Albany; E. Burbank (Conway) and M. Colby (Eaton)
Frank, d. 3/18/1917 at 64/2/6; carcinoma, etc.; Thomas Annis and Mary Allen
Mark, d. 8/8/1931 at 62/8/1; myocardial insufficiency
Sarah J., d. 4/6/1913 at 50/6/23; chronic endocarditis; Andrew J. Tibbetts and Lucinda Knox

ANTINOPOULOUS,
Constantine, d. 12/29/1907 at 38; pneumonia

ANTON,
Elias, d. 3/14/1937 at 58; coronary thrombosis
Mary, d. 11/25/1913 at 66; acute bronchitis; Assan Shibbly and Merter Reter
Nagchite, d. 6/4/1916 at 1/2; ac. dilatation of heart; Elias Anton and Teresa Alexander
Rosaline, d. 3/29/1937 at 26; general peritonitis

APOSTOLOPULOS,
Efthemios, d. 5/7/1909 at 18/0/8; pneumonia acute; K. Apostolopulos and Sophia -----
George, d. 3/5/1917 at 2/11/9; entero colitis; Kostos Apostolopoulos and Theoni Katopoulos

APOSTOPOULOS,
Sophia, d. 2/21/1920 at 2/0/16; influenza; Kostos Apostopoulos and
   Theona -----

APPLEBEE,
Arthur F., d. 4/25/1893 at 24; phthisis; b. Dover; (Milton; Strafford)
Linville T. S., d. 9/4/1896 at 21; phthisis pulmonalis; b. Dover; PH
Mary A., d. 10/23/1936 at 88/7/21*
Theodore S., d. 1/16/1928 at 87/3/20 in Lawrence, MA; arterio sclerosis
Viola, d. 2/7/1894 at 4; tubercular meningitis; b. Dover; PH

APPLEBY,
Allen, d. 2/22/1934 at 52/0/5; acute appendicitis

APPLETON,
Howard C., d. 12/31/1937 at 69/2/26; heart disease

ARBOUR,
Therese A., d. 10/9/1925 at 0/0/4; patent foramen; Wilfred Arbour and
   Odelie Grenier

ARCHAMBAULT,
Arthur, d. 12/12/1933 at 66/2/10; pyelonephritis

ARGAROGANIS,
Manuel, d. 12/21/1935 at 63; coronary thrombosis

ARLAND,
James, d. 8/7/1893 at –; cholera infantum; b. Dover; (Dover; Canada)

ARLIN,
Abigail, d. 12/3/1914 at 75; chronic myocarditis
Addie F., d. 9/21/1895 at 1; cholera infantum; b. Dover; PH
Burleigh E., d. 11/6/1916 at 59/11/12; carcinoma of liver; John W. Arlin
   and Sarah Hoyt
Cora Belle, d. 1/3/1893 at –; pneumonia; b. Dover; (Barrington; Dover)
Dorothy M., d. 12/22/1910 at 12/6/21; broncho-pneumonia; B. E. Arlin and
   Addie Clark
Edward A., d. 4/26/1912 at 59/8/19 in Barrington; neuritis; John W. Arlin
   and Sarah Hoyt
Frank, d. 6/1/1919 at 23/5/22; pulm. tuberculosis; Burleigh Arlin and Addie
   Clark
Hannah, d. 3/3/1925 at 76; apoplexy
Jesse F., d. 10/20/1932 at 65/0/3 in Rochester; apoplexy

John, d. 11/6/1936 at 82/8/6; cerebral embolism
John W., d. 8/26/1908 at 83/4/25; epithelioma; John Arlin and Polly Cater
Laura E., d. 9/8/1930 at 65; cancer of stomach; Wilber Freeman and Melissa Waterhouse
Lewis, d. 6/16/1909 at 55; pernicious anemia
Priscilla A., d. 12/25/1925 at 79/10/22 in Barrington; nephritis; William Bodge
Sarah, d. 5/7/1908 at 75/4/24; pneumonia; Benjamin Hoyt and Mahala Giles
Walter E., d. 9/16/1931 at 60/6/23; chronic endocarditis
William, d. 9/4/1887 at 66; laborer; widower; b. Barrington

ARMIEN,
Joseph, d. 2/26/1903 at 18; acute general tuberculosis

ARMSTRONG,
George, d. 8/30/1889 at 3/8; b. Dover; ----- (Ireland) and May McCabe (Ireland)

ARNO,
Anna G., d. 1/1/1935 at 82/4/9; cerebral hemorrhage
Hannah H., d. 10/10/1887 at 58/3 in Boston, MA; married
Harry E., d. 4/30/1887 at 31/1/21
John, d. 6/--/1891 at --
William E., d. 6/8/1922 at 61 in Brentwood; chronic nephritis

ARNOLD,
Dwight P., d. 10/7/1930 at 21/4/24; ulcer of stomach; Eudell M. Arnold and Adele M. Parker
Rodney O., d. 2/19/1933 at 75/7/25; cholelithiasis

ARNSTEIN,
Louis, d. 12/5/1924 at 74; angina pectoris; Jacob Arnstein

ARRANTES,
Mary, d. 12/1/1923 at --; premature birth; Socrates Arrantes and Angelina Marge

ARSENAULT,
Joseph L., d. 6/30/1932 at 66 in Portland, ME; chronic myocarditis

ARTEMUS,
Timothy, d. 8/15/1936 at 21/1/2; accidental drowning

ASH,
Charles H., d. 12/24/1918 at 72/2/11; cerebral hemorrhage
Joseph, d. 1/13/1929 at 73/4/25; valvular heart dis.; Edmund Ash and Celeste Miller

ASHBURN,
James, d. 1/28/1907 at 57/1/22; accident

ASHBY,
Albert E., d. 5/28/1891 at 0/0/6; Albert E. Ashby (England) and Rose Dalton (Nottingham)
Rose M., d. 7/10/1933 at 73/2/17; acute appendicitis

ASHNAULT,
Catherine, d. 1/3/1932 at 61/9/18; senile dementia

ASHTON,
Amelia E., d. 9/1-/1902 at 59; phthisis pulmonalis; PH
Elizabeth L., d. 6/8/1906 at 62/1/8 in Bristol; tuberculosis of urinary tract
James, d. 8/16/1893 at 89; chronic bronchitis; b. Manchester, England

ASTON,
Mary, d. 9/30/1891 at 49; Pat Agnew (Ireland) and Kate Grimes (Ireland)

ATHERTON,
Clara J., d. 8/8/1912 at 65/8/20 in Boston, MA; pernicious anemia
George W., d. 4/8/1895 at 29; consumption; b. Unity, ME; PH
Lenora J., d. 3/8/1895 at 26; heart disease; PH
Tyleston W., d. 6/19/1905 at 64/9/17; chronic bronchitis; PH

ATKINS,
Mary E., d. 11/14/1931 at 72/11/7; natural causes

ATKINSON,
Georgia, d. 11/30/1923 at 70 in Boston, MA; cerebral hemorrhage

ATWATER,
Gertie, d. 9/17/1887 at 6/7/23; b. ME; B. Frank Atwater (ME) and Carrie L. (ME)

ATWOOD,
Lucy A., d. 2/10/1909 at 73/4/18; old age; Ezekiel Carter and Fannie Kimball

AUBRIS,
Aldge, d. 10/23/1912 at 49; hemorrhage of lungs; Fredele Leveille and Philomene -----

AUCLAIR,
Martha J., d. 1/6/1922 at 46 in Danvers, MA; gen. paralysis of in.

AUDETTE,
Mary F., d. 8/18/1893 at 16; typhoid fever; b. Canada; (Canada; Canada)

AUJIM,
Shedid, d. 10/20/1917 at 60; valvular heart dis.

AUSTEY,
James Corson, d. 3/23/1928 at 0/0/20; acute gastritis; Alice Haskell

AUSTIN,
Ai, d. 3/5/1920 at 85; gastro enteritis
Albert, d. 5/27/1903 at 66/2/20; peritonitis; PH
Albert J., d. 3/14/1896 at –; catarrhal pneumonia; b. Dover; PH
Alphonso B., d. 12/16/1904 at 54/6/17; consumption; buried in Austin Cem.
Arthur S., d. 12/3/1888 at 18/11/19; farmer; single; b. Dover; Stephen Austin (Dover) and Sarah F. Erew (Dover)
Charles E., d. 11/11/1925 at 68; chronic myocarditis
Earle F., d. 3/28/1897 at 0; congestion of brain; b. Dover; PH
Eliza J., d. 8/13/1908 at 70; valv. disease of heart
Ethel Irene, d. 12/3/1902 at 1/8/5; brain lesion; PH
Frank, d. 3/15/1897 at 19; diphtheria; b. Dover; PH
Fred B., d. 1/1/1930 at 66/6/15; lobar pneumonia; Ai Austin and Susan Austin
Joseph C., d. 12/18/1920 at 52/11/20 in Portsmouth; phthisis pulmonalis
Lillie M., d. 10/25/1888 at 5; b. Dover; Edward Austin (Dover) and Mary Agnes (Ireland)
Mary E., d. 8/17/1888 at 62/2/26; single; b. Dover; James Austin (Farmington) and Elizabeth Varney (Farmington)
Nancy, d. 9/2/1893 at 86; enlarged liver, dropsy; b. Bristol, ME; (Rochester; Portsmouth)
Nellie M., d. 4/24/1937 at 74/7/10; coronary thrombosis
Sarah F., d. 5/14/1910 at 73/1/19; probably heart disease; Joseph Drew and Adeline Spurling
Sarah J., d. 8/4/1933 at 75/10/22; carcinoma rectum
Stephen, d. 11/12/1902 at 75/11/5; disease of heart; PH
Susan M., d. 12/24/1914 at –; senility

AVARD,
Peter, d. 12/27/1928 at 51; fract. 5th cerv. vert.; Pierre Avard and Zoi Bauvin

AVERILL,
James W., d. 3/28/1905 at 82/1/20 in Kittery, ME; valvular heart disease; PH
Joseph B., d. 2/24/1920 at 70/5/4 in Holderness; paralytic shock
Justin, d. 11/21/1892 at 43; heart failure; b. ME

AVERY,
Carrie, d. 12/23/1895 at 59; shock; b. NB; PH
Charles B., d. 12/19/1894 at 1; pneumonia; b. Dover; PH
Eliza G. T., d. 2/17/1917 at 78/3/12; broncho pneumonia; Lemuel G. Trickey and Maria Goodhue
George W., d. 6/8/1911 at 72/2/2; ch. pulm. tuberculosis; Daniel E. Avery and Abigail L. Richardson
Harry B., d. 8/11/1892 at –; cholera infantum; b. Dover; (Dover; Dover)
Idella May, d. 6/16/1917 at 46/0/22; cerebral apoplexy; Willoughby Mason and Lydia M. Cook
Louisa Friars, d. 7/23/1912 at 62/9; paralysis agitans; Charles Bunce
Mabel, d. 5/4/1919 at 32/8; carcinoma of uterus; Charles Jones and Julia Lougee
Mark, d. 12/–/1892 at 39; heart disease; b. Newfield
Mary E., d. 4/11/1898 at 74; cerebral paralysis; b. Strafford; buried in S. Barnstead
Ralph J., d. 12/24/1903 at 6/2/5; pneumonia; PH
Susan, d. 4/17/1887 at 48; widow; b. Farmington (see following entry)
Susan, d. 4/17/1888 at 48; b. Farmington (see preceding entry)
William K., d. 3/22/1891 at 30; single

AXWORTHY,
Clara L., d. 12/21/1918 at 27/6/3; influenza; Thomas Axworthy and Sarah M. Green
Sarah M., d. 11/17/1924 at 67; lobar pneumonia; John Green

AYER,
child, d. 12/27/1911 at –; premature birth; Maulea Ayer and Mary A. Hughes
Mary A., d. 5/6/1932 at 55/9/3; arterio sclerosis
Mary J., d. 8/–/1900 at 2; cholera infantum; SM
Warren P., d. 1/6/1890 at 37/11/2; married; Albert Ayer (NH) and Ann Hoyt (NH)

BABB,
Carrie A., d. 2/7/1911 at 66/5/9; diabetes; Cyrus W. Nute and Almira Banfield
Elizabeth A., d. 10/24/1926 at 64/5/24; cerebral hemorrhage; Charles Henderson and Elizabeth Chesley
Frank H., d. 4/11/1935 at 71/8/4; septicemia
Freeman, d. 12/10/1895 at 60; Brights disease; b. NH; PH
Harry K., d. 10/18/1935 at 57/3/14; fractured skull
Horace T., d. 11/26/1911 at 69/2/18; acute indigestion; Joseph R. Babb and Mary B. Tibbetts
Jennie S., d. 12/20/1893 at 32; phthisis pulmonalis; b. Dover; (Strafford; Madbury)
John D., d. 6/25/1936 at 78/11/0; myocarditis
Mary H., d. 7/8/1901 at 65/11/18; carcinoma; PH
Mary L., d. 5/6/1909 at 22/7/9; phthisis pulmonalis; George E. Marsden and Mary McLaughlin
Willie S., d. 3/14/1933 at 72/9/23; angina pectoris

BACKUS,
Mary F., d. 3/4/1919 at 0/0/5; unknown; Arthur Backus and Ada Drew

BACON,
Charles E., d. 6/10/1898 at 65 in Strafford; heart failure; b. Biddeford, ME; PH
Edward S., d. 4/8/1913 at 50/1 in Providence, RI; Charles E. Bacon
Richard O., d. 3/15/1928 at 78/0/11; accidental; Isaac Bacon and Marion Douglas
Susan, d. 8/4/1908 at 69/10/5; cerebral hemorrhage; Joseph Clark

BADGER,
child, d. 3/14/1894 at –; stillborn; b. Dover; SM
Annie I., d. 9/28/1930 at 68/11/8; natural causes; William Wilkinson and Jane Walker
Daniel M., d. 1/16/1902 at 63/6/8; general paresis; PH
Florence A., d. 12/2/1927 at 78/5/13; apoplexy; Joseph D. Allen and May Shorey
Margaret M., d. 10/15/1906 at 64/2/16 in Lebanon; angina pectoris; PH
Marie Aurelie Cote, d. 6/28/1909 at 34; suicide by drowning; Edward Cote and Desange Couture
Minnie E., d. 1/13/1937 at 76/2/12; angina pectoris
Robert, d. 10/5/1910 at 52; general tuberculosis
Victoria, d. 8/23/1911 at 0/3/23; infantile diarrhea; Archie Badger and Mary A. Cote

BAER,
Alfred, d. 1/5/1917 at 0/0/21; septicemia; Joseph Baer and Gertrude Severson

BAILEY,
Charles H., d. 2/11/1913 at 62/7/14; heart disease; Joseph Bailey and Martha Hough
Cora M., d. 9/13/1926 at 51; apoplexy
Daniel, d. 10/3/1905 at 50; nephritis; PH
Frank P., d. 3/24/1916 at 70; Bright's disease
John W., d. 10/11/1931 at 86; arterio sclerosis
Lucy, d. 11/19/1915 at 60/8; acute bronchitis; Lyman Tibbetts and Mary J. Whitehouse
Marcia S., d. 11/4/1917 at 54/2; carcinoma of liver; Louis Turner and Luella Hastings
Mildred M., d. 7/22/1911 at 0/1/16; Edgar Rowe and Mary Bailey
Nellie F., d. 9/22/1905 at 37/8/6 in Westboro, MA; paresis
Thomas H., d. 8/18/1929 at 64/4 in Newburgh, ME; carcinoma; Henry B. Bailey and Mary Curtis

BAILY,
Hammond, d. 4/27/1920 at 38; lobar pneumonia

BAIN,
Sadie, d. 6/28/1924 at 55/3/10; carcinoma of intestine; Alexander Matherson and Mary McKeigan

BAIRD,
Delia F., d. 12/23/1933 at 88/6/20; cerebral hemorrhage

BAKER,
Asa S., d. 6/19/1911 at 80/1/25; old age; Sharanton Baker and Mary A. Varney
Charles O., d. 10/22/1923 at 76/0/20; septicaemia; Samuel W. Baker and Lydia Blake
Effie M., d. 10/11/1930 at 71/8 in Sangerville, ME; chr. bronchitis; Richard Philbrick
Elizabeth, d. 12/26/1930 at 76/8/27; heart failure; Swain Drew and Matilda Richardson
George M., d. 4/30/1926 at 71/0/26; pneumonia; Otis Baker and Lavinia Hayes
John N., d. 1/15/1911 at 79/0/14; uraemia; Brown Baker and Phoebe Collins

John Priest, d. 3/30/1891 at 35/5/28 in East Weymouth; married; John
    Baker (England) and Emily A. Priest (Nottingham)
Lorraine, d. 3/15/1933 at 4/11/1; empyema
Lydia P., d. 2/4/1899 at 76 in Whitman, MA; bronchitis; PH
Martha, d. 3/6/1895 at 16 in Boston, MA; chronic nephritis; buried in Dover
Mary, d. 8/13/1890 at 67; widow; Enoch Place (Rochester) and Sally
    Demerritt (Barrington)
Otis, d. 5/5/1892 at 74; heart disease, valvular; b. Rochester; (Rochester; Rochester)
Samuel B., d. 5/26/1935 at 75/6/27 in Somerville, MA; chronic endocarditis
Sarah F., d. 3/15/1916 at 70/8/23; carcinoma of uterus; Levi Meader and
    Amanda Eastman
Warren L., d. 1/12/1890 at 60/0/23; married; Brown Baker (Litchfield, ME)
    and ----- (Gloucester, ME)

BALCH,
George, d. 11/3/1915 at 64; cerebral embolism; John Balch

BALDWIN,
Charles M., d. 7/9/1919 at 60/9/19; Brights disease; William Baldwin and
    Mary -----

BALL,
Edward Moses, d. 9/5/1925 at 72/0/5; prostatic carcinoma; Amos Ball and
    Jane Little
Elizabeth Ann, d. 11/4/1911 at 71/3/7 in Stoneham, MA; pneumonia
Elmira, d. 9/17/1893 at 72; old age - heart disease; b. NH; (NH; NH)
Harry E., d. 11/11/1934 at 54/4/24; paraplegia
Ida L., d. 5/28/1916 at 55/11/4; excessive alcoholism; Simeon B. Converse
    and Emma Gleason
Mary E., d. 9/20/1934 at 80/4/28; diabetes mellitus

BALLANTYNE,
Gordon E., d. 8/9/1931 at 29/4/5; suicide by gas

BANAIAN,
John, d. 4/3/1933 at 43/6/9; lobar pneumonia

BANALAN,
Edward, d. 4/27/1927 at --; asphyxia of labor; Hagop Banalan and
    Margaret Haladjian

BANFIELD,
Elizabeth L., d. 1/21/1915 at 91/11 in Milton; pneumonia

Esther P., d. 11/7/1898 at 88 in Portsmouth; paralysis; PH

BANGS,
Ellen, d. 1/3/1913 at 76/3/20; old age; Cyrus Bangs and Matilda Varney
Mary, d. 11/8/1920 at 83/2/18 in Malden, MA; illuminating gas

BANKS,
John, d. 7/2/1895 at 14; accident; b. Dover; SM
John, d. 9/18/1898 at 42; valvular disease of heart; b. Ireland; SM
Joseph S., d. 4/8/1916 at 32/0/3; acute pneumonia; John Banks and Julia Conneran

BARBER,
William A., d. 7/15/1909 at –; unknown; William Barber and Elizabeth Burder

BARDEN,
John, d. 1/17/1920 at 0/0/1; malformation; James H. Barden and Edna E. Daggle
Lavinia M., d. 4/21/1887 at 82/5; housewife; married; b. Rochester; Shadrach Chesley and Jennie Ham

BARDSLEY,
David T., d. 10/8/1901 at 3 in New Bedford, MA; burn; PH
Nellie C., d. 2/1/1906 at 40/3/23 in New Bedford, MA; opium poisoning - suicide; PH
Simeon J., d. 12/26/1904 at 34/8/23 in Exeter; pulmonary tuberculosis; PH

BARKER,
Archie P., d. 10/31/1933 at 43/3/18; alcoholism
Charles A., d. 12/22/1887 at 29/5/22; single; b. Exeter, ME; John Barker (Exeter, ME) and Clara Robinson (Exeter, ME)
Charles L., d. 6/30/1902 at 69/4 in Biddeford, ME; phthisis pulmonalis; PH
Fannie W., d. 9/18/1906 at 63 in Malden, MA; heart disease; PH

BARLOW,
Mary, d. 12/9/1904 at 58; apoplexy; PH

BARNARD,
Ada W., d. 12/16/1910 at 52/8/16; anaemia; A. T. Pierce and Rachael N. Cushman
Henry F., d. 7/8/1901 at 46 in Nashua; ulcer of stomach; PH

BARNES,
child, d. 5/8/1932 at –; stillborn
Annie R., d. 8/25/1929 at 57/3/20; chronic gastroenteritis; Robert Porter and Rose Martin
Arland S., d. 11/29/1931 at 56/9/2; myocarditis
Benjamin, d. 4/11/1914 at 75/11/26 in Brookline, MA; acute oedema of lungs
Edith Alice T., d. 4/12/1937 at 50/9/8; strep'cus meningitis
Harriet E., d. 11/6/1931 at 84/7/10; chronic endocarditis
Margaret E., d. 2/11/1933 at –; arteriosclerosis
Mary E., d. 3/25/1928 at 84/2/21; arterio sclerosis; Isaac Meader and Nancy Berry
William H., d. 6/19/1932 at 77/11/2; chronic endocarditis

BARNEY,
Frank, d. 5/6/1911 at –; comp. fracture skull

BARON,
Ferdinia, d. 1/26/1907 at 18; destroyed by fire; Alfred Baron and Victoria Cyr
Samuel, d. 7/20/1932 at 67/3/26; arterio sclerosis
Victoria, d. 12/28/1929 at 63; chr. myocarditis; Francis Cayer and Clafe Labonville

BAROUNIS,
George, d. 7/9/1918 at 0/5/12; meningitis tubercular; Satirios Barounis and Avezo Dianatopoulon

BARRETT,
child, d. 2/8/1899 at – in Rollinsford; infancy; PH
child, d. 11/21/1923 at –; premature birth; Clarence E. Bennett (sic) and Alice M. Drew
child, d. 10/21/1924 at –; premature birth; C. E. Barrett and Alice M. Drew
Frank L., d. 9/28/1904 at 39 at sea; heart failure
George D., d. 7/20/1924 at 59/7/16; carcinoma of esophagus; John Barrett and Jerusha C. Denning
H., d. 2/4/1900 at <1; peritonitis; SM
Helen, d. 3/17/1903 at 0/0/2; premature birth; buried in Edmeston, NY
John, d. 9/30/1916 at 87 in Wakefield, MA; ingravescent apoplexy; ----- Barrett and ----- Brennan

BARROWCLOUGH,
Mary J., d. 6/28/1931 at 66/8/5; coronary thrombosis
Sarah A., d. 10/27/1912 at 78/5/27; old age; Jonathan Bathys and Mary ---

William, d. 3/1/1910 at 67/8/14; cerebral apoplexy; James Barrowclough and Ann Senior

BARRY,
Ellen, d. 5/9/1912 at 69/11/24; cerebral embolism; Coleman Driscoll and Annie McCarthy
Honora, d. 5/14/1936 at 57; chr. myocarditis
James, d. 3/22/1897 at 5; scarlet fever; b. Dover; SM
John, d. 1/25/1914 at – in Tewksbury, MA; lobar pneumonia; ----- Barry
John A., d. 9/11/1911 at 38; tuberculosis; ----- Barry and Ellen Driscoll
John F., d. 1/10/1917 at 33; accidental; Thomas J. Barry and Mary E. Rosnihan
Maggie, d. 3/5/1893 at 25; phthisis; b. Ireland; (Ireland; Ireland)
Maria A., d. 1/6/1936 at 59; chronic nephritis
Patrick, d. 7/9/1916 at 50; alcoholism; ----- Barry and Ellen Driscoll
Patrick J., d. 3/1/1915 at 67; lobar pneumonia; John Barry and Mary Kennedy
Timothy, d. 4/16/1919 at –; stillborn; Jeremiah Barry and Nora Daley

BARSTOW,
S. Austin, d. 12/29/1935 at 54/9/20; gunshot wound

BARTELS,
Edward A., d. 7/30/1915 at 0/0/9; cong. atelectasis; George A. Bartels and Mary E. McAdam
George, d. 12/5/1917 at 29/11; septic endocarditis; Alto Bartels and Louise

BARTER,
Ruth C., d. 3/8/1915 at 29 in Tewksbury, MA; tubal pregnancy

BARTLE,
Helen, d. 12/7/1937 at 85/0/0; gangrene of foot
William, d. 2/19/1927 at 65/2 in Lawrence, MA; angina pectoris

BARTLETT,
Abbie H., d. 10/17/1888 at 61/6/1; married; b. Epping; Samuel (Epping) and Sally Haley (Nottingham)
H. E. W. T., d. 3/9/1892 at 84; old age; b. Portsmouth; (Portsmouth; Greenland)
Hannah C., d. 5/4/1900 at 64; inanition; PH
James, 2nd, d. 6/25/1895 at 28 in Plymouth, MA; Brights disease; SM
James W., d. 11/5/1906 at 73/6/21 in Portsmouth; tuberculosis of stomach and bowels; PH

Jennie, d. 1/28/1920 at 70/6/4 in Rye; cancer of stomach
John, d. 2/1/1903 at 79/8/25 in Madbury; valvular disease of heart; buried in Lee

BARTON,
Leonora Grace, d. 5/15/1925 at 35/5/18 in Binghamton, NY; carcinoma of pelvic

BASFORD,
Emeline C., d. 5/20/1904 at 49/0/3; heart failure; PH

BASSETT,
Alberta M., d. 9/13/1906 at 0/2/2; marasmus; PH
Bernice M., d. 4/19/1924 at 47/9; secondary anaemia; Edgar Palmer
Bernice M., d. 10/22/1932 at 30/0/16; chr. intestinal nephritis
Bert, d. 3/30/1907 at 24/8/19; pleuro-pneumonia; Toussaint Bassett and Susan Hamel
George W., d. 6/11/1935 at 45; fracture 5 ribs - rupture lung
May, d. 5/16/1916 at 0/0/½; premature birth; George W. Bassett and Sarah Oates
Robert F., d. 3/20/1904 at 0/2/6; pneumonia; buried in Dover
Susan, d. 9/25/1928 at 88/0/24 in S. Stukely, Can.; angina pectoris; ----- Hamel
Thomas A., d. 5/15/1928 at 60/8/24; carcinoma of larynx; Toussaint Bassett and Susan Hamel
Walter W., d. 1/8/1921 at 27/8/24; oedema of lungs; Henry Bassett and Mary A. Boissie

BATCHELDER,
Edgar R., d. 11/20/1932 at 55/8/2; cerebral hemorrhage
Emma M., d. 1/19/1930 at 62/9/27; chronic myocarditis; Augustus Swanson and Hannah -----
Justus, d. 1/19/1930 at 79/2; cerebral hemorrhage; Samuel Batchelder and Nancy Trafton
Louis S., d. 11/7/1931 at 85/10/7; chronic endocarditis
Magda E., d. 1/18/1888 at 8/9/2; b. S. Berwick, ME; J. Batchelder (Shapleigh, ME) and Sarah O. Grant (Acton, ME)
Mary E., d. 11/24/1936 at 83/3/3; cerebral hemorrhage
Maud, d. 4/21/1910 at –; premature birth; Asa Batchelder and Georgianna Healey
Sarah O., d. 5/10/1937 at 81/9/21; coronary occlusion

BATEMAN,

Martha L., d. 1/1/1926 at 75/3/29; arterio sclerosis; Samuel Leighton and Adeline Winkley
Mary, d. 11/19/1892 at 7; purpura hemorhagica
W. M., d. 11/22/1905 at 55/7/24 in Strafford; pneumonia; PH
William M., d. 3/1/1926 at 3/1/1926 at 46/5; chronic inter. nephritis; Woodbury Bateman and Martha Leighton

BATES,
Fred N., d. 11/15/1934 at 59/2/8; acute myocarditis
William H., d. 5/5/1925 at 25/11/14; pulmonary tuberculosis; Henry W. Bates and Margaret A. Tansey

BATLEY,
John W., d. 5/8/1905 at 52/10/7; Bright's disease; PH
Sarah A. O., d. 4/5/1932 at 79/6/22 in Milford, MA; arterio sclerosis

BATTLES,
Ann, d. 3/1/1887 at 49/9; single; b. Ireland; Harry Battles (Ireland) and Bridget (Ireland)
Eliza J., d. 9/2/1896 at 50; gastric catarrh; b. Dover; SM
Henry R., d. 3/1/1923 at 83 in Taunton, MA; heart disease
John, d. 10/30/1937 at –; cerebr. hemorrhage

BATTYE,
Joshua, d. 3/4/1929 at 68/10/28 in Kingston; arthritis deformans
Richard, d. 10/4/1909 at 72/8/19; heart disease; Jonathan Battye and Mary Dearnley

BATY,
Mary A., d. 5/20/1925 at 67; chr. pulm. tuberculosis; John B. Sanders and Mary A. Randall

BAXTER,
Abbie M., d. 8/3/1894 at 39; phthisis pulmonalis; b. Milton; PH
Hannah, d. 7/30/1888 at 67/3; married; b. Gilmanton; ----- Lougee (Wheelock, MA) and Dorethy Hull (London, ME)
John M., d. 4/26/1920 at 73/7/1 in Haverhill, MA; cerebral hemorrhage
Joseph E., d. 5/11/1909 at 1/1/3; burned to death; Walter I. Baxter and Annie W. Burley
Naham, d. 1/26/1927 at 78/3/13 in Concord; erysipelas; Abel Baxter and Hannah Lonsey
Philip B., d. 2/10/1922 at 15/0/15 in Madbury; cerebral meningitis; Nahum N. Baxter and Alta Maddox
Walter I., Jr., d. 7/21/1905 at 0/6/13; whooping cough; PH

BEACH,
Alice B., d. 4/30/1931 at 67/4/20; food poisoning
Catherine, d. 12/2/1887 at 68/10/5; single; b. Torrington, CT; Samuel
    Beach (Torrington, CT) and Constance Hall (Wallington, CT)
Laura, d. 8/14/1897 at 85; old age; b. Dover; PH

BEALE,
Lucy S., d. 2/23/1937 at 89/4/7; myocarditis - arteriosclerosis

BEAN,
child, d. 1/21/1920 at –; premature birth; Lloyd L. Bean and Laura Brock
Agnes, d. 3/13/1915 at 63/11/13; mitral regurgitation; Sylvester McNally
    and Ann Hughes
Albert James, d. 7/3/1929 at 76/11/25 in Taunton, MA; angina pectoris
Alexander, d. 9/24/1913 at 52/7/11; acute nephritis; Alexander Bean and
    Lena Gadbois
Alger C., d. 4/22/1896 at 41 in West Newton, MA; pneumonia
Frances, d. 3/13/1902 at 40 in Lowell, MA; uraemia; PH
Horace J., d. 9/16/1896 at –; suicide by drowning; buried in West
    Kennebunk
Jenson H., d. 1/27/1917 at 62/1/11; pneumonia; Lewis Bean and Clara
    Downs
John, d. 6/8/1888 at 40/7 in Nottingham
John F., d. 4/23/1899 at 53; inflammation of bowels; PH
Lura B., d. 6/30/1931 at 32/9/15; septicemia; Arthur N. Brock and Mary B.
    Jones
Miriam N., d. 12/4/1905 at 76/5/29 in Lexington, MA; pneumonia; PH
Samuel A., d. 9/18/1908 at 76/1/3 in Rochester
Walter C., d. 4/18/1900 at 38 in Boston, MA; tuberculosis; PH

BEARD,
Abby R., d. 10/2/1905 at 76/1; senility; buried in Farmington
Arthur L., d. 4/18/1910 at 82/7/28; burns; William Beard and Isabel
    McCauley
George M., d. 5/28/1914 at 55/6/9; pneumonia; Arthur L. Beard and Abbie
    R. Sanborn
Hannah E., d. 6/30/1924 at 67/1/17; apoplexy; Rufus Bolo and Susan
    Young
Mary, d. 9/7/1900 at –; cholera infantum; SM
Mary Jane, d. 9/5/1933 at 22/3/1; pulmonary tuberculosis

BEARDSLEY,
Mary, d. 1/11/1890 at 75/11/10 in Lynn, MA

BEARDSWORTH,
Margaret, d. 1/23/1908 at 68/6/3; phthisis pulmonalis; James Beardsworth and Ann Sargent

BEATLEY,
Annie, d. 9/26/1896 at 70 in Saco, ME; heart disease

BEATTIE,
James F., d. 8/2/1931 at 16/10/30; accidental drowning

BEAUCHAMP,
John H., d. 7/30/1897 at 49; dilation of stomach; b. Lynn, MA; buried in Lynn, MA

BEAUDET,
Doris, d. 3/17/1926 at 3/10/11; pleuritic effusion; Dissire Beaudet and Camilia Provencher
Mary L., d. 5/9/1898 at 0; premature birth; b. Dover; SM

BEAUDETTE,
Adolph, d. 11/29/1928 at 68 in Boston, MA; carcinoma

BEAUDREAU,
Mary, d. 7/24/1908 at --; nephritis

BEAULEAIR,
Annie, d. 9/5/1888 at 0/1/10; b. Dover; William Beauleair (Canada) and Ellen Ballange (Canada)

BEAULIEU,
Emma A., d. 3/26/1931 at 66; carcinoma
Evangeline Rita, d. 5/20/1925 at 1/7/17; broncho pneumonia; Eugene A. Beaulieu and Olivene M. LaRoche
Helene E., d. 2/22/1903 at 24/0/7; typhoid fever
Laurent, d. 9/4/1914 at 0/10/20; cholera infantum; Emelio Beaulieu and Ida Morin

BEAUPEE,
Mary H., d. 8/30/1901 at 0/2/5; cholera infantum

BEAUPERE,
Marie, d. 5/14/1888 at 31; married; b. Canada; C. Couprie (Canada) and Merance Vaseur (Canada)

BEAUPRE,
daughter, d. 5/8/1888 at –; b. Dover; Jules Beaupre (Canada) and Minie Cauillion (Canada)
daughter, d. 5/8/1888 at –; b. Dover; Jules Beaupre (Canada) and Minie Cauillion (Canada)
Alfred, d. 8/16/1891 at 0/1/20; Jules Beaupre (Canada) and Melanise St. Jean (Canada)
Minnie, d. 10/13/1922 at 50/11/26; cerebral hemorrhage; Edward Hall and Mary -----

BEAVINS,
Annie M., d. 10/26/1922 at 73/4; valvular heart disease; William Beavins and Mary J. Southwick
James T., d. 5/4/1926 at 72 in Lynn, MA; myocarditis
Mary A., d. 6/2/1899 at 80; heart disease; PH
Rev. William, d. 7/2/1892 at 72; heart disease; b. England; (England; England)

BECK,
Addie, d. 10/30/1935 at 60/3/2; pulmonary embolus
Iva May, d. 9/12/1908 at 0/1/17; entero colitis; William Beck and Addie Lewis
William, d. 12/21/1933 at 55/8/24; heart disease

BECKETT,
Benjamin, d. 2/22/1893 at 78; disease of the heart - dropsy; b. Salem, MA; (Salem, MA; Salem, MA)

BECKINGHAM,
Catherine, d. 4/18/1927 at 60; cerebral apoplexy; Thomas Beckingham
Pat. J., d. 4/27/1933 at –; arteriosclerosis
Thomas, d. 8/2/1901 at 40; tuberculosis; PH

BECKLEY,
Gertrude E., d. 8/26/1893 at –; phthisis; b. Dover; (England; Dover)

BEDANTE,
Marie F., d. 9/3/1887 at 7; b. Canada; Bartholomew Bedante (Canada) and Arrie (Canada)

BEDARD,
Daniel, d. 11/7/1935 at 0/0/1; premature
H., d. 7/25/1888 at 0/4/21; b. Dover; Cassimir Bedard (Canada) and Saleme Bedard (Canada)

John, d. 7/11/1888 at 0/4/2; b. Dover; Tallus Bedard (Canada) and
Sophronia Grenier (Canada)
Prexcede, d. 4/23/1918 at 73/0/27 in Lawrence, MA; mitral stenosis

BEDELL,
Ella L., d. 7/1/1912 at 61/6/1; spinal sclerosis; Benjamin Buzzell and
Fannie Smith
Jane, d. 4/7/1894 at 72; heart disease and pneumonia; b. Rochester; PH
Joseph, d. 8/20/1904 at 79/11; disease of prostate gland; PH
Martha, d. 4/12/1917 at 72/10/19; chr. interstitial nephritis; James Bedell
and Theodate Baker
Olive M., d. 2/15/1899 at 83; paralysis; PH
P. W., d. 6/10/1899 at 80; paralysis
Parker W., d. 2/10/1897 at 80; paralytic shock; b. New Durham; PH

BEEBE,
Marriet F., d. 1/7/1926 at 70/2/26 in Newmarket; cerebral hemorrhage

BEEDE,
A. Elizabeth, d. 2/8/1915 at 85 in Portland, ME; senile gangrene
Abbie B., d. 8/21/1921 at 76/0/9; chr. Brights disease; ----- Smith
Augustus H., d. 6/18/1910 at 83/3/15; catarrhal pneumonia; John Beede
and Tamson -----
Frances E., d. 6/29/1927 at 55/1 in E. Braintree, MA; mitral insufficiency;
Augustus H. Beede
Harvey A., d. 1/17/1908 at 34/1/5; suicide by hanging; William H. Beede
and Abbie Smith
William H., d. 10/24/1931 at 80/3/15 in Braintree, MA; carcinoma of
stomach

BEEDLE,
Rufus, d. 12/1/1901 at 83/8/25; gastric catarrh; buried in Rollinsford

BEGLEY,
Daniel F., d. 6/30/1932 at 72; cerebral hemorrhage
Doris A., d. 9/20/1920 at 17/3/13; peritonitis; Daniel F. Begley and Susan
M. Rice
Susan M., d. 11/10/1917 at 36/1/20; broncho pneumonia; Edwin E. Rice
and Margaret I. Taylor

BEHAN,
Andrew, d. 4/17/1916 at 40; acute pneumonia; Patrick Behan and Mary
Betton

Pearl Eva, d. 11/14/1923 at 17/4/5; septicemia of face; George W. Behan and Laura H. Kearney

S. Kathleen, d. 6/23/1921 at 17/11/28; pulmonary tuberculosis; George W. Behan and Loura H. Kearney

BELANGER,
Edmond A., d. 3/18/1929 at 0/0/11; premature birth; Eugene L. Belanger and Rosanna Deroy

Jane N., d. 7/2/1934 at 1/6/8; broncho pneumonia

Luc, d. 11/30/1903 at 30/10/26; typhoid fever

Mary J. I., d. 10/17/1924 at 0/4/6; athrepsia; Alzear Belanger and Mary J. Dupre

BELCHER,
Mary E., d. 10/20/1896 at 64 in So. Framingham, MA; la grippe; PH

BELGER,
James E., d. 4/21/1889 at 0/8/16; b. Dover; William H. Belger (Natick, MA) and Kate Feenan (New York City)

John Francis, d. 8/10/1891 at 0/7/20; William H. Belger (Natick, MA) and Kate Feenan (New York, NY)

William H., d. 2/2/1909 at 48; paresis; Patrick Belger and Mary Fox

BELL,
George W., d. 12/25/1914 at 71/4; heart disease

Hattie Ada, d. 6/24/1896 at –; infantile debility; b. Dover; PH

Julia E., d. 1/22/1913 at 72/11/6; pneumonia; Jedediah Felch and Mary Hill

BELLEFEUILLE,
Joseph O., d. 8/7/1899 at –; diarrhea infantile; SM

BELLEVIAN,
A. Eva, d. 8/30/1913 at 0/2; marasmus; George W. Bellevian and Merilda Cormier

BELLIVEAU,
Alice, d. 12/8/1935 at 37/10/7; chronic myocarditis

BELMEKE,
Sophia, d. 12/21/1902 at 41/5/29 in W. Newton, MA; chronic tuberculosis

BELWARE,
Edith, d. 1/6/1921 at 0/11/27; pneumonia; George Belware and
   Georgianna Cote

BEMIS,
Elizabeth Frye, d. 11/27/1936 at 80/7/26*
Florence R., d. 9/26/1919 at 38/2 in New Durham; septic endocarditis
George W., d. 8/12/1918 at 59/10/24 in Marlboro, MA; cardio renal
   disease

BENEDICT,
William H. W., d. 10/21/1932 at 68/11/25; chronic nephritis

BENJAMIN,
Mary E., d. 9/20/1903 at 65/2/15; fatty degeneration of heart; buried in
   Barre, VT

BENN,
Abby E., d. 5/2/1922 at 91/7/27; old age; Isaac Benn and Deborah
   Emerson
Deborah E., d. 1/13/1892 at 87; pneumonia; b. Dover; (Dover; Dover)
Elizabeth J., d. 4/11/1930 at 66/8/3; chronic myocarditis; Edward Benn
   and Elizabeth Woodward
George William, d. 8/30/1910 at 78/1/27; heart disease; Isaac Benn and
   Deborah Emerson
Letitia, d. 4/6/1887 at 59/8/29; housewife; married; b. NY; Elijah Shaw
   (Kensington) and Lydia True (Andover)

BENNET,
Almira, d. 7/27/1912 at 63; abdominal carcinoma; John Droulet

BENNETT,
child, d. 7/21/1891 at –; Martin P. Bennett (Dover) and Mary E. Abbott
   (Dover)
child, d. 5/27/1906 at –; stillborn; SM
child, d. 8/18/1909 at –; stillborn; William Bennett and Bertha Surles
child, d. 8/20/1909 at –; stillborn; John Bennett and Mary Mulcahy
Abbie C., d. 10/9/1929 at 81/4/26; apoplexy; Freeman Drew and Abigail L.
   Watson
Abby P., d. 4/8/1889 at 63/8/18; housewife; widow; b. Somersworth;
   Moses Straw (Somersworth) and Sabra Stackpole (Somersworth)
Amanda M., d. 10/24/1887 at 71/0/2; married; b. Alton; John Chamberlin
   (Alton) and Abigail Stevens (New Durham)
Andrew, d. 5/12/1906 at 2/0/15; drowned; SM

Andrew B., d. 5/12/1906 at 60/11/27; phthisis; PH
Arthur, d. 6/11/1916 at 57; cerebral apoplexy; John Bennett and Rose Lavin
Betsey N., d. 12/11/1910 at 88/5/11 in New Durham; cerebral hemorrhage
Catherine, d. 5/20/1903 at 1; meningitis; SM
Cedric, d. 2/1/1919 at 21 in Hartford, CT; influenza
David L., d. 6/17/1918 at 68/4/1; organic int'al obstruction; David Bennett and Judith Elliott
Delia F., d. 4/7/1891 at 37/4/7; married; James S. Young (Gilmanton) and Mary A. Nute (Alton)
Dennis, d. 8/17/1900 at <1; measles; SM
Edna I., d. 3/5/1932 at 73/7/23; chronic myocarditis
Ella, d. 6/6/1937 at 72/4/26; cerebr. hemorrhage
Ellen, d. 1/15/1908 at --; premature birth; John Bennett and Mary Mulchy
Ellen H., d. 11/25/1912 at 54; chronic gastric ulcer; Francis Hughes and Bridget Rooney
Ellery I., d. 1/7/1917 at 66/1/7 in Exeter; cerebral hemorrhage; James Bennett
George A., d. 8/17/1896 at --; cholera infantum; b. Dover; PH
George H., d. 11/17/1913 at 43/9/9 in New York, NY
George W., d. 2/8/1929 at 75/2/29 in Farmington; cardiac dilatation
Grace Althea, d. 9/8/1891 at 0/10/26; Charles F. Bennett (Dover) and Edith A. Jenkins (New Durham)
Henry, d. 4/20/1908 at 86/10/9; old age
Honora, d. 8/2/1900 at <1; cholera infantum; SM
James, d. 11/21/1894 at 78; apoplexy; b. New Durham; PH
James M., d. 10/28/1892 at 73; apoplexy
Jeremiah, d. 6/15/1911 at 10/6/15; acute tuberculosis; John Bennett and Mary Mulcahy
John, d. 8/3/1934 at 66; cirrhosis of liver
John L., d. 3/28/1910 at 56/2/10; killed by bull; Sylvestre Bennett and Olive Lang
Joseph W., d. 1/25/1892 at 74; la grippe; b. Farmington; (Farmington; Farmington)
Josephine H., d. 3/17/1921 at 46/5/8; cerebral hemorrhage; Harvey G. Tetford and Nellie Gowdy
Leon E., d. 4/13/1896 at 12; chronic rheu. arthritis; b. NH; buried in Rollinsford
Lydia J., d. 5/24/1902 at 85/10/13; heart disease; buried in Meredith
Martin P., d. 6/30/1932 at 70/7/2 in S. Berwick, ME; cerebral hemorrhage
Mary, d. 9/22/1932 at 70; chronic endocarditis
Mary C., d. 9/8/1919 at 86; acute enterocolitis
Mary E., d. 3/7/1908 at 50/5/12; heart disease; John W. Abbott and Emily B. Cheswell
Mary E., d. 2/1/1932 at 69/11/1; cancer of stomach

Michael J., d. 11/7/1928 at 34/6/30; natural causes; John Bennett
Rachel E., d. 11/29/1897 at 11; diabetes mellitus; b. Dover; PH
Robert, d. 2/2/1922 at 42/9/2; cancer of stomach; James Bennett and
 Mary Caldwell
Roland G., d. 3/15/1932 at 6 in Boston, MA; cer. spinal meningitis
Samuel, d. 12/30/1913 at 86/3/27; chronic endocarditis
Sophronia T., d. 3/22/1896 at 73; consumption; b. Pittsfield; PH
Susan, d. 3/15/1905 at 81/10/24; apoplexy; PH
Thomas, d. 10/22/1893 at 83; old age - bronchitis; b. New Durham;
 (Durham; South Newmarket)
Thomas, d. 1/5/1929 at 62; lobar pneumonia
William, d. 9/6/1931 at 60 in Concord; chronic myocarditis

BENSON,
child, d. 6/29/1935 at – in Medford, MA; intracranial hemorrhage
Anton H., d. 12/27/1908 at 58/2/19 in Stonington, ME

BENTLEY,
Elijah, d. 6/14/1906 at 67/8; acute gastritis; PH

BENTLY,
Rebecca, d. 2/4/1890 at 52/2/14; married; James Dudley (England) and
 Elizabeth Fenner (England)

BERARD,
Joseph, d. 3/9/1929 at 60/11/19; cerebral hemorrhage; Joseph Berard and
 Georgianna -----

BERG,
Karen H., d. 6/10/1927 at 85/7/12; arterio sclerosis; Peter Paulsen
William, d. 11/9/1935 at 64/6/18; coronary thrombosis, acute myocarditis

BERGERON,
daughter, d. 5/23/1890 at –; Joseph P. Bergeron (Canada) and Hannah
 Hallworth (MA)
Cored, d. 4/29/1916 at 0/6/16; lobar pneumonia; Edward Bergeron and
 Delia Cayer
Joseph, d. 2/20/1929 at 59 in Concord; broncho pneumonia; Arsone
 Bergeron and Mary Dion
Joseph A., d. 6/13/1910 at –; premature birth; Achille Bergeron and
 Marianne Cote
Louis D., d. 7/22/1932 at 48/7/11; sarcoma of left femur
Marie, d. 6/29/1918 at 68/10/27; acute gastro enteritis; Augustus Dionne
 and Mary -----

Mary, d. 11/3/1908 at 48 in Concord; strangulation; Tim Bergeron and Mary N. Heath
Napoleon, d. 1/5/1926 at 51; cerebral hemorrhage; Urbin Bergeron and ---- - Crampoux
Raymond O., d. 3/11/931 at 2/0/4; convulsions
Urbain, d. 10/25/1936 at 81/1/11; chr. endocarditis
Valiere, d. 4/2/1900 at 1; pneumonia

BERMAN,
Grace B., d. 4/13/1903 at 29 in Worcester, MA; pneumonia; PH

BERMINGHAM,
J. J., d. 1/23/1896 at 1; infantile convulsions; b. Dover; SM

BERNARD,
Alphonse, d. 1/3/1915 at 55 in MA; bronchial pneumonia; Enoch Bernard and Silimon Loulin
Augustine, d. 2/6/1922 at 83/0/24; arterio sclerosis
Jacque, d. 6/24/1890 at 69/6; widower; (Canada; Canada)
Leo A., d. 3/20/1922 at 16/4/15; tuberculosis (lungs); Arthur Bernard and Elmina Leclair
Mattie, d. 10/11/1918 at 31/7/7; pneumonia; Adelard Loisel and Hermine Langelin
Oliver, d. 9/6/1910 at 64; gangrene
Philomene, d. 9/15/1915 at 75/0/19; general debility; Francis Fredette and Lucy Beaudoin
Timothy, d. 10/2/1891 at 17/2/14; single; Augustin Bernard (Canada) and Philamene Fredette (Canada)
Timothy, d. 3/11/1919 at 66 in Lowell, MA; cerebral hemorrhage

BERNIER,
Charles, d. 12/10/1927 at 70/3/25; arterio sclerosis; Charles Bernier and Cecelia Cote
Jennie, d. 12/26/1896 at 2; scarlet fever; b. Dover; SM

BERRY,
child, d. 5/1/1925 at –; stillborn; Thomas J. Berry and Margaret Gallant
child, d. 3/3/1926 at 0/0/4; hemorrhage of membrane; Thomas J. Berry and Margaret Gallant
child, d. 6/9/1935 at –; stillborn
Abbie F., d. 7/6/1927 at 88/10/23 in Wells Beach, ME; valv. heart disease; Charles Felker and Polly Swain
Abigail, d. 2/2/1891 at 72; widow; Richard Berry (Barrington) and Abigail Evans (Strafford)
Alonzo F. W., d. 12/10/1904 at 64/11/9; cancer of mouth and tongue; PH

Alonzo W., d. 7/21/1894 at 4; accidental drowning; b. Dover; PH
Amanda E., d. 4/1/1890 at 35/0/16; widow; Lyford T. Buzzell (Barrington) and Lydia F. Cushing (Tamworth)
Amanda H., d. 12/8/1922 at 78/6/3 in Brockton, MA; cerebral hemorrhage
Andrew E., d. 12/7/1922 at 68 in Berwick, ME; heart disease
Ann M., d. 9/8/1887 at 48/4; single; b. Dover; Richard Berry and Ann M. Meader
Anthony M., d. 2/19/1932 at 61; gastro enteritis
Artezena I., d. 9/25/1937 at 84/9/9 in Somersworth; old age and general disability
Benjamin T., d. 8/10/1896 at — in Minneapolis, MN; cancer of stomach
Charles F., d. 5/20/1934 at 71/11/17 in Concord; arteriosclerosis
Charles H., d. 9/5/1928 at 71; chr. Brights dis.
Charles L., d. 9/6/1930 at 79/9/20; lobar pneumonia; Lemuel Berry and Olive Hoyt
Clara A., d. 8/22/1912 at 56; diabetic coma; Holman Haskell and Mary Harris
Clark T., d. 3/5/1897 at 71 in Rollinsford; general debility; PH
Cora Lane, d. 1/21/1931 at 68 in New Orleans, LA; chronic nephritis
Eben C., d. 3/20/1911 at 77/3/1; nephritis; Nicholas Berry and Abigail Connell
Edward M., d. 6/2/1924 at 25/11/4; accidental; Edward M. Berry and Mary Alice Gray
Emily, d. 2/7/1904 at 76/10/18 in Rochester; cancer of stomach; PH
Emma P., d. 5/27/1908 at 0/10/4; tubercular meningitis; William C. Berry and Emma Rhoades
George G., d. 5/17/1907 at 69 in Boston, MA; probably heart disease
George O., d. 1/12/1931 at 61/2/14; arterio sclerosis
Gertrude, d. 8/21/1926 at 31/5/27; epilepsy; Frank C. Ham and Adeline Ross
Gladys I., d. 10/5/1905 at 0/2/26; acute indigestion
Ida Esther, d. 12/26/1901 at 1/10/17; laryngeal diphtheria; PH
J. Frank, d. 8/2/1934 at 89/2/9; cerebral hemorrhage
Jason A., d. 12/18/1887 at 29/1/17; clerk; single; b. Strafford; Samuel Berry (Barrington) and Margaret F. (Strafford)
Jennette E., d. 3/28/1897 at 38; ascites; b. Milton; PH
John, d. 1/17/1899 at 74; old age, general breakdown; buried in Manchester
John A., d. 1/16/1906 at 0/2/5; marasmus from innutrition; SM
John E., d. 6/12/1918 at 65/7/4 in Brockton, MA; urinary suppression
Josephine M., d. 7/14/1925 at 82 in Methuen, MA; cerebral hemorrhage
Judith, d. 5/6/1898 at 72; valvular disease of heart; b. Sheffield, VT; PH
Laura A., d. 5/5/1925 at 61 in Concord; broncho pneumonia; Freeman Berry and Judith -----
Louisa, d. 2/10/1904 at 80/0/20 in Chester; PH

Margaret A., d. 6/23/1900 at 75 in Pittsfield; pneumonia; PH
Margaret F., d. 4/17/1910 at 86/1/4; senility; John Berry and Rachel Hayes
Marilla M., d. 12/21/1910 at 77/9/12 in Rollinsford
Martha J., d. 1/4/1918 at 90/1/14 in Minneapolis, MN; senility
Mary A., d. 6/20/1897 at 85 in Boston, MA; paralysis
Mary J., d. 3/21/1908 at 0/0/2; premature birth; James Berry
Mary J., d. 11/23/1933 at 44/2/7 in Somersworth; chronic nephritis
Mary Susan, d. 7/6/1913 at 60/3/22 in Brockton, MA; ch. ulcer of leg
Rosa C., d. 11/25/1907 at 75/6/7; pneumonia; Thomas Pinkham and
    Sarah -----
Roscoe E., d. 6/11/1936 at 66/7/2; cirrhosis of liver
Ruth Lois, d. 11/20/1919 at 0/0/13; atelectasis; Harry O. Berry and Mary
    A. Meserve
Sarah E., d. 5/12/1919 at 64/10/27; carcinoma of liver; Elbridge Snow and
    Olive J. Day
Stephen, d. 2/13/1930 at 58 in W. Swanzey; cerebral hemorrhage
Thomas L., d. 9/23/1899 at 68; heart disease; PH
Viana, d. 12/24/1890 at 89/4/1 in Boston, MA
Vienna F., d. 3/29/1912 at 67/3/28 in Lowell, MA; tumor of kidneys
Wilfred, Jr., d. 2/8/1937 at –; miscarriage

BERUBE,
Joseph W., d. 2/16/1932 at 81/4/21; arterio sclerosis

BESON,
Fred., d. 8/3/1889 at 0/3/27; b. Dover; Joseph Beson (Canada) and
    Josephine Mettera (Canada)

BESSEY,
Eli P., d. 10/21/1937 at 61/5/18*

BICKFORD,
Abbie M., d. 4/8/1895 at 71; pulmonary consumption; b. New Durham; PH
Ansel R., d. 10/17/1909 at 62/9/1; acute nephritis; Edward Bickford and
    Melissa Thompson
Ansel R., d. 1/9/1913 at 0/5/23; natural causes; Albert R. Bickford and
    Florence V. Grant
Benjamin F., d. 12/12/1898 at 84; heart disease; b. NH; PH
Charlotte, d. 3/18/1889 at 62/6 in Newton, MA
Clara J., d. 4/4/1893 at 34; Bright's disease; b. Rochester; (Rochester;
    Tuftonboro)
Clemantina, d. 2/9/1891 at 82/0/9; widow; Daniel Randall (Great Falls) and
    ----- Hussey (Great Falls)
Edward T., d. 11/5/1933 at 66/0/15; angina pectoris

Eliza, d. 7/5/1887 at 83/7; widow; b. ME; Jonathan Cushing (Dover) and
   Hannah M. (ME)
Ella C., d. 2/7/1926 at 72/3/10; lobar pneumonia; Stephen H. Bickford and
   Abigail Chamberlain
Elmina P., d. 10/27/1908 at 79/1/24; cerebral paralysis; Daniel Canney
Emma J., d. 11/7/1913 at 62/6/29; ruptured appendix; William F.
   Pennington and Elizabeth Bradley
Emma M., d. 1/17/1929 at 55/8/21; carcinoma of rectum; George W.
   Milliner and Hannah M. Brooks
Eunice R., d. 9/25/1889 at 64/2/5 in Farmington
Fanny M., d. 1/1/1902 at –; stillborn
Francis M., d. 6/19/1926 at 67/8 in Boston, MA; endocarditis
Herbert L., d. 2/7/1897 at 52 in Boston, MA; heart disease; PH
Jackson C., d. 4/28/1908 at 64; nephritis
James W., d. 11/3/1888 at 0/0/20; b. Dover; Ansel B. Bickford (NH) and
   Mary Sprague (ME)
Jennie, d. 10/12/1937 at 88/2/22; cardiac insufficiency
John T., d. 2/27/1904 at 56/9/11 in Rollinsford; probably continued
   syncope; PH
Judith A., d. 11/18/1906 at 64/8/3 in So. Berwick, ME; PH
Kezia V., d. 1/19/1890 at 73/8/14; married; Samuel Nason
Louisa A., d. 1/18/1905 at 55/2/18; phthisis; PH
Marion E., d. 12/21/1934 at 46/4/1; cerebral hemorrhage
Mary J., d. 12/26/1896 at 75; paralysis; b. Durham; PH
Mary J., d. 12/1/1916 at 55/8/8; pneumonia; Sloan Sprague and Mary
   Greenough
Moses H., d. 6/25/1894 at 71; suicide with knife; buried in Austin Cem.
Olive A., d. 9/8/1919 at 67/6/30 in Boston, MA; paralysis from brain tumor
Stephen H., d. 8/4/1911 at 88/9/23 in Rochester; David Bickford and
   Elizabeth Jenness
Susan E., d. 9/28/1888 at –; widow; b. Dover; Moses Paul (Alfred, ME)
   and Susan Hodsdon
Susan J., d. 12/16/1901 at 24/0/4 in Effingham; PH
William H., d. 12/2/1913 at 58/11/9; chronic nephritis; William H. Bickford
   and Emeline -----

BICKINGHAM,
Charles, d. 6/11/1897 at 1; meningitis; b. Dover; SM

BICKLEY,
William H., d. 7/11/1894 at –; malnutrition; b. Dover; SM

BIEDERMAN,
child, d. 1/3/1907 at –; prolonged labor; August Biederman and Catherine
   Gailey

August, d. 11/11/1917 at 74/9/11 in Madbury; bronchitis
August W., d. 3/18/1918 at 43/9/21; toxemia of gangrene; August C.
   Biederman and Augusta Machel
Augusta H., d. 11/30/1929 at 85/9/26 in Worcester, MA; arterio sclerosis

BILBLAN,
Angeline, d. 1/17/1929 at 79/4/2; chronic myocarditis; Joseph Foster and
   Sophie Baker

BILLADON,
Mary C., d. 4/5/1896 at –; marasmus; b. Dover; SM

BILLINGS,
Charles W., d. 11/17/1922 at 64/3/6 in Dracut, MA; myocarditis
Lillicore T., d. 11/25/1912 at 61/3/10; uremia; Henry R. Frary and Mary A.
   Richardson
Lizzie A., d. 7/3/1905 at 57 in Cambridge, MA; obstructed gall bladder; PH
Marina W., d. 4/21/1929 at 61/1/3 in Laconia; cardiac insufficiency
Rosella M., d. 8/29/1921 at 54/11/18 in Billerica, MA; cerebral hemorrhage
Sarah E., d. 3/22/1896 at 68 in Concord; pul. oedema
Sarah P., d. 12/4/1916 at 72/4/4 in Boston, MA; pneumonia
Warren, d. 3/27/1887 at 60/5/25; stone cutter; married; b. Canton; Dudley
   Billings (Foxboro, MA) and Achsa (Foxboro, MA)
Warren T., d. 10/27/1933 at 65 in Concord; chronic alcoholism

BILLS,
William C., d. 5/7/1926 at 75/9/12; cancer of test. and cord

BILODEAU,
Beatrice, d. 2/1/1914 at 2/11; scalds; Paul Bilodeau and Vetaline Fortin
Napoleon, d. 1/15/1933 at 74/6/20; lobar pneumonia
Theodore, d. 10/23/1937 at 73/4/27; cerebr. hemorrhage

BINETTE,
child, d. 11/17/1919 at –; stillborn; Henry Binette and Minnie Simoneau
Joseph, d. 5/24/1912 at –; stillborn; Henri Binette and Minnie Simoneau
Marie, d. 4/30/1914 at –; stillborn; Henri Binette and Minnie Simoneau

BINGHAM,
Ann, d. 2/16/1929 at 76 in Rochester; senility; James Quinn and Susie
   Hamel
George A., d. 6/16/1930 at 77/2/13 in Rochester; cancer of throat; John
   Bingham and Ellen Kelley

Jennie, d. 12/27/1889 at 4; George E. Bingham (US) and ----- Quinn
   (England)
Joanna, d. 1/18/1888 at 59/9 in Salmon Falls; married; b. Ringabella Isl.;
   David Doiram (Ringabella I.) and Bridget Callahan (Bingabella I.)
John B., d. 12/2/1922 at 34/9/0 in Rochester; starvation

BINKS,
son, d. 9/29/1888 at 0/1; b. Dover; Benjamin Binks (England) and Sarah
   Holdsworth (England)
child, d. 1/10/1892 at –; asphyxia; b. Dover; (England; England)
Archibald H., d. 9/12/1914 at 24/11/12 in Springvale, ME; pulmonary
   tuberculosis
Benjamin, d. 10/19/1894 at 39; chronic bronchitis; b. England; PH
Mary Jane, d. 7/20/1921 at 35/8/16 in Springvale, ME; convulsions;
   Benjamin Binks and Sarah Holdsworth
Sarah, d. 3/10/1916 at 57/0/29 in Springvale, ME; Bright's disease; Joseph
   Holdsworth and Mary -----

BIRCHSTEAD,
Alonzo, d. 11/9/1935 at 60/11/5; heart disease

BIRMINGHAM,
Annie T., d. 3/29/1909 at 0/1/2; pneumonia; Patrick Birmingham and Delia
   Devining
Kate, d. 4/16/1900 at <1; stillborn; SM

BIRON,
Adolph, d. 8/15/1931 at 58; lobar pneumonia

BISHOP,
Addie C., d. 3/3/1909 at 70/4/24 in Brooklyn, NY; burns
Nellie M., d. 10/23/1931 at 81/0/3; cerebral hemorrhage
Rupert G., d. 3/21/1929 at 85/7/14; cerebral hemorrhage; Leander L.
   Bishop and Rebecca Burbridge

BISSET,
Robert, d. 5/13/1921 at 79; arterio sclerosis

BISSON,
Napoleon J., d. 5/15/1914 at 34/11; gen. miliary tuberculosis; Joseph
   Bisson and Sara Turmelle

BLACKBURN,
child, d. 6/1/1918 at –; stillborn; Thomas E. Blackburn and Bertha Gray

James, d. 12/8/1893 at 75; heart disease; b. England; (England; England)
Thomas, d. 10/11/1918 at 64/5/6; uraemia, etc.; James Blackburn

BLACKMAR,
Charles A., d. 2/16/1911 at 38 in Laconia; septicaemia

BLAIR,
child, d. 8/10/1894 at –; premature birth; b. Dover; buried in Dover
child, d. 4/27/1899 at –; stillborn; SM
Frank, d. 5/31/1892 at 38; Bright's disease; b. Canada; (Canada; Canada)
Helen, d. 4/17/1931 at 48; "see card"
Robert C., d. 5/1/1930 at 49/10/18; biliary calculi; John Blair and Martha
    Collins

BLAIS,
Albert, d. 10/6/1930 at 66/6; chr. endocarditis; Celestin Blais and Marie
    Chabot
Joseph, d. 5/24/1914 at –; stillborn; Arthur Blais and Marianne Gouin
Mary E., d. 7/28/1895 at 0; gastro enteritis; b. Dover; SM
Omer, d. 10/11/1936 at 63/7/9; cerebral hemorrhage

BLAISDELL,
child, d. 8/29/1917 at – in Somersworth; stillborn
child, d. 10/6/1930 at –; stillborn; George H. Blaisdell and Hazel Lewis
child, d. 12/4/1937 at –; asphyxia of labor
Cora W., d. 9/17/1912 at 52/6/10; cancer colon; Thomas L. Wilson and
    Octavia L. Carney
Edward, d. 9/16/1905 at 87/7/11; old age; buried in Somersworth
Eliza A., d. 3/13/1912 at 88/8/17; senility; Abigail Kenniston
Elizabeth, d. 9/2/1894 at 63; cancer; b. Lebanon, ME; PH
Elizabeth C., d. 4/15/1922 at 66/7/17; chronic appendicitis; Thomas Curtis
    and Elizabeth Ann Abbott
Ellman E., d. 12/28/1924 at 0/6/18; premature birth; Roy L. Blaisdell and
    Annie C. E. Smith
Elmer E., d. 5/8/1917 at 52/10/27; pulmonary oedema; Thomas Blaisdell
    and Mary J. Manson
Everett W., d. 6/5/1926 at 71/11/18; natural causes; Uriah Blaisdell and
    Rebecca Moore
Florence, d. 10/16/1914 at 26/5/5; acute nephritis; Charles Clark and Lena
    Stevens
Frank E., d. 12/5/1933 at 77 in Orlando, FL; chronic myocarditis
Fred, d. 9/23/1936 at 77/10/21; coronary thrombosis
Gertrude, d. 12/5/1889 at 8 in Durham
Hannah L., d. 1/23/1911 at 79/10/29; heart disease; Millett Shapleigh and
    Betsey Lord

Herbert G., d. 9/21/1914 at 47/4/4; pulmonary tuberculosis
Herbert H., d. 11/18/1897 at 43 in Rochester; accident; PH
Irving, d. 12/21/1904 at 36/4 in Manchester; laudanum poisoning; PH
Jacob H., d. 11/13/1889 at 56/4/14; carpenter; married; b. Lebanon, ME; Edward Blaisdell (Lebanon, ME) and Betsey Hanson (Rochester)
John E., d. 11/6/1896 at 67; Bright's disease; b. ME; PH
John L., d. 9/5/1911 at 1/0/23; diarrhea; R. C. Blaisdell and Mary Durnin
Mamie, d. 11/9/1930 at 55/0/23 in Rollinsford; intest. obstruction
Manfield, d. 4/19/1919 at 66; dilatation of heart; John E. Blaisdell and Elizabeth J. Shapleigh
Mary A., d. 3/18/1919 at 57/4/23; carcinoma of uterus; Edward H. Green and Maria Bennett
Mary H., d. 7/10/1902 at –; valvular heart disease; PH
Mary J. D., d. 9/11/1897 at 78; old age; b. Pittsfield; buried in Moultonboro
Maude Etta, d. 8/26/1893 at –; cholera infantum; b. Dover; (Dover; Chicopee, MA)
Muriel F., d. 7/11/1914 at 11/0/22; accidental; Harry F. Blaisdell and Jennie E. Fuller
Onslow S., d. 12/20/1930 at 61/8/17; nephritis, etc.; John A. Blaisdell and Elizabeth Shapleigh
Roderic B., d. 4/12/1929 at 28/4/14; suicide; Onslow S. Blaisdell and Jane Black
Rose I., d. 10/24/1932 at 65/1/6; coronary thrombosis
Sarah E., d. 3/25/1898 at 64 in Boston, MA; pneumonia; PH
Sarah T., d. 7/13/1915 at 91/2; paralytic shock; Samuel Tyler and Annie Willey
Sumner E., d. 10/18/1918 at 9/0/28; lobar pneumonia; John D. Blaisdell and Bertha Cote
Viola E., d. 1/21/1906 at 7/6/13 in Somersworth; burns; PH

BLAKE,
Anna F., d. 2/1/1931 at 82/9/14 in Worcester, MA; carcinomatosis
Clara Ida, d. 12/24/1922 at 48; pneumonia; William Rousseau and Sophie Brooks
David A., d. 3/26/1912 at 82; senility
George F., d. 10/2/1918 at 73/7/21; probably pneumonia; Samuel Blake and Abigail Babcock
Harry, d. 9/25/1932 at 73/6/8 in Haverhill, MA; arterio sclerosis
John, d. 9/7/1899 at 87; general paralysis; buried in Somersworth
Mary, d. 7/24/1930 at 89/8/23 in Newport; cardio renal
Susan, d. 12/18/1900 at 83; grip, pneumonia; buried in Somersworth
Thomas C., d. 1/29/1888 at 84/7; carpenter; widower; b. Ireland; Thomas Blake (Ireland) and Martha C. Lord (Ireland)

BLANCHARD,
Abbie L., d. 8/18/1906 at 82/10/1; fracture of hip; buried in Saco, ME
Gordon F., d. 8/27/1935 at 27/6/6; acute poliomyelitis
John H., d. 12/25/1916 at 75/1/23; chro. val. dis. of heart; Lowell
    Blanchard and Dianna -----
Laura H., d. 5/18/1915 at 64/11/7; pelvic carcinoma; Zina H. Hodgdon and
    Rinda B. Reed
Luretta F., d. 11/29/1898 at 50; catarrhal pneumonia; b. Dover; PH
Mary B., d. 7/29/1888 at 0/5/10 in Chelsea, MA; b. Dover; Joseph
    Blanchard (Canada) and Rachel Isabel (Canada)
Reginald S., d. 12/18/1906 at 3/5/4; cerebral lesion; PH
Susan E., d. 7/1/1913 at 65/9/17; ch. intestitial nephritis; Joseph Caswell
    and Mary A. Wilson

BLANCHET,
Elmire, d. 12/26/1898 at 17; oedema of lungs; b. Canada; SM
Fredeline, d. 8/11/1901 at 31/3/1; tuberculosis of lungs

BLANCHETT,
Alma Y., d. 5/14/1900 at <1; broncho-pneumonia

BLANCHETTE,
Eva, d. 9/3/1891 at 0/4/5; Frank Blanchette (Canada) and Flore Gouin
    (Canada)
Joseph, d. 11/22/1895 at 41; accident; b. Canada; SM

BLANT,
Rose E., d. 8/19/1907 at 0/8/10; cholera infantum; Victor Blant and Rose --

BLAZO,
Charles, d. 2/5/1912 at 35 in Denver, CO; nephritis
Elizabeth C., d. 12/3/1903 at 34; uraemia; SM
Ivan, d. 9/1/1921 at 48 in Pembroke; pulmonary tuberculosis; Ivan Blazo
    and Adeline Brown

BLETCHER,
Lizzie S., d. 3/4/1892 at 4; convulsions, cerebral; b. MA; (England;
    England)
Rena, d. 3/31/1899 at 6; bronchitis, laryngitis; PH

BLISS,
Blanche M., d. 11/25/1922 at 43/2/21; myocarditis; Frank C. Snow and
    Alma M. Varney
Sarah J., d. 4/29/1898 at 80; hepatitis; b. Milton; buried in Rehoboth, MA

BLIXT,
John, d. 6/1/1903 at –; premature birth; SM

BLOGURAS,
Kristesta, d. 4/18/1913 at 0/11/12; broncho pneumonia; Charles Bloguros (sic) and Dimannto Politz

BLOOD,
child, d. 5/28/1925 at –; asphyxia of labor; Theodore Blood and Hattie Swain
Elmer E., d. 9/22/1930 at 66/8/3 in York, ME; angina pectoris
Philip H., d. 6/19/1896 at 4; peritonitis; b. Dover; PH

BLOOMER,
Mary, d. 4/13/1906 at 62; apoplexy; SM

BLOUGOURA,
Geanoula K., d. 3/12/1921 at 0/8; fibrinous bronchitis; Kostos Blougoura and Theanando Polite

BLOUGOURAS,
Demetro, d. 8/22/1921 at 0/4/2; septic colitis; Gust Blougouras and Diamanto Poulatis

BLOUIN,
child, d. 12/15/1928 at –; stillborn; Alfred Blouin and Ilda Labonte
George, d. 12/31/1935 at 52/2/20 in Laconia; cerebral hemorrhage

BLUM,
Merton E., d. 1/15/1910 at 0/2/3 in Worcester, MA; malnutrition

BLYE,
Joseph S., d. 7/17/1892 at 51; suicide by shooting; (Dummerston, VT; Roxbury, MA)

BOARDMAN,
Theodore E., d. 11/25/1920 at 0/7/27 in York Beach, ME; bronchial pneumonia

BODGE,
Clarence W., d. 6/9/1910 at 55; Brights disease; Daniel W. Bodge and Sarah Smith
George E., d. 7/11/1910 at 67/6/10 in Madbury; valvular disease of heart
Henry F., d. 12/15/1899 at 51; cancer of stomach; PH

James A., d. 1/3/1910 at 67/7/18; chronic nephritis; Benjamin Bodge and
   Harriet C. Glidden
Sarah A., d. 12/7/1913 at 68; pneumonia

BOFORD,
Arthur, d. 10/2/1896 at –; marasmus; b. Dover; SM

BOGAN,
Charles, d. 7/29/1895 at 51; acute dysentery; b. Ireland; SM
Elizabeth, d. 6/4/1895 at 65; heart disease; b. Ireland; SM
Elizabeth, d. 8/15/1912 at 64 in Gloucester, MA; carcinoma uterus; Patrick
   Congley and Elizabeth Shanahan

BOGRAKOS,
George, d. 11/8/1918 at 0/5; convulsions; Anthony Bograkos and Caliope
   Coutralakos

BOHAN,
child, d. 1/14/1894 at –; asphyxia
Angelina, d. 2/15/1935 at 61/1/22; chronic myocarditis
Ellen, d. 7/1/1916 at 70/1; chronic nephritis; Timothy Hourahan and
   Catherine Sullivan
Frank, d. 1/24/1911 at 49/1/15; cancer of groin; John Bohan and Ellen
   Hourihan
John, d. 1/7/1911 at 77; pneumonia
Peter, d. 12/8/1935 at 77/7/6; hypertensive heart dis.

BOIS,
child, d. 6/23/1902 at –; stillborn
Albertha D., d. 9/27/1927 at 26/2/19; pulmonary tuberculosis; Ferdinand
   Dagenais and Louise Beaudreau
Claudia, d. 7/19/1921 at 39/4/5; embolism right lung; Alphonse Dube and
   Philomene Mitayer
Ferdinand, d. 12/15/1926 at 76/8/18; secondary anemia

BOISSONEAU,
Clarisse, d. 9/15/1905 at 15/9/17; abscess of brain

BOISVERT,
Alphonsine, d. 7/5/1892 at –; cholera infantum; b. Dover; (Canada;
   Canada)
Emile, d. 10/6/1918 at 29/4/9; acute lobar pneumonia; Samuel Boisvert
   and Arline Lemaire

George G., d. 10/27/1930 at 48; heart disease; Joseph Boisvert and Mary Dossier
Joseph E., d. 7/27/1932 at 73/6/5; cerebral hemorrhage

BOKATUK,
Allek, d. 6/14/1915 at 23; appendicitis; Kornilio Bokatuk and Polaszka -----

BOKER,
Curtis L., d. 2/27/1922 at 50; heart failure

BOLDUC,
Henri, d. 4/10/1931 at 42/6/16; fracture of skull

BOLO,
Charles F., d. 2/4/1907 at 72/11; paralysis; Rufus Bolo and Susan Young
Elizabeth H., d. 7/14/1915 at 78/11/24 in Whitman, MA; carcinoma of uterus
Emma, d. 8/1/1915 at 65 in Portland, ME; typhoid
Frederick E., d. 2/19/1907 at 37 in Cambridge, MA; acute laryngitis
George N., d. 5/23/1909 at 64 in Cambridge, MA; carcinoma of bowels
Hannah E., d. 6/11/1911 at 77/5/25; abdominal carcinoma; Elisha Abbott and Harriet Tate
Orrin T., d. 10/18/1915 at 63/4/8; fibroid myocarditis; Rufus Bolo and Susan Young
Susan, d. 3/23/1902 at 85/1/15; apoplexy; PH
Winnie, d. 5/19/1890 at 14/0/18; Amon Bolo and Sarah Mechan

BOLUS,
Louis, d. 11/6/1936 at 40/8/11*

BOND,
Florence M., d. 7/6/1933 at 63/11/6
Priscilla D., d. 2/21/1890 at 79/10; married; ----- Diman (NH) and Mercy Kenniston (NH)

BONNEAU,
Albert, d. 3/13/1932 at 19/5/25; influenza
Beatrice H., d. 9/10/1936 at 27/11/26; tox. of pregnancy
Eleanor, d. 5/2/1936 at 3 hrs.; prematurity
Geraldine T., d. 12/8/1937 at –; stillborn
Jacqueline, d. 5/2/1936 at –; prematurity
Mary, d. 8/21/1936 at –; prematurity
Robert J., d. 3/10/1927 at 0/4; malnutrition; Conrad J. Bonneau and Beatrice H. Brooks

BONNEY,
George C., d. 12/3/1911 at 61/0/24; cerebral hemorrhage; Roland B. Bonney and B. Jane Record

BONSER,
Douglass W., d. 3/14/1909 at 1/7/2 in Berwick, ME
Emma, d. 6/20/1903 at 67/9/26; abscess of liver; PH
Frederick, d. 9/21/1907 at 25/10/20; tuberculosis; Samuel Bonser and Emma Potter
Samuel, d. 3/8/1909 at 75/11/9 in Concord; cerebral hemorrhage
Samuel, d. 11/3/1913 at 49/3/9 in Lynn, MA; probably heart disease
Sarah E., d. 9/13/1889 at 20/9/23; mill girl; single; b. Dover; Samuel Bonser (England) and Emma Pottar (England)
Thomas, d. 7/30/1893 at 26; phthisis pulmonalis; b. Dover; (England; England)
William H., d. 7/9/1912 at 36/7/3; phthisis pulmonalis; Samuel Bonser and Emma Potter

BOODY,
Charles S., d. 8/22/1933 at 78/6/6; general carcinomatosis
Eunice G., d. 5/30/1929 at 76/2/23; carcinoma of stomach; Charles Moulton and Olive Ayers

BOOMER,
E. Frank, d. 10/30/1917 at 48/11/22; osteo sarcoma l. scapula; Ephraim Boomer and Annie L. Hevey
Ina G., d. 3/13/1936 at 66/4/8; cerebral hemorrhage

BOOS,
Lena, d. 8/18/1898 at 77; old age; b. Germany; PH

BOOTH,
Bella, d. 10/14/1925 at 95; arterio sclerosis
John, d. 1/26/1908 at 41; pneumonia
Lula M., d. 3/7/1929 at 56/8/1; carcinoma of uterus; George Gray
Maurice L., d. 11/7/1905 at 3/5/1; membraneous croup; PH
William A., d. 7/11/1934 at 73/3/20; intestinal obstruction

BOOTHBY,
Ardis, d. 9/27/1919 at 0/2/23; spina bifida ruptured sac; John L. Boothby and Susie Davis
John, d. 2/5/1905 at 57/11/2; ulcer of stomach; PH
John L., d. 7/19/1930 at 57/3/4; typhoid; Amasa Boothby and Annette Benson

BOOTHROYD,
child, d. 1/6/1901 at 1 hr.; premature birth

BORASH,
Rachael, d. 3/11/1910 at 0/7/28; capillary bronchitis; Maurice Borash and Etta Goldberg

BORAZAKES,
Arthur, d. 3/30/1916 at 0/1/14; pneumonia; George Borazakes and Mary Pappas

BORROUGHS,
Nancy B., d. 1/4/1888 at 63/1/18; married; b. Strafford; Samuel Clark (Strafford) and Esther Howard (Strafford)

BOSSE,
George, d. 6/16/1934 at 21 in S. Berwick, ME; railroad accident
Sympharosa, d. 5/18/1931 at 82/7/26; cerebral hemorrhage

BOSSIE,
Teressa, d. 6/16/1914 at 1/11/29 in Tamworth; shock; Paul Bossie and Rena Drew

BOSTON,
child, d. 4/24/1935 at –; stillborn
Almira S., d. 5/13/1901 at 21/8/24 in Barrington; consumption; PH
Esther E., d. 12/28/1908 at 34/0/10; phthisis; Henry Lee and Esther Thurston
Everett F., d. 2/24/1923 at 1; intestinal obstruction; Mark A. Boston and Mabel F. Hasty
Fannie R., d. 6/30/1914 at 81/0/2; hemorrhage from stomach
Gertrude E. M., d. 5/2/1904 at 0/0/14; convulsions; PH
Harry P., d. 10/3/1906 at 0/1/14; cholera infantum; PH
Joseph, d. 3/13/1929 at –; premature birth; Ernest Boston and Elsie Drowne
Lucy A., d. 8/10/1903 at 70/3/15; heart disease; buried in Shapleigh, ME
Nettie Blanche, d. 1/31/1922 at 40/10/23; cancer of uterus; William H. H. Foss and Fannie D. -----
Sarah E., d. 11/21/1896 at 62; heart disease; b. Springvale, ME; buried in Springvale, ME

BOSWORTH,
Charles M., d. 1/31/1910 at 59/5/6 in Berwick, ME; uraemia

Fanny H., d. 9/19/1887 at 42/2/29; married; b. Farmington; Ephraim
    Perkins (Rochester) and Susan Wentworth (Milton)
Mabel I., d. 12/11/1896 at 6; scarlatina; b. Dover; PH

BOUCHAINE,
Emily A. J., d. 12/9/1918 at 0/0/28; lobar pneumonia; Adelard Bouchaine
    and Mary Levesque

BOUCHARD,
child, d. 11/30/1915 at –; stillborn; Joseph Bouchard and Rachel LeBlanc
child, d. 5/23/1917 at –; miscarriage; Celestin Bouchard and Mary
    Champoux
child, d. 9/13/1917 at –; miscarriage; Joseph Bouchard and Rochelle L.
    Blane
Alice, d. 7/2/1907 at 0/1/14; marasmus; Celestin Bouchard and Mary
    Champux
Frank, d. 5/30/1904 at 4/1/18; meningitis
Henry, d. 9/22/1903 at 0/3/5; cholera infantum
Henry, d. 3/7/1912 at 0/0/22; athrepsia; Celestine Bouchard and Mary
    Champoux
Joseph, d. 8/28/1899 at 44; consumption; SM
Joseph, d. 7/1/1913 at 1 hr.; premature birth; Celestin Bouchard and Mary
    Champoux
Joseph, d. 2/19/1919 at 38/3/6; tuberculosis of lungs; Frank Bouchard and
    ----- Cote
Lucien J., d. 7/25/1911 at 1/4/9; pneumonia; Celestin Bouchard and Mary
    Champoux
Mary A., d. 4/5/1907 at 0/0/17; athrepsia; Octave Bouchard and Emilia
    Martel
Pierre A., d. 10/29/1922 at 45; parametric abscess; Antoine Bouchard and
    Marie Pelletier
Robert, d. 8/21/1909 at 0/6/19; cholera infantum; Joseph Bouchard and
    Racheal Leblanc

BOUCHER,
Alfred, d. 7/25/1921 at 28/2/10 in Concord; accidental drowning; Henry
    Boucher and Melvina Devonier
Antoinette, d. 1/31/1929 at 42/0/11; cerebral meningitis; Theodore
    Tanguay and Mary Fredette
Bertha, d. 10/17/1918 at 28/1/6; broncho pneumonia; Peter Legace and
    Albina Bouchard
Elsie M., d. 12/13/1937 at 41/9/29 in Portland, ME; heart failure
Henry, d. 6/14/1923 at –; asphyxia of labor; Arthur Boucher and Elcic
    Duford

Raymond, d. 9/27/1920 at 2/11/25 in Rochester; Arthur Boucher and Beula Legace

BOUCHOIT,
Pauline, d. 10/3/1887 at 2/8; b. Canada; Frank Bouchoit (Canada) and Almira Cote (Canada)

BOUDREAU,
Katherine M., d. 7/26/1916 at 10/1/17 in Lawrence, MA; valv. disease of heart

BOUFFARD,
Joseph G., d. 10/26/1928 at 0/0/13; premature birth; Joseph G. Bouffard and Josephine Demers
Xavier, d. 8/8/1936 at 43/10/4 in Rochester; per. gastric ulcer

BOUFFORD,
Louis E., d. 10/6/1918 at 0/9; pneumonia; George Boufford and Josephine Demers

BOUGOUIN,
Louis L., d. 11/28/1916 at 0/4/23; infantile atrophy; Lewis P. Bougouin and Mabel A. Gillan

BOULANGER,
child, d. 11/26/1926 at –; miscarriage; William Boulanger and Victoria Cote
Joe, d. 1/18/1937 at 0/2/7; entero-colitis
Marie E., d. 10/10/1918 at 27/0/2; broncho pneumonia; Paul Labonte and Adeline Labonte

BOULIER,
Mary J., d. 7/31/1888 at 0/2/14; b. Dover; William Boulier (Canada) and Silvia Bilayer (Canada)

BOULTER,
Amaziah H., d. 1/23/1901 at 82/11/17; heart disease; buried in Unity, ME
Carrie H., d. 6/13/1936 at 76/5/2*; b. Salmon Falls (see following entry)
Carrie Hayes, d. 6/13/1936 at 76/5/2 in Portsmouth; cerebral hemorrhage (see preceding entry)

BOUPREY,
George, d. 3/20/1907 at 52 in No. Berwick, ME; intestinal obstruction

BOURDEAU,
Marc, d. 12/13/1916 at 75/7; mitral insufficiency; Pierre Bourdeau and Angelique Leisor

BOURGOIN,
Celia M., d. 10/4/1920 at 0/0/22 in Durham; infantile jaundice
Joseph Louis, d. 8/2/1899 at –; diarrhoea infantile; SM

BOURKE,
William J., d. 10/9/1904 at 1/10 in Lowell, MA; cholera infantum; SM

BOURQUE,
Edward R., d. 11/10/1929 at 4/2/11; Vincent's angina; Arthur Bourque and Yvonne Baron
Joseph N., d. 5/18/1910 at 21/10/13; pulmonary tuberculosis; Napoleon Bourque and Emily Roberge
Napoleon J., d. 3/19/1922 at 64/3/24; apoplexy; Uldaric Bourque and Henrietta Richard

BOUTIETTE,
Octave, d. 7/22/1887 at 45; shoemaker; married; b. Canada; Julian Boutiette (Canada)

BOUTIN,
Madeline R., d. 12/27/1928 at 25/9/6; pulm. tuberculosis; Gilbert Boutin and Hannah Murray
Marion, d. 2/21/1934 at 37 in Pembroke; pulmonary tuberculosis

BOUTWELL,
child, d. 2/20/1932 at –; abrupt placenta

BOUVIA,
Ray S., d. 9/23/1918 at 30/11/19; probably influenza

BOUZES,
Nicholas, d. 1/1/1920 at 0/7/1; broncho pneumonia; James Bouzes and Stavroula -----

BOVILLE,
Annie N., d. 8/21/1900 at 29; phthisis pulmonalis; PH

BOWDOIN,
Daniel, d. 3/28/1889 at 81/6 in W. Warren, MA
Eliza, d. 3/30/1889 at 77 in W. Warren, MA

Eliza B., d. 3/1/1899 at 48 in Haverhill, MA; heart disease and pul. apoplexy; PH

BOWEN,
child, d. 1/30/1934 at –; prematurity
child, d. 1/30/1934 at –; prematurity
Alfred W., d. 4/5/1927 at 48/10/7 in Concord; broncho pneumonia; William Bowen and Eliza Smith
Bridget, d. 5/22/1928 at 87; chronic nephritis; Patrick Ryan and Mary Quinn
Jeremiah, d. 6/28/1934 at 49/5; cancer of rt. cheek

BOWERS,
George, d. 7/17/1896 at 66; chronic bronchitis; b. Germany; PH
Hannah, d. 10/11/1919 at 95/6/23; sarcoma of left hand; Robert Willey and Hannah Temple
John, d. 3/15/1909 at 65 in Somerville, MA; cerebral hemorrhage
Katherine, d. 3/19/1907 at 83; chronic endocarditis; Thomas Murray and Katherine -----
Margaret, d. 3/1/1888 at 54 in Chelsea, MA
Maurice L., d. 7/20/1904 at 0/3/12; marasmus; buried in Rollinsford

BOWES,
George A., d. 4/23/1910 at 53/9/16 in Malden, MA; surgical shock
George E., d. 5/8/1893 at 4

BOWLEN,
Fannie B. P., d. 7/12/1896 at 40; septicaemia; b. Dover; PH

BOWLES,
Erwin, d. 12/28/1925 at 77/4/26; strangulated ing. hernia; Alpheus Bowles and ----- Howe
Louis C., d. 7/6/1935 at 79/4/5; myocarditis

BOYD,
son, d. 5/29/1888 at –; b. Dover; Henry Boyd (Ireland) and Rosanna Brennan (Ireland)
child, d. 12/30/1895 at 0; stillborn; b. Dover; SM
Annie, d. 5/31/1928 at 75; chronic myocarditis; John Murphy
Arthur, d. 4/25/1921 at 34/0/18 in San Diego, CA; fracture base of skull
Emily, d. 2/7/1904 at 0/1/10; capillary bronchitis; PH
Esther M., d. 6/26/1925 at 29; brain abscess; James Riley and Catherine Asleford

Henry, d. 10/9/1918 at 60; chronic endocarditis; John Boyd and Ann Tamany
John, d. 10/15/1935 at 64; chronic myocarditis
John W. McK., d. 2/28/1903 at 1/5/21; pneumonia; PH
Joshua, d. 3/3/1904 at 45; cirrhosis of liver; buried in Ellsworth, ME

BOYDEN,
Frank J., d. 11/5/1930 at 71/3/5; cerebral hemorrhage; George W. Boyden and Sophia Davis
Rose S., d. 11/30/1932 at 75/2/5; carcinoma of uterus
Sophia R., d. 11/23/1915 at 84/8/10; bronchial pneumonia; Jacob Davis and Lois Kelley

BOYLE,
child, d. 6/25/1895 at 0; stillborn; b. Dover
child, d. 10/1/1900 at –; stillborn; SM
Catherine, d. 11/30/1912 at 82; broncho pneumonia; ----- McLaughlin
Daniel, d. 5/18/1931 at 61/10/2; natural causes
Ellen, d. 8/2/1892 at –; convulsions; b. Dover; (Scotland; Dover)
Hugh, d. 7/24/1901 at 30/11/14; consumption; SM
Mary Ellen, d. 10/2/1900 at 35; heart failure; SM
Patrick J., d. 3/5/1933 at 67/11/26; chronic myocarditis

BRACEWELL,
Mary A., d. 3/7/1887 at 19 in N. Adams, MA

BRACKETT,
child, d. 8/13/1916 at –; premature; John Brackett and Annie -----
Basil, d. 2/14/1887 at 0/2/2; b. Goffstown; Ezra G. Brackett (Acton, ME) and Cora J. Foot (Goffstown)
Elizabeth Q., d. 1/5/1924 at 62/9/20; chronic myocarditis; William Quinlan and Mary Brackett
Emily J., d. 8/6/1917 at 78/11/29; chronic nephritis; Samuel Goodwin and Pauline Cooper
Emma, d. 10/14/1914 at 52/8/19; cancer of breast; James Newton and Ann Silcock
Frank, d. 5/22/1933 at 74/0/10; chronic nephritis
Helen C., d. 9/23/1896 at 19; intra-pelvic inflammation; b. Dover; buried in Acton, ME
John H., d. 4/2/1915 at 77/10/20; fatty degen. of heart; Nathan Brackett and Mary Hurd
Leonie, d. 2/23/1890 at 0/7/19; Frank Brackett (NH) and Elizabeth Quinlan (NH)
Luther J., d. 2/1/1903 at 74/2/4; paralysis and gangrene; buried in Acton, ME

Rachael, d. 2/21/1914 at 35/5/2; heart failure; Thomas Boyce and Mary ---

BRACY,
Lydia K., d. 2/27/1923 at 77/9/14; cerebral hemorrhage; Oliver K. Hayes and Eliza H. Ham

BRADBURY,
Annie S., d. 11/17/1893 at 34; marasmus; b. Dover; (Dover; Durham)
Ellen A., d. 11/11/1931 at 77 in Framingham, MA; myocarditis
Frederick A., d. 2/2/1931 at 78 in Framingham, MA; cerebral hemorrhage
William H., d. 8/4/1910 at 4/6/18; ileo-colitis; Fred Bradbury and Harriet Maud

BRADEEN,
Austin, d. 11/4/1925 at 64/1/2; cancer of rectum
Mary J., d. 6/30/1936 at 63/10/13; fracture, skull

BRADFORD,
Hannah, d. 12/13/1892 at 67; heart disease; b. Canaan; (Canaan; Cohasset)
John M., d. 12/2/1891 at 68/2/10; married; Daniel Bradford (Salem) and Abigail Emerson
John W., d. 2/24/1888 at 24/11/14; cloth inspector; married; b. Dover; John Bradford (Salem) and Hannah Gould (Canaan)
Maria, d. 12/16/1892 at 29; consumption; b. Madbury; (England; England)

BRADLEY,
Alice Mary, d. 9/10/1913 at 19/9/20; prel. tuberculosis; James Bradley and Catherine Cox
Annette W., d. 11/14/1920 at 89/8/26; fracture of right hip; Jonathan P. Baker and Clementine R. Gordon
Annie, d. 2/7/1916 at 72/2; chron. int. nephritis; Michael Brady and Bridget Carr
Clementine, d. 2/28/1932 at 70/1/14; arterio sclerosis
Daniel F., d. 7/2/1921 at 62/6/2; cancer of larynx; Daniel Bradley and Johanna Bingham
Ellen, d. 1/17/1916 at –; burned
Emma F., d. 7/22/1906 at 30/10/24; pulmonary tuberculosis; buried in Wells Beach, ME
Harry F., d. 10/13/1904 at 19/9/1 in Rutland, MA; railroad accident; PH
John J., d. 4/18/1926 at 66/1/21; chronic myocarditis; Maurice Bradley and Ellen Connor
Jonathan, d. 4/13/1898 at 77 in Boston, MA; uraemia; PH
Martha S., d. 12/17/1937 at 86/9/14; hemorrhage
Mary S., d. 4/4/1897 at 30; pneumonia; b. MA; buried in Danville

William, d. 2/5/1908 at 72; acute nephritis
William H., d. 5/5/1929 at 62; acute endocarditis
Winfield Scott, d. 4/10/1928 at 80/0/18; chronic endocarditis; Benjamin Bradley

BRADY,
Catherine, d. 12/17/1903 at 56/2/1; heart disease
Mary, d. 1/7/1892 at 61; gastritis; b. Ireland; (Ireland; Ireland)

BRAGDON,
Georgia A., d. 11/1/1890 at 20/5/25; married; Daniel P. Seaver (Kingston) and Dolly Seaver (Kingston)
Eliza A., d. 3/8/1910 at 79/10/8; senility; William Sanborn and Sally Crockett
John, d. 6/26/1889 at 82; single
John H., d. 1/5/1934 at 64/1/7 in Plaistow; heart disease
Mildred G., d. 7/24/1911 at 0/2/2; cholera infantum; William H. Bragdon and Cora E. Welch

BRAGINSKY,
William, d. 7/–/1891 at 0/7/15; William Braginsky (Russia) and Martha Perham (Labrador)

BRANCH,
Sophia, d. 4/11/1932 at 86/4/3 in Milford, MA; arterio sclerosis

BRANDEIS,
Karl E., d. 7/16/1908 at 1/8/17 in Seymour, CT; entero colitis

BRANDOIN,
child, d. 2/24/1913 at 0/0/2; premature birth; Ernest Brandoin and Alice Goodreau

BRAWN,
Joseph, d. 2/12/1907 at 84; senility

BREED,
Emma L., d. 6/16/1900 at 63 in Brookfield, MA; heart failure; PH
Stephen, d. 4/11/1913 at 81/5/20 in Brookfield, MA; cerebral apoplexy

BREEN,
Arthur, d. 4/29/1898 at 30; capillary bronchitis; b. Ireland; SM
Frank, d. 4/13/1934 at 62/9/13; chronic myocarditis
Margaret V., d. 3/9/1896 at –; acute bronchitis; b. Dover; SM

Mary, d. 6/17/1895 at 10; accidental drowning; b. Ireland; SM
Michael, d. 4/19/1902 at 48; pulmonary phthisis; SM
Thomas J., d. 3/5/1896 at –; malnutrition; b. Dover; SM

BRENNAN,
son, d. 6/14/1887 at –; b. Dover; Patrick Brennan (Ireland) and Mary
  Murray (Ireland)
son, d. 8/18/1888 at –; b. Dover; Sarah Brennan
daughter, d. 8/25/1888 at 0/0/6; b. Dover; Sarah Brennan
Alice, d. 7/2/1923 at 52; ac. intest. obstruction; John McCooey and Rose
  McShane
Andrew, d. 4/5/1918 at 49/8/21; chronic appendicitis; Patrick Brennan and
  Margaret Rooney
Ann, d. 1/20/1903 at 57/0/26; cardiac hypertrophy; SM
Bernard, d. 12/30/1913 at 38; tuberculosis
Bridget, d. 3/9/1905 at 21; tuberculosis; SM
Catherine, d. 1/16/1909 at 70; burned; Michael Farrell
Christopher, d. 7/15/1890 at 50 in Boston, MA
Cora M., d. 8/15/1907 at 0/4/3; indigestion; Edward Brennan and Ethel M.
  Ross
Elizabeth, d. 4/8/1900 at 63; catarrhal pneumonia; SM
Elizabeth, d. 6/13/1922 at 56 in Haverhill, MA; myocardial degeneration
Elizabeth M., d. 11/25/1933 at 63/5/11 in Lebanon; arteriosclerosis
Frank, d. 6/22/1901 at 31; heart disease
Frank P., d. 5/3/1901 at 23/3/9 in Rochester; heart failure; PH
James, d. 2/22/1903 at 55; chronic nephritis; buried in Rollinsford
James, d. 3/27/1926 at 72; myocarditis
James, d. 1/17/1935 at 73; carcinoma of axilla
James H., d. 5/19/1927 at 45; cerebral hemorrhage; James Brennan and
  Mary Duffy
John Joseph, d. 1/25/1912 at 16/9; pulmonary tuberculosis; Bernard
  Brennan and Mary Cavano
Kate, d. 10/17/1904 at 65 in Concord; mitral insufficiency
Leo, d. 9/6/1899 at 1; cholera infantum; SM
Margaret, d. 1/31/1929 at –; broncho pneumonia; Anthony Rooney and
  Kate Morgan
Mary, d. 12/13/1904 at 60; cancer
Mary, d. 6/9/1922 at 75 in Boston, MA; chronic myocarditis
Mary, d. 8/29/1925 at 62; acute myocarditis; Terrence McGonnell and
  Annie McShane
Mary E., d. 2/14/1892 at 20; peritonitis; b. Dover; (Ireland; Ireland)
Mary E., d. 2/8/1928 at –; pernicious anemia; James Brennan and Ellen
  McArdle
Mary E., d. 9/27/1931 at 64/3/10; carcinoma larynx
Michael, d. 1/30/1906 at –; chronic nephritis; SM

Michael, d. 10/7/1914 at 76/2/6; cardio vascular febrosis; James Brennan
   and Rose -----
Patrick, d. 6/2/1898 at 0; bronchitis; b. Dover; SM
Patrick, d. 6/4/1898 at 33; phthisis; b. Ireland; SM
Patrick, d. 9/12/1901 at 4; brain fever
Patrick, d. 1/21/1912 at 65; paresis; Cornelius Brennan and Sarah Markey
Philip, d. 2/15/1916 at 64; strangulated hernia
Rose A., d. 1/21/1897 at –; scarlet fever; b. Dover; SM
Teresa M., d. 1/7/1894 at 16; peritonitis; b. Ireland; SM
Thomas, d. 5/11/1908 at 37/9; ascites; J. Brennan and Catherine Smith
Thomas, d. 6/30/1932 at –; chronic myocarditis
Thomas B., d. 11/20/1901 at 0/3; cholera infantum; SM

BRENT,
James C., d. 12/2/1915 at 24/6/20; asphyxiated - illuminating gas

BRETON,
Joseph, d. 6/3/1897 at 22; typhoid fever; b. Canada; SM

BRETTON,
Bertha E., d. 11/11/1922 at 42/8/17; chronic endocarditis; Alfred Dupras
   and Emma E. Quimby

BREWETT,
Ernest L., d. 11/7/1896 at 2; scarlet fever; b. Dover; PH

BREWITT,
Della, d. 10/19/1897 at 28; phthisis; b. NS; PH

BREWSTER,
Anna A., d. 3/14/1928 at 74 in Orlando, FL; hypertention
Charles E., d. 4/7/1894 at 39 in So. Newmarket; struck by locomotive; b.
   Dover; buried in Wakefield
Comfort A., d. 6/24/1894 at 80; heart disease; b. Strafford; PH
Eli V., d. 3/18/1903 at 78/11/24; disease of prostate gland; PH
Freelove J., d. 1/27/1908 at 82/9/15; senile decay; Joseph Hayes and
   Sarah Chesley
Harold W., d. 12/30/1899 at 0 in Somersworth; pneumonia; PH
Helen W., d. 2/12/1893 at 8; peritonitis; b. Dover; (Dover; Wakefield)
J. Smith, d. 5/13/1919 at 65/10/3; cardiac hypertrophy; Charles Brewster
   and Lydia A. Chamberlain
Jonathan D., d. 1/7/1890 at 87/9/12; widower; William Horn (Durham) and
   Susan Worth (VT)
Lucy A., d. 9/21/1912 at 73/6/29 in Strafford; arterio sclerosis

Lydia A., d. 10/27/1919 at 61/8/20; neoplasm - thyroid
Mary A., d. 10/25/1887 at 69/0/16; widow; b. Dover; Jeremiah Libbey
    (Wolfeboro) and Esther Smith (Alton)
Mary A., d. 10/21/1919 at 82/11/12; abdominal cancer; John Stevens and
    Hannah Gilman
Sarah, d. 3/21/1888 at 49; mill operative; widow; b. Ireland; Owen Curry
    (Ireland) and Ellen Cassily (Ireland)

BRIDE,
Clara B., d. 5/19/1903 at 24/2/12; phthisis; PH
George H., d. 5/19/1926 at 56/2/9 in Portland, ME; organic heart disease
Sarah E., d. 10/5/1906 at 47/4/28; cancer of uterus; PH

BRIDGE,
Coradon S., d. 11/21/1914 at 73/7; acute indigestion; Beziel Bridge and ---
    --- Lamson

BRIDGES,
Etta B., d. 10/20/1926 at 83/8/18 in Liberty, ME; broncho pneumonia;
    Patrick Mallen and Alice McTearney
Hannah F., d. 4/20/1925 at 81 in St. Petersburg, FL; heart failure

BRIERE,
Andrew J., d. 6/25/1937 at 41/4/11 in Hooksett; heart disease
Robert J., d. 11/7/1924 at 0/8/4; infectious diarrhea; Andrew J. Brien (sic)
    and Sarah Fox

BRIERLEY,
Alice J., d. 1/22/1895 at –; marasmus; b. Dover; PH
Benjamin, d. 11/6/1917 at 69/3/17 in Stratham; carcinoma of stomach
George Eric, d. 5/7/1892 at –; gastric and intestinal catarrh; b. Dover;
    (Manchester, England; Manchester; England)
Robert, d. 7/7/1889 at 0/2/2; b. Dover; Benjamin Brierley (England) and
    Harriet Tarbuck (England)

BRIERLY,
Clifton A., d. 8/3/1897 at 0; diarrhea; b. Dover; buried in So. Berwick, ME

BRIGGS,
Alice M., d. 12/23/1902 at 42/10/29; phthisis; PH
James, d. 5/10/1923 at 71/9/10; Brights disease; Jonas Briggs and Ann ---
Lydia F., d. 5/2/1889 at 54/11/18 in Grafton; housewife; b. VT; Sewell
    Miles (VT)

BRIGHAM,
E. T., d. 11/5/1895 at 45; disease of heart; b. England; buried in Lawrence, MA
Emma J., d. 7/21/1934 at 83/1/21; angina pectoris
Frank E., d. 8/28/1925 at 76/11/7; pyelonephritis; H. H. Brigham
Rebecca C., d. 11/9/1903 at 76/5/8; pneumonia; PH

BRINE,
Sarah, d. 1/23/1889 at --

BRISARD,
Almandiria, d. 8/6/1899 at --; diarrhea infantile; SM

BRISSETTE,
Toussaint, d. 11/26/1887 at 50/10/11; laborer; married; b. Canada; John Brissette (Canada) and Josette (Canada)

BROADBENT,
Bertha, d. 9/12/1916 at 60; cerebral hemorrhage; Stephen Wren and Diana Rand
Helen P., d. 8/8/1897 at 0; gastro enteritis; b. Dover; PH
Mark, d. 7/21/1889 at 1/8/0; b. Dover; Mark Broadbent (Biddeford, ME) and Sarah Casey (Dover)
William, d. 1/8/1898 at 51 in Concord; brain disease; PH

BROCHU,
Blanche, d. 8/5/1893 at --; cholera infantum; b. Dover; (Canada; Canada)
Fannie W., d. 10/13/1916 at 68/6; apoplexy; John Brochu and Nancy Wallace
Leon L., d. 4/24/1936 at 45/2/5; lobar pneumonia
Leonel, d. 7/12/1928 at 2/9; acute lobar pneum.; Leonard Brochu and Rose Larochelle
Marie R. P., d. 7/15/1926 at 1/9/28; acute meningitis; Leon Brochu and Anna Larochelle

BROCK,
Annie, d. 6/30/1930 at 59/8/15; typhoid fever; Charles A. Dyer and Martha Drew
Edna E., d. 2/4/1924 at 81/3/26 in Lynn, MA; arterio sclerosis
Edwin H., d. 12/4/1904 at 62/4/26 in Lynn, MA; apoplexy; PH
Josiah B., d. 5/26/1893 at 45; pneumonia
Rose, d. 1/18/1890 at 40 in Rollinsford; widow; Samuel Leighton (Danville, VT) and Cynthia Heath (Danville, VT)
William H. H., d. 7/24/1923 at 66/2/27; coronary thrombosis

BRONSON,
Oscar J., d. 11/24/1927 at 85/5/22; chronic endocarditis

BROOKS,
Bickford G., d. 3/16/1908 at 0/7/16; broncho-pneumonia; Guy Brooks and Mary Malone
Francis, d. 3/11/1910 at 78/3/21; inflammation of brain; William Brooks and Miriam Cressey
Frank P., d. 11/2/1912 at –; tuberculosis
Guy Melvin, d. 12/25/1933 at 46/4/20; pulmonary tuberculosis
Harold, d. 2/25/1896 at –; spina bifida; b. Dover; buried in Newington
Ida May, d. 12/1/1888 at 29/7; married; b. Dover; Benjamin Hussey (Dover) and Emily Battles (Sanford, ME)
Ina Gertrude, d. 10/3/1911 at 42/8/24; pulmonary tuberculosis; Alpheus Littlefield and Atsy L. Pierce
Irena C., d. 8/23/1911 at 85/6/8; cancer of bowels; Winthrop Hayes and Hannah Clough
Isaac, d. 11/10/1900 at 81; old age; PH
John, d. 3/25/1893 at 70; intestinal catarrh; b. New Durham; (Buxton, ME; New Durham)
Julia, d. 8/15/1900 at 77; apoplexy; PH
Mary L., d. 11/2/1923 at 83/2/2; pneumonia; John Hanscom and Eunice Estes
Sarah, d. 4/17/1894 at 68; congestion of lungs; PH
Thomas, d. 5/9/1900 at 1; apoplexy; buried in Mystic, CT
Tyler, d. 5/17/1924 at 0/0/2; atelectasis; Guy Brooks and Mary Malone
William, d. 10/29/1917 at 92; arterio sclerosis

BROPHY,
George William, d. 8/19/1901 at 0/4/9; cholera infantum; PH
Georgia Etta, d. 6/29/1901 at 1/9/16; convulsions; PH
Thomas, d. 4/3/1893 at 3; burned by fire; b. Salmon Falls; (England; Salmon Falls)

BROSNAHAN,
Margaret, d. 9/10/1918 at 77; diabetes mellitus; John Hennessy and Mary Splaine

BROWN,
child, d. 12/9/1895 at 0; stillborn; b. Dover; PH
child, d. 10/9/1918 at –; stillborn; Ida Brown
Abigail F., d. 5/26/1915 at 58/6/1; cancer of ileum; Nathaniel Horn
Addie S., d. 4/15/1934 at 65/8/19; cerebral degeneration
Alexander, d. 1/8/1903 at 62; apoplexy; PH

Alphonso M., d. 10/17/1906 at 34/9/24 in Newburyport, MA; myocarditis; PH
Amelia A., d. 9/12/1920 at 74; articular rheumatism; Joseph Lewis and Sophronia A. Lear
Andrew H., d. 5/19/1891 at 59/11/12 in Strafford
Annie, d. 7/1/1900 at 52; apoplexy
Annie G., d. 4/20/1935 at 65/9/8; bronchial pneumonia
Arthur R., d. 4/18/1929 at 46/1/8 in Andover, MA; chronic nephritis
Arthur W., d. 7/17/1934 at 45/1/2; suicide by gas
Belmont W., d. 4/3/1927 at 23 in Gatun, Canal Zone; drowned
Betsey E. W., d. 1/18/1908 at 90/6/11; cerebral hemorrhage; Eliphalet Willey and Sally S. Henderson
Catherine S., d. 9/15/1909 at 78/1/9; senile dementia; Remembrance Smith and Sarah A. Bunker
Catherine V. H., d. 1/6/1926 at 55/1/22; aneurysm of aorta; Henry Van Horenburg and Mary E. Pease
Charles, d. 6/6/1907 at –; drowned; a/k/a Charles Sias
Charles Allen, d. 7/15/1901 at 2/6/15; meningitis; PH
Charles E., d. 8/21/1931 at 53/3/5; chronic endocarditis
Charles H., d. 10/16/1920 at 80/9/12; arterio sclerosis
Charles H., d. 3/11/1922 at 75/7 in Medford, MA; organic heart disease
Charles J., d. 3/20/1895 at 68; diabetes mellitus; b. Boston, MA; PH
Charles M., d. 6/1/1936 at 68/5/13 in Portsmouth; ch. cardio-renal dis.
Charles O., d. 1/5/1912 at 65; heart disease
Clara A., d. 1/24/1907 at 72/4/19; valvular heart disease; John Hall and Nancy Whitehouse
Clara M., d. 5/15/1928 at 72/7/3; natural causes; Timothy C. Gordon
Clarinder A., d. 11/12/1919 at 65/4; valvular heart disease; Joseph B. Wakeham and Polly West
Edward E., d. 10/2/1888 at 44/0/11; laborer; married; b. Canada; Octavius Brown (Canada) and Argie Amond (Canada)
Edward E., d. 1/11/1919 at 60 in Boston, MA; heart disease
Eleanor H., d. 12/24/1898 at 76; pneumonia; b. NH; PH
Elisha R., d. 12/25/1922 at 75/8/28; cerebral hemorrhage; Colville D. Brown and Mary E. Rhodes
Eliza M., d. 8/23/1912 at 37/6/6 in Bristol; pulmonary tuberculosis
Elizabeth, d. 3/12/1889 at 74; housewife; married; b. NH
Elizabeth, d. 12/21/1932 at 95/8/5 in Rochester; acute bronchitis
Elizabeth S., d. 1/10/1914 at 0/0/11; premature birth; Charles H. Brown and Susan L. Sterling
Ella B., d. 8/17/1928 at 76/3/16; chronic endocarditis; Dominicus Warren and Matilda McLucas
Ella M., d. 4/29/1898 at 37; penumonia; b. Dover; PH
Ellen, d. 12/25/1933 at 84; broncho pneumonia
Ellen A., d. 12/7/1898 at 65; paralysis; b. Union, ME; PH

Elmer A., d. 7/21/1925 at 54/6/4 in Somerville, MA; pernicious anemia
Emily, d. 8/14/1908 at 11/10; severe burns; Theodore Brown and Marie Pedade
Emma, d. 11/20/1891 at 22/5/10; widow; John H. Hanscom (Great Falls) and Mary E. Whittier (Tamworth)
Emma M., d. 7/30/1897 at 46; phthisis pulmonalis; b. Barrington; buried in Barrington
Fanny H., d. 9/1/1901 at 73/8; inanition; buried in Waterford, ME
Finetta C., d. 3/13/1925 at 82/7/3; lobar pneumonia; George Meserve and Climena Chesley
Flora, d. 11/18/1921 at 52; carcinoma of uteus; Philip Douchette and ----- Myocarditi
Frances E., d. 11/10/1918 at 68/8/27; acute cardiac dilation; Alphonso Bickford and Mary J. Smith
Frank E., d. 11/20/1931 at 73/9/8; angina pectoris
Fred A., d. 6/4/1896 at 34; heart clot; b. Dover; PH
Fred D., d. 3/16/1890 at 33/8/21; married; William R. Brown (Portsmouth) and Martha Allen (Barrington)
Frederick E., d. 1/1/1932 at 70/6/15; carcinoma of stomach
Freeman L., d. 9/7/1924 at 73 in Bristol; valvular heart disease
George, d. 3/28/1920 at 70/6/5; chronic nephritis; Isaac Brown and Susan E. Dame
George Austin, d. 4/26/1935 at – in N. Providence, RI; bronchial pneumonia
George W., d. 11/9/1917 at 90/1/29; acute indigestion; Robert Brown and Esther Jenness
Jacob F., d. 5/4/1921 at 99/6/15; senility; John Brown and Sally Goodwin
Jacob K., d. 7/20/1917 at 84/0/12; senility; James W. Brown and Abigail Hanson
James O., d. 4/8/1916 at 57/3/15; angina pectoris; James E. Brown and Clara A. Hall
John, d. 1/6/1903 at 35; mitral disease of heart
John, d. 4/8/1909 at 84/6/29; erysipelas; John Brown and Sarah Hanson
John E., d. 9/28/1901 at 21/10/1 in Boston, MA; pneumonia; PH
John E., d. 4/20/1905 at 68/8/18; chronic nephritis; PH
John F., d. 3/1/1896 at 76 in Brookfield; heart disease
John F., d. 12/14/1928 at 76 in Brentwood
John Frank, d. 8/1/1887 at 53/4/11; farmer; married; b. Moultonboro
John M., d. 12/23/1923 at 77/4/28 in Ossipee; valv. heart disease
Joseph, d. 2/27/1908 at 21; cancer of gall bladder; Theodore Brown
Josephine A., d. 2/25/1891 at 51/8/23 in Concord; single; William B. Brown (Germany) and Matilda Reed (Medford, MA)
Leola, d. 12/26/1887 at 0/0/4; b. Dover; William M. Brown (Northfield, VT) and Rose E. Hanscom (Rollinsford)
Leon B., d. 2/20/1897 at 1; convulsions; b. Dover; PH

Lester G., d. 5/1/1899 at –; pneumonia; PH
Lizzie J., d. 4/4/1906 at 60/2/10 in Farmington; la grippe
Lucena J., d. 3/3/1905 at 73/2/17 in Belmont, MA; heart failure
Lydia B., d. 9/4/1912 at 78/7/22; uraemia; Jonathan M. Johnson and
   Mehitable Dearborn
Mabel Mary, d. 9/16/1927 at 37/5/30; embolism; George M. Brown and
   Mary T. McDermot
Margaret A., d. 11/10/1909 at 44/1/22 in Portsmouth; typhoid fever
Margaret A., d. 9/20/1921 at 69/6/17 in Somerville, MA; pernicious anemia
Maria, d. 11/8/1908 at 64/0/4; Bright's disease
Marie F., d. 5/7/1923 at 42/8/29; pulmonary oedema; George Haffner and
   Mina Dosch
Mark F., d. 9/3/1913 at 62/1/26; acute Brights disease; Dennis Brown and
   Matilda Evans
Martha A., d. 1/12/1901 at 76/7/7 in Boston, MA; malignat disease of
   bowels; PH
Martha A., d. 12/15/1904 at 72/7/19; pneumonia; buried in family lot
Mary, d. 5/23/1903 at 30/2/13; phthisis; PH
Mary A. F., d. 5/12/1923 at 18 in Franklin; gastro enteritis
Mary Agnes, d. 3/12/1930 at 60/0/11; lobar pneumonia; Thomas Dobbins
   and Joanna Costigan
Mary E., d. 10/28/1891 at 72; married; ----- Allard (NH)
Mary E., d. 6/27/1921 at 64/7/27; intestinal tuberculosis; Abel W. Baxter
   and Hannah M. Lougee
Mary J., d. 10/20/1894 at 64; pneumonia; b. Sheffield, VT; PH
Mary R., d. 1/18/1908 at 21; asphyxia; Joseph Brown and Rose Rouleaux
Maxine L., d. 9/30/1915 at 1/9/27; tubercular meningitis; Albert R. Brown
   and Emma E. Neal
May L., d. 8/12/1911 at 0/3/11; cholera infantum; John B. Brown and
   Minnie E. Duprey
Melinda M., d. 3/1/1899 at 70 in Boston, MA; pneumonia; PH
Moses, d. 4/22/1889 at 64; farmer; widower; b. NH; James Brown (NH)
   and Abigail Hanson (NH)
Nicholas, d. 9/26/1899 at 79 in Barrington; heart failure; PH
Olive, d. 1/18/1904 at 82/2/18 in Wells, ME; old age; buried in Dover
Olive W., d. 10/8/1892 at 81; heart disease; b. Thornton; (NH; Durham)
Patrick H., d. 3/17/1900 at 37 in So. Berwick, ME; phthisis
Pauline E., d. 11/23/1919 at 91/10; senility; Thomas W. Tibbetts and Mary
   -----
Philander C., d. 9/14/1904 at 75; valvular disease of heart; PH
Philip A., d. 2/3/1901 at 0/3/15; probably suffocation; PH
Raymond G., d. 10/23/1932 at 47/1/26 in Concord; Schilder's disease
Robert M., d. 2/2/1932 at 11/3/13; cardiac dilatation
Rosa M., d. 12/12/1930 at 79/6/27; acute bronchitis; John Larkin and
   Betsey -----

Rose, d. 9/3/1916 at 86 in Waltham, MA; lobar pneumonia; Charles Brown and Susan ——
Ruth M., d. 5/4/1930 at 16/5/26; con. malformation heart; E. W. Brow (sic) and Eleanor C. Berry
Samuel, d. 12/24/1891 at 76
Sarah M., d. 7/11/1911 at 76/9; senility; Joseph Sanborn and Mary Abbott
Susan E., d. 4/6/1900 at 81; disease of spine; PH
Susan L., d. 1/1/1914 at 32/10/4; pneumonia catarrhal; Wesley B. Sterling and Lizzie M. Foss
Syrena J., d. 4/2/1905 at 76/9/20; repeated syncope
Thomas, d. 10/7/1909 at 79 in Boston, MA; mitral regurgitation; William Brown
Thomas F., d. 12/10/1922 at 67/5/22; lobar pneumonia; Jeremiah Brown
Thomas S., d. 11/12/1925 at 40/8/29; pulmonary oedema; Robert M. Brown and Annie Hanley
Wilbur, d. 9/19/1907 at 0/8/23; cholera infantum; John Brown and Minnie Dupres
William A., d. 1/14/1930 at 63/7/28; cong. heart failure; Joseph Brown and Jeannette Kirk
William H., d. 9/24/1908 at 50/1/25; hepatitis; John Brown and Paulie E. Tibbetts
William H., d. 11/12/1913 at 54/8/22; cancer of rectum; Robert Brown and Sarah Smiley
William L., d. 5/23/1894 at 71 in Wells, ME; consumption; PH
William M., d. 8/13/1891 at 35/8; married; Albert H. Brown (Waterbury, VT) and Fanny C. Fisk (Williamstown, VT)
William O., d. 11/13/1917 at 66/3/25; apoplexy; Hezekiah H. Brown and Augusta Sylvester
William R., d. 8/30/1888 at 54/1/8; stable keeper; married; b. NH; Joseph Brown (NH) and Margaret Barden (NH)
Winfield W., d. 11/1/1923 at 79; gastro enteritis
Woodbury, d. 2/27/1906 at 18/11 in West Bath, ME; explosion steam boiler; PH

BROWNE,
Diana, d. 4/24/1909 at 88/7/24 in Rochester; paralysis

BROWNELL,
Amaziah, d. 9/11/1913 at 79/8/17; cerebral apoplexy; William Brownell and Lydia Clark
Benjamin C., d. 7/15/1895 at 70 in Somerville, MA; senile gangrene; buried in Dover
Charles H., d. 6/11/1920 at 64; diabetes mellitus; Amaziah J. Brownell and Mary J. Burley
Eliza J., d. 3/16/1905 at 77/11/13; heart disease; PH

Eliza J. M., d. 5/4/1896 at 70; pneumonia; b. Dover; PH
Fannie, d. 5/1/1915 at 78; septicemia; William Brownell and Lydia Clark
Frederick, d. 8/17/1922 at 72 in Boston, MA; valvular heart disease
Harry H., d. 8/10/1927 at 61/11/9 in Greenland; chronic myocarditis
Lydia C., d. 4/27/1902 at 73/4/24 in Somerville, MA; fractured hip and debility; PH
Mary J., d. 2/16/1903 at –; chronic nephritis; PH
Samuel H., d. 11/3/1910 at 83/3/11; heart disease; William Brownell and Lydia Clark
William A., d. 1/4/1927 at 69/2/12; diabetes; Amaziah Brownell and Mary J. Burley
William B., d. 5/12/1914 at 92; chronic ulcer foot

BROWNING,
Frances, d. 5/3/1931 at 91/2/18 in Cambridge, MA; cerebral hemorrhage
Francis, d. 12/5/1905 at 75/6/9 in Cambridge, MA; broncho pneumonia; PH
John S., d. 8/9/1916 at 56/6/23 in Cambridge, MA; pulmonary embolism

BRUCE,
Hattie A., d. 3/18/1894 at 27 in Lowell, MA; pulmonary tuberculosis; buried in Dover
John B., d. 2/17/1897 at 81 in Hooksett; gangrene; PH

BRUNELLE,
Ernest, d. 6/26/1930 at 62/4/3 in Manchester; myocarditis; Leon Brunelle and Julia Boisvert
Norman, d. 7/11/1928 at 2 hrs.; asphyxia of labor; Wilfrid E. Brunelle and Laura E. -----

BRUNO,
M., d. 12/14/1889 at 3; b. Dover; ----- (Canada) and ----- Vallit (Canada)
Pride, d. 5/1/1914 at 20/6/15; cerebral injuries; Louis Bruno

BRYANT,
Edwin, d. 3/20/1909 at 75/9/15 in Medford, MA; carcinoma of intestines
Elizabeth M., d. 12/29/1900 at 75; brain disease; buried in Exeter
Frank H., d. 3/31/1926 at 72/11/4; chr. inter. nephritis; Samuel Bryant and Eunice Thurston
George A., d. 7/11/1925 at 52; com. fracture skull; Charles F. Bryant and Lizzie Hanson
Grace Davis, d. 1/17/1925 at 44; pulmonary embolism; Ben F. Davis and A. Flora Thompson
Joseph A., d. 6/25/1928 at 80/6/14; chronic endocarditis; David Bennett (sic) and Judith Allard

Katie, d. 4/17/1910 at 50; pulmonary tuberculosis; James Johnson and
    Katie -----
Lena E., d. 3/2/1919 at 73/9/8; cerebral hemorrhage; Christian Bauer and
    Christina Timkins
Mary W., d. 6/1/1892 at 25; peritonitis; b. Woburn, MA; (Durham; Dover)
Roger D., d. 6/22/1928 at 17 in Portland, ME; acute Hodkins dis.
Sarah R., d. 10/27/1902 at 70/3/23 in Portsmouth; heart disease; PH

BUCHANAN,
Emmabelle, d. 5/29/1937 at 65; heart disease

BUCK,
Frank, d. 9/30/1924 at 68; apoplexy

BUCKLEY,
child, d. 10/27/1891 at -; John Buckley (Ireland) and Rose Cooley
    (Ireland)
child, d. 10/3/1911 at -; premature birth; Daniel J. Buckley and Mary C.
    Sherry
Adelaide S., d. 4/23/1910 at 65/10/6 in Norristown, NJ; Levi G. Hill and A.
    B. Shackford
Ben, d. 8/25/1888 at 0/2; b. Dover; John W. Buckley (England) and Martha
    Aglett (England)
Catherine, d. 6/8/1890 at 77; widow; Daniel Mahoney (Ireland) and
    Elizabeth Flynn (Ireland)
Catherine, d. 10/12/1914 at 72; cerebral hemorrhage
Charles, d. 5/6/1937 at 51/4/17; acute lob. pneumonia
Daniel, d. 3/31/1896 at 26; typhoid pneumonia; b. Ireland; SM
Daniel, d. 1/17/1925 at 44 in Portland, ME; degeneration of heart; Daniel
    Buckley and Catherine Mahoney
Fr. Henry, d. 8/7/1891 at 0/4/11; ----- (England) and Martha Greyson
    (England)
James J., d. 11/4/1930 at 53/8/16; carcinoma bladder; Daniel Buckley and
    Catherine McCarthy
James M., Rev., d. 2/8/1920 at 83/1/20 in Morristown, NJ; broncho
    pneumonia; John Buckley and Abbie L. Munroe
John D., d. 6/12/1897 at 38; fracture of spine; b. Ireland; SM
Martha, d. 2/10/1894 at 42; phthisis pulmonalis; b. England; buried in
    Exeter
Mary Ann, d. 10/12/1890 at 0/0/10; John Buckley (Ireland) and Rosan C.
    (Ireland)
Rose, d. 3/30/1899 at 30; septicaemia; SM
Seth, d. 5/12/1896 at 44; phthisis pulmonalis; b. England; buried in Exeter

BUCKMAN,
A. H., d. 5/29/1895 at 55; suicide; b. Salem; buried in Rochester

BUCKNELL,
Benjamin W., d. 10/14/1902 at 71/0/12; valvular disease of heart; PH

BUCKNER,
Mary, d. 4/19/1928 at 100/3/25; cancer of bowel; ----- Whittier

BUDLONG,
Florence J., d. 11/25/1909 at 29/2/10 in Bridgeport, CT; fibroids of uterus; Charles E. Joy and Effie B. Bunker

BUKER,
William F., d. 6/3/1935 at 70; cerebral embolism

BULLA,
James, d. 6/4/1936 at 64 in Concord; arteriosclerosis

BUMFORD,
child, d. 6/18/1901 at –; stillborn; PH
child, d. 4/28/1909 at – in Somersworth; stillborn; Frank W. Bumford and Lucinda B. Goodwin
Beatrice E., d. 9/15/1913 at 13/10/3 in Somersworth; diarrhea and enteritis
Forrest G., d. 12/25/1915 at 36/7/11; cirrhosis of liver; Charles W. Bumford and Nellie Hodgdon
George, d. 2/3/1904 at 0/4/9; convulsions; PH
Marie G., d. 3/21/1914 at 0/3/3 in Somersworth; gastro enteritis; Frank W. Bumford and Lucinda B. Goodwin
Sarah J., d. 6/11/1921 at 33/11/6; gall stones
Verna M., d. 9/16/1905 at 0/6/2; ilio-colitis; PH

BUNCE,
Charles C., d. 8/31/1925 at 82/5/4 in Sanford, ME; myocarditis; George Bunce and Ann Simkins
Charles H., d. 1/30/1887 at 63; widower; b. England
George F., d. 10/9/1913 at 63/8/1 in Old Orchard, ME; result cerebral apoplexy
Sarah E., d. 6/16/1913 at 61/7 in Old Orchard, ME; cancer in abdomen

BUNKER,
Bernice A., d. 6/12/1894 at –; meningitis; b. Dover; buried in Durham
Charles A., d. 1/30/1888 at 44/4 in Haverhill, MA

Edna A., d. 6/22/1924 at 64/2/26; arterio sclerosis; Israel Demeritt and
    Fannie ----
Eliza Jane, d. 7/6/1907 at 71/11/19 in Cambridge, MA; James V. Clark and
    Elizabeth Nute
Elizabeth T., d. 6/2/1919 at 30/2/13 in New London, CT; cerebral apoplexy
Ernest H., d. 5/27/1904 at 38/4/6 in Malden, MA; endocarditis; PH
Eveline F., d. 1/1/1914 at 68/5/20 in Merrimac, MA; cancer - abdominal
Frances, d. 5/15/1934 at 80/4/18 in S. Berwick, ME; cerebral hemorrhage
Frank J., d. 4/6/1929 at 77 in S. Berwick, ME; angina pectoris
Fred M., d. 11/17/1916 at 55/6/24; carcinoma of face; William H. Bunker
    and Abbie G. Thompson
Gladys T., d. 8/11/1899 at 6; peritonitis; PH
James F., d. 5/11/1911 at 51/7/29 in Revere, MA; tubercular laryngitis
James M., d. 7/12/1905 at 74/10/24 in Rollinsford; chronic bronchitis
Martha A., d. 4/5/1936 at 91/11/3; arteriosclerosis
Rebecca, d. 5/22/1888 at 76/8/20 in Durham
Thomas R., d. 1/17/1890 at 56/11; Rufus Bunker (Roxbury, ME) and
    Hannah Flanders (So. Hampton)

BURBANK,
Elizabeth W., d. 8/26/1911 at 76/2/11; nephritis; Daniel M. Christie and
    Dorothy Wheeler
Melissa, d. 11/25/1932 at 90/9/19; fracture of femur
Phoebe H., d. 12/7/1902 at 91/9/23; angina pectoris; buried in Saco, ME
Robert S., d. 5/8/1893 at 75; heart disease

BURCH,
Amos, d. 12/19/1910 at 73/9/21; apoplexy

BURGESS,
Evora M., d. 4/24/1927 at 64/8/3; chronic myocarditis; Charles Messer and
    Emily Leathers
Frank H., d. 9/24/1933 at 70/11/17; chronic nephritis
Vernon R., d. 12/28/1924 at 66/8/22; heart syncope; Benjamin Burgess
    and Emeline Taft
Walter P., d. 2/19/1919 at 0/0/10; hemophilia; Walter P. Burgess and Lucy
    Colpritt

BURKE,
Catherine, d. 9/7/1899 at --; cholera infantum; SM
Elizabeth, d. 9/13/1895 at 0; marasmus; b. Dover; SM
Ephraim, d. 6/21/1903 at 63; la grippe
Frank, d. 9/3/1889 at 1/2/18; b. Charlestown, MA. Peter Burke (Milford,
    MA) and Mollie O'Brion (Dover)
Hannah, d. 12/4/1895 at 59; heart disease; b. Ireland; SM

James, d. 3/31/1926 at 69; myocarditis; Owen Burke and Catherine Cartney
Jennie, d. 6/23/1919 at 67; cancer of liver; John Hale and Elizabeth Jackson
John, d. 12/27/1896 at –; b. Dover; SM
John, d. 3/23/1925 at 52/7; lobar pneumonia; Patrick Burke and Eliza Keenan
John H., d. 3/5/1898 at 3; scarlet fever; b. Dover; SM
Julia, d. 11/14/1893 at 27; consumption; b. Ireland; (Ireland; Ireland)
Katie, d. 11/12/1897 at 25; heart trouble; b. Ireland; SM
Mary, d. 7/20/1897 at 35; consumption; b. Ireland; SM
Mary, d. 3/3/1907 at 70; apoplexy; Thomas Griffin
Mary, d. 5/26/1914 at 79; apoplexy; James McKone and Nancy Reynolds
Mary Ann, d. 7/17/1895 at 0; cholera infantum; b. Dover; SM
Sarah, d. 7/23/1893 at –; cholera infantum; b. Dover; (Ireland; Ireland)
Sarah, d. 3/5/1897 at 25; phthisis pulmonalis; b. Ireland; SM
Thomas J., d. 3/9/1898 at 4; scarletina maligna; b. Dover; SM

BURLEIGH,
Albina N., d. 9/10/1928 at 76/0/20 in Manchester; hemiplegia; Albert Edgerly and Nancy Hersey
Bridget M., d. 11/10/1911 at 48; pul. tuberculosis; Daniel Corrigan and Alice Flanagan
Cora L., d. 10/21/1931 at 76/8/8; lobar pneumonia
Etha F., d. 1/18/1890 at 0/4/3; Walter Burleigh (America) and Mary Bee (Ireland)
George, d. 11/28/1933 at 76/9/20 in Concord; arteriosclerosis
Hiram J., d. 8/1/1906 at 39 in Warwick, RI; pulmonary tuberculosis; PH
James F., d. 9/24/1895 at 58; alcoholism; b. Wakefield; buried in E. Wakefield
Jennie F., d. 4/23/1888 at 0/10/23; b. Dover; W. Burleigh (Dover) and Mary Battles (Ireland)
Job H., d. 1/22/1922 at 93/11/24; pneumonia; Job Burleigh and Susan Frost
Katie, d. 10/4/1888 at 0/4/8; b. Dover; Walter Burleigh (Dover) and Mary Battles (Ireland)
Laura A., d. 11/29/1924 at 45/6/5; endocarditis; Edward Lauzon and Elmira Jormeau
Maranda W., d. 3/24/1916 at 87/10/6; the grip; Jeremiah Marston and Anna Young
Mary, d. 1/17/1890 at 29/9; married; Thomas Battles (Ireland) and Katie Prime (Ireland)
Mary, d. 3/29/1934 at 54; broncho pneumonia
Mina E., d. 5/12/1901 at 29/6; anemia and innutrition; buried in Tuftonboro
Susan H., d. 4/3/1895 at 82; pneumonia; b. Dover; PH

Veronica I., d. 11/1/1898 at 2; bronchitis; b. Dover; PH
Walter, d. 10/15/1925 at 65; natural causes; Charles H. Burleigh and Mary E. McGaugh

BURLEY,
Alfred, d. 4/12/1917 at 0/0/10; premature birth; Joseph Burley and Annie Roy
Alice, d. 4/3/1904 at 7/8/16; pneumonia; PH
Annie, d. 3/14/1919 at 23; phthisis pulmonalis; John Roy and Phoebe St Germain
Charles Henry, d. 10/29/1915 at 85/7/6; senility; John Burley and Lydia Caverly
Charles Hiram, d. 5/17/1921 at 81 in E. Greenwich, RI; arterio sclerosis
Ernest J., d. 8/10/1887 at 0/6/13; b. Dover; Hiram Burley (Dover) and Mary A. Sawtelle (NY)
Ernest W., d. 1/11/1898 at 0; pneumonia; b. Dover; PH
Ethel R., d. 2/1/1898 at 0; b. Dover; PH
Flora R., d. 12/19/1892 at 30; phthisis
Fred W., d. 3/25/1898 at 0; bronchitis; b. Dover; PH
Frederick W., d. 8/18/1901 at 0/7/5; peritonitis; PH
James R., d. 4/21/1889 at 4/6/7; b. Dover; Charles H. Burley (Dover) and Mary E. Burley (Dover)
Jennie May, d. 12/4/1894 at 2; tubercular meningitis; b. Dover; PH
Lydia S., d. 6/10/1893 at 79; heart disease; b. Effingham; (Parsonsfield, ME; Parsonsfield, ME)
Martha, d. 7/2/1889 at 78/2; housewife; married; b. Madbury; Jere. Ham (Madbury) and May Twombly (Madbury)
Mary E., d. 3/29/1899 at 53; phthisis; PH
Parkman, d. 5/11/1894 at 83; disease of heart; b. Brookfield; PH
Samuel D., d. 2/10/1902 at 53/5/20; PH
Sarah J., d. 5/22/1912 at 87/0/16; pneumonia; Moses Moulton and Mary Sargent
Stella, d. 7/19/1894 at 1; pneumonia; b. Dover; PH

BURNHAM,
Abby, d. 11/17/1896 at 60; disease of brain; b. Dover; PH
Alice C., d. 3/21/1919 at 64/6/21 in Whitman, MA; senile dementia
Amos B., d. 8/2/1922 at 63/5/12 in Epping; mitral insufficiency
Anna F., d. 12/13/1902 at 42/3/6 in York, ME; heart disease and dropsy; PH
Annie, Mrs., d. 8/30/1937 at 70; cerebr. hemorrhage
Asenath, d. 3/4/1897 at 79; pneumonia; b. So. Berwick, ME; PH
Belle D., d. 1/7/1919 at 64/0/24; broncho pneumonia; Gideon S. Burnham and Almira Giles
Benjamin, d. 6/23/1906 at 82/8/3; senility; buried in Portland, ME

Charles E., d. 12/30/1928 at 79/0/25; arterio sclerosis; Benjamin Burnham and Mary Foster
Charles H., d. 4/5/1934 at 69/5 in Boston, MA; pulmonary embolism
Edwin L., d. 3/2/1915 at 64/3/3; dementia paralytica; Royal R. Burnham and Mary A. Vickery
Eliza J., d. 3/28/1892 at 67; brain lesion; b. Barnstead; (Barnstead; Barnstead)
Elizabeth J., d. 4/2/1912 at 69/5/12; morphine habit; Samuel Burnham and Eliza J. Foye
Ella A., d. 6/1/1922 at 73/8/17; pernicious anaemia; Gilman Vickery and Julia Clements
Ellen, d. 2/13/1920 at 42 in Worcester, MA; broncho pneumonia
Fannie J., d. 8/22/1926 at 74/0/28; cerebral hemorrhage; Leonard Corson and Maria ----
Freeman G., d. 10/13/1912 at 40/2/12 in Plymouth, MA; fracture cervical vertebrae
Gideon, d. 4/20/1909 at 60/1/12 in Plymouth, MA; heart disease
Hannah S., d. 3/28/1892 at 66; consumption
Harriet C., d. 12/27/1888 at 82/9; single; b. Nottingham; Moses Burnham (Nottingham) and Zipporah Straw (Newfield, ME)
John M., d. 6/1/1900 at 57; pul. oedema; PH
Joseph R., d. 12/10/1937 at 53/9/28 in Winchester, MA; lobar pneumonia
Mary E., d. 1/7/1908 at 56/11/18; brain disease; G. S. Burnham and Almira Giles
Mattie F., d. 5/11/1931 at 74/9/26 in Gardiner, ME; fracture left femur
Royal B., d. 4/5/1902 at 65/0/4; chronic cerebral softening; PH
Walter S., d. 5/27/1899 at 51; heart disease; PH
William E., d. 4/9/1932 at 55 in Chelsea, MA; oedema of brain
Winthrop, d. 8/13/1890 at 83

BURNS,
Ann, d. 11/15/1893 at 48; acute cerebritis; b. Ireland; (Ireland; Ireland)
Ann, d. 5/5/1897 at 59; paralysis; b. Ireland; SM
Annie, d. 6/27/1935 at 61; cerebral apoplexy
Charles, d. 9/28/1892 at 13; typhoid fever; b. Hancock; (Ireland; Ireland)
Dennis, d. 7/20/1893 at –; diarrhea; b. Dover; (Ireland; Ireland)
Ella Maria, d. 2/7/1929 at 78/4/14 in Vernon, VT; cerebral hemorrhage; Warren Billings and Sara L. Smith
Frank W., d. 12/24/1890 at 22/8/2; single; Thomas Burns (Ireland) and Ann Murray (Ireland)
Jack, d. 5/12/1891 at 40; married
John E., d. 3/8/1894 at 16 in Lowell, MA; phthisis
John H., d. 10/2/1889 at 18/3/17; print works; single; b. NH; John Burns (Ireland) and Mary Cuddihy (Ireland)

Kate, d. 10/30/1887 at 40/3; married; b. Ireland; Daniel Murray (Ireland) and Kate (Ireland)
Martin, d. 4/21/1890 at 0/1; Michael Burns (Ireland) and Sarah Lannon (Ireland)
Mrs. P., d. 4/16/1889 at 57; weaver; widow; b. Ireland; James Duffy (Ireland) and Bridget Duffy (Ireland)
Nancy, d. 12/11/1917 at 95/10/7; arterio sclerosis; John Clancy and Elizabeth Ahern
Sarah, d. 2/13/1929 at –; acute indigestion
Thomas, d. 6/9/1896 at 33; heart disease; b. New Britain, CT
Thomas, d. 10/29/1902 at 73; shock; SM

BURNSIDE,
Annie D., d. 9/2/1908 at 39/6/8 in Lawrence, MA; post-operative shock

BURPEE,
Helen B., d. 12/23/1890 at 1/6/5 in Bradford
Henry W., d. 3/23/1924 at 70/9/23 in Haverhill, MA; angina pectoris
Julia Brooks, d. 4/23/1924 at 70/0/1 in Haverhill, MA; cerebral hemorrhage

BURR,
Edwin, d. 2/21/1915 at 67/5/18; cerebral congestion; William Burr and Frances McDonald
Etta J., d. 9/10/1918 at 58/3/27; diabetes; Miles P. Buzzell and Almira Arland
Frances S., d. 11/25/1895 at 85; old age; b. Limerick, ME; PH
Frank M., d. 4/2/1909 at 58/0/7; carcinoma of throat; William Burr and Francis McDonald

BURROUGHS,
Barbara E., d. 9/23/1903 at 1/0/5; peritonitis; PH

BURROWS,
Evelyn M., d. 1/1/1930 at 0/11/4; secondary anaemia; Walter W. Burrows and Hattie M. Magoon
Mercy A., d. 10/8/1930 at 91/2/5; senility; Paul Howard and Sarah E. Annis
Richard S., d. 11/29/1926 at 0/4/25; atrophy; Wallace H. Burrows and Marie Roper

BURWELL,
Augustus B., d. 10/14/1892 at 57; railroad accident; b. Boston, MA; (West Indies; Boston, MA)
Martha A., d. 11/20/1899 at 62; cerebral apoplexy; buried in Chelsea, MA

BUSBY,
Sarah Page, d. 8/8/1937 at 85/10/24; arteriosclerosis
William H., d. 11/16/1928 at 76/1 in Boston, MA; cellulitis left leg; John Busby

BUSFIELD,
John G., d. 3/29/1917 at 85/6/21; cerebral hemorrhage; Thomas Busfield and Mary Gibson

BUSH,
daughter, d. 6/18/1888 at –; b. Dover; Oliver Bush and Phoebe Bush
Joseph, d. 10/19/1924 at 63/5/13; chr. Brights disease

BUSHEY,
Joseph, d. 3/8/1900 at 70; organic disease of heart; SM
Julia, d. 6/1/1892 at 67; general debility; (Canada; Canada)

BUSHWAY,
Josephine, d. 6/15/1935 at 68; lobar pneumonia

BUTLAND,
Charles W., d. 8/3/1909 at 53/6/20; endocarditis; Thomas Butland and Pemelia Littlefield
Myra, d. 4/15/1910 at 73 in Concord; myocarditis; John M. Gallison and Elvira Hall

BUTLER,
Albert, d. 7/3/1895 at 0; gastric enteritis; b. Dover; SM
Annella A., d. 9/30/1889 at 27/6/1; married; b. Millsbury, IA; J. S. Cowan (ME) and Ruth Tanner (NY)
Benjamin S., d. 1/23/1895 at 71 in Boston, MA; tuberculosis; buried in Dover
Carrie E., d. 8/6/1888 at 0/6/25; b. Rochester; Thomas Butler (Newfield, ME) and Julia A. Watson (Portland, ME)
Charles, d. 3/5/1927 at 77/0/1 in Boston, MA; myocarditis
Christiana A., d. 10/5/1904 at 74/1/23 in Old Orchard, ME; cancer of uterus; PH
Edgar W., d. 3/17/1896 at 42; pleurisy; b. NH; PH
Emily, d. 12/20/1896 at 69; old age; b. Durham; PH
Emily J., d. 10/2/1926 at 72/8/15 in Portsmouth; cerebral hemorrhage
Everett M., d. 2/16/1891 at 0/4; Frank A. Butler (Eliot, ME) and Bernice M. Flynn (Haverhill, MA)
Frank J., d. 10/25/1892 at 32; asthma; b. Durham; (Durham; Durham)

George W., d. 9/1/1902 at 76/5/19 in Old Orchard, ME; chronic heart disease; PH
James, d. 5/31/1896 at 72; general exhaustion; b. Durham; PH
James E., d. 8/6/1896 at 48 in New York City; apoplexy
John Edwin, d. 12/8/1911 at 92/9/7 in Portsmouth; senility
John S., d. 9/17/1892 at 89; old age; b. Gloucester, MA; (Gloucester; Gloucester)
Julia A., d. 1/23/1890 at 25; married
Lucinda J., d. 11/15/1896 at 73 in Portsmouth; apoplexy; PH
Martha A., d. 10/17/1932 at 56
Martha E., d. 7/2/1927 at 56/10/9; cancer liver; Walter G. Colbath and Elmira Hussey
Nettie, d. 11/7/1920 at 54/2/9; interstitial nephritis; John McGlone and Diadana James
Phebe Y., d. 1/31/1893 at 69; stricture of intestines; b. So. Berwick, ME; (So. Berwick, ME; Berwick, ME)
Sarah E., d. 2/10/1920 at 70; apoplexy; Sumuel Butler and Sarah Hanson
Sarah Elizabeth, d. 3/20/1927 at 81/8/20 in Portsmouth; cerebral hemorrhage
Sarah Jane, d. 12/10/1922 at – in Haverhill, MA; bronchial pneumonia
Thomas, d. 3/22/1937 at 36; intestinal obstruction

BUTTERCUP,
Eva A., d. 11/3/1908 at 3; pneumonia; Abraham Buttercup and Mary McAdam

BUTTERFIELD,
child, d. 12/19/1928 at –; premature birth; Helene Butterfield
Blanche C., d. 6/28/1937 at 61/8 in Portland, ME; mediastinal cancer (see following entry)
Blanche C., d. 6/28/1937 at 61/8* (see preceding entry)
Ira A., d. 3/8/1898 at 71 in Fremont; chronic int. catarrh; PH
Sarah J., d. 2/27/1887 at 57 in Boston, MA
Welbee, d. 7/30/1911 at 30/10/28 in Saco, ME; pulm. tuberculosis; Ira A. Butterfield and Eliza Granville
Welbee J., d. 11/28/1891 at 63/7/10; widower; Welbee Butterfield (Topsham, VT) and Eliza Brown (Newbury, VT)

BUXTON,
Kate, d. 7/21/1903 at 31; vegetable growth of stomach; SM

BUZZELL,
Alice G., d. 3/21/1912 at 1/9/18; acute catarrhal laryngitis; Roy W. Buzzell and Maud Hanson

Alice Welch, d. 8/16/1887 at 20/5/8; married; b. Dover; Samuel M. Welch (Middleton) and Dorothy O. Gray (New Durham)
Almira W., d. 1/1/1911 at 85/3/0; heart disease; Richard Arland and Lois Drew
Caroline E., d. 2/13/1932 at 82/10/18 in Durham; carcinoma of breast
David O., d. 2/10/1928 at 88/7/3; arterio sclerosis; David Buzzell and Lois Leighton
Edna May, d. 10/25/1912 at 0/1/15; diarrhea, enteritis; Roy Buzzell and Maud Hanson
Esther, d. 6/24/1909 at 91/1/12 in Durham; old age
Hattie W., d. 5/8/1927 at 68/5/3; cerebral hemorrhage; Charles E. Whitehead and Mary Bailey
John E., d. 1/13/1896 at – in Durham
John P., d. 5/29/1930 at 78/1/24; lobar pneumonia; Samuel T. Buzzell and Susan Pierce
Mary A., d. 3/4/1889 at 59/11/26 in Lynn, MA
Maud, d. 10/21/1912 at 26/7/5; catarrhal dysentery; George Hanson and Arabella Drew
Miles R., d. 11/22/1905 at 87/10/17; pneumonia; PH
Rhoda, d. 6/3/1887 at 47/1/23; married; b. Etna, ME; Luke Emerson (Gorham) and Lucy Munch (Bangor, ME)
Roger M., d. 4/15/1897 at 2 in Weymouth, MA; gastric enteritis; PH
Sarah A., d. 6/9/1920 at 65/0/15 in Merrimac, MA; arterio sclerosis

BYERS,
James H., d. 8/11/1907 at 46/4/9; heart disease; George Byers and Margaret -----

BYRNE,
Mary, d. 10/30/1912 at 94/9/13; cerebral hemorrhage; Martin Byrne and Huldah Bradford

CADA,
Albert, d. 5/27/1922 at 44; tubercular arthritis; Oliver Cada and Agatha Macey

CADORETTE,
Marie R. A., d. 7/28/1914 at 0/5; cholera infantum; Peter Cadorette and Rose A. Mailhot
Mary P., d. 9/27/1915 at 25/6/15 in Atkinson; pulmonary tuberculosis; Carroll W. Chase and Lucy Tarr

CADY,
George W., d. 6/24/1911 at 23; meningitis; George B. Cady and Margaret A. Donahue

CAFKAS,
Stavroula, d. 9/16/1919 at 0/0/16; premature birth; Chris Cafkas and Elena Costopoulos
Stileani, d. 9/16/1919 at 0/0/16; premature birth; Chris Cafkas and Elena Costopoulos

CAHILL,
Ann, d. 10/1/1915 at 58/5/1; acute dilar. of heart; John Cahill and Mary Ackley
Edward, d. 12/17/1889 at 46/5; laborer; married; b. Dover; Mathew Cahll (Ireland) and Ann (Ireland)
John, d. 8/26/1893 at 80; old age; b. Ireland
Mary A., d. 7/6/1904 at 65/6/12; heart disease; SM

CAIG,
Elizabeth, d. 11/26/1910 at 46/3/15; apoplexy; James McNice and Jane ---
William R., d. 8/26/1914 at 56; cancer of liver

CAIN,
Juliet A., d. 8/11/1927 at 77/6/27; angina pectoris; Noah Cummings and Mary -----

CALCUTT,
Annie, d. 12/18/1891 at 18/11/18; single; Henry Calcutt (England) and Emma Srtone (England)
John B., d. 12/16/1929 at 67/11/29 in Boston, MA; cancer prostate

CALDWELL,
Clara E., d. 9/24/1935 at 71/0/27 in Barrington; coronary thrombosis
Mary S., d. 3/17/1909 at 75/2/19 in Lawrence, MA; uraemia; Israel Swain and Susan Bennett
Samuel, d. 10/29/1892 at 39; insane - complication diseases; b. England

CALKINS,
Addie, d. 3/23/1930 at 79; angina pectoris

CALL,
child, d. 12/29/1923 at 0/0/½; premature birth; Fred Call and Annie E. McLin
Arthur, d. 7/13/1890 at --; George G. Call (Gloucester, MA) and Bertha M. Moulton (Berwick, ME)
Bertha M., d. 10/6/1935 at 67/11/5 in Rochester; heart disease
George G., d. 8/8/1914 at 48/10/8; acute dilitation of heart; Ezekiel Call and Annie Sylvester

Lizzie L., d. 2/16/1895 at 23 in Lynn, MA; typhoid fever; buried in Dover

CALLAHAN,
Michael, d. 10/4/1902 at 35; accident; SM
Michael A., d. 12/25/1928 at 27; acute gastritis; Thomas Callahan
Patrick, d. 4/25/1896 at 29; suicide by hanging; b. Ireland; SM
Thomas J., d. 3/2/1922 at 54; carcinoma of larynx; Thomas Callahan and Catherine Mahoney
Thomas J., d. 9/8/1937 at 65; car. colon (rectum)

CALONGIANIS,
child, d. 12/20/1920 at –; premature birth; Andrew Calongianis and Julia Kostopoulos

CALVAL,
Vivian Rose, d. 2/22/1923 at 15; pulmonary tuberculosis; Peter Calval

CAMERON,
Gertrude M., d. 9/25/1889 at 0/10/3; b. Dover; P. B. Cameron (Ireland) and Mary E. Rafferty (Woburn, MA)
Ida Ellen, d. 12/21/1937 at 73/7/16; appendicitis - acute perforated
Isabella, d. 1/6/1890 at 75/11/25; widow; John Galbraith (Scotland) and Margaret Phillips (Scotland)
John, d. 2/24/1890 at 74/3/13; widower; John Cameron (Scotland) and Kate Cameron (Scotland)

CAMMAL,
George A., d. 9/30/1922 at 63; chronic nephritis

CAMPBELL,
Agnes, d. 9/25/1896 at 33; heart disease; SM
Catherine, d. 11/28/1912 at –; acute nephritis; John Scanlon and Mary Mitchell
Eileen E., d. 12/12/1937 at 26/4/20; cancer of lung
Ernest C., d. 9/13/1919 at 51/2/19; Brights disease; Edward Campbell and Phoebe -----
Evelyn R., d. 1/20/1930 at 4/6/19; pneumonia; Clinton Campbell and Lucy E. Hill
James, d. 8/15/1893 at –; stillborn; b. Dover; (Ireland; Ireland)
James, d. 6/23/1907 at 45/1/12; phthisis; George Campbell and Mary Evans
Mary, d. 11/21/1907 at 66; old age
Mary E., d. 12/22/1915 at 1/1/8; intersussception; James Campbell and Anna Maria Breen

Nancy, d. 4/29/1905 at 74; broncho pneumonia
Robert J., d. 12/18/1905 at 15/9/1; general tuberculosis; PH
William Henry, d. 1/25/1917 at 18/2/12; phthisis pulmonalis; James
    Campbell and Alice McNeice

CANDAN,
Ellen, d. 1/8/1911 at 77; old age; Henry Battles and Mary Welch

CANDISH,
Maude, d. 9/11/1927 at 48/9 in Cedar Grove, NJ; cerebro spinal syphillis

CANNAVAN,
Addie A., d. 6/24/1909 at 65/4/14; carcinoma of liver; Martin H. Cannavan
    and Clarica Waldron
Lizzie H., d. 1/7/1924 at 77/9/15; cancer neck of bladder; Martin H.
    Cannavan and Clarissa Waldron

CANNEY,
Adaline B., d. 1/31/1896 at 79; chronic pneumonia; b. Stratham; buried in
    Meaderboro
Albert M., d. 2/20/1916 at 78/8/26; angina pectoris; Thomas J. Canney
    and Sarah Waldron
Andrew J., d. 7/28/1918 at 74/8/7; diabetes mellitus; Isaac D. Canney and
    Matilda Reed
Benjamin L., d. 5/6/1934 at 72/10/21; diabetes mellitus
Benjamin R., d. 9/26/1912 at 59/10/3; pneumonia; Benjamin R. Canney
    and Adeline B. Merrow
Betsey, d. 10/3/1903 at 92/2/10; valvular heart disease; PH
Charles A., d. 2/17/1931 at 78/1/25 in Madbury; diabetes
Charles E., d. 5/15/1923 at 80/10/8; cerebral hemorrhage; James Canney
    and Betsey J. -----
Clyde E., d. 9/11/1928 at 22/1/10; pulm. tuberculosis; Frank S. Canney
    and Ida M. Gavel
Cynthia, d. 3/1/1922 at 71/4 in Pepperell, MA; cirrhosis of liver
Ella C., d. 7/28/1934 at 82/11/18 in Madbury; embolism
George F., d. 4/24/1914 at 78/2/8 in Boston, MA; bronchitis
Grace W., d. 11/11/1932 at 67/0/13 in Pepperell, MA; pulmonary asthma
Hannah J., d. 12/3/1894 at 77; worn out, heart failure; b. Blue Hill, ME; PH
Hannah M., d. 5/27/1900 at 68; brain disease; PH
Harold E., d. 6/7/1914 at 0/5; acute pneumonia; Frank S. Canney and Ida
    M. Gaville
Helen L., d. 1/19/1931 at 4/5/19 in Madbury; erysipelatous
Henrietta, d. 6/2/1936 at 63/4/0; diabetic gangrene
Herbert A., d. 1/9/1910 at 61/3/22 in Rochester; apoplectic shock
Herbert B., d. 10/9/1901 at 18/9/20; typhoid fever; PH

Herman E., d. 4/29/1932 at 81/1/23; cerebral concussion
Isaac B., d. 10/18/1912 at 70/4/22; uraemia; Isaac D. Canney and Matilda Reed
Jerome B., d. 1/21/1897 at 78; uraemia; b. Strafford; PH
John, d. 1/24/1923 at 77/1/8; carcinoma of intestines; Isaac Canney and Betsey Decatur
John H., d. 4/18/1929 at 70; apoplexy; George Canney and Asenath Nason
John N., d. 9/20/1887 at 81/2/24; painter; single; b. Madbury; Jacob Canney (Durham) and Sarah Jenness (Rochester)
Laura L., d. 9/29/1923 at 64/10/21 in Revere, MA; carcinoma of bladder
Lavina, d. 2/27/1898 at 90; old age; PH
Marguerite, d. 7/30/1928 at 0/0/4; cong. mal. of heart; Herman C. Canney and Cora M. James
Marjorie B., d. 2/22/1905 at 2/6/17; cerebro spinal meningitis; PH
Mary F., d. 1/13/1910 at 66/3/4; la grippe; Benjamin R. ----- and Adeline B. Merrow
Minnie, d. 6/29/1934 at 48/0/11; carcinoma of stomach
Nancy P., d. 4/7/1903 at 82/11/2; old age; PH
Sarah, d. 5/9/1913 at 44/9/16; pulmonary tuberculosis; Franklin Grant and Elizabeth Earle
Sarah A., d. 12/12/1926 at 84/10/22; chronic myocarditis; James Woodus and Marabah -----
Sarah H., d. 4/10/1922 at 77/2/10; senility; Daniel Norris and Caroline Warner
Susan E., d. 4/16/1922 at 80/7/21; heart syncope; Benjamin R. Canney and Adeline B. Merrow

CANOVAN,
Clarissa, d. 7/27/1887 at 72/7/28; widow; b. Barrington; John Waldron and Elizabeth Gray (Barrington)

CANTIN,
Bertrand, d. 8/27/1932 at 11/2/16; fracture of skull
Josephine, d. 5/7/1935 at 45/4/24; hydatidiform-cupt

CAPELINIS,
Alexander, d. 4/29/1929 at 48 in Portsmouth; ac. cardiac dilation

CAPEN,
Augustus, d. 4/14/1913 at 1/2/26; pneumonia; Theodore Capen and Elizabeth Hanscom
Chester, d. 4/27/1918 at 0/11/21; acute lobar pneumonia; Theodore Capen and Elizabeth Hanscom
Clara, d. 1/14/1916 at –; cirrhosis of liver; Wilbur Freeman

Frank, d. 6/6/1918 at 0/0/4; premature birth; Ethel M. Capen
May, d. 11/15/1931 at 38/5/14; chronic myocarditis
May E., d. 6/29/1916 at 21/5/2; eclampsia; John Freeman and Mamie
    Richardson
Ned, d. 1/24/1937 at 42 in Springvale, ME; coronary thrombosis

CAPIN,
George, d. 7/6/1917 at 55; gastro enteritis

CARABELAS,
Louis D., d. 9/13/1911 at 18/5/15 in Rumford, ME; typhoid pneumonia
Venita, d. 5/23/1914 at 0/0/19; marasmus; James Carabelas and
    Stavroula Aloupolos

CARBERRY,
Bridget, d. 5/15/1905 at 75; old age and apoplexy; SM
Catherine, d. 10/10/1929 at 74 in Watertown, MA; chr. myocarditis
Frank W., d. 11/29/1906 at 17/0/27; pulmonary tuberculosis; SM
Jane F., d. 2/23/1931 at 0/4/11; marasmus
John W., d. 8/23/1936 at 76/3/26; carcinoma intestines
Margaret, d. 11/4/1888 at 55; mill operative; widow; b. Ireland; John
    Carberry (Ireland) and Ann Riley (Ireland)
Mary, d. 12/6/1907 at --; asphyxia; John W. Carberry and Nellie Linehan
Philip, d. 8/24/1909 at 3/1/13 in Cambridge, MA; tubercular meningitis;
    John Carberry and Ellen Linnehan

CARCELL,
John T., d. 5/23/1929 at 5; acute peritonitis; James Carcell

CARD,
Andrew P., d. 8/1/1909 at 72/4/11 in Lynn, MA; cerebral hemorrhage
Anna M., d. 4/10/1889 at 29/6/6; housewife; married; b. Quebec; S.
    Empey (England) and Julia Shurtleff (Canada)
Annie E., d. 7/24/1931 at 83/5/18; cerebral softening
Azubah, d. 1/18/1894 at 70; malignant disease of stomach; b. Kennebunk,
    ME; buried at Dover Point
Daniel, d. 4/18/1889 at 81/1/3; farmer; married; b. Dover; Thomas Card
    (Dover) and Phoebe Trefethen (Dover)
Edcil P., d. 3/20/1929 at 74/10/18; arterio sclerosis; Thomas H. Card and
    Deborah P. Hayes
Elmer W., d. 7/4/1912 at 28 in Beardstown, IL; cerebral hemorrhage
Fred D., d. 5/30/1937 at 62*
George A., d. 12/19/1923 at 65 in San Diego, CA; suicide
George H., d. 9/6/1922 at 79/1/24; pneumonia; William Card and Martha
    Roberts

Ida F., d. 6/12/1914 at 22/10/26; acute mania; George H. Card and Annie
   E. Gage
James H., d. 2/24/1904 at 78/9/17; apoplexy; buried at Dover Point
John P., d. 6/8/1913 at 39 in Concord; renal tuberculosis; George Card
Marion D., d. 8/13/1895 at 0; cholera infantum; b. Dover; PH
Martha A., d. 12/5/1889 at 69/2/23; housewife; married; b. Farmington; I.
   Roberts (Farmington) and Elsie Pinkham
Mary E., d. 11/25/1892 at 52; cancer
Raymond Carl, d. 9/1/1923 at 0/1/7; marasmus; Ernest L. Card and
   Pauline A. Williams
Sylvester, d. 3/21/1917 at 81/6/23; pneumonia; Daniel Card
Willard J., d. 12/3/1890 at 30/7/27; widower; James H. Card (Dover) and
   Azubah Cousens (Kennebunk, ME)
William, d. 11/29/1904 at 86/0/25; humaturia; buried at Dover Point

CARDEN,
child, d. 6/17/1825 at –; miscarriage; Charles J. Carden and Iva E. Davis
Melvin James, d. 5/19/1921 at –; asphyxia of labor; Charles J. Carden and
   Iva E. Davis

CAREW,
Vicey E., d. 8/2/1925 at 77/8; arterio sclerosis; James D'Arcy and Phoebe
   Titus

CAREY,
Bridget, d. 7/17/1930 at 60/1/13; chronic nephritis; Dennis Carey and Mary
   Shea

CARHART,
George E., d. 11/25/1906 at 58/6/21; chronic Bright's disease; buried in
   Somersworth

CARIGNAN,
Edmond N., d. 1/13/1925 at 43/3/6; lobar pneumonia; Zephiran Carignan
   and Mary Blais
Joseph, Jr., d. 11/24/1933 at 20 mins.; asphyxia of labor
Zepherin, d. 9/18/1914 at 66/8/12; carcinoma of rectum; Valire Carignan
   and Olive Poisson

CARLELOST,
A. Maria, d. 12/3/1906 at 62/9/14 in Brockton, MA; exhaustion from
   apoplexy; PH

CARLETON,
Fred C., d. 10/30/1913 at 38/3/20 in Brockton, MA; pulm. tuberculosis
James, d. 2/15/1902 at 65/6/3; cerebral softening; PH

CARLOW,
Vera, d. 6/17/1932 at 35 in New York, NY; cancer

CARLSON,
Carl, d. 5/18/1899 at – in Manila, P.I.; gun-shot wound; PH

CARLTON,
Ernest, d. 1/5/1902 at 3/2/27; convulsions and exhaustion; SM
Kenneth P., d. 6/1/1910 at 0/7/14; bronchitis; Walter Carlton and Minnie E. Pinkham

CARNEY,
Frank B., d. 5/19/1923 at 61/16/4 (sic); acute nephritis; John Carney and Mary Jones
Lizzie, d. 11/5/1919 at 62; arthritis deformans; George Moore and Anne Cassidy
Martha J., d. 8/17/1895 at 67 in Newburyport, MA; cancer; buried in Dover
Mary, d. 10/7/1901 at 68; old age; SM
Thomas, d. 6/5/1899 at 38; la grippe and acute phthisis; SM

CARON,
Lucienne, d. 2/6/1936 at 13/2/22; aplastic anemia
Philippe, d. 4/19/1934 at 52/5/16; peritonitis

CARPENTER,
child, d. 1/28/1891 at –; Joseph Carpenter (Canada) and Sarah Sharkey (Canada)
child, d. 9/1/1896 at –; stillborn; b. Dover; SM
Charles S., d. 9/4/1890 at 0/8/23; Joseph Carpenter (Canada) and Arsile Charretier (Canada)

CARR,
Ann, d. 2/9/1893 at 50; died in Strafford Co. Asylum fire
Charles J., d. 8/10/1892 at –; cholera infantum; b. Dover; (Lancaster; Ireland)
Edwin M., d. 3/25/1936 at 69/6/19; cerebral hemorrhage
J. Frank, d. 1/15/1890 at 40/5/16; married; Josiah Carr (Hebron, ME) and Elizabeth Bridgham
Mrs. Hugh, d. 11/14/1891 at 28; married; (Ireland; Ireland)
Sarah A., d. 9/16/1907 at 69 in Concord; exhaustion

Sarah F., d. 8/24/1913 at 73 in Boston, MA; valv. heart disease

CARRAGHER,
Mary, d. 4/15/1913 at 70; broncho pneumonia; James Garvey and Mary Riley

CARREGHER,
Catherine, d. 12/16/1917 at 45; acute lobar pneumonia; Patrick Bradley and Alice -----
Frank, d. 7/2/1937 at 72/11/26*; b. New Durham
Henry, d. 4/2/1892 at 65; heart disease; b. Ireland; (Ireland; Ireland)

CARRIER,
child, d. 7/8/1901 at –; stillborn
Adrienne L., d. 6/15/1913 at 7/3/6; acute pneumonia; Edmond Carrier and Maria Bergeron
Bernadette, d. 8/10/1911 at 6/11/15; ileo colitis; George Carrier and Mary Leger
Earl, d. 1/4/1909 at 0/0/17; bronchitis; Melvin Carrier and Mabel H. Morton
Edmond, d. 3/2/1934 at 62/1/26; carcinoma of stomach
Emily, d. 2/9/1921 at 1/9/14; gastro enteritis; Alphonse Carrier and Dianna Pola
George, d. 8/31/1919 at 42 in Concord; drowning
Gerard, d. 1/8/1914 at 5/10/13; acute pneumonia; Edmond Carrier and Maria Bergeron
Jacques, d. 11/8/1918 at 75; general arterio sclerosis; Charles Carrier and Marie Tremblay
Joseph L., d. 1/9/1914 at 0/10/9; acute gastro enteritis; Edmond Carrier and Maria Bergeron
Leonore, d. 11/30/1901 at 65; Bright's disease; SM
Lucien, d. 10/9/1914 at 6/7/11; appendicitis; Edmond Carrier and Maria Bergeron
Robert, d. 12/16/1909 at 0/4/11; marasmus; George Carrier and Marie Leger

CARRIGAR,
Edmund J., d. 11/28/1893 at –; anaemia; b. Dover; (Canada; Canada)

CARROLL,
son, d. 5/3/1888 at –; b. Dover; John Carroll (Portland, ME) and Mary E. Hughes (Dover)
child, d. 1/19/1900 at –; meningitis; SM
child, d. 7/9/1908 at –; stillborn; Michael Carroll and Mary Dailey
Ann, d. 1/8/1892 at 50; heart disease; b. Ireland; (Ireland; Ireland)

Barbara Louise, d. 2/2/1928 at 2/8; scarlet fever; John F. Carroll and Bessie Lewis

Bridget, d. 1/6/1897 at 65; heart disease; b. Ireland; SM

Bridget E., d. 8/3/1889 at 46; dressmaker; married; b. Ireland; Pat. Riley (Ireland) and Sarah Grimes (Ireland)

Catherine, d. 3/20/1901 at 91/0/19; Bright's disease; SM

Catherine, d. 5/19/1916 at 70; carcinoma of stomach

Catherine, d. 12/26/1934 at 68; chronic myocarditis

Daniel, d. 9/23/1917 at 87; gen. arterio sclerosis

Dennis, d. 4/29/1902 at 72; heart disease; SM

Dennis, d. 9/2/1914 at 44; mitral insufficiency; Dennis Carroll and Catherine Cavanaugh

Edwin M., d. 1/5/1932 at 52/7/4; angina pectoris

Eileen E., d. 1/12/1920 at 36/5/26; infantile paralysis; Patrick Carroll and Catherine Flanagan

Elizabeth, d. 8/14/1911 at 80 in Exeter; entero colitis

Eva B., d. 8/1/1933 at 37; chronic myocarditis

Florence Arlene, d. 7/3/1923 at 0/0/24 in Rochester; marasmus

Gertrude E., d. 1/20/1936 at 43/4/23; angina pectoris

Henry, d. 11/22/1917 at –; accidental asphyxiation

James, d. 3/3/1901 at 65; cerebral meningitis

James, d. 12/26/1908 at 67; chronic nephritis; Dennis Carroll and Catherine Cavanaugh

James J., d. 9/22/1918 at 44/9/29 in Portsmouth; accident; Patrick Carroll and Catherine Flanagan

John, d. 3/31/1913 at 43 in Brentwood; pneumonia

John, d. 2/9/1931 at –; carcinoma of colon

Julia, Mrs., d. 7/24/1937 at 70; temicious anaemia

M., d. 6/4/1902 at 28; uremia; SM

Madeline B., d. 1/25/1929 at 0/0/5 in Rochester; atelectasis; George Carroll and Madeline Laroche

Margaret F., d. 11/15/1902 at 0/10/5; whooping cough; SM

Mary D., d. 4/27/1926 at 47; pernicious anemia; Patrick Carroll and Catherine Flanagan

Patrick, d. 1/29/1922 at 84; chr. inter. nephritis

Thomas F., d. 10/15/1904 at 28; general tuberculosis; SM

Thomas H., d. 4/10/1904 at 0/2/13; eczema; SM

Thomas S., d. 1/12/1910 at 42/0/1; hemorrhage; James ----- and Anne Cavanaugh

CARRUTH,
child, d. 1/14/1895 at 0; infancy; b. Dover; PH

CARTEN,
Mary P., d. 11/23/1887 at 94/6/5; b. Dover; Andrew Tuttle and Martha Dame

CARTER,
child, d. 9/9/1893 at –; stillborn; b. Dover; (Canada; Canada)
Bridget, d. 1/15/1906 at 38; alcoholism; SM
Edward, d. 10/29/1908 at 1/8/23; convulsions; Frank Carter and Mary E. Hughes
Frank, d. 7/28/1913 at 54/0/26; uraemia; Theophile Carter and Phoebe Lannier
Henry M., d. 5/16/1933 at 21/8/23; accidental drowning
Josephine E., d. 3/31/1926 at 73/2/28; influenza; William Greenleaf and Sarah Hanson
Lillian, d. 3/18/1909 at 52; pneumonia; William H. Allen and Maria Cobb
Lucy, d. 6/27/1890 at 88/0/4; widow; ----- Smith (Sandwich)

CARTERY,
Patrick, d. 3/19/1890 at 28/9; single; Patrick Cartery (Ireland) and Bridget Ward (Ireland)

CARTLAND,
Charles W., d. 9/9/1925 at 37 in Paris, France; non-contagious
Elizabeth, d. 4/7/1909 at 88/3/25; valv. heart disease; Tobias Cartland and Hannah Marden
Elizabeth, d. 8/18/1937 at 20/0/26; diabetes mellitus
Florence F., d. 3/27/1935 at 49/6/4; angina pectoris
Jennie, d. 4/5/1923 at 60 in Orlando, FL; chronic myocarditis
Julia H. W., d. 6/13/1894 at 43; acute cerebritis; b. Dover; PH
Mary E., d. 2/4/1936 at 86/8/15; hypostatic pneumonia
Moses H., d. 12/14/1923 at 47/9/15; suicide, shooting; Rufus W. Cartland and Mary F. Philpot
Rufus M., d. 5/24/1908 at 63/2/26; cerebral apoplexy; John Cartland and Nancy Milliken
Vara L., d. 8/3/1919 at 48/5/27; sarcoma of femur; Ira Libby and Mary Gilpatrick
William F., d. 12/16/1932 at 72/11/11; myocarditis

CARVER,
Catherine A., d. 6/15/1923 at 59/7/3; pernicious anemia; James Crennan and Ellen Lawlor
John J., d. 11/3/1917 at 23/7/3; diabetes mellitus; Simon Carver and Catherine Crennan
Simon, d. 12/15/1916 at 69; apoplexy; John Carver and Honora Houligan

CARVILLE,
child, d. 4/15/1906 at 0/0/2; inanition; SM
Robert W., d. 8/29/1924 at 1/0/15; Hierschsprung disease; Joseph W. Carville and Carrie A. Stevens

CASE,
child, d. 12/16/1902 at –; compression of cord; PH
Charles W., d. 4/12/1915 at 32/4/16; run over by train; Herman Case and Catherine Skillings
Nathan, d. 12/6/1911 at 72 in Togus, ME; croupous pneumonia; ----- Case and Annie -----

CASEY,
son, d. 11/13/1889 at –; b. Dover; James Casey (Dover) and Maggie Casey (Dover)
child, d. 7/1/1900 at –; stillborn
child, d. 7/18/1900 at <1; immaturity; SM
child, d. 2/4/1904 at 0/3; SM
child, d. 2/13/1905 at –; premature birth
child, d. 2/13/1905 at –; premature birth
child, d. 4/24/1913 at 0/0/2; premature birth; Margaret Casey
Ann, d. 7/29/1895 at 55; heart disease; b. Ireland; SM
Anne, d. 11/30/1901 at 80; heart failure; SM
Bridget, d. 3/12/1917 at 75; cerebral hemorrhage
Catherine, d. 1/27/1903 at 66; pneumonia; SM
Catherine, d. 1/13/1929 at 78; ch. interst. nephritis; John Cronin
Catherine M., d. 10/11/1931 at 71; angina pectoris
Ellen, d. 4/8/1911 at 36; cerebral hemorrhage
George F., d. 4/29/1925 at 27/10/3; pulmonary tuberculosis; Michael Casey and Susan Hughes
James, d. 4/3/1892 at 25/4; married; James Casey (Ireland) and Mary McNally (Ireland)
James, d. 6/14/1891 at 56; married; John Casey (Ireland) and Sarah Quinn (Ireland)
James, d. 10/14/1906 at 0/3; brain disease; SM
James, d. 12/17/1937 at 70/0/0; chronic nephritis
James E., d. 4/13/1931 at 15/5/28; pulmonary odema
James J., d. 7/11/1917 at 44 in Boston, MA; pulm. tuberculosis
John, d. 5/29/1899 at 55; pneumonia; SM
John, d. 6/23/1903 at –; tumor cancerous; SM
John S., d. 8/9/1917 at 40; apoplexy; John Casey and Annie Kelley
John W., d. 2/25/1911 at 45/9/17; cancer of the stomach; William Casey and Mary A. Carberry
Maggie, d. 11/13/1889 at 23; housewife; married; b. New Durham; P. Cassidy (Ireland) and Mary McGuiness (Ireland)

Mary S., d. 4/27/1887 at 22; single; b. Ireland
Michael, d. 2/9/1893 at 49; died in Strafford Co. Asylum fire
Susan M., d. 11/25/1918 at 45/4/25; chr. parenchymatous neph.; Thomas Hughes and Margaret Murray
Thomas F., d. 7/14/1930 at –; fracture of skull; Thomas F. Casey and ----- Coffey

CASH,
Dennis, d. 1/11/1903 at 53; diabetes; SM
James, d. 11/10/1924 at 64/8/12; gastric carcinoma; Thomas Cash and Margaret Mithen
John, d. 3/27/1921 at 54/11; myocarditis; Thomas Cash and Margaret Mithen
Margaret, d. 10/7/1906 at 80/4; old age; SM
Mary, d. 9/28/1907 at 0/1; marasmus; Thomas Cash and Annie Quigley
Mary E., d. 10/14/1927 at 73; cerebral embolism
Michael, d. 4/1/1912 at 74; acute dilitation of heart; Patrick Cash and Paulina Connors
Susan, d. 8/10/1922 at 80; strangulated hernia; John Macklin
Teresa B., d. 10/23/1902 at 19/9/13; ulcer of stomach; SM
Thomas, d. 2/17/1925 at 73/8/16; chronic myocarditis; Thomas Cash and Margaret Mithen
Thomas P., Jr., d. 6/16/1932 at 24 in Boston, MA; acute nephritis

CASHEM,
Daher J., d. 10/11/1913 at 48; peritonitis; Joseph Cashem

CASSELL [see Cassels],
child, d. 7/10/1927 at –; miscarriage; Dominick Cassell and Anna Robideau
child, d. 8/3/1929 at –; breech presentation; Dominick Cassell and Annie Robideaux
David, d. 11/20/1922 at 53/0/15; apoplexy; David Cassell and Ellen Brown
Dominick, d. 12/9/1932 at 60; coronary thrombosis
Irene C., d. 5/5/1931 at 29/11/22; eclampsia
James, d. 1/4/1923 at 0/10/17; lobar pneumonia; Dominick Cassells (sic) and Annie Roberdeaux
John, d. 1/16/1935 at 74/4/22 in Concord; probably organic disease of heart (a/k/a Castles)
Myra M., d. 8/24/1931 at 49/11; leukemia
Rose B., d. 6/16/1931 at 60/11/12 in Belmont, MA; carcinoma stomach

CASSELS [see Cassell],
child, d. 6/8/1923 at –; stillborn; Dominick Cassells and Anna Robideoux
Ellen, d. 6/23/1912 at 57 in Saugus, MA; cerebral hemorrhage

CASSERLY,
Ann, d. 1/4/1890 at 40; married; P. Brennan (England) and ----- (England)
James E., d. 5/15/1896 at 27; nephritis; b. US; SM

CASSIDY,
Alice, d. 12/6/1887 at 20/6/20; mill operative; single; b. Amesbury, MA; Patrick Cassidy (Ireland) and Mary McGuinness (Ireland)
Annie, d. 4/29/1903 at 57; cerebral thrombosis; SM
Bernard J., d. 10/2/1893 at –; inanition; b. Dover; (Ireland; Rochester)
Charles, d. 2/12/1892 at 24; pneumonia; b. New Durham; (Ireland; Ireland)
Edward, d. 2/9/1893 at 26; died in Strafford Co. Asylum fire
Elizabeth, d. 9/4/1892 at 34; chronic diarrhoea; (Ireland; Ireland)
Ellen F., d. 10/16/1918 at 50 in Lowell, MA; cancer of liver, bile ducts
Frank E., d. 11/15/1893 at 32; pulmonary tuberculosis; b. Ireland; (Ireland; Ireland)
James, d. 4/3/1897 at 36; pneumonia; b. Dover; SM
James, d. 2/10/1899 at 36; apoplexy; SM
James, d. 9/12/1904 at 33/3; consumption; SM
James J., d. 6/7/1896 at –; intersusception; b. Dover; SM
John, d. 5/15/1898 at 39; phthisis; b. Waltham, MA; buried in Waltham, MA
Margaret M., d. 9/18/1892 at 2; brain disease; b. Lowell, MA; (Dover, Ireland)
Mary, d. 10/24/1936 at 70; carcinoma of colon
Mary A., d. 1/20/1902 at 25/0/26; phthisis pulmonalis; SM
Nellie V., d. 9/20/1892 at –; cholera infantum; b. Dover; (Dover; Ireland)
Olide P., d. 1/27/1922 at – in Lowell, MA; premature birth
Patrick, d. 5/20/1887 at 46; laborer; married; b. Ireland; Peter Cassidy (Ireland) and Ann Brennan (Ireland)
Patrick, d. 3/7/1893 at 19; typhoid fever; b. at sea; (Ireland; Ireland)
Patrick, d. 7/28/1900 at 73; pericorditis; SM
Patrick, d. 8/18/1916 at 78; chronic Bright's dis.; Patrick Cassidy
Peter J., d. 2/7/1915 at 26/5 in Somersworth; pulmonary oedema
Philip, d. 6/27/1888 at 39; married; b. Dover; Philip Cassidy (Ireland) and Mary Wood (Ireland)
Raymond V., d. 5/22/1901 at 0/15 in West Derry; congestion of lungs
William, d. 12/16/1892 at 21; consumption; b. Dover; (Ireland; Ireland)
William T., d. 9/21/1931 at 40/11/7 in New Haven, CT; acute myocarditis

CASSILY,
Alice, d. 12/30/1891 at 76; widow; George McNally (Ireland)
Bridget, d. 5/14/1889 at 25; weaver; single; b. Ireland; Patrick Cassily (Ireland) and Bridget McAdam (Ireland)
Catherine, d. 1/18/1925 at 93; angina pectoris; Michael Donnelly and Margaret McShane

Catherine, d. 11/25/1925 at 82; angina pectoris; Lawrence McGlone
Charles, d. 4/13/1925 at 48; chronic bronchitis; Edward Cassily and Elizabeth Moran
Edward, d. 5/3/1900 at 50; la grippe; SM
Elizabeth, d. 1/26/1893 at 39; heart failure; b. ME; (Ireland; Ireland)
Frank, d. 5/5/1899 at 60; apoplexy; SM
Frank E., d. 2/2/1931 at 59 in Concord
Frank P., d. 3/12/1935 at 43; lobar pneumonia (double)
James, d. 12/13/1897 at 44; phthisis; b. Dover; SM
Jennie, d. 4/10/1903 at 26; apoplexy, cerebral; SM
Jennie, d. 12/10/1931 at 56; carcinoma of stomach
John, d. 6/15/1888 at 26/1/28; clerk; single; b. Dover; Patrick Cassily (Ireland) and Catherine Dormilly (Ireland)
John, d. 11/5/1898 at 3; laryngitis; b. Dover; SM
Margaret, d. 3/28/1920 at 56/1/27; cerebral hemorrhage; Peter Duffy and Mary Murphy
Margaret A., d. 6/7/1934 at 73/4/9; heart disease
Mary, d. 1/22/1891 at 42/3/5; married; Patrick Judge (Ireland) and Mary Lavin (Ireland)
Mary, d. 10/28/1897 at 55; apoplexy; b. Ireland; SM
Mary, d. 10/13/1901 at 71; heart disease; SM
Mary, d. 8/30/1907 at 66; heart disease; Patrick McMahon
Mary A., d. 10/11/1918 at 28/9/3; pneumonia; Hugh Cassily and Mary A. Lennon
Mary Ann, d. 1/3/1913 at 48; cerebral embolism; John Lennon and Susan Hughes
Patrick, d. 5/11/1895 at 52; phthisis pulmonalis; b. Dover; SM
Patrick, d. 3/14/1935 at 71; arteriosclerosis
Rose, d. 9/25/1916 at 23/4/29; tuberculosis of lungs; Christopher Leavitt and Mary A. Mallen
Thomas J., d. 1/22/1906 at 61; old age; SM

CASTLE,
James W., d. 1/3/1904 at 50 in Pawtucket, RI; pneumonia; buried in Dover

CASTLES,
John, d. 1/16/1935 at 74/4/22 in Concord; probably organic disease of heart (a/k/a Cassell)

CASTONGUAY,
child, d. 6/6/1927 at –; miscarriage; John Castonguay and Albertine Gregoire

CASWELL,
Alice, d. 1/14/1917 at – in Freeport, ME; stillborn; Roland A. Caswell and Alice Smith
Betsey T., d. 11/4/1896 at 84; apoplexy; b. Wolfeboro; PH
Charles A., d. 7/15/1902 at 58/1/11 in Haverhill, MA; acute nephritis
Charles C., d. 8/15/1919 at 83; gen. arterio sclerosis; Thomas Caswell and Sarah Evans
Charles E. T., d. 3/3/1932 at 67/1/28; lobar pneumonia
Charles F., d. 11/21/1907 at 56 in Denver, CO; apoplexy
Charles H., d. 2/7/1932 at 72/11/2; arterio sclerosis
Deborah, d. 12/23/1900 at 74; heart disease; buried in Strafford Center
Edgar, d. 11/12/1918 at 6 in Haverhill, MA; acute nephritis
George W., d. 12/14/1904 at 85/6/23; heart disease; PH
George W., d. 10/26/1914 at 66/2/11; pernicious anemia; Timothy Caswell and Hannah Hall
Mary A., d. 4/1/1906 at 88/10/12; pneumonia; PH
Mary Ann, d. 5/10/1904 at 83/3/28; gangrene; PH
Mary E., d. 8/10/1928 at 67/10/8; cerebral hemorrhage; William Waldron and Mary Peavey
N. F., d. 2/14/1903 at 56 in Charlottesville, VA; cerebral apoplexy; PH
Scott W., d. 9/21/1919 at 58/3/4; myelitis; Joseph O. Caswell and Martha Libbey
Smith W., d. 10/17/1933 at 76/0/29; carcinoma of eye
Sophronia A., d. 12/24/1918 at 84/9/29 in Somerville, MA; chr. valvular heart dis.
Thomas E., d. 5/2/1936 at 41/8/21; pulmonary tuberculosis
Viola U., d. 4/14/1912 at 3/9/3; nervous shock; William Caswell and Edna F. Earle

CATE,
Alice M., d. 10/16/1927 at 52/0/29; probably heart disease; David O. Cate and Emily A. Gilman
Charles A., d. 3/7/1887 at 0/3/11; b. Dover; David W. Cate (NH) and Belle V. Huckins (NH)
David H., d. 2/24/1937 at 2/10/23; acute appendicitis - rupture
Emily A., d. 6/21/1892 at 55; abscess; b. Alton; (Alton; Alton)
Frank, d. 7/23/1888 at 0/1/9; b. Dover; Charles Cate (Canada) and Amelia Meehean (Canada)
Frank, d. 7/7/1895 at 0; gastro enteritis; b. Dover; SM
Harriet R., d. 1/27/1890 at 58/11/27; married; Jesse Kimball (Lyman, ME) and Ruth Smith (Lyman, ME)
John, d. 8/29/1888 at 1/1/15; b. Dover; John Cate (Canada) and Rosa Beaupre (Canada)
Joseph A., d. 12/27/1903 at 77/11/30; pneumonia; PH
Joseph A., d. 8/29/1926 at 79/11/15 in Alton; cerebral hemorrhage

Joseph W., d. 12/19/1905 at 74/3/19; valvular heart disease
Lydia B., d. 5/30/1920 at 91/0/2 in Boston, MA; valvular heart disease
Mary E., d. 5/20/1904 at 72/5/26; disease of liver; PH
Nathaniel S., d. 12/19/1904 at 72/6/18; Bright's disease; PH
Sadie G., d. 8/5/1917 at 46/11/23 in Derry; chr. intes. nephritis
Sarah A., d. 3/28/1914 at 79/3/24; pernicious anaemia; Lemuel Drew and Lydia H. Twombly

CATER,
Abbie S., d. 2/22/1905 at 47; chronic nephritis; buried in Alton
Annie May, d. 6/18/1917 at 47/10/6; apoplexy; Aaron Farnham and Mary Ellis
Charles A., d. 6/1/1927 at 95; arterio sclerosis
Elmira O., d. 6/27/1913 at 70/1/29; cerebral hemorrhage; Ephraim K. Meader and Lavinia Otis
Emma L., d. 12/22/1906 at 49/10/2; intestinal tuberculosis; PH
Forest A., d. 6/2/1892 at –; diarrhoea; b. Dover
Frank H., d. 5/14/1922 at 66/10/3; pericarditis; Charles Cater and Maria B. Babb
Fred L., d. 12/13/1905 at 27/3/29; nephritis; PH
George F., d. 1/18/1899 at 59; progressive pernicious anaemia; PH
Isaac J., d. 3/10/1905 at 47/5/22; blood lesion; buried in Barrington
Mariam, d. 10/20/1901 at 77/8/27; osteo-sarcoma; buried in Barrington
Walter V., d. 4/16/1918 at 63/1/7 in Concord; arterio sclerosis; Isaac W. Cater and Marion Rowe

CATES,
child, d. 7/16/1926 at –; stillborn; Gladys Cates
James, d. 9/4/1922 at 54/7/6; interstitial nephritis; Bernard Cates and Eliza Fields

CATON,
Sarah, d. 8/12/1911 at 73/11/27 in Beverly, MA; entero colitis

CATONS,
James, d. 9/17/1893 at 50; rheumatism and heart disease; b. Ireland; (Ireland; Ireland)

CAULEY,
child, d. 8/2/1894 at –; stillborn; b. Dover; SM

CAVANAUGH,
child, d. 3/1/1899 at –; inanition; SM
child, d. 12/14/1899 at 0; stillborn; SM

Bridget, d. 5/23/1897 at –; Brights disease; b. Ireland; SM
Bridget, d. 7/7/1901 at 56; carcinoma of breast; SM
Bridget M., d. 10/24/1930 at 69; pyelo nephritis; Patrick McKernan and Catherine Murray
Catherine, d. 2/5/1896 at –; inanition; b. Dover; SM
Christopher, d. 2/23/1917 at 85; chronic cystitis; John Cavanaugh and Mary McKernan
Ellen, d. 10/24/1892 at 60; gastric ulcer; b. Ireland; (Ireland; Ireland)
F. Paul, d. 4/10/1917 at 9/2/15; membranous croup; Edward Cavanaugh and Julia Murphy
James, d. 9/7/1932 at 72; pernicious anemia
Julia, d. 9/27/1937 at 74/4/26; carcinoma of colon
Mary, d. 9/10/1917 at 70; carbuncle of neck; Thomas Cavanaugh and Mary Sinnott
Mary A., d. 3/26/1898 at 32; heart disease; b. Ireland; SM
Mary J., d. 3/7/1912 at 6/2/7; cerebral meningitis; Michael Cavanaugh and Bridget McKernan
Mathew, d. 7/3/1902 at 64; heart disease; SM
Michael, d. 10/22/1921 at 59/10/16; uraemia; Mathew Cavanaugh and Bridget Howland
Michael, d. 3/30/1924 at 80; apoplexy; Thomas Cavanaugh and Mary Sinnott
Rosanna, d. 8/4/1908 at 70; cholecystitis; Peter Couley and Anna M. Kelley
Sarah, d. 5/26/1890 at 30/11; married; Patrick Carbury (Ireland) and Bridget Ward (Ireland)
Stasia G., d. 6/22/1916 at 47/9/6; pernicious anemia; William Holden and Anna Schahian
Thomas, d. 9/17/1898 at 40; cancer of stomach; b. Dover; SM
Thomas J., d. 3/–/1903 at 0/8; meningitis; SM
William H., d. 6/11/1911 at 16/11/24; sarcoma; James Cavanaugh and Stasia Holden

CAVANO,
Catherine, d. 5/15/1922 at 70; myocarditis; Michael Hessian and Catherine ----
James, d. 6/19/1917 at 62; acute dilitation of heart; John Cavano and Katherine McConnell
Margaret, d. 5/19/1904 at 62 in Concord; erysipelas; buried in Dover
Sarah, d. 3/31/1919 at 46/0/28; intestinal indigestion; Felix M. Kone and Margaret McLin

CAVENO,
Ida, d. 10/21/1918 at 78/1/24 in Portsmouth; chronic nephritis

CAVERLY,
Abbie A., d. 12/8/1902 at 73/5/23 in Portsmouth; chronic gastritis
Abra C., d. 3/16/1895 at 91; old age with heart disease; b. Barrington; PH
Augusta W., d. 10/6/1926 at 68/7/1; carcinoma of intestine; Allen G. White and Elizabeth R. Lougee
Charles M., d. 7/14/1890 at 29/8/1 in Fort Payne, AL; single; John S. Caverly (Orford) and Nancy J. Ricker (Lebanon, ME)
Clara S., d. 5/22/1926 at 68/3/21; myocarditis; George W. Churbuck and Harriet Lunnell
Edgar, d. 2/28/1927 at 72/2/16; probably heart disease; George H. Caverly and Salome Hubbard
Francis E., d. 9/20/1894 at 37; typhoid fever; b. Barrington; PH
Fred, Dr., d. 5/15/1935 at 52/11 in Clifton, NJ; cardiac failure
Frederick A., d. 2/21/1924 at 78/10/26 in Stratham; valvular heart disease
George H., d. 2/17/1912 at 88/5/29 in Everett, MA; arterio sclerosis
Henry V., d. 5/12/1900 at 45; cerebral congestion; PH
John Colby, d. 6/4/1891 at 38/10/1; married; John S. Caverly [ ] and Nancy J. Ricker (Lebanon, ME)
John H., d. 11/5/1909 at 83/5/3; cerebral hemorrhage; Daniel Caverly and Nancy Hill
John W., d. 5/3/1914 at 67/3/21 in Lynn, MA; oedema of lungs
Luther M., d. 3/5/1909 at 69/2/20; disease of heart; John Caverly and Nancy French
Mary D., d. 7/8/1916 at 61/4/16; carcinoma of uterus; Benjamin Wiley and Mary C. Hutchins
Mary E., d. 1/20/1921 at 73/11/24 in Lynn, MA; myofibrocarditis
Salome, d. 2/17/1894 at 64; Bright's disease; b. Glenburn, ME; PH
Sarah E., d. 7/19/1937 at 74/8/24; chr. myocarditis
Scott W., d. 10/29/1931 at 29/2/5; accidental
Susan A., d. 4/12/1894 at 67; Bright's disease; b. Dover; PH
Thomas, d. 3/21/1935 at 75/4/17; coronary thrombosis
Valmore Homer, d. 7/9/1926 at 66/2/17; suicide, illuminating gas; George H. Caverly and Salome Hubbard

CAVERNO,
Eliza A., d. 4/19/1898 at 74; pneumonia; b. New Durham; PH
George S., d. 10/21/1916 at 74/3/20 in Durham; dementia
John W., d. 3/29/1917 at 46/6/1; cerebral hemorrhage; James Caverno and Catherine Hession

CAYER,
Adeloniska, d. 12/20/1905 at 18/9; acute enteritis
Lazare, d. 10/12/1890 at 44/3; married; J. Bte. Cayer (Canada) and Sophia Cote (Canada)
Leonie, d. 1/7/1898 at 0; diarrhoea infantile; b. Dover; SM

Ludmille, d. 1/24/1933 at 63/2/20; cerebral hemorrhage
Wilfred, d. 5/7/1900 at <1; broncho pneumonia
William, d. 2/22/1937 at 76/1; chr. myocarditis

CEDER,
George L., d. 8/3/1915 at 0/5/30 in Newburyport, MA; premature birth

CEDRAS,
Adolphe, d. 7/10/1927 at 73/9/3; gen. arterio sclerosis; Louis Cedras and
   Mary L. Rondeau
Albert, d. 3/23/1937 at 46/3/14; chr. myocarditis
Lumina, d. 3/16/1937 at 79/1/19 in Manchester; carcinoma of uterus

CEMAL,
Frandill, d. 1/16/1919 at 22; influenza

CESEY,
James Peter, d. 1/11/1890 at 0/11/7; James Cesey (Ireland) and Eliza
   Cesey (Ireland)

CHABOT,
Joseph J., d. 9/11/1897 at 0; diarrhea infantile; b. Dover; SM
Louis, d. 12/28/1926 at 49; acute nephritis
Pierre, d. 7/5/1919 at 85; natural causes

CHABUT,
Peter, d. 6/12/1901 at 0/4/23; pneumonia

CHADBOURNE,
Cora J., d. 2/3/1918 at 54/6/8; acute bronchitis; Aaron R. Willey and
   Susan W. Pease
Flora M. C., d. 6/10/1927 at 21 in Biddeford, ME; pernicious vomiting;
   Perley W. Gray and Ruby H. Ellis
Leonard K., d. 12/22/1925 at 26/4/7; natural causes; Henry Chadbourne
   and Cora J. Willey
Moses W., d. 10/24/1916 at 74/5/27; cerebral hemorrhage; George G.
   Chadbourne and Eunice Boston
Plavent., d. 8/24/1932 at 91/6/9; chronic myocarditis
Susan H., d. 3/25/1929 at 78/0/28; fracture of femur; Seth Philpot and
   Ruth Nutter
William E., d. 4/22/1901 at 39/9/25 in Cambridge, MA; phthisis -
   tubercular enteritis; PH

CHADBURNE,
Nellie, d. 5/30/1888 at 47

CHADWICK,
Arabella H., d. 3/23/1902 at 43/11/2; paranoia; PH
Edward A., d. 9/24/1905 at 65; Bright's disease; buried in Rockport, MA
Grace M., d. 9/13/1934 at 53 in Melrose, MA; carcinoma of breast
Louisa, d. 5/31/1918 at 91/9/27; shock due to fall; Isaac Seavey and Dolly Twombly
Luther, d. 4/16/1907 at 70/10/10 in Tilton; organic disease of heart
Mahala H., d. 4/30/1901 at 50/5/16; pachymeningitis; PH
Olive M., d. 4/7/1887 at 48/1/10; married; b. Gilmanton; Nehemiah Lougee (Gilmanton) and Dorothy Hull (Moultonboro)
Sarah E., d. 11/6/1899 at 41; traumatic peritonitis; SM
William Kirk., d. 11/14/1915 at 68/11/1; angina pectoris; Daniel Chadwick and Louisa Seavey

CHAISSON,
Joseph, d. 6/29/1937 at 71/3/20; massive hemorrhage of heart

CHALFAUT,
Esther J., d. 10/15/1920 at 0/0/1; unknown; Ivan M. Chalfaut and Anna L. Smith

CHAMBERLAIN,
Charles, d. 4/14/1924 at 75; arterio sclerosis
Clarence H., d. 12/24/1925 at 74/9/20 in Rochester; gangrene
Ethel M., d. 10/16/1932 at 37/1/15; carcinoma
Frank A., d. 3/30/1929 at 50 in Raymond; ch. parench. nephritis
Frank H., d. 5/3/1926 at 67; ac. gastro enteritis; Edward B. Chamberlain and Abigail Colcord
George E., d. 12/12/1899 at 0; convulsions; PH
George W., d. 5/10/1924 at 78/5/4 in Raymond; cancer of throat
Hannah P., d. 4/23/1908 at 84/2/17; senility; John Pillsbury and Hepzibah Smith
Henry, d. 10/19/1892 at 50; paralysis
J. Franklin, d. 11/23/1899 at 62 in Malden, MA; railroad accident; PH
John B., d. 10/8/1898 at 82 in Lawrence, MA; debility from old age
Joseph H., d. 12/24/1919 at 47/4/7; pulm. tuberculosis; George W. Chamberlain and Mary Mansur
Mary A., d. 10/3/1891 at 78/1; widow; George Wendell
Melissa, d. 1/9/1911 at 79/4 in Boston, MA; paralysis
Nellie A., d. 10/15/1934 at 76/1/26 in Rochester; carcinoma of sigmoid
William E., d. 10/12/1932 at 74/3/7; arterio sclerosis

CHAMBERLIN,
Abby D., d. 7/18/1904 at 84 in West Newton, MA; apoplexy; PH
D. T. P., d. 7/21/1892 at 45; apoplexy; b. Lebanon, ME; (Lebanon, ME; Lebanon, ME)
Edward B., d. 2/17/1901 at 88/11/11; senility; PH
Mary E., d. 9/2/1901 at 53/10/28; acute toxaemia from ptomaines; PH

CHAMBERS,
Sarah Jane, d. 9/3/1890 at 0/5/17; Charles Chambers (Fall River, MA) and Sarah Charpentier (Woonsocket)

CHAMPION,
John N., d. 1/1/5/1894 at 82; heart failure; b. Effingham; PH

CHAMPLIN,
William H., d. 5/19/1917 at 58/9/26; diabetes mellitus; George Champlin and Mary Lake

CHANDLER,
Chester S., d. 3/28/1921 at 38 in Pembroke; pulmonary tuberculosis; Arthur Chandler and Belle Foss
Daniel W., d. 6/1/1917 at 54/10/28; phthisis pulmonalis; Ichabod W. Chandler and Mary R. Mackenzie
David H., d. 11/13/1921 at 70/2/17; endocarditis; Hiram Chandler and Lucy Peters
Lucy L. H., d. 10/15/1915 at 74 in Warren; chr. intest. myocarditis; John P. Hale and Lucy H. Lambert
Mary, d. 9/24/1896 at 89; old age; b. Dover; PH
Melvin J., d. 5/16/1887 at 23; laborer; single; b. Ripley, ME; Harvey Chandler (ME)
William L., d. 6/18/1887 at 82/0/20; merchant; widower; b. Dover; Philemon Chandler (Andover, MA) and Betsey Torr (Dover)

CHANEY,
Benjamin F., d. 12/1/1937 at 81/5/1; carcinoma bladder
Frederick A., d. 1/11/1925 at 15/11/16 in Portsmouth; sarcoma of neck

CHAPDELAIN,
William, d. 4/16/1925 at 48; pulmonary tuberculosis

CHAPDALOINE,
Lewis J., d. 2/13/1907 at 0/10/10; tuberculosis; Michael Chapdaloine and Mary H. Campbell

CHAPIN,
Derrick W., d. 11/14/1894 at 84 in Boston, MA; old age; buried in Dover
George W., d. 3/18/1909 at 65 in Littleton; chronic Brights disease

CHAPMAN,
Abigail C., d. 3/12/1925 at 10/1/3; encephalitis; Frank V. Chapman and Christine Bordeen
Amelia, d. 10/22/1905 at – in New York City; peritonitis
Benjamin F., d. 8/13/1899 at 69 in Boston, MA; carcinoma of liver; PH
Charles L., d. 1/18/1887 at 55/7/21; watchman; married; b. Sanford, ME; Charles L. Chapman and Margaret Gaivell (Lebanon, ME)
Hazel M., d. 8/8/1934 at 24/0/20 in Middleton, MA; pulmonary tuberculosis
Mary E., d. 6/30/1913 at 19/7/20; cerebral hemorrhage; Frank E. Chick and Annie F. Stanton
Nathan D., d. 1/27/1908 at 75/0/20; bronchial ashthma; Nathan Chapman and Abigail Dearborn
Sarah, d. 2/7/1910 at 78/10/24; valv. heart disease; Alexander Witham and Mehitable Moody
Thama, d. 11/27/1920 at 89/7/4; valvular heart disease; Thomas Garland and Mahala Varney
Thomas C., d. 10/22/1925 at 87/8/5 in York, ME; exhaustion
William G., d. 6/27/1916 at 60/0/23; mitral regurgitation; William Chapman and Sarah Davis

CHAPPELL,
Edward, d. 4/29/1891 at 4/0/6; Lister Chappell (England) and Ann Garratt (England)
Lister, d. 4/9/1915 at 54/4/27; angina pectoris; Edward Chappell and Hannah Tatterson

CHARBONNEAU,
Albert, d. 3/27/1907 at 18/4/28; typhoid fever; Joseph Charbonneau and Anna Leveillee

CHAREST,
Cleopatra A., d. 8/10/1922 at 58/6; angina pectoris; Oliver Charest
Jennie, d. 10/25/1891 at 0/1/16; Fred Charest (Canada) and Jennie Reney (Great Falls)
Paul E., d. 10/1/1911 at 15/7/24; perforation of intestines; Cleophas Charest and Rosalie Deloge
Philias L., d. 5/9/1909 at 41/2/6; pul. tuberculosis; Oliver Charest and Henriette Paradis
Rosalie M., d. 5/9/1936 at 75/3/22; cer. arteriosclerosis
Wilfred, d. 7/4/1923 at 18/9/15; struck by locomotive

CHARETTE,
Angelina, d. 2/14/1923 at 50/3/12; typhoid fever; Treffle Fillion and
  Celunire Roussin
Henry, d. 9/27/1930 at 54/5/15; peritonitis; Elisee Charrette (sic) and Marie
  Mailloux

CHARLES,
Jennie F., d. 2/6/1932 at 53/6/15; endocarditis

CHASE,
child, d. 1/14/1892 at –; pneumonia; b. Dover; (Dover; Chesterfield)
child, d. 2/28/1898 at 0; brain trouble; b. Dover; PH
child, d. 10/7/1900 at <1; immaturity
Abbie, d. 3/10/1913 at 79; natural causes; ----- Thompson and ----- Boston
Abbie E., d. 6/19/1893 at 40; Bright's disease; b. Farmington;
  (Farmington; Milton)
Alan Card, Jr., d. 6/19/1935 at 4 hrs.; hemorrhage - new born
Alice J. F., d. 10/13/1917 at 52/0/29; dementia; John C. Farrington and
  Mary A. Banfill
Audrey M., d. 2/6/1929 at 8/5; brain abscess; Charles W. Chase and Cora
  M. Wilkinson
Benjamin F., d. 9/2/1887 at 0/10/26; b. Dover; Frank Chase (Danvers, MA)
  and ----- (Middleton)
Betsey, d. 3/18/1911 at 80/11/17; pneumonia; Hiram Goodwin and Draxy
  Gowell
Charles H., d. 7/3/1931 at 74/3/6; chronic myocarditis
Eliza A., d. 12/26/1915 at 90/9/19; pneumonia; John Hill and Lydia
  Brackett
Emma V., d. 12/31/1915 at 52; pneumonia; Jacob Chase and Abigail
  Thompson
Florence A., d. 1/13/1922 at 62/10/24; apoplexy; John H. Hayes and Eliza
  J. Andrews
Frank H., d. 11/6/1923 at 70 in Coos; cancer of prost. gland; Mark W.
  Chase and Mary A. Fowler
Frank K., d. 7/2/1923 at 74/10 in Maple Shade, NJ; oedema of brain
Georgie, d. 1/6/1892 at ½; disease of brain; b. Lawrence, MA; (No.
  Berwick, ME; Ossipee)
James F., d. 7/27/1911 at 80/7/27; senility; John Chase and Jehoaddan
  Piper
Jehoaddan, d. 7/18/1895 at 82; disease of heart; b. Middleton; PH
Lizzie, d. 9/1-/1902 at 65/10/15 in Sanford, ME; heart disease; PH
Louisa B., d. 8/23/1895 at 77; senile asthma; b. York, ME; buried in York,
  ME
Maria H., d. 6/20/1901 at 59/1 in Middleboro, MA; heart disease; PH
Mark, d. 7/24/1937 at 85/1/4; coronary thrombosis

Nellie H., d. 4/9/1921 at 58/11/8; chr. int'st'l nephritis; ----- Crosby
Pamelia A., d. 6/7/1895 at 62; paralysis; b. Wolfeboro; PH
Parmelia A., d. 12/21/1899 at 4; disease of brain; PH
Paul F., d. 6/28/1927 at 0/0/3; hem. dis. of new born; Alan C. Chase and Catherine Hughes
Perley F., d. 12/7/1887 at 0/3/15; b. Dover; George S. Chase (Danvers, MA) and Lizzie McKenna (PEI)
Plummer I., d. 8/16/1905 at 0/11/16; convulsions; buried in East Rochester
Robert W., d. 5/19/1900 at 70 in Newton, MA; heart disease; PH
Rosalie A., d. 12/29/1887 at 35/3/17; married; b. Rochester; Plummer Horne and Mary Waldron

CHASSE,
August, d. 1/13/1931 at 40/10/12 in Kittery, ME; atelectasis
Robert, d. 11/24/1937 at –; stillborn

CHASSEE,
John D., d. 11/30/1931 at 60; angina pectoris

CHEBOT,
child, d. 6/3/1899 at –; pneumonia

CHELLIS,
Henry, d. 1/16/1928 at 75; apoplexy; Ira Chellis and Betsy Clark

CHEMIKLIS,
Helen, d. 9/11/1924 at 0/4/16 in Manchester; septicemia

CHENARD [see Chenaud],
Aurelian, d. 4/28/1933 at 52/4/25; chronic myocarditis
Henri, d. 3/14/1915 at 0/8/17; entero colitis; Amelien Chenard and Alice Dube
Joseph, d. 7/4/1926 at 3 hrs.; miscarriage; Aurelien Chenard and Alice Dube

CHENAUD [see Chenard],
Robert, d. 3/2/1923 at 0/1/20; ileo colitis; Amelian Chenaud and Alice Dube

CHENEVERT,
Mary, d. 11/20/1928 at –; malformation; William Chenevert

CHENEY,
Alphonso A., d. 9/22/1903 at 52/3/16; broken neck; PH

George H., d. 4/11/1928 at 58/0/11; hypertrophy of prostate; Ira Cheney and Sarah A. York
Irene C., d. 12/17/1891 at 73/9/28 in Chelsea, MA
Joseph, d. 12/17/1901 at –; laryngeal tuberculosis; buried in Somersworth
Josiah H., d. 7/29/1928 at 63/6; cancer of face; Ira Cheney and Sarah A. York
Person Colby, d. 6/19/1901 at 73/3/25; pernicious anemia; buried in Manchester
Sarah A., d. 11/26/1925 at 83/7/29; lobar pneumonia; Josiah York and Catherine Davis
William G., d. 7/15/1921 at 54/6/18 in Lynn, MA; pulmonary tuberculosis

CHEREST,
Philip, d. 6/21/1889 at 23; laborer; married; b. Canada; Lawrence Cherest (Canada)

CHERRETTE,
Lois F., d. 4/14/1932 at 5/0/16; cerebral hemorrhage

CHESLEY,
Anastasia, d. 9/21/1935 at 74/7/29; chronic myocarditis
Arthur P., d. 10/5/1915 at 55/0/6; intestinal ulcer; Philip Chesley and Mary J. Meserve
Edith May, d. 10/10/1902 at 0/3/28; malnutrition; PH
Frank A., d. 2/2/1893 at 37; pneumonia; b. Madbury
Harold W., d. 3/31/1934 at 38/7/16; erysipelas
James C., d. 11/19/1893 at 70; shock - apoplexy; b. Barrington
James S., d. 3/26/1927 at 63/0/5; endocarditis; John S. Chesley and Adeline N. Sanborn
Jennie S., d. 8/30/1914 at 41/5/19; diabetes
John B., d. 10/3/1890 at 71; single; Joseph Chesley and Mary Hull
John F., d. 11/18/1911 at 74/4/28; nephritis; John M. Chesley and Sarah Jenkins
John S., d. 10/13/1896 at 57 in Durham; heart failure; PH
Liza F., d. 11/21/1912 at 65; broncho pneumonia; John Layne
Mary A., d. 12/31/1916 at 77/7/5 in Durham; angina pectoris
Mary A., d. 3/12/1918 at 69 in Boston, MA; la grippe
Mary H., d. 9/20/1895 at – in Durham; PH
Samuel, d. 6/27/1887 at 83/7; carpenter; widower; b. Madbury; Paul Chesley (Durham)
Stephen P., d. 12/20/1937 at 75/3/27*
Susan A., d. 8/30/1924 at 61/9; myocarditis; George W. Horne and Nancy Mason
Wilbert S., d. 11/20/1935 at 69/10/24 in Durham; bronchial aylbria
William, d. 2/9/1893 at 42; died in Strafford Co. Asylum fire

CHESSIA,
Namoi, d. 3/28/1908 at 11/5; typhoid fever; John B. Chessia and Jenny M. Abbott

CHESWELL,
Sophronia J., d. 9/19/1914 at 65 in Somersworth; heart trouble
Thomas E., d. 3/23/1923 at 79/11/23 in Manchester; mitral regurgitation

CHEVERETTE,
Maud S., d. 1/8/1926 at 51; angina pectoris; John B. King and Mary Abbott

CHICK,
Annie B., d. 3/29/1924 at 78/0/8; hemiplegia; Thomas Clough and Ruth Whitehouse
Byron S., d. 6/22/1930 at 82/5/23; chronic myocarditis; Stephen Chick and Sarah A. Pillsbury
Dorothea A., d. 12/3/1930 at 26/4/17; acute nephritis; D. O'Neil and Mary Carnes
Ellen C., d. 12/15/1925 at 0/0/3; umbilical hemorrhage; Charles E. Chick and Martha E. McGlone
George, d. 2/24/1892 at 4; diphtheria; b. Dover; (Eliot, ME; Ireland)
George A., d. 8/19/1911 at 55 in Concord; gastro enteritis; Thomas Chick and Mary A. Hersom
George E., d. 11/24/1895 at 49; compression of brain; b. Berwick, ME; buried in Berwick, ME
George T., d. 8/30/1906 at 15; accidental drowning; SM
Ina E., d. 8/8/1905 at 1/0/17; cholera infantum; buried in East Rochester
Nellie May, d. 3/4/1920 at 29/10/28 in Laconia; lobar pneumonia; George Chick and Maggie -----

CHICOINE,
child, d. 12/28/1903 at –; unknown
Alexander, d. 4/30/1937 at 86/4/1; cerebral embolism
James M., d. 8/9/1898 at 0; diarrhea infantile; b. Dover; SM
William N., d. 8/16/1902 at 0/9/11; cholera infantum

CHILDS,
Jennie M., d. 10/21/1915 at 47 in Kansas City, MO; shock

CHIMIKILIS,
Athanasios, d. 4/3/1920 at 0/10/8; Peter Chimikilis and Ellen Mocacos
Francena, d. 11/5/1929 at 38 in Pembroke; pulm. tuberculosis
Helen, d. 6/4/1924 at 38; diarrhea and enteritis; Charles Markos
Mary, d. 11/22/1936 at 22/3/7*

Peter, d. 3/16/1925 at 46/2/16 in Benton; pulmonary tuberculosis; Arthur C. Chimiklis and Annie S. Kostis

CHIPMAN,
Edwin S., d. 9/13/1933 at 66/0/20; fractured skull

CHOUINARD,
Albert, d. 6/5/1923 at 3/6/26; peritonitis; Lazare Chouinard and Clara Pelletier

CHRISENTEN,
Cora, d. 12/19/1917 at 53/8/2 in Newburyport, MA; lobar pneumonia

CHRISENTON,
Charles W., d. 9/20/1888 at 0/1/6; b. Dover; Charles Chrisenton (MA) and Cora S. Milliken (ME)

CHRISOPOULOS,
Stephen, d. 10/16/1918 at 34; influenza; Louis Chrisopoulos and Jeannette
-----

CHRISTENSON,
Charles E., d. 12/11/1928 at 65/0/12 in Newburyport, MA; cancer of stomach

CHRISTIE,
child, d. 10/11/1894 at –; stillborn; b. Dover; PH
Annie W., d. 9/21/1933 at 65/6/27; broncho pneumonia
Edward M., d. 3/2/1901 at 62/10/14; apoplexy; PH
Fred Abbott, d. 8/11/1930 at 85/11/1; cerebral hemorrhage; Ira Christie and Ann Collier
James I., d. 4/6/1889 at 46/10/27 in Washington; b. NH
Thomas C., d. 9/27/1902 at 69/0/18 in Kittery, ME; cardiac dropsy; PH

CHRISTY,
Robert, d. 12/22/1891 at 88/0/22; widower; Jesse Christy (ME) and Olive Whitehouse (NB)

CHURBUCK,
George H., d. 12/18/1914 at 62/2/9; heart dilitation; George W. Churbuck and Harriet Linnell
Harriet E., d. 2/5/1897 at 63; pneumonia; b. Centreville, MA; PH
Jennie R., d. 4/12/1935 at 72/8/20; some form of heart disease
Orlando L., d. 5/22/1934 at 75/0/7 in Madbury; cerebral hemorrhage

CHURCHILL,
E. P., d. 7/25/1903 at 38/3/8; gastric cancer; PH
Martha J., d. 1/29/1895 at 64 in Boston, MA; nevritis; buried in Dover
Nathaniel W., d. 5/8/1903 at 75/6/27 in Boston, MA; senile dementia; PH

CILLEY,
Abraham, d. 2/4/1902 at 72/9/27; cerebral hemorrhage; SM
Benjamin F., d. 1/19/1912 at 85; chronic nephritis
Eliza E., d. 2/27/1934 at 92/7/25; bronchitis
Horace L., d. 8/17/1897 at 64 in Hamilton, MA; apoplexy; PH
L. Etta, d. 7/1/1935 at 73/7/4; cerebral hemorrhage
Octavia M., d. 11/24/1913 at 80/9/1; angina pectoris; Mark Chase and -----
    Taylor

CISCO,
Mary J., d. 1/8/1900 at 74; chronic Bright's disease; PH

CLAGGETT,
Delana M., d. 11/29/1936 at 53/9/13; gen. carcinomatosis

CLAMPET,
George R., d. 3/30/1909 at 0/9/29; convulsions; John H. Clampet and
    Bessie B. Williams

CLANCEY,
child, d. 1/1/1909 at –; stillborn; James Clancey and Rosanna Moran
James, d. 11/15/1895 at 22; peritonitis; b. Dover; SM

CLANCY,
Bridget, d. 11/17/1899 at 101; old age; SM
Ellen, d. 6/8/1904 at 51; heart disease; PH
James Francis, d. 9/13/1912 at 0/3/3; cholera infantum; Sylvester Clancy
    and Margaret Markey
James W., d. 4/24/1904 at 1/10/8; spinal meningitis
John A., d. 8/22/1907 at 0/6/21; cholera infantum; John Clancy and Eva
    McKenna

CLARK,
child, d. 1/12/1897 at 0; stillborn; b. Dover; PH
child, d. 2/23/1900 at <1; PH
child, d. 2/27/1913 at 0/0/1; apnoea neonatorum; Frank Clark and Agnes
    Bather
child, d. 9/23/1923 at – in Cambridge, MA; stillborn
Abigail T., d. 7/9/1887 at 78/3/01; widow; b. Dover; Edward Cotton

Alfred C., d. 8/22/1893 at 65; hernia; b. Strafford; (Strafford; -----)
Annie F., d. 11/19/1936 at 57/8/15; intestinal obstruction
Annis C. H., d. 4/4/1891 at 62/11/9; married; Chipman Hodgkins (Portland, ME) and Abigail Thurlow (Portland, ME)
Aphia P., d. 4/8/1890 at 62; widow; Daniel Johnson (Berwick, ME) and Philenia Ford (Berwick, ME)
Benny P., d. 6/7/1908 at 24/5/29 in Rollinsford; accidental drowning
Bernard, d. 8/28/1891 at 32/5/16; married; Francis Clark (Ireland) and Catherine McCabe (Ireland)
Catherine, d. 1/7/1906 at 79/5/12; old age; SM
Charles, d. 3/25/1895 at – in Rochester; PH
Charles E., d. 5/27/1907 at 48/9/4; diabetes; Charles E. Clark and Martha Vining
Charles E., d. 9/7/1913 at 61/7/29; cancer of bladder; Charles L. Clark and Sarah Guptill
Charles H., d. 9/30/1918 at 67/8/9; carcinoma of rectum; John S. Clark and Lucinda Gilman
Charlotte, d. 10/1/1896 at 91; old age; b. Barrington; buried in Newmarket
Daniel J., d. 2/13/1921 at 67/7/19 in Jersey City, NJ; pneumonia
David C., d. 12/30/1908 at 81/2/25; old age; Joseph Clark and Mary Cate
E., d. 9/2/1893 at 82; apoplexy; b. Berwick, ME; (Berwick, ME; Berwick, ME)
Elizabeth, d. 11/21/1888 at 18/1/16; mill; single; b. Ireland; Patrick Clark (Ireland) and Mary Farrin (Ireland)
Elizabeth A., d. 11/7/1935 at 82/7/28; chronic interstitial nephritis
Elizabeth C., d. 11/21/1929 at 70/3 in Boston, MA; angina pectoris; James Crawford and ----- McPherson
Elizabeth L., d. 4/27/1914 at 94/8/7 in Boston, MA; bronchitis
Elizabeth N., d. 2/9/1892 at 83; pneumonia, la grippe; b. Dover; (Dover; -----)
Ellen B., d. 12/3/1929 at 81 in Hingham, MA; cereb. hemorrhage
Emma F., d. 10/22/1916 at 55/8/16; nephritis; Joshua Foss
Emma M., d. 2/28/1910 at 55; diabetes mellitus; Seorus Whitcomb and M. J. Brown
Emma M., d. 10/16/1918 at 21/4/6 in Somersworth; pneumonia; F. Metivier and Celina Labbe
Frank Burns, d. 3/17/1928 at 76/9/27 in Los Angeles, CA; chronic myocarditis; Robert Clark and Alvira G. Stevens
Frank H., d. 3/21/1912 at 59 in Portland, ME; chronic nephritis
Frank H., d. 7/12/1926 at 65/4/3; chronic endocarditis; John M. Clark and Annice Hodgkin
Fred, d. 5/24/1903 at 0/0/2; atelactasis
George B., d. 6/14/1934 at 67/10/7; chronic myocarditis
George F., d. 11/23/1936 at 70/7/11*; b. Dover

George W., d. 11/1/1910 at 43 in Wakefield, MA; suicide; John S. Clark and Lucinda Gilman

George W., d. 5/24/1912 at 77/11/20 in Hingham, MA; apoplexy

Grace G., d. 5/18/1897 at 19; acute tuberculosis; b. Somerville, MA

Harry, d. 12/23/1895 at –; heart disease; b. Dover; buried in Oxford, MA

Helen, d. 6/27/1926 at 73/11/23; diabetes mellitus; Charles Estes and Mercy Varney

Ida G., d. 5/11/1901 at 43/0/22; surgical shock; PH

Irene O., d. 1/27/1917 at 69/6/10 in Haverhill, MA; myocarditis

James, d. 9/27/1928 at 53; natural causes; Patrick Clark and Mary Farnham

John, d. 7/26/1887 at 50/9/6; loom fixer; married; b. Scotland; James Clark (Scotland) and Margaret (Scotland)

John P., d. 2/6/1922 at 30/8/12; phthisis pulmonalis; Elmer Clark and Bertha Fernald

John S., d. 1/27/1910 at 35/11/24; apoplexy; Jonathan Clark and Sophia D. -----

Joseph L., d. 11/21/1923 at 78/1/19; myocarditis; Charles Clark and Martha A. Leighton

Laforest C., d. 12/9/1932 at 82/10/26; cerebral hemorrhage

Lovie D., d. 4/20/1926 at 79/11/1; broncho pneumonia; Charles H. Hayes and Nancy J. -----

Margaret J., d. 6/16/1910 at 1/10/21; drowning; William J. Clark and Mary R. Dearborn

Martha A., d. 3/17/1921 at 99/2/4; natural senile changes; Levi Leighton and Hannah Peavey

Martha S., d. 8/26/1893 at 57; heart disease; b. Farmington; (Eliot, ME; Dover)

Martin V. B., d. 10/9/1909 at 75/6/26 in Framingham, MA; cerebral embolism

Mary, d. 5/2/1907 at 67; rheumatism; Patrick Farran

Mary Buell, d. 1/16/1891 at 82/7/29; widow; James Rollins (Rollinsford) and Dorothy Folsom (Portsmouth)

Mary E., d. 12/14/1897 at 84; old age; b. Portsmouth; PH

Mary E., d. 11/14/1903 at 74/0/16; septicaemia; PH

Mary E., d. 2/14/1906 at 80/6/11; pneumonia; PH

Mary E., d. 7/8/1916 at 60/8/10; disease of liver; John McDonald

Mary Ellen, d. 10/27/1887 at 0/5/6; b. Dover; Bernard Clark (Philadelphia, PA) and Sarah Riley (Ireland)

Mary F. E., d. 10/27/1909 at 57/1/8; cancer of uterus, bladder; Sampson Locke and Sarah Canney

Mary P., d. 1/9/1905 at 52 in Portland, ME; pneumonia; PH

Mary W., d. 10/3/1898 at 78; senility; b. Dover; PH

Matilda, d. 12/6/1927 at 59; carcinoma of uterus; John Lynch

Minnie M., d. 5/20/1922 at 47/4/27; uterine carcinoma; John E. Durgin and Cassandria E. -----
Nancy, d. 9/20/1901 at 80/5/18; old age; PH
Oliver J., d. 2/8/1907 at 55/4/14; strangulated hernia; Alfred C. Clark and Mary E. Horn
Orin, d. 6/10/1901 at 48/4/28; primary lobar pneumonia; buried in Tuftonboro
Orrin R., d. 8/16/1913 at 65; indigestion; John S. Clark and Lucinda W. Gilman
Patrick, d. 10/25/1892 at 55; typhoid fever; b. Ireland; (Ireland; Ireland)
Philip R., d. 1/8/1931 at 9/0/3 in Framingham, MA; acute nephritis
Phyllis Eileen, d. 4/15/1923 at 1/5/19 in Haverhill, MA; diarrhea, enteritis
Rachel, d. 5/24/1904 at 76 in Concord; cerebral hemorrhage; buried in Dover
Renselaer E., d. 10/28/1892 at 76; inanition; b. Parsonsfield, ME; (Sturbridge, MA; Sturbridge, MA)
Richard O., d. 2/10/1926 at 71; chronic myocarditis; Robert B. Clark and Elvira G. Stevens
Robert B., d. 3/2/1890 at 72/0/4; widower; Robert B. Clark (NH) and ----- Currier (NH)
Robert W., d. 8/12/1911 at 1/6/25; hit by team; J. Walter Clark and Viola A. Webster
Rosella M., d. 9/23/1918 at 38/0/30; acute uraemia; Alexander McWilliams and Susan Egleson
Ruth E., d. 8/4/1924 at 31/6/1 in Haverhill, MA; pulmonary tuberculosis
Samuel, d. 5/1/1932 at 73; apoplexy
Sarah A., d. 6/16/1914 at 76/7/4; diabetes; Oliver Clark and Ruth Delano
Sarah B., d. 12/9/1922 at 83/6/23; arterio sclerosis; David Huntington and Clarissa Osgood
Sarah J., d. 7/16/1923 at 55/9/4; cancer of uterus
Sarah M., d. 4/18/1904 at 70/1/8 in Cambridge, MA; cancer of liver; PH
Susan F., d. 9/29/1920 at 87 in Berwick, ME; grip cold, old age
Susie A., d. 9/11/1887 at 0/8; b. Dover; William R. Clark (Dover) and Mary E. McDonald (Bath, ME)
Thatcher R., d. 5/1/1936 at 54/10/8*
William A. H., d. 8/17/1918 at 35/10/7 in E. Providence, RI; railroad accident; William R. Clark and Lizzie M. -----
William H., d. 11/22/1903 at 61/7 in Boston, MA; pneumonia; PH
William R., d. 12/31/1923 at 74/11/6; chronic myocarditis; John S. Clark and Lucinda Gilman
Zelia W., d. 1/25/1899 at 73 in Concord; bronchial pneumonia; PH

CLARKE,
Ann M., d. 1/29/1906 at 55/0/15; chronic diffuse nephritis; buried in Jamaica Plain, MA

Clarissa D., d. 12/19/1893 at 73; pneumonia; b. Barrington; (Barrington; Rochester)
Edward S., d. 8/27/1918 at 59/0/16; chronic nephritis; Everett C. Clarke and Sarah A. Bean
Emma A., d. 12/31/1928 at 70/11/24; prim. lateral sclerosis; Benjamin F. Clark and Mary Gray
George F., d. 11/17/1935 at 84/5/19; arteriosclerosis
Isaac W., d. 9/2/1924 at 71 in Boston, MA; intestinal obstruction
John M., d. 5/10/1892 at 70; chronic bronchitis; b. Alton; (Middleton; Farmington)
Mary E., d. 6/3/1890 at 50; widow
Mary S., d. 2/16/1900 at 63 in Blue Hill, ME; cancer; PH
Mary Towle, d. 11/9/1926 at 68/2; cerebral hemorrhage; Gilman D. Towle and Jane Edgerly
Susan M., d. 4/3/1894 at 90; old age; PH

CLAY,
Daniel, d. 6/12/1911 at 81 in Concord; organic heart disease; R. Parker Clay and Harriet Spurling
Elizabeth L., d. 6/15/1921 at 63/8/23; carcinoma of liver; Leonard Cole and Mary E. Harris
Flora Bell, d. 1/1/1888 at 4; b. Somersworth; Nellie Clay
Harry P., d. 11/30/1934 at 67/0/10; cerebral hemorrhage
Mary V., d. 3/18/1905 at 82/6/23 in Strafford; cardiac dropsy; PH

CLEAVES,
Nancy W., d. 12/9/1895 at 86; senility; b. Alton; PH
Ursula T., d. 7/9/1903 at 71/6/17; rheumatic arthritis; buried in Kennebunk, ME

CLEE,
Walter F., d. 2/8/1902 at 20/2/28; acute lobar pneumonia; buried in No. Andover, MA

CLEMENT,
child, d. 2/21/1916 at –; congenital atelestasis; George E. Clement and Bertha Norman
Benjamin, d. 12/25/1888 at 60/6/17
Catherine, d. 10/5/1935 at 51; cerebral apoplexy
Leonora, d. 1/8/1910 at 50 in Concord; valv. disease of heart; J. N. Rogers and Naomi Hall

CLEMENTS,
child, d. 12/30/1917 at –; stillborn; John H. Clements and Kate O'Neil
Abigail, d. 9/6/1899 at 85; inanition; buried at Dover Point

Addie F., d. 6/5/1923 at 68/10/29; cystitis; Charles Pinkham and Adeline Card
Annie C., d. 10/14/1892 at –; typhoid fever
Eliza F., d. 8/24/1933 at 18/2/1 in S. Berwick, ME; cerebral hemorrhage
John, d. 11/6/1887 at 77/1/21; farmer; married; b. Dover; William Clements (Dover) and Nancy Tripe (Dover)
John B., d. 6/1/1932 at 68/5/24; arterio sclerosis
John Wesley, d. 1/26/1922 at 70/11/9; cancer of lip; John Clements and Abigail Dow
Olive H., d. 3/2/1895 at 78; la grippe; b. Waterboro, ME; buried in Somersworth

CLEUTIER,
John, d. 12/1/1924 at 31 in Portsmouth; lobar pneumonia

CLIFFORD,
Charles G., d. 5/6/1912 at 13/4/12 in S. Berwick, ME; pneumonia
Elizabeth, d. 11/17/1912 at 72; broncho pneumonia; Thomas Clifford and Mary Breen
George, d. 6/1/1937 at 63/8/23 in Rollinsford; heart disease (see following entry)
George W., d. 6/1/1937 at 63/9/8* (see preceding entry)
Helen M., d. 11/2/1925 at 85/3/11; angina pectoris; Joseph B. Skinner and Eunice Slocum
Margaret A., d. 1/1/1914 at 85/3/9; cerebral hemorrhage; Joseph Hawkins and Harriet Lougee
Mary J., d. 4/26/1918 at 52/9/11; acute gastritis; Thomas Lee and Mary O'Connor
Stuart, d. 2/20/1887 at 82/2/10; dyer; married; b. Newburyport, MA; Benjamin Clifford (Rumney) and ----- Currier (S. Hampton)

CLINTON,
Farnham D., d. 3/8/1928 at 76/4/6; broncho pneumonia

CLOUCHER,
Lena, d. 8/6/1906 at 0/9/3; cholera infantum

CLOUGH,
Betsey A., d. 4/19/1905 at 65/4/20; diabetes mellitus; buried in Newfields
Burt E., d. 8/11/1896 at 24 in Londonderry; blood poisoning
Charles H., d. 7/26/1926 at 85/7/18 in Portsmouth; uremia
Charles W., d. 11/30/1894 at 26; overdose of aconite; buried in Kennebunk, ME
Clarence Edward, d. 2/6/1923 at 1/0/4; broncho pneumonia; Perley G. Clough and Jennie M. Freeman

Emily R., d. 8/23/1908 at 79; cancer of stomach; D. D. Bennett and Sarah T. Collins
Frank B., d. 10/21/1905 at 57/7/7; pneumonia; PH
Frank W., d. 10/10/1905 at 46; heart disease; PH
George F., d. 11/14/1918 at 81/2/18; arterio sclerosis; John Clough
Gladys Belle, d. 4/20/1921 at 0/0/6; convulsions; Perley G. Clough and Jennie Freeman
Grace P., d. 2/25/1922 at 50/7/12; cerebral hemorrhage; George F. Clough and Hannah D. Bedell
Hannah D., d. 7/5/1916 at 77/5/11; cancer of bowel
Hattie A., d. 3/6/1934 at 69/8/10 in Brentwood; arteriosclerosis
Ida C., d. 4/22/1927 at 69/11/19; broncho pneumonia; Bela H. Emerson and Mary J. Clough
James E., d. 8/7/1928 at 76/4/23 in Wolfeboro; prob. ac. heart failure
Jonathan A., d. 4/28/1893 at 63; paralysis; b. Moultonboro; (Gilmanton; Gilmanton)
Joseph, d. 8/30/1898 at 65; dysentery; b. England; PH
Joseph A., d. 6/10/1911 at 88/7/25; ch. intestinal nephritis; Richard Clough and Rhoda Elkins
Julia A., d. 3/19/1913 at 57 in Portland, ME; apoplexy
Mary D., d. 5/3/1915 at 44/2/24; suicide - cutting throat; Wells Pinkham and Martha J. Grey
Mildred J., d. 2/9/1925 at 2 in Fremont; Perley Clough and Jennie -----
Nathaniel, d. 7/25/1907 at 63/5/24; Bright's disease; John Clough and Mary Howe
Sarah, d. 9/14/1897 at 73; paralysis; b. Eliot, ME; PH

CLOUTIER,
Angelina, d. 7/31/1891 at 0/6/25; Thomas Cloutier (Canada) and Georgiana Gagnon (Canada)
John, d. 5/9/1927 at 81/11/17 in Portsmouth; eraemia
Magloire, d. 11/25/1936 at 50/10/3; cerebral hemorrhage
Mary, d. 11/6/1930 at 80 in Portsmouth; chr. myocarditis
Romeo, d. 8/19/1917 at 0/2/14; athrepsia; Joseph Cloutier and Nora Fournier

CLOUTMAN,
Addie L., d. 2/26/1914 at 63/9/20; acute bronchitis; Amos P. Caswell and Lucy Spring
John H., d. 2/10/1910 at 76/6/21; senile gangrene; Asa Cloutman and Syrena Hanson

CLUFF,
Asa F., d. 3/28/1936 at 74/3/25; cerebral hemorrhage

Luella R., d. 10/31/1930 at 72/5/23; eraemia; Enoch Roberts and Hannah Jellison
Miriam Weed, d. 6/25/1891 at 66/7/11; widow; William Weed (Topsham, VT) and Susan Davis (Topsham, VT)

CLUKEY,
Eugene R., d. 10/20/1917 at 1/7/15 in Portsmouth; gastro enteritis; Lea Clukey

COAKLEY,
Bridget A., d. 1/16/1937 at 74; chr. endocarditis
James, d. 9/22/1916 at 50; hem. of spinal cord

COBB,
Marcellus L., d. 12/2/1892 at 56; Brights disease; b. Union, ME; (MA; Union, ME)

COBBETT,
Eugenia L., d. 4/1/1926 at 83/7/26; cerebral hemorrhage; James Aborn and Sarah J. Brown

COBURN,
Clara E., d. 9/10/1916 at 59/7/21; can. cirrhosis of liver; Gilman Ham and Hannah E. Hanscom
Gladys H., d. 9/3/1893 at –; peritonitis; b. Dover; (Exeter; No. Berwick, ME)
Herbert A., d. 2/25/1931 at 73/8/24; lobar pneumonia
Nancy C., d. 4/10/1925 at 86/10/8 in Haverhill, MA; broncho pneumonia

COCHRAN,
Ella L., d. 5/31/1912 at 52/11; epithelioma (abdominal); William Hayes and Lavina Williams

COCHRANE,
child, d. 8/3/1934 at –; stillborn
William H., d. 1/21/1916 at 32/2/18; puncture of duodenum; Joseph L. Cochrane and Charlotte Kitchen

COCHREN,
George F., d. 6/27/1890 at 7/9; Henry Cochren (US) and Effie E. Ford (Dover)

COCKERING,
Albert R., d. 12/26/1891 at 1/4; Dean Hale (NH) and Susan Cockering (Scotland)

COCKIN,
Charles R., d. 3/11/1902 at 59/2 in Madbury; nephritis; PH

COCKING,
Edward H., d. 3/29/1894 at 49; Bright's disease; b. Dover; PH
Mary A., d. 12/16/1920 at 73/7/18 in S. Berwick, ME; valvular heart disease
Priscilla A., d. 8/21/1917 at 84/5/15; cerebral hemorrhage; John H. Abbott and Adeline Doloph

CODY,
Mary, d. 7/3/1911 at 77; myocarditis; Bernard Rand and Ann Hughes
Mary, d. 11/4/1936 at 65; chr. myocarditis
William, d. 5/20/1890 at 25/5/26; single; Daniel Cody (Ireland) and Mary Ann Rand (Dover)

COFFEE,
Eugene, d. 6/5/1909 at 68; epitheliona
Mary, d. 5/23/1906 at 65; liver disease; SM
Patrick, d. 4/7/1893 at 50; organic disease of heart; b. Ireland

COFFEY,
Albert E., d. 7/27/1933 at 32/4/19; valvular disease of heart
Bridget, d. 4/15/1911 at 69; elephantiasis; John Rodden and Mary McCarron
Michael J., d. 10/4/1937 at 67/5/25; coronary thrombosis

COFFIN,
child, d. 12/24/1919 at –; stillborn; George W. Coffin and Edith Barenforth
Edith, d. 3/24/1923 at 35/5/8; cerebral hemorrhage
Fred, d. 6/3/1935 at 67/9/7; pernicious anemia
George W., d. 4/2/1932 at 51/1/19; chronic nephritis
Nathan, d. 12/21/1930 at 58; natural causes; James H. Coffin and Caroline ----
William M., d. 3/31/1903 at 50 in St. Paul, MN; nephritis; PH

COFFY,
Mary, d. 1/31/1913 at 57 in N. Chelmsford, MA; myocarditis

COGLEY,
Frank P., d. 8/21/1897 at 48 in Pike's Station; cerebral hemorrhage; b. Richmond, PQ; PH

COGNEY,
Mary, d. 2/9/1893 at 40; died in Strafford Co. Asylum fire

COLBATH,
Caroline S., d. 12/19/1933 at 73/0/15; angina pectoris
Carrie E., d. 9/17/1920 at 52/10/2; diabetes mellitus; George W. Colbath and Lucinda Trafton
Clara E., d. 5/23/1937 at 79/8/20; cerebral embolism
Clarence, d. 3/30/1932 at 74/7/9; chronic endocarditis
Dudley, d. 2/17/1893 at 55; paralysis
Edwin C., d. 12/8/1931 at 69/2 in Lowell, MA; chronic myocarditis
Emily, d. 10/12/1899 at 69; cancer of bowels; PH
Emma Inez, d. 6/29/1891 at 8/9/27 in Rochester
Emma Inez, d. 4/21/1894 at 2 in Somerville, MA; cerebro meningitis; buried in Dover
George W., d. 6/14/1895 at 63; sudden; b. Alton; PH
Guy Hamilton, d. 6/4/1887 at 15/2/29; b. Dover; Lafayette Colbath (Milton) and S. A. Langley (Strafford)
Jennie M., d. 9/8/1896 at 49 in Somerville, MA; val. dis. of heart
King, d. 11/25/1904 at – in Porter, ME; angina pectoris; PH
Lafayette, d. 4/5/1895 at 66; phthisis pulmonalis; b. Middleton; PH
Lucinda F., d. 4/29/1890 at 56/11/16 in Concord
Martha H., d. 11/8/1887 at 21/8/26; married; b. Dover; Rufus B. Emery (S. Berwick, ME) and Mary E. Hervey (S. Berwick, ME)
Nellie G., d. 12/9/1910 at 41/4/2; myxodema; Charles H. Jackson and Martha Senard
Neriah S., d. 2/8/1893 at 58; phthisis pulmonalis; b. Farmington; (Middleton; Rochester)
Sadie A., d. 6/15/1893 at 52; phthisis pulmonalis; b. Strafford; (Deerfield; -----)
William, d. 12/3/1894 at 70; heart disease; b. Alton; PH

COLBURN,
Helen J., d. 4/5/1917 at 0/3/4; pneumonia; Fred A. Colburn and Dena V. King

COLBY,
child, d. 9/4/1921 at –; stillborn; Allston G. Colby and Flossie L. Hatch
Allston G., Jr., d. 6/23/1920 at 1; athrepsia; Allston G. Colby and Flossie L. Hatch

Edwin F., d. 10/19/1916 at 82/9/19; angina pectoris; Benjamin Colby and Dolly ——
John R., d. 9/27/1896 at 62; consumption; b. Wolfeboro
Julia F., d. 10/17/1900 at 58 in Medford, MA; cancer; PH
Melissa J., d. 5/17/1923 at 77/10/16; dilatation of heart; Jonas A. Lundberg and Mellissa Deminich

COLE,
child, d. 5/18/1903 at –; stillborn; SM
child, d. 10/23/1910 at – in Madbury; at birth; Joseph Cole and Rose Ann Morgan
Abbie R., d. 6/5/1896 at 63; paralysis; b. Brookfield; buried at Dover Point
Ann, d. 3/1/1901 at 65 in Madbury; la grippe; SM
Anna E., d. 4/3/1928 at 0/0/1-4; premature birth; Samuel Cole and Anna Daley
Annie L., d. 9/23/1918 at 24/9 in Bartlett; uraemia
Annie M., d. 9/6/1889 at 25/2/21; mill operative; single; b. Portsmouth; Franklin Cole (Madbury) and Eliza A. Cole (Dover)
Bernice R., d. 2/25/1909 at 36/0/18; tuberculosis; Michael G. Cole and Catherine Doherty
Blanche, d. 6/29/1925 at 51; cancer of uterus
Blanche S., d. 7/6/1888 at 0/1/10; b. Dover; Edwin Cole (Portsmouth) and Cora W. Witham (S. Berwick, ME)
Catherine, d. 7/29/1924 at 54; cancer of liver; Arthur Tomney and Ann Hughes
Charles, d. 10/26/1905 at 45; heart disease; SM
Charles A., d. 8/27/1919 at 67/2/10; intestinal obstruction; John W. Cole
Charles T., d. 11/28/1910 at 73/1/27 in Haverhill, MA; cerebral hemorrhage
Clara P., d. 5/27/1912 at 57/5/21; pneumonia; Abel Baxter and Hannah Lougee
Eliza A., d. 1/14/1897 at 58 in Kittery, ME; peritonitis; PH
Franklin, d. 11/10/1906 at 73/6/7; bronchitis; PH
George H., d. 8/15/1901 at 0/7/25; cholera infantum; PH
J. Frank, d. 9/3/1928 at 68/9/12 in Haverhill, MA; toxemia, urinary ob.
James Buchanan, d. 1/8/1937 at 80/1/30 in S. Berwick, ME; cerebr. hemorrhage (see following entry)
James Buchanan, d. 1/8/1937 at 80/1/30* (see preceding entry)
Jeremiah E., d. 8/1/1935 at 72/9/16; hypertrophy of prostate
Jesse, d. 9/8/1902 at 73/2/28 in Hiram, ME; cardiac dropsy
Mary A., d. 2/24/1897 at 80; old age; b. Pittsfield, ME; PH
Mary A., d. 2/5/1932 at –; broncho pneumonia
Mary Kelley, d. 10/4/1929 at 60 in Rollinsford; pulm. tuberculosis
Michael G., d. 12/25/1907 at 75; pneumonia; Richard Cole and Catherine Draper

Nancy E., d. 11/4/1897 at 57; paralysis; b. Dover; PH
Nellie A., d. 10/17/1936 at 75/1/15*
Rachael A., d. 4/26/1894 at 62; old age; b. Sandwich; buried in Madbury
Ralph H., d. 10/28/1918 at 25/8/13 in Baltimore, MD; pulmonary
    thrombosis
Robert, Jr., d. 7/1/1915 at –; meningitis; Robert J. Cole and Hannah J.
    Swailes
Rose Ann, d. 8/21/1928 at 56 in Boston, MA; cancer of intestine
Tobias, d. 10/2/1896 at 75; paralysis; b. Dover; SM
Tobias, d. 5/16/1906 at 43 in Madbury; pneumonia; SM
Winthrop S., d. 11/13/1937 at 89/0/21; arteriosclerosis - general intestine

COLELL,
George Peter, d. 5/12/1920 at 0/0/12; intestinal obstruction; Peter Colell
    and Annie Peter
Najeet Peter, d. 5/8/1917 at 0/3/15; cholera infantum; Peter Colell and
    Mary Peter

COLEMAN,
child, d. 2/26/1914 at – in Boston, MA; spina bifida; Raymond Coleman
    and Gladys B. Corson
A. Evans, d. 10/7/1889 at 0/2/28; b. Dover; John C. Coleman (Dover) and
    Abby Card (Dover)
Abbie F., d. 10/8/1897 at 49; peritonitis; b. Dover; buried at Dover Point
Ada Minnie, d. 6/10/1901 at 37/10/17; cancer; PH
Angie, d. 8/7/1887 at 0/0/13; b. Dover; Frank P. Coleman (Durham) and S.
    M. Philpott (Rollinsford)
Annie, d. 1/30/1900 at 50; angina pectoris; PH
Asenath H., d. 8/18/1919 at 82/5/1; senility; Samuel Cushing and Asenath
    Hyde
Augustus T., d. 4/13/1897 at 64; heart disease; b. Dover; PH
C. Herbert, d. 11/8/1908 at 37/11/10; chronic inflammation of brain; John
    C. Coleman and Abbie F. Card
Charles A., d. 12/5/1903 at 3/0/5; convulsions; buried at Dover Point
Charles A., d. 9/15/1911 at 43/11 in Eliot, ME; dilitation of heart
Charles C., d. 9/17/1891 at 56/10/23; widower; Joseph Coleman (Durham)
    and Dorothy Card (Dover)
Daniel, d. 5/6/1932 at 72/4/13; arterio sclerosis
Dorothy, d. 9/21/1899 at 93; old age; PH
Emma L., d. 2/21/1912 at 66/9/13; cerebral apoplexy; Henry D. Davis and
    Ann M. ----
Esabell, d. 6/4/1921 at 53/7/22; heart failure; William Cooper
Florence R., d. 4/3/1900 at 18; pneumonia; PH
Frank C., d. 2/18/1933 at 56/9/14; arteriosclerosis

Frank P., d. 2/5/1929 at 76/9/17 in Boston, MA; obstructing prostate; Oliver Coleman and Mehitabel Clark
Fred O., d. 2/14/1904 at 33 in Concord; exhaustion from acute mania; buried in Dover
J. Henry, d. 8/10/1912 at 83/1/24; broncho pneumonia; Joseph Coleman and Dorothy Card
John C., d. 1/15/1929 at 87/3/18; arterio sclerosis; Calvin Coleman and Phoebe Card
Lillie M., d. 12/17/1888 at 32/4/13; married; b. Rollinsford; I. R. Philpot (Rollinsford) and Ruth A. Dore (Rollinsford)
Louisa A., d. 3/6/1904 at 72/4/3; cerebral thrombosis; PH
Mary E., d. 12/21/1896 at 24; pneumonia; b. Dover; PH
Mehitable, d. 2/9/1892 at 83; heart disease, valvular; b. Strafford
Michael McC., d. 8/14/1897 at 70; apoplexy; b. Dover; buried in Exeter
Oliver D., d. 1/7/1937 at 65/2/0*
Oliver W., d. 1/15/1912 at 73/8/18; chronic endocarditis; Oliver Coleman and Mehitable Clark
Perley S., d. 9/2/1911 at 15/8/17; Luther H. Coleman and Luella L. Durgin
Phoebe, d. 2/28/1887 at 88/3/5; Thomas Card
Sarah E., d. 8/7/1888 at 53/1/26; married; b. Boston, MA; James Haines
Sophia J., d. 2/7/1906 at 71/6/0; cerebral hemorrhage; buried at Dover Point
Thomas C., d. 1/12/1906 at 79/11/20; cerebral hemorrhage; PH
Walter L., d. 1/2/1909 at 9/7/16; rickets; Charles A. Coleman and Maud E.

COLLETT,
Albert P., d. 8/4/1902 at 1/0/28; diarrhea; PH
Charles H., Rev., d. 11/11/1937 at 49/1/14*

COLLIN,
Rahoul, d. 3/21/1910 at 25/8/22; fracture of skull; Eleazer Collin and Melvina Cote

COLLINS,
Ann, d. 9/5/1897 at 66; cancer of liver; b. Ireland
Annie, d. 8/22/1920 at 70/8; valvular disease of heart; Edward McDonald and Bridget Loughlin
Arthur D., d. 1/17/1898 at 54 in Salem, MA; embolism; buried in Rollinsford
Benjamin, d. 3/24/1906 at 85/2/3; old age; PH
Eliza F., d. 1/4/1919 at 92/5/5; chr. valv. dis. of heart; John T. Parker and Sally Seavey
Ellen, d. 11/25/1936 at 80; cerebral embolism
John J., d. 2/24/1937 at 78; broncho pneumonia

Julia E., d. 5/31/1915 at 65 in Wakefield; heart disease; John Collins and
  Elizabeth -----
Kate, d. 2/24/1904 at 46; pulmonary tuberculosis; SM
Leroy M., d. 3/28/1900 at 40; suicide; buried in Troy, NY
Lydia A., d. 5/7/1896 at 76; marasmus; b. Dover; PH
Margaret, d. 11/22/1936 at 80; chr. myocarditis
Mary E., d. 2/4/1890 at 3/11/3; Lawrence Collins (Ireland) and Catherine
  Murray (Ireland)

COLOMY,
child, d. 6/9/1920 at –; ateloctasis; William R. Colomy and Ethel Rodden
Abram, d. 7/27/1892 at 75; old age; b. New Durham
Andrew D., d. 11/23/1897 at 87; apoplexy; b. New Durham; PH
Annie, d. 8/16/1897 at 45 in Haverhill, MA; heart disease; PH
Augustus A., d. 2/17/1928 at 81/7/1; arterio sclerosis; Andrew A. Colomy
  and Mary Pinkham
Cora L., d. 6/25/1897 at 42; peritonitis; b. Milton; buried in Milton
Dorothy S., d. 8/11/1906 at 74/1/23; old age; PH
Emma F., d. 12/13/1916 at 65; anaemia; Daniel Colomy and Dorothy S.
  Locke
Frank, d. 11/17/1908 at 60; chronic nephritis
Frank, d. 10/22/1918 at 69/10/22; Brights disease; Nehemiah Colomy and
  Hannah Dame
James D., d. 9/15/1925 at 74 in Haverhill, MA; myocarditis
John K., d. 11/18/1931 at 71/2/22; cardiac renal disease
Leon, d. 4/24/1926 at 58; paralysis agitans
S. Edwin, d. 1/19/1924 at 72/10/6; chronic endocarditis
Stephen, d. 7/18/1916 at 82; apoplexy
William E., d. 8/8/1931 at 72/3/3; acute myocarditis
William H., d. 5/17/1901 at 57/2/7; phthisis; buried in Rochester

COLONY,
Frank L., d. 12/14/1936 at 81*

COLPOIT,
child, d. 8/28/1935 at – in Winchester, MA; stillborn

COLPRIT,
Everett E., d. 10/2/1918 at 26; influenza; Daniel D. Colpritt and Jennie
  Vanner
James H., d. 11/9/1915 at 59/2/12 in Madbury; cancer of rectum; Charles
  Colprit and Louisa Daggett

COLPRITT,
Barbara, d. 4/9/1920 at –; stillborn; Charles E. Colpritt and Mildred Hobby

Nettie S., d. 7/3/1937 at 73/5/29; cancer of spine
Richard, d. 4/23/1922 at – in Portsmouth; stillborn
Warren C., d. 4/19/1922 at 0/8/19; cere. spinal meningitis; Charles Colpritt and Mildred Hobby

COLT,
Jennie E., d. 2/5/1892 at 8; peritonitis

COLTON,
Richard P., d. 2/11/1929 at 0/6/3; lobar pneumonia; Chester A. Colton and Anne Mone

COMINGS,
Emma J., d. 10/22/1911 at 59/9/15; peritonitis; Gordon B. Dow and Elizabeth -----

COMISKY,
Julia, d. 3/13/1932 at 58; cerebral hemorrhage

COMTOIS,
George Arthur, d. 6/21/1923 at 5/9/21; peritonitis; Arthur Comtois and Emily Martel

CONDON,
Annie, d. 12/9/1926 at 81; unknown

CONELLY,
Catherine, d. 5/23/1890 at 67/8/12; widow; Bernard Duffey (Ireland) and Sarah McMahon (Ireland)

CONGROVE,
Bridget, d. 3/10/1919 at 34 in Cumberland, RI; pleuro pneumonia

CONKLIN,
Robert T., d. 9/5/1933 at –; stillborn

CONLEN,
child, d. 9/4/1895 at 0; undevelopment; b. Dover; PH
Michael, d. 12/12/1919 at 71/8/9; carcinoma, neck and throat; Michael Conlen and Mary A. Finn

CONLEY,
child, d. 2/16/1892 at –; stillborn; b. Dover; (Ireland; Ireland)
Arthur J., d. 10/20/1902 at 22; acute nephritis; SM

Catherine, d. 11/14/1898 at 45; cirrhosis of liver; b. Ireland; SM
Elizabeth, d. 11/24/1904 at 43; anaemia; SM
James, d. 4/26/1891 at 55; married; (Ireland; Ireland)
Mary E., d. 10/19/1897 at 27; consumption; SM

CONNELL,
Florence M., d. 8/11/1906 at 29 in St. Johnsbury, VT; suicide by shooting
Johannah, d. 2/17/1891 at 52; married; Thomas Roach (Ireland) and Hannah Machoney (Ireland)
John, d. 12/13/1914 at 61/9/20; pulmonary embolism; Patrick Connell and Martha McNeil
Martha, d. 9/22/1900 at 17 in So. Kingston, RI; dysentery; PH
Mary, d. 8/17/1890 at 58; married; Timothy O'Connell (Ireland) and Julia Flynn (Ireland)
Mary J., d. 5/22/1922 at 71; carcinoma of face; Robert Kerr and Annie Fleming

CONNELLY,
Elizabeth, d. 3/4/1922 at 43 in Pembroke; pulmonary tuberculosis; James Connelly and Elizabeth Carroll
Elizabeth, d. 10/8/1936 at 65/0/20; chr. nephritis
James, d. 12/11/1894 at 69; heart disease; b. Ireland; SM
Margaret B., d. 3/14/1925 at 43/11/12; suicide - illuminating gas; Michael Connelly and Catherine Fox
Mary, d. 6/30/1888 at 0/11/20; b. Dover; John Connelly (Ireland) and B. McLaughlin (S. Berwick, ME)
Mary E., d. 1/10/1923 at 68; pneumonia; John Hughes and Mary A. Griffin
Peter, d. 6/7/1924 at 60/6/16; hemorrhage of lungs; Patrick Connelly and Katherine ----

CONNER,
John A., d. 12/9/1888 at 1/5/9; b. Dover; John Conner (Ireland) and Kate Conley (Ireland)
Lydia E., d. 5/12/1917 at 77/0/16; mitral regurgitation; James Goodwin and Elizabeth Seavey

CONNERS,
Mary, d. 8/9/1907 at 0/6; cholera infantum; Patrick Conners and Delia Mulligan

CONNISS,
Patrick J., d. 5/19/1907 at 46 in Winooski, VT; angina pectoris

CONNOLLY,
Bridget, d. 11/14/1893 at 37; consumption; b. US; (Ireland; Ireland)
Ed., d. 5/4/1889 at 68; laborer; widower; b. Ireland; James Connolly (Ireland) and Mary McDonough (Ireland)
Elizabeth, d. 9/16/1918 at 63; cerebral apoplexy; ----- Carroll and Bridget Riley
Ellen, d. 1/30/1891 at 0/3; Jonathan Connolly (Ireland) and Bridget McLaughlin (US)
Jno. P., d. 3/23/1892 at –; marasmus; b. Dover; (Ireland; US)
John, d. 4/15/1918 at 43/8/5; general arterio sclerosis; Michael Connolly and Catherine Fox
Joseph, d. 6/29/1927 at 45; angina pectoris
Mary, d. 11/2/1913 at –; stillborn; James Connolly and Elizabeth Grimes
Mary, d. 5/10/1915 at 65; broncho pneumonia; Owen Connolly and Ann Brennan
Mary, d. 1/24/1917 at 54; cancer of stomach; Charles Connolly and Elizabeth Comiske
Michael, d. 12/24/1892 at 33; phthisis pulmonalis
Michael, d. 3/24/1908 at 54; endocarditis; John Connolly and Mary O'Connell
Michael, d. 2/24/1913 at 49; ch. Brights disease

CONNOR,
Annie T., d. 10/9/1927 at 52/10/9; carcinoma of rectum; Patrick Murray and Sarah McKone
Edward James, d. 10/5/1918 at 28/11/5; influenza; John Connor and Margaret F. Sheehan
Elizabeth G., d. 3/18/1909 at 70/3/7; cirrhosis of liver; Neb. Goodwin and Mary Ham
Isaiah C., d. 6/14/1901 at 76/5/9 in Providence, RI; catarrh of stomach; PH
John, d. 8/18/1919 at 75; entero colitis
John A., d. 12/29/1926 at –; angina pectoris; John Connor and Ann Foley

CONNORS,
Bernard J., d. 11/30/1932 at 48; heart disease
Edward, d. 5/29/1910 at 0/3/15; gastro-enteritis chronic; Patrick Connors and Delia Mulligan
Ellen, d. 4/24/1905 at 53; chronic interstitial nephritis
Ellen, d. 4/19/1931 at 67; cerebral apoplexy
Felix J., d. 3/29/1935 at 56/11/16; heart disease
James E., d. 3/8/1892 at 11; congestion of the lungs; b. MN; (Ireland; Zanesville, OH)
James H., d. 9/13/1927 at 73; carcinoma of stomach
John, d. 9/9/1909 at 45; mitral regurgitation

John F., d. 2/4/1917 at 1/6/26; lobar pneumonia; Bernard Connors and Sarah Donnelly
Margaret, d. 10/29/1912 at 4/3/18; diphtheria; Patrick Connors and Delia Mulligan
Margaret A., d. 12/26/1934 at 77/1/20; arteriosclerosis
Owen, d. 9/11/1911 at 0/0/20; athrepsia; Patrick Connors and Delia Mulligan
Patrick, d. 12/23/1911 at 0/4/1; gastro int. indigestion; Patrick Connors and Delia Mulligan
Sarah, d. 11/15/1923 at 65; chr. inter. nephritis; John Murphy
Thomas F., d. 9/23/1933 at 46; chronic tuberculosis

CONROY,
John, d. 2/6/1913 at 65; chronic nephritis
Mary A., d. 9/13/1904 at 49/3; carcinoma of breast; SM
Sadie, d. 9/23/1915 at 0/0/1-4; premature birth; George J. Conroy and Mary -----
Thomas, d. 5/4/1920 at 64/11/26 in Tewksbury, MA; cancer of stomach

CONSTANTAKOS,
child, d. 6/22/1916 at –; prolapse of umbilical cord; William Constantakos and Constantina Karimiri
child, d. 3/15/1927 at –; stillborn; Vasil Constantakos and Constantine Carmerce

CONSTANOPOULIS,
P., d. 8/23/1913 at 7/4/2; accidental drowning; V. Constanopoulos (sic) and Aristitsa -----

CONSTANTOPOULOS,
Exini, d. 10/15/1918 at 1/2/8; broncho pneumonia; C. Constantopoulos and Stavoula -----

CONVERSE,
Joshua, d. 4/5/1891 at 77/9/21 in Rollinsford; married; Joshua Converse (Rindge) and Polly Piper (New York, NY)

CONWAY,
Catherine, d. 7/5/1924 at –; natural causes; Charles Ackley and Ann -----
Emily J. A., d. 4/8/1889 at 16/8/28 in Pawtucket, RI
John, d. 4/16/1899 at 62; heart disease; buried in Amesbury, MA
Mary J., d. 2/7/1923 at 63 in Boston, MA; carcinoma of liver
Michael, d. 1/17/1914 at 54; septicaemia, general
Michael, d. 10/10/1933 at 63; fracture of skull

Patrick, d. 1/30/1894 at 45; heart disease; b. Halifax, NS; SM

COOGAN,
Margaret, d. 2/28/1892 at 47; cancer; b. Ireland; (Ireland; Ireland)
Michael, d. 10/19/1917 at 69; diabetes mellitus; Owen Coogan and Ann Hughes
Owen, d. 12/22/1937 at 66/0/0; chr. endocarditis
Sarah A., d. 4/6/1933 at 55/1/21; carcinoma of breast

COOK,
Abbie J., d. 10/18/1906 at 63/3/7; organic heart disease; PH
Alden B., d. 1/16/1910 at 77/3/26; chronic endocarditis; Joseph Cook and Roxanna Haskell
Ann W., d. 2/27/1905 at 87/10/13; old age; PH
Annette M., d. 11/18/1897 at 49 in Haverhill, MA; heart disease; PH
Arseneth, d. 5/7/1936 at 77/10/21*
Carrie A., d. 4/29/1896 at – in Boston, MA; heart clot
Charles, d. 12/26/1909 at 42/6/1; valvular dis. of heart; John H. Cook and Martha A. Young
Daniel E., d. 1/31/1907 at 57/8/19 in Haverhill, MA; fatty degeneration heart
Dench W., d. 8/23/1891 at 26/1/1; single; John H. Cook (Milton) and Martha A. Young (Farmington)
Eaton, d. 1/23/1924 at 29/1/7; staphylococcus infection; Elisha Cook and Gertrude Kaine
Emily J., d. 1/22/1892 at 76; congestion of lungs - grippe; b. Stark, ME
Eugene E., d. 3/15/1904 at 46/6/15; paresis; PH
Harry E., d. 11/21/1934 at 1/2/2 in Boston, MA; respiratory disease
Harry R., d. 6/29/1935 at 74/8/25; fractured skull
Isabelle F., d. 1/26/1932 at 74/8/17; arterio sclerosis
James, d. 7/11/1897 at 55; sunstroke; b. Dover; PH
Joel E., d. 9/7/1906 at 74/3/17; cancer; buried in Newmarket
John H., d. 3/31/1907 at 62/0/27; typhoid pneumonia; Robert Cook and Jane Taylor
Lucinda, d. 3/19/1895 at 81 in Weston, MA; influenza; buried in Dover
Margaret A., d. 3/25/1926 at 55/1/13; myocarditis; Richard P. Hoyt and Margaret Hutchins
Martha A., d. 10/2/1924 at 78; angina pectoris
Maurice C., d. 1/30/1917 at 1/5/29; pneumonia; Carl Cook and Delia M. Bean
Rosetta T., d. 12/7/1910 at 61/11/29; intestinal obstruction; D. W. Leighton and Thurza Poppy
Sarah A., d. 7/9/1895 at 81; old age; b. Shapleigh, ME; PH
Warren, d. 3/4/1921 at 39/6/24; lobar pneumonia; Henry Cook and Mary Babb

Weston, d. 2/11/1916 at 44/8/14; chronic enteritis; John H. Cook and Martha A. Young

Will O., d. 10/–/1914 at 57/5/13; lobar pneumonia; John A. Cook and Cynthia Johnson

COOKE,
Almira J., d. 2/1/1891 at 47/3; single; Jonas Cooke (Great Falls) and Mahala Horne (Great Falls)

Charles H., d. 6/27/1894 at 41; consumption; b. Boston, MA; PH

James W., d. 4/23/1927 at 74/4/7; strangulated hernia; James Cooke and Margaret Turnbull

Maria, d. 9/30/1890 at 57; married

COOLEY,
Joseph H., d. 4/24/1901 at –; SM

COOMBS,
Henry B., d. 5/21/1894 at 59; Bright's disease; b. Readfield, ME; buried in Readfield, ME

COOPER,
Comfort, d. 4/24/1920 at 88/10 in San Antonio, TX; cancer of stomach

Evon A., d. 5/21/1923 at 2/11/28; ac. gastro enteritis; William H. Cooper and Mary J. Ellsmore

George E., d. 1/19/1921 at 72 in New York, NY; chronic myocarditis

Jennie M., d. 4/8/1923 at 76/10; fatty degen. of heart; Josiah Wentworth and Betsey Lucas

Levi C., d. 1/15/1907 at 81/10/21; congestion of lungs; Moses Cooper and Francis H. Goodwin

Mercy H., d. 3/18/1900 at 84; erysipelas; PH

William H., d. 6/8/1921 at 40/2/8 in Portsmouth; hemorrhage of spinal cord

COPACZUISKI,
Jurka, d. 9/17/1917 at 30 in Haverhill, MA; suicide by drowning

COPE,
child, d. 2/3/1892 at –; stillborn; b. Dover; (England; Ireland)

COPELAND,
David, d. 7/4/1911 at 65; arteriosclerosis

COPP,
Abbie, d. 5/28/1906 at 90; cerebral thrombosis

H. Parker, d. 1/8/1890 at 55/6/13; married; Samuel Copp (Lebanon, ME) and Abbie Staples (Shapleigh, ME)
Moses W., d. 3/10/1904 at 21/11/15; typhoid fever; buried in Magog, Canada

CORAN,
Julia, d. 7/19/1918 at 0/1/20; acute lobar pneumonia; Joseph Coran and Bertha Simoneau
Nellie, d. 1/16/1914 at 34; tuberculosis; Joseph Drew and Catherine McGuinness

CORBIN,
Eva, d. 10/27/1900 at 2; laryngeal obstruction; SM

CORCORAN,
Harrietta, d. 9/8/1919 at 3/5/3; acute entero colitis; Walter J. Corcoran and Annie Kenney

CORDES,
Caroline, d. 3/30/1918 at 67/11/15; acute myocarditis; Joseph Hesse and Magdalene -----
Florence K., d. 5/20/1932 at 44 in Winthrop, MA; coronary embolism
Henry O., d. 12/10/1935 at 89/3/26; arteriosclerosis

COREY,
child, d. 10/11/1918 at –; premature birth; George J. Corey and Mary D. Corey
child, d. 10/11/1918 at –; premature birth; George J. Corey and Mary D. Corey
Mary, d. 1/31/1918 at –; premature birth; George Corey and Mary Skamon
Mary, d. 7/17/1922 at –; premature birth; George J. Corey and Mary -----

CORLISS,
Charles W., d. 5/10/1918 at 63/10/27; Brights disease; Samuel Corliss and Harriet Titcomb
Mary W., d. 2/19/1923 at 65/10/25; angina pectoris; Warren D. Jones and Ruth R. Smith

CORMAN,
Leo, d. 8/18/1932 at 42; auto accident

CORMIER,
Edgar, d. 9/20/1921 at 0/2/2; acute entero colitis; Joseph Cormier and Sylvia Babineau

Joseph J., d. 3/17/1929 at 55/7; acute myocarditis; Joseph O. Cormier and
  Philomene M. Gingras
Marguerite, d. 2/2/1903 at 70; cerebral hemorrhage
Stella, d. 5/31/1913 at –; premature birth; Stella Cormier

CORNELL,
Ellen L., d. 12/25/1932 at 27/4/28; broncho pneumonia
James W., d. 10/23/1904 at 12/9/27; shock from crushing thigh; PH
John, d. 4/29/1925 at 63/2/3; diabetes mellitus; Daniel Cornell and Mary
  Smith
Lillian, d. 4/24/1896 at –; pneumonia; b. Dover; PH

CORRAN,
Amos S., d. 8/24/1890 at 0/3/16 in Raymond

CORRY,
Frank, d. 6/10/1932 at 63/10/2 in Somersworth; broncho pneumonia

CORSON,
Anna L., d. 2/16/1937 at 74/5/12; mycl'gen's leukemia
Annie E., d. 5/23/1931 at 80/2/23; lobar pneumonia
Blanch V., d. 1/21/1891 at 0/8; Sterns E. Corson (New Durham) and Rose
  B. Hilton (Wells, ME)
Blanche V., d. 5/29/1894 at –; pneumonia; b. Dover; buried in family lot
Charles B., d. 7/18/1903 at 27/7/15; phthisis pulmonalis; PH
Charles M., d. 1/16/1930 at 73/1/28; carcinoma colon; Zimri Corson and
  Dorothy Wentworth
Edith E., d. 6/8/1889 at 11/11/6; b. Dover; Charles M. Corson (Rochester)
  and Ellen Corson (Dover)
Elizabeth T., d. 10/2/1887 at 40/1/10 in Boston, MA
Ellen S., d. 9/26/1917 at 64 in Concord; ac. bacilliary dysentery; Cornelius
  Sullivan and Mary -----
Emma, d. 8/26/1889 at 35/4; single
Emma J., d. 6/5/1934 at 59/10/27; coronary thrombosis
Frank H., d. 9/3/1933 at 65/1/6; coronary thrombosis
Frank I., d. 4/4/1924 at 72/3/28; chronic endocarditis; Hiram Corson and
  Hannah J. Ham
Hannah J., d. 12/4/1904 at 77/4/13 in Rochester; senile debility; PH
Henry D., d. 9/28/1922 at 68/7/15; apoplexy; Dow Corson and Malinda
  Allen
Hiram, d. 10/8/1893 at 73; congestion of brain; b. New Durham; (New
  Durham; Somersworth)
Hiram H., d. 6/26/1922 at 65 in Boston, MA; oedema of brain
Ida May, d. 6/29/1937 at 6/5/21; carcinoma of cervix

John Henry, d. 6/23/1928 at 54/3/9; angina pectoris; Leonard Corson and Sarah S. Ring

John M., d. 8/6/1935 at 62/6/20; pulmonary embolism

Leonard Z., d. 2/20/1937 at 84/4/23; broncho pneumonia

Mary A., d. 5/2/1919 at 61/8/4; shock; John B. Decatur and Abbie Woodus

Philip, d. 2/17/1888 at 1/5/11; b. Boston, MA; Walter Corson and Elizabeth Tomkins

Sarah S., d. 8/23/1920 at 80/1/10; myocardial insufficiency; Jerry King and Phoebe Ellis

Stearns E., d. 2/15/1897 at 36; heart disease; b. Ireland; buried in family lot

Wilbur W., d. 10/2/1934 at 59/5/20; myocarditis

William A., d. 12/26/1929 at 57/10/24; fracture of skull; William H. Corson and Mary Gilbert

COSGROVE,

James, d. 8/12/1912 at 13/9/7; cerebral meningitis; Dominick Cosgrove and Mary Tierney

John, d. 12/7/1898 at 4; pneumonia; b. Dover; SM

COSKER,

Annie, d. 4/18/1907 at 41/4; chronic endocarditis; Patrick Cosker and Catherine Brennan

Catherine, d. 3/14/1891 at 70; married; Patrick Brennan (Ireland) and Rose Fox (Ireland)

Catherine, d. 4/14/1897 at 51; acute yellow atrophy of liver; b. Ireland; SM

Charles, d. 10/12/1918 at 86; chronic rheumatism; Hugh Cosker and Ann McAtavey

Eliza, d. 1/22/1890 at 52; married; J. Riely (Ireland)

Francis, d. 1/3/1931 at –; chr. val. heart dis.

Frank, d. 3/2/1893 at 17; meningitis; b. Dover; (Ireland; Ireland)

Patrick, d. 9/27/1902 at 75; heart disease; SM

Patrick J., d. 7/7/1931 at 53 in Lynn, MA; phthisis (?)

COSKORAN,

John, d. 1/26/1907 at 16; destroyed by fire; Michael Coskoran and Ellen Redden

Raymond, d. 2/7/1913 at –; stillborn; Patrick Coskoran and Sarah Breen

COSKRAN,

James, d. 1/12/1919 at 33; lobar pneumonia; Thomas Cochran (sic) and Mary Redden

COSTORAS,
John, d. 6/12/1919 at 0/0/3; premature birth; Harry Costoras and A. Metsolon

COTE,
child, d. 3/27/1901 at 3 hrs.; premature birth
child, d. 3/27/1901 at 5 hrs.; premature birth
child, d. 8/29/1928 at –; miscarriage; Samuel Cote and Margaret -----
Alda, d. 2/9/1928 at 33/5/2; tuberculosis of lungs; Eusebe Dionne and Justina Lafont
Alfred, d. 1/16/1916 at 0/0/1; premature birth; Saul Cote and Marie Demers
Alice, d. 12/10/1894 at 19; phthisis pulmonalis; b. Canada; SM
Almond L., d. 1/13/1932 at 19/2/22; accidental drowning
Amedee, d. 3/31/1931 at 50/4/9; ac. lobar pneumonia
Angeline, d. 9/20/1901 at 0/0/24; cholera infantum
Arsene, d. 7/21/1901 at 0/2/14; diarrhea infantile
Arthur, d. 8/27/1911 at 0/4/19; cholera infantum; Samuel Cote and Margaret -----
Arthur, d. 12/11/1920 at 20/0/18 in Benton; tuberculosis of lungs; Philip Cote and Alix Baril
Atherline, d. 8/19/1930 at 34/6/21; acute myocarditis; Fred Lundeville and Mina -----
Bernadette, d. 3/15/1930 at 40/10/16; pulmonary embolism; Theophile Leblanc and Eleonard Provencher
Celina, d. 6/13/1906 at 32/11/17; pyelo nephritis
Celina, d. 11/23/1913 at 22 in Concord; exhaustion in acute mania; Paul Cote and Valentine Michael
Edward, d. 4/10/1917 at 39; broncho pneumonia; Edward Cote and Desanges Couture
Edward F., d. 3/4/1932 at 38/7/19; angina pectoris
Eliza, d. 2/18/1911 at 48; tuberculosis; Joseph Gagnon and Victoria Gardner
Eugene, d. 8/14/1909 at 27; tuberculosis; James Cote and Elizabeth Gagnon
Ferdinand, d. 5/5/1928 at 25; ac. lobar pneumonia; Joseph Cote and ----- Gagnon
George, d. 2/10/1910 at 6/7/13; cerebral hemorrhage; Edward Cote and Mary Drouin
J. Henry, d. 8/13/1896 at –; cholera infantum; b. Dover; SM
John A., d. 5/3/1899 at 3; measles
Joseph, d. 5/13/1917 at 57/7 in Loudon; burn of entire body; Etienne Cote and Margaret Thibeault
Joseph A., d. 5/3/1897 at 2; la grippe; b. Dover; SM
Joseph Alfred, d. 2/15/1903 at 0/5; convulsions

Joseph H., d. 10/21/1893 at –; entero-colitis; b. Dover; (Canada; Canada)
Justin, d. 4/12/1928 at 70; natural causes; Joseph Lafond
Lena, d. 7/6/1911 at 0/6/14; cholera infantum; Etienne Cote and Mary Gregoire
Lodia, d. 10/27/1909 at 4/3/22; meningitis; Edward Cote and Mary Drouin
Lydia, d. 5/31/1912 at 1/5/12; tubercular meningitis; Calixte Cote and Bernadette Leblanc
Marie Desanges, d. 3/7/1916 at 70/11/23; chronic bronchitis; Louis Couture
Marie Louise, d. 7/13/1891 at 0/15/7; Joseph Cote (Canada) and Elise Gagnon (Canada)
Mary, d. 8/20/1904 at 15/10/12; gastro-enteritis
Mary Irene, d. 8/10/1914 at 0/2; cholera infantum; Louis Cote and Odina Deroy
Odile, d. 7/30/1894 at 1; diarrhea; b. Dover; SM
Ovila, d. 1/15/1916 at 4 hrs.; premature birth; Saul Cote and Marie Demers
Oweles, d. 1/31/1891 at 0/0/20; Jonathan Cote (Canada) and Emma Denaureque (Canada)
Paul, d. 9/15/1926 at 77/5/1; cerebral hemorrhage; Etienne Cote and Margaret ——
Philip, d. 4/23/1910 at 26/11; shock; Joseph Cote and Elizabeth Gagnon
Philippe, d. 5/23/1921 at 60; phthisis pulmonalis; Vincent Cote and Emily Beaulac
Raymond, d. 9/11/1909 at 0/5/9; cholera infantum; Seraphin Cote and Marguerite Curran
Robert, d. 4/8/1928 at 8/7/20; accidental drowning; Napoleon Cote and Victoria ——
Rosanna, d. 7/31/1893 at –; cholera infantum; b. Dover; (Canada; Canada)
Urbin, d. 5/25/1919 at 15/7; pulm. tuberculosis; Philip Cote and Alex. Barel
Valentine, d. 11/1/1920 at 68/7; diabetes; Jean B. Michaud and Valentine Bernier
Wilfred A., d. 5/23/1905 at 0/8/5; marasmus
Wilfrid, d. 7/18/1908 at 0/2; cholera infantum; Fred Cote
Wilfrid Arthur, d. 8/21/1892 at –; entero-colitis; b. Dover; (Canada; Canada)

COTTER,
Bridget, d. 2/2/1920 at 89 in Lawrence, MA; cerebral hemorrhage
Daniel, d. 8/6/1904 at 58; dysentery
Elizabeth, d. 7/25/1903 at 55; nervous prostration; SM
Ellen, d. 6/20/1888 at 88; widow; b. Ireland; (Ireland; Ireland)
Pat., d. 8/27/1890 at 46; James Cotter (Ireland) and Mary McFarlan (Ireland)

Sarah H., d. 1/14/1892 at 23; anaemia; b. Dover; (US; Ireland)

COTTON,
Albert W., d. 4/9/1895 at 67 in Madbury; heart disease; b. Wolfeboro; PH
Benjamin D., d. 2/19/1917 at 55; senile gangrene of foot; Richard R.
    Cotton and Abbie Nute

COUCHEN,
Napoleon, d. 10/14/1908 at --; accidental

COUCHESNES,
child, d. 12/30/1902 at --; stillborn
Mary, d. 9/17/1916 at --; asphyxia of labor; Phila. Courchesnes and
    Obeline Gregoire

COUGHLIN,
Susan, d. 9/21/1932 at 56; carcinoma of larynx

COUHIG,
Ethel May, d. 1/21/1892 at 4; influenza with brain disease; b. Dover; (Lynn,
    MA; Berwick, ME)
Eugene, d. 1/19/1892 at 2; influenza - brain complications; b. Dover;
    (Lynn, MA; Berwick, ME)

COUILLARD,
Vina C., d. 11/20/1932 at 55/2/19; angina pectoris

COULANGES,
Leonitine, d. 12/1/1914 at 0/1/27; acute oedema of lungs; N. G. Coulanges
    and Vasela Kard

COURCHENE,
child, d. 2/18/1912 at --; miscarriage; Philadelpha Courchene and Obeline
    Gregoire
Eva, d. 1/28/1912 at 3/2/5; diphtheria; Philadelpha Courchene and Ibeline
    Gregoire

COURCHESNES,
Alberic, d. 8/26/1902 at 0/4/3; ileo-colitis
Emma, d. 8/31/1902 at 0/5/12; pneumonia
Joseph, d. 1/11/1909 at --; asphyxia; Philadelpe ----- and Obeline Gregoire
William, d. 8/23/1905 at 0/4/13; gastroenteritis

COURIER,
Peter, d. 2/7/1904 at 80; senility

COURSER,
Jessie, d. 1/28/1926 at 71/1/3; fatty degen. of heart; Richard Foss and Ann Sanborn
Leroy J., d. 11/30/1937 at 50/5/3*; b. Dover
Mary E., d. 1/30/1925 at 81/11/11; lobar pneumonia; James J. Wentworth and Clarissa Hall
Robert J., d. 7/15/1910 at 0/0/3 in Manchester; Leroy J. Courser and Alberta M. Lodge
William W., d. 7/12/1901 at 25/1/21; phthisis; PH

COURSON,
George L., d. 5/23/1895 at 46; meningitis; b. Lewiston, ME; buried in Lewiston, ME
James M., d. 4/5/1913 at 66/2/21; heart disease; James Courson and Eunice Hill

COURT,
John, d. 10/18/1918 at 50/1/28; lobar pneumonia

COURTEAN,
Mary R., d. 4/29/1897 at 2; abscess of the brain; b. Canada; SM

COURTEAU,
Fred, d. 1/23/1923 at 71/1/7; lobar pneumonia; Pierre Courteau
Paul A., d. 10/29/1922 at 0/2/17; ileo colitis; George A. Courteau and Emma Grenier
Paul E., d. 5/5/1934 at 0/0/4; cerebral hemorrhage

COURTNEY,
Bridget, d. 5/1/1907 at 39; heart dilation
Catherine, d. 12/27/1903 at 36/11/27 in Lawrence, MA; alcoholism and exposure
Elizabeth, d. 11/9/1910 at 65; chronic uraemia; Michael Howland and Bridget Shale
Frances, d. 7/25/1891 at 0/3/7; James Courtney (England) and Mary Farmer (Ireland)
Hannah, d. 12/12/1897 at 70; old age; b. Ireland; SM
Hannah, d. 9/27/1924 at 65/6; chronic endocarditis; Dennis Grady and Ellen Burke
James E., d. 9/6/1895 at 3; brain fever; b. Dover; SM
John, d. 12/18/1896 at 3; pneumonia; b. Dover; SM

Martin, d. 12/16/1931 at 77/1; arterio sclerosis
Mary E., d. 6/1/1888 at 4/5; b. Dover; Patrick Courtney (Ireland) and Elizabeth Howland (Ireland)
Mary J., d. 10/6/1918 at 25/6/25; influenza; Thomas Courtney and Catherine Clark
Patrick, d. 4/26/1914 at 66; acute uraemia; James Courtney and Mary ----
Patrick, d. 1/20/1923 at 55; influenza
Thomas, d. 3/30/1909 at 47; pneumonia; Patrick Courtney and Hannah Kearns

COURY,
Mary, d. 9/30/1936 at 47/9/10; chr. par. nephritis

COUSENS,
Elizabeth T., d. 3/21/1927 at 76/4/4 in Fremont; arterio sclerosis; John Tully
Myrtie W., d. 5/29/1906 at 20/10/4 in Portsmouth; heart failure
William G., d. 11/21/1904 at 66/7/4 in Portsmouth; cancer of stomach; PH

COUSINS,
Caroline M., d. 6/14/1894 at 77; sudden; b. Kennebunk, ME; buried at Dover Point
Eva M., d. 3/9/1896 at –; b. Dover; PH

COUSSOULE,
George, d. 3/15/1926 at 41; lobar pneumonia; John Coussoule and Elizabeth Maravelis

COUTU,
Lillian, d. 6/17/1935 at 37/4/15; cerebral hemorrhage

COUTURE,
child, d. 2/21/1931 at 0/0/1-3; premature birth
Annie V., d. 9/9/1892 at –; asthenia and premature birth; b. Great Falls; (Canada; Canada)
Edward, d. 7/2/1915 at 0/2; acute pneumonia; Joseph Couture and Mary Bisson
Margaret, d. 3/31/1918 at 1/9/14; tuberculous meningitis; Joseph Couture and Mary C. Bisson
Marie, d. 2/19/1912 at 0/0/½ ; miscarriage; Joseph Couture and Marie Bisson
Marie F., d. 3/6/1927 at –; premature birth; Alice Couture

COWAN,
Annie, d. 4/5/1899 at 2; thrush; SM
Bridget, d. 1/18/1906 at 53/7; Bright's disease; SM
Carl J., d. 9/13/1889 at 0/6/7; b. Dover; John R. Cowan (Oxford, MA) and Eugenie Copeland (Pascoag, RI)
Edie, d. 8/28/1897 at 1; worms; b. Dover; SM
John James, d. 10/7/1891 at 0/1/27; William G. Cowan (Dover) and Bridget Conley (Millersburg, IA)
Joseph A., d. 9/18/1920 at 62 in Wakefield, MA; carcinoma of sigmoid
Joseph C., d. 4/21/1929 at 40 in Medford, MA; illuminating gas
Lenora L., d. 11/13/1897 at – in Wales, MA; PH
William, d. 9/18/1913 at 63; sarcoma of jaw; Joseph Cowan and Mary -----

COWEN,
John R., d. 2/8/1908 at 62/10/14 in Danvers, MA; arteriosclerosis

COX,
child, d. 10/11/1934 at –; stillborn
Catherine, d. 12/10/1910 at 66; influenza; Edward Hughes and Mary Evans
Elizabeth, d. 2/24/1912 at 26/0/20; tuberculosis general; Henry Cox and Catherine Hughes
Elizabeth J., d. 7/18/1935 at 81/7/23; carcinoma of stomach
Henry, d. 2/14/1904 at 59/1/25; chronic catarrhal gastritis; SM
Howard, d. 1/28/1911 at 0/2/25; intestinal indigestion; Lizzie Cox
Margaret, d. 8/18/1930 at 52; carcinoma; John Lappin and Sarah J. Jackson
Margaret J., d. 5/28/1915 at 4/2/3; convulsions; Thomas H. Cox and Margaret A. Lappin
Mary, d. 5/5/1920 at 69/5/12; pulmonary oedema; Patrick Cunningham and Bridget Lang
Sarah, d. 7/1/1907 at 0/0/26; hemophilia; Thomas H. Cox and Margaret R. Lappen
Thomas, d. 1/6/1911 at 55/6/29; heart disease; Thomas Cox and Sarah Colvin

CRAGIN,
child, d. 1/28/1897 at 0; inanition; SM
Annie, d. 10/21/1889 at 6/0/16; b. Dover; Patrick Cragin (Ireland) and Kate Sweeney (Ireland)
Catherine, d. 10/9/1914 at 54/4; chr. intestitial nephritis; Eugene Sweeney and Mary McAuliffe
John, d. 10/9/1889 at 4/3/13; b. Dover; Patrick Cragin (Ireland) and Katie Sweeney (Ireland)

Kate, d. 10/15/1889 at 2/2/21; b. Dover; Patrick Cragin (Ireland) and Kate Sweeney (Ireland)
Patrick, d. 10/2/1933 at 86/9/23; chronic nephritis
Sarah, d. 4/29/1918 at 74 in Rochester; arterio sclerosis

CRAIG,
Adelaide E., d. 12/23/1915 at 28/8/25; acute dil. of heart; William H. Brown and Emily Duncan
Elizabeth, d. 5/28/1925 at 80/0/16 in W. Toronto, Can; myocarditis
James, d. 8/11/1919 at 78/2/18; cerebral hemorrhage; Robert Craig and Jennie Parker

CRAM,
Helen B., d. 1/9/1928 at 77/11/15; pulmonary oedema; Dean R. Tilton and Susan S. Jordan
John C., d. 2/7/1891 at 66/4/17; married; ----- (Laconia) and Sallie Russell (Gilford)
Sarah E., d. 3/30/1934 at 63/11/24; erysipelas of face

CRANE,
Eli W., d. 3/21/1906 at 39/7/16; pulmonary tuberculosis
Isabel, d. 8/25/1905 at 0/8/6; gastroenteritis
John H., d. 9/12/1897 at 75 in Freeport, NY; cerebral hemorrhage; PH

CRANNAN,
John P., d. 8/23/1899 at – in Stoneham, MA; PH
Mary, d. 3/28/1903 at 56 in Concord; tuberculosis; SM
Michael, d. 11/14/1890 at 57; married

CRANNON,
Helen F., d. 9/8/1898 at 0 in Stoneham, MA; PH
Joseph W., d. 8/20/1898 at 25 in Stoneham, MA; PH
Mary A., d. 3/25/1898 at 8 in Stoneham, MA; PH

CRANON,
Annie M., d. 10/10/1887 at 0/1; b. Dover; James W. Cranon (Dover) and Nora King (Ireland)

CRANSHAW,
Edward, d. 3/9/1895 at 43; grippe - pneumonia; b. England; PH

CRASSON,
Kate, d. 7/1/1901 at 52; heart disease; SM

CRATEAU,
Henry, d. 4/18/1929 at 1 hr.; premature birth; Wilfred Crateau and Alice Genest
Ludger J., d. 12/27/1935 at 57/2/29; encephalitis

CRAWFORD,
Alexander B., d. 8/22/1910 at 61/0/25 in Newmarket; apoplexy
Erastus A., d. 10/21/1898 at 74; peritonitis; b. Norfolk, NY; buried in Somersworth
Jane S., d. 3/14/1896 at 76; apoplexy; b. Conway; buried in Somersworth
Marion F., d. 6/27/1923 at 79/9/7 in Danvers, MA; broncho pneumonia
Sarah J., d. 5/25/1929 at 87/7/3; myocarditis; Aaron S. Crawford and Elizabeth Locke

CREDIFORD,
Addie L., d. 5/24/1931 at 65/7/5; cerebral hemorrhage
Edna May, d. 12/18/1890 at 5/7/25; Asa R. Crediford (Kennebunkport) and Addie Huntress (Shapleigh, ME)

CREIGHTON,
John, d. 5/5/1904 at 45; R. R. accident

CRENNAN,
Daniel M., d. 8/20/1890 at 22/3/9; single; Martin J. Crennan (Ireland) and Ann Lane (Ireland)

CRESSEY,
Amy R., d. 5/16/1916 at 55 in Boston, MA; cancer; ----- Robinson and Mary A. Twombly
Asenath C., d. 7/1/1920 at 97/11/23; old age; Isreal Swain and Susan Bennett
Irwin P., d. 12/24/1910 at 60/0/19; locomotor ataxia; Thaddeus P. Cressey and Asenath C. Swain
Thaddeus P., d. 2/22/1895 at 69; mitral disease of heart; b. Gorham, ME; PH

CRICHTON,
Frances J., d. 7/20/1897 at 0; cholera infantum; b. Dover; SM

CRISSELL,
Albert H., d. 6/16/1911 at 3/6; tubercular meningitis; Andrew Crissell and Esther Riddle
Esther R. G., d. 1/28/1924 at 54; tuberculosis lungs
Mary, d. 7/30/1892 at 2; meningitis; b. Dover; (Portsmouth; Lawrence, MA)

Mary, d. 1/26/1902 at 34/11/26; uraemic poisoning; PH

CROCKETT,
Ann E., d. 12/28/1928 at 95/0/4 in Boston, MA; broncho pneumonia
Annie Mabel, d. 4/20/1890 at 28; single; Charles H. Crockett (Dover) and
    Ellen J. Mooney (Belmont)
Benjamin T., d. 5/23/1887 at 57/3 in Boston, MA; single; b. Dover
Charles W., d. 1/31/1931 at 52/6/11; fracture of skull
Chesley H., d. 6/14/1921 at 1/3/16; broncho pneumonia; Fred J. Crockett
    and Helena R. Cother
Elizabeth A., d. 2/5/1904 at 72 in Fort Smith, AR; pneumonia; PH
Harriet, d. 9/14/1912 at 83/6 in Stuart, IA; fracture of hip
Jacob G., d. 11/6/1893 at 65; pulmonary oedema; b. NH; (Barnstead;
    Dover)
Lydia A., d. 11/5/1899 at 78 in Boston, MA; paralysis; PH
Mary E., d. 9/3/1891 at 41/11/36 in Bradford, MA
Mary Jane, d. 1/18/1892 at 68; la grippe; b. Ossipee
Nathaniel B., d. 7/4/1892 at 15; accidental drowning
William D., d. 8/5/1899 at 79 in Boston, MA; paralysis; PH

CROFT,
Florence Mary, d. 12/18/1933 at 0/0/½; premature birth
Jean Marc, d. 8/20/1925 at 9/6/9; accidental drowning; William Croft and
    Olivine Dodier
John, d. 8/2/1921 at 84; dilatation of heart; Joseph Croft and Mary Socier

CROMIER,
Charles, d. 9/28/1936 at 45/1/12*

CRONIN,
John B., d. 12/6/1926 at 41/10; chr. parench. nephritis; John Cronin and
    Julia McCarthy
Julia, d. 7/1/1934 at –; fracture hip
Patrick F., d. 9/30/1914 at 28/9/3; pulmonary tuberculosis; Robert Cronin
    and Johanna McCarthy
Robert, d. 8/15/1933 at 86; chronic nephritis

CROOKER,
Anna Brooks, d. 1/3/1903 at 64; pneumonia; buried in Saco, ME

CROSBY,
Charles R., d. 1/9/1923 at 79; apoplexy; Archibald Crosby and Mary N.
    Ferry
Christopher, d. 5/29/1900 at 59; paralysis; PH

Dixie L., d. 3/21/1912 at 51/3/10; uraemic convulsions; Dixie J. Crosby and Martha S. Fairbanks
Harry L., d. 2/14/1929 at 38/1/12 in Cambridge, MA; broncho pneumonia
Ida B., d. 10/13/1925 at 74/7/24; valv. heart disease; Samuel H. Mathes and Mary Perkins
Jennie M., d. 2/11/1916 at 66/8/24; chronic nephritis; Freeman Williams and Betsy Demton
John M., d. 4/21/1919 at 77/0/27 in Cambridge, MA; arterio sclerosis

CROSS,
Charles W., d. 1/30/1890 at 44/1/27; single; Isaac Cross (Salem) and ----- Low (Georgetown)
David, d. 5/16/1907 at 41 in Somersworth; gastritis
Florence M., d. 3/6/1896 at 39 in Santa Barbara, CA; pul. tuberculosis
Mary A. L., d. 1/12/1917 at 94/0/11; bronchitis; Samuel Hatch
Mary E., d. 1/17/1929 at 70/4/21; broncho pneumonia; Gilman Upham and Abigail Twombly
Winthrop W., d. 7/20/1908 at 0/2/21 in Burlington, VT; acute enteritis

CROSSAN,
Margaret, d. 7/23/1911 at 0/5/23; cholera infantum; Philip Crossan and Mary A. Timmons

CROSSEN,
Evelyn, d. 3/12/1917 at 7/7/13; acute endocarditis; Patrick Crossen and Alice O'Hare

CROSSLEY,
Amelia J., d. 3/9/1908 at 29/5/20; phthisis; John Booth and Jane Jackson
Joseph C., d. 9/6/1892 at –; dysentery; b. Dover; (England; England)

CROSSLY,
child, d. 10/14/1893 at –; stillborn; b. Dover; (Manchester, England; Manchester, England)

CROSSON,
Philip, d. 8/20/1910 at 0/7; diarrhea; Philip Crosson and Mary Tomney

CROTEAU,
child, d. 3/21/1901 at 3 hrs.; premature birth
child, d. 10/7/1906 at –; stillborn
child, d. 3/12/1928 at 0/0/½; miscarriage; Wilfrid Croteau and Alice Genest
Alice, d. 10/25/1924 at 0/3; entero colitis; Wilfred Croteau
Joseph, d. 7/29/1927 at 4 hrs.; premature birth; Wilfred Croteau

Mary A., d. 9/12/1934 at –; miscarriage
Sara, d. 3/23/1901 at 40/5; eclampsia

CROUCH,
Winifred S., d. 8/9/1930 at 59/3/24; Albert S. Kingman

CROUSE,
Annabelle, d. 9/3/1935 at 55/2/10; intestinal obstruction

CROWE,
Olive L., d. 6/21/1935 at 20/5/28; rupture uterus (hemorrhage)

CROWELL,
child, d. 2/10/1924 at –; stillborn; Milton Crowell and Esther A. Dairy
Emily F., d. 6/21/1929 at 66/6/24; apoplexy; Sylvanus Howes and
    Diadema E. Edwards
Henry S., d. 7/12/1922 at 71/5; heart disease

CROWLEY,
Michael J., d. 8/25/1937 at 85; chronic bronchitis
Nora, d. 12/22/1909 at 51; chronic nephritis; Cornelius Hourihan and Mary
-----

CULLEN,
child, d. 12/3/1913 at –; stillborn; James F. Cullen and Elizabeth M. Tardiff
child, d. 12/4/1923 at 4 hrs.; premature birth; Marion C. Cullen
Frank A., d. 8/18/1913 at 38/2/17; myocarditis; James Cullen and Delia
    Dolphin
Helen L., d. 2/7/1911 at 1/5/11; pneumonia; George Cullen and Ida
    Southerland
Louis A., d. 5/1/1916 at 38/1/18; frac. lumb. vertebrae; James H. Cullen
    and Sarah J. Lemora
William W., d. 3/25/1932 at 78/6/12; cerebral hemorrhage

CUMMINGS,
Albert L., d. 5/31/1924 at 34/1/11 in Madbury; asphyxia - accidental; Frank
    H. Cummings and Carrie J. -----
Almira R., d. 12/5/1905 at 68/5/9 in Somerville, MA; cerebral hemorrhage
Betsey, d. 8/8/1887 at 67 in Somerville, MA
Carrie J., d. 6/26/1937 at 80/0/29; gen. arteriosclerosis
Charles A., d. 12/11/1915 at 76/6/18 in Somerville, MA; chr. valv. heart
    disease
Frank H., d. 7/5/1927 at 67/5/7; tubercular peritonitis; Charles Cummings
    and Elmira Hussey

Frank M., d. 11/18/1913 at 61/3/4 in Somerville, MA; senility
George E., d. 12/2/1891 at 0/0/12; Frank H. Cummings (Dover) and Carrie J. Nourse (Fox Lake, WI)
Harrie R., d. 9/16/1936 at 73/0/2*; b. Dover
Lamey, d. 1/1/1924 at 52; apoplexy
Olive A., d. 7/29/1914 at 83/0/9; old age; William Abbott and Olive Hodgdon

CUMMISKY,
child, d. 7/9/1913 at –; stillborn; Thomas Cummisky and Annie McCabe
Annie, d. 7/21/1913 at 43/3; uraemia; Patrick McCabe and Susan Moan
James, d. 10/24/1910 at 23/2/7; peritonitis; Thomas Cummisky and Bridget Fitzgerald
Mary, d. 4/3/1932 at 86/6; chronic endocarditis

CUNNINGHAM,
child, d. 9/12/1917 at –; stillborn; M. A. Cunningham and Mary Foley
child, d. 6/12/1921 at –; stillborn; Alfred Cunningham and Mary A. Foley
Ann, d. 4/19/1937 at 79/1/19; carcinoma liver
Bridget, d. 2/24/1897 at 65; apoplexy; b. Ireland; SM
Catherine, d. 2/4/1905 at 93; pneumonia
Elizabeth, d. 12/9/1932 at 76/9/11; cardiac decomposition
Frank, d. 5/10/1926 at 76 in Concord; arterio sclerosis; Frank Cunningham
James, d. 3/20/1915 at 63; cancer of oesophagus; Patrick Cunningham and Rose -----
John, d. 8/23/1889 at –; b. Dover; John Cunningham (Ireland) and M. McGrory (Ireland)
John, d. 4/4/1894 at 45; paralysis; b. Ireland; SM
John J., d. 10/26/1888 at 0/0/27; b. Dover; John A. Cunningham (Ireland) and M. McGrotty (Ireland)
Margaret, d. 4/23/1917 at 53; pulm. tuberculosis; John Gallagher and Sarah Mullin
Mary, d. 2/26/1923 at 70 in Haverhill, MA; myocarditis; Edward McArdle and Nellie Collins
Michael, d. 12/4/1923 at 73; apoplexy
R., d. 3/31/1892 at –; pneumonia; b. Dover; (Ireland; Dover)
Rosanna, d. 12/1/1893 at 74; acute bronchitis; b. Ireland; (Ireland; Ireland)
William, d. 3/29/1897 at 25; b. Dover; SM
William J., d. 8/4/1935 at 84; angina pectoris

CURLEY,
John, d. 7/5/1909 at –; stillborn; John F. Curley and Mary Chapman

CURRAN,
Georges, d. 7/5/1900 at 1; convulsions

CURRIE,
child, d. 6/29/1899 at –; stillborn; PH
Sarah J., d. 3/10/1900 at 65 in Malden, MA; la grippe; PH

CURRIER,
child, d. 4/2/1919 at –; stillborn; Mary Currier
Adeline, d. 2/4/1921 at 93/6/27; senility; Daniel C. Tuttle and Sarah Drew
Benjamin F., d. 5/3/1937 at 82/1/25; cerebral embolism
Dorothy Grace, d. 10/16/1909 at 0/2/29; marasmus; William H. Currier and Jennie Douglass
Edward L., d. 9/27/1927 at 79/5/1; apoplexy; Thomas Currier and Harriet Smith
Ella S., d. 3/1/1932 at 76/4/21; arterio sclerosis
Ellen S., d. 11/20/1921 at 78/0/24; fatty degen. of heart; Joseph Snow and Asenath Ladd
Fred H., d. 9/25/1916 at –; fracture of spine; Andrew J. Currier and Mary Daniels
Hannah M., d. 6/4/1897 at 59; Bright's disease; b. Dover; PH
Mary A., d. 8/29/1928 at 88/3/12; apoplexy
Raymond H., d. 8/14/1907 at 0/1/25; marasmus; William H. Currier and Jennie E. Douglass
Thomas, d. 5/22/1897 at 65; Brights disease; b. NY; PH
William, d. 12/9/1935 at 67/6/17; chronic myocarditis

CURRY,
Catherine, d. 6/22/1906 at 12/8; accidental drowning; SM
Catherine, d. 3/14/1935 at 63; acute pulmonary edema
Emma May, d. 5/6/1908 at 0/3/17; tuberculosis meningitis; John F. Curry and Mary Chapman
Francis, d. 8/6/1908 at 41; lightning stroke; Francis Curry and Ann Loughlin
Thomas, d. 7/19/1921 at 58; cancer of stomach; Francis Curry and Ann Loughlin
William E., d. 3/23/1917 at 50; traumatic shock

CURTEY,
Emily, d. 11/11/1920 at 21 in Boston, MA; toxaemia pregnancy

CURTIS,
Eliza, d. 2/27/1901 at 65; la grippe; SM
Mary M., d. 3/19/1920 at 80/8/28; chronic nephritis; Samuel Remick and Abagail Dearborn
William R., d. 6/9/1926 at 71/7/27; lobar pneumonia

CUSHING,
Charles, d. 1/4/1914 at 83/5/15; old age; Peter Cushing and Sarah Austin
Charles H., d. 10/22/1918 at 67/2/23; cerebral hemorrhage; Samuel W. Cushing and Asenath Hyde
Exilda, d. 10/18/1928 at 65/1 in Concord; diabetes; Rami Roch and Rosalie Gilbert
Hannah M., d. 1/6/1894 at 56; catarrhal pneumonia; b. MA; buried in family lot
Jennie, d. 2/16/1906 at 39/1/10 in Clinton, MA; septicemia; PH
Mabel, d. 7/5/1937 at 76/0/0; pulmonary tuberculosis

CUSHMAN,
Helen M., d. 6/29/1929 at 87 in New Haven, CT; aortic regurgitation
Olive S., d. 5/13/1891 at 79/11/11; widow; Greely Sturdivant (Cumberland, ME) and Deborah York (Cumberland, ME)
Thomas K., d. 6/18/1914 at 75/4/28; syncope of heart; Joseph E. F. Cushman and Olive Sturdivant
William W., d. 2/3/1910 at 68/11/8; uraemia; William C. Cushman and Sarah Rollins

CUSKER,
M., d. 1/24/1890 at 55; married; Bernard Cusker (Ireland) and Bridget (Ireland)
Mary, d. 1/21/1896 at 62; cancer; b. Ireland; SM

CUSSON,
Charles, d. 3/5/1920 at 69/10/5; interstitial nephritis; Michael Cusson and Lucie Desforges

CUSTEAU,
Zephia, d. 10/14/1926 at 52/6/28; locomotor ataxia; George Custeau and Florence Thibodeau

CUTLER,
Euphemia J., d. 10/7/1919 at 39/9/1; tuberculosis pulmonary; Andrew Stevenson and Henrietta McFarlane
Harriet B., d. 11/16/1895 at 82; resulting from injury; b. Conway; buried in Conway
Nellie F., d. 2/19/1921 at 68; apoplexy; Henry Taylor and Olive Randall

CUTTING,
Henrietta, d. 6/1/1924 at 74/0/18; apoplexy; Argyl Potter and Mary Roberts

CUTTS,
Lavina C., d. 4/3/1917 at 74/11/4 in Malden, MA; lobar pneumonia

CYR,
Jenny, d. 12/3/1891 at 30; single
Joseph, d. 10/13/1918 at 31/6/19; influenza; John Cyr and Josephine Levine

D'ARCY,
Gerald Joseph, d. 8/31/1937 at 53/5/18; coronary thrombosis
Michael, d. 7/9/1920 at 72/6/14; cerebral hemorrhage; Daniel D'Arcy and Sarah Fenton

DABNEY,
child, d. 4/24/1919 at 0/0/½; premature birth; Vaughan Dabney and Ruth E. Burdette

DAERIS,
John, d. 11/11/1918 at 39; gangrene of leg; Constantine Daeris and Athanasia -----

DAGENAIS,
child, d. 10/20/1924 at 0/0/7; atelectasis; Edward Dagenais and Delia St. Laurent
Alcide, d. 3/18/1921 at 11/10/16; uraemia; Ferdinand Dagenais and Louise Bomdeau
Ferdinand, d. 3/30/1928 at 66/5; natural causes; Cezaire Dagenais and Philomene Bedard

DAGONAIS,
Mary L., d. 10/22/1932 at 68/1/25; acute myocarditis

DAHER,
child, d. 1/2/1907 at –; stillborn; Joseph Daher and Sarah Sheval
Mary, d. 3/23/1904 at 0/0/1; premature birth

DAIGLE,
Madeleine T., d. 3/21/1930 at 0/5/15; ac. lobar pneumonia; Telesphore Daigle and Parmelia Mailhot
Madeline Rita, d. 3/4/1925 at 0/2/23; marasmus; Telesphore Daigle and Parmelia Mailhot

DAILEY,
child, d. 3/7/1891 at –; Francis Dailey (Ireland) and Annie Armstrong (Ireland)
Charles F., d. 5/22/1910 at 2/3/1 in Madbury; malignant diphtheria
James H., d. 1/18/1929 at 71/9/10 in Madbury; ac. cardiac dilatation
Mary, d. 2/14/1890 at 38; married; Hugh Gallagher (Ireland) and Ellen Doherty (Ireland)

DAILY,
Bridget, d. 4/19/1904 at 83 in Madbury; erysipelas; SM
Mary A., d. 7/31/1907 at –; acute tuberculosis; ----- McKone
Patrick, d. 6/3/1887 at 32; laborer; married; b. Ireland; Patrick Daily (Ireland) and Mary (Ireland)

DALE,
George, d. 5/5/1893 at 22; phthisis pulmonalis

DALEY,
Annie E., d. 8/9/1892 at –; anaemia; b. Dover; (Ireland; Ireland)
Bernard, d. 9/30/1918 at 53; mitral regurgitation; Bernard Daley and Mattie Kelley
Bridget T., d. 1/3/1915 at 54 in Concord; acute dilatation of heart; Eugene Daley and Julia Downing
Catherine M., d. 2/1/1936 at 25/1/13; pulmonary tuberculosis
Charles Francis, d. 9/19/1912 at 8/3/7; diphtheria; Daniel Daley and Mary Berry
Daniel, d. 1/1/1926 at 71; cancer of face
Daniel J., d. 8/11/1925 at 50; frac. cervical vertebrae; Michael Daley and Mary Collins
Edward, d. 11/14/1937 at –; carcinoma large intestine
Elizabeth A., d. 12/20/1915 at 0/0/7; pneumonia, acute; Daniel Daley and Mary Berry
Elizabeth C., d. 6/26/1912 at 82/5/29; senility; Charles P. Holton and Lydia Crockett
Ellen, d. 8/9/1907 at 0/5/15; cholera infantum; Michael Daley and Elizabeth Sullivan
Ellen, d. 2/21/1908 at 55; heart disease; Daniel Maloney and Bridget Herlihy
James, d. 4/6/1903 at 51; uremic coma; PH
John, d. 5/15/1888 at 88/6/8 in Madbury; railroad; married; b. Ireland; (Ireland; Ireland)
Joseph, d. 12/21/1937 at 55/9/2; cerebr. hemorrhage
Margaret P., d. 12/20/1915 at 0/0/7; pnuemonia; Daniel Daley and Mary Barry

Mary, d. 9/7/1911 at 24/10/24; acute appendicitis; Michael Daley and
   Elizabeth Sullivan
Michael J., d. 1/22/1931 at 71/0/27; uraemia
Patrick, d. 5/6/1898 at 29; Bright's disease; b. Ireland; SM
Rose, d. 8/13/1918 at 58; cerebral hemorrhage; Patrick Morgan and
   Katherine Donnelly
Rose B., d. 10/9/1889 at 2/2/2; b. Dover; Patrick Daley (Ireland) and Rose
   Morgan (Ireland)
Sarah J., d. 6/16/1893 at 1; cerebral meningitis; b. Dover; (Ireland; Ireland)

DALTON,
child, d. 7/22/1910 at –; stillborn; William Dalton and Lillian Hall
Frank, d. 2/23/1909 at 0/0/2; atelectasis; William Dalton and Lily Hall
John J., d. 11/17/1927 at 74; angina pectoris; Samuel Dalton and Sarah A.
   Bean
Samuel B., d. 1/9/1891 at 71/10/13; married; James J. Dalton (Deerfield)
   and Betsey Rand (Deerfield)
Sarah A., d. 3/3/1898 at 75; heart disease; b. Nottingham; buried in
   Nottingham

DALY,
Annie, d. 1/21/1937 at 80; chronic nephritis
Frances, d. 5/14/1929 at 61; cerebral apoplexy
Mary, d. 1/5/1897 at 7; diphtheretic scarletina; b. Dover
Mary, d. 1/3/1926 at 60; angina pectoris; John Fagen and Ann Flanagan

DAM,
Daniel, d. 12/13/1887 at 82/3/13; widower; b. Newfield, ME; Joseph Dam
   (Dover) and Margaret Nelson (Portsmouth)

DAME,
Abbie M., d. 11/30/1900 at 68; meningitis; PH
Bessie F., d. 12/10/1928 at 69/5/7 in Agawam, MA; cancer of breast;
   William Slattery and Catherine Martin
Betsey Canney, d. 10/30/1905 at 76/4/10; meningitis; PH
Carrie E., d. 3/19/1923 at 57/0/28; cerebral hemorrhage; Moses Dame and
   Abigail Mitchell
Charles, d. 6/26/1892 at 82; cerebral hemorrhage
Charles E., d. 11/18/1929 at 71/11/10; arterio sclerosis; Samuel H. Dame
   and Mary E. Henderson
Charles G., d. 1/29/1926 at 64/11/24; valvular heart disease; Israel S.
   Dame and Mary Hanson
Charles H., d. 11/1/1896 at 34; paraplegia; b. Dover; PH
Druscilla, d. 9/23/1895 at 71; insanity; b. Effingham; PH

Edith May, d. 4/6/1915 at 35/10/18; cerebral hyperemia; John W. Batley and Sarah A. Ogden

Edward E., d. 2/7/1919 at 55/10/10; cerebral hemorrhage; Israel S. Dame and Mary Hanson

Edwin Forest, d. 12/10/1928 at 73/1/5; cancer of tongue

Eliza S., d. 2/4/1896 at 65; heart disease; b. Ossipee; PH

F. H., d. 1/9/1887 at 32/5/27; jeweler; married; b. Dover; S. Hiram Dame (Dover) and Mary E. Henderson (Dover)

Frank H., d. 1/18/1892 at 3; congestion of lungs; b. Dover; (Lee; Eliot, ME)

Franklin P., d. 11/27/1894 at 50; R.R. accident; b. Farmington; PH

Grace G., d. 11/28/1917 at 47/9/10; mitral regurgitation; Charles Coleman and Mary Pinkham

Harriet Walker, d. 7/3/1890 at 71/10/3; single; Jabez Dame (Rochester) and Elizabeth Cushing (Rochester)

Ida May, d. 5/28/1907 at 30/6/22; confinement; Richard A. Pinkham and Mary A. Hart

Israel S., d. 3/22/1931 at 63/1/6 in Lee; heart disease

John Edward, d. 1/28/1914 at 74/1/17; chronic gastro enteritis; John N. Dame and Caroline H. Parker

John H., d. 11/7/1936 at 77/11/16; heart disease

John S., d. 9/19/1918 at 77/10/24; prob. cerebral hemorrhage; Joseph Dame and Mehitabel Burrows

Lucy M., d. 2/17/1921 at 50/2/14; accidental burns; Horace Joy and Cynthia Knowles

Lydia H., d. 10/3/1932 at 91/8/12; chronic myocarditis

Martin L., d. 11/19/1901 at 84; cerebral embolism; buried in Rochester

Mary E., d. 12/6/1887 at 59/7/7; married; b. Dover; Samuel Henderson (Dover)

Norman C., d. 6/3/1917 at 7/6/25; epilepsy; John E. Dame and Grace Sterling

Rose Ann, d. 4/18/1937 at 1/3/3; stoph meningitis

Samuel H., d. 2/22/1907 at 84/6/19; senile dementia; Samuel Dame and Phoebe Wentworth

Sarah Elizabeth, d. 4/11/1890 at 4/10/12 in Newburyport

Sarah O., d. 9/7/1931 at 87/4/7; chronic myocarditis

William, d. 7/27/1887 at 59/10; trader; married; b. Acton, ME; Joseph Dame (Farmington) and Anna Palmer (Rollinsford)

William F., d. 2/26/1906 at 78/5/6; arterial sclerosis; PH

DAMES,
child, d. 9/17/1921 at –; stillborn; George Dames and Poulina Daube

DAMM,
Johanna D., d. 4/4/1931 at 82/8/14; arterio sclerosis

DAMON,
Everett E., d. 4/13/1922 at 46/0/3; lobar pneumonia; Franklin Damon and Angie Goodrich
George W., d. 2/27/1914 at 76/10/12; acute uraemia

DAMSELL,
Benjamin F., d. 6/8/1911 at 56/9/1; nervous prostration; ----- Damsell and Jane -----

DANA,
Thomas, d. 3/31/1888 at 37; laborer; married; b. Dover; Fanny Trefethen

DANDENEAU,
Blanche, d. 5/18/1911 at 0/4/2; athrepsia; Isaac Dandeneau and Mary Boissoneau
Catherine T., d. 7/25/1931 at 48/4; arterio sclerosis
Mary Anna, d. 5/23/1915 at 0/2; athrepsia; Isaac Dandeneau and Mary Bresineau
Oliva, d. 8/29/1925 at 66; cerebral hemorrhage; Louis Lavoie

DANEY,
Ovilla, d. 2/12/1934 at 86/10/29 in Sacramento, CA; chronic myocarditis

DANFORTH,
Alice, d. 4/3/1890 at 1/3/6 in Rochester; George Danforth (Rollinsford) and Julia A. Lutolf (Switzerland)
Eliza J. C., d. 2/18/1897 at 78 in Westfield, MA
James E., d. 2/5/1931 at 45/4/29; suffocation
Stephen A., d. 6/26/1915 at 77/3/21; acute indigestion; John Danforth and ----- Atwood
Vera, d. 2/27/1930 at 8; diphtheria; James E. Danforth and Ida Whittier

DANGERFIELD,
child, d. 8/19/1933 at – in Durham; stillborn
Catherine, d. 11/6/1930 at 82/4/27; cerebral apoplexy; Murdock Campbell and Isabel Fraser
Ethel E. I., d. 2/21/1913 at 33/5/19; heart disease; Charles E. Dangerfield and Catherine L. Campbell
Lionel S., d. 1/12/1919 at 30/2/30; influenza; Charles E. Dangerfield and Catherine L. Campbell

DANIELS,
child, d. 8/8/1928 at –; stillborn; Forrest Daniels and Annie M. Desautels
Betsey, d. 7/21/1895 at 98 in Lawrence, MA; old age; buried in Dover

George E., d. 7/8/1935 at 70/0/1; peritonitis
Mary E., d. 9/3/1919 at 85; pneumonia; William E. Coner and Mary E. McDonald
Miles D., d. 4/8/1925 at 64/10/1 in Boston, MA; carcinoma of stomach; Nathaniel Daniels and Miriam Foss

DARVILL,
Ella F., d. 4/15/1920 at 71/10/24; neurasthenia; Edmund Tibbetts and Sophronia Blake
Joseph, d. 7/16/1936 at 81/10/9*; b. England

DARVILLE,
Euphemia G., d. 3/15/1933 at 76/8/5; carcinoma pyloris

DASHA,
Florence, d. 4/15/1888 at 38; single; b. Great Falls (see Dashe)

DASHE,
Horace, d. 4/15/1887 at 38; b. Great Falls (see Dasha)

DAUDREAU,
Simeon, d. 5/9/1893 at 38; pleuritis com. by peritonitis; b. Quebec; (Quebec; Quebec)

DAUPHIN,
Clara Theresa, d. 10/28/1937 at 88/10/12; generalized arterios.
Gabriel, d. 1/17/1933 at 79; broncho pneumonia

DAVEY,
child, d. 12/17/1933 at –; mother's bro. pneumonia
Annie, d. 7/17/1887 at 0/4/10; b. Dover; James Davey (Ireland) and Mary (Ireland)
Bertha, d. 12/18/1902 at 0/0/10; valvular disease of heart
Mary, d. 10/18/1901 at 50; heart disease; SM
Mary A., d. 2/16/1893 at 38; congestion of brain; b. England; (England; England)
Mary A., d. 6/19/1925 at 51/6/1; myocarditis; Chris. Cavanaugh and Rosanna Connelly
Thomas, d. 7/11/1887 at 0/4/4; b. Dover; James Davey (Ireland) and Mary (Ireland)

DAVIAN,
Alice, d. 9/13/1913 at –; stillborn; Alphonse Davian and Mary Gracey

DAVIDSON,
Benjamin H., d. 6/22/1925 at 69/0/21; angina pectoris; Alexander Davidson and Eliza Hoffman

DAVIS,
child, d. 3/20/1907 at –; stillborn; William C. Davis and Martha L. White
child, d. 2/9/1917 at –; premature birth; Iva Davis
Abbie J., d. 4/27/1923 at 73/3/15; burns, accidental; Freeman Gowell and Mary Gowen
Abbie L., d. 12/14/1929 at 76/8/2; chr. myocarditis; Benjamin Hurd and Lydia Billings
Ada F., d. 3/28/1900 at 35; pul. phthisis; PH
Albert S., d. 5/13/1887 at 65/1/5; florist; married; b. NH; Beniah Davis (NH) and Abigail Gilman (NH)
Alexzene S., d. 12/31/1915 at 58/0/1; pneumonia; Enoch Davis and Taulina Staples
Amanda, d. 8/7/1935 at 88/11/12; fracture of hip
Annie M., d. 8/28/1896 at 73 in Durham; neuralgia of the heart; PH
Annie P., d. 10/21/1922 at 62; heart syncope; Augustus Perkins and Abigail Plummer
Arthur L., d. 9/27/1933 at 63/1/26 in Boston, MA; cardiac failure
Augustus A., d. 12/6/1906 at 66/9/12; diabetes; PH
Ben, d. 7/12/1929 at 77 in Portland, ME; erythema nodosum; Obadiah ----- and Elizabeth A. Dow
Carrie O., d. 2/4/1931 at 73/9/16; cerebral thrombosis
Catherine, d. 3/29/1909 at 63/10; la grippe with pneumonia; James McGuire and Margaret Seniott
Charles A., d. 10/27/1922 at 64/9/19; carcinoma of bladder; Henry Davis and Sarah Willey
Charles A., d. 5/16/1930 at 78/3/10; embolism; Albert S. Davis and Mary F. Stevenson
Charles F., d. 7/1/1930 at 67/4/18; angina pectoris; Charles W. Davis and Emily E. French
Charles W., d. 8/26/1906 at 70/7/21; heart disease; PH
Daniel W., d. 5/4/1920 at 74/7 in Acton, ME; arterio sclerosis
David, d. 7/8/1904 at 14/11; accidental drowning; buried in Somersworth
Edgar Alonzo, d. 12/26/1937 at 57/10/22 in Kittery, ME; appendicitis, acute
Edward, d. 9/10/1914 at 60/3/17; suicide by hanging; Edward Davis and Elizabeth Law
Edward E., d. 5/21/1922 at 12/10; locomotor ataxia; William C. Davis and Martha L. White
Edwin R., d. 12/17/1897 at 55; alcoholism; b. Farmington; PH
Eleazer, d. 1/16/1895 at 79; heart disease; b. Alton; PH
Eliza, d. 2/9/1913 at 82/0/4 in Brooklyn, NY; ch. endocarditis
Eliza J., d. 10/19/1902 at 61/6/1; cerebral hemorrhage; PH

Elizabeth, d. 9/17/1904 at 77/5/4; toxic poisoning of bowels; PH
Emily B., d. 10/8/1927 at 65/0/8; cerebral hemorrhage; Charles O. Brown and Mary Piper
Emily E., d. 5/11/1924 at 86/8; arterio sclerosis; Charles E. French and Betsey Bunker
Emma A., d. 1/31/1896 at 31; result of miscarriage; b. Barrington; PH
Emma F., d. 7/22/1920 at 56/2/19; uterine cancer; John Watson
Fannie, d. 12/27/1933 at 82/11/23; myocarditis
Fannie M., d. 7/3/1917 at 51/11/10; surgical shock; Edwin B. Stevens and Mary A. Pike
Filena P., d. 3/17/1928 at 64/1; cerebral hemorrhage; George W. Murray and Hannah Chick
Florence V., d. 11/12/1922 at 25/11/18; pulmonary tuberculosis; Henry G. Hutchins and Elizabeth Spencer
Frank, d. 12/24/1935 at 66/6/17; chronic endocarditis
Frank E., d. 9/22/1929 at 70/3/14; cerebral hemorrhage; William Davis and Sarah F. Libby
Frank J., d. 1/20/1935 at 80 in Brentwood; myocarditis
Franklin F., d. 9/5/1901 at 65/3/6; cerebral apoplexy; PH
Fred C., d. 1/24/1887 at 1/4/16; b. Madbury; Frank E. Davis and Emma A. Willey
Frederick W., d. 7/21/1917 at 55/8/4; locomotor ataxia; Albert Davis and Mary Stevenson
Freeman N., d. 6/5/1934 at 83/11/13; cerebral hemorrhage
Hannah E., d. 2/12/1908 at 63/7/10 in Lowell, MA; rheumatism of heart
Hannah I., d. 7/18/1922 at 51/9/13; typhoid fever; Andrew J. Lang and Mehitable Sanborn
Harriet E., d. 4/16/1916 at 57/5/6; cerebral hemorrhage; Joseph W. Cate and Harriet Kimball
Harry A., d. 5/4/1890 at 1/2/21 in Epping
Harry D., d. 10/17/1894 at 85 in Durham; pneumonia; PH
Harry D., d. 9/14/1897 at 0; cholera infantum; b. Malden, MA; buried in Moultonboro
Harry G., d. 7/20/1933 at 62/5/12; erysipelas
Hazel M., d. 12/18/1931 at 36/1/9; carcinoma uterus
Henry, d. 12/14/1912 at 64/3/17; probably heart disease; Edward Davis and Elizabeth J. Law
Henry S., d. 4/8/1893 at –; rheumatism
Herbert A., d. 1/19/1904 at 0/0/10; inanition; buried in Somersworth
Herbert G., d. 1/25/1914 at 54/8/7; pneumonia; Charles F. Davis and Sarah A. Drew
Herbert M., d. 7/3/1937 at 83/11/18; chronic myocarditis
Ira, d. 1/1/1892 at 77; old age; b. Barnstead
Ira A., d. 5/11/1923 at 74/6/10; apoplexy
James, d. 12/15/1921 at 73; arterio sclerosis

James H., d. 11/19/1899 at 71; fibroid phthisis; PH
Jennie Eliza, d. 5/1/1929 at 84/5/1 in Apponaug, RI; senility
Joanna M., d. 9/18/1888 at 74/11/19; widow; b. ME; ----- Morrill
Laura A., d. 2/11/1893 at 44; phthisis; b. Farmington; (NH; NH)
Lizzie E. M., d. 11/24/1922 at 52/6/2; cancer of small intes.; Jonathan C. Chesley and Sarah A. Chesley
Louisa, d. 2/19/1917 at 79; broncho pneumonia
Louise M., d. 3/2/1891 at 0/8/12; George H. Davis (NH) and Emily B. Brown (NH)
Lucetta M., d. 2/6/1908 at 85/3/10; old age; Nathaniel Davis and Susan Ford
Lydia, d. 7/16/1891 at 83; widow
Lydia, d. 10/18/1897 at 98; old age; b. Milton; PH
Mabel E., d. 6/29/1904 at 29/6/26; phthisis pulmonalis; buried in Newmarket
Margaret J., d. 11/15/1896 at 67; diabetes; b. Wakefield; PH
Martha L., d. 3/7/1934 at 54/0/23; carcinoma of uterus
Mary A. R., d. 2/6/1901 at 38/10/12; tuberculosis; PH
Mary Amanda, d. 2/21/1922 at 79/10/4 in Durham; pneumonia
Mary E., d. 12/31/1915 at 100/10/21 in So. Berwick, ME; general debility
Mary E., d. 10/11/1918 at 6/10/14; pneumonia; Harper Davis and Bertha Tyler
Mary F., d. 10/17/1907 at 76/4/17; chronic bronchitis; Thomas Stevenson and Sarah W. Bickford
Mathilda M., d. 7/10/1908 at --; stillborn; Harry S. Davis and Maria Michel
Meander H., d. 5/16/1931 at 70/7/10 in Farmington; arterio sclerosis
Newell C., d. 8/12/1902 at 70/9/26; debility of old age; PH
Reuben A., d. 12/7/1926 at 67/3/29 in Haverhill, MA; chr. valv. heart disease
Sadie, d. 8/13/1904 at 52/0/7; septicaemia; buried in Nottingham
Samuel C., d. 3/11/1891 at 57/10; single; Samuel Davis (ME) and Lidia Davis (ME)
Samuel P., d. 7/1/1936 at 48/9*; b. Boston, MA
Sarah E., d. 10/10/1905 at 64/5/22 in Amesbury, MA; Bright's disease; PH
Sarah E., d. 7/18/1924 at 84/6/11; chronic myocarditis; Benjamin Randall and Melinda Stillings
Sarah H., d. 5/20/1908 at 38/8/23; pulmonary tuberculosis; James H. Davis and Margaret J. Bickford
Sarah J., d. 3/28/1911 at --; pneumonia; Mathew Scully and Margaret E. Fitzgerald
Stephen C., d. 4/11/1911 at 90/3/6 in W. Newbury, MA; cerebral hemorrhage
Susan P., d. 3/8/1891 at 42/1/17 in Brockton, MA
Thomas A., d. 2/28/1913 at 20/10; typhoid fever; Fred W. Davis and Mary A. Ransom

Walter C., d. 10/20/1928 at 70/11/14; carcinoma of prostate; Charles S. Davis and Sarah Butler
William, d. 1/6/1898 at 84; old age; b. NH; PH
William H., d. 10/12/1899 at 31; alcoholic heart disease; PH
William H., d. 8/10/1911 at 48/11/21; apoplexy; Jeremiah Davis and Mary J. Glidden

DAVY,
child, d. 8/24/1916 at –; stillborn; Bernard Davy and Mary J. Ford
Carl Joseph, d. 9/13/1913 at 0/1/26; cholera infantum; Bernard H. Davy and Mary Ford
Edward A., d. 6/7/1922 at 21/5/27; pulmonary tuberculosis; Stephen Davy and Mary Cavanaugh
Ellen F., d. 7/15/1916 at 51; valvular heart disease; James Dasey and Mary Candam
James J., d. 6/10/1932 at 59/2/27; angina pectoris
Mary B., d. 11/4/1916 at 51; acute bronchitis; James Davy and Mary Condon
Stephen, d. 6/21/1910 at 0/0/6; perpura hemorrhagica; Stephen Davy and Mary Cavanaugh

DAWSON,
William Francis, d. 4/23/1910 at 0/2/18; convulsions; George Dawson and Margaret H. Clements

DAY,
Catherine M., d. 8/19/1914 at 85/4/3; senility; John Day and Anne Bagley
Emma J., d. 10/31/1915 at 61/1/10; cerebral hemorrhage; Josiah Morrill and Elizabeth Tozier
John L., d. 1/6/1923 at 76/7/24; arterio sclerosis; Benjamin Day

DEAN,
Lydia M., d. 9/3/1898 at 47; Brights disease; b. Taunton, MA; PH
Roscoe C., d. 10/12/1927 at 42/10/16; septic tonsilitis; Charles Dean and Delia Allen

DEANANTES,
child, d. 8/26/1920 at –; stillborn; George Deanantes and Panageota Douves

DEARBORN,
Charles H., d. 6/18/1916 at 60/0/2; fatty heart; Thomas J. Dearborn and Sarah A. Dame

Helen, d. 12/27/1887 at 0/7/27; b. Dover; Charles H. Dearborn (Wakefield) and Mary J. Hartford (Dover)
Horace E., d. 3/8/1925 at 69/0/29; mitral stenosis; John C. Dearborn and Harriet Leland
John S., d. 6/5/1896 at 9; cerebral meningitis; b. Dover; PH
John S., d. 12/2/1896 at 72; heart disease - pneumonia; b. Northfield; buried in Tilton
Laura E., d. 12/5/1921 at 70/0/26 in Methuen, MA; carcinoma of uterus
Mary J., d. 4/4/1923 at 70/8/2; mitral regurgitation; James W. Hartford and Phoebe Hayes
Nathan L., d. 3/11/1887 at 37/9/17; physician; b. Wakefield; Thomas L. Dearborn (Wakefield) and Sarah A. Dame (Rochester)
Sarah A., d. 4/23/1912 at 86/3/8; heart disease; William Dame and Anne Fogg
Thomas H., d. 12/30/1932 at 72/4/9; Paget's disease

DEBIEU,
Eugene, d. 9/3/1891 at 0/6; Joseph Debieu (Canada) and Delia Ramzay (Canada)

DEBLOIS,
Erwin W., d. 11/19/1933 at 41/7/18; angina pectoris

DECATER,
Caroline, d. 10/20/1909 at 88/11/8; old age; Samuel Nutter and Marion Clark

DECATUR,
child, d. 9/25/1904 at –; stillborn
Abbie A., d. 1/23/1930 at 77/10/29; cerebral hemorrhage; Theophilas Barnes and Abbie H. Staples
Abbie H., d. 1/23/1891 at 60/5/28; widow; John F. Woodus (Dover) and Helen Eastman (Dover)
Commodore, d. 9/19/1893 at 112 (sic); apoplectic shock; b. Albany, NY
Herman F., d. 12/5/1905 at 44/0/4; typhoid fever; buried in Barrington

DECLOS ,
Philomene, d. 7/6/1897 at 50; disease of spine; b. Canada; SM

DEGARDON,
Annie M., d. 8/27/1905 at 0/1/7; mal-assimilation; SM

DEGLER,
child, d. 8/30/1931 at –; convulsions

DEJADON,
Leon, d. 9/16/1905 at 1/10/9; anaemia; SM

DEJARDIN,
Joseph S., d. 3/28/1911 at –; intestinal hemorrhage; Alexander De Jardin and Georgiana Devereaux

DEJARDON,
Mary E., d. 2/21/1909 at 17; acute nephritis; Joseph DeJardon and Mary E. Barry

DELAND,
Ephraim J., d. 4/20/1897 at 61; phthisis; b. So. Wolfeboro; PH
Sarah C., d. 2/10/1930 at 85/5/10; ch. val. dis. of heart; James Littlefield and Sarah Bean

DELANEY,
Elizabeth, d. 2/29/1904 at 53/0/3; gangrene and cerebral embolism; PH
Fred, d. 8/22/1892 at 32; railroad accident; b. Dover; (Ireland; England)
John, d. 3/8/1893 at 83; old age - injury; b. Ireland; (Ireland; Ireland)
John, d. 2/21/1902 at 72; heart disease
John W., d. 5/26/1896 at 56; ch. rheumatic arthritis; b. Dover; PH
Joseph, d. 10/27/1893 at 73; disease of liver; b. England; (Ireland; Ireland)
Joseph H., d. 8/23/1929 at 72; cancer of rectum
Margaret L., d. 1/25/1897 at 79; old age; b. England; PH
Mary E., d. 10/11/1889 at 48/3/2; housewife; married; b. Dover; Isaac Jacobs (Dover) and Elizabeth Waldron (Barrington)
Mary J., d. 10/13/1934 at 65/5/3 in Portland, ME; cerebral hemorrhage
Nell, d. 12/23/1930 at 65 in Hartford, CT; broncho pneumonia
Owen, d. 7/26/1912 at 66/7/10; cancer of inferior maxillar; John Delaney and Margaret Leyland
Patrick, d. 5/25/1895 at 23; accidental drowning; b. Ireland; SM
Walter, d. 6/7/1921 at 65/8/5; arterio sclerosis; John Delaney and Margaret Layland

DELISLE,
Henry, d. 1/11/1919 at 27/5; lobar pneumonia; David Delisle
Marie, d. 12/20/1930 at 34/2; rheum. heart dis.; Francis Berry
Orin, d. 3/–/1902 at 10; drowned in Cocheco River; SM
Zoe, d. 6/17/1901 at 43/4/7; eclampsia

DELOCK,
Napoleon, d. 5/13/1925 at 78; chronic Brights disease

DELUCAS,
John, d. 1/7/1929 at 54/4/6; chronic myocarditis

DELYSLE,
Barbara L., d. 3/16/1924 at 0/9/24 in Sanford, ME; pneumonia

DEMARS,
Delfinus, d. 2/4/1906 at 38; acute nephritis; SM
Francois, d. 6/12/1901 at 41/2; accidental drowning; buried in Lewiston, ME
Thomas, d. 11/30/1918 at 15/4/2; accidentally shot; Joseph Demars and Margaret Cushing

DEMBOREIAN,
Peter, d. 7/16/1905 at –; accidental drowning; SM

DEMERITT,
Alaric B., d. 1/17/1908 at 78/0/10; cerebral hemorrhage; J. B. Demeritt and Martha V. Barron
Amanda J., d. 3/27/1898 at 51; heart disease; b. Dover; PH
Charles W., d. 2/17/1917 at 72/1/5 in Portland, ME; Charles Demeritt and Ann Young
Elizabeth P., d. 3/19/1932 at 67/5/18 in Durham; angina pectoris
Emma F., d. 12/2/1930 at 76/2/14; myocarditis, etc.; T. F. Kennedy and Mary J. Cook
Fannie A., d. 12/25/1890 at 44/7/9; married; Samuel Joy (So. Berwick, ME) and Eliza Moulton (York, ME)
Fannie W., d. 3/8/1901 at 69/11/9; heart disease; buried in Lee
Forrest, d. 10/4/1929 at 66; chr. myocarditis; Israel Demeritt and Fannie --
Frances A., d. 1/17/1906 at 63/9/2; heart disease; PH
Frances E., d. 12/2/1936 at 86/7/7; ar. heart-kid. disease
George H., d. 2/1/1901 at 53/7/20; cerebral thrombosis; PH
George H., d. 8/26/1937 at 80/4/20; cerebral apoplexy
George P., d. 3/20/1917 at 75/6 in Durham; arterio sclerosis; William Demeritt and Frances Wilson
Idella W., d. 12/18/1925 at 60/5/1; carcinoma of brain; Andrew Neal and Almira Hatch
James H., d. 4/30/1926 at 85/7/25; arterio sclerosis; Jacob Demeritt and Marcia Fernald
James Y., d. 6/28/1913 at 67/6/9; ch. intestitial nephritis; James Y. Demeritt and Matilda Rowe
Lewis I., d. 10/25/1930 at 73/5/23; cerebral embolism; Israel DeMeritt and Fannie W. -----
M. Ida, d. 3/4/1920 at 34/2/3; pneumonia; George H. Demeritt and Emma H. Kennedy

Martha W., d. 6/17/1927 at 80/0/27 in Plymouth; chronic myocarditis
Samuel M., d. 5/23/1890 at 79/0/16; married; Andrew DeMeritt (Madbury) and Susanna Hill (Barrington)
Seorim, d. 4/10/1908 at 70/3/16; paralysis; Jacob J. Demeritt and Marcia H. Fernald

DEMERITTE,
Laura A., d. 1/11/1927 at 81/5/2; arterio sclerosis; James Y. Demeritt and Matilda Rowe

DEMERRITT,
Katherine, d. 4/14/1923 at 36/0/24 in Chicago, IL; chronic appendicitis

DEMERS,
child, d. 6/17/1899 at 0; stillborn
child, d. 7/17/1899 at –; stillborn; SM
child, d. 5/11/1928 at –; asphyxia of labor; Joseph A. Demers and Elsie Charest
child, d. 2/13/1934 at –; stillborn
Benoit Joseph, d. 3/12/1916 at 1; pneumonia; Arsene Demers and M. Nedeau
Elzar, d. 8/1/1936 at 64/5/19; carcinoma of stomach
Ernest, d. 3/21/1902 at 0/3/24; broncho-pneumonia
Ferdinand, d. 5/5/1895 at 0; typhoid fever; b. Canada; SM
Gedeon, d. 1/28/1931 at 0/1/25; lobar pneumonia
Harve, d. 10/23/1937 at 16/5/29; fracture of spine
J. D., d. 4/9/1901 at 0/2/12; pneumonia
Joseph A., d. 9/5/1907 at 3/7/3; meningitis; ----- Demers and Delphine Fountaine
Joseph W. A., d. 10/11/1924 at 0/3/2; ac. lobar pneumonia; Gedeon Demers and Alphonsine Clement
Justine, d. 7/3/1916 at 74/8; chronic nephritis; Pierre Contari and Charlotte Bisson
Louis Philippe, d. 3/6/1903 at 0/7/9; marasmus
Louisa, d. 11/8/1913 at 3/9/3; typhoid fever; William Demers and Mary E. Norman
Mary R., d. 7/10/1900 at <1; diarrhea infantile
Octave, d. 6/13/1920 at 64/2/19 in Boston, MA; cancer of stomach
Victor, d. 10/2/1935 at 83/5; arteriosclerosis
William, d. 2/24/1901 at 0/3; pneumonia

DEMIER,
William, d. 2/5/1887 at 1/6; b. Dover

DEMING,
Elsie E., d. 2/16/1897 at 4; scarletinal nephritis; b. Dover; PH

DEMPSEY,
Bridget, d. 11/6/1935 at 63/10/13; broncho pneumonia
Grace, d. 11/5/1914 at 30; syphillis
James, d. 3/25/1895 at 61; pulmonary phthisis; b. Ireland; SM
Margaret, d. 10/3/1914 at 79/1/18; old age; John Howland and Mary Whelan
Mary, d. 12/2/1928 at 66/9/14; pulm. tuberculosis; James Dempsey and Margaret Howland
Moses, d. 11/21/1925 at 61/3; alcoholic poisoning; James Dempsey and Margaret Howland
Peter, d. 4/15/1893 at 34; Bright's disease; b. Dover; (Ireland; Ireland)

DENNETT,
Horace B., d. 2/18/1903 at 61; valvular disease of heart; PH
William H., d. 2/10/1928 at 69/2/20; pulmonary embolism; John Dennett and Jane H. Hubbard

DENNING,
Eliza, d. 7/16/1920 at 72/4/3; chronic nephritis; John Bartle and Sarah -----
Ella, d. 10/12/1918 at 34/6/16; lobar pneumonia; Michael O'Callaghan and Mary A. Ryan
Ethel G., d. 3/12/1937 at 50/10/8; lobar pneumonia
Matthew, d. 8/7/1893 at 75; old age, inanition; b. England; (England; England)
Thomas, d. 8/26/1924 at 69/3; hypernephroma; Joseph Denning and Mary -----
Warren F., d. 2/2/1926 at 0/4; broncho pneumonia; Harry Denning and Theresa Axworthy

DENNIS,
Ann, d. 10/21/1916 at 65; acute pneumonia; James White and Ann McKenna
Benjamin F., d. 2/12/1890 at 40/4/23; married; Benjamin Dennis (Marblehead) and Deliverence McPhillips (Marblehead)
James, d. 3/27/1937 at 68; acute cardiac failure
James J., d. 10/27/1905 at 0/4; cholera infantum; SM
James Joseph, d. 6/6/1913 at 0/2/1; marasmus; John Dennis and Mary Welch
John T., d. 10/4/1917 at 3/2/1; lobar pneumonia; John P. Dennis and Mary Welch
Katherine, d. 1/23/1914 at 5/3/13; broncho pneumonia; James Dennis and Mary Morgan

Leah H., d. 6/1/1917 at 68/9/14 in Washington, DC; myocarditis
Margaret, d. 10/25/1925 at 55; myocarditis
Mary, d. 2/19/1915 at 41/10/13; pulmonary oedema; M. McGuigan and Alice McNally
Patrick, d. 12/22/1926 at –; angina pectoris
Paul F., d. 2/13/1909 at 0/9; cholera infantum; James F. Dennis and Mary McGuigan

DENSMORE,
Charles S., d. 11/22/1927 at 69/5/28; chronic endocarditis; John Densmore and Sophia Nichols

DEPHEN,
Mary, d. 8/24/1888 at 64; b. England

DERMODY,
Margaret, d. 12/3/1908 at 21; typhoid fever; Richard Dermody and Annie Stevens

DEROCHEMONT,
child, d. 9/21/1923 at –; stillborn; John DeRochemont and Elspy Shorey

DEROSIER,
child, d. 8/17/1910 at 0/0/1; premature birth; George Derosier and Ann Bergeron
Joseph, d. 5/9/1911 at 17; general peritonitis; Antoine Derosier and Amanda Cournoyer

DEROY,
Albani, d. 6/4/1910 at –; asphyxia; Arthur Deroy and Aurelie Kirouack
Arthur, d. 11/26/1934 at 71/10/17 in Rollinsford; acute myocarditis
Audelie, d. 1/20/1930 at 65 in Rollinsford; angina pectoris
Theodore, d. 12/31/1909 at 10/9/4; leucocythemia; Arthur Deroy and Aurelie Kiroicac

DERSOCHORS,
Angelina, d. 8/9/1919 at 34 in Peabody, MA; auto accident
Roland, d. 8/9/1919 at 1/6 in Peabody, MA; auto accident

DERY,
Alice, d. 7/3/1911 at 0/4/13; cholera infantum; Laureat Dery
Joseph, d. 6/29/1912 at –; anencephalus; Laureat Dery and Rosanna Huot

DESAUTEL,
Robert H., d. 2/24/1912 at 0/9/24; pneumonia; F. Desautel and Margaret McArdle

DESAUTELLE,
child, d. 7/22/1901 at 0/9; cholera infantum; SM
child, d. 11/26/1902 at –; premature birth; SM
child, d. 4/19/1904 at –; stillborn; SM
child, d. 12/5/1904 at –; stillborn; buried in private
child, d. 7/3/1908 at --; unknown; Peter J. Desautelle and Inez M. Young
child, d. 4/18/1910 at –; premature birth; Peter T. Desautelle and Inez M. Young
child, d. 5/7/1936 at –; prematurity
B. M., d. 7/24/1901 at 0/6/4; cholera infantum; SM
Inez M., d. 11/12/1910 at 28/5/24; tubercular meningitis; N. H. Young and Ella M. Hodgdon
Louis, d. 8/20/1905 at 0/6/5; cholera infantum
Theophilus, d. 5/7/1927 at 86; acute hepatitis; Francis Desautelle and Victoria Senner

DESHAIES,
M. W., d. 7/25/1900 at <1; cholera infantum

DESJARDIN,
Rose A., d. 8/28/1919 at 3/5/7; peritonitis; Alsine Desjardin and Anna Jodion

DESJARDINS,
Ilna, d. 12/29/1901 at 4/5; scald
Marie, d. 2/18/1921 at 66/1/15; surgical shock; Juillaume Berube and Marie -----
Paul, d. 3/3/1913 at 2/11/26; convulsions; Adele Desjardins
Philippe, d. 1/11/1903 at 4/2/26; membranous croup

DESMARAIS,
child, d. 11/2/1922 at –; stillborn; Wilfred Desmarais and Anne M. Savoie

DESORTELS,
Michael, d. 10/5/1909 at –; stillborn; Ovilor Desortels and Bridget King

DESOTELL,
child, d. 7/30/1899 at –; stillborn; SM

DESOTELLE,
Bridget, d. 12/2/1934 at 68/10/21; acute myocarditis
Eva, d. 3/17/1900 at <1; marasmus; SM

DESOTELS,
child, d. 6/12/1906 at –; unknown
child, d. 11/9/1924 at –; stillborn; Frank E. Desotels and Margaret V. Keenan
John, d. 4/24/1911 at –; stillborn; Ovilor Desotels and Bridget King
Wilfred, d. 3/6/1916 at –; premature birth; Wilfrid Desotels and Rose Benoit

DESROSIERS,
Desnieges, d. 2/21/1901 at 49/7/22; cerebral hemorrhage; SM

DEVAN,
child, d. 5/14/1901 at –; stillborn; SM
child, d. 1/21/1905 at –; stillborn; SM
Susan A., d. 6/29/1897 at 37; anaemia; b. Dover; SM
William, d. 12/5/1909 at 69; broncho pneumonia; William Devan and Margaret Powers

DEVARNEY,
David, d. 2/16/1922 at 60/6/3; hyper. cirr. of liver; Joseph DeVarney and Sarah -----
Sarah, d. 4/25/1928 at 67/0/6; carcinoma intestine; George W. Wicks and Hannah Freestone

DEVENNE,
Alice M., d. 10/17/1902 at 23/6/25; appendicitis; PH
Hugh, d. 4/17/1936 at 82/8/16; cerebral hemorrhage

DEVEREAU,
Mary, d. 9/30/1926 at 43 in Lowell, MA; carcinoma of stomach

DEVEREAUX,
Philip B., d. 9/19/1937 at 11; acute appendicitis
Thomas, d. 2/28/1921 at 91; gen. arterio sclerosis; James Devereaux and Elizabeth Barry

DEVIAU,
Leo Joseph, d. 2/10/1916 at 0/7/19 in Manchester; marasmus; Alphonse Deviau and Mary E. Gracey

DEVIN,
Annie E., d. 2/24/1926 at 90/2/19; chronic myocarditis; Oliver Wyatt and Hannah Foss

DEVINE,
Catherine G., d. 6/6/1901 at 1/8; cholera infantum; SM
Ellen, d. 11/13/1910 at 40/1; alcoholism; James Loughlin and Mary Ann ---
Hannah L., d. 11/7/1931 at 60/1/2; chronic myocarditis
John, d. 4/10/1889 at 27; married; b. Ireland
Lucy P., d. 5/25/1925 at 48/1/16; fracture of skull; Moses A. Parker and Eliza E. Hale
Michael T., d. 11/4/1930 at 68/9; carcinoma stomach; Timothy Devine and Norah Ash

DEVINNE,
Jane, d. 1/7/1923 at 75/6/7; cerebral hemorrhage; John White and Jane Smith

DEVLIN,
Edward P., d. 9/1/1894 at 8; endocarditis; b. Dover; SM
Elizabeth, d. 3/9/1893 at 70; carcinoma of stomach; b. Ireland; (Ireland; Ireland)
Ellen, d. 1/21/1914 at 65/6/15; cancer of rectum; Daniel Mahoney and Ellen Drew
Margaret, d. 10/10/1924 at 53/6/16; cancer of stomach; Patrick O'Brien and Margaret Carberry
Patrick, d. 1/28/1913 at 67/10/16; mitral regurgitation; Patrick Devlin and Fannie Doherity
Philip T., d. 8/1/1926 at 27/11 in Andover; fracture of skull

DEVOE,
James, d. 2/26/1911 at 71; endocarditis (see following entry)
James, d. 2/26/1912 at 65 (see preceding entry)

DEWITT,
Dorothy M., d. 7/31/1929 at 0/0/24; premature birth; Carroll K. DeWitt and Flora Brown

DEXTER,
child, d. 10/4/1920 at –; stillborn; Pardon N. Dexter and Marion W. Seavey
Margaret E., d. 8/13/1924 at 61/8/28; cancer of thigh; Cornelius McDonald and Nora O'Brien
Pardon Newell, d. 7/23/1917 at 66; apoplexy cerebral; Pardon N. Dexter and Abbie Wilbur

Rose, d. 5/10/1937 at 24*

DEZOTELLE,
Edward, d. 4/21/1931 at 61/4/23 in Barre, VT; cancer of lip

DHIRREN,
Louisa, d. 4/19/1901 at 3/6; pneumonia; SM

DIAKAKIS,
John, d. 3/5/1934 at 42/2/21; carcinoma of stomach

DICICCO,
Rudolph, d. 4/12/1935 at 0/6/14; bronchial pneumonia

DICK,
George, d. 8/26/1889 at 21/9; laborer; single; b. Canada; George Dick (Canada) and Sara Beaulieu (Canada)

DICKERMAN,
Sarah E., d. 8/18/1915 at 76/10/11; broncho pneumonia; Charles Ham and Abigail D. Bartlett

DICKERSON,
Amanda A., d. 5/27/1931 at 81/4/7; angina pectoris

DICKSON,
Frank, d. 9/15/1934 at 50; acute cardiac failure

DILLON,
child, d. 6/24/1905 at 0/0/11; spasms; SM
child, d. 8/29/1907 at --; stillborn; Patrick Dillon and Margaret Bradley
Alice M., d. 7/15/1905 at 1/6/22; whooping cough; SM
Annie R., d. 2/4/1903 at 44/4/22 in Bristol, RI; pneumonia; PH
Charles, d. 8/14/1906 at 0/0/1; cong. malformation of heart; SM
Elizabeth, d. 5/8/1930 at 77/5/17 in Rochester; acute nephritis
Ellen, d. 9/11/1925 at --; chronic endocarditis
James P., d. 7/19/1905 at 2/9/22; whooping cough; SM
Jerrold C., d. 2/25/1915 at 69/4/13 in E. Rochester; arterio sclerosis
Joseph L., d. 12/30/1904 at 0/0/½; lack of vitality
Patrick, d. 10/14/1921 at 60/6/27; angina pectoris; Michael Dillon and Sarah Rooney

DINEAKOS,
Kaliope V., d. 3/20/1936 at 53*; b. Greece

DINSMORE,
Frank L., d. 6/25/1926 at 71/6/9; burns; William Dinsmore and Eliza Fickett
Onslow, d. 5/29/1912 at 60/7/24; accidental burns; William Dinsmore and Eliza Feckett

DION,
child, d. 1/23/1894 at –; premature birth; b. Dover; SM
child, d. 6/6/1923 at –; premature birth; Frank Dion and Ora Lapointe
Agenard, d. 8/18/1921 at 25/11/22 in S. Berwick, ME; electrocuted; Prudent Dion and Rose Rousseaux
Celina, d. 4/4/1928 at 71/0/21; senile gangrene; Narcisse Dion and Oberline Giroux
Eva, d. 9/23/1904 at 0/1/23; gastro-enteritis; SM
Evarest, d. 10/6/1910 at 5/11/10; infantile paralysis; Prudent Dion and Rose Rousseau
Louis, d. 10/8/1918 at 42/9/13; influenza; Marcis Dion and Oberline Luri
Louis P., d. 12/13/1902 at 1/4/23; entero-colitis
Mary, d. 2/2/1905 at 30/5; tuberculosis intestinal; SM
Mary, d. 2/8/1934 at 78; cerebral hemorrhage
Narcisse, d. 7/19/1900 at 75; heart disease; SM
Obeline, d. 5/8/1918 at 85/9/8; general arterio sclerosis; Pierre Leroux and Theatisse Cote
Prudent, d. 9/22/1912 at 56; hemorrhage of lungs; Nazaire Dion
Yvonne M., d. 6/22/1904 at 0/0/16; marasmus

DIONNE,
Albert, d. 9/17/1932 at 40 in Danvers, MA; auto accident
Anna, d. 6/25/1912 at 4/10/18; ptomaine poisoning; Joseph Dionne and Aulda Gingras
Arthur, d. 6/9/1928 at 27 in Pembroke; pulm. tuberculosis
Eusebe, d. 12/30/1909 at 48/6/22; pulmonary tuberculosis; Augustine Dionne and Julie Maillotte
Eva Lena, d. 11/6/1928 at 0/0/5; poisoning; George P. Devine (sic) and Rose Bourbeau
Francis, d. 10/9/1915 at 70/8/14; general septicemia; August Dionne and Julie -----
Harvey, d. 9/17/1932 at 4 in Danvers, MA; auto accident
John B., d. 4/27/1905 at 73/7; cerebral hemorrhage
Joseph, d. 7/13/1915 at 75; softening of brain
Laura, d. 2/12/1903 at 0/4/17; pneumonia
Magloire, d. 2/9/1893 at 54; died in Strafford Co. Asylum fire
Marie, d. 6/9/1925 at 73/1/10; acute myocarditis; Pierre Burgeron and Teressa -----
Robert, d. 6/30/1934 at 2/0/28; myxedema

Rosanna, d. 8/25/1904 at 0/3/22; cholera infantum; SM
Rosanna, d. 11/22/1917 at 9/6/13; tubercular meningitis; Nestor Dionne and Mary Gingras
Rose, d. 5/8/1928 at 35 in Pembroke; pulm. tuberculosis
Victor, d. 5/22/1893 at –; bronchitis; b. Dover; (Canada; Canada)

DIXON,
Cora B., d. 6/14/1900 at 45 in Boston, MA; cerebral hemorrhage; PH
Ethel A., d. 2/24/1893 at 8; meningitis
Forrest H., d. 6/1/1932 at 57/6/29; post operative
Jane, d. 6/21/1889 at 79 in Lowell, MA
Julia A., d. 3/12/1920 at 58/3/18; pulmonary tuberculosis; William F. Wentworth and Armine Hall
Mary A., d. 6/17/1894 at 83 in Everett, MA; old age; PH

DOBBINS,
Frederick F., d. 6/23/1924 at 34/9/7; chronic myocarditis; James Dobbins and Alice Cassidy
James, d. 10/12/1898 at 67; diarrhoea; b. Ireland; SM
Margaret A., d. 8/30/1889 at 2/4/6; b. Dover; James Dobbins (Dover) and Alice Cassidy (Dover)
Mary A., d. 4/5/1929 at 45 in Lowell, MA; "see card"
Patrick, d. 10/17/1932 at 58/7; carcinoma
Rose, d. 2/13/1915 at 80; nephritis; James Cassidy and Alice McKernan
Thomas, d. 7/5/1900 at –; pistol wound; SM
Walter J., d. 8/10/1889 at 0/8/12; b. Dover; James Dobbins (Dover) and Alice Cassidy (Dover)

DOBSON,
James, d. 9/3/1919 at 91; acute gastroenteritis

DODGE,
Carl L., d. 4/21/1918 at 26/10/20 in Benton; tuberculosis of lungs; William L. Dodge and Ida M. Jacques
Chester E., d. 1/3/1935 at 47/9/22; angina pectoris
Clayton E., Jr., d. 5/3/1916 at 0/8/23; ac. dilitation of heart; Clayton E. Dodge and Dorothy A. Horr
Harry S., d. 5/16/1909 at 28 in Norristown, PA; tuberculosis of lungs
Herbert W., d. 12/6/1922 at 1/3/16; lobar pneumonia; Ernest Dodge and Bernice Freeman
Ida M., d. 1/28/1936 at 64/11/25; angina pectoris
Lenora, d. 12/25/1928 at 83/5/9; fractured hip; William Burleigh and Gertrude E. Kennard
Martha, d. 2/24/1901 at 79; old age; buried in Rochester
Mary E., d. 4/10/1928 at 55; diabetes; John Cusack and Mary Moffat

Mary E. R., d. 7/4/1932 at 90/5/17; cerebral hemorrhage
Oliver A., d. 4/21/1891 at 52/5/4; married; George H. Dodge (Hampton Falls) and Mary Keley (England)
William C., d. 8/25/1916 at 76/10/14; ac. nephritis uraemia; Robert G. Dodge and Pairne Lang
William L., d. 6/2/1933 at 63/9; lobar pneumonia

DODSON,
Annie, d. 11/17/1932 at 66/6/29; intestinal paralysis

DOE,
Eben F., d. 12/2/1917 at 89/6/20; old age; Joshua Doe and Nancy Torr
Frank E., d. 9/2/1931 at 75/7/14; arterio sclerosis
Lorin, d. 7/5/1918 at 47; cancer of stomach
Robert, d. 10/22/1925 at 50/3/1 in Rollinsford; angina pectoris

DOEG,
Gilman, d. 9/17/1892 at 44; heart disease; b. Durham; (Portsmouth; Lee)

DOFA,
Delia, d. 7/1/1889 at 6/1; b. Malone, NY; Gabe Dofa (Canada) and Clara Sears (Canada)

DOHERTY,
Ann F., d. 1/7/1920 at 77; broncho pneumonia; Ann Murphy
Daniel, d. 9/30/1923 at 62/11/2 in Provo, UT; cerebral hemorrhage
Dennis, d. 2/23/1907 at –; bullet from revolver
Mary, d. 7/9/1937 at 67/2/3; heat exhaustion
Nancy, d. 12/24/1903 at 80; senile dementia
Rose, d. 10/6/1897 at 70; cancer of stomach; b. Ireland
Vivian V., d. 1/24/1911 at 8/9/11; acute cardiac dilitation; Frank J. Doherty and Dora A. Wallingford

DOLAN,
John F., d. 11/9/1913 at 43/10/9; peritonitis; John Dolan and Nancy Flynn
Nellie E., d. 1/26/1925 at 51; acute myocarditis; George W. Evans and Elmira Rounds

DOLBEARE,
Celia, d. 12/31/1934 at 85/0/11 in W. Newbury, MA; apoplexy

DOLLOFF,
George S., d. 8/28/1927 at 55/9/2; chronic myocarditis; Levi Dolloff and Susan Callan

DONAHUE,
Catherine, d. 1/11/1924 at 80; accidental; Dennis Donahue and Mary -----
Mary Ann, d. 10/23/1937 at 68/7/14; cerebr. hemorrhage

DONALDSON,
Raymond G., d. 1/5/1921 at 1/9/30; diphtheria; George A. Donaldson and
    Clara I. Twombly

DONDERO,
child, d. 9/11/1921 at –; stillborn; Frank J. Dondero and Ellen Smith
child, d. 5/8/1924 at –; stillborn; Frank J. Dondero and Ellen Smith
Charlotte M., d. 1/24/1895 at 3; hydrocephalus; b. Dover; SM
Joseph F., d. 6/6/1916 at 78 in Buffalo, NY; lobar pneumonia; Rose -----
Nora F., d. 3/29/1911 at 31/4/6; ac. tuberc. broncho pneumonia; Timothy
    Connors and Hannah Mahoney
Philip A., d. 8/31/1890 at 0/6/4; Francis A. Dondero (Italy) and Mary C.
    Cahill (Dover)
Sarah E., d. 5/17/1925 at 72/6/6; cerebral apoplexy; Valentine Byrnes and
    Eleanor Keogh

DONGAN,
James, Jr., d. 12/15/1890 at 30/1/15; single; James Dongan (Ireland) and
    Mary T. (Ireland)

DONNELLY,
Annie, d. 7/25/1892 at –; cholera infantum; b. Dover; (Ireland; Ireland)
Annie, d. 9/23/1892 at –; consumption; b. Ireland; (Ireland; Ireland)
Annie M., d. 10/3/1913 at 48/5/24; chronic endocarditis; George Marston
    and Sarah Cheswell
Catherine, d. 2/26/1916 at 78 in Beverly, MA; arterio sclerosis
Ethel B., d. 11/30/1915 at 30; acute dilatation of heart; Thomas Donnelly
    and Mary Hennessey
Frances, d. 4/13/1902 at 63; uraemic shock; SM
Henry, d. 12/27/1891 at 21/3/8; single; Patrick Donnelly (Ireland) and Mary
    Carregher (Ireland)
Hugh, d. 12/29/1916 at –; premature birth; John F. Donnelly and Susan
    Grimes
James, d. 10/22/1912 at 44; oedema of lungs; James Donnelly and
    Margaret McMahon
James, d. 9/23/1930 at 60 in Rollinsford; phthisis pulmonalis
James Patrick, d. 2/15/1920 at 6/8/17; empyema of chest; John Donnelly
    and Susie Grimes
Kate, d. 8/16/1887 at 0/1/17; b. Dover; Michael Donnelly (Ireland) and
    Annie Hughes (Ireland)

Margaret, d. 1/4/1888 at 18/9/17; dressmaker; single; b. Ireland; F. Donnelly (Ireland) and Margaret Hickey (Ireland)
Margaret, d. 9/13/1908 at 67; asphyxia; James Hickey and Rose ----
Mary, d. 4/4/1911 at 60; diabetes; Owen Kelly and Ann Markey
Mary, d. 4/13/1929 at 67; chronic endocarditis; John Hennessy and Ann Foley
Mary Ann, d. 7/13/1912 at 0/1/24; marasmus; John Donnelly and Susan Grimes
Maud D., d. 2/25/1923 at 49/4 in Lowell, MA; hemorrhage from mouth
Michael, d. 11/14/1920 at 58; myocarditis
Peter, d. 4/4/1912 at 72 in Madbury; chronic endocarditis; Patrick Donnelly and Margaret Burns
Rose A., d. 12/26/1936 at 52 in Rollinsford; cerebral apoplexy
Sarah J., d. 1/1/1924 at 55; chr. inter. nephritis
Thomas, d. 6/5/1933 at 76/5/27; arteriosclerosis

DONNOLLY,
Patrick, d. 7/21/1891 at 29/11/6; single; Francis Donnolly (Ireland) and Margaret Hackay (Ireland)

DONOVAN,
Agnes, d. 9/26/1920 at 42; pulmonary tuberculosis; James Hughes
Daniel J., d. 3/7/1901 at 81 in Amesbury, MA; SM
James E., d. 9/10/1915 at 0/11/25; tuberculous meningitis; Michael Donovan and Agnes Hughes
John C., d. 10/18/1937 at 65*
Joseph H., d. 5/16/1932 at 61/7/6; cerebral hemorrhage
Michael, d. 8/15/1914 at 0/11/20; cholera infantum; Michael Donovan and Agnes Hughes

DOOLEY,
child, d. 12/5/1937 at –; asphyxia liver (sic)

DOPHEIM,
Sarah E., d. 3/19/1894 at 51; ovarian tumor; b. Gilmanton; PH

DOPHERY,
Ramie, d. 3/25/1925 at 80/9/27 in Wakefield; paralysis of heart

DORAN,
Charles H., d. 7/17/1927 at 66/3/14 in Berwick, ME; vernacu. dis. of heart
Harry W., d. 4/28/1927 at 65/0/29; acute alcoholism; Andrew Doran and Maria M. Farrar
John, d. 8/21/1928 at 78 in Berwick, ME; endocarditis

Lilla Eliza, d. 7/13/1901 at 38/6/14; septicaemia; buried in Laconia
Mary, d. 4/27/1899 at 72; heart disease; SM

DORE,
Annie E., d. 10/5/1897 at 23 in Brockton, MA; ulcerative laryngitis
Augusta E., d. 8/29/1923 at 69/2/25; surgical shock; Jonas Runnels and Hannah Corson
Bertrand L., d. 1/28/1896 at 15 in Brockton, MA; uraemia
Charles A., d. 3/26/1910 at 70/4/4; pneumonia; Oliver Dore and Frances --
Charles O., d. 12/11/1931 at 59/6/9 in Wolfeboro; pneumonia
Charles W., d. 5/15/1923 at 73/6/4 in Brockton, MA; cerebral hemorrhage
Eliza N., d. 2/5/1890 at 50/0/12; widow; John G. Chick (Ossipee) and Eliza Hyde
Elmer H., d. 11/15/1904 at 29/2/19 in Madbury; tuberculosis; PH
Elsie D., d. 3/21/1915 at 87/2/2; old age; Enoch Stimpson and Nancy Payson
Ezekiel, d. 8/13/1909 at 89/2/27; senility; Beniah Dore and Eunice Dore
Frances, d. 2/23/1904 at 90/9/24; inanition; PH
George Edwin, d. 9/29/1912 at 0/0/18; athrepsia; George Edward Dore and Mary E. Wentworth
James E., d. 4/16/1931 at 77/0/10; cerebral hemorrhage
Mary A., d. 1/19/1914 at 78/0/2; cyst of kidneys; Michael Murphy and Esther Stackpole
Oliver, d. 7/20/1887 at 80/5; machinist; married; b. Lebanon, ME; Benjamin Dore (Lebanon, ME) and Betsey Lord (Lebanon, ME)
Sarah A., d. 8/20/1904 at 84; senility; buried in Milton

DORR,
Charles C., d. 1/28/1921 at 78/9/25; emypema; Charles Dorr and Sarah Chase
Elizabeth E., d. 1/16/1929 at 86/8; arthritis deformans; Timothy Emerson and Sarah Homer
Lucinda P., d. 8/23/1926 at 86/5/6; senility; John Dorr and Mary P. Richmond
Mary P., d. 2/23/1888 at 77/9/18; widow; b. Bridgewater, MA; A. Richmond (Middleboro, MA) and ----- Pierce
Stephen, d. 5/14/1916 at 85; dilatation of heart; George W. Dorr and Jane Frost

DORSEY,
Mary, d. 5/6/1922 at 51 in Tewksbury, MA; dermatitis exfoliative

DORT,
Eliza A., d. 5/23/1929 at 79/5/23; chronic nephritis; William Dort and Eliza

-----

DOSCHER,
Eliza, d. 12/26/1928 at 76; chr. intest. nephritis; ----- Keenan

DOTY,
Eliza, d. 12/17/1906 at 75/10/9 in Swampscott, MA; hemorrhage; PH
Simeon W., d. 11/10/1900 at 76; old age; PH

DOUGAN,
Elizabeth J., d. 9/6/1907 at 0/2/17; marasmus; Robert D. Dougan and Martha Lappan

DOUGHTEY,
Sidney P., d. 4/6/1891 at 0/2 in Strafford

DOUGLASS,
Daniel H., d. 4/7/1909 at 74/0/27; senile gangrene; James Douglass
June H., d. 9/13/1924 at 0/2/28; entero colitis; William L. Douglass and Ruth Cottrell
Sarah, d. 4/25/1910 at 57; cancer of stomach; William Bingham and Jane McNally

DOUGLE,
Richard, d. 9/29/1902 at 41; shock; PH

DOW,
Charlotte, d. 6/24/1910 at 40/2/8; cancer of the face; James Heeney and Charlotte Yates
Edwin C., d. 11/26/1926 at 43/11/30; chronic endocarditis; Luther C. Dow and Mary E. Millard
Florence B., d. 11/21/1896 at 4; scarlet fever; b. Dover; buried in Farmington
Florence N., d. 7/23/1930 at 72/5/24 in Old Town, ME; carcinoma of uterus; William Carney and M. Karney
Helen I., d. 3/31/1903 at 0/9/28; meningitis; buried in Moultonborough
Henry, d. 8/18/1889 at 84; physician; married; b. Dover; Jabez Dow (Kensington) and Hannah Waite (Boston, MA)
Jane J., d. 3/10/1914 at 88/2/9; pneumonia; George Quint and Mary J. Bran
Mary E. H. G., d. 8/24/1914 at 70/8/9; intestinal obstruction; Nathaniel E. Hill and Esther Ela
Zebulon, d. 7/31/1922 at – in Rochester; chronic nephritis

DOWALIBY,
Alexander, d. 7/19/1924 at 64; acute myocarditis; Colell Dowaliby and Sardi Bellish
Asa E., d. 1/20/1918 at 18; pleurisy with effusion; Elias A. Dowaliby and Saliney -----
Freida, d. 3/30/1925 at 64; chronic endocarditis; David Dowaliby and Takla Wehbee
Martha, d. 12/7/1915 at 61; cancer of stomach; George Dowaliby and Martha -----
Mary, d. 8/18/1925 at 16/6/18 in Pembroke; pulmonary tuberculosis; Elias Dowaliby and Saleney -----
Waldi, d. 1/1/1917 at 13/6; paralysis; Elias Dowaliby and Howley Akley

DOWLING,
child, d. 2/19/1915 at –; stillborn; Albert J. Dowling and Lillian Foss
Charles, d. 12/15/1932 at 53/6/10; carcinoma of larynx

DOWNEY,
Catherine, d. 8/16/1917 at 67; chr. intestitial nephritis; Jeremiah Hickey and Nora Costello
Minnie, d. 10/27/1887 at 19; b. Chelsea, MA; (Ireland)

DOWNING,
child, d. 1/23/1897 at 0; stillborn; b. Dover
Catherine, d. 2/9/1906 at 50 in Manchester; cardiac hypertrophy; PH
Hazel G., d. 6/7/1901 at 0/0/8; malnutrition; buried in So. Berwick, ME
James, d. 10/16/1903 at 0/2/21; meningitis; PH
Lovey M., d. 12/13/1910 at 92/2 in Boston, MA; old age
Matilda C., d. 4/6/1904 at 55/1/26; cancer of brain; buried in Eliot, ME
Waldo P., d. 12/2/1905 at 83 in Boston, MA; cerebral hemorrhage

DOWNS,
Charles M., d. 1/9/1928 at 34/3/11; mastoid operation; John E. Downs and Melissa Guptil
Clara S., d. 8/1/1912 at 38/4/27; cirrhosis of liver; John H. Downs and Ellen L. Staniford
Jennie, d. 4/22/1919 at 8; septic endocarditis; Stephen Downs and Bridget Coury
John H., d. 12/31/1935 at 87/7/15; chronic endocarditis
Mary J., d. 10/14/1896 at – in Concord; organic heart disease; PH
Mary J., d. 2/11/1903 at 77/6/4 in Rochester; influenza with bronchitis; PH
R. Eliza, d. 9/27/1933 at –; fracture of spine
Richard C., d. 6/9/1921 at 0/2/13; congenital syphillis; Edmund G. Downs and Mae E. Goddard
Roland, d. 1/23/1937 at –; stillborn

DOYAN,
Lucipe, d. 12/16/1932 at 69/0/18; acute myocarditis

DOYLE,
Lucretta B., d. 1/14/1893 at 15; rheumatic fever - heart comp.; b. Gt. Village, NS; (Five Islands, NS; Truro, NS)
Michael T., d. 5/27/1916 at 55; chron. intes. nephritis; Stephen Doyle and Ann Riley

DOYON,
Elmire, d. 6/27/1913 at 58; pulmonary tuberculosis; John Jeneau and Elmire Croteau

DRACUP,
Daniel, d. 11/19/1937 at 69/4/24; coronary thrombosis

DRAGO,
Antonio, d. 2/23/1930 at 86/10/16; cancer of throat; John Drago

DRAKE,
Abram M., d. 10/1/1895 at 72; paralysis; b. Effingham; PH
Amanda H., d. 12/8/1890 at 52/9 in Portsmouth
Anna C., d. 11/17/1894 at 15 in Laconia; pulmonary tuberculosis; PH
Attie, d. 9/25/1927 at 89 in Lawrence, MA; apoplexy
Evelyn C., d. 1/22/1903 at 28/8/2 in Boston, MA; pulmonary tuberculosis
George A., d. 5/8/1932 at 65/0/28 in Rollinsford; valv. heart disease
Gordon C., d. 5/12/1925 at 0/3/17; malnutrition; Elmer C. Drake and Catherine Elliott
Mercy, d. 10/27/1903 at 84/0/5 in Farmington; old age; PH
Phoebe J., d. 2/14/1914 at 76 in Grand Junction, CO; cancer of breast
Ruth E., d. 11/29/1900 at 30 in Portsmouth; phthisis; PH

DRAPEAU,
Albert Joseph, d. 3/26/1910 at 0/3/15; whooping cough; William Drapeau and Mary Drolet
Delina L., d. 9/27/1906 at 1/5/9; pneumonia
Ernest, d. 5/1/1904 at 3/3/2; broncho-pneumonia
Frank, d. 3/17/1915 at 79/4; lateral sclerosis
Honore, d. 2/4/1925 at 71/6/10; cerebral hemorrhage; Pierre Drapeau and Adele Gagnon
James A., d. 9/7/1895 at 0; peritonitis; b. Dover; SM
Lydiane, d. 3/7/1937 at 38*
Pauline, d. 5/19/1923 at 21/4/11; tuberculosis of lungs; Thomas Vachon and Marie Silvain

Rita I., d. 12/4/1923 at 1/3; tuberculous meningitis; George Drapeau and Pauline Vachon

Wildrey P., d. 1/1/1935 at 39/1/30 in Boston, MA; lobar pneumonia

DRAUGHTON,
Woodworth P., d. 3/6/1919 at 62/11; chronic nephritis; W. P. Draughton

DREW,
daughter, d. 11/21/1890 at –; Johnny Drew (Canada) and Mary McGinnis (Dover)

child, d. 1/22/1913 at – in Rollinsford; stillborn; John W. Drew and Mary A. Farrell

child, d. 8/7/1932 at –; stillborn

Aaron W., d. 8/5/1929 at 76/2/7; chr. interst. nephritis; Martin V. B. Drew and Sarah W. Watson

Adele, d. 2/4/1894 at 29; pulmonary phthisis; b. Canada; SM

Adeline, d. 12/5/1893 at 79; bronchitis - heart disease; b. Madbury; (Madbury; Dover)

Alfred P., d. 10/21/1917 at 81/10/27; cerebral apoplexy; Jeremiah Drew and Elizabeth -----

Alice S., d. 3/3/1920 at 86/3/20; erysipelas of head; Aaron Crosby and Eleanor Dunphry

Alice W., d. 2/27/1936 at 90/11*

Almira A., d. 4/5/1909 at 76/5/16; phthisis; James J. Wentworth and Clarissa J. Hall

Annie E., d. 4/17/1904 at 66/5/16; softening of brain; PH

Annie W., d. 9/27/1912 at 37/11/28; pulmonary tuberculosis; Jonathan Wentworth and Mary E. -----

Ansel A., d. 6/15/1933 at 63/0/5; angina pectoris

Barbara Ruth, d. 1/2/1928 at 6/4/10; tonsilitis, septic; Freeman Drew and Doris R. Pray

Betsey, d. 8/13/1894 at 82; old age; b. Dover; PH

Carrie B., d. 4/24/1931 at 68/0/1; pneumococcus

Catherine, d. 6/29/1894 at 41; pernicious anaemia; b. Dover; SM

Charles, d. 5/29/1895 at 0; malnutrition; b. Dover; SM

Charles A., d. 6/13/1908 at 64/4/11; heart disease; Lemuel Drew and Lydia H. Twombly

Charles E., d. 6/7/1891 at 25/2/11; married; Charles A. Drew (Newmarket) and Mary E. Foss (Durham)

Charles F., d. 3/19/1902 at 41/3/19; consumption; PH

Charles U., d. 5/26/1915 at 72/4/9 in So. Berwick, ME; influenza

Charles W., d. 12/31/1914 at 56/6/2 in Ware, MA; heart disease

Chesley, d. 12/4/1918 at 65 in N. Andover; uraemia

Clarinda, d. 3/7/1902 at 81/3/22 in Southborough, MA; apoplexy; PH

Dana L., d. 11/24/1915 at 70/6/16; bronchial pneumonia; Hezekiah Drew and Mary Martin
Daniel W., d. 9/26/1910 at 73/6; occlusion of bowels; John T. Drew and Alice Waterhouse
David, d. 5/9/1898 at 67; phthisis; b. Madbury; PH
David L., d. 3/28/1889 at 80/11; mason; married; b. Newington; William Drew (Dover) and Martha Pickering (Newington)
David P., d. 11/6/1892 at 64; apoplexy; b. Dover; (Dover; Newington)
Dolly M., d. 2/23/1908 at 81/4/27 in Swampscott, MA
Eddie L., d. 5/5/1898 at 30 in Strafford; consumption; PH
Edward F., d. 5/2/1901 at 0/7/29; pneumonia; SM
Edwin F., d. 1/26/1903 at 42/6 in St. Louis, MO; pneumonia; PH
Eliza V., d. 1/24/1905 at 83/5/25; apoplexy; buried in Union
Elizabeth M., d. 5/19/1925 at 57/2/20; acute myocarditis; Charles K. Drew and Emily Fife
Ellen Francis, d. 6/30/1917 at 72/1/29; diabetes mellitus; Robert Pitman and Susan Pearl
Emeline, d. 11/5/1910 at 73/3/4; carcinoma of liver; James M. Clark and Susan Twombly
Ethel M., d. 8/11/1888 at 1/3/17; b. Dover; Nelson A. Drew (Boston, MA) and Delia Mahoney (Ireland)
Fannie A., d. 1/8/1928 at 82/8/15; arterio sclerosis; Isaac Drew and Betsy Tuttle
Francis A., d. 9/8/1888 at 0/1/10; b. Dover; Joseph Drew (Canada) and Catherine McG's (Dover)
Fred W., d. 8/2/1912 at 53/6/25; chronic myocarditis; Asa B. Drew and Hannah Pinkham
George D., d. 3/13/1930 at 0/0/2; cong. malformation; George D. Drew and Honora Donahue
George K., d. 4/8/1915 at 87/0/27 in Lancaster; senile heart
Georgianna A., d. 5/3/1902 at 0/1/8; pneumonia
Gerrish P., d. 12/28/1894 at 61; b. Dover; buried at homestead
Grace D., d. 5/20/1888 at 22/10/5; milliner; single; b. Barrington; William Drew (Newmarket) and Susan L. Ayer (Barrington)
Harrison, d. 1/20/1910 at 69/8/27; heart disease; William P. Drew and Eliza H. Demeritt
Harrison, d. 7/13/1911 at 85; lobar pneumonia
Harrison B., d. 1/4/1903 at 11/6/26; heart disease; PH
Henry, d. 11/15/1906 at 23; pleuro pneumonia
Henry A., d. 6/10/1916 at 90/8; acute endocarditis
Henry C., d. 4/4/1911 at 78 in Boston, MA; broncho-pneumonia; Nicholas Drew and Eliza Chesley
Jennie S., d. 12/2/1930 at 82/6/4; chr. endocarditis
John Henry, d. 10/25/1892 at 19; typhoid fever; b. Dover; (Canada; Dover)
John S., d. 9/13/1937 at 77/8/9; thrombosis femoral artery

John T., d. 5/5/1902 at 6/3/29; diphtheria; PH
John W., d. 5/13/1901 at 63/3/24; locomotia ataxia; PH
Joseph, d. 8/23/1899 at 75; chronic bronchitis; PH
Joseph, d. 9/25/1914 at 78; chronic diarrhea
Joseph W., d. 9/2/1923 at 85; arterio sclerosis
Lavina H., d. 6/24/1925 at 89/3/24 in Calais, ME; senility; Hurd Twombly and Lavina Tuttle
Lillian A., d. 12/25/1899 at 64 in Amesbury, MA; heart disease; PH
Lucinda B., d. 11/20/1888 at 48/10/17; married; b. Dover; Thomas L. Cook (Rochester) and Sarah A. Emery (Shapleigh, ME)
Mabel A., d. 6/19/1892 at 1; diphtheria; b. Dover; (Dover; Dover)
Martin V. B., d. 4/7/1908 at 68/0/27; heart disease; PH
Mary, d. 8/9/1887 at 56/6/14; married; b. Dover; Samuel Hanson (Dover) and Clarissa Varney (Milton)
Mary A., d. 8/14/1898 at 31 in Portsmouth; consumption; PH
Mary A., d. 5/1/1900 at 78; brain disease; PH
Mary A., d. 9/19/1917 at 62; chr. inter. nephritis; Patrick McGuinness and Susan Connolly
Mary E., d. 12/3/1898 at 54; cerebral apoplexy; b. Durham; PH
Mary F., d. 5/3/1893 at 85; pneumonia
Mary J., d. 3/30/1920 at 79/8/27 in Clinton, MA; natural causes
Mary T., d. 1/13/1921 at 74/6; mitral regurgitation; Timothy G. Langley and Louisa Dow
Mary Y. C., d. 11/2/1911 at 88/4/7; pneumonia; Simon Chase and Sarah Wingate
Matilda, d. 5/30/1905 at 88/11/8; heart disease; buried in Barrington
Nathaniel, d. 8/29/1898 at 50 in Nashua; consumption; PH
Nellie P., d. 1/4/1912 at 67/3/14; heart disease; Benjamin F. Preston and Olive Hill
Nelson R., d. 10/5/1908 at 0/4/16; gastro enteritis; Nelson U. Drew and Delia Maloney
Nelson U., d. 6/24/1917 at 53/0/27; intestinal obstruction; Daniel W. Drew and Lavinia H. Twombly
Richard A., d. 9/13/1909 at 72/7/1; broncho-pneumonia; Swain Drew and Matilda Hall
Rose C., d. 7/20/1923 at 65; John Collins and Mary Morgan
Sabra B., d. 4/19/1916 at 68/0/12 in S. Berwick, ME; acute endocarditis
Samuel F., d. 2/25/1918 at 65/9/3 in Quincy, MA; acute cardiac dilatation
Sarah E., d. 2/25/1910 at 98/0/15; senility; John McDuffee and Abigail Torr
Sarah J., d. 1/8/1918 at 79/8/5; bronchial pneumonia; William P. Drew and Eliza Demeritt
Sarah W., d. 4/3/1892 at 66; chronic bronchitis; b. Dover; (Dover; Dover)
Susan Lydia, d. 4/9/1922 at 77/6/9 in Quincy, MA; broncho pneumonia
Thomas F., d. 12/13/1898 at 56; phthisis; b. Dover; PH

Thomas P., d. 2/17/1917 at 73 in Concord; lobar pneumonia; William P.
    Drew and Eliza Demeritt
William, d. 12/22/1899 at 19; pleurisy with effusion; SM
William, d. 4/19/1924 at 77/6/19 in Quincy, MA; chronic myocarditis
William H., d. 12/14/1896 at 72 in W. Newton, MA; heart disease; b.
    Brookfield; PH

DRINKWATER,
Emma M., d. 6/20/1922 at 85/3/1 in Haverhill, MA; chronic myocarditis
Farrar, d. 2/5/1931 at 80/11/21; cerebral hemorrhage
Hannah, d. 4/8/1901 at 82/4 in Woodsville; old age; PH
Harry F., d. 3/14/1925 at 48/1/23; acute alcohol poisoning; Farrar
    Drinkwater and Julia A. Goodwin
James, d. 1/29/1905 at – in Norristown, PA; cardiac asthenia
Julia A., d. 8/3/1923 at 72; fatty degen. of heart; Elisha Goodwin and Julia
    Hanscom

DRISCOLL,
Dennis J., d. 8/20/1911 at 58; cerebral hemorrhage; Coleman Driscoll and
    Anna McCarthy
Edna E., d. 3/13/1895 at 2; peritonitis; b. Dover; PH
James Henry, d. 8/29/1892 at –; diphtheria sequelae; b. Dover; (Ireland;
    Ireland)
John J., d. 7/18/1889 at 1/1; b. Dover; John Driscoll (Ireland) and Mary
    Hickey (Ireland)
John R., d. 5/12/1937 at 72; cerebral apoplexy

DROLET,
Annie, d. 10/15/1898 at 23; pulmonary tuberculosis; b. Canada; SM
Arthur, d. 5/13/1892 at –; membranous croup; b. Dover; (Canada;
    Canada)
Charles, d. 3/27/1926 at 58/2/21; lobar pneumonia; Charles Drolet and ----
    -- Bernard
Edward, d. 12/23/1891 at 2/4/21; Henry Drolet (Canada) and Odelia
    Roberge (Canada)
John, d. 10/19/1924 at 77; arterio sclerosis; Joseph Drolet and Phebe
    Fitzgerald
Nellie, d. 2/7/1924 at 55; carcinoma; Patrick McGuinness and Susan
    Connelly
Sophronia, d. 1/24/1912 at 65/9/12; oedema of lungs; Jacques Bernard
    and Genevieve -----
William H., d. 12/9/1936 at 17/4/3; chr. myelitis

DROUIN,
child, d. 10/4/1900 at <1; premature birth

Alfred Joseph, d. 9/15/1901 at –; cholera infantum; SM
Alphonse, d. 3/11/1905 at 0/0/15; pneumonia
Archie, d. 3/12/1927 at 49/0/10; chronic bronchitis; Thomas Drouin and Zilda Richard
Beatrice, d. 3/31/1915 at 19/4/19 in Lewiston, ME; auto intoxication, etc.; Leon Drouin and Gorgianna Morrissette
Charles W., d. 2/21/1904 at 3/2/21; acute gastritis; SM
Edwin, d. 6/27/1903 at –; marasmus; SM
Emma, d. 9/12/1896 at –; purpura hemorrhagica; b. Dover; SM
Eva, d. 9/14/1889 at 0/9/9; b. Dover; Thomas Drouin (Canada) and Zilda Richards (Canada)
George R., d. 4/8/1918 at 3/7/7; acute articular rheumatism; Fred Drouin and Mary Labonte
Georgianna, d. 1/12/1923 at 61; chronic endocarditis; Gon'gue Morrissette
Glorianna, d. 3/27/1913 at 0/1/17; marasmus; Arthur Drouin and Yvonne Noel
Joseph, d. 2/19/1918 at 42; acute peritonitis; Thomas Drouin and Zelda Richard
Leanore, d. 10/30/1903 at 32/4/24; pulmonary tuberculosis
Margaret, d. 12/18/1914 at 79/5/11; cancer of stomach; Antoine Turgeon and Soulanges Talbot
Marie, d. 11/21/1929 at 54/7/3; carcinoma of colon; Paul Labonte and Adeline Dion
Osmond D., d. 8/11/1908 at 0/1/20; gastro enteritis; Louis P. Drouin and Blanche Dufort
Richard, d. 4/7/1928 at 31/1/21; acute nephritis; Perin Drouin and ----- Routhier
Wilfred, d. 11/12/1901 at 0/0/2; premature birth; SM
Wilfred, d. 11/2/1929 at 49; Wilfred Drouin and ----- Richard

DROULET,
Arthur A., d. 6/18/1931 at 16/10/3; accidental drowning
Charles, d. 6/19/1913 at 70/5/24 in Lowell, MA; cerebral hemorrhage
Joseph, d. 8/27/1903 at 22/1/25; tuberculosis; SM

DRUELET,
Joseph, d. 4/3/1892 at 50; shock; b. Canada; (Canada; Canada)

DRUIN,
Louis, d. 2/23/1892 at 1; pneumonia; b. Dover; (Canada; Canada)

DRYSDALE,
Stanis J., d. 4/4/1934 at 58/10/21; dilatation of heart

DUBE,
Annie, d. 7/4/1923 at 15/7/8; accident; Louis Dube and Artimese Boucher
Dominique, d. 3/13/1930 at 58/3; cerebral hemorrhage; Alphonse Dube
    and Philomena Metoyer
Emma, d. 3/9/1905 at 61/11/25; heart failure
Francois, d. 7/11/1888 at 21; single; b. Canada; Aimeble Dube (Canada)
    and Mary Beaupreau (Canada)
Ida, d. 7/5/1923 at 18/2; accident; Louis Dube and Artimese Boucher
Isadore, d. 5/23/1934 at 57/1/22; coronary thrombosis

DUBOIS,
Albion, d. 9/17/1914 at 25; cerebral thrombosis
Alexander, d. 2/21/1926 at 60; softening of brain
Antonio, d. 7/20/1909 at 2/0/18; cholera infantum; Narcisse Dubois and
    Alphonsine Cote
Honore, d. 2/14/1930 at 77/4/4; thrombosis; Modiste Dubois and Adele St.
    Hilaire
Irene, d. 7/15/1902 at 0/10/13; cholera infantum
Irene, d. 7/22/1909 at 0/1/12; cholera infantum; Narcisse Dubois and
    Alphonsine Cote
Narcisse, d. 3/4/1906 at 0/23; pneumonia

DUBREUIL,
Angeline, d. 3/11/1899 at 0; laid over

DUCHAMP,
son, d. 2/27/1890 at –; Paul Duchamp (Canada) and Olivia Martin
    (Canada)

DUCHARME,
Paul, d. 7/23/1908 at 49; ascites; Calix Ducharme

DUCHARNE,
Charles E., d. 9/25/1889 at 2/9/15; b. Barrington; Joseph Ducharne
    (Canada) and Alice S. Ducharne (Canada)

DUCHENNE,
Dora, d. 1/11/1891 at 2/5/22; Joseph Duchenne (Canada) and Alice
    Duchenne (Canada)

DUDALIS,
Hepokretis, d. 1/28/1918 at 41; carcinoma of liver; Michael Dudalis and
    Mary -----

DUDLEY,
Mildred L., d. 5/7/1893 at 1; tubercular meningitis; b. Bradford, MA; (Dover; Biddeford, ME)
Walter, d. 10/4/1907 at 3/0/16; meningitis; Frank M. Dudley and Florence Colburn

DUFAULT,
David, d. 12/13/1921 at 56/11/12; carcinoma of stomach; Charles Dufault and Edwidge Dowal
Jean S., d. 2/14/1919 at 0/4/18; asthenia; David Dufault and Lydia Savoie
Jeanne L., d. 2/11/1919 at 0/4/14; asthenia; David Dufault and Lydia Savoie
Lucille Marie, d. 7/19/1910 at 0/2/11; athrepsia; David Dufault and Lydia Savoie

DUFFEE,
Edward W., d. 2/1/1892 at –; railroad accident
Susan, d. 11/15/1898 at 65 in Concord; heart disease

DUFFEY,
Annie, d. 2/14/1907 at 25; pneumonia; John Roy and Mary Poulit
Edward, d. 1/24/1908 at 73; cancer of face; Edward Duffy

DUFFY,
daughter, d. 1/30/1888 at –; b. Dover; William Reynolds (Dover) and Bridget Duffy (Ireland)
child, d. 2/5/1901 at 6 hrs.; premature birth
child, d. 2/5/1901 at 5 hrs.; premature birth
child, d. 10/13/1901 at 0/0/1-6; premature birth
child, d. 7/4/1911 at –; dystocia; Bernard Duffy and Mary Finnigan
child, d. 11/1/1919 at –; premature birth; Peter J. Duffy and Ethel M. Lunk
child, d. 5/4/1924 at –; stillborn; Peter J. Duffy and Ethel L. Lunk
Alice, d. 2/16/1907 at 70; cerebral hemorrhage
Alice, d. 12/21/1908 at 0/5/21; pneumonia; Michael Duffy and Sarah Sheehy
Anastasia, d. 3/28/1916 at 0/3; intestinal indigestion; Michael Duffy and Sarah Shuley
Annie, d. 9/16/1891 at 28/1/4; married; Thomas Laughlin (Ireland) and Susan Laughlin (Ireland)
Bernard, d. 10/9/1889 at 32; barber; married; b. Ireland; Luke Duffy (Ireland) and Bridget Quinn (Ireland)
Bernard J., d. 1/9/1921 at 53/3/15; angina pectoris; Bernard Duffy and Rose Scanlon
Bridget, d. 1/21/1893 at 60; diabetes; b. Ireland; (Ireland; Ireland)
Bridget E., d. 3/25/1900 at <1; overlaid by mother; SM

Catherine, d. 7/22/1912 at 0/0/11; debility; Michael Duffy and Sarah Sheehy
David E. C., d. 4/3/1904 at 30/8/7; apoplexy; buried in Farmington
Edward F., d. 8/25/1911 at 0/2/2; marasmus; Michael Duffy and Sarah Sheehy
Elizabeth I., d. 10/9/1918 at 40; influenza; Henry Duffy and Margaret Duffy
Ellen, d. 2/14/1910 at –; tuberculosis
Francis, d. 8/5/1888 at 0/6/25; b. Dover; Michael Duffy (Ireland) and Annie Laughlin (Ireland)
Hugh, d. 10/2/1904 at –; SM
Hugh, d. 11/20/1915 at 50; acute alcoholism; Patrick Duffy and Alice Morse
James, d. 5/18/1905 at 2/1; malnutrition; SM
James, d. 10/27/1905 at 32; pulmonary tuberculosis; SM
James J., d. 10/1/1918 at 43 in Providence, RI; pneumonia - influenza
Joseph E., d. 5/24/1936 at 49/3/24; pul. tuberculosis
Kate, d. 2/9/1893 at 34; died in Strafford Co. Asylum fire
M. [daughter], d. 9/3/1890 at 1/0/14; Michael Duffy (Ireland) and Annie Laughlin (Ireland)
Margaret A., d. 12/5/1924 at 40/5/9; pernicious anemia; Henry Duffy and Margaret -----
Margaret T., d. 4/18/1910 at 0/2; marasmus; Michael Duffy and Sarah Sheehy
Mary, d. 11/4/1928 at 57; carcinoma of breast; Michael Finnegan and Julia -----
Michael M., d. 2/20/1934 at 63/1/26; chronic myocarditis
Patrick, d. 11/18/1893 at 66; heart disease; b. Ireland; (Ireland; Ireland)
Patrick, d. 10/13/1904 at 0/2/10; gastro enteritis; SM
Rose, d. 3/3/1910 at 61; tuberculosis; Michael Scanlon
Sarah, d. 7/17/1914 at 27/8 in Richmond, VA; meningitis
Thomas, d. 10/5/1891 at 0/0/27; Michael Duffy (Ireland) and Annie Loughlin (Ireland)

DUFORD,
Lumina, d. 9/26/1919 at 61/8/12; cancer of stomach and liver; Octave Chabot and Clarence Cheney
Roland, d. 11/15/1918 at 0/4; phthisis; Charles Duford and Ida Mailhiot

DUFOUR,
Alfred, d. 4/14/1916 at 37; typhoid fever; Zoel Dufour and Mary Trembley
Edith, d. 1/11/1923 at 23 in Haverhill, MA; gangrene of intestines

DUFRESNE,
Ellen, d. 9/15/1917 at 53/7/23; cancer of womb; Joseph Cote and Mary Richard

DUGAN,
Edward P., d. 5/10/1905 at 35; gastric ulcer of stomach; buried in Bangor, ME
James W., d. 10/30/1892 at 1; cholera infantum; b. Dover; (Iowa; Lebanon, ME)

DUGGAN,
John R., d. 6/27/1927 at 65; acute nephritis
Mary, d. 1/18/1890 at 3/1/4; John Duggan (Ireland) and Mary Goggin (Dover)
Mary, d. 11/4/1928 at 69; arterio sclerosis; Michael Goggin and Julia -----
Richard, d. 7/26/1890 at 2/3; John Duggan (Ireland) and Mary Goggin (Dover)

DUKE,
James R., d. 9/30/1918 at 3/1/4; intersusseption intestinal; William Duke and Mary Doscher
Margaret, d. 9/26/1908 at 0/1; cholera infantum; William Duke and Mary Desher

DUMAIS,
Albert J., d. 7/16/1936 at 36/7/7; shock, frac. skull
Alside, d. 4/3/1929 at 12/0/19; peritonitis; Philip Dumais and Oulamine Lamb
Wilfred L., d. 7/1/1912 at 15; appendicitis; Thomas Dumais

DUNCAN,
Burnice M., d. 11/19/1888 at 0/0/14; b. Dover; Eugene Duncan (Lincolnville) and Catherine Carter (Dover)
Ernest A., d. 9/1/1917 at 53 in Haverhill, MA; natural causes
Katherine, d. 2/11/1899 at 32 in Beverly, MA; chronic nephritis; PH

DUNHAM,
Alta S., d. 6/12/1921 at 47/7/24 in Framingham, MA; cerebral hemorrhage
Clifton D., d. 1/6/1919 at 38/6/28 in Framingham, MA; influenza, pneumonia

DUNLAP,
Albert, d. 2/9/1919 at 63/8; influenza; John Dunlap and Sarah Jones
Carrie Bell, d. 12/7/1893 at 23

DUNN,
Annie, d. 5/21/1888 at 1/8/9; b. Dover; Julia Dunn (Newburyport, MA)

Catherine T., d. 4/30/1915 at 82/10/13; senility; John Waldron and
 Elizabeth Gray
Deborah, d. 5/14/1900 at 62; PH
Eliza, d. 3/18/1895 at 80; old age; b. ME; PH
Ellen M., d. 9/25/1895 at 8; pulmonary tuberculosis; SM
Farrell, d. 2/3/1910 at 26; pneumonia; James Dunn and Eliza Caton
George, d. 7/31/1890 at 57/9/14; Enoch Dunn (Gorham, ME) and Eliza
 Fullington (Wolfeboro)
John J., d. 2/28/1895 at 62; heart disease; b. Dover; buried in Taunton,
 MA
Mary, d. 7/9/1892 at 80; old age - hemorrhage stomach; b. ME; (ME; ME)
Mary J., d. 12/2/1910 at 60; general paresis
Samuel, d. 1/27/1890 at 85/9/28; widower; Samuel Dunn (ME) and Mary
 Johnson (ME)
Samuel T., d. 11/3/1905 at 72/10/14; mitral insufficiency; PH

DUPEREY,
Elise, d. 8/9/1904 at 47/5/5; concussion of brain, etc.; PH

DUPONT,
Alexander, d. 8/24/1898 at –; diarrhea infantile; b. Dover; SM
Alphonse, d. 1/15/1901 at 0/3/11; heart failure
Joseph P., d. 11/5/1902 at 0/4/20; marasmus
Marie, d. 3/5/1904 at 27/2/3; chronic phthisis
Mary A., d. 9/2/1906 at --
Mary L., d. 7/28/1905 at 0/6/16; cholera infantum
Mary M., d. 8/7/1901 at 0/0/20; cholera infantum

DUPRAS,
Theophile, d. 5/13/1933 at 79/9/29; chronic endocarditis

DUPREE [see Dupries],
Frank, d. 11/14/1926 at 71/1/19; arterio sclerosis; Andre Dupries and
 Maraie Paradis

DUPRIES [see Dupree],
Alfred J., d. 9/3/1905 at 0/4/13; atherepsia; SM
Emma, d. 2/28/1907 at 49/1/5; chronic endocarditis; Frank E. Quimby and
 Abbie Wallis
Philomene, d. 9/3/1920 at 44/11/17; oedema of lungs; Alphonse Dube and
 Philomene Mataryer

DUPUIS,
child, d. 9/3/1934 at –; stillborn

DUQUETTE,
Delphine, d. 10/9/1892 at 16; acute pulmonary phthisis; b. So. Boston, MA; (Canada; Canada)
Octave, d. 8/25/1893 at 43; typhoid fever; b. Canada; (Canada; Canada)

DURANT,
Mary, d. 4/30/1913 at 28/0/7; tuberculosis; Frank J. Vaillancourt and Demerise Allen
Peter, d. 6/16/1917 at 37; cirrhosis of liver

DURELL,
Mary S., d. 11/28/1906 at 63/3/10; fatty degeneration of heart; PH

DURFEE,
Frank P., d. 12/23/1915 at 37/1; bronchitis - asthma

DURGIN,
Almira P., d. 7/4/1887 at 48/9; married; b. Dover; Jonathan (Dover) and Lydia H. Goodrich (Lebanon, ME)
Angelina, d. 10/16/1932 at 42/5/30; heart disease
Annie B., d. 6/23/1914 at 59/3/21; arcitis; John Young and Sarah Dunnells
Arthur C., d. 11/5/1888 at 0/10/1; b. Dover; Sylvester L. Durgin (Greenland) and Lillie K. Lincoln (Lowell, MA)
Cassandra E., d. 10/11/1916 at 84/7/19; chronic endocarditis; Ephraim Durgin and Annie Furlong
George E., d. 9/30/1904 at 73/4/17; cerebral apoplexy; PH
George M., d. 5/19/1898 at 66; paresis; b. Farmington; buried in Farmington
George W., d. 2/19/1907 at 72 in Boston, MA; apoplexy
Gilman Y., d. 1/18/1918 at 73/3/4 in Lee; uraemia
John, d. 1/21/1900 at 1; croup; SM
John Elliott, d. 10/26/1891 at 59/3/27; married; Joshua Durgin (Limerick, ME) and Rebecca Elliott (Parsonsfield, ME)
Lewis A., d. 6/16/1924 at 62 in Haverhill, MA; tuberculosis of intestine; Alpheus Durgin and Harriet N. Daly
Lorenzo, d. 1/17/1909 at 55; heart disease; A. W. Durgin and Melissa Spurling
Lydia Ann, d. 8/5/1893 at 62; carcinoma; b. Lee; (Lee; Lee)
Mary F., d. 10/11/1919 at 76/7/1 in Lee; acute bronchitis
Mary Jane, d. 7/15/1887 at 62/4/18; weaver; single; b. Dover; Daniel Derrigio (New Durham) and Betsey Folsom (New Durham)
Sarah E. D., d. 8/24/1897 at 65 in Boston, MA; heart disease; PH
Seward, d. 9/4/1915 at 54; carcinoma of stomach; Benjamin Durgin and Dorcas -----

DURKIN,
child, d. 5/4/1909 at –; stillborn; Patrick J. Durkin and Elizabeth Breen
child, d. 1/9/1918 at –; stillborn; John J. Durkin and Catherine Carroll
child, d. 8/20/1918 at –; miscarriage; John Durkin and Katherine Carroll
child, d. 12/5/1934 at –; stillborn
Alice, d. 8/12/1898 at –; cholera infantum; SM
Bridget, d. 12/25/1933 at – in Somersworth; cerebral apoplexy
Catherine, d. 9/5/1907 at 10/0/28; Edward Durkin and Catherine Scanlon
Dominick J., d. 4/26/1910 at 54; uraemia; John Durkin and Mary Welsh
Edward, d. 9/10/1905 at 42; accidental drowning; SM
John C., d. 3/5/1922 at 0/0/2; premature birth; John Durkin and Kate Carroll
Katherine, d. 11/11/1922 at 38/7; uraemia; Patrick Durkin and Katherine Flanagan
Mary, d. 9/12/1913 at 62; chr. catarrhal gastritis; Michael Welch and Sabina McNally
Mary, d. 1/26/1917 at –; stillborn; John Durkin and Katherine Carroll
Thomas, d. 9/10/1905 at 3/3; accidental drowning; SM

DURLIN,
Susie, d. 6/16/1895 at --; Brights disease; b. Dover; buried in Rollinsford

DURNIN,
Alice McE., d. 11/17/1906 at 47; heart disease; SM
Charles B., d. 11/4/1923 at 35; peritonitis; Edward Durnin and Susan A. Wesley
George P., d. 11/28/1893 at –; anaemia; b. Dover; (Lewiston, ME; So. Berwick, ME)
Isabel, d. 8/4/1893 at –; cholera infantum; b. Dover; (Lewiston, ME; Berwick, ME)
James, d. 2/23/1912 at 0/0/1; atelectasis; James Drouin (sic) and Margaret Sunderland
John H., d. 10/2/1887 at 0/0/1-4; b. Dover; Edward Durning (Lewiston, ME) and Susan A. Wesley (S. Berwick, ME)
Margaret V., d. 8/14/1921 at 33/7/29; cancer of stomach; John Sunderland and Catherine McGrory
Mary A., d. 11/7/1910 at 34/8/26; heart disease; Terrence Durnin and Mary E. Brennan
Owen, d. 3/26/1935 at 84; gen. arteriosclerosis
Peter, d. 1/23/1904 at 36/11/20; acute tuberculosis of lungs; buried in Dover

DURRELL,
Dorothy, d. 6/2/1893 at 80; grippe

DURROLL,
Lebanon, d. 4/6/1893 at 83; paralysis

DURWARD,
Alexander, d. 6/21/1936 at 49/7/29; broncho-pneumonia

DUSSAULT,
Alma, d. 11/17/1937 at 34/3/11; cerebral embolism
Mark F., d. 11/24/1930 at 68/11/3; rupture; Abrian Dussault and Mary Morren
Matilda, d. 7/5/1937 at 72/9/15; coronary thrombosis

DUSTIN,
Grace H., d. 10/16/1928 at 68/11 in York, ME; lobar pneumonia

DUTTON,
Alvin P., d. 8/23/1897 at 52; cerebral hemorrhage; b. Billerica, MA; PH

DUXBURY,
Emily V., d. 8/24/1906 at 69/2/14; chronic nephritis; PH
George A., d. 6/22/1922 at 50/11/15 in Monson, MA; epilepsy
John J., d. 10/16/1889 at 78/5/18; broker; widower; b. England; James Duxbury (England) and Elizabeth Collier (England)
Juliette, d. 6/17/1888 at 77/2/5; married; b. Dover; John Wheeler (Howard, MA) and Elizabeth Crosby (Bellview, MA)
Mary F., d. 11/25/1912 at 65/5/9; cancer of womb; John J. Duxbury and Juliette -----
Nancy, d. 10/31/1894 at 81 in Concord; apoplexy; buried in Dover

DWYER,
Catherine, d. 4/29/1898 at 82 in Exeter; heart disease
Mary, d. 7/–/1905 at – in Exeter; Bright's disease
Mary J., d. 4/9/1915 at 74; chronic endocarditis

DYAR,
Carrie E., d. 2/2/1919 at 58/4/27; syncope of heart; John S. Clark and Lucinda Gilman
George E., d. 7/9/1914 at – in York Village, ME; infantile paralysis
George H., d. 5/27/1925 at 79/6 in York, ME; lobar pneumonia

DYER,
Annoth, d. 8/8/1890 at 0/2; John Dyer (England) and Catherine Higgins (England)
Michael J., d. 5/31/1903 at 28; phthisis pulmonalis; SM

EAGAN,
James J., d. 12/26/1927 at 59/4/4 in Concord; general paresis

EARLE,
Louise M., d. 4/1/1922 at 88/6/7; pneumonia; John Earle and Betsy Roberts

EARLY,
Anthony, d. 2/6/1898 at 59; paralysis; b. Ireland; SM
Jeremiah F., d. 11/20/1902 at 35/2/2; heart disease; SM
Josephine, d. 11/10/1934 at 60 in Portsmouth; intestinal perforation
Margaret L., d. 7/9/1937 at 60/11/15; cancer uterus
Mary E., d. 11/26/1922 at 78/3/11; chronic endocarditis; Jeremiah Meskill and Johanna Drinan
Mary V., d. 4/2/1937 at 65/4/21; cancer bladder

EASTMAN,
Elvira, d. 12/16/1891 at 66/8/15; ----- McCollister (ME)
Florence E., d. 4/27/1901 at 6/5/11 in Lynn, MA; idiopathetic - infantile paralysis; PH
Ida May, d. 3/13/1902 at 43/3/18; chronic nephritis; PH
John F., d. 11/1/1893 at 69; accident; b. Peacham, VT
John F., d. 3/7/1925 at 72/2/23; carcinoma of stomach; John F. Eastman and Elvira McColester
Lydia E., d. 7/17/1901 at 84; heart disease; PH

EATON,
Adeline, d. 2/19/1911 at 67/9/15; old age; William Eaton and Mary E. Ham
Benjamin F., d. 10/2/1917 at 81/0/16; cerebral embolism; Moses Eaton and Betsey Jones
Doris B., d. 10/27/1923 at 33/10/19 in Rochester; acute uremia
Ethel, d. 11/21/1898 at 0; pneumonia and petrissis; b. Dover; buried in family lot
Frank F., d. 5/21/1930 at 59/10/2; chr. val. heart dis.; Walter Eaton and Lucanna Chadbourne
Hannah Susan, d. 10/28/1891 at 54/2/26; single; William Eaton (Woburn) and Mary Elizabeth Ham (Dover)
Harriet, d. 1/27/1911 at 73/0/10; cancer of stomach; John C. Eaton and Dorcas J. Jacobs
Helen Gertrude, d. 7/30/1930 at 44/10/17 in Lynn, MA; carcinoma
Helen N., d. 3/1/1921 at 87/9/25; old age; John Kennard and Lydia Merrow
James C., d. 4/20/1931 at 6/7/5; cong. malformation
John E., d. 6/4/1896 at 87; old age; b. Wells, ME; buried in Wells, ME
Lois E., d. 11/10/1912 at 4/11/16; membraneous croup; Oscar E. Eaton and Nellie V. Lomas

Lucy M., d. 11/22/1922 at 54/3/3; carcinoma of uterus; Henry Paul and Mary A. Hayes
Mary E., d. 2/3/1900 at 74; chronic nephritis; PH
Nathaniel H., d. 7/7/1903 at 75/11/10; old age; buried in family lot
Polly, d. 4/15/1898 at 86; bronchitis; b. Wells, ME; PH

ECKLUND,
Oscar, d. 5/13/1933 at 70/3; carcinoma of stomach

EDGECOMB,
child, d. 10/1/1935 at –; stillborn

EDGERLY,
Charles J., d. 12/22/1890 at 45/11/6 in Somersworth; married; Dudley Edgerly (Wolfeboro) and Eliza Hackett (Wolfeboro)
Charles P., d. 6/3/1904 at 51/7/7; pneumonia
Charles R., d. 2/16/1907 at 81/6/1; old age; John Edgerly and Fannie -----
E., d. 10/21/1889 at 84; farmer; widower; b. Durham
Eliza J., d. 1/21/1925 at 89/9/14; arterio sclerosis; Ira Andrews and Sarah Wentworth
Emma L., d. 12/21/1888 at 28/7; married; b. Kennebunk, ME
Frank E., d. 10/5/1919 at 64/11/12 in Providence, RI; subdiaphraghmatic cancer
Henry I., d. 2/6/1923 at 84/3/2; senility; Jonah B. Edgerly and Cordelia Waldron
Hiram O., d. 2/23/1904 at 60/10/8 in Chelsea, MA; chronic nephritis; PH
J. Homer, d. 10/17/1915 at 71/5/12 in Boston, MA; endocarditis
James A., d. 2/8/1908 at 61/8/24; uraemia; James Edgerly and Nancy Wedgewood
Jennie L., d. 7/28/1927 at 71/5/22; gen. arterio sclerosis; Samuel Hussey and Susan Horne
Leroy M., d. 1/31/1922 at 26/3/15 in Kittery, ME; broncho pneumonia
Lucy M., d. 6/20/1912 at 88/7/15 in Boston, MA; carcinoma
Maria M., d. 7/6/1914 at 57; diabetes mellitus; James Boland and Mary ----
Mary A., d. 4/23/1889 at 5/1/13; b. Dover; Frank E. Edgerly (Durham) and Jennie L. Hussey (Dover)
Mary A., d. 3/19/1919 at 88/1/24; arterio sclerosis; John Ferguson and Grace -----
Mary E., d. 4/22/1896 at 53; shock; PH
Mary T., d. 4/11/1898 at 97; old age; b. New Durham; buried in New Durham
Rose L., d. 6/17/1925 at 83; myocarditis; Ezekiel Hayes and Sarah Sanborn
Sarah A., d. 3/11/1936 at 87/3/10; arteriosclerosis

Sarah J., d. 11/29/1898 at 71; paralysis; b. Limington, ME; buried in Dixmont, ME
Susan M., d. 1/20/1911 at 70/5/24; locomotor ataxia; David Rand and Nancy Edgerly
Walter S., d. 9/3/1927 at 57/6/24; peritonitis; John O. Edgerly and Annie E. Palmer
William H., d. 9/26/1912 at 79/7/2; carcinoma of jaw; Jacob Edgerly and Susan Chapman
Winnifred, d. 5/27/1920 at 51/7/22 in N. Reading, MA; chronic parenchymatous

EDWARDS,
Frederick L., d. 4/1/1924 at 77/8/7; nephritis; Eli Edwards and Julia Clapp
William R., d. 8/25/1888 at 0/6; b. Lowell, MA; John L. Edwards (England) and Mary Welsh (Fall River, MA)

EGAN,
Mary A., d. 4/15/1888 at 0/1/19; b. Dover; William Egan (NH) and Susie Shaw (Ireland)

EGELTON,
John, d. 11/6/1903 at 41; kidney and heart disease; SM

EGGLESTON,
Corilla C., d. 9/16/1913 at 29/8/10; fracture of skull and ribs; Ezra S. Eggleston and Nettie F. Bates

EGLESTON,
Mary A., d. 7/11/1896 at 3; convulsions; b. Dover; SM

ELDER,
Dorothy P., d. 4/7/1919 at 3/6 in S. Portland, ME; lobar pneumonia; Fred L. Elder and Mildred C. Collins
Edith M., d. 3/28/1910 at 48/5/19; nephritis; David W. Pierce and Olive Allbee
Fred L., d. 8/14/1933 at 46/7/28 in Portland, ME; enteritis thrombosis
Gertrude L. V., d. 10/7/1918 at 40/6/16; acute dilatation of heart; Herman Vyth and Dora Salinger
H. Foster, d. 1/12/1935 at 73/0/29; chronic myocarditis
Mary E., d. 5/1/1905 at 72/9/9; diabetic coma; PH
Nellie E., d. 11/9/1915 at 51/7/4 in Worcester, MA; postoperative shock
William L., d. 8/13/1928 at 63/2/19 in Worcester, MA; chronic nephritis

ELDREDGE,
Mary, d. 1/3/1928 at 75; carcinoma of stomach

ELEURIE,
Pierre, d. 11/21/1931 at 76; pulmonary embolism

ELIOPULOS,
Constantine, d. 1/26/1907 at 19; destroyed by fire

ELKINS,
Berte, d. 3/27/1890 at 4
Laura, d. 12/30/1935 at 78/0/29; coronary thrombosis
Perry P., d. 7/28/1914 at 67/10/13; cerebral hemorrhage; Ebenezer Elkins and Emily Glidden

ELLARD,
Natalie H., d. 10/29/1936 at 26/8/5*

ELLIOT,
Arthur F. R., d. 1/31/1890 at 63/11/12; widower; Joseph Elliot

ELLIOTT,
Alonzo W., d. 8/21/1924 at 76/8/19; strangulated hernia; Henry G. Elliott and Nancy B. Clark
Ann T., d. 12/22/1888 at 62/7/22; married; b. Pittsfield; Isaac Twombly (Pittsfield) and Martha Durga (Pittsfield)
Christine, d. 1/4/1923 at 80; apoplexy
Ellen F., d. 7/4/1921 at 71/7/12; gen. arterio sclerosis; Charles C. Hayes and Elizabeth W. Pollard
George E., d. 5/24/1910 at 57/9/4 in Rochester; endocarditis
Gertrude F., d. 4/2/1918 at 0/0/17; malnutrition; George F. Elliott and Flora B. Miller
Gladys, d. 6/18/1922 at 0/0/1; premature birth; George F. Elliott and Flora B. Miller
James, d. 12/14/1887 at 45; married; b. Somersworth
Mary J., d. 3/31/1889 at 54/7/6; dresser; single; b. Dover; Henry S. Elliott (Barnstead) and Sarah A. Cushing (Dover)
Sarah A., d. 4/10/1887 at 83/1/6; widow; b. Dover

ELLIS,
child, d. 6/1/1922 at –; stillborn; Samuel A. Ellis and Mildred Tucker
child, d. 2/1/1935 at –; prematurity (7 mos.)
child, d. 2/8/1935 at 0/0/8; prematurity
Annie, d. 2/24/1922 at 44 in Augusta, ME; general paralysis

Arthur W., d. 6/10/1919 at 7/4/6; diphtheria; Arthur G. Ellis and Georgianna Herrick
Benjamin C., d. 7/17/1922 at 72/4/4; gastro enteritis; Joshua Ellis and Maria J. Foss
Bessie A., d. 12/2/1911 at 2/3/10; naso laryngo phoryngitis; Arthur S. Ellis and Mildred Tucker
Doris, d. 8/10/1920 at 7/3; ileocolitis; Florence Colomy
Dorothy E., d. 3/30/1934 at –; prematurity
Edna Annie, d. 3/13/1911 at 0/3; indigestion; Henry Ellis and Florence Colomy
Eli, d. 1/16/1926 at 69/8/19; cancer of tongue; John Ellis and Hannah Lonsdale
Esther L., d. 6/1/1889 at 71; dressmaker; single; b. Middleton; Reuben Ellis and Esther N. Buzzell
John A., d. 8/13/1915 at 75; senility
John L., d. 11/2/1934 at 51/3/17; cerebral apoplexy
Laura, d. 2/9/1893 at 71; died in Strafford Co. Asylum fire
Lizzie, d. 2/9/1893 at 43; died in Strafford Co. Asylum fire
Maggie, d. 7/5/1892 at 36; cancer; b. PEI; (PEI; PEI)
Thomas C., d. 8/9/1901 at 4/7/11; ptomaine poisoning; PH

ELLISON,
Bertha P., d. 7/18/1925 at 66; cancer of sternum
Charles H., d. 10/20/1933 at 78/10/8; gangrene
Jacob, d. 9/3/1899 at 67 in Haverhill, MA; disease of heart; PH

ELLMORE,
child, d. 10/9/1920 at –; premature birth; Catherine Ellmore

ELLSMORE,
William H., d. 12/4/1933 at 76/4/18; fracture of skull

ELLWOOD,
Annie, d. 1/17/1935 at 67 in New Bedford, MA; cerebral hemorrhage

ELWELL,
Eileen H., d. 10/6/1926 at 35/2/1; pernicious anaemia; Harry E. Hodgdon and Edith Johnson
Elizabeth, d. 2/22/1931 at 61/11/8; cholelithiasis

EMERSON,
Arthur R., d. 5/16/1903 at 20/8/21; tuberculosis; buried in Saco, ME
Arvilla M., d. 12/16/1933 at 77/6/28; carcinoma of stomach
Asenath W., d. 9/25/1900 at 79; disease of brain; buried in Dover Neck

Charles E., d. 4/21/1893 at –; pneumonia; b. Dover; (New Durham; Rochester)
Charles G., d. 2/1/1907 at 39/7/14 in Haverhill, MA; carcinoma of stomach
Daniel E., d. 5/11/1893 at 67; Bright's disease; b. Northwood; (Northwood; Northwood)
Dimion A., d. 6/23/1925 at 63/11/5; angina pectoris; Washington Emerson and Asenath Cousens
Ella E., d. 1/13/1935 at 77/10/4; cerebral hemorrhage
Emery W., d. 5/13/1917 at 66/4/28; apoplexy; Joseph D. Emerson and Eliza Wakefield
Frank H., d. 7/10/1929 at 73/10/2; carcinoma of stomach
Fred H., d. 4/22/1905 at 47/0/4; pneumonia; buried in Saco, ME
George Bowen, d. 2/5/1890 at 36/7/11; married; Jefferson Emerson and Vienna Cilley
George H., d. 9/6/1918 at 48/11/9 in Portsmouth; fracture of spine; John Emerson and ----- Brewster
George W., d. 3/19/1916 at 77/8/8; acute indigestion; Benjamin Emerson and Sally Vincent
Gracie B., d. 3/23/1890 at 12/1/17; Herbert S. Emerson (Alton) and Mary Emma Hobbs (Biddeford, ME)
Hannah, d. 12/7/1904 at 89/6/23; senility; buried in Alton
Harold S., d. 10/15/1896 at 1; inanition; b. Dover; PH
Herbert S., d. 5/17/1931 at 79/8/28 in Haverhill, MA; chr. valv. heart dis.
Horace, d. 2/6/1914 at 80/10/19; prostatitis; Nathaniel Emerson and Patience Clark
Isabelle, d. 1/18/1902 at 74/9/5 in Durham; chronic Bright's disease; PH
John, d. 12/4/1897 at 64 in Durham; senile gangrene; PH
Lewis H., d. 4/15/1919 at 43/1/24 in Newton; acute nephritis; Herbert S. Emerson and Eunice Hobbs
Marilla, d. 5/25/1928 at 84/0/2; pulmonary oedema; Samuel Charles and Malinda Abbott
Mary E., d. 3/1/1906 at 48/1/18 in Alton; multiple nauritis; PH
Mary J., d. 1/9/1912 at 72/8; senility
Samuel, d. 3/5/1900 at 61 in Durham; acute bronchitis; PH
Sarah, d. 10/11/1889 at 89/9/22; widow; b. Boston, MA; Joseph W. Homer (Amherst) and Sarah Rae (Boston, MA)
Verna B., d. 7/1/1907 at 13/7/18 in Alton; diphtheria; Herbert S. Emerson
William L., d. 6/15/1932 at 67/2/17 in Boston, MA; dermatitis

EMERY,
Annie L., d. 8/22/1924 at 61/3/16; tuberculosis of lungs; Henry Hutchinson and Virginia Hadley
Clarence D., d. 6/15/1898 at 43 in Tacoma, WA; pistol shot wound; PH
Clifton E., d. 11/5/1912 at –; alcoholism and exposure; E. A. Emery and Francis S. Jenkins

Ellen Estelle, d. 8/24/1902 at 47/2/1 in Everett, MA; pulmonary tuberculosis; PH
Everett A., d. 3/6/1905 at 53/4/24 in Everett, MA; intestitial nephritis; PH
Frank H., d. 10/21/1888 at 19/3/20; clerk; single; b. Portsmouth; Reuben B. Emery (S. Berwick, ME) and Mary E. Harvey (Portsmouth)
Hermina Jennie, d. 5/16/1921 at 54/0/1; dementia; Simon Emery and Mary A. Ehrlacher
Jacob, d. 11/22/1905 at 76/6/14; angina pectoris; buried in Kennebunk, ME
James Y., d. 5/28/1912 at 56/4/4; accident; Timothy K. Emery and Irena P. Merrill
John Bernard, d. 6/3/1921 at 35/9/19 in Orleans, VT; cerebral meningitis; Woodbury Emery and Luella E. Edgerly
Lizzie E., d. 9/17/1898 at 11 in Chelsea, MA; appendicitis; PH
Luetta E., d. 10/6/1935 at 75 in Chelsea, MA; chronic endocarditis
Mary A., d. 3/6/1924 at 74/7/14 in Somerville, MA; arterio sclerosis
Mary Anna, d. 2/26/1910 at 78/2/16; cerebral hemorrhage; Martin Ehrlacher and Mary A. Zimmerman
Mary H., d. 12/6/1907 at 83/6 in Somersworth; bronchitis
Philomela, d. 7/4/1919 at 73/5/26; heart exhaustion; John Stackpole and Mary L. Gray
Rufus B., d. 4/20/1887 at 62/5/13; carpenter; married; b. S. Berwick, ME; Rufus Emery (S. Berwick, ME) and ----- Hamilton (S. Berwick, ME)
Simeon, d. 5/7/1895 at 65; pneumonia; b. England; PH

EMMONS,
Mary B., d. 11/3/1894 at 2; pneumonia; b. Dover

EMMOTT,
Amelia A., d. 2/10/1917 at 79/4/15 in Haverstraw, NY; chronic nephritis
John, d. 10/29/1916 at 83/10/12 in N. Adams, MA; valvular heart disease

ENGLAND,
Ellen F., d. 8/5/1931 at 81/7/10 in Natick, MA; cerebral hemorrhage
Mary A., d. 3/16/1931 at 67; uremia
Thomas, d. 2/1/1915 at 81/4/11; senility; Michael England and Mariam Duckles

ENGLISH,
Harold C., d. 10/1/1918 at 25/3/28; lobar pneumonia

ERWIN,
Dorothy H., d. 7/25/1910 at 0/0/19 in Madbury; whooping cough

ESCHMAN,
child, d. 11/26/1922 at –; premature birth; Werner Echman (sic) and Yula Bridges

ESTES,
daughter, d. 4/1/1887 at –; b. Dover; Stephen A. Estes (China, ME) and Emma F. Stevens (Boston, MA)
Alice Rebecca, d. 6/6/1894 at 41; some unknown toxic agent; b. Dover; PH
Benjamin F., d. 7/24/1925 at 74 in Detroit, MI; dilatation of heart
Charles, d. 1/31/1920 at 89/2/10; senility; John Estes and Abia Green
Elizabeth C., d. 2/10/1909 at 65/6/24; cirrhosis of liver; Stephen P. Estes and Pamelia C. Dame
Esther F., d. 1/27/1901 at 50/6/20 in Revere, MA; PH
Josephine F., d. 10/16/1894 at 26 in Lynn, MA; salpingitis; buried in Dover
Leonard, d. 3/19/1897 at 64; chronic brain disease; b. Kennebunk, ME; PH
Mary M., d. 7/16/1899 at 52; carcinoma posterior to rectum; buried in Rochester

ESTEY,
Thomas W., d. 11/18/1931 at 66/6/2; carcinoma of colon

ESTY,
Elizabeth A., d. 2/13/1922 at 61/2/26; chronic endocarditis; William Raliston and Mary Montieth

EUCONOMUS,
Charles, d. 3/3/1913 at –; burned to death

EVANS,
child, d. 5/23/1934 at –; stillborn
Abram, d. 4/3/1905 at 78; cerebral thrombosis
Albion, d. 6/5/1896 at 51; alcoholism; b. Lovell, ME; buried in Fryeburg, ME
Almira P., d. 7/12/1912 at 78/6/15; endocarditis and senility; James Evans and Nancy Davis
Ann, d. 10/12/1929 at –; cancer of stomach; Patrick Lennon and Nancy Murray
Eugene I., d. 11/29/1924 at 70/5/23; natural causes; John Evans and Rhoda Twombly
Fannie L., d. 3/27/1920 at 58/11/19; mediastinal carcinoma; David H. Evans and Catherine Hill
Frank, d. 12/17/1931 at 69/11/5; lobar pneumonia
Junia E., d. 10/26/1927 at 72/10/28 in Rochester; abdominal carcinoma
Louis W., d. 10/15/1898 at 2; diphtheria; b. Dover; PH

Martha, d. 2/4/1890 at 80; widow
Mary H., d. 7/30/1900 at 59; apoplexy; PH
Nancy, d. 2/1/1897 at 88; old age; b. Barnstead; PH
Peter H., d. 12/24/1905 at –; convulsions; PH
Robert, d. 7/11/1893 at 76; heart disease
Sarah C., d. 6/17/1896 at 64 in Boston, MA; pulmonary tuberculosis
Sylvester, d. 12/18/1913 at 70/0/13; acute uremia; ----- Evans and Mary ---

EVEREST,
Bert L., d. 9/16/1899 at –; marasmus; buried in Brattleboro, VT

EVERETT,
Abbie M., d. 2/4/1907 at 73/1/20; uraemia; Stephen P. Palmer and Abigail
    Horne
Charles E., d. 4/24/1892 at 63; apoplexy; b. Dover; (MA; MA)
Charles E., d. 12/17/1893 at 1; acute cerebral meningitis; b. Dover;
    (Dover; NY)
Jennie R., d. 3/28/1903 at 42/4/12; heart disease; PH
Walter P., d. 12/7/1887 at 4/6/7; b. Dover; John Evertt (Dover) and Jenrie
    R. Golding (New York City)

EWER,
Isaac Everett, d. 9/12/1930 at 67/7/22 in Portsmouth; carcinoma
Jennie P., d. 12/28/1933 at 60/5/21 in Worcester; apoplexy

EXAS,
child, d. 12/1/1922 at –; miscarriage; Christos Exas and Angelica
    Koupritzes
Christos, d. 4/21/1936 at 57; apoplexy

FAGAN,
Arthur, d. 3/23/1935 at 77; cerebral embolism
Joseph A., d. 4/30/1935 at 39/7/8 in Altamont; pulmonary T. B. (chronic)
Patrick, d. 1/31/1916 at 45; acute nephritis

FAIRBANKS,
Charles A., d. 4/30/1932 at 82/4/13; chronic myocarditis
Emma Belle, d. 5/28/1888 at 30/3/23; b. Dover; Cornelius E. Fairbanks
    (Strafford) and Betsey T. Chase (Wolfeboro)
Lydia L., d. 1/19/1892 at 70; influenza; b. Barrington; (Barrington;
    Barrington)

FAIRBROTHER,
Harold H., d. 5/31/1916 at 0/10 in Lowell, MA; lobar pneumonia

Isabelle, d. 9/29/1933 at 55/1/11 in Lowell, MA; diabetes

FAIRBURN,
Marion T., d. 3/27/1933 at 73/0/26; chronic nephritis

FALEY,
Hugh F., d. 4/22/1888 at 0/8; b. Dover; Hugh Faley (Bangor, ME) and Ann McKee (Ireland)

FALL,
George C., d. 3/4/1929 at 75/9/28; arterio sclerosis; Joseph Fall and Sarah Brown
George S., d. 5/4/1910 at 64/4/5; dementia paralitica; Jacob Fall and Melissa Jones
Horace P., d. 10/17/1924 at 61/7/12; valvular heart; Otis Fall and Mary Evans
Jane L., d. 8/17/1918 at 70/9/8 in Concord; hepatitis; Abraham Hill and Lydia Barton
Martha D., d. 4/12/1925 at 92/11; lobar pneumonia; Moses Warren and Susan Peckham
Mary A., d. 1/3/1898 at 63; neurasthenia; b. Shapleigh, ME; buried in Rochester
Mary Ann, d. 12/21/1909 at 79/4/10; old age; William Beck and Sarah Bickford
Rodney E., d. 9/15/1916 at 56/1/15; accidental poisoning; Otis W. Fall and Rosanna Evans
Vivian Mildred, d. 11/30/1901 at 0/6/17; marasmus; buried in Farmington

FALLON,
Francis, d. 7/21/1912 at 0/1/1 in Durham; inanition; John Fallon and Katherine -----

FALVEY,
Margaret, d. 3/7/1912 at 68; senility; Jere Sullivan and Abigail -----

FARLEY,
Barbara C., d. 8/3/1919 at 0/0/19; whooping cough; Benjamin L. Farley and Emily J. Kisterman
Carrie Sophia, d. 7/25/1921 at 63/9/23 in Dedham, MA; arthritis deformans
Edward D., d. 2/13/1896 at 69; typhoid fever; b. Ireland; SM
Francis, d. 4/21/1916 at 0/0/5; purpura hemorrhagica; Francis J. Farley and Annie G. Buckley
John Q., d. 12/14/1912 at 59/1/22; phthisis; Benjamin L. Farley and Elizabeth Howe

Mary, d. 6/23/1912 at 60; gastritis and cholecystitis; James Rehill and
   Mary Cremer
Nancy R., d. 3/25/1930 at 74/10/9; carcinoma of stomach; Thomas Robb
   and Anna Carr
Patrick, d. 4/12/1890 at 68; (Ireland; Ireland)
Robert K., d. 8/18/1925 at 9/1/29 in S. Portland, ME; lobar pneumonia;
   Benjamin L. Farley and Emily J. Kistermann
Thomas W., d. 8/26/1892 at –; catarrh of bowels; b. Dover; (Ireland; -----)
Wilda P., d. 2/24/1915 at 22/2/24; tuberculosis of lungs; Thomas Peltier
   and Alice E. Cartier

FARMER,
Sarah M., d. 2/13/1893 at 41; tumor on brain; b. Strafford; (Barrington;
   Strafford)

FARNHAM,
child, d. 5/28/1931 at –; stillborn
Alice S., d. 8/27/1932 at 74/7/7; cerebral hemorrhage
Betsey, d. 6/3/1891 at 70/7/6; single; David Farnham (Lebanon, ME) and
   Elizabeth Burrows (Lebanon, ME)
Charles H., d. 11/7/1935 at 80/9/11 in Boston, MA; cancer of stomach
Elizabeth A., d. 12/11/1933 at 73/6/5; coronary embolism
Fred L., d. 4/16/1920 at 61/11/12; natural causes; Daniel Farnham
Fred L., d. 11/19/1923 at 78/2/9; chr. inter. nephritis; Frederick Farnham
   and Olive Whitten
George W., d. 5/9/1916 at 97/1/25; senility; Jeremiah Farnham and
   Martha Perkins
Henry C., d. 4/6/1935 at 87/7/11 in Brentwood; senility
Horace A., d. 11/8/1919 at 63/6/18 in Malden, MA; chr. interstitial nephritis
James M., d. 5/18/1923 at 87; chr. inter. nephritis; John Farnham and
   Fanny Wood
Martha M., d. 4/11/1935 at 74/5/16; accidentally burned
Mary F., d. 3/16/1905 at 64/6/25; acute congestion of lungs; PH
Mary M., d. 11/–/1902 at – in Manchester; gastro-enteritis; SM
Moses P., d. 4/18/1911 at 86/6/18; bronchitis; Jeremy Farnham and
   Martha Perkins
Rose B., d. 12/24/1922 at 69 in Berwick, ME; dbl. lobar pneumonia
Susan Frances, d. 2/24/1920 at 67 in Somersworth; chronic myocarditis
Walter E., d. 8/25/1929 at 59/3/20; nar. of portal veins; Edwin P. Farnham
   and Mary C. Ricker

FARNUM,
Lydia R., d. 7/31/1925 at 82/11/5; senility; David Farnum and Rhoda C.
   Rolfe

FARRAN,
Mary E., d. 7/7/1904 at 51/6/12; valvular disease of heart

FARRAND,
Edward E., d. 12/28/1926 at 56/4; pulmonary tuberculosis; Leander Farrand and Elizabeth Rogers
Horace L., d. 12/11/1932 at 65/8/7; coronary embolism
Ruth H., d. 4/7/1925 at 1/11/1; catarrhal pneumonia; Horace L. Farrand and Adeline M. Daniels

FARRAR,
Annie F., d. 7/27/1927 at 73/0/12 in San Diego, CA; arterio sclerosis; Joseph E. Kimball and Annie Bennett
Leander C., d. 4/16/1931 at 84/8/20; cerebral embolism
Orris W., d. 6/10/1916 at 65 in Gaylord, MI; suicide
Ralph W., d. 10/28/1915 at 28/2/11; pulmonary tuberculosis; Leander Farrar and Emma Perkins
Sarah E., d. 4/11/1931 at 81/6/8; cerebral hemorrhage

FARRELL,
Ann, d. 7/8/1889 at 42; mill operative; single; b. Ireland; Peter Farrell (Ireland) and Elizabeth Murray (Ireland)
Annie, d. 3/15/1936 at 56; carcinoma of liver
Annie L., d. 1/29/1908 at 28/10 in Haverhill, MA; Bright's Disease
Bridget, d. 7/2/1919 at 51; disease of heart; John Gilhuly and Ann -----
Elizabeth, d. 11/16/1895 at 28; typhoid fever; b. Ireland; SM
Ida, d. 8/31/1934 at 78; cerebral hemorrhage
Maurice, d. 2/24/1890 at 45 in Boston, MA
Michael, d. 2/14/1913 at –; heart dilitation; Peter Farrell and Elizabeth Murray
Peter, d. 3/21/1905 at 2 in Quebec, Canada; collapsus
Rose, d. 2/19/1913 at 67; carcinoma uteri; Patrick McBennett and Mary McNally
Thomas, d. 2/11/1909 at 53 in Concord; enterocolitis; Thomas Farrell and Liza Hughes

FARREN,
Albert H., d. 10/9/1906 at 0/4/15; tubercular meningitis; PH

FARRINGTON,
Mary A., d. 7/30/1892 at 66; pulmonary phthisis

FARRON,
Jane, d. 2/8/1928 at –; chronic endocarditis

Joseph, d. 7/8/1914 at 59; aneurism of aorta
Joseph J., d. 8/30/1906 at 25/7; acute catarrhal enteritis; SM

FARROW,
Elizabeth, d. 6/6/1925 at 64; chr. inter. nephritis; John Cassidy and Marg. McCarragher

FAULKNER,
Christine, d. 7/23/1920 at 0/0/1 in Lawrence, MA; marasmus
Martha, d. 2/27/1900 at 86; pneumonia; PH

FAXON,
Charles A., d. 11/7/1910 at 70/2/18; acute indigestion; Ebenezer Faxon and Olive Thompson
Ellen A., d. 6/23/1913 at 70/7/25; chronic myocarditis; Walter Ham and Nancy Morrill
Ellen F., d. 1/7/1932 at 87/11/13 in Auburn, ME; chronic myocarditis
Ruby A., d. 6/9/1924 at 73/0/8 in Auburn, ME; cerebral hemorrhage

FAY,
Mary V., d. 8/28/1934 at 48/3/19; acute uraemia

FEATHER,
Herbert, d. 10/11/1937 at 54/9/12; acute ang. pectoris

FECTEAU,
Arthur, d. 7/7/1926 at 66/2/6; chronic myocarditis; Rephael Fecteau and --- -- Bourgeois
Desange M., d. 6/14/1935 at 75/4/9; cerebral hemorrhage
Edwedge, d. 9/11/1914 at 48; carcinoma of stomach; Prudent St. Jean and A. Tremblay
Fred, d. 8/14/1887 at 0/11/16; b. Dover; Michael Fecteau (Canada) and Emma (Canada)
George, d. 1/29/1892 at 2; diarrhoea; b. Dover; (Canada; Canada)
Michel, d. 6/4/1934 at 81/3; arteriosclerosis

FEENAN,
Mary, d. 2/12/1908 at 74; bronchitis, heart disease

FEENEY,
child, d. 10/--/1895 at -- in Wolfeboro; PH
child, d. 11/20/1901 at --; stillborn; SM
child, d. 3/4/1914 at --; stillborn; Edward J. Feeney and Louise A. Goodwin
Bernard, d. 4/20/1928 at 77; broncho pneumonia

Catherine, d. 12/4/1909 at 45/5; rheumatism; Thomas Battles and
   Catherine Clarke
Catherine C., d. 4/22/1921 at 52/3/8 in Boston, MA; post operative shock
Dominick, d. 2/11/1915 at 40; alcoholic gastritis; Dominick Feeney and
   Margaret Haley
Edward J., d. 1/29/1930 at 45; acute endocarditis; Owen Feeney and Mary
   Neville
James J., d. 4/27/1926 at 61 in Portsmouth; lobar pneumonia
Katie, d. 7/1/1898 at –; meningitis; b. Dover; SM
Mary, d. 5/23/1887 at 27; married; b. Ireland; Edmund Neville (Ireland)
   and Margaret McMahon (Ireland)
Nellie B., d. 2/3/1891 at 0/6/19; ––––– (Ireland) and K. Nettles (Ireland)
Nora E., d. 9/4/1930 at 61/5/9; cancer of liver; Patrick Feeney and
   Margaret Fay
Winnifred, d. 11/10/1905 at 64; heart disease; SM

FEINBERG,
child, d. 11/20/1931 at –; stillborn

FELCH,
Frederick T., d. 8/11/1890 at 7/10/23; Frank Felch (MA) and Dora Simpson
   (Dover)

FELKER,
child, d. 12/29/1936 at –; prematurity
Albert H., d. 6/18/1895 at 41; chronic alcoholism; b. Rochester; buried in
   Rochester
Elias V., d. 7/5/1909 at 58; acute nephritis
Eliza W., d. 9/3/1913 at 81/11/22; diabetes mellitus; Ebenezer Hanson and
   Polly Hanson
Ellery M., d. 12/6/1925 at 57/10/1; gangrene of hand; Martin V. B. Felker
   and Cordelia J. Locke
John Frank, d. 11/11/1914 at 55/9/7; tuberculosis; John W. Felker and
   Mary J. Page
John W., d. 8/30/1913 at 77/1/22; injury; John Felker
Jonathan K., d. 6/12/1914 at 86/4/19; ch. valvular disease; Levi Felker and
   Sally F. Nichols
Mary J., d. 4/6/1909 at 75; old age; James Page and Mary Furber
William P., d. 8/9/1934 at 69 in Haverhill, MA; arteriosclerosis

FELLOWS,
Cora E., d. 5/30/1887 at 15/11/15; b. Barrington; Charles S. Fellows
   (Wakefield) and Anna L. Sherburne (Barrington)
Eleanor K., d. 7/27/1917 at 0/0/1; premature birth; Carroll E. Fellows and
   Ruth V. Kane

Oscar F., d. 1/6/1934 at 83/9/5; broncho pneumonia

FELOMES,
Margaret, d. 12/7/1911 at –; purpura hemorrhagica; George Felomes and Starv'a Coragairoula

FENDERSON,
Cora W., d. 10/23/1924 at 51/3; carcinoma of intestine; Oliver Elwell and Martha Brown

FENIKER,
Ann T., d. 4/8/1899 at 64; Bright's disease; PH

FENNER,
Albert Gallatin, d. 3/3/1891 at 77/3/3; married; Elhanan W. Fenner (Providence, RI) and Julia A. White (Taunton, MA)
Benjamin W., d. 1/14/1905 at 58 in St. Louis, MO; dilitation of heart
Frank, d. 11/2/1893 at 21; accident
Mary H., d. 4/18/1899 at 89 in Lewiston, ME; Bright's disease; PH

FENNESSY,
Mary, d. 2/3/1922 at – in Providence, RI; chronic nephritis

FENTON,
child, d. 8/24/1920 at –; asphyxia of labor; John Fenton and Ellen Piper
Annie, d. 6/3/1922 at 50 in Manchester; strangulated hernia
Catherine M., d. 2/23/1918 at 0/2/2; athrepsia from malnutrition; Daniel J. Fenton and Mary F. Rossiter
Daniel, d. 8/12/1893 at 50; concussion of the brain; b. Ireland; (Ireland; Ireland)
Joseph E., d. 7/5/1919 at 0/0/21; premature birth; Daniel J. Fenton and Mary F. Rossiter
Julia, d. 2/2/1905 at 65; la grippe
Madeline D., d. 6/14/1919 at –; premature birth; Daniel J. Fenton and Mary F. Rossiter
Patrick H., d. 4/26/1936 at 76/9/3; cerebral apoplexy
William, d. 7/11/1891 at 0/9; William Fenton (NH) and Annie Riley (Dover)
William D., d. 6/17/1921 at 54; probably alcoholic poisoning; Daniel Fenton and Julia McCabe

FENUCANE,
William E., d. 11/6/1889 at 8/7/20; b. Lawrence, MA; Daniel Fenucane (Ireland) and Kate Cash (Ireland)

FERGUSON,
Charles T., d. 1/25/1936 at 92/8/5; gen. arteriosclerosis
David P., d. 5/15/1929 at 81/1/13; arterio sclerosis; Alexander Ferguson and Phoebe Peacock
Herbert, d. 8/30/1928 at 48/3/15; angina pectoris; Isaac Ferguson and Louise Dill
Jane, d. 10/10/1908 at 72; cerebral hemorrhage
John W., d. 5/21/1890 at 39/7/11; single; John Ferguson (Sandwich) and Hannah Wallace (Moultonboro)
Reuben, d. 8/17/1900 at 75; old age and paralysis; PH
Sabina W., d. 9/30/1926 at 86/5/11; lobar pneumonia; Daniel Wingate and Sabina Tibbetts
William, d. 6/2/1928 at 71/9/13; arterio sclerosis

FERMANI,
Anastasia, d. 1/22/1913 at –; acute pneumonia; Starvos Fermani and Georgia Katsui

FERMINE,
Mary A., d. 7/8/1933 at 72/10/23; pernicious anemia

FERNALD,
Alice M., d. 5/19/1922 at 82/1/29; nephritis; Isaac Leighton and Abigail Lougee
Alpheus, d. 12/29/1893 at 71; inanition following la grippe; b. Newfield, ME; (Newfield, ME; ----)
Arthur Herbert, d. 4/5/1924 at 23/5/2 in Boston, MA; peritonitis
Avis M., d. 10/30/1887 at 71/8/16 in Tuftonboro; married
Charles A., d. 6/29/1915 at 77/0/21; valvular heart disease; Issac Furnald (sic) and Mary Drew
Cylena A. D., d. 12/3/1919 at 61/5/22 in Lee; acute bronchitis
Edwin L., d. 5/4/1890 at 44/7/21; married; William H. K. Fernald (Kittery, ME) and Martha S. Perkins (Barrington)
Elizabeth L., d. 10/11/1901 at – in Lyman, ME; paralysis; PH
Ella Adelia, d. 8/21/1913 at 62/6; carcinoma of stomach; Ephraim M. Jones and Adelia A. Moulton
Emma J., d. 8/30/1935 at 80/4/19; coronary thrombosis
Enoch F., d. 8/4/1901 at 74/1/8 in Madbury; diabetes mellitus; PH
Ernest W., d. 3/6/1902 at 26/9/18; erysipelas; buried in Kittery, ME
Fannie, d. 12/17/1925 at 65; arterio sclerosis; William Ham
Hancy M., d. 5/30/1921 at 87/8/22; mitral insufficiency; Dorman Burrill and Hannah P. Copeland
Isa B., d. 5/10/1913 at 66/5/23; cerebral hemorrhage; George W. Caswell and Mary A. Kenniston
James E., d. 7/9/1935 at 82/7/10; carcinoma of colon

Joseph H., d. 3/1/1904 at 74/11/10; apoplexy, cerebral; PH
Julia A., d. 10/28/1927 at 82; chr. intest. nephritis
Julia Alice, d. 6/22/1936 at 71/9/12; arteriosclerosis
Juliette, d. 10/10/1926 at 84/11/2 in Madbury; chronic arthritis
Kingman, d. 6/10/1918 at 70/11/26; fatty degeneration of heart; William H.
    K. Fernald and Martha S. Perkins
Laura I., d. 11/21/1935 at 56/4/22; intestinal obstruction
Loren S., d. 1/4/1935 at 75/2/16 in Lee; apoplexy
Martha S., d. 6/17/1894 at 75; ovarian tumor; b. Somersworth; buried in
    family lot
Mary A., d. 5/18/1899 at 87 in Boston, MA; old age; PH
Mary A., d. 3/24/1922 at 72/3/21; cirrhosis of liver; Lewis Thompson and
    Elizabeth Locke
Matthew C., d. 10/12/1931 at 91/9/8; chronic myocarditis
Oscar L., d. 11/18/1921 at 67 in Lynn, MA; pulmonary tuberculosis
Percival H., d. 12/24/1926 at 51/9/10 in Newburyport, MA; angina pectoris
Sarah A., d. 8/12/1921 at 79/0/4; cerebral hemorrhage; Robert Fernald
    and Aphia Coffin
Sarah E., d. 2/17/1902 at 51/3/2; cerebral hemorrhage; PH
Shepleigh T., d. 2/19/1926 at 68; myocarditis; William H. K. Fernald
William Edgar, d. 5/21/1937 at 68/4/0; empy. gall bladder

FERNS,
child, d. 9/21/1911 at –; stillborn; Elizabeth Ferns
Alice A., d. 8/10/1905 at 2/6/13; whooping cough
Mary, d. 10/18/1907 at 1/10/10; pneumonia; Augustine Ferns and
    Elizabeth Sunderland

FERRIN,
Abbie S., d. 1/28/1899 at 63 in Natick, MA; la grippe; PH
Allen J., d. 5/23/1899 at –; cerebral congestion; PH
Allen J., d. 10/16/1900 at <1; catarrhal pneumonia; PH
Delphine, d. 7/18/1907 at 52; typhoid fever; —— Boufford
Emma I., d. 3/4/1914 at 39/4/9 in Rollinsford; valvular disease of heart
Levi E., d. 11/30/1904 at 68/8 in New Ipswich; valvular disease of heart;
    PH

FERRIS,
Annie, d. 12/5/1922 at 59; gangrenous hernia; Robert Ferris and Mary
    McNichol
John, d. 12/17/1926 at 70/2/10 in Concord; senility
Peter, d. 7/6/1911 at 47; heart failure; William Ferris and Mary Ferris

FFROST,
Margaret B., d. 10/6/1916 at 70/6/12 in Durham; anaemia pernicious; William P. Ffrost and Mary N. Hoole

FIDDER,
Mary A., d. 12/13/1925 at 85/9/6; diarrhea and enteritis; Stephen Eaton and Almira Hatch

FIFE,
John, d. 4/1/1896 at 66; heart disease

FILES,
William J., d. 2/9/1893 at 38; died in Strafford Co. Asylum fire

FILTEAU,
Eugene, d. 3/16/1928 at 56/11/14; intercranial hemorrhage; Fortunat Filteau and Sara Coulombe

FINDLEY,
Margaret R., d. 12/24/1930 at 93/8/25; cerebral hemorrhage; Thomas Reed and Jane Walker

FINLEY,
Harold, d. 3/12/1897 at 0; pneumonia; b. Dover; PH
Wallace S., d. 2/3/1897 at 8; catarrhal pneumonia; b. East Cambridge, MA; PH

FINN,
child, d. 1/10/1907 at –; stillborn; William Finn and Annie -----
William P., d. 9/22/1936 at 77; chr. fib. tuberculosis

FINNEGAN,
Hilda H., d. 2/12/1929 at 30/11/18 in Portsmouth; pneumonia, oedema
Susan, d. 3/8/1923 at 71/7/7 in Concord; mitral regurgitation

FINNIN,
Marlene J., d. 10/14/1934 at 0/1/4; prematurity

FINNUCANE,
Cornelius, d. 5/10/1899 at 24; phthisis; SM

FINUCANE,
Catherine P., d. 10/30/1914 at 70; acute bronchitis; Edward Cash

Daniel, d. 4/2/1908 at 56; gastric ulcer; William Finucane and Catherine Ryan
Mary, d. 9/5/1921 at 71; neurasthenia; Thomas Sheehy and Mary Geaney
Mary, d. 5/27/1923 at 38/10; peritonitis
Michael J., d. 12/18/1926 at 43/8/29 in Lawrence, MA; tubercular meningitis
Thomas J., d. 9/17/1937 at 60*

FIRTH,
Harold, d. 6/26/1905 at 14/8; heart failure; PH

FISH,
Bertha N., d. 12/5/1915 at 41/0/16; tuberculosis of lungs; Charles Gowen and Sarah E. Littlefield
Susan, d. 2/18/1901 at 84; senility; buried in New Castle

FISHER,
child, d. 4/7/1897 at 0; infancy; b. Dover; PH
Albert C., d. 11/5/1933 at 24/5/21; fracture of skull
Andrew, d. 6/30/1913 at 12/9/7; cerebral meningitis; Andrew Fisher and Margaret Connell
Andrew, d. 2/19/1918 at 55/6/4; mitral insufficiency; William J. Fisher and Betsy White
Charlotte E., d. 4/14/1898 at 18; consumption; b. Dover; PH
Frank Y., d. 11/26/1914 at 76/10/7 in Boston, MA; Francis H. Fisher and Laura L. -----
Margaret A., d. 5/15/1905 at 0/4/12; tuberculosis; PH
Margaret A., d. 1/26/1937 at 70/0/0*; b. Ireland
Mary, d. 6/27/1901 at 27; typhoid fever
Mary L., d. 1/18/1924 at 70/3/5 in Hudson, MA; chr. Brights disease
Samuel C., d. 7/10/1909 at 86/7/12; senility; Mathew Fisher and Jane C. Christie
Sarah J., d. 2/2/1898 at 67; apoplexy; b. Dover; PH

FISKE,
George W., d. 12/9/1929 at 77/6/23; valv. heart disease; John Fiske and Elizabeth Warren
Moses W., d. 3/24/1887 at 58 in Dayton, OH; actor; married

FITZGERALD,
Dennis J., d. 2/28/1919 at 24/5/14; pulmonary tuberculosis; John Fitzgerald and Ellen McCarty
Elizabeth A., d. 10/5/1909 at 31; pulmonary tuberculosis; James Fitzgerald and Honora Sweeney
Ellen, d. 8/4/1928 at –; myocarditis; Dennis McCarthy and Julia Drew

Frank W., d. 8/31/1898 at 0; cholera infantum; b. Dover; SM
Grover B., d. 6/19/1924 at 39/4/7 in Stoneham, MA
Honora, d. 1/25/1910 at 71/8/5; senility; John Sweeney and Mary Horrigan
James, d. 1/27/1890 at 2/7/5; John Fitzgerald (Ireland) and Ellen McCarty (Ireland)
Jno., d. 4/11/1890 at 3; ----- (US) and Nellie Ford (US)
John, d. 10/12/1899 at 40; typhoid fever; SM
Leo. P., d. 8/14/1933 at 27/1/14 in Kittery, ME; gastric hemorrhage
Patrick, d. 8/21/1898 at –; railroad accident; buried in Lowell, MA
Thomas, d. 4/18/1890 at 1/1; Pat Fitzgerald (US) and N. Hughes (Ireland)
William, d. 8/30/1890 at 28; single; Edmund Fitzgerald (Ireland) and ----- (Ireland)

FITZHARRIS,
child, d. 4/4/1891 at –; John FitzHarris (Dover) and Margaret Hughes (Dover)
Edward, d. 1/2/1910 at 20/4/2 in Stoneham, MA; consumption
John D., d. 2/9/1898 at 0; anaemia; b. Dover; SM
Margaret, d. 3/20/1899 at 71; pneumonia; SM
Margaret, d. 1/6/1935 at 62 in Andover, MA; endocarditis
Mary, d. 11/13/1907 at 33; pulmonary tuberculosis; Thomas Finucane and Mary Sheehy
Mary T., d. 1/25/1907 at 0/6/18; chronic pneumonia; Stephen Fitzharris and Mary Finucane
Patrick, d. 11/28/1903 at 30 in New York; phthisis
Stephen, d. 12/19/1913 at 54/2/18; oedema of lungs; Patrick Fitzharris and Margaret -----

FITZPATRICK,
Edward, d. 9/8/1889 at 0/0/14; b. Dover; John B. Fitzpatrick (NB) and Mary E. Sweeney (MA)
Lula, d. 8/19/1890 at 0/3/22; James Fitzpatrick (England) and Maria Smith (England)

FLAGG,
Edward H., d. 4/9/1911 at 47/3/6; pneumonia; Joshua G. Flagg and Emily C. Hussey
Ellen Frances, d. 3/14/1916 at 75/11/12 in Somerville, MA; William Flagg and Harriet Heard
Emily C., d. 8/21/1909 at 72/2/16 in Milton; pulmonary oedema; Moses Hussey and Clarissa Ham
Emily M., d. 8/23/1895 at 41 in Pawtucket, RI; pulmonary tuberculosis; buried in Dover
Emma D., d. 12/6/1922 at 85/0/6 in Portsmouth; cerebral embolism
Helen V., d. 12/2/1931 at 66/3/13 in Providence, RI; cerebral hemorrhage

Joshua G., d. 4/3/1907 at 72/3/29; posterior poliomyelitis; William Flagg
   and Harriet Getchell
Mahala F., d. 4/11/1906 at 78; heart disease; PH

FLAHERTY,
Catherine, d. 2/10/1936 at 80; pernicious anemia
Della T., d. 10/15/1936 at 75*
Martin M., d. 1/25/1897 at 7; scarletina; b. Lynn, MA; SM
Mary, d. 2/26/1897 at 5; scarlet fever; b. Dover; SM
Mary, d. 1/30/1918 at 51; ascites; Michael Hughes and Mary Murray
Patrick R., d. 4/18/1936 at 43/7/19 in Northampton, MA; tuberculosis,
   pulmonary

FLANAGAN,
child, d. 3/3/1920 at –; premature birth; S. A. Flanagan and Ellen M. White
Catherine, d. 6/1/1897 at 40; pulmonary phthisis; b. Ireland; SM
Catherine J., d. 7/8/1894 at –; cholera infantum; b. Dover; SM
James, d. 2/17/1931 at 65; chronic endocarditis
John, d. 10/15/1894 at 46; tuberculosis mesentry; b. Ireland; SM
John A., d. 4/14/1922 at 56/5/9; uraemia; John Flanagan and Mary
   Mahoney
John Joseph, d. 1/13/1921 at 0/0/7; hemophilia; Joseph F. Flanagan and
   Alice McCoole
John M., d. 4/16/1924 at 50/11/18; carcinoma of colon; John Flanagan
   and Mary Powers
John P., d. 8/24/1911 at 0/7/26; atelectosis; James Flanagan and Rose
   McDonnell
Joseph, d. 7/24/1901 at 27; tuberculosis; SM
Leo, d. 3/31/1914 at 15/10/19; electrocution; James Flanagan and Mary
   Gallagher
Margarette, d. 8/3/1922 at 51; cancer of stomach; Patrick McManus and
   Mary Quinn
Mary, d. 1/1/1906 at 61 in Brookline, MA; carcinoma of uteri; SM
Mary C., d. 12/30/1894 at –; pneumonia; b. Dover; SM
Owen, d. 1/31/1937 at 79/3/18*
Robert, d. 11/14/1932 at 6/4/13; septicaemia
Rose, d. 2/19/1926 at 64; broncho pneumonia; Patrick Hughes and Sarah
   Barrett
Rose B., d. 1/28/1910 at 0/2/23; broncho-pneumonia; James Flanagan
   and Rose McDonald

FLANAHAN,
James, d. 12/4/1909 at 38; tuberculosis; Frances ----- and Alice Carragher

FLANDERS,
child, d. 6/24/1924 at –; stillborn; Earle S. Flanders and Margaret ----
Abbie C., d. 3/17/1910 at 86/5/9; hemiplegia; ---- Champion and Elizabeth Nudd
Asenath W., d. 4/27/1906 at 70/7/29; hematemesis; PH
Emma J., d. 9/16/1928 at 72; arterio sclerosis; Job Flanders and Abbie ----
Eva E., d. 8/1/1918 at 21/11/9 in S. Berwick, ME; puerperal albuminuria
George H., d. 4/2/1915 at 81/7/8; cerebral hemorrhage; Ezekiel Flanders and Rosalie Glidden
Job, d. 9/15/1893 at 74; paralysis; b. Chelsea, VT; (Salisbury; Eaton)

FLANIGAN,
Alton B., d. 9/10/1905 at 0/10; chronic entero-colitis; SM

FLANNAGAN,
Annie J., d. 3/26/1922 at 53; cancer of uterus; Owen Callahan
Cornelius, d. 5/31/1899 at 3; membraneous croup; SM
Hugh, d. 9/26/1901 at 54; SM
Richard, d. 2/1/1909 at 53; heart disease

FLANNIGAN,
Anne E., d. 10/5/1895 at 0; anaemia; b. Dover; SM
Edward, d. 7/27/1893 at –; heart disease; b. Dover; (ME; Ireland)
John, d. 4/24/1899 at 4; membraneous croup; SM
John P., d. 1/15/1890 at 0/4/24; John Flannigan (Berwick, ME) and Rose Hughes (Ireland)
Mary, d. 7/27/1905 at 0/9/5; cholera infantum

FLARETY,
Thomas E., d. 11/24/1926 at 67 in Lynn, MA; apoplexy

FLAVARIS,
Dorothy C., d. 9/6/1934 at 28/0/12; pueperal sepsis

FLAYHAN,
child, d. 11/1/1932 at –; asphyxia of labor
Mary, d. 3/28/1934 at 70; cerebral hemorrhage

FLAYHEM,
Nossif, d. 4/9/1926 at 0/7/1; broncho pneumonia; Michael Flayhem and Elizabeth ----

FLEER,
child, d. 10/17/1894 at –; faulty development; b. Dover; PH

FLEMING,
James H., d. 12/7/1912 at 0/4/1; pneumonia; George E. Fleming and
  Deborah M. Swain
Martin, d. 2/12/1899 at 38; chronic alcoholism; SM
Nellie, d. 11/6/1890 at 21; single
Onora, d. 2/13/1890 at 56/2/19; married; Michael Sheon and Leonora D.
Robert, d. 3/11/1895 at 32; pneumonia; b. Dover; SM

FLEURIE,
Alice, d. 1/31/1934 at 67/0/22; carcinoma of bladder

FLINN,
Alfred R., d. 12/3/1900 at 44; brain tumor; PH

FLINT,
Mary A., d. 1/14/1909 at 62 in Tewksbury, MA; ileocolitis
Richard L., d. 2/13/1927 at 0/9; malnutrition; Daniel Flint and Hazel M. Hill
Walter H., d. 9/28/1896 at 6; scarlet fever; b. Portsmouth; buried in
  Portsmouth

FLOOD,
Homer, d. 10/13/1917 at 2/3/15; toxemia; Homer Flood and Mamie
  Cummings
John J., d. 12/21/1888 at 30/8/17; laborer; married; b. Dover; John Flood
  (Ireland) and Eliza Cooey (Ireland)

FLOWERS,
Robert, d. 11/28/1931 at 0/4/11; acute bronchitis

FLOYD,
Kathryn E., d. 6/23/1917 at 24/0/4; septicemia; LeB. S. Floyd and Jennie
  B. Geldart

FLUET,
Mary Ann, d. 6/6/1911 at 93/11; cerebral apoplexy; John Ewing and
  Elizabeth Ritter

FLYNN,
child, d. 8/17/1903 at –; stillborn; SM
Annie E., d. 8/14/1936 at 44/9/23; acute appendicitis
Charles, d. 7/22/1926 at 64/2/25; cancer of rectum
Daniel, d. 1/23/1924 at 64; angina pectoris; David Flynn and ----- Brennan
David, d. 6/5/1918 at 62/11/23; traumatic injury; David Flynn and Joanna
  Drew

Dennis M., d. 6/25/1905 at 18/7/6; pulmonary tuberculosis
Ellen, d. 9/24/1921 at 71/6/20; cerebral apoplexy; Michael Rossiter and
    Mary Kelley
Gertrude, d. 9/20/1890 at 11/3/4; William A. Flynn (St. Andrews) and Mary
    Shea (Portland, ME)
Hannah C., d. 9/26/1930 at 50; lobar pneumonia; David Flynn and Ellen
    Rossiter
Helen C., d. 10/5/1915 at 21/7/18 in Georgetown, MA; phthisis pulmonalis;
    Thomas Flynn and Mary Rhodes
Helen Therese, d. 7/20/1927 at 0/0/2; atelectasis; William N. Flynn and
    Bessie G. Finucane
Honora, d. 3/26/1917 at 53; cerebral hemorrhage; Colman Driscoll and
    Anna McCarthy
Imelda M., d. 1/14/1922 at 0/0/7; cephalahematoma; William N. Flynn and
    Bessie G. Finucane
John, d. 9/4/1900 at 55; pneumonia; SM
Joseph G., d. 2/16/1907 at 1/0/11; bronchitis; Daniel Flynn
Joseph J., d. 1/12/1911 at 11/4/9 in Rollinsford; pulmonary hemorrhage;
    Thomas Flynn and Mary Rhodes
Mabel, d. 1/26/1935 at 48; bronchial pneumonia
Mary A., d. 7/20/1889 at 0/8/21; b. Amesbury, MA; Daniel Flynn (Ireland)
    and Mary Cameron (Ireland)
Nellie, d. 1/23/1935 at 81/3 in Concord; arteriosclerosis
Norman, d. 11/17/1924 at 0/0/1; premature birth; Raymond D. Flynn and
    Alice Grenier
Timothy, d. 2/26/1925 at 66; chr. int. nephritis; John Flynn and Mary
    Quinn

FODY,
Bridget, d. 3/7/1888 at 0/9; b. Dover; Patrick Fody (Ireland) and Mary
    Finnerance (Ireland)
Elizabeth, d. 2/24/1908 at 57; intestinal obstruction; Philip Mooney and
    Elizabeth McCone
Mary, d. 4/28/1902 at 52/4; pneumonia; SM
Mary B., d. 9/19/1900 at 23; typhoid fever; SM
Patrick, d. 4/14/1927 at 69; arterio sclerosis; Patrick Fody and Mary Dyer
Sarah E., d. 9/29/1934 at 42; carcinoma gastric
Thomas, d. 3/30/1922 at 37 in Lawrence, MA; over stim. alcoholism
Thomas, d. 4/7/1930 at 82; chr. int. nephritis; Patrick Fody and Mary Dyer

FOGARTY,
Martin J., d. 11/6/1932 at 45/8/18; Ludwig's angina

FOGERTY,
child, d. 10/28/1920 at –; premature birth; William C. Fogerty and
   Elizabeth A. Donavan
child, d. 10/4/1922 at –; stillborn; Leonard Fogerty and Laura Plourde
James, d. 3/27/1904 at 63; angina pectoris; SM
John, d. 5/28/1912 at 64/6/18; general debility; Edward Fogerty and Mary
   Ennis
Mary A., d. 7/11/1908 at 69/10/21 in Manchester; acute enteritis
Richard Henry, d. 4/12/1923 at 2/2/23; mastoiditis - operated; John E.
   Fogerty and Elizabeth R. Mason

FOGG,
Eliza J., d. 8/27/1905 at 83/7/22; nephritis; PH
Elmer W., d. 6/13/1917 at 55/5/9; pneumonia; Hilliard F. Fogg and Ann M.
   Bennett
Fred, d. 10/15/1931 at 71/2/17; apoplexy
John W., d. 7/11/1899 at 63; softening of the brain; PH

FOLDS,
Bridget, d. 9/29/1906 at 63 in Manchester; heart disease; SM
Christopher J., d. 8/26/1902 at 48/8/4 in Newmarket; consumption; SM

FOLEY,
Ann, d. 9/24/1889 at 29; housewife; b. Ireland; P. McKee (Ireland) and
   Cath. McNally (Ireland)
Emma, d. 11/7/1908 at 0/0/21; cholera infantum; Emma Foley
Francis, d. 11/27/1889 at 0/10; b. Dover; Hugh Foley (Dover) and A.
   McKee (Ireland)
Joseph, d. 10/1/1918 at 33/2; lobar pneumonia; Joseph Foley and Mary
   Lacombe
Lignare, d. 10/3/1918 at 36; lobar pneumonia; William Foley and Mary
   Lacombe
Mary, d. 1/22/1888 at 48; weaver; married; b. Ireland; P. Carraghan
   (Ireland) and C. Flannagan (Ireland)
Mary, d. 9/30/1918 at 55; influenza; Henry Lacombe and ----- Doyon
Michael, d. 10/1/1935 at 63; arteriosclerosis
William, d. 4/28/1889 at 40; laborer; widower; b. Ireland; (Ireland; Ireland)
William, d. 10/8/1918 at 62; influenza; Michael Foley

FOLLAND,
child, d. 6/24/1903 at –; stillborn
Bridget, d. 12/4/1920 at 64 in Kennebunk, ME
Charles, d. 7/16/1908 at –; premature birth; Charles Folland and Eva M.
   Baker
Charles E., d. 3/5/1906 at 2/1/17; pneumonia

Charles Henry, d. 8/27/1912 at 36/11/26; accident; John Folland and Mary Hanna
Elizabeth, d. 3/8/1904 at 22/8/30; phthisis pulmonalis; SM
John, d. 12/12/1933 at 84/6/25; chronic myocarditis

FOLLETT,
Aaron H., d. 8/8/1890 at 0/10; James Follett (Dover) and Eliza Miller (Dover)
Andrew J., d. 10/16/1899 at –; croup; PH
Arthur E., d. 10/23/1918 at 24/9/27 in Thomaston, ME; pneumonia; Sadie Lindsay
Clarence A., d. 1/25/1900 at 3; pneumonia; PH
Elizabeth, d. 12/7/1913 at 32; tuberculosis; John Haughey and Margaret Murray
Eva Lillie, d. 12/13/1891 at 0/5; Frank Follett (Dover) and Sarah Miller (Dover)
Frank, d. 9/28/1887 at 1/6/28; b. Dover; Frank Follett (Dover) and Sarah Miller (Dover)
Frank W., d. 6/20/1907 at 58/2/29; bronchorrhoea; James Follett and Sarah Giles
Herbert, d. 8/1/1893 at –; cholera infantum; b. Dover; (Dover; Dover)
James, d. 6/21/1893 at 5; accidental drowning; b. Dover; (Dover; Dover)
James W., d. 6/6/1893 at 76; pneumonia; b. Durham
James W., d. 7/26/1898 at 43; alcoholism; b. Dover; PH
M. May, d. 9/30/1891 at 0/5; ----- (Dover) and Eliza Miller (Dover)
Mary E., d. 11/25/1920 at 36/7/5; cancer of bowels; James ----- and Bridget Flemming
Nellie G., d. 1/28/1891 at 1/3/11; William Follett (Dover) and Sarah Miller (Dover)
Wilfred, d. 8/1/1907 at 0/0/25; cholera infantum; George Follett and Delvina Bisson

FOLSOM,
A. Wilbur, d. 8/17/1894 at 52 in Boston, MA; apoplexy
Andrew P., d. 7/18/1910 at 47/9/29; duodenal ulceration; Josiah B. Folsom and Olive B. Pierce
Annie B., d. 6/19/1926 at 53/2/27; lobar pneumonia; Josiah B. Folsom and Olive P. Pierce
Ernest B., d. 3/19/1915 at 41/1/3; apoplexy; Simeon B. Folsom and Susan A. Abbott
Frances Olive, d. 3/5/1915 at 0/0/3; pneumonia; William M. Folsom and Beulah Kimball
George L., d. 6/9/1915 at 72/0/25 in Manchester; apoplexy
Grace O., d. 4/11/1896 at 42 in Boston, MA; pneumonia
Harrison A., d. 2/22/1901 at 30 in Berlin, CT; suicide by pistol; PH

Harry L., d. 3/24/1930 at 63 in Brookline, MA; cerebral hemorrhage; Simeon B. Folsom and Clovia Mason

James L., d. 7/13/1937 at 83 in Boston, MA; carcinoma of colon (see following entry)

James L., d. 7/13/1937 at 83/5*; b. Somerville, MA (see preceding entry)

Josiah B., d. 8/17/1889 at 73/5/15; merchant; married; b. Stratham; Simeon Folsom (Exeter) and Mary Leavitt (Effingham)

L. Ellen, d. 5/9/1903 at 65/8/7 in Boston, MA; cerebral apoplexy; PH

Mary Leavitt, d. 4/3/1914 at 74/5/11; cerebral apoplexy; Abraham Folsom and Abigail S. Pierce

Olive B., d. 12/22/1921 at 92/6/22; senility; Andrew Pierce and Abigail Osborne

Simeon B., d. 10/11/1892 at 55; apoplexy, probably; b. E. Bridgewater; (NH; NH)

Susan A., d. 11/8/1918 at 76/5/18; asphyxiation, etc.; ----- Abbott and Elizabeth Robinson

William H., d. 2/6/1887 at 18/5/2; printer; single; b. Dover; Simeon B. Folsom (E. Bridgewater, MA) and Susan A. Abbott (Lowell, MA)

FONTAINE,
Leo, d. 10/5/1906 at 0/7/27; gastro-enteritis
Rose, d. 2/13/1935 at 45/9/13; acute lobar pneumonia
Zephir O., d. 3/9/1909 at 0/0/2; atelectasis; George Fontaine and Marie L. Dube

FOOTE,
George E., d. 12/14/1893 at 53; rheumatic meningitis, cerebral; b. Dover; (Danbury, CT; Londonderry)
J. Elmer, d. 5/10/1888 at 16/8/26; school boy; b. Dover; George E. Foote (Dover) and Sarah A. Rollins (Dover)
Margaret P., d. 8/25/1915 at 81; frac. cervical verterbrae; William L. Foote and Mary Wood
Sarah A., d. 8/27/1908 at 60/1/19 in Kennebunk, ME; chronic nephritis

FORBES,
Albert O., d. 10/30/1918 at 0/1/25; athrepsia; Robert H. Forbes and Frances Cunningham
Clara E., d. 3/14/1909 at 0/1/8; premature birth; James S. Forbes and Gladys L. Abbott
Patricia, d. 11/10/1934 at –; stillborn

FORCIER,
Annette, d. 7/11/1908 at 1/7/3; whooping cough; Arthur Fortier and Celina Carrier

FORD,
Alice Baker, d. 1/5/1931 at 50/7/15; lobar pneumonia
Anna Cornelia, d. 1/5/1921 at 0/6/21; cerebro-spinal men'gi's; Cornelius J. Ford and Mary I. McGlone
Betsey A., d. 6/16/1914 at 84/6/4; spondylitis; Jacob Ford and Sarah Mitchell
C. Baker, d. 5/22/1934 at 22/4/25; suicide carbon mon.
Carrie E., d. 6/13/1931 at 73; chronic endocarditis
Chester M., d. 11/26/1916 at 32/9/23; accident; Charles A. Ford and Lillian M. Diamond
Daniel, d. 4/24/1904 at 68/0/19; cancer of stomach; PH
Eva Gertrude, d. 4/8/1892 at –; pertussis - convulsions; (Lebanon; Lebanon)
George M., d. 1/10/1887 at –; pattern maker; married; b. VT; Gurdin Hamlet (VT) and Susan Ford
George W., d. 5/20/1910 at 85/0/12; heart disease; Benjamin A. Ford and Sally York
Gladys H., d. 11/9/1906 at 13/2/23; typhoid fever; buried in Berwick, ME
Hollis P., d. 12/12/1933 at 84/6/25; chronic myocarditis
Jacob S. M., d. 5/22/1920 at 84/6/28; natural causes; Jacob Ford and Sarah Mitchell
James W., d. 12/31/1920 at 71/8/21; mitral regurgitation; George W. Ford and Martha S. Cate
Jane, d. 8/28/1906 at 80/4/2; cholera morbus; PH
Mabel Isabel, d. 4/4/1925 at 30/9/12; tuberculosis of lungs; James McGlone and Mary A. Hester
Margaret S., d. 10/9/1926 at 64/5/16; chronic endocarditis; James Williamson and Margaret Irwin
Martha S., d. 2/15/1896 at 72; apoplexy; b. Barrington; buried at Dover Point
Richard, d. 12/8/1914 at 51; cancer of the liver; John Ford and Mary Hamilton
Sadie, d. 3/19/1908 at 38/10/20; pulmonary tuberculosis; George Knox and Hannah L. Cole
William H., d. 5/21/1907 at 66/7/25 in Milton; abscess of lung; Jacob Ford and Sarah Mitchell

FOREST,
John W., d. 7/12/1897 at 72 in Conway; Brights disease
Lydia, d. 12/22/1911 at 80/7; senility; Richard Arland and Louise Winkley

FORREST,
child, d. 9/16/1898 at 0; icterus neonatorum; b. Dover
John L., d. 1/28/1927 at 42/11/8; natural causes; John L. Forrest and Josephine Mills

FORSAITH,
Lizzie H., d. 6/1/1922 at 69/10/20; cerebral hemorrhage; Benjamin F. Evans and Mary E. Hall

FORTEALE,
Rasolet R., d. 3/27/1892 at 42; pneumonia; b. Canada; (Canada; Canada)

FORTIER,
child, d. 3/8/1902 at –; premature birth
Alphonsine, d. 1/17/1898 at 0; gastritis; b. Dover; SM
Arthur, d. 5/25/1902 at 22 in Salmon Falls River; accidental drowning; buried in Lawrence, MA
Elzear, d. 3/20/1900 at 4; influenza
George, d. 1/31/1912 at 56; gangrene of the lungs; Joseph Fortier and Julienne Marceau
Joseph, d. 3/15/1921 at 42/8 in Rochester; struck by train; George Fortier and Celina Duquette
Joseph, d. 7/8/1922 at –; premature birth; Theodule Fortier and Eva Dagenais
Joseph L. A., d. 11/26/1919 at 0/0/2; premature birth; Theodule Fortier and Eva Dagenais
Thomas, d. 10/5/1931 at 0/2/26; acute dermatitis

FORTIN,
Oviline, d. 1/22/1934 at 44; gangrene

FOSS,
child, d. 3/19/1897 at 0; inanition; b. Dover; buried in family lot
Ada, d. 1/14/1929 at 76/6 in Washington, DC; fracture of skull
Albert S., d. 7/7/1931 at 71/4/25; carcinoma intestines
Aletta Jane, d. 10/22/1935 at 71/9/1; coronary thrombosis
Alice, d. 2/28/1894 at 85; b. Strafford; PH
Alice, d. 7/25/1918 at 49/0/14 in Concord; mitral regurgitation, chr.; James W. Foss and Julia A. Littlefield
Alice J., d. 3/31/1898 at 67; nephritis; b. Strafford; PH
Almira N., d. 2/20/1893 at 63; paralysis; b. Rochester
Alonzo Melvin, d. 8/31/1922 at 75/1/8; carcinoma of prostate; Dennis Foss and Hannah Peavy
Alvah, d. 2/25/1909 at 60/3/22 in Rochester; cerebral hemorrhage
Ann M., d. 2/2/1905 at 82/4/26; gastric ulcer; PH
Annie, d. 3/5/1900 at 58 in Haverhill, MA; paralysis; PH
Annie H., d. 12/25/1898 at 38; nephritis; b. Biddeford, ME; PH
Annie M., d. 12/17/1930 at 71/8/9; intestinal flu; George Wicks and Hannah Freeman

Arthur, d. 12/29/1929 at 78/2/3; chr. Brights dis.; Ivory H. Foss and Harriet Quimby

Betsey B., d. 11/23/1909 at 73/2/18; acute nephritis; Andrew Huckings and Mary L. Jenness

Calixta A., d. 1/3/1927 at 93/2 in Stratham; cerebral hemorrhage

Carrie E., d. 8/24/1930 at 73 in Swanzey; valv. heart disease

Carrie G., d. 1/13/1929 at 79/2/27; chronic myocarditis; Walter Garside and Elizabeth Chadderton

Carroll, d. 9/11/1935 at 54/6/28; heart disease - angina ?

Catherine, d. 11/19/1934 at 64; intestinal obstruction

Charles H., d. 6/14/1934 at 83/2/12; chronic myocarditis

Charles K., d. 4/26/1924 at 67/3/5; chr. paren. nephritis; Charles R. Foss and Mary A. Squires

Charles R., d. 8/5/1906 at 70/5/4; paralysis, hemiplegia; PH

Clark, d. 8/27/1896 at 70 in Farmington; haematemesis

Clayton C., d. 7/5/1927 at 74/4/28; carcinoma of stomach; Stephen D. Foss and Mary A. Leighton

Clayton E., d. 6/14/1892 at 37; epilepsy; b. Barrington; (Great Falls; Strafford)

Cynthia D., d. 1/15/1889 at 71/10/11; housekeeper; widow; b. New Durham; Ambrose Tuttle (Middleton) and Nancy Frost (Milton)

Darius, d. 4/29/1898 at 68; cerebral apoplexy; b. Strafford; PH

Dennis, d. 12/24/1899 at 81; old age; PH

Dorothy E., d. 7/26/1920 at 8/9/5; acute appendicitis; Howard E. Foss and Millie Grant

Drew, d. 11/29/1919 at 89/2/18 in Plaistow; influenza

Edgar, d. 11/27/1931 at 78/8/23 in Kittery, ME; chronic myocarditis

Edith, d. 1/25/1924 at 28/7/9 in Concord; broncho-pneumonia; John L. Foss and Nellie Osgood

Edwin H., d. 9/6/1926 at 65/4/7 in Augusta, ME; diabetes mellitus

Eliza J., d. 1/22/1897 at 50; spinal paralysis; b. So. Berwick, ME; PH

Elizabeth, d. 12/2/1897 at 83 in Strafford; disease of heart; PH

Ella C., d. 6/5/1933 at 84/2/4; acute bronchitis

Ella M., d. 7/19/1912 at 29/11/5; cardiac embolism; Frank W. Grant and Lizzie J. Hoitt

Ella M., d. 8/16/1927 at 67/2/17; cancer of stomach; Samuel Hersom and Eliza Hodgdon

Ellen C., d. 1/1/1900 at 62; pneumonia; PH

Elmer Locke, d. 9/3/1898 at 28; septicemia; b. Dover; PH

Elmira P., d. 10/31/1924 at 82; pulmonary pneumonia; Nathaniel Perry and Eliza Perkins

Emery W., d. 3/9/1918 at 80/2/13 in Mystic, CT; arterio sclerosis

Emma S., d. 6/23/1905 at 54/10/19; heart disease; PH

Enos G., d. 11/14/1908 at 92/3/23; catarrhal pneumonia; E. B. Foss and Polly Grant

Etta M., d. 1/13/1917 at 48/5/8 in Farmington; chronic pancreatitis

Eugene B., d. 10/1/1923 at 65/1/20; carcinoma of liver; Joshua B. Foss and Eliza Foss

Eunice A., d. 5/10/1900 at 87; old age; PH

Everett O., d. 3/1/1916 at 85/2/7; senility

Fannie M., d. 2/4/1907 at 28/8/20; cancer of stomach; Henry M. Foss and Elcenah Thompson

Frank W., d. 6/4/1912 at 55/4/24; hemiplegia; Clark Foss, Jr. and Harriet Shepard

Frederick H., d. 7/24/1913 at 63/7/18; heart disease; Joel S. Foss

George H., d. 7/5/1921 at 60/11/23 in Boston, MA; valvular heart disease

George W., d. 8/14/1915 at 13/10/8; accidental drowning

Grace E., d. 10/13/1928 at 75; arterio sclerosis; Asa Smith and Eliza Venner

Ham, d. 4/18/1916 at 86/1/7; fatty deg. of heart; Daniel Foss and Mary A. Tebbets

Hannah, d. 4/28/1904 at 80/8/7; pneumonia; PH

Hannah E., d. 5/11/1907 at 79/5/23 in Malden, MA; weak heart

Harriet, d. 12/30/1890 at 63/9/21; widow; Robert Quimby (Ossipee) and Mary Young (Ossipee)

Harriet A., d. 8/26/1901 at 70/9/16 in Farmington; Bright's and heart disease; PH

Harry N., d. 5/27/1893 at 22; injury from cars

Harry W., d. 7/7/1908 at 2/5/10 in E. Hartford, CT; extensive burns; Clarence E. Foss and Maude Benjamin

Helen K., d. 1/30/1916 at 0/3/27; acute indigestion; Mary Foss

Herbert E., d. 9/9/1933 at 66/10/2; gastric ulcer

Hollis E., d. 9/30/1918 at 24/6/9; lobar pneumonia; Elmer Foss and Mattie J. Spurlin

Ida B., d. 7/31/1891 at 31/5/8; married; Alvin Goodwin (Berwick, ME) and Ann Roberts (Gorham, ME)

Ida M., d. 9/18/1936 at 57/1/8 in Rochester; shock, hemorrhage

Jacob K., d. 1/20/1913 at 76/2/28; ch. endocarditis; John B. Foss and Alice Parshley

James W., d. 10/5/1903 at 64/6/8; pneumonia; PH

John B., d. 3/21/1889 at 78/8; farmer; married; b. Strafford; John Foss (Strafford) and Dorothy Babb (Strafford)

John Louis, d. 7/17/1921 at 54/7/24 in York Village, ME; diabetes mellitus

Julia A., d. 9/28/1900 at 61; tuberculosis; PH

Kenneth E., d. 10/9/1915 at 0/0/6; premature birth; May Foss

Laura J., d. 2/7/1928 at 72/8/3; gastro enteritis; Azariah Foss and Sarah A. Foss

Laurentine R., d. 10/24/1930 at 89/5/5; arterio sclerosis; John C. Farnham and Esther Kelley

Lillian E., d. 6/5/1897 at 18; laryngal phthisis; b. Dover; PH

Lucinda, d. 1/1/1907 at 82/6/22; senility; John Smith and Lucy Brown
Luther B., d. 3/6/1901 at 67 in Lowell, MA; apoplexy; PH
Lydia A., d. 10/8/1908 at 65/5/17 in Rochester; cancer in bowels
Maggie May, d. 8/22/1892 at –; cholera infantum; b. Dover; (Dover; Rochester)
Mandana P., d. 3/15/1916 at 77/0/8; old age; John L. Pickering and Mary J. Berry
Maria M., d. 12/31/1923 at 91/5/29; fracture of right hip; Nathaniel Locke and Maria Otis
Marie E., d. 7/27/1917 at 67/6/29; cerebral hemorrhage; Benjamin M. Nealley and Abbie Pray
Mary, d. 3/24/1896 at 83 in Haverhill, MA; heart disease
Mary A., d. 11/13/1913 at 79/8/3 in New Salem, MA; cancer of left eye
Mary C., d. 2/10/1907 at 81/10/10; old age; Benjamin Waldron and Rosella Paul
Mary E., d. 12/6/1913 at 65; valv. disease of heart; Patrick Riley and Catherine McIntire
Mary P., d. 3/25/1893 at 60; paralysis; b. Dover; (Dover; Dover)
Mattie J., d. 12/26/1925 at 55 in Concord; gen. paralysis of insane; Charles Spurling and ---- Cook
Melinda J., d. 9/4/1899 at 58; nephritis; PH
Mercy E., d. 8/3/1931 at 84/8/24; chronic myocarditis
Miah Raymond, d. 1/8/1899 at 1; marasmus; buried in Rochester
Moses, d. 1/24/1905 at 83; cerebral thrombosis
Nathaniel, d. 3/22/1892 at 42; paralysis; b. Newmarket
Nehemiah, d. 12/19/1903 at 85/5/8; old age; buried in Strafford
Ralph W., d. 3/5/1887 at 0/1/5; b. Dover; George H. Foss (Dover) and Ida B. Goodwin (Dover)
Robert H., d. 7/28/1893 at 79; apoplexy - heart failure; b. NH; (NH; NH)
Russell S., d. 8/6/1909 at 43/10/25 in Somerville, MA; uraemia
Sarah, d. 12/28/1894 at 91; old age; b. Parsonsfield, ME; PH
Sarah J., d. 2/7/1890 at 60/3/7; married; James Haines (Wolfeboro) and Hannah Lord (Parsonsfield)
Sarah J., d. 2/17/1912 at 84/0/13; senility; Joseph Buswell and Hannah Harvey
Stephen D., d. 8/23/1895 at 77; heart disease; b. Barrington; PH
Walter D., d. 12/28/1918 at 58/8/26; cerebral hemorrhage; Drew Foss and Betsy Hawkins
Warren, d. 1/6/1893 at 77; dropsy cardiac; b. Strafford; (Strafford; Strafford)
Warren, d. 3/5/1931 at 82; coronary thrombosis
Warren F., d. 2/23/1900 at 45 in Rochester; railroad accident; buried in Dover
Warren H., d. 3/4/1887 at 0/1/13; b. Dover; George H. Foss (Dover) and Ida B. Goodwin (Dover)

Wilhelmina M., d. 2/24/1937 at 62/5/13; influ. pneumonia
William B., d. 12/1/1896 at 78; old age; b. Strafford; PH
William P., d. 6/24/1934 at 62 in Concord; arteriosclerosis
Xena, d. 1/12/1926 at 41/7; lobar pneumonia; Charles C. Beaton and Eliza A. Hill

FOSTER,
Albert S., d. 1/7/1914 at 66/4/14; acute pneumonia; Jonathan Foster and Margaret A. Munsey
Anna C., d. 4/6/1922 at 67/5/21; apoplexy; Seth H. Clark and Clarisa Clark
Caleb C., d. 7/4/1914 at 77/2/22 in Oxford, ME; arterio sclerosis; Moses B. Foster and Eliza A. Benson
Caroline J., d. 10/4/1929 at 77/4/16; chr. endocarditis; E. Barton Foster and Mary E. Noyes
Charles G., d. 10/27/1907 at 48/3/19; heart disease; Joshua L. Foster and Lucretia A. Gale
Doris J., d. 3/10/1900 at <1; marasmus; PH
Emily, d. 7/13/1926 at 17/5/11 in Ware, MA; acute endocarditis
George J., d. 6/21/1928 at 74/4/7; chronic nephritis; Joshua L. Foster and Lucretia Gale
James M., d. 2/27/1914 at 9/3/25; pernicious anemia; Albert D. Foster and Annie Schuman
Jane W., d. 6/11/1935 at 83/10/25; cancer of breast
Joshua L., d. 1/29/1900 at 75; heart disease; PH
Lucretia A., d. 5/6/1905 at 79/1/6; catarrhal pneumonia; PH
Margaret, d. 1/12/1925 at 89/6/22; chronic endocarditis; Charles Pelkey
Marianna, d. 9/6/1933 at 86/9/21 in Portland, ME; broncho pneumonia
Martha B., d. 3/7/1907 at 90/3/15; acute dilation of heart; ----- Davis and --- Babbage
Mary A., d. 2/26/1917 at 81/11; myocarditis; George Dodge and Mary D. Whipple
Mary J., d. 11/26/1896 at 68; uterine tumor - peritonitis; b. Madison; PH
May Belle C., d. 9/3/1911 at 50/1/11; acute nephritis; Benjamin Clement and Sarah C. Scruton
Reginald Keyser, d. 1/22/1910 at 1/2/24 in Otisfield, ME; tubercular meningitis; George A. Foster and Lula E. Keysar
Richard S., d. 11/13/1925 at 0/1/20; hemophilia; Fred R. Foster and Alice Jenness

FOUNTAIN,
Catherine, d. 11/20/1926 at 52 in Boston, MA; natural causes
Daniel, d. 5/17/1892 at 2; drowned by accident; b. Canada; (Canada; Canada)
John, d. 6/21/1907 at –; degeneration of cord; Alexander Fountain and Mary Tardy

Margaret, d. 11/5/1903 at 56; heart disease; SM

FOURNIER,
William, d. 10/12/1892 at 2; cholera infantum; b. Dover; (Canada; Canada)

FOWLER,
Frank W., d. 3/29/1907 at 50 in Worcester, MA; general paralysis
George, d. 8/9/1912 at 79/8/6; cancer of breast; John Fowler and Abigail Dame
John N., d. 10/21/1925 at 60 in Reading, MA; diabetes mellitus
Stephen D., d. 3/28/1909 at 78/6/26 in Foxborough, MA; mitral insufficiency

FOX,
Charles H., d. 4/13/1903 at 48/0/11; angina pectoris; PH
Henry S., d. 6/3/1914 at 78/7/25; ch. intestitial nephritis; George Fox and Drusilla E. Hussey

FOYE,
Ann E., d. 1/4/1895 at 54 in Durham; cancer of the stomach; b. Strafford; PH
Carl F., d. 1/31/1912 at 23/8/17; pulmonary tuberculosis; Frank Foye and Helen A. Locke
Elizabeth, d. 9/28/1904 at 90/0/11 in Durham; shock; PH
Frank, d. 4/4/1934 at 71/10/17 in N. Andover, MA; diabetes coma
Georgia A., d. 9/13/1915 at 59/2/9; endocarditis; Frederick Foye
Helen A., d. 11/2/1935 at 73 in Newburyport, MA; rheumatic heart disease
Lucy H., d. 12/27/1915 at 72/8/10; pneumonia; Joshua Hurd and Lucy Roberts
Roxanna H., d. 4/4/1909 at 83/11/25; chr. valvular dis. of heart; Benjamin Hayes and Phebe Syms
Solomon H., d. 4/14/1905 at 86/2/5; senility; PH
Susan, d. 11/25/1934 at 55 in Lawrence, MA; angina pectoris
Susan E., d. 3/19/1893 at 75; dilation of the heart; b. Dover; (Dover; Dover)
Thomas, d. 11/29/1894 at 79; disease of brain; b. Berwick, ME; PH
Warren, d. 2/9/1890 at 64/2/15 in Strafford; married; Aaron Foye (Strafford) and Susan James (Durham)
William P., d. 5/4/1915 at 69/3/7; valvular heart disease; Thomas Foye and Susan E. Horne

FRAMBAY,
Martha, d. 9/29/1906 at 29; general tuberculosis

FRANCES,
Delia, d. 10/19/1897 at –; alcoholism

FRANCIS,
Alice, d. 7/30/1887 at 82; married; b. Ireland; (Ireland; Ireland)
Freedom F., d. 12/23/1920 at 62/7/26; phthisis pulmonalis; Joseph Francis and Angeline Moore
Ina A., d. 11/25/1888 at 1/11/8; Freedom Francis and Hattie R. Palmer

FRANK,
Florence, d. 8/22/1911 at 8/11/2; typhoid fever; Joseph Trank (sic) and Alphonsine Legasse

FRANKLIN,
William H., d. 1/25/1932 at 69/3/26; cerebral hemorrhage

FRARY,
Fred D., d. 12/19/1918 at 61/10/7; angina pectoris; Dexter Frary and Clarissa -----
Mary E., d. 2/19/1923 at 51/8/6; lobar pneumonia; William T. Pinkham and Elizabeth A. Ricker

FRAZIER,
Alexander, d. 8/17/1893 at 68; erysipelas; b. Dover
Ann S., d. 6/30/1923 at 91/8/26 in Rochester; gen. fail. vital force

FREAMAN,
Annie, d. 12/30/1933 at 92; chronic myocarditis

FRECHETTE,
Joseph, d. 6/7/1929 at 28/11/12; septicaemia; Misaie Frechette and Mary Robideaux

FREDETTE,
Alto, d. 12/7/1921 at 71; apoplexy
Fred, d. 12/14/1893 at –; grippe; b. Dover; (Canada; Canada)
Inez, d. 2/13/1920 at 56; ascites
Lorenzo R., d. 2/25/1903 at 0/1; pneumonia
Mabel, d. 2/18/1891 at 1/7/3; Elmer Fredette (Canada) and Agnes Bergeron (Canada)
Mary, d. 2/2/1902 at 2/7; croup
Victoria, d. 2/18/1891 at 3; Elmer Fredette (Canada) and Agnes Bergeron (Canada)

FREEHETT,
Amore, d. 9/23/1919 at 16; tumor of brain; Misai Freehette (sic) and Mary Robidoux

FREEMAN,
child, d. 3/2/1922 at –; stillborn; John E. Freeman and Florence Little
Arthur D., d. 8/12/1906 at 47/11/6 in Newbury, MA; heart disease; PH
Carrie L., d. 2/16/1895 at 30; phthisis pulmonalis; b. Dover; PH
Charles R., d. 5/13/1922 at 1/2/25; accidental burning; Earl S. Freeman and Eva May Sanborn
Edmund, d. 1/1/1894 at 82 in Philadelphia, PA; bronchitis; b. Wellfleet, MA; PH
Ernest E., d. 4/12/1931 at –; slow delivery
Esther E., d. 5/13/1922 at 3/7/26; accidental burning; Earl S. Freeman and Eva May Sanborn
Henry D., d. 1/2/1894 at 59; heart disease; b. Wellfleet, MA; PH
Jennie P., d. 9/16/1911 at 77/1/18 in Concord; mitral insufficiency; Thomas J. Palmer and Louisa F. Ayers
John F., d. 9/16/1935 at 74; dropsy- heart failure
Joshua F., d. 1/17/1936 at –; stillborn
Mary E., d. 10/21/1918 at 11/6/16; lobar pneumonia; Walter Freeman and Effie Tyler
Phebe, d. 9/19/1924 at 90/4/23; arterio sclerosis; Peter Nason and Sarah Goodwin
Raymond W., d. 3/30/1925 at 10/9/5; fracture of skull; Walter Freeman and Effie E. Tyler
Stephen R., d. 5/9/1929 at 81/7/27; arterio sclerosis; David Freeman and Hannah Gray
Willis G., d. 4/17/1937 at 67/4/19; cerebr. hemorrhage

FREER,
son, d. 12/2/1890 at –; Frank H. Freer (Vineland, NJ) and Zennia W. Willand (Dover)

FRENCH,
Arthur W., d. 10/10/1918 at 36/1/13; pneumonia; Clarence E. French and Addie Winkley
Edith E., d. 5/9/1892 at 18; peritonitis
Elizabeth, d. 10/1/1905 at 82/4/24 in Bath, ME; dysentery
Ellen S., d. 8/14/1900 at 48; cancer; PH
Emily J., d. 12/1/1913 at 64/8/20 in Lynn, MA; uraemia
Eunice, d. 2/16/1895 at 89; old age; b. Dover; buried in family lot
Fannie Dow, d. 5/30/1930 at 71/7/11; chronic endocarditis; Daniel Dow and Sarah E. Bartlett
Frank, d. 8/27/1892 at 4; dropsy; b. Dover; (Ireland; Ireland)

Frank, d. 1/25/1929 at 69/3; broncho pneumonia; Richard French and Bridget Bryan
Frank N., d. 12/29/1930 at 70/4/2; angina pectoris; Sperry French and Harriet Robinson
George F., d. 7/13/1897 at – in Minneapolis, MN; cerebral hemorrhage; PH
George O., d. 10/30/1921 at 62/9/17; softening of brain; John S. French and Charlotte Tucker
Hannah P., d. 9/22/1898 at 87; old age; b. Portsmouth; buried in Portsmouth
Harry W., d. 2/25/1932 at 56/2/24; carcinoma of rectum
Hazel E., d. 10/22/1935 at 36/11/6; Hodgkin's disease
Helen, d. 4/2/1892 at 40; consumption; b. Ireland; (Ireland; Ireland)
James, d. 2/20/1917 at 73; broncho pneumonia; James French and Sally French
John, d. 10/3/1893 at 65; shock; b. Newmarket
John M., d. 10/25/1904 at 76/8/9; old age; buried in Somersworth
Joseph, d. 5/9/1897 at 0; cerebral hemorrhage; b. Dover; buried in family lot
Joseph R., d. 6/27/1934 at 63/6/24; coronary occlusion
Marquis D., d. 3/20/1929 at 79/2/19 in Lynn, MA; left hem. of brain
Martha F., d. 12/9/1907 at 70/10/25 in Lynn, MA; acute bronchitis; Elijah French and Sarah Spinney
Mary A., d. 3/22/1903 at 67/11/16; intestinal cancer; PH
Mary E., d. 12/23/1903 at 85 in Ipswich, MA; organic heart disease
Mary E., d. 2/17/1909 at 75/10/17; apoplexy; Edgar Hood and Mary Avery
Mary J., d. 10/10/1934 at 65 in Springfield, MA; carcinoma of breast
Mary W., d. 5/17/1888 at 0/6/5; b. Dover; Arthur E. French (Danvers, MA) and Edith Faulkner (Cape Elizabeth, ME)
Richard, d. 1/16/1899 at 18; accident, blow on abdomen; SM
Sarah, d. 2/24/1928 at 61; carcinoma of colon; Patrick Riley and ----- Finnigan
Washington J., d. 5/11/1890 at 47/11/28; married; F. S. French (US) and Amelia Ennis (US)

FREWEN,
Sarah, d. 12/20/1930 at 80; cancer stomach; Owen Frewen and Catherine Kayer

FREY,
George, d. 2/11/1935 at 58/0/21; chronic myocarditis

FRIARS,
Alfred, d. 6/16/1892 at 46; disease of brain; b. England; (England; England)
Annie M., d. 5/27/1935 at 60/7/21; fibroid tumor of uterus

Harold F., d. 3/7/1932 at 30/10/22 in Kittery, ME; pulmonary tuberculosis

FRIEL,
Lucy L., d. 8/2/1926 at 71/3/18; cerebral hemorrhage

FRIMEGHAN,
K., d. 2/4/1890 at 89; widow; John Griffin (Ireland) and Catherine Brennan (Ireland)

FRISBEE,
Annie M., d. 7/30/1926 at 68/10/5; chronic myocarditis; William Ray and Abbie Golden
Elmer F., d. 10/11/1937 at 58/0/4; lobar pneumonia
Jesse E., d. 12/11/1916 at 79/8/18; dropsy; Daniel Frisbee and Parmelia Parker

FROST,
Ann S., d. 8/11/1912 at 78/10/29; paralysis; David Frost and Rachael York
Anna P., d. 11/23/1909 at 60/10/15 in Durham; cancer
Annie L., d. 7/22/1929 at 76/1/26; cerebral hemorrhage; Henry Bond and Mary E. Graves
Annie S., d. 7/3/1920 at 75/4/26 in Madison; chronic myocarditis
Anthony I., d. 2/14/1931 at – in Madison; chr. arterio sclerosis
Catherine, d. 8/5/1922 at 70/3/20; cerebral hemorrhage; Michael McBennett and Mary Haughey
Charles C., d. 12/3/1918 at 24/6 in Portsmouth; pulmonary tuberculosis; William E. Frost and Mabel Spencer
Curtis J., d. 11/6/1896 at 32; phthisis pulmonalis; b. Wolfeboro; buried in Wolfeboro
David E. D., d. 10/13/1903 at 78/4/6; valvular disease of heart; PH
Edward A., d. 2/12/1926 at 58/11/11 in Westborough, MA; myocarditis
Edwin H., d. 8/11/1929 at 75/5/14; cerebral hemorrhage; Joseph D. Frost
Elizabeth C., d. 9/16/1906 at 94/6/13 in Newburyport, MA; cancer of breast; PH
Emery, d. 5/28/1916 at 74/0/14; ecterus; ----- Frost
Emily M., d. 5/22/1891 at 49/4/27; married; Alva A. Darling (New Durham) and Elizabeth E. Fernald (New Durham)
Emma P., d. 3/3/1910 at 69/9/5 in So. Berwick, ME; enteritis
George A., d. 3/28/1923 at 81/11/26 in Somerville, MA; arterio sclerosis
George S., d. 5/7/1931 at 86/11/7; myocardial insufficiency
Hiram P., d. 2/1/1891 at 27/7/5 in Middleton; married; David E. D. Frost (Middleton) and Phoebe A. Ellis (Middleton)
Jane, d. 7/15/1891 at 80/5/13; widow; John Graham (England) and Elizabeth Woodman (ME)

John Fred, d. 4/28/1920 at 65/4/29 in Haverhill, MA; chronic nephritis; David E. D. Frost and Phoebe A. Ellis

John G., d. 4/15/1919 at 77/10/27; cerebral hemorrhage; John R. Frost and Jane Graham

Laura O., d. 5/21/1888 at 26/10/2 in Amesbury; b. East Kingston; William F. Cater (Exeter) and Sarah T. Smith (Franconia)

Martha Hale, d. 9/20/1925 at 84/3/7; gangrene of foot; Nathaniel Low and Mary Ann Hale

Nancy, d. 12/22/1898 at 69; heart failure; b. Madbury; PH

Phoebe Ann, d. 4/1/1896 at 70 in Middleton; apoplexy; b. Middleton

Ralph Carter, d. 2/29/1924 at 63/11 in Providence, RI; heart disease

William E., d. 8/8/1923 at 56/5/14 in Portsmouth; intestinal obstruction

William P., d. 5/20/1893 at 90; old age

FRY,

Albert Sterns, d. 4/14/1891 at 0/1/8; Moses Fry (NY) and Bella J. Sterns (Ireland)

Bella J., d. 10/27/1934 at 72; coronary occlusion

Moses, d. 4/20/1914 at 62/8/14; acute congestion of kidneys; Benjamin Fry

FRYE,

Angie B., d. 7/21/1889 at 19/2/25; dressmaker; single; b. Kingston; Joseph W. Frye (Eliot, ME) and Clara J. Locke (Barrington)

Catherine E., d. 6/6/1892 at 73; old age; b. NH; (NH; NH)

Clara J., d. 7/30/1904 at 64/2/22; paralysis and insanity; PH

Clarence B., d. 10/21/1896 at 27 in Newmarket; consumption; PH

Elizabeth, d. 9/14/1894 at 84; old age; b. Milton; PH

Emily O., d. 9/21/1897 at 53 in Newmarket; pulmonary tuberculosis; PH

Frank O., d. 9/7/1904 at 60 in Portland, ME; rupture of urethra; PH

George L., d. 1/10/1897 at 21 in Newmarket; consumption; PH

Gertrude A., d. 2/24/1900 at <1 in Augusta, ME; pneumonia

Grace M., d. 1/13/1894 at 11 in Berwick, ME; scarlet fever; buried in Dover

John E., d. 10/25/1887 at 45; clerk; single; b. Dover; James Frye (Limerick, ME) and Elizabeth Burroughs (Milton)

Joseph W., d. 1/13/1928 at 78/9/10; chr. intest. nephritis; Joseph Frye and Hannah Berring

Keziah, d. 12/25/1916 at 82/11/22; senility; Briant Peavey and Anna Twombly

Lizzie M., d. 8/28/1897 at 32 in Somersworth; gen. peritonitis; PH

Lydia A., d. 2/13/1912 at 74; senility; Joseph Elliott

Mae G., d. 10/18/1927 at 55/2/4 in Augusta, ME; Graves disease; Lafayette Ricker and Nellie Goodwin

Martin E. O'N., d. 3/15/1902 at 74/0/14; dropsy - heart failure; PH

Nellie F., d. 6/6/1902 at 36/7/2; phthisis; PH

Sarah M., d. 10/6/1903 at 88/9/9; capillary bronchitis; buried in Rochester
William A., d. 10/8/1906 at 87 in Boston, MA; senility; PH

FULLER,
child, d. 11/23/1916 at –; stillborn; Perley H. Fuller and Marion A. Hanscom
Dianthia J., d. 9/14/1916 at 90/7/5; senility; James K. Jordan and Nancy Corson
Elmer A., d. 3/28/1918 at 54/3/1; acute pulmonary oedema; Levi A. Fuller and Elvira L. Bemis
Elsie K., d. 4/3/1933 at 51/6/27; P. O. surgical shock
Henry F., d. 2/26/1896 at 66 in Portsmouth; goitre
Sarah J., d. 11/3/1920 at 80/6/17; senility; Zachariah Chickering and Sally Sleeper

FULLERTON,
Susan F., d. 4/5/1922 at 86/10/20; lobar pneumonia; James Fullerton and Sophia B. Wiggin

FULWILER,
James H., d. 7/26/1923 at 79/7/7; apoplexy; Henry Fulwiler and ----- Fellows

FURBER,
Bernice DeM., d. 2/21/1891 at 15/9 in Hamilton, MA; Frank B. Furber (Lee) and Isabelle DeMeritte (Barrington)
Charles A., d. 2/5/1910 at 85/11/20; capillary bronchitis; Augustus Furber and Sarah -----
Cora E., d. 3/23/1917 at 67/2/16; carcinoma spinal cord; Ralph Carlton and Amanda M. Pearl
Dudley L., d. 12/1/1914 at 66/3/13; intestinal nephritis; Haley Furber and Mary Leavitt
Katie E., d. 11/3/1934 at 81 in Weymouth, MA; myocarditis
Louisa A., d. 1/6/1907 at 84/4/8; cerebral apoplexy; Samuel Cate and Catherine Jenkins
Rosa B., d. 8/18/1924 at 79/10/7; angina pectoris; Jethro Furber and Susan Ellison
Susan G., d. 7/2/1894 at 76 in Hooksett; paralysis; buried in Dover
William L., d. 1/23/1897 at 80; heart disease; b. Wolfeboro; PH

FURBISH,
Charles E., d. 2/16/1931 at 44/9/26; typhoid fever
Charles F., d. 5/7/1916 at 60/5/10; sar. in mus. of thigh; Joseph Furbush (sic) and Caroline Baker
Edith A., d. 7/13/1900 at 21; cerebral hemorrhage; PH

Edith B., d. 2/6/1896 at 25; peritonitis; b. IN; buried in Gloucester

FURBUR,
Susan J., d. 6/19/1895 at 59 in Boston, MA; acute gastritis; buried in Dover

FURBUSH,
child, d. 1/17/1919 at –; stillborn; Joseph Furbush and Myra W. Worster
Elizabeth R., d. 7/26/1923 at 61/1/27 in Pawtucket, RI; chr. inter. nephritis
Levi L., d. 1/27/1892 at 66; heart disease; b. ME; (ME; ME)

FURLONG,
Winnifred H., d. 6/15/1927 at 64/2/27; diabetes; Timothy B. Hubbard and Avelene Boston

GAFFNEY,
James, d. 5/10/1910 at –; premature birth; Charles Gaffney and Annie Galloghy
John, d. 4/3/1933 at 56/1/19; chronic myocarditis
Peter John, d. 10/26/1910 at 0/0/16; congenital syphilis; John Gaffney and Sarah McCourt
Susan G., d. 10/21/1935 at 57/8/29; chronic myocarditis

GAGE,
child, d. 8/22/1901 at –; stillborn
child, d. 8/16/1904 at –; stillborn; buried in private
Abigail B., d. 1/25/1900 at 77; heart disease; PH
Adelaide, d. 6/30/1936 at 93/8/5 in Concord; chr. myocarditis (see following entry)
Adelaide, d. 6/30/1936 at 93/8/5* (see preceding entry)
Albert D., d. 3/7/1903 at 22/9/18 in Somersworth; typhoid pneumonia; PH
Amanda J., d. 1/5/1916 at 62/11/24; lobar pneumonia; E. A. Sterling and Susan Ham
Ava L., d. 8/31/1913 at 31/1; pul. tuberculosis; Clarendon Hardy and ----- Haskell
Carrie R., d. 2/11/1921 at 55; endocarditis; Gerry R. Gage and Abigail B. Tuttle
Daniel, d. 7/4/1899 at 71; valvular disease of heart; PH
Daniel A., d. 12/5/1926 at 73/9/10; natural causes; Daniel Gage and Sarah J. Hersom
David H., d. 7/16/1900 at 80; heart disease; PH
Elbridge Gerry, d. 2/1/1925 at 68/11/17; arterio sclerosis; Gerry K. Gage and Abigail B. Tuttle
Fred B., d. 2/3/1900 at 33; pulmonary phthisis; PH
George F., d. 9/6/1906 at – in Minneapolis, MN; PH

George Fred, d. 5/20/1891 at 18/7/26; single; George Wesley Gage (Dover) and Sarah J. Lucas (England)
Gerry R., d. 7/22/1895 at 70; atrophy of liver; b. Dover; PH
Ida F., d. 9/28/1932 at 78/10/16 in Portsmouth; chronic myocarditis
John M., d. 4/26/1918 at 57; lobar pneumonia; Moses Gage and Sarah A. Marston
John P., d. 2/28/1923 at 70/10/9; acute indigestion; Gerry R. Gage and Abigail B. Tuttle
Moses, d. 1/13/1911 at 92/4/20; old age; Jonathan Gage and Betsey Ham
Moses W., d. 8/26/1889 at 42/8/24; brickmaker; b. Dover; Moses Gage (Dover) and Elizabeth Hussey (Dover)
Robert W., d. 11/10/1891 at 9/11; Moses W. Gage (Dover)
Sarah J., d. 7/25/1907 at 78/11/9; senility; Mark Hanson and Sarah Hodgdon
Sarah J., d. 1/19/1920 at 68/9/28; mitral regurgitation; James Lucas and Nancy Lee
Thomas F., d. 10/8/1918 at 67/10/10 in Portsmouth; pneumonia
Walter F., d. 2/21/1909 at 60/4/12; cancer of liver; Daniel Gage and Sarah Hersom
Warren N., d. 2/26/1895 at 38 in Lynn, MA; consumption; buried in Dover
Zelma I., d. 3/25/1924 at 31 in Portland, ME; intestinal obstruction; William Letch and Ida Tibbetts

GAGIN,
Julia, d. 7/12/1923 at 62; apoplexy; Patrick Gagin
Mary, d. 11/29/1930 at 74; chr. endocarditis

GAGNE,
child, d. 6/24/1927 at –; stillborn; Alfred A. Gagne and Mary Coron
Alside, d. 9/23/1917 at 28/3/15; accidental gas asphyxiation; George Gagne and Matilda Plante
Ernest, d. 6/14/1929 at 0/0/2; premature birth; Alfred Gagne and Jeannette Letourneau
Fred, d. 10/15/1902 at 75 in Fall River, MA; parasis
Frederick, d. 3/11/1935 at 77/0/17; gen. arteriosclerosis
George, d. 5/22/1932 at 65; accidental drowning
Joseph, d. 5/10/1905 at 23/9/28; meningitis
Joseph, d. 10/22/1928 at 73/6/7; diabetes
Laura P., d. 6/15/1910 at 25/6/14; pulmonary tuberculosis; Charles M. Newton and Addie M. White
Paul H., d. 10/22/1920 at 0/0/20; erysipelas; John M. Gagne and Elsie Cyr

GAGNER,
Edward, d. 4/18/1918 at 66/3; chronic nephritis; Peter Gagner and Mary Boileau

John, d. 7/25/1910 at 32 in Concord; valvular disease of heart; James Gagner and Mary Cavanaugh

GAGNON,
Andre, d. 4/20/1932 at 79/4/16; chronic myocarditis
Antonio, d. 1/8/1911 at 3; pneumonia; Narcissi Gagnon and Eva Charest
Henriette, d. 12/4/1926 at 68/11/16; cerebral embolism; Toussain Mailloux and Desange Robert
Irene Marie, d. 6/10/1934 at 0/3/23; lobar pneumonia
Joseph H. O., d. 8/28/1893 at –; cholera infantum; b. Dover; (Quebec; Quebec)
Maria C., d. 11/19/1894 at 18; la grippe; b. Canada; SM
Rita, d. 1/20/1919 at 0/1/13; convulsions; Edmond Gagnon and Eugenia Ouellette
Rosanna, d. 11/19/1907 at 0/0/10; gastritis acute; Delphis Gagnon and Marie Louise Roy
Rose Anna, d. 11/26/1925 at 33/6/22; puerperal septicemia; Andre Gagnon and Henriette Mailloux
Victoria, d. 6/8/1912 at 74; broncho pneumonia; Noah Desjardins and Marie Beaupre

GAILEY,
Eleanor M., d. 1/6/1936 at 19/7/22; pulmonary tuberculosis
Hugh, d. 3/30/1927 at 47/8/4; suicide by hanging; John Gailey and Mary Gallagher
John, d. 5/3/1901 at 28; pulmonary phthisis; SM
Nellie, d. 9/24/1896 at –; cholera infantum; b. Dover; PH

GAINEY,
Patrick Joseph, d. 6/23/1917 at –; stillborn; Timothy Gainey and Mary E. --

GAJDA,
John, d. 4/26/1916 at 0/5/19 in Manchester; acute indigestion; K. Gajda and Rosalie Pelc
Rosalie, d. 3/12/1916 at 22; ac. pulm. tuberculosis; Valentine Pelc and Mary Felyn

GALAN,
child, d. 7/6/1921 at –; stillborn; Ernest Galan and Stavroula Bloura

GALANIS,
Arthur, d. 1/11/1931 at 0/4 in Biddeford, ME; broncho pneumonia

GALE,
Betsey J., d. 1/2/1904 at 51/8/17; cerebral apoplexy; buried in Saugus, MA
Daniel B., d. 3/26/1891 at 48; single
Laura E., d. 4/17/1910 at 34; accidental poisoning; ----- Cassidy

GALERRIZZI,
Emillio, d. 7/15/1906 at 28; accidental drowning; SM

GALIBOIS,
Joseph, d. 8/17/1917 at 34/8/17; muscular rheumatism; Octave Galibois
  and Sanaghie -----

GALLAGHER,
child, d. 6/18/1910 at --; stillborn; John E. Gallagher and Ida J. Gage
Bridget, d. 8/28/1908 at --; cancer of throat; Mathew Gallagher and Mary
  Davy
Ellen, d. 10/14/1921 at 76 in Boston, MA; aortic insufficiency
Ida J., d. 6/18/1910 at 34/0/4; placenta praevia; Moses W. Gage and
  Sarah W. Lucas
Mary R., d. 11/7/1898 at 34; peritonitis; b. Dover; PH
Patrick, d. 9/6/1921 at 75 in Boston, MA; cardiovascular disease

GALLEY,
Thomas W., d. 6/30/1903 at 50/2/4; apoplexy; PH

GALLIGAN,
Alta C., d. 4/19/1906 at 89/5/23; cancer of the rectum; PH
Matthew J., d. 3/12/1919 at 63/2/18; chronic nephritis; John M. Galligan
  and Bridget McMullen

GANNON,
Joseph F., d. 5/28/1898 at 0; pneumonia; b. Dover; PH

GARDINER,
James W. F., d. 10/19/1912 at 85/8/19; bronchitis, acute

GARDNER,
Alta A., d. 4/19/1913 at 66/8/7 in W. Newton, MA; gall stones, myocarditis
Anna, d. 5/24/1889 at 65 in S. Berwick, ME
Catherine E., d. 9/14/1906 at 0/7; gastro enteritis; SM
Flora W., d. 4/11/1937 at 69/7/18; coronary thrombosis
James A., d. 6/8/1925 at 83/7/14 in Newton, MA; valv. heart disease
Margaret, d. 1/3/1923 at 80/11; apoplexy; Samuel Phillips and Mary -----
Mary P., d. 2/24/1909 at 42/9/1 in Haverhill, MA

Warren W., d. 9/16/1896 at 48; organic disease of heart; b. Newark, NJ; PH
William, d. 9/15/1911 at 60 in Boston, MA; heart failure

GARGIN,
Katherine, d. 1/27/1915 at –; lobar pneumonia; Patrick Gargin and Ellen ---

GARLAND,
Adeline C., d. 7/13/1913 at 72/11/9; fracture of hip; Bishop Tibbetts
Alfred K., d. 8/26/1915 at 65/10/2; interstitial nephritis; Thomas B. Garland and Harriet Kimball
Caroline H., d. 6/24/1933 at 79/4/30; cerebral hemorrhage
Darius E., d. 9/9/1910 at 75/2/28 in Farmington; mitral insufficiency
Ellen J., d. 1/23/1890 at 44/3/13; married; Joel W. Holmes (Cambridge, VT) and Abigail E. Elliott (Barnstead)
George H., d. 7/12/1934 at 74; suicide by hanging
George M., d. 8/7/1930 at 57/9/8 in Portsmouth; cerebral hemorrhage
Harriet K., d. 1/13/1900 at 76; pneumonia; PH
Herbert A., d. 3/23/1930 at 72/1/25; chronic myocarditis; John F. Garland and Susan Hall
J. F., d. 11/11/1895 at 62; Brights disease; b. Loudon; buried in Newmarket
Jacob P., d. 6/30/1896 at 72 in Wolfeboro; chronic nephritis
John F., d. 2/14/1926 at 71/5/22; broncho pneumonia
Julia A., d. 2/6/1934 at 78/11/6; carcinoma of stomach
Sarah A., d. 4/2/1933 at 97/5/18; old age
Thomas B., d. 5/9/1901 at 83/8/19; pyelo-nephritis; PH

GARMON,
Velma J., d. 4/3/1896 at 32; paralysis; b. Watson, NY; PH

GARNETT,
Flora E., d. 1/25/1891 at 0/2/7; John Garnett (England) and Annie Lancaster (England)

GARNEY,
Maggie, d. 10/25/1887 at 2/0/16; b. Dover; James Garney (Ireland) and Bridget Cassidy (Ireland)

GARRETT,
Tony, d. 9/6/1919 at 68 in Concord; chr. interstitial nephritis

GARSIDE,
Addie M., d. 5/21/1912 at 48/9/14; goitre; Orimel C. Ingraham and Mary E. Hanson
Agnes, d. 7/17/1890 at 88/0/27 in Southbridge; widow; David Ferrier (Scotland) and Agnes (Scotland)
Elizabeth, d. 4/25/1909 at 84/0/13; senility; Frederick Chadderton and Sarah Mayall
George F., d. 10/29/1923 at 77 in Norristown, PA; hemiplegia
Ida A., d. 1/3/1903 at 43/5/19; heart disease; PH
Lizzie, d. 12/24/1894 at 18; typhoid fever; b. Dover; PH
Matilda, d. 8/9/1926 at 79/10/18; carcinoma intestines; James Drinkwater and Hannah Ingham
Walter, d. 2/10/1906 at 81/9/25; cardiac asthma; PH

GARVEY,
Bridget, d. 11/14/1908 at 56; intestinal occlusion; John Cassidy and Margaret M. Carragher
Hannah, d. 9/26/1893 at 30; phthisis pulmonalis; b. Dover; (Ireland; Ireland)
James, d. 8/26/1899 at 58; progressive pneumonia; SM
James H., d. 8/6/1899 at 24 in Lynn, MA; drowning; SM
Joseph, d. 2/12/1929 at 50/3/10; chronic endocarditis; James Garvey and Bridget Cassidy
Katie, d. 12/17/1890 at 0/4; James Garvey (Ireland) and Bridget Cassidy (Ireland)
Thomas, d. 11/23/1888 at 33; grocer; married; b. Ireland; Joseph Garvey (Ireland) and C. McDonough (Ireland)

GARVIN,
Donald, d. 3/11/1923 at 23/3/20; pulmonary tuberculosis; William R. Garvin and Mary E. Staples
James H., d. 4/27/1912 at 75/6/24 in Rollinsford; chronic intestinal nephritis
John, d. 12/11/1903 at 69/5/24 in Rollinsford; valvular heart disease
Marion N., d. 9/6/1924 at 30/9/7 in Glencliff; pulmonary tuberculosis
Sherwood H., d. 4/26/1925 at 3/10/10 in S. Berwick, ME; lobar pneumonia
Susan H., d. 3/9/1917 at 89/0/27 in Rollinsford; atheroma
Timothy, d. 4/11/1902 at 25; cerebral hemorrhage; buried in Malden, MA

GASSES,
Assed, d. 3/21/1924 at 40; pulmonary oedema; Gasses Rized and Annie Abdella

GASSIS,
Annie, d. 4/5/1934 at 69; chronic myocarditis

GAUDREAU,
Joseph H., d. 5/3/1923 at 51/3/4; intestinal obstruction; Paul Gaudreau and Victoria Beaulieu

GAUDREAULT,
Alphonse, d. 5/19/1918 at 20/8; fracture base skull; Philip Gaudreault and Odile Twombly

GAULET,
Alcide J., d. 1/8/1925 at 40/6/21; myocarditis; Jacques Goulet (sic) and Adelie Bilodeau

GAULIN,
Celina, d. 4/18/1926 at 49; chronic nephritis; Louis Pincince

GAUNYA,
Francis R., d. 12/31/1934 at 63/6/5; chronic endocarditis
Nancy B., d. 11/11/1936 at 0/0/4 in Barrington; gastro-enteritis

GAUTHIER,
Cora, d. 11/10/1923 at 44/8/18; carcinoma of omentum; Alphonse Legacy and Vitalene Seveille
George, d. 4/20/1908 at 60; natural causes

GAUVIN,
Eva, d. 10/20/1889 at 1/7; b. Manchester; Frank Gauvin (Canada) and Louise (Canada)
Laura, d. 9/27/1892 at 3; entero-colitis; b. Dover; (Canada; Canada)
Louise, d. 12/18/1914 at 60/0/22; traumatic shock; Alexander ----- and Marie -----

GAWEY,
Daniel, d. 7/26/1889 at 0/0/2; b. Dover; James Gawey (Ireland) and Bridget Cassidy (Ireland)

GEAR,
Ida B., d. 10/17/1909 at 54/7/22; cancer of liver; John B. Burley and Lydia Caverly
John M., d. 1/16/1895 at 61; abdominal cancer; b. Stratham; buried in Concord
Rosina, d. 4/14/1920 at 87/0/8; influenza; Nathaniel Brock and Mary Drew

GEARY,
Daniel, d. 1/7/1930 at 75; hemiplegia; Daniel Geary

GEBAILEY,
Josephine, d. 1/21/1911 at 0/9/6; pneumonia; Farris Gebailey and Maggie Abud

GEBBARD,
Annie L., d. 7/10/1923 at 76/5/6 in Mt. Vernon, NY; chr. intest. nephritis

GEGHAN,
John, d. 3/29/1891 at 35/5/14; married; Patrick Geghan (Ireland) and Ellen Lannigan (Ireland)

GELDERT,
Blanchford, d. 5/8/1935 at –; fractured skull

GELINAS,
Isabelle, d. 9/29/1932 at 56/10/23; cerebral embolism
Joseph A., d. 6/11/1905 at 0/4/25; entero-colitis
Joseph H., d. 5/4/1935 at 65/4/7; coronary thrombosis

GENEST,
Aldea, d. 1/14/1920 at 33/4/14; paralysis of op. and f. nerves; Esube Dionne and Justina Lafond

GENTLEMAN,
Hannah, d. 3/20/1897 at 0; pneumonia; b. Dover; SM
Isabel A., d. 1/22/1906 at 70/7/21; heart disease; PH

GEORGE,
child, d. 4/21/1916 at 0/0/½; premature birth; Elias George and Mary Peters
child, d. 4/27/1916 at 0/0/6; premature birth; Elias George and Mary Peters
child, d. 1/23/1926 at –; stillborn; Michael George and Martha Anton
child, d. 1/15/1927 at –; premature birth; Bolus George and Adele Chded
Annie E., d. 6/2/1935 at 65/11/29 in Haverhill, MA; cerebral hemorrhage
Eugene, d. 2/17/1919 at 2/11/7; ac. lobar pneumonia; Peter George and Salisna Luzion
Fred W., d. 1/24/1924 at 49/10/17; asphyxia by smoke; Charles P. George and Eliza Gilman
Joseph, d. 12/27/1923 at 4/9/24; acute nephritis; Charles George and Martha Dowaliby
Joseph, d. 4/11/1931 at 21 in Pembroke; pulmonary tuberculosis
Peter, d. 2/24/1919 at 0/0/17; ac. lobar pneumonia; Peter George and Salisna Luzion

Rolland, d. 12/8/1925 at 0/4/22; retropharyngeal abscess; Albert George and Emma Flayhenn

Stephen W., d. 1/5/1907 at 50/1/20; thrombosis; James W. George and Diadama Butterfield

GEORGELAS,
Nellie, d. 7/6/1930 at 6/0/21; burns; Tom Georgelas and Sophie Dragormanos

GERO,
Robert, d. 8/5/1898 at 9; accidental drowning; b. Dover; SM

GERRISH,
Bridget, d. 10/28/1902 at 47/6/20; tuberculosis of lungs; SM
Charles H., d. 4/3/1919 at 77 in Madbury; arterio sclerosis
Claribel, d. 9/15/1931 at 91/0/1 in Haverhill, MA; arterio sclerosis
Edgar H., d. 10/25/1898 at 29; peritonitis; b. Madbury; PH
Edwin, d. 2/16/1926 at 81/0/14 in Madbury; cerebral hemorrhage
Elizabeth, d. 11/8/1935 at 81/9/1 in Madbury; cerebral hemorrhage
Elmer F., d. 12/15/1897 at 0; pneumonia; b. Dover; PH
Forrest E., d. 7/13/1893 at 32; fracture of skull
Gardner E., d. 5/11/1925 at 72/2/7; intestinal volvulus; Samuel Gerrish and Catherine Elliott
George, d. 9/24/1899 at 75; cancer of face; buried in Lee
Joseph A., d. 4/26/1929 at 70; fracture of skull; Nathaniel Gerrish and Harriet Poore
Matilda, d. 8/27/1887 at 60/11 in Bradford, MA; single
Melinda C., d. 2/27/1899 at 82 in Madbury; old age; PH
Melvin J., d. 4/14/1936 at 51/9/15 in S. Berwick, ME; uremia
Sarah E., d. 3/26/1917 at 64; endocarditis aortic; Freeman Shepard and Susan Leighton

GETCHELL,
Abram, d. 9/28/1888 at 0/9/23; b. Lisbon, ME; James Getchell and Elizabeth
Bertha R., d. 1/10/1919 at 29/0/20; pneumonia; John Raitt and Sarah Newton
Stephen O., d. 4/9/1899 at 74; angina pectoris; buried in Salem, MA

GEVELIN,
Johnna, d. 5/20/1889 at 69/5; housewife; married; b. Ireland; Heneri (Ireland)

GIBBS,
Ellen M., d. 5/10/1892 at 51; sapraemia; b. Barnard, VT; (VT; VT)
Frederick Azro, d. 11/1/1924 at 49/8/17; tuberculosis of lungs; Oliver A. Gibbs and Susan M. Scates
George Scates, d. 2/15/1914 at 21/9/14; pulmonary tuberculosis; Oliver A. Gibbs and Susan M. Scates
Harold C., d. 7/25/1908 at 22/3/27 in Woodstock, VT; tuberculosis
Oliver A., d. 11/23/1893 at 76; apoplexy; b. Bridgewater, VT; (MA; MA)
Oliver Azro, d. 5/10/1922 at 79/0/27; valvular heart disease; Oliver A. Gibbs and Betsy Perkins
Susan Mary, d. 9/18/1913 at 60/10/3; chronic nephritis; Zimri Scates and Susan M. W. Clark

GIBSON,
child, d. 5/22/1920 at –; stillborn; Charles R. Gibson and Caroline E. O'Neil
Ruth, d. 10/17/1905 at 1/7/16; tuberculosis; PH

GIGNAULT,
child, d. 12/5/1899 at 0; premature birth; SM
child, d. 12/5/1899 at 0; premature birth; SM

GILBERT,
Albert, d. 4/22/1906 at 1/4/26 in Durham; tuberculosis; SM
Alphonse J., d. 5/11/1931 at 58/3/3; angina pectoris
Hattie C., d. 3/11/1894 at 24 in Newton, MA; septicaemia
Martha A., d. 10/9/1913 at 79/11/24 in New Bedford, MA; enteritis - exhaustion

GILBERTSON,
child, d. 9/2-/1902 at –; stillborn; PH

GILE,
Abbie C., d. 7/15/1899 at 75 in Milton; paralysis; PH
Mary Abby, d. 5/15/1903 at 59/11/10 in Webster, ME; pneumonia; PH

GILES,
Hiram, d. 5/29/1922 at –; broncho pneumonia
Julia E., d. 1/14/1919 at 63; apoplexy; George W. Fish and Mary Elliott
Ruth Ellen, d. 9/30/1910 at 74/6/24 in Lewiston, ME; sarcoma
William F., d. 11/26/1888 at 2/5/9; b. Dover; Mathew Giles (Ireland) and Annie Brady (Ireland)

GILL,
Francena H., d. 9/7/1935 at 41/8/18 in Melrose, MA; pulmonary embolism
Rachel M., d. 12/15/1911 at 81/10/17; pneumonia; Robert Wood and Ann Bottomley

GILLETT,
Alice A., d. 4/15/1896 at –; catarrhal enteritis; b. Dover; PH
Bertie, d. 7/18/1898 at 0; overlaid by mother; b. Dover; PH

GILLETTE,
Hazel B., d. 1/11/1898 at 0; inanition; b. Dover; PH

GILLINGHAM,
Myra J., d. 2/14/1908 at 52/10/15 in Warner; cancer in lower bowels; William B. Miles and Kezia Morrill

GILLIS,
Catherine, d. 7/27/1922 at 52/3/24; myocarditis; Patrick McEneaney and Mary Mone
Elizabeth, d. 8/25/1912 at 87/5/18; senility; Robert Murey and Isabella –––––
Elizabeth, d. 2/28/1926 at 48; accidental burning; John Guthrie and Sarah I. Grady
Frances E., d. 10/16/1916 at 59/5/19; paralysis; Luke B. Willey and Mary E. Ellis
James W., d. 4/22/1925 at 68/10/27; acute lobar pneumonia; William P. Gillis and Elizabeth Murray

GILMAN,
Ai T., d. 11/19/1891 at 71/8/3; widower; David Gilman and Rhoda Hurd
Anna E., d. 2/14/1893 at 77; paralysis
Asaph, d. 8/21/1897 at 78; old age; b. Wakefield; PH
Hayson, d. 2/6/1903 at 70/10/28; heart disease; buried in Somersworth
Henry A., d. 7/9/1927 at 67/1/9; arterio sclerosis; Micajah Gilman and Lydia Libby
Ida A., d. 11/21/1925 at 73/7/4; cerebral hemorrhage; Micajah Gilman and Lydia Libby
Jacob O., d. 11/25/1906 at 75/0/11 in Rochester; Bright's disease; PH
James M., d. 10/5/1932 at 53/1/3 in Reading, MA; cerebral hemorrhage
Jeannette S., d. 2/3/1919 at 70/11/17; endocarditis; Andrew J. Nealley and Lydia H. Hodsdon
Joseph L., d. 6/24/1935 at 72/6/4 in Conway; myocarditis
Lydia L., d. 2/7/1900 at 76; apoplexy (cerebral); PH
Lydia S., d. 2/21/1892 at 69; pneumonia; b. Rollinsford; (Rollinsford; -----)

Mary E. F., d. 1/9/1913 at 80/6/14; paralytic shock; Jedediah Felch and
    Mary Hill
Mary Jane, d. 3/24/1903 at 71/8/25; heart disease; buried in Somersworth
Micajah, d. 11/18/1895 at 71; heart disease; b. Strafford; PH
Nancy A., d. 5/23/1891 at 53/11/11; married; James McDuffee (Alton) and
    Sally Gilman (Alton)
Nellie M., d. 6/9/1917 at 62/9/24 in Concord; cerebral hemorrhage; Samuel
    Gilman and Christina Bunker
Randolph A., d. 12/25/1902 at 39/2; prob. disease of heart; buried in No.
    Sandwich
Sadie W., d. 11/6/1931 at 42/8/17; membraneous croup
Samuel D., d. 4/3/1900 at 73; pneumonia; PH
Sarah L., d. 12/25/1898 at 69; neurasthenia; b. Orford; PH
Sarah M., d. 1/9/1906 at 49/10/19; pneumonia; PH
William A., d. 11/1/1910 at 63/11; cerebral apoplexy; George Gilman and
    Susan Plummer

GILMETTE,
Ermina L. D., d. 3/8/1915 at 61/7/15 in Montreal, Can.; paralysis

GILPATRICK,
Donabelle M., d. 5/15/1917 at 0/1/8 in Boston, MA; blue baby
Edna E., d. 5/28/1914 at 26/0/9; pulmonary tuberculosis; Joseph Gosselin
    and Ella Rowe
George F., d. 6/2/1909 at 0/2/15; pneumonia; Jasper Gilpatrick and Edna
    Gosselin
Mary, d. 3/28/1917 at 34/8/11; pulm. tuberculosis; Luther Varell and Sarah
    McDonald
Nettie F., d. 3/28/1912 at 0/0/5; malformation; Jasper Gilpatrick and Edna
    Gosselin

GILSON,
Melissa J., d. 1/3/1892 at 60; general debility (see following entry)
Melissa J., d. 1/3/1893 at 60; general debility (see preceding entry)
William E., d. 10/12/1923 at 96/9/9; fracture of femur; Ralph Gilson and
    Eliza Bailey

GINGRAS,
Mabel L., d. 9/10/1934 at 38/11/10; frac. of skull (acc.)
Philomene, d. 1/8/1914 at 54; diabetes insipidus; Joseph Breton and Lucy
    Merchant
Pierre, d. 12/18/1934 at 78/5/5 in Concord; chronic myocarditis

GIRCORAKOS,
Dimotroula, d. 5/13/1916 at 24/2; drowning - suicide; George Gircorakos and Stavoula -----

GIROUARD,
Mae E., d. 6/20/1935 at 26/9/20; puerperal septis

GIROUX,
Hilda B., d. 8/28/1937 at 75/3/23 in Rochester; cerebr. hemorrhage
Joseph, d. 1/29/1907 at –; premature birth; David Giroux and Marie J. Faucher
Osborn J., d. 6/26/1917 at 24/4/29 in Methuen, MA; accidental fall; Robert Giroux and Hilda ----
Robert, d. 11/29/1919 at 0/0/30; malnutrition; Louise Giroux
Robert J., d. 10/1/1911 at 48/5/6; carcinoma; John Giroux and Jeanne Downing
Theresa, d. 8/10/1932 at 0/9/17 in Rochester; electrocution

GITCHIER,
Ann, d. 3/10/1923 at 1/4/27; tuberculous meningitis; Herman Gitchier and Catherine V. Kelley

GITSCHIER,
Herman, d. 1/10/1937 at 74/8/22; acute myocarditis

GIVIENS,
Shirley, d. 7/5/1927 at 0/0/4; con. malformation; Robert W. Giviens and Edna T. Selby

GLASS,
Albert M., d. 3/3/1922 at 62 in Concord; apoplexy; Samuel Glass and Mary Waldron
George W., d. 6/25/1902 at 39/9/10; shot with revolver; PH
John S., d. 4/12/1897 at 74; inanition; b. Nottingham; PH
Mary F., d. 10/14/1908 at 74/1/16 in Hartford, CT; apoplexy
Samuel D., d. 6/25/1890 at 64/4/11 in Madbury; married; Samuel Glass and Susan Demerett (Madbury)
Sarah A., d. 4/3/1900 at 62; grip; PH

GLEASON,
James L., d. 11/21/1904 at 43/6/3; chronic dementia; PH
Mary, d. 2/2/1887 at 78; housewife; married; b. Ireland; James Murray (Ireland) and Ann Shaughnessy (Ireland)

Patience, d. 6/5/1913 at 76; mitral insufficiency; John Milne and Jane Trotter
Rose, d. 10/4/1902 at 62; heart disease; SM

GLIDDEN,
Alonzo F., d. 7/10/1902 at 60/5/15; cerebral hemorrhage; PH
Augusta C., d. 9/19/1919 at 66/2/2 in Beverly, MA; cerebral hemorrhage
Ellen B., d. 9/10/1928 at 82/5/10 in Melrose, MA; carcinoma of descending colon
Frank, d. 10/29/1927 at 60/6/4; arterio sclerosis; Charles A. Glidden and Cherry A. Robinson
Harriett L., d. 1/29/1925 at 88/1/18 in Croghall, NY; lobar pneumonia
Henry P., d. 6/3/1916 at 82/9/21; cerebral hemorrhage; John Glidden and Pluma B. Dame
Ida H., d. 3/7/1925 at 77; arterio sclerosis
Jennie C., d. 10/29/1918 at 59 in Concord; broncho pneumonia; Alonzo Glidden and Harriet Canney
John A., d. 2/2/1913 at 76/10/18; cerebral hemorrhage; John A. Glidden and Phema B. Dame
Margaret E., d. 5/8/1914 at 57/11/18 in Beverly, MA; shock after operation; Jeremiah O'Sullivan and Katherine Brick
Mary A., d. 9/16/1891 at 48/3/6; married; James Manson (Barrington) and Zerviah Sherburne (Barrington)
Sarah, d. 3/12/1909 at 71/5/28; cerebral apoplexy; William Lucas and Mary T. Kimball
Sarah E., d. 1/13/1930 at 81/6/11; chronic myocarditis; Stephen Walker and Lydia A. Ham
Walter H., d. 8/6/1898 at 0; diarrhea; b. Dover

GLINES,
George W., d. 2/9/1894 at 65; chronic bronchitis; b. Wolfeboro; PH
Margaret D., d. 12/11/1893 at –; heart failure; b. Alton; (NH; NH)

GLOVER,
Katherine A., d. 9/2/1936 at 67*; b. Portsmouth

GODDARD,
child, d. 4/11/1912 at –; stillborn; Adam J. Goddard
child, d. 6/4/1925 at –; stillborn; Herbert H. Goddard and Bridie Lawlor
Annie M., d. 2/24/1894 at 33; consumption; b. Holliston, MA; SM
Bridget, d. 4/13/1894 at 30; consumption; b. Northbridge, MA; SM
Doris Alice, d. 7/20/1904 at 0/0/12; convulsions; buried in Austin Cem.
Harriet Ann, d. 3/17/1925 at 60/6/2 in Uxbridge, MA; myocarditis
James, d. 3/30/1892 at 64; railroad accident; b. Ireland; (Ireland; Ireland)
John, d. 4/1/1931 at 78 in Concord; chronic myocarditis

Mary, d. 1/31/1893 at 66; carcinoma of liver; b. Ireland; (Ireland; Ireland)
Mary, d. 12/3/1899 at 47; myetitis; SM
Robert H., d. 10/5/1932 at 71/5/9; angina pectoris
William S., d. 11/21/1915 at 62; pulmonary tuberculosis

GODFREY,
child, d. 5/4/1919 at –; stillborn; Edward C. Godfrey and Bertha Snow
James E., d. 11/7/1895 at 45; disease of heart; b. England; PH
John R., d. 12/24/1899 at 0; immaturity
Mary O., d. 1/7/1907 at 52/8/28; carcinoma; Jere M. Hackett and Mary Ann York

GODREAU,
Amelia, d. 9/25/1893 at 42; phthisis pulmonalis; b. Canada; (Canada; Canada)
Florence, d. 10/10/1918 at 15/5/22; acute lobar pneumonia; Napoleon Godreau and Marilla Beauleau

GOGGIN,
child, d. 3/–/1902 at 0/11; drowned
Annie, d. 2/19/1907 at 40; heart disease; Edward Mulligan and Ann Duffy
Catherine, d. 5/9/1900 at 62; shock; SM
Eugene, d. 5/17/1893 at 25; convulsions; b. Dover; (Ireland; Ireland)
Jeremiah, d. 11/2/1908 at 49; Bright's disease; Jeremiah Goggin
Julia, d. 1/16/1902 at 59; congestion of lungs; SM
Marguerite R., d. 12/17/1919 at 25/2/19 in Boston, MA; intestinal adhesion; Jeremiah Goggin and Annie Mulligan
Michael, d. 5/29/1890 at 65; married; Jere. Goggin (Ireland) and Mary Mahoney (Ireland)

GOINGS,
C. Everett, d. 9/6/1915 at 34/7 in Pleasantville, NJ

GOLDEN,
Mary Ann, d. 3/2/1888 at 19/11/18; mill operative; single; b. Dover; M. Golden (Ireland) and Rosanna Rodden (Ireland)
Rose, d. 6/21/1900 at 65; phthisis; SM

GOLDSTEIN,
Abraham, d. 6/8/1919 at –; premature birth; Barney Goldstein and Minnie Goldstein
Bessie, d. 5/14/1914 at 0/0/2; premature birth; Barney Goldstein and Minnie -----
David, d. 9/11/1912 at 0/0/3; hemophilia; Bernard Goldstein and Minnie ---

David, d. 9/14/1913 at 0/0/½; premature birth; Barney Goldstein and Minnie Goldstein

GOLDTHWAITE,
Ephraim J., d. 5/2/1916 at 66; valv. heart disease; Timothy Goldthwaite and Hannah Jones
William, d. 2/24/1907 at 80; senile dementia

GONET,
Victoria, d. 7/1/1925 at 13/6/9; acute gastritis; John Gonet and Julia Velus

GOOCH,
Hartley R., d. 8/18/1922 at 64/6/3; cerebral hemorrhage; Alonzo Gooch and Martha Freeman
Robert G., d. 10/21/1918 at 34/5/15 in Baltimore, MD; influenza

GOODALL,
Annie E., d. 11/26/1899 at 64 in Lawrence, MA; cancer; PH
Hiram, d. 2/4/1888 at 50/9/5; shoemaker; married; b. Northwood; H. Goodall and Martha York

GOODCHILD,
Lizzie M., d. 6/14/1887 at 34/9/8; b. Hampstead; John Arnold (NH) and Mary A. Gleason (NH)

GOODHUE,
Josiah, d. 1/22/1887 at 87/10/28; switchman; married; b. Brookfield; Josiah Goodhue and Hannah
Mary J., d. 3/12/1906 at 89/10/11 in York, ME; chronic bronchitis; PH

GOODIE,
Mary Lucille, d. 6/8/1919 at 0/0/2; atelectasis; Frank J. Goodie and Mary T. Monroe

GOODMIN,
Joyce, d. 6/27/1933 at 2/0/4; acute appendicitis

GOODREAU,
Albert, d. 9/5/1906 at 0/0/2; premature birth
Alfred, d. 9/7/1906 at 0/0/4; premature birth
Ameralda, d. 11/12/1912 at 40/14/26 (sic); pernicious vomiting
Daniel, d. 5/12/1916 at 12/2/21; pleurisy with effusion; Daniel Goodreau and Admena Mailhot

GOODRICH,
Mary J., d. 12/1/1918 at 85/1/20; lobar pneumonia; Burt T. Cook and Dorcas Guptill

GOODWIN [see Googins],
child, d. 6/12/1898 at 0; brain disease; b. Dover; PH
Abbie H., d. 4/23/1937 at 78/5/28; fabu. heart disease
Abbie Martha, d. 1/17/1920 at 58 in New York, NY; cardiac
Addie F., d. 2/19/1929 at 78/7/30; chronic myocarditis; Jacob M. Hatch and Flavilla Russell
Adelaide F., d. 11/17/1923 at 74/10/3; ulcer of stomach; Isaiah F. Connor
Albion N., d. 6/16/1910 at 65/6/23; cancer of stomach; Asa Goodwin and Mary A. Newell
Alice E., d. 1/31/1891 at 28/1/6; single; Edward Goodwin (Ireland) and Catherine Printy (Ireland)
Annie, d. 9/8/1889 at 11/3/12; b. Kennebunk, ME; ----- Herman and Emma Gerrish
Annie M., d. 2/10/1922 at 88 in Brockton, MA; old age
Annie Mildred, d. 5/20/1904 at 20 in Malden, MA; diabetes; PH
Belle S., d. 9/6/1893 at 91; septicemia
Bessie C., d. 8/21/1893 at –; meningitis; b. Dover; (Dover; Barrington)
Catherine P., d. 4/15/1907 at 85/5; old age; Owen Printy and ----- Mooney
Charles A., d. 1/30/1920 at 76/1/22; acute nephritis; Charles E. Goodwin and Dorcas Libby
Charles B., d. 3/1/1890 at 40/2/18 in Magnolia, FL; married; Jonathan B Goodwin (West Lebanon) and Emily Piper (Wolfeboro)
Charles E., d. 8/6/1900 at 84; heart disease; buried in Rollinsford
Charles W., d. 3/5/1897 at – in Manchester; acute cerebral meningitis; FH
Clyde M., d. 8/5/1899 at –; cholera infantum; buried in Eliot, ME
Clyde W., d. 3/24/1923 at 0/0/4; undeveloped; Frank E. Goodwin and Eva Williams
Ellen, d. 10/12/1917 at 45; chronic endocarditis; William McNulty and Catherine Dacey
Emma M., d. 11/18/1936 at 71/6/12 in S. Berwick, ME; cerebral hemorrhage
Ezra C., d. 3/27/1927 at 86/1; senility; Samuel Goodwin and Pauline Goodwin
Ezra M., d. 5/13/1909 at 73/5/5; pneumonia; Elisha J. Goodwin and Martha Mills
Francena, d. 1/17/1903 at 50/1/16; cerebral hemorrhage; buried in Salem
Fred, d. 11/12/1937 at 73/2/12 in Concord; chr. myocarditis
George W., d. 4/25/1903 at 75/8/11 in Strafford; pneumonia; PH
George W., d. 6/7/1912 at 54/7/15; chr. intestinal nephritis; James L. Goodwin and Lucinda H. Stevens
Harvey B., d. 1/19/1931 at 62 in Concord; erysipelatous

Hattie, d. 10/1/1932 at 62/2/11 in Concord; conflagration
Hattie L., d. 9/22/1888 at 25/8/28 in Brockton, MA
Hazel B., d. 5/27/1896 at –; disease of brain; b. Dover; PH
Helen, d. 9/7/1937 at 69/4/28*; b. Dover
Helen E., d. 5/31/1907 at 63 in Lowell, MA; paralytic shock
Irving E., d. 4/11/1936 at 70/5/24; chronic nephritis
Ivory L., d. 4/1/1918 at 75/11/2; endocarditis; Charles E. Goodwin and Dorcas Libby
James F., d. 12/28/1911 at 64/3/13; heart disease; Neb. Goodwin and Mary Ham
Jason M., d. 9/28/1911 at 67/11/13; pneumonia; Reuben Goodwin and Mary Goodrich
John Alvah, d. 8/21/1907 at 62/10/4; chronic nephritis
John E., d. 5/31/1893 at 72; paralysis of the heart
John M., d. 7/30/1887 at 34 in Boston, MA
John O., d. 10/24/1937 at 32/4/5 in S. Berwick, ME; accidental drowning
Jonathan B., d. 12/29/1887 at 69/4; mechanic; b. Lebanon, ME; Thomas Goodwin (Lebanon, ME) and Nellie (Lebanon, ME)
Joseph, d. 11/27/1890 at 46/2; married; Joseph H. Goodwin (Rollinsford) and Mary Callaghan (Ireland)
Katharine, d. 12/13/1892 at 19; typhoid fever
Lizzie M., d. 6/13/1908 at 70; inanition; Levi Hoyt and Margaret Lord
Lottie M., d. 6/24/1931 at 40/2/1; septicaemia
Margaret, d. 1/22/1898 at 22 in Boston, MA; septi pentenitis; PH
Mariette C., d. 4/17/1893 at 71; paralysis
Marjorie L., d. 4/20/1908 at 0/10/5; pneumonia; Frank E. Goodwin and Mabel V. Tuttle
Mary E., d. 10/14/1889 at 43/3/5; operative; married; b. Kennebunk, ME; Charles Webster (Sanford) and Rachel Hulls (Long Island)
Mary F., d. 4/25/1889 at 34/7/21; housewife; widow; b. Dover; George Decatur and Betsey Burnham
Mildred L., d. 4/28/1904 at 0/3/23; pneumonia; buried in Berwick, ME
Nancy J., d. 3/10/1909 at 74/9/13; injury from fall; James Evans and Nancy Davis
Oliver L., d. 11/11/1908 at 68/3/10; pulm. tuberculosis; Charles E. Goodwin and Dorcas P. Libby
Pamelia N., d. 10/11/1904 at 75/6/23 in Malden, MA; cerebral hemorrhage; PH
Rose, d. 2/10/1908 at 57; uraemia; Edward Goodwin and Catherine Printy
Samuel H., d. 1/13/1918 at 73/5/23 in Harvard, MA; lobar pneumonia
Samuel H., Jr., d. 12/20/1910 at 30/4/28 in Boston, MA; pul. tuberculosis
Sarah, d. 11/12/1892 at 76; heart disease; (MA; -----)
Sarah A., d. 11/12/1904 at 68/3/10; phthisis pulmonalis; buried in Rollinsford

Sarah E., d. 10/15/1915 at 70/3/16; cerebral apoplexy; Daniel Goodwin and Eliza Jellison
Sophia M., d. 8/26/1927 at 80/5/25; leukemia; Joseph Weare and ----- Sweet
Thomas, d. 12/31/1909 at 43/8/26 in Lawrence, MA; overstimulation; Edward Goodwin and Catherine Printy
Thomas J., d. 1/29/1891 at 83/5/20; married; Samuel Goodwin (Shapleigh, ME)
William E., d. 7/16/1932 at 53/9/28; aortic aneurism
William H., d. 2/8/1931 at 72/7/7 in Brockton, MA; broncho pneumonia

GOOGINS [see Goodwin],
Frank, d. 2/11/1926 at 76/1/25; arterio sclerosis; Samuel Goodwin (sic) and Martha Smith

GORDON,
Catherine L., d. 6/30/1928 at 73/0/27; chronic endocarditis; Thomas Adair and Isabelle McCordic
Duncan S., d. 6/27/1905 at 55/0/1; Bright's disease; buried in Newington
Edith W., d. 5/6/1909 at 37/6/28; puerperal peritonitis; Samuel E. Wyman and Alicia Hall
Edward A., d. 11/26/1912 at 56/6/16; intersusseption; Charles S. Gordon and Mary Spencer
Edward A., d. 11/13/1936 at 61/5; chr. endocarditis
Harriett N., d. 11/26/1909 at 81/0/3; senility; Thomas Hodgdon and ----- Cromwell
Ida, d. 10/25/1926 at 74; fracture of skull; Herman Snierson and Martha ---
Leonard A., d. 2/26/1921 at 68/7/18; gangrene left foot; Alonzo Gordon and Abigail Carrier
Marguerite V., d. 11/14/1924 at 25 in Providence, RI; lobar pneumonia
Mary, d. 12/22/1900 at 25; phthisis pulmonalis; buried in New Durham
Sarah J., d. 12/5/1915 at 60; carcinoma of breast; George W. Hall and Lucinda -----
Susie E., d. 7/22/1937 at 86/10/24; pneumonia

GORHAIN,
Alfred, d. 9/2/1937 at 89/7/23*

GORHAM,
Ella Josephine, d. 3/17/1923 at 65/10 in Cambridge, MA; brain tumor

GORMAN,
child, d. 5/8/1898 at 0; anaemia; b. Dover; SM
child, d. 5/11/1923 at –; premature birth; James B. Gorman and Agnes White

Ann, d. 11/14/1920 at 75/3/4; tuberculosis of lungs; James Riley and Mary Hughes
Bridget, d. 3/2/1901 at 38; malignant jaundice
Bridget E., d. 7/17/1894 at –; cholera infantum; b. Dover; SM
Catherine, d. 7/7/1900 at 70; old age; SM
Catherine, d. 9/17/1903 at 43/0/12; phthisis
Catherine, d. 10/16/1903 at 65; heart disease; PH
Catherine H., d. 9/7/1933 at 50/9/3; hernia
Daniel E., d. 12/8/1929 at 49 in Lowell, MA; lobar pneumonia
Edward J., d. 12/25/1906 at 20/11/23; phthisis
Eliza J., d. 12/24/1926 at 73; chronic endocarditis; John Campbell and Ann Haughey
Elizabeth, d. 8/25/1889 at 6/2/18; b. Dover; Patrick Gorman (Ireland) and Ann Riley (Ireland)
Fr., d. 2/18/1889 at 2; b. Dover; John Gorman (Ireland)
Francis C., d. 5/27/1919 at 61; acute nephritis
George W., d. 9/1/1902 at 1/1; cholera infantum
James, d. 9/7/1917 at 56; cerebral hemorrhage; Peter Gorman and Mary Murray
John, d. 7/3/1900 at <1; malnutrition; SM
John Francis, d. 8/30/1914 at 61; mitral insufficiency; Patrick Gorman and Catherine McCooey
John J., d. 1/31/1919 at 67; general arterio sclerosis; Patrick Gorman and Margaret Hughes
Joseph L., d. 10/31/1888 at 2/7/1; b. Dover; John F. Gorman (NY) and Eliza Campbell (Dover)
Margaret, d. 5/24/1918 at 56; acute oedema of lungs; Jeremiah Goggin and Abbie Sullivan
Margaret J., d. 8/9/1894 at 52; heart disease; b. Ireland; SM
Mary, d. 12/7/1889 at 0/0/2; b. Dover; John F. Gorman (NY) and Eliza Campbell (Dover)
Patrick, d. 11/1/1919 at 71/9/18 in Concord; chronic myocarditis; Patrick Gorman and Margaret Hughes
Patrick F., d. 5/30/1921 at 65; pulmonary oedema; John Gorman and Mary McArdle
Peter, d. 10/21/1900 at 32; tuberculosis; SM
Rose, d. 1/5/1918 at 64; acute oedema of lung; Bernard Donnelly
William H., d. 4/12/1901 at – in Rollinsford; SM

GORMELY,
Patrick, d. 1/31/1890 at 62; married; Daniel Gormely (Ireland) and Nancy McMahon (Ireland)

GOSNELL,
Clara B., d. 6/2/1896 at 22 in Somerville, MA; pulmonary consumption

Roger, d. 12/19/1895 at 2 in Somerville, MA; diphtheria; PH

GOSS,
Charles Carpenter, d. 5/4/1915 at 69/3/7; valvular heart disease; John A. Goss and Electa Carpenter

GOSSELIN,
Henri, d. 9/13/1906 at 0/3/19; entero colitis
William, d. 12/2/1931 at 43 in Rollinsford; tubercular meningitis

GOTHA,
Emily, d. 2/19/1905 at 87; valvular heart disease

GOTHAM,
Minnie F., d. 3/16/1912 at 32/11/7; carcinoma; Jethro E. Horne and Laura E. -----

GOUDREAU,
Marie B., d. 11/27/1895 at 0; whooping cough; b. Dover; SM
Richard, d. 1/28/1933 at 4/11/27; acute mastoiditis

GOUGH,
Susan M., d. 7/12/1915 at 74; cancer of liver; Nahum Ferguson and Mary Chadbourne

GOUIN,
Celina, d. 7/13/1901 at 54/2/8; cerebral embolism
Edward, d. 1/18/1905 at 63/5/18; pneumonia; SM
Edward F., d. 9/11/1905 at 0/0/9; cholera infantum

GOULATOS,
John, d. 4/15/1912 at 58; gastric carcinoma

GOULD,
Anna L., d. 11/13/1928 at 74/7/8 in Brockton, MA; cerebral hemorrhage
Annie W., d. 10/22/1916 at 76/5/12; dropsy; Samuel Whitehouse and Deborah Brown
Arthur J., d. 10/22/1910 at 66/9/9 in Taunton, MA; arterio sclerosis
Carrie I., d. 5/18/1915 at 52/9/18 in Methuen, MA; cancer of uterus
Charles W., d. 5/20/1916 at 68/5/11 in Amesbury, MA; chronic nephritis
Edward, d. 11/4/1888 at 86/11/15; expressman; widower; b. Eliot, ME
Edward H., d. 10/6/1920 at 80/11/3; valvular heart disease; Edward Gould and Lucy Nason
Edwin J., d. 10/6/1899 at 32; drowned; buried in Wilton

John, d. 2/27/1891 at 81/2/20; married; John Gould (Bath, ME) and Mary Hinckley (Lisbon, ME)
Lucy Jane, d. 10/21/1921 at 86/5/20 in Manchester; endocarditis; John Gould
Martha A., d. 5/22/1907 at 78/8/20; uraemia; George W. Lilly and Rebecca M. White
Martha E., d. 2/7/1911 at 75/3/8; heart disease; George W. Patterson and Elizabeth Hall
Mary A., d. 2/22/1902 at 76/5/22; cardiac asthma; buried in Portsmouth
Minnie L., d. 11/7/1920 at 78/4/7 in Manchester; dilated heart; Benjamin Davis and Eunice M. Gilbert
Sarah S., d. 4/15/1900 at 85 in Taunton, MA; senile debility; PH

GOUPIL,
James, d. 11/12/1936 at 87/2/5; cerebral hemorrhage
Raymond, d. 10/7/1933 at 18/2/10 in Barrington; fracture of skull

GOURDOUSOS,
Maria, d. 4/11/1930 at 35; ac. lobar pneumonia; George Gourdousos and Antonia -----

GOWAN,
Margaret L., d. 12/6/1915 at 35; pul. and laryng. tuberculosis; Patrick Keenan and Margaret Hughes

GOWELL,
Freeman, d. 6/6/1895 at 76; apoplexy; b. Sanford, ME; buried in Sanford, ME
Freeman, d. 6/6/1898 at 76; apoplexy

GOWEN,
child, d. 4/14/1903 at –; stillborn; SM
Edith A., d. 12/2/1933 at 66/8/9; lobar pneumonia
Eleanor V., d. 5/13/1906 at 79/10/9; senility; PH
Harry A., d. 2/4/1935 at 49/7/12; abscess of right lung
Jacob, d. 5/8/1926 at 74; chronic endocarditis
John L., d. 3/2/1929 at 0/0/1; premature birth; Harry A. Gowen and Nancy A. Rowe
John P., d. 4/12/1892 at 66; cancer; b. ME; (ME; ME)
Lewis, d. 4/13/1903 at 75/7; mitral disease of heart; PH
Loretta S., d. 11/3/1911 at 1/1/18 in Portsmouth; tuberculosis general
Luther K., d. 6/12/1896 at 36 in Springvale, ME; Brights disease; b. Dover

GOWIN,
Ed., d. 4/29/1904 at 0/0/4; umbilical hemorrhage; SM

GOWITZKE,
child, d. 7/23/1925 at –; stillborn; Howard Gowitzke and Amy Coldwell

GRACEY,
Ann, d. 1/19/1922 at 72 in Lowell, MA; broncho pneumonia
Bridget, d. 11/3/1897 at 39; la grippe; b. Ireland; SM
James, d. 2/1/1922 at 73; broncho pneumonia; Thomas Gracey and
  Catherine McKenna
Thomas J., d. 1/26/1895 at 14; typhoid fever; b. Rochester; SM

GRADY,
child, d. 5/12/1895 at 0; marasmus
child, d. 3/6/1898 at 0; stillborn; b. Dover; SM
child, d. 10/12/1921 at –; stillborn; Thomas L. Grady and Annabel Ryan
Annabel R., d. 1/6/1924 at 37/3/24; cancer of stomach; Mary Hennessey
Annie, d. 12/8/1913 at 55/9 in Manchester; cancer of breast; Thomas Parle
  and Mary Howland
Charles J., d. 10/26/1930 at 73 in Boston, MA; lobar pneumonia
Dennis L., d. 7/18/1919 at 31/9/27 in Somersworth; valvular heart disease;
  John Grady and Ellen Donahue
Ellen, d. 8/27/1892 at 70; old age; b. Ireland; (Ireland; Ireland)
Ellen, d. 10/11/1915 at 56; cerebral apoplexy; Timothy Donohoe and Mary
  O'Brien
James, d. 5/12/1897 at 0; marasmus; b. Dover
John, d. 9/5/1919 at 72; endocarditis; Dennis Grady and Ellen Burke
Maggie, d. 9/5/1887 at 19/3; mill operative; single; b. Ireland; ––––– (Ireland)
  and Mary (Ireland)
Mary, d. 2/28/1908 at 55; apoplexy; Dennis Grady and Mary –––––
Mary, d. 5/31/1925 at 61; cancer of uterus; Patrick Grady and Marguerite -
Patrick, d. 8/20/1923 at 80; arterio sclerosis; Dennis Grady and Ellen
  Burke
Richard, d. 11/18/1921 at 70; myocarditis; Dennis Grady and Ellen –––––
Richard J., d. 4/7/1893 at –; acute bronchitis; b. Dover; (Ireland; Ireland)
Thomas, d. 2/27/1925 at 70/2; apoplexy; Dennis Grady and Ellen Burke
Thomas, Jr., d. 2/17/1932 at –

GRANGER,
Rosaire J. A., d. 4/20/1911 at 0/10/21; pneumonia; Ferdinand Granger and
  Elizabeth Comtois

GRANOCOPOULOS,
Antonio, d. 9/14/1918 at 45; apoplexy

GRANT,
Abbie, d. 3/31/1898 at 35 in Salem, MA; apoplexy; PH
Annie C., d. 5/6/1913 at 75/11/2 in Douglass, MA; cancer of liver
Caroline M., d. 11/16/1895 at 66; exhaustion; b. Tuftonboro; buried in Tuftonboro
Charles, d. 11/7/1933 at 46; fracture of skull
Charles E., d. 5/25/1912 at 75/6/26 in Cambridge, MA; sclerosis, etc.
Charles H., d. 10/5/1905 at 52; fracture; buried in Rollinsford
Elijah M., d. 10/7/1893 at 51; heart disease; b. Saco, ME; (Saco, ME; Limerick, ME)
Elizabeth, d. 1/11/1920 at 75; broncho pneumonia; Owen Hughes and Ann Hughes
Elmer E., d. 7/8/1932 at 69/0/6; uraemia
Frances M., d. 10/8/1918 at 85/3/5; senility; Josiah F. Heath and Hannah Grant
Frank L., d. 4/9/1921 at 0/0/1; premature birth; George L. Grant and Nettie H. Eaton
Frederick T., d. 6/4/1929 at 55/5/28 in Beverly, MA; broncho pneumonia; Lucien Grant and Emily Witham
Genevieve H., d. 10/14/1920 at 51/1/18; valvular heart disease; Norman Squires and Hannah Jenkins
George B., d. 7/26/1929 at 71/10/8; acute nephritis; Eli Grant and Pamelia A. Varney
George H., d. 4/16/1890 at 45/3/16; married; George W. Grant (Acton, ME) and Charlotte H. Shaw (Springfield, ME)
George Louis, Jr., d. 12/27/1919 at 0/0/1; premature birth; George L. Grant and Nettie H. Eaton
Jennie G., d. 3/7/1930 at 65/11/8; chronic myocarditis; Eli Grant and Parmelia A. Varney
John L., d. 3/21/1905 at 64/1/14; cancer; PH
Julia Ann, d. 10/20/1909 at 38/9/17; chronic nephritis; Eli Grant and Permelia Varney
Lewis, d. 4/3/1898 at 68; apoplexy; b. West Lebanon, ME; buried in Lawrence, MA
Lucien H., d. 9/21/1899 at 59; heart disease; PH
Maria L., d. 8/31/1910 at 69/5/7; heart disease; Edward Chase and Louisa Bragdon
Mary E., d. 3/22/1915 at 60/1/26; pneumonia; Samuel Hanson and Melinda J. Hurd
Moses V., d. 9/10/1891 at 36/1/3; married; Eli Grant (ME) and Pamelia Varney (Dover)
Nellie E., d. 5/14/1936 at 69/6/12*

Nellie Florence, d. 6/30/1910 at 36/11/22; cerebral hemorrhage; Eli Grant and Pamelia A. Varney
Pamelia A., d. 1/26/1895 at 64; paralysis; b. Dover; PH

GRASON,
James M., d. 8/21/1894 at 4; convulsions; b. Dover; SM

GRASSE,
child, d. 10/2/1937 at –; stillborn

GRATEY,
child, d. 11/15/1932 at 00; premature birth

GRAVES,
Elizabeth Q., d. 3/27/1916 at 97/0/14 in Reading, MA; myocarditis
George, d. 2/19/1904 at 61; valvular disease of heart; PH

GRAY,
child, d. 9/27/1932 at –; stillborn
Albert, d. 8/10/1891 at 0/2; Aaron Grey (sic) (VT) and Lizzie Grey (NH)
Almira, d. 5/26/1889 at 59; married; b. Strafford
Anna M., d. 2/12/1911 at 73/9/16 in Bow; broncho-pneumonia
Arthur P., d. 12/29/1935 at 65/3/14; acute lobar pneumonia
Bernice B., d. 6/17/1937 at 52/5/13; acute myocarditis
Carrie E., d. 12/30/1922 at 78; intestinal obstruction
Charles, d. 12/17/1936 at 73/0/12; diabetic gangrene
Charles, d. 12/26/1937 at 61/11/29; angina pectoris
Cora Alice, d. 9/13/1933 at 75/6/16; cholecystitis
Delia A., d. 11/18/1902 at 61/2; pneumonia; PH
Della M., d. 6/3/1931 at 63/0/15; diabetes
E. Ida, d. 11/9/1930 at 75; asphyxiation; Nathaniel S. Cate
Eben T., d. 7/3/1888 at 50/9/15 in Waltham, MA; laborer; single; b. Barrington; William Gray (Barrington) and Mary Thompson (Barrington)
Emily J., d. 2/20/1891 at 46/0/27; married; Luther Lord (Lebanon, ME) and Sally Sheldon (Beverly, MA)
Emma L., d. 6/26/1933 at 70/9/26; acute cholecystitis
Francis, d. 9/22/1934 at 71/6/29 in Barrington; cancer of bladder
Francis C. W., d. 4/25/1905 at 73/3/21; la grippe; PH
George F., d. 7/27/1901 at 1 in Somersworth; phthisis
George M. J., d. 11/11/1891 at 44/2/7; married; George Gray (England) and Eliza Scott (England)
George W., d. 1/13/1907 at 28/2/11 in Groveton; pneumonia
George W., d. 5/12/1907 at 64/8/17; cerebral hemorrhage; Henry Gray and Joanna Hall

George W., d. 7/2/1911 at 74/0/20; carcinoma of face; James Gray and Joanna Gray

Gerald W., d. 12/8/1929 at 2/2/8; suffocated; George S. Gray and Helen C. Wellington

Gertie N., d. 10/31/1891 at 11/2/5; John N. Gray (Little Compton, RI) and Kattie F. (New London, CT)

Hannah A., d. 5/16/1899 at 56; arthritis difornus with intercurrent phthisis; buried in Rollinsford

Hannah H., d. 7/19/1891 at 75/7/9; married; Samuel Mitchell (New Durham) and Betsey Edgerly

Ira, d. 1/6/1887 at 37; laborer; single; b. Barrington

James H., d. 4/24/1915 at 62; chronic Brights disease; James M. Gray and Cordelia Perkins

James M., d. 8/26/1893 at 78; old age - heart failure; b. Barrington; (Barrington; Barrington)

Joanna, d. 6/16/1898 at 84; paralysis; b. Sandwich; PH

John H., d. 4/21/1937 at 71/5/21; pneumonia lobar

John S., d. 7/30/1928 at 73/8/23; chronic endocarditis; Simon Gray and Lovey -----

John W., d. 3/16/1911 at 43/3/29; typhoid fever; Smith W. Gray and Delia A. Tuttle

John W., d. 3/20/1926 at 69/8/20; cerebral hemorrhage; William H. Gray and Clara D. Woodes

Joseph, d. 11/24/1898 at 0; stillborn; b. Dover; SM

Leonard S. R., d. 9/5/1895 at 72; uraemia from nephritis; b. Portsmouth; PH

Lilla Belle, d. 5/17/1892 at –; whooping cough; b. Dover; (Rochester; Lowell, MA)

Mary A., d. 9/30/1912 at 86/8/16; fracture femur; Moses Davis and Deborah Emerson

Mary Addie, d. 10/19/1910 at 66 in Haverhill, MA; cancer of liver

Mary E., d. 4/3/1900 at 74; Bright's disease; PH

Mary H., d. 6/14/1918 at 49; tuberculosis of intestines; Charles F. Gray and Lavina Clay

Mary S., d. 8/13/1892 at 46; heart failure

Nancie C., d. 12/19/1915 at 69/11/29; pneumonia; Parker Bedell and Olive Griffin

Orrin W., d. 9/30/1923 at – in Lynn, MA; heart disease

Ralph, d. 1/3/1932 at 58; cerebral tumor

Samuel L., d. 11/27/1896 at 73; shock; b. Barrington; PH

Sidney A., d. 12/4/1934 at 75/3/20; chronic myocarditis

Sidney T., d. 2/14/1906 at 10/7/6; rheumatic endocarditis; PH

Smith Albert, d. 7/12/1894 at –; cholera infantum; b. Dover; PH

Smith W., d. 7/8/1910 at 72/6/11; pulmonary tuberculosis; John Gray and Sarah Jenness

Vella Trask, d. 7/17/1910 at 25/7/18; pulmonary tuberculosis; Charles
    Trask and Hattie Chase
William, d. 9/23/1887 at 83/8/27; farmer; widower; b. Barrington; Eben
    Gray (Barrington) and Deborah Hodgdon (Barrington)
William H., d. 1/28/1907 at 83/7/7; old age; Henry Gray and Dorothy Otis

GRAZIANO,
child, d. 2/12/1913 at –; stillborn; Fred Graziano and Ellen Courtney

GREAR,
John, d. 4/30/1930 at 58; lobar pneumonia; John Grear and Mary -----

GREELEY,
James A., d. 6/4/1914 at 70/2 in Everett, MA; pneumonia
Mary C., d. 7/31/1918 at 75 in Winthrop, MA; arterio sclerosis

GREEN,
Charles H., d. 12/9/1898 at 45 in Boston, MA; nephritis; PH
Frances A., d. 6/23/1895 at 64; chronic nephritis; b. Dover; PH
Frank I., d. 11/2/1935 at 76/10; cerebral hemorrhage
Jessie, d. 4/4/1894 at 52; pleurisy and heart disease; SM
Mary A., d. 8/26/1887 at 0/3/21; b. Dover; John Green (Ireland) and Mary
    (Ireland)
Samuel, d. 6/8/1915 at 69; peritonitis
Samuel H., d. 12/27/1894 at 70; abdominal cancer; b. Tamworth; PH
Thomas, d. 9/19/1917 at 3/11/3; membranous colitis; Patrick Green and
    Hannah McCarthy
Victoria May, d. 8/30/1888 at 0/3/6; b. Dover; William Green (England)
    and Emily Clark (England)
William, d. 9/9/1912 at 38; drowning; Michael Green and Mary White

GREENAWAY,
child, d. 4/11/1919 at –; asphyxia of labor; Harold L. Greenaway and
    Adelaide M. Whitehouse
Charles Edward, d. 3/19/1918 at 4/2/11; acute gastro int. infection; John
    Greenaway and Ethel Burham
Chester A., d. 10/2/1918 at 22/6/25; influenza; Edward Greenaway and
    Ellen Wilson
Edward, d. 9/18/1923 at 70/9/8; gen. arterio sclerosis; Robert Greenaway
    and Sarah Tartin
Samuel, d. 1/2/1914 at 63/6/10; epithelioma; Robert Greenaway and
    Sarah -----

GREENEY,
Eva May, d. 8/2/1901 at 0/1/29; infantile diarrhea; SM

GREENLAW,
Margaret R., d. 5/8/1921 at 39/8/11 in Winthrop, MA; natural causes; Rufus S. Atkinson and Margaret J. Shannon

GREENWOOD,
Catherine, d. 4/14/1891 at 47; married; (Ireland; Ireland)
Clara, d. 7/–/1892 at –; cholera infantum; b. Dover; (Canada; Canada)
John, d. 10/16/1889 at 38; laborer; married; b. Canada; Edward Greenwood (Canada) and Margaret (Canada)
Mary A., d. 8/3/1888 at 0/2/19; b. Dover; John Greenwood (Canada) and Ellen Muligan (Dover)
Mary E., d. 7/26/1890 at 0/3; John Greenwood (Canada) and Ellen Mucragan (US)
Maxine, d. 8/8/1924 at 75; burns, legs and feet
Rose, d. 8/23/1931 at 32 in Danvers, MA; tuberculosis

GREGOIRE,
Aime, d. 6/4/1934 at 56/8/3; coronary thrombosis
Georgianna, d. 11/13/1918 at 35/0/19; acute mania; Paul Cote and Velantine Merchant
Joseph, d. 7/11/1928 at 0/0/1; premature birth; Marie Gregoire
Joseph G., d. 8/15/1918 at 0/0/1-4; premature birth; Aime Gregoire and Georgianna Cote
Louis, d. 10/2/1933 at 45/1; carcinoma of stomach
Oliva, d. 2/5/1903 at 0/0/15; athrepsia
Rena, d. 12/21/1925 at 4/2/19; membraneous croup; Albert Gregoire and Regina Crateau

GREGORAKOS,
George, d. 9/23/1931 at 69; acute myocarditis

GRENIER,
Adeline, d. 1/23/1935 at 57/8/26; cancer of uterus
Albert, d. 11/9/1931 at 63/2/24; acute myocarditis
Eugene, d. 3/14/1909 at 0/10; pneumonia; Eugene Grenier and Olivine Fortier
Flora, d. 5/12/1914 at 39; status epilepticus
Ida, d. 10/9/1918 at 20/2/9; acute lobar pneumonia; Ernest Brunelle and Odeli Renaud
Joseph E., d. 5/1/1896 at –; premature birth; b. Dover; SM

Marie F., d. 3/2/1908 at --; premature birth; Josaphat Grenier and
    Rosanna Martin
Odelie, d. 8/1/1896 at 25; tuberculosis of the lungs; b. Canada; SM
Odiana, d. 3/1/1908 at --; premature birth; Josaphat Grenier and Rosanna
    Martin

GREY,
John W., d. 7/10/1910 at 66/0/28 in Concord; uraemia; George W. Grey
William B., d. 11/11/1891 at 86; widower

GRIFFIN,
Abner C., d. 10/13/1918 at 64/8/15 in Concord; Abner C. Griffin and
    Harriet Flagg
Alice M., d. 3/9/1897 at 15 in Boston, MA; phthisis; PH
Anna Elizabeth, d. 7/22/1937 at 31/7/26*; b. Dover
Cordelia W., d. 9/26/1891 at 33/1/10; widow; Andrew Tetherly and Eliza A.
    Roberts (Dover)
Grace G., d. 7/22/1897 at 22; consumption; b. Dover; PH
John H., d. 5/11/1916 at 46; amputation right leg; John Griffin and Julia
    Sheehan
Margaret, d. 1/8/1898 at 63; old age; b. Ireland; SM
Margaret, d. 5/21/1910 at 15/5/26; pulmonary tuberculosis; Thomas Griffin
    and Mary Cosker
Martha A., d. 6/20/1914 at 80/5/21 in W. Springfield, MA; carcinoma of
    kidneys
Mary, d. 7/20/1901 at 2/2; meningitis cerebral; SM
Mary, d. 8/9/1909 at 37; tuberculosis; John Cosker and Mary Margan
Maud H., d. 2/18/1920 at 23 in Boston, MA; pneumonia - influenza
Michael, d. 10/21/1905 at 39/2/18; pneumonia
Minnie B., d. 5/31/1899 at 18; paresis; PH
Rose, d. 4/15/1917 at 71; apoplexy; Patrick Carroll
Ruby L., d. 3/19/1932 at 27/1/24; cer. spinal meningitis
Sarah A., d. 8/6/1911 at 85/8/23 in Lawrence, MA; paralytic shock
Sarah R., d. 4/20/1893 at 71; heart failure
Thomas, d. 12/10/1891 at 0/7/9; Michael Griffin (Ireland) and Katie Grimes
    (Ireland)
Thomas, d. 1/11/1895 at 50; accident - heart disease; b. Ireland; SM
Thomas, d. 10/6/1914 at 35 in Boston, MA; cirrhosis of liver
Thomas J., d. 11/12/1905 at 31/10/14; pulmonary tuberculosis
Timothy W., d. 5/4/1937 at 79/6/16*

GRIME,
Evelyn, d. 12/6/1915 at 28/11/21; burns; George Saxon and Mahlia Owens
Herbert C., d. 6/16/1926 at 59 in New York, NY; hypertrophy of prostate
Mary, d. 10/11/1900 at 65; diabetes; buried in Portsmouth

GRIMES,
child, d. 9/22/1894 at –; stillborn; b. Dover; SM
child, d. 12/20/1894 at –; stillborn; b. Dover; SM
Ann, d. 3/28/1925 at 84/7/17; carcinoma of breast; Christopher Hughes and Ellen Keating
Bridget, d. 1/22/1892 at 28; consumption; b. Dover; (Ireland; Ireland)
Bridget, d. 5/27/1913 at 85; old age; James Grimes and Catherine Trainor
Catherine, d. 1/30/1887 at –; b. Ireland
Catherine, d. 10/19/1901 at 58; diabetes; SM
Edward F., d. 2/12/1916 at 48; lobar pneumonia; Francis Grimes and Mary McDonald
Elizabeth, d. 11/9/1908 at 52; cerebral hemorrhage
Elizabeth, d. 4/23/1909 at 40; scarlet fever; James A. Grimes and Bridget Grimes
Eva, d. 8/17/1892 at –; cholera infantum; (Ireland; Ireland)
Evangeline, d. 12/17/1888 at 0/3/7; b. Dover; Patrick Grimes (Ireland) and M. Cunningham (Ireland)
Francis, d. 10/21/1906 at 69; heart disease; SM
Francis, d. 5/11/1927 at 56 in Lawrence, MA; chronic myocarditis; Owen Grimes and Mary Mullen
Francis A., d. 12/16/1895 at 0; convulsions; b. Dover; SM
Frank, d. 6/24/1904 at 57; locomotor ataxia; SM
Frank, d. 8/19/1934 at 67; carcinoma of sigmoid
Frank E., Jr., d. 6/23/1918 at 13/9/1; acute nephritis; Frank E. Grimes and Grace Hill
Grace H., d. 1/18/1931 at 61/0/18 in Boston, MA; cong. heart failure
Henry, d. 2/26/1892 at –; asthenia; b. Dover; (Dover; Dover)
Henry, d. 8/30/1912 at 34 in Goffstown; pulmonary tuberculosis; Owen Grimes and Mary Mullen
Henry J., d. 6/12/1913 at 60/5/15; arterio-sclerosis; Henry Grimes and Sarah Barker
Herbert, d. 9/30/1889 at 1; b. Dover; Henry J. Grimes (Dover) and Mary Ryan (CT)
James, d. 12/30/1893 at 67; softening of brain; b. Ireland; (Ireland; Ireland)
James, d. 4/30/1904 at 75; cardiac asthma; SM
James, d. 1/25/1917 at 66; valvular dis. of heart
James A., d. 2/9/1924 at 80; nephritis; Robert Grimes and Sarah Donnelly
James F., d. 4/11/1928 at 18/8/1; meningitis; George Grimes and Ella Good
James H., d. 11/5/1926 at 63; apoplexy; James A. Grimes and Bridget -----
John, d. 3/21/1891 at 39/9; married; Owen Grimes (Ireland) and Alice McReough (Ireland)
John, d. 12/23/1898 at 51; apoplexy; b. Ireland; SM

John, d. 10/29/1907 at 36/2/4; disease of brain; James A. Grimes and
   Bridget -----
John, d. 1/9/1916 at 65; cirrhosis of liver
John H., d. 3/30/1915 at 56/7/13; cerebral hemorrhage; James Grimes
   and Mary Riley
Joseph F., d. 10/1/1932 at 44; heart disease
M., d. 6/26/1901 at 29; compression of lungs; SM
Mabel A., d. 10/9/1907 at 23/6/5; diabetes; Francis Grimes and Tressa
   Finnegan
Maggie, d. 6/23/1898 at 27; Addison's disease of liver; b. Georgetown,
   MA; SM
Margaret, d. 3/15/1899 at 50; phthisis; SM
Margaret, d. 4/15/1903 at 69; dysentery; SM
Margaret, d. 10/5/1915 at 71; strangulated ing. hernia; John McNally and
   Catherine Grimes
Margaret, d. 1/18/1916 at 72; apoplexy
Mary, d. 8/3/1892 at 13; phthisis; b. Rochester; (Ireland; Ireland)
Mary, d. 8/5/1898 at 60; cancer; b. Ireland; SM
Mary, d. 3/11/1902 at 71/0/25; cerebral softening; SM
Mary, d. 4/20/1906 at 77; old age; SM
Mary, d. 2/23/1911 at 61/1/24; nephritis; John Cassidy and Margaret
   Carragher
Mary A., d. 12/24/1908 at 35; phthisis pulmonalis
Mary A., d. 12/7/1920 at 86 in Elizabeth, NJ; bronchitis, old age
Mary A., d. 3/9/1922 at 59; ac. lobar pneumonia; James Grimes and Mary
   Riley
Mary Ann, d. 4/10/1920 at 62; uraemia; Terrance Grimes and Mary Vallely
Mary C. C., d. 3/17/1904 at 76/2/18; atropsy of liver; PH
Mary E., d. 10/18/1889 at 17/11/20; single; b. Dover; John Grimes
   (Ireland) and Mary Cassily (Ireland)
Mary M., d. 10/29/1891 at 49; widow; Michael Mullen (Ireland) and Ann
   McKone (Ireland)
Mary S., d. 3/17/1890 at 36/7/17; married; James Ryan (Ireland) and Mary
   Phelan (Ireland)
Mary T., d. 8/30/1901 at 0/4/17; acute intestinal catarrh; PH
Michael, d. 10/31/1897 at 62; congestion of lungs; SM
Nellie, d. 8/16/1908 at 8; typhoid; Frank Grimes and Mary Hollor
Owen, d. 4/6/1912 at 35; natural causes; Owen Grimes and Mary Mullen
Patrick, d. 10/29/1916 at 77/10/4; ac. lobar pneumonia; James Grimes
   and Catherine Trainor
Robert, d. 10/17/1896 at 75; pneumonia; b. Ireland; SM
Robert, d. 2/12/1929 at 69; angina pectoris
Sara E. A., d. 4/4/1928 at 42/5/21; natural causes; Henry J. Grimes and
   Mary Ryan
Sarah, d. 11/19/1894 at 82; dropsy of chest; b. Ireland; SM

Sarah, d. 7/14/1897 at 61; heart disease; SM
Sarah, d. 4/24/1927 at –; arterio sclerosis
Sarah A., d. 8/21/1925 at 71; cerebral hemorrhage; Owen Hughes and Catherine Mooney
Susan M., d. 9/16/1906 at 51/4; heart disease; SM
Theresa, d. 2/4/1909 at 65/3/4; broncho pneumonia; Dennis Finnegan and Catherine Gribben
Walter D., d. 2/11/1903 at 0/8/29; pneumonia
Winifred, d. 5/22/1937 at –; acute cholecyolitis

GRIMSHAW,
Cecilia, d. 7/10/1902 at 9/0/27; pneumonia
Edward, d. 3/17/1926 at 88 in Lawrence, MA; chronic myocarditis
Jane A., d. 5/14/1888 at 56; married; b. England; John Sager (England)

GRINMILLARO,
Salvatore, d. 4/7/1913 at 26; cerebral tumor; Leo Grinmillaro and Nina

GROARKE,
Mary E., d. 3/30/1935 at 74/0/19 in Portsmouth; chronic interstitial nephritis
Mary M., d. 5/28/1900 at 45; int. nephritis; SM

GROCHMAL,
Albina, d. 5/14/1925 at 12; chr. discharge left ear; Andrew Grochmal and Annelia Sergaryd

GROURKE,
John T., d. 9/14/1891 at 5/3/22; John T. Grourke (Ireland) and Mary Muney (Ireland)
Sarah J., d. 12/2/1889 at 5/5/11; John Grourke (Ireland) and Mary Murray (Ireland)

GROVER,
child, d. 3/8/1932 at –; asphyxia of labor
Albert T., d. 1/29/1906 at 57/2/25; phthisis pulmonalis; buried in Waterville, ME
Daniel, d. 6/10/1887 at –; widower; b. Dover; (Berwick, ME; Berwick, ME)
Frank H., d. 2/23/1925 at 0/0/29 in Kittery, ME; bronchial pneumonia
Jennie M., d. 3/11/1911 at 71/8/21; cerebral hemorrhage; Ellen Littlefield
John H., d. 5/20/1919 at 76/1; mitral insufficiency; Daniel Grover and Olive Hubbard
Kate S., d. 10/6/1914 at 58/6/2; chronic morphinism
Margery, d. 9/17/1936 at 91/2/5; myocarditis

Mary J., d. 8/25/1936 at 90/6/26; chr. nephritis
Olive, d. 5/11/1895 at 89; carcinoma; b. Berwick, ME; PH
Walter S., d. 9/26/1912 at 67/1/11; cerebral hemorrhage; John Grover and Sarah Woodus
William A., d. 9/1/1934 at 59/4/16; frac. of skull (acc.)

GROVES,
Martha H., d. 6/2/1903 at 65/6/26; hemiplegia; buried in Wiscasset, ME

GRUPE,
child, d. 10/21/1923 at –; stillborn; Karl G. Grupe and Dorothy M. Shequen

GRYNES,
Monika, d. 7/18/1908 at 0/1/7; cholera infantum; Charles Grynes and Mary Sickmark

GUENARD,
M. A. E., d. 10/23/1894 at –; spina bifida; b. Dover; SM

GUIGNARD,
Lucien, d. 12/17/1928 at 12/8/13; post operative; Philip Guignard and Melanie Hamel

GUILFOYLE,
James, d. 2/17/1907 at 80 in Somerville, MA; bronchitis

GUILMET,
Blanche A., d. 4/8/1915 at 28/5/21; locomotor ataxia; Rodney E. Fall and Eva C. Reynolds

GUILMETTE,
child, d. 5/27/1924 at –; premature birth; Alfred J. Guilmette and Yvonne C. Bois
child, d. 9/10/1929 at –; stillborn; Yvonne Guilmette
Charles D., d. 10/11/1924 at 2/11/1; accident; Charles W. Guilmette and Nellie L. Goupil
Leona E., d. 4/20/1936 at 0/2/7; suffocation, accidental
Louis, d. 7/16/1922 at 64/10/21; cholecystitis; Pierre Guilmette and Marie Charier
M. I., d. 2/24/1900 at <1; unknown
Wilfred G., d. 1/1/1897 at 48 in Concord; brain disease

GUINARD,
Eleazer, d. 10/1/1918 at 20/8/10; influenza; Joseph Guinard and Marie Henault
Joseph, d. 9/30/1918 at –; premature birth; Ludger Guinard and Laura L'Hemeux
Laura, d. 10/1/1918 at 25/0/12; influenza; Peter L'Hemeux and Georgianna
-----
Marie, d. 10/2/1918 at 54/6; influenza; Joseph Henault
Marie, d. 10/
Odelie, d. 5/16/1904 at 11/9/4; epilepsy

GULBRANDSEN,
child, d. 11/5/1917 at –; stillborn; Trygve Gulbrandsen and Ingel Martinsen
Anna C., d. 11/14/1922 at 54/10/24 in Beverly, MA; pulmonary embolism; Eric Occersen
Eleanor B., d. 5/17/1918 at –; stillborn; Reidar Gulbrandsen and Gladys A. Nelson
G. A., d. 9/22/1933 at 38/2/2; peritonitis
Herman K., d. 4/30/1936 at 69/1/23 in Beverly, MA; silicosis
Reidar, d. 8/30/1922 at 29/1/29; perf. duodenal ulcer; H. K. Gulbrandsen and Anna Ottersen

GULLINE,
Joseph S., d. 3/26/1892 at –; convulsions; b. Dover; (Fall River, MA; England)
Mary A., d. 7/4/1914 at 54/0/13; abdominal carcinoma; Joseph Oldroyd and Margaret Tomlinson
Robert N., d. 1/19/1915 at 65/0/6; apoplexy; Stewart Gulline and Mary C. Ogden

GUPPEY,
child, d. 6/30/1901 at – in Saugus, MA; stillborn; PH
Albert, d. 1/26/1903 at 51 in Lee; crushing wound of head
Charles, d. 1/12/1899 at 59 in Brentwood; paralysis; PH
Comfort, d. 4/5/1900 at 78 in Boston, MA; pneumonia; PH
George W., d. 3/20/1914 at 74/6/16 in Portsmouth; chronic Brights
Louise A., d. 1/16/1917 at 71/7/12 in S. Berwick, ME; cancer of uterus
Margaret E., d. 6/30/1901 at 32/0/4 in Saugus, MA; heart failure; PH
Susan, d. 10/19/1913 at 66/11/24; acute nephritis; James Perkins and Susan Downs

GUPPY,
child, d. 10/16/1924 at 0/0/1; atelectasis; George A. Guppy and Mary E. Courtney

child, d. 3/23/1929 at –; premature birth; George A. Guppy and Mary Courtney
child, d. 8/29/1937 at –; stillborn
George, d. 2/16/1903 at 0/1/24; stoppage of bowels; PH
George E., d. 9/20/1906 at 62/1/26 in So. Berwick, ME; cerebral apoplexy; PH
George N., d. 3/8/1897 at 59 in Pittston, ME; b. Dover; PH
Hannah C., d. 4/13/1913 at 84/8/13; pneumonia; John Guppy and Hannah Dame
Hazel R., d. 4/24/1907 at 0/4/6; pneumonia; George A. Guppy and Sarah A. Cronshaw
J. Belnap, d. 3/16/1917 at 85/11/10; pneumonia; John Guppy and Hannah Dame
James E., d. 11/10/1901 at 65/8/23 in Portsmouth; cirrhosis of liver; PH
John, d. 12/16/1915 at 72/11/28 in Haverhill, MA
Joseph D., d. 6/3/1890 at 67/3/23; single; John Guppy (Portsmouth) and Hannah Dame (Kittery, ME)
Joshua J., d. 12/8/1893 at 73; pneumonia
Langdon, d. 4/15/1889 at 57; single; b. Brookfield; Benjamin F. Guppy (Wolfeboro) and Martha A. Warren (Wolfeboro)
Mable Ellen, d. 5/13/1914 at 0/4/26; acute pneumonia; Henry M. Guppy and Ethel M. Bailey
Sophia, d. 11/27/1892 at 77; old age - apoplexy; b. Dover; (NH; NH)

GUPTILL,
Alvena W., d. 1/26/1918 at 40/8/12; carcinoma of uterus; Alvin Littlefield and Charlotte Simes
Charles, d. 6/3/1927 at 63/2; chronic Brights disease; James Guptill and Elizabeth Dearborn
Damon B., d. 7/7/1911 at 50/9/18; gored by bull; Robert Guptill and Lucy -
Elizabeth, d. 2/2/1911 at 78/6/23; heart disease; William Dearborn and Evelina Drew
James H., d. 2/25/1906 at 78/5/6; cerebral hemorrhage; buried in Rollinsford
Mary J., d. 7/22/1935 at 69/10/29 in N. Berwick, ME; dropsy

GUSIN,
Ed, d. 1/19/1890 at 71; W. Gusin (Canada) and Julia Shabant (Canada)

GUY,
Edward T., d. 6/4/1926 at 17/4/23; hemorrhage; Michael Guy and Bridget Holland

HACKET,
John Willie, d. 10/29/1894 at –; marasmus; b. Dover; SM

HACKETT,
child, d. 4/1/1908 at 0/2; marasmus; Jaspar E. Hackett and Mary E. Remick
Clara A., d. 9/16/1901 at 39/4/22 in Boston, MA; diabetes mellitus; PH
Etta May, d. 3/27/1892 at –; meningitis, cerebral; (Danvers, MA; England)
Fred C., d. 6/20/1894 at 23; killed by lightning; b. Danvers, MA; PH
George S., d. 2/6/1891 at 38/6/25; married; Jeremiah H. Hackett (Gilmanton) and Mary A. York (Rochester)
Ince F., d. 8/15/1934 at 73/6/29; angina pectoris
Jasper E., d. 7/20/1911 at 53/5/10; suicide by shooting; Jeremiah M. Hackett and Mary A. York
Jeremiah, d. 2/7/1899 at 76 in Berwick, ME; asthma, with la grippe
Marion G., d. 4/6/1896 at 1; b. Dover; PH
Mary A., d. 12/6/1895 at 65; failure of the vital forces; b. Barnstead; PH
Mary A. Y., d. 8/28/1895 at 74; consumption; b. Rochester; PH
William E., d. 9/18/1905 at 0/5; marasmus; SM

HACKING,
Addie M., d. 7/27/1899 at 26; hepatic abscess; PH
Alice, d. 1/3/1906 at 76/1/25; bronchitis and old age; buried in Farmington
Elizabeth G., d. 11/20/1934 at 53/8/11 in Brighton, NY; carcinoma of breast
Emma S., d. 8/16/1932 at 81/2/24; coronary thrombosis
William, d. 8/3/1906 at 56/4/3; cerebral apoplexy; PH

HAEARD,
Louis, d. 3/9/1888 at 77/2/23; farmer; married; b. St. Johns, Canada; Louis Haeard (St. Johns) and Mary Reboye (St. Johns)

HAFFNA,
George, d. 9/24/1922 at 71/10/22 in Boston, MA; org. disease of heart; George Haffna and Mary -----

HAFFNER,
Mina, d. 8/9/1917 at 66; rheumatoid arthritis; George Dosck

HAFFY,
Ann, d. 11/6/1907 at 70; tuberculosis; Daniel McBennett and ----- Hughes

HAGAR,
Abbie L., d. 6/9/1924 at 79/0/30 in Boston, MA; cardiac
Hayward B., d. 6/13/1927 at 45/5/15 in Boston, MA; myocarditis; Warren Hager (sic) and Abbie Littlefield
Warren G., d. 8/10/1901 at 64/3/19; heart disease; PH

HAGGER,
Georgianna, d. 9/21/1924 at 77/9/29 in Boston, MA; arterio sclerosis

HAGGERTY,
John J., d. 9/8/1922 at 49; pulm. embolism; Charles Haggerty and Mary ---
Julia M., d. 6/30/1891 at 23/4/9; Jeremiah Hagerty (Ireland) and S. A.
    McSorley (Ireland)

HAIGH,
Emily, d. 6/13/1935 at 76/1; angina pectoris
Harold T., d. 8/30/1892 at --; cholera infantum; b. Dover; (England; Dover)
Joseph, d. 9/30/1937 at --; stillborn infant

HAINES,
Charlotte P., d. 10/6/1889 at 36/9/6; housewife; married; b. Dover; James
    M. (Wolfeboro) and Nancy Mathews (Gilmanton)

HALE,
child, d. 12/31/1893 at --; stillborn; b. Dover; (Lee, ME; Ireland)
Abbie, d. 6/26/1927 at 78/6/25; apoplexy
Ann Mary, d. 8/29/1909 at 40/0/22 in Wellesley, MA; cerebral hemorrhage
Belle C., d. 6/2/1919 at 67/0/22 in Gilford; chronic nephritis
Calvin, d. 5/16/1887 at 71/4/19; bank cashier; married; b. Rochester;
    Moses Hale (Bradford, MA) and Elizabeth Demerritt (Durham)
Charles H., d. 4/28/1931 at 67 in Portland, ME; coronary thrombosis
Elizabeth, d. 12/7/1893 at 70; old age; b. Ireland; (Ireland; Ireland)
Eva C., d. 4/24/1937 at 82/6/5; arteriosclerosis
Francis W., d. 10/18/1896 at 69; valvular dis. of heart; PH
George, d. 10/25/1907 at 50/3/11 in Boston, MA; ruptured spleen
George L., d. 8/7/1896 at --; meningitis; b. Dover; buried in Wolfeboro
George W., d. 3/12/1931 at 82/5/7; apoplexy
Janet E., d. 7/12/1937 at 66/1/23; paralysis agites
Lucy Hill, d. 5/29/1902 at 89 in Washington, DC; chronic bronchitis; PH
Martha, d. 11/16/1908 at 79 in Boston, MA; pneumonia
Martha C., d. 3/17/1924 at 92/4/18 in Newton, MA; acute bronchitis
Severine D., d. 4/30/1922 at 36/7/7; shock; Joseph Perreault and Emma
    Juneau
Susan Lord, d. 3/15/1909 at 82/4/8 in Gloucester, MA; pneumonia
Thomas W., d. 1/26/1911 at 85/0/20; arterio-sclerosis; William Hale and
    Eliza A. Shackford
William, d. 6/1/1893 at 88; failure on account of age; b. Dover;
    (Portsmouth; Rollinsford)

HALEY,
Allen E., d. 5/8/1921 at 74/1/20; obstruction of bowels; John D. Haley and Phoebe Gromaugh
Annie, d. 6/24/1898 at 25; peritonitis; b. St. John, NB; PH
Bridget, d. 5/27/1913 at 34; aortic stenosis; John Haley and Ellen Wethers
Catherine, d. 2/9/1893 at 48; died in Strafford Co. Asylum fire
Charles, d. 12/14/1887 at 0/2; b. Dover; Dennis Haley (England) and Catherine Cassiley (Dover)
Edmund J., d. 11/4/1923 at 12/10/13; hemorrhage; John J. Haley and Eunice Vallely
Edward, d. 11/24/1892 at 34; drowned; b. Dover; (Lee; Dover)
Ella M., d. 5/3/1889 at 4/6/14; b. Dover; W. Monson (NS) and Ellen J. Stevens (NS)
Ellen, d. 3/27/1901 at 7/6/4; meningitis; SM
Ellen, d. 11/9/1934 at 64/10 in Salem, MA; cerebral hemorrhage
Frank G., d. 2/18/1909 at 38/6/1; alcoholism; Rufus Haley and Jennie M. Tredick
George D., d. 4/23/1889 at 2/7/4; b. Dover; Morrison Haley (NS) and Ella Stevens (NS)
Gertrude, d. 8/3/1897 at 0; diarrhea; b. Dover; PH
Harrison, d. 5/26/1906 at 80/11/26; septicemia; PH
Hattie E., d. 5/15/1888 at 0/2/10; b. Dover; W. M. Haley (NS) and Ellen J. Stevens (NS)
Hattie P., d. 10/9/1887 at 13/8/13; b. Madbury; Allen E. Haley (NS) and Mary E. Robinson (Halifax)
Hattie P., d. 9/11/1895 at 0; cholera infantum; b. Dover; PH
James, d. 2/28/1926 at 59/0/10; sarcoma of thyroid; John Haley and Ellen -----
Jeanette, d. 4/4/1902 at 0/0/6; PH
Jennie, d. 4/13/1906 at 77/7/12; old age; PH
Jennie G., d. 10/1/1909 at 75; acute gastritis; James Gordon and Sally Massey
John Edmund, d. 9/29/1923 at 3/3/4; pneumonia; Dennis J. Haley and Lillian G. Benn
John J., d. 12/8/1934 at 51/3/29 in Concord; poly. rubra vera
Julia, d. 11/14/1914 at 60; broncho pneumonia; ----- Callahan and Nora Carroll
Kate, d. 2/6/1894 at 20; pneumonia; b. Dover; SM
Lillian, d. 7/8/1931 at 76/3/8 in Exeter; hypertension
Martha W., d. 4/20/1887 at 48/1/3; teacher; single; b. Exeter; Gilman Haley (Exeter) and Sarah Smith (Exeter)
Rufus, d. 3/26/1895 at 71; old age; b. NH; PH
Samuel, d. 8/10/1914 at 74/11/20; angina pectoris; John D. Haley and Phoebe A. Greene
Sarah J., d. 3/12/1931 at 85/9/24 in York, ME; chr. valv. heart dis.

Sarah R., d. 2/26/1903 at 63; paralysis; PH
Thomas M., d. 5/17/1931 at 73 in Cambridge, MA; hypostatis pneumonia
Willie, d. 10/1/1889 at 0/1/1; b. Dover; William Haley (NS) and Eliza J. Stevens (NS)

HALFPENNY,
Elizabeth, d. 7/9/1937 at 41/6/5*

HALL,
child, d. 7/29/1897 at 0; stillborn; b. Dover; PH
Abbie A., d. 7/8/1909 at 72 in Rochester; paralysis; William Tuttle and Abigail Perkins
Alonzo, d. 1/16/1911 at 63/4/22 in Albany, NY; pneumonia
Alva A., d. 6/15/1912 at 73/1/29; cerebral hemorrhage; William Hall and Lydia Hall
Andrew S., d. 11/5/1925 at 75/2/13; chronic endocarditis; Winslow Hall and Sophia Stevenson
Benjamin H., d. 3/30/1905 at 66/5/15; heart disease; buried in New Castle
Bertram Eldred, d. 12/31/1937 at 36/9/8 in Valentine, NE; found dead on street
Carrie A., d. 9/10/1914 at 67/2/21; fatty degeneration of heart; Richard Gale and Sally Downing
Carrie D., d. 2/19/1928 at 85/9/5; carcinoma of intestine; Jonathan Hall and Lydia Demeritt
Carrie N., d. 3/18/1924 at 59/5/12; cerebral apoplexy; Joseph W. Nairn and Alice L. Finckle
Charles A., d. 12/9/1918 at 58/8/1; natural causes; George W. Hall
Charles A., d. 6/8/1925 at 68/6/12; cerebral hemorrhage; Joel S. Hall and Lydia -----
Charles A., d. 4/12/1927 at 55/7/21; ch. int. nephritis; John F. Hall and Sarah Merrill
Charles F., d. 2/23/1916 at 72/8/23; haemoptysis; Elisha S. Hall and Mary Bickford
Charles H., d. 12/25/1898 at 71; epithetical cancer; b. Strafford; PH
Charles S., d. 2/22/1918 at 62/0/29 in Boston, MA; lobar pneumonia
Charles W., d. 3/8/1900 at <1; whooping cough; PH
Clara Elliott, d. 3/16/1937 at 87/1/4; arteriosclerosis
Cora H., d. 7/22/1920 at 57/11/22; cerebral hemorrhage; Louis Wiggin and Cordelia Decater
Daniel, d. 1/8/1920 at 87/10/11; old age; Gilman Hall and Eliza Tuttle
Daniel Gilman, d. 4/29/1927 at 50/4/14 in Middleton, MA; pulmonary tuberculosis
David O., d. 7/23/1899 at 57; fatty degeneration of heart; PH
E. Forest, d. 8/2/1908 at 38 in Concord; exhaustion in dementia; D. O. Hall and S. M. Tuttle

E. Melvin, d. 5/1/1925 at 79/1/2 in Concord; broncho pneumonia; Eri Hall and Mary Bunker
Edwin, d. 1/17/1898 at 48 in Brockton, MA; rheu. dis. of heart asthma; PH
Edwin F., d. 11/15/1917 at 76/7/19 in Haverhill, MA; chronic myelitis
Effie May, d. 3/25/1919 at 20/11/25; tuberculosis of lungs; John B. Chasse and Jennie M. Abbott
Eliza, d. 11/9/1888 at 85/6/1; widow; b. Dover; David Tuttle (Dover) and Esther Bunker (Durham)
Eliza, d. 10/13/1900 at 72; acute peritonitis; PH
Eliza D., d. 4/19/1919 at 74/1/24; cerebral hemorrhage; Jonathan Hall and Lydia Demeritt
Elizabeth A., d. 6/26/1930 at 91/2/23 in Somerville, MA; pneumonia
Elizabeth C., d. 1/7/1892 at 51; grippe (see following entry)
Elizabeth Chapman, d. 1/7/1893 at 51; grippe (see preceding entry)
Elizabeth G., d. 10/30/1911 at 63/1/24 in Haverhill, MA; umbilical hernia
Elizabeth W., d. 11/29/1907 at 69/4/21 in Taunton, MA; bronchial la grippe
Ella F., d. 11/3/1920 at 63/11/22 in Haverhill, MA; broncho pneumonia
Eri E., d. 7/19/1935 at 51/6/7; myocarditis
Etta B., d. 8/12/1897 at 29; consumption; b. Durham; PH
Eunice C., d. 4/10/1919 at 71/11 in Providence, RI
Everett, d. 2/5/1894 at 76; bronchitis following grippe; b. Barrington; PH
Frank H., d. 2/20/1935 at 85/11/17; cerebral hemorrhage
Fred E., d. 10/15/1908 at 17/4/15; cerebral hemorrhage; Edward Hall and Ora -----
Fred L., d. 11/14/1912 at 39/3/16 in Bridgeport, CT; chronic heart disease; David O. Hall and Sophronia M. -----
George A., d. 4/2/1929 at 85/3/26 in S. Berwick, ME; cerebral hemorrhage
Gertrude E., d. 4/19/1908 at 0/4/8; bronchitis; Harry B. Hall and Gertrude M. Walker
Gilman, d. 9/7/1917 at 76/7/12; chr. valv. dis. of heart; Gilman Hall and Eliza Tuttle
Gilman, d. 2/9/1926 at 80; broncho pneumonia
Hannah A., d. 10/1/1911 at 78/1/8; cerebral hemorrhage; ----- Willey and Sarah Roberts
Hannah J., d. 12/23/1918 at 80/4/14; cerebral hemorrhage; Stephen Reynolds and Sally Garland
Henry, d. 9/24/1899 at 78; heart disease; PH
Hiram H., d. 5/24/1930 at 83/6/19; organic heart dis.; Jacob H. Hall and Lydia Quimby
Howard, d. 9/4/1905 at 0/0/16; marasmus; PH
Hubbard W., d. 6/2/1894 at 30 in Barrington; tuberculosis; buried in Dover
Ida M., d. 5/7/1923 at 50/7/24 in Worcester, MA; arterio sclerosis
Isaac G., d. 1/4/1911 at 83/1/7; chronic nephritis; David Hall and Mary Giles
James C., d. 3/7/1934 at 84/2/14; lobar pneumonia

Joel S., d. 7/12/1909 at 80/10/18; arteriosclerosis; Israel Hall and Mary Sanders
John C., d. 9/15/1919 at 84/8/15; endocarditis; William P. Hall and Louisa C. Durgin
John Clayton, d. 8/29/1915 at 0/3; marasmus; John C. Hall and A. Mary Bergeron
John W., d. 10/13/1900 at 70 in Durham; PH
Joseph, d. 4/23/1921 at 71/9/3 in Concord; cerebral arterio sclerosis; Joseph I. Hall and Mary Libby
Joseph D., d. 10/5/1908 at 74/9/4; entero colitis; Joseph Hall and Sarah Sanborn
Joshua G., d. 10/31/1898 at 69; peritonitis; b. Wakefield; PH
Kate B., d. 12/10/1917 at 64/11/27; uraemia; John S. Buzzell and Olive J. Young
Laura G., d. 9/4/1927 at 60 in Danvers, MA; arterio sclerosis
Leonra F., d. 2/27/1912 at –; chronic myelitis; ----- Barden
Leonard, d. 11/16/1892 at 75; heart disease; b. NH; (NH; NH)
Livona S., d. 2/24/1909 at 73/5/20; hemiplegia; Aaron Morrill and Abigail Sargent
Lizzie H., d. 12/3/1920 at 73/2/5; lobar pneumonia; William P. Hall and Louisa Durgin
Lola N., d. 9/30/1916 at 34/1/21; pulmonary tuberculosis; Fred Noble and Rose Hatch
Loraine N., d. 10/12/1918 at 0/4/15; influenza; James E. Hall and Effie M. Chase
Lucy H., d. 10/27/1930 at 75/7/18; chr. mit. heart dis.; James Boston and Elizabeth Carter
Lydia, d. 12/12/1892 at 98; old age; b. Strafford; (Portsmouth; Lee)
Lydia S., d. 11/18/1913 at –; heart disease; Aaron Willey and Susan Mills
Marie F., d. 10/12/1918 at 51/7; malnutrition; Moses N. Bartlett and Louisa M. Fitts
Martha J., d. 5/10/1909 at 60/4/28; cerebral apoplexy; John C. Varney and Margaret Brock
Mary, d. 3/7/1906 at 92/2/27 in Barrington; senility; PH
Mary A., d. 1/11/1909 at 69; apoplexy; Stephen Richardson and Abigail Hanscom
Mary A., d. 8/9/1909 at 72/10/20 in Boston, MA; hemiplegia
Mary E., d. 1/9/1892 at 75; la grippe; b. Rochester; (Rochester; Rochester)
Mary E., d. 7/3/1896 at 44; phthisis; b. NY; buried in Newmarket
Mary F., d. 11/15/1911 at 85/7/11; cerebral apoplexy; Obediah Moody and Mary Bean
Mrs. Andrew, d. 7/11/1889 at 42/10/14; housewife; married; b. Dover; H. G. Hanson (Dover) and Irene Corson (Lebanon)
Nancy Libby, d. 11/30/1901 at 79/4/15; cancer; PH
Nellie M., d. 3/22/1901 at 33/0/20; apoplexy; PH

Olive N., d. 7/15/1901 at 50/10/19 in Brockton, MA; apoplexy; PH
Oram R., d. 12/7/1901 at 75/0/25; paralytic shock; PH
Orinda A., d. 11/13/1931 at 81/7/23 in W. Newbury; arterio sclerosis
Phoebe, d. 4/12/1887 at 67; b. Barrington (see following entry)
Phoebe, d. 4/12/1888 at 67; widow; b. Barrington; Catherine Smith (see preceding entry)
Samantha E., d. 8/30/1926 at 76/5; pleurisy with effusion; George Wiggin and Sophia Hayes
Sophia, d. 10/9/1896 at 79; liver complaint; b. Wolfeboro; PH
Sophia D., d. 12/1/1918 at 76/3/14; locomotor ataxia; Jonathan T. Dodge and Sarah Hanson
Sophronia M., d. 4/5/1912 at 71/5/15; acute uraemia; James W. Tuttle and Sally Middleton
Stephen T., d. 9/20/1906 at 64/0/7; dysentery, chronic; PH
Susan E. B., d. 8/6/1894 at 57; blood poisoning; b. Boston, MA; PH
Thomas, d. 7/22/1897 at 18 in Manchester; exhaustion; SM
Thomas D., d. 2/2/1909 at 59/5/26; haemoptysis; Ezra T. Hall and Abbie J. Howe
Ursula W., d. 2/21/1920 at 68/5/14; chronic nephritis; Oram R. Hall

HALLAM,
Daniel W., d. 5/31/1925 at 87/3/6; senile gangrene; Daniel Hallam and Martha Purrglove
Edwin, d. 1/2/1918 at 65 in Philadelphia, PA; myocarditis
Elizabeth Ann, d. 11/26/1919 at 82/5/2; disease of spine; Daniel Hallam and Martha Purseglove
Sarah L., d. 4/25/1919 at 77/0/28; pneumonia, lobar; Daniel Hallam and Martha Purseglove

HALLIDAY,
Frank C., Jr., d. 8/12/1934 at 38/3; Bright's disease
Frank W., d. 1/16/1935 at 68/2/3; chronic myocarditis

HALLORAN,
Hannah, d. 12/31/1904 at 65; heart failure
Jeremiah, d. 12/9/1902 at 36; valvular disease of heart; SM
Matthew, d. 7/26/1887 at 24/7; shoemaker; single; b. S. Newmarket; Patrick Halloran (Ireland) and Elizabeth Hoye (Ireland)
Matthew J., d. 3/2/1935 at 63 in Springfield, MA; chronic myocarditis

HALLOWAY,
child, d. 4/1/1936 at –; stillborn

HALLWORTH,
James A., d. 8/11/1887 at 19/9/2; shoemaker; single; b. NH; Henry
    Hallworth (England) and Harriet Cowan (England)
Louise H., d. 4/17/1920 at 33/11/10; phthisis pulmonalis; Henry Hallworth
    and Harriet Cowan

HAM,
son, d. 12/18/1890 at –; George W. Lyons and Sadie J. Ham (Dover)
child, d. 3/19/1925 at –; stillborn; Harold R. Ham and Judith Jenness
Abigail Dame, d. 11/29/1890 at 82/6/8; widow; William Bartlett (Lee) and
    Sarah Dame (Lee)
Adeline E., d. 4/22/1937 at 82/10/14; heart disease
Alpha, d. 5/9/1933 at 75/8/20; cerebral embolism
Alta E., d. 6/1/1930 at 70/7/29; carcinoma uterus; Henry Paul and Mary A.
    Hayes
Ann S., d. 1/15/1902 at 72/2/11; pneumonia; PH
Anna Kate, d. 9/6/1926 at 66/4/3 in Barrington; cerebral hemorrhage
Aramantha E., d. 4/3/1935 at 84/5/18 in Springfield, VT; cerebral
    arteriosclerosis
Asa Giles, d. 11/9/1910 at 82/4/12 in Manchester; cancer of lip
Augusta DeM., d. 10/30/1919 at 83/4/18 in W. Newton, MA; broncho
    pneumonia
Charles, d. 2/19/1930 at 76; arterio sclerosis; Moses Ham and Elizabeth
    Nutter
Charles A., d. 1/27/1927 at 75/0/2 in Rollinsford; cerebral hemorrhage
Charles E., d. 2/12/1923 at 72/9/6; chr. inter. nephritis; Benjamin M. Ham
    and Sarah O. Hall
Charles F., d. 2/28/1890 at 50/8/12; married
Charles F., d. 8/19/1908 at 73/7/19; progressive paralysis; Daniel Ham
    and Sarah Bickford
Charles W., d. 2/25/1900 at 43 in Ashland, MA; primary tuberculosis; PH
Charlotte A., d. 6/10/1935 at 85/11/10; cerebral hemorrhage
Ellen A., d. 7/22/1926 at 80/3/21; acute myocarditis; William Ham and
    Tamson Davis
Ellen B., d. 1/23/1908 at 88/4/13; pneumonia; Joseph D. Pollard and
    Susan Cook
Emily C., d. 8/7/1909 at 66/6/19 in Malabar, FL; ind. com. by weak heart
Ephraim, d. 3/1/1913 at 76/6/21; organic disease of heart; Charles Ham
    and Abigail D. Bartlett
Ethel J., d. 8/14/1888 at 0/9/22 in S. Berwick; b. Dover; George W. Ham
    (Newfield, ME) and Emma Jones (Saco, ME)
Fannie E., d. 7/2/1934 at 75/4/29 in Attleboro, MA; carcinoma of liver
Guy Leslie, d. 5/10/1915 at 24/8/4; acute Brights disease; Charles E. Ham
    and Addie Hackett

Helen J., d. 12/25/1922 at 76/0/14; senility; Charles Ham and Abigail D. Bartlett
J. Edward, d. 8/15/1906 at 59/7/18; meningitis; PH
John E., d. 1/15/1931 at 73/3/15 in Attleboro, MA; lobar pneumonia
John R., d. 10/20/1889 at 60/8/20; watchman; married; b. Rollinsford; Nathaniel Ham (Portsmouth) and Betsey Fry (Berwick, ME)
John R., d. 10/31/1928 at 78/0/8 in Palmer, MA; cardio vascular dis.
John S. F., d. 12/2/1903 at 73/9/28; fatty degeneration of heart; PH
John T. W., d. 8/22/1925 at 87/1/22; lob. pneu. traumatic; John Ham and Martha Wentworth
Joseph, d. 8/5/1929 at 91/9/3; arterio sclerosis
Joseph, 3rd, d. 6/16/1896 at 84; old age; b. Dover; PH
Joseph A., d. 6/14/1922 at 37/7/12; endocarditis; William F. Ham and Mary Jane Lynes
Joshua M., d. 11/19/1888 at 47/6/27; farmer; married; b. Dover; Walter Ham (Milton) and Nancy Morrill (Salisbury, MA)
Julia A., d. 10/19/1902 at 72/5/6; Bright's disease; PH
Lillian E., d. 1/5/1937 at 57/4/24*; b. England
Lola T., d. 12/17/1932 at 54 in Radnor, PA; carcinoma
Lona M., d. 12/14/1910 at 33/4/21; phthisis pulmonalis; Eli Varney and Abbie Ellis
Louisa M., d. 8/31/1895 at 55 in Exeter; apoplexy; buried in Dover
Lurana Jane, d. 2/1/1903 at 68/0/1; cancer of bowel; buried in Barrington
Margaret, d. 7/2/1910 at 49/10; cerebral hemorrhage; Florence Driscoll and Mary Haley
Maria Theresa, d. 12/31/1919 at 79/9/4; bronchitis; Joseph Ham and Mary Randall
Marilla M., d. 3/11/1902 at 65/10/6; thrombi in heart; PH
Martha A., d. 3/9/1909 at 79/3/17; pneumonia; Charles Ham and Abigail Bartlett
Martha J., d. 8/20/1898 at 74; paralysis; b. Barrington; PH
Mary A., d. 1/17/1929 at 80/3/6; myocarditis; George Wiggin and Sophia Hayes
Mary J., d. 7/27/1905 at 75; carcinoma; PH
Maude L., d. 6/15/1934 at 59/9/11 in York, ME; cerebral hemorrhage
Nancy M., d. 9/8/1898 at 89; senility; b. Salisbury; buried in family lot
Olive A., d. 4/1/1921 at 84 in S. Portland, ME; cerebral hemorrhage; James W. Dana
Orren F., d. 12/4/1898 at 19; phthisis pulmonalis; b. Newfields; buried in Newfields
Paul, d. 4/21/1917 at 84; apoplexy
Rebecca J., d. 7/13/1902 at 19/3/6; pulmonary phthisis; buried in Newfields
Sally B., d. 9/27/1890 at 82/8/19; single; Joshua Ham (Dover) and Mehitable Horne (Dover)

Sarah B., d. 1/10/1911 at 80/5/20; nephritis and heart disease; John Richards and Phoebe McDuffee

Sarah M., d. 8/19/1887 at 76/5/14; housekeeper; widow; b. Parsonsfield, ME; Nicholas Morrill (Parsonsfield, ME) and Abigail Bickford (Parsonsfield, ME)

Tamsen, d. 9/14/1911 at 90/4/3; old age; Isaac Davis and Betsy Davis

William, d. 9/14/1904 at 82/10/23; heart disease; PH

William H., d. 12/5/1906 at 53/3; pnuemonia; SM

HAMEL,
Alfred, d. 9/22/1929 at 84; chr. endocarditis

Dora, d. 7/26/1913 at 17/7/4; septicemia; Nelson Hamel and Clara Begin

Eleonard, d. 2/18/1920 at 63/10/14; endocarditis acute; Louis Provencher and Rosalie Hebert

Hector, d. 11/11/1934 at 18/1/15; laryngeal edema

Onesime, d. 11/7/1916 at 67/10/1; chron. gastro enteritis; ----- Hamel and ----- Pepin

Pierre, d. 7/31/1930 at 75/8/20; fracture of neck; Joseph Hamel and Marie Provencher

HAMILTON,
child, d. 1/18/1929 at –; stillborn; Raymond L. Hamilton and Emma C. Rickert

Agnes C., d. 3/6/1888 at 16/2/13; student; b. Scotland; R. Hamilton (Scotland) and Sarah Campbell (Scotland)

Carrie F., d. 4/24/1916 at 63/10/13; chronic endocarditis; James Hamilton and Rhoda L. Allen

David, d. 10/28/1916 at 64/1/10 in Worcester, MA; tuberculosis

Henry E., d. 7/20/1889 at 52 in Stratham

Robert A., d. 11/11/1916 at 73/9/28; carcinoma of intestines; Thomas Hamilton

Sarah C., d. 2/14/1910 at 63/6/28; heart disease; John Campbell and Catherine McFarland

Simeon B., d. 5/6/1904 at 77/5; paralysis; PH

HAMM,
Ethel M., d. 3/31/1937 at 42*

HAMMOND,
Agnes, d. 7/9/1888 at 21/11 in Durham; mill operative; married; b. Boylston, MA; Alfred (England) and Susan (W. Brookfield, MA)

Almeda C., d. 9/7/1925 at 72/10/17; pernicious anemia; Newell C. Davis and Mary A. Emerson

Amasa H., d. 1/31/1889 at 72/9/26; farmer; married; b. Phippsburg, ME; David Hammons and H. Batchelder

Charles F., d. 5/28/1931 at 79/0/23; diabetes mellitus
David A., d. 4/30/1920 at 66/5/8; lobar pneumonia; David Hammond and
    Sarah J. Buzzell
Doris M., d. 2/24/1923 at 1/4/21 in Lawrence, MA; endocarditis
John A., d. 12/9/1902 at 81/10/26; senility; buried in Portsmouth
Lua M., d. 4/18/1907 at 46/4/29; typhoid fever; John W. Felker and Mary J.
    Page
Lydia F., d. 1/9/1887 at 30/0/7; housewife; married; b. Dover; Enoch
    Brown and Abbie Brown
M. B., d. 9/15/1895 at 41 in Kennebunk, ME; organic disease of heart; b.
    Albion, ME; buried in Albion, ME
Mary E., d. 1/24/1897 at 72; gangrene; b. Epping; PH
Susan E., d. 1/1/1908 at 74/0/27; cerebral hemorrhage; C. H. Wentworth
    and Harriet Thompson
William B., d. 6/13/1924 at 76/2/18 in Ossipee; cerebral hemorrhage
Willie W., d. 10/18/1932 at 62/9/4; diabetes

HAMMONS,
Caroline A., d. 6/12/1909 at 82/4/9; senility; Mark Plummer and Sally Lary
Caroline S., d. 9/15/1935 at 81/5/27; arteriosclerosis

HAMPSON,
Henry, d. 12/16/1891 at 29; single; (England; England)

HANAFORD,
Deborah, d. 9/10/1906 at 87/1/29; senile decay; PH

HANAGHAN,
John, d. 2/10/1917 at 75; cerebral hemorrhage; James Hanaghan and
    Mary A. Flannery
Thomas E., d. 10/28/1936 at 69/10/28 in Manchester; carcinoma
    oesophagus

HANAHAN,
Mary, d. 5/18/1892 at –; bronchitis; b. Dover; (Dover; Dover)

HANGION,
Stavroula, d. 6/12/1913 at 0/10/22; whooping cough; William Hangion and
    Demetro Phiskelley

HANKE,
Henrietta, d. 4/25/1932 at 72 in Danvers, MA; arterio sclerosis

HANLEY,
Adelia E., d. 4/30/1934 at 57/1/13 in Berwick, ME; angina pectoris

HANLON,
Annie, d. 12/22/1893 at 1; croup; b. Dover; (Dover; Lewiston, ME)
Catherine, d. 8/8/1926 at 60 in Concord; senility
Charles, d. 2/22/1916 at 49 in Tewksbury, MA; cerebral hemorrhage
James E., d. 7/2/1887 at 1/9/20; b. Dover; John Hanlon (Dover) and Sarah A. Holland (Dover)
James P., d. 2/19/1905 at 26/11/2 in Marlboro, MA; Bright's disease
Joseph, d. 2/11/1896 at 53; heart disease; b. Ireland; SM
Joseph, d. 10/5/1924 at 55; probably heart disease
Julia S., d. 1/29/1914 at 63; general apoplexy; Eugene Sullivan and Margaret Flynn
Rose, d. 9/4/1887 at 0/3/7; b. Dover
Roseanna, d. 7/27/1896 at 55; cholera morbus; b. Ireland; SM
Sarah J., d. 2/15/1902 at 41; peritonitis; SM

HANNA,
Bridget, d. 5/3/1896 at 42; organic dis. of heart; b. Ireland; SM
Catherine, d. 2/12/1917 at 72/3/1; cerebral apoplexy; Owen Curry and Ellen Cassily
Elizabeth, d. 3/23/1937 at 62/11/22 in Concord; cere. arteriosclerosis
James, d. 8/25/1887 at 60; laborer; married; b. Ireland; John Hanna (Ireland) and Margaret Smith (Ireland)
James P., d. 2/2/1932 at 57/2/13; chronic nephritis
Janet, d. 6/30/1901 at 80/6; paralysis; PH
John, d. 10/10/1893 at 67; inflammation stomach & bowels; b. Ireland; (Ireland; Ireland)
John, d. 2/26/1925 at 76/11/18; arterio sclerosis; John Hanna and Catherine Cassily
John A., d. 2/24/1934 at 52/8/21; heart disease
Katherine, d. 8/3/1895 at 64; cholera morbus; b. Ireland; SM
Katherine, d. 5/31/1918 at 42; carcinoma of stomach; John Hanna
Patrick, d. 3/18/1927 at 50/7/14; diabetes mellitus; John Hanna and Catherine Curry
Sarah, d. 1/1/1920 at 85/7/12; cancer of stomach; James Toner and Nancy Haggan
William, d. 5/--/1919 at –; accidental drowning
William B., d. 12/10/1918 at 66/3/4 in Lawrence, MA; chronic endocarditis, etc.

HANNAFIRE,
Annie L., d. 9/11/1899 at –; pneumonia; buried in Lowell, MA

HANNAN,
Nellie, d. 2/5/1906 at 33; pneumonia

HANNON,
Dennis J., d. 3/20/1935 at 61/8/4 in Concord; chronic myocarditis
Frank, d. 8/16/1894 at 1; cholera infantum; b. Dover; SM
John, d. 4/11/1906 at –; malaria; SM

HANRATTY,
Alice, d. 6/28/1918 at 67/7/28; cancer of mouth; James Garvey and Mary Riley
Catherine, d. 11/7/1910 at 59/3/6; pulmonary embolism
Elizabeth, d. 4/10/1895 at 0; cerebral meningitis; b. Dover; SM
Frank, d. 2/1/1912 at 64; carcinoma of stomach
James, d. 7/6/1898 at 23; acute mania; b. Dover; SM
James J., d. 6/23/1912 at 83/2/28; ptomaine poisoning; Frank Hanratty and Mary Donnelly
John, d. 7/11/1895 at 18; phthisis pulmonalis; b. Dover; SM
John, d. 10/15/1917 at 64; myocarditis
Mary, d. 1/21/1901 at 45/7; la grippe; SM
Patrick, d. 9/28/1925 at 81; uraemia; Rose O'Neil
Patrick, d. 6/1/1928 at 67/11/2; natural causes; Owen Hanratty and Rose Duffy

HANRATY,
Mary C., d. 8/8/1909 at 22; tuberculosis; Patrick ----- and Catherine -----

HANSCOM,
son, d. 5/18/1888 at –; b. Dover; Frank A. Hanscom (NH) and Fannie Glidden (ME)
child, d. 1/14/1918 at –; miscarriage; Julia Hanscom
child, d. 5/28/1920 at –; stillborn; Fred Hanscom and Mary I. Robinson
Albert S., d. 5/27/1891 at 2/7/21; Henry L. Hanscom (Dover) and Jennie Bailey (MN)
Alice C., d. 5/29/1891 at 10/5/24; Henry Hanscom (Dover) and Jennie Bailey (MN)
Annie E., d. 5/6/1932 at 67/2/18; cerebral hemorrhage
Arabella, d. 10/28/1919 at 68/11/11; cancer of liver; Jeremiah Moulton and Abigail Stackpole
Catherine, d. 7/11/1924 at 43; myocarditis; John Connors and Catherine --
Charles M., d. 6/6/1889 at 34/1 in Underhill; shoe cutter; b. Cape Elizabeth, ME; Josiah Swett (Casco, ME) and Nancy Newbegin (Casco, ME)
Clara D., d. 5/1/1914 at 93/6/17; old age; William Gray and Sarah Rowe

Edgar L., d. 11/24/1890 at 1/0/5; Henry L. Hanscom (Malden, MA) and Jennie E. Bailey (MN)
Ellen A., d. 3/8/1930 at 83/6/22; cerebral myocarditis; John S. Jordan and Amelia Bell
Fannie E., d. 1/21/1923 at 58/11/27; ulcers of intestines; Reuben Dorrell and Caroline Kane
Fred, d. 5/18/1920 at 55/8/18; typhoid fever; John E. Hanscom and Julia Dorr
George W., d. 8/11/1923 at 85/3/9; senility; John Hanscom and Nancy Jellison
Henry L., d. 10/14/1925 at 76/1/7 in Berwick, ME; acute alcoholism
James M., d. 1/18/1926 at 77/7/21; angina pectoris; Micajah J. Hanscom and Clarissa Gray
John H., d. 7/3/1909 at 66 in Tilton; pulmonary phthisis
Kate E., d. 4/24/1915 at 56; tuberculosis of lungs; Jessie J. Giles and Isabel Drew
Kingsbury, d. 11/19/1905 at 70/0/19; cerebral hemorrhage; PH
Leon R., d. 7/1/1896 at – in Exeter; tuberculosis; PH
Lizzie A., d. 1/22/1890 at 31/2/10; single; Robert Hanscom (ME) and Susan Staples (ME)
Lorenzo, d. 2/28/1895 at 76; cystitis; SM
Mary, d. 4/6/1914 at 64; broncho pneumonia
Mary E., d. 11/10/1905 at 64/0/26; carcinoma; PH
Micajah S., d. 3/20/1909 at 90/0/24; senility; Jeremiah Hanscom and Sarah Swaine
Ruben M., d. 3/18/1897 at 0; scrofula; b. Dover; PH
Samuel, d. 11/18/1906 at 65/0/5; chronic interstitial nephritis; buried in Barrington
Sylvina P., d. 10/21/1906 at 76/11/1 in Melrose, MA; pneumonia; PH
Willie B., d. 5/27/1891 at 6/4/26; Henry L. Hanscom (Dover) and Jennie Bailey (MN)

HANSON,
child, d. 1/4/1896 at –; stillborn; b. Dover
child, d. 2/13/1898 at 0; stillborn; b. Dover
Adeline E., d. 4/12/1897 at 70; shock; b. Alton; PH
Alice B., d. 11/15/1897 at 0; convulsions; b. Dover; PH
Alice I., d. 7/20/1930 at 61/0/2; chronic myocarditis; John I. Hall and Lucy Murphy
Andrew, d. 4/1/1901 at 76/11/9; nephritis; PH
Ann E., d. 3/25/1891 at 46/5/25; married; Stephen Kendell (Groton, MA) and Jane Harlow (Boston)
Annie C., d. 4/1/1931 at 67/8/4 in Somersworth; carcinoma uteri
Burnham, d. 6/5/1916 at 91/1/5; senility; James Hanson and Hannah M. Place

Caroline, d. 5/16/1909 at 84; phthisis; Joseph Banks and Mary Smith
Carrie Belle, d. 1/21/1901 at 18; consumption; PH
Carrie K., d. 8/30/1890 at 19/10/17; George W. Hanson (Dover) and Annie Kimball (Dover)
Carrie L., d. 12/10/1933 at 72/2/3; cerebral hemorrhage
Carrie S., d. 5/13/1919 at 55/9/6; chronic endocarditis; James W. Hanson and Margaret Simmons
Catherine, d. 2/18/1927 at 68; cerebral thrombosis
Catherine F., d. 1/31/1907 at 80/4/29; sclerosis spinal cord; William Frye and Anne Buffum
Charles A., d. 1/28/1899 at 83; pneumonia; PH
Charles E., d. 1/30/1926 at 62/6/17; broncho pneumonia; Samuel R. Hanson and Elizabeth C. Fowler
Charles W., d. 5/9/1904 at 0/8/17; bronchitis; buried in Austin Cem.
Christine, d. 1/2/1887 at 83/2; housewife; married; b. Lee; ----- Daniels (Lee) and Polly Daniels (Lee)
Clara A., d. 7/20/1913 at 75/1/10; mitral regurgitation; Samuel Hanson and Clarissa Varney
Daniel E., d. 10/28/1902 at 68/0/2; abdominal cancer; PH
David S., d. 4/7/1907 at 70/7/13; pneumonia; Samuel Hanson and Clarissa Varney
Edith H., d. 8/14/1906 at 39/4/29; pulmonary tuberculosis; PH
Eliza A., d. 1/11/1925 at 82/10/6; chronic gastritis; William Holt and Ann Thornton
Elizabeth A., d. 9/2/1911 at 86/3/5; heart disease; David R. Stevens and Susan Young
Elizabeth E., d. 11/7/1910 at 62/10/26 in Haverhill, MA; chronic nephritis
Ella E., d. 9/8/1925 at 78 in Portsmouth; chr. intest. nephritis
Ellen C., d. 10/6/1926 at 76/5/24; chronic endocarditis; William Main and Susan Rollins
Ellen M., d. 12/20/1895 at 55; pneumonia; b. Dover; PH
Emeline, d. 10/17/1889 at 74/2/11; housekeeper; single; b. Dover; Benjamin Hanson (Dover) and Elizabeth Willand (Dover)
Emily J., d. 11/10/1913 at 76/7/27 in Lynn, MA; pul. tuberculosis
Emma J., d. 4/27/1926 at 68; angina pectoris
Enoch True, d. 4/2/1912 at 71/0/1; chron. articular rheumatism; Charles H. Hanson and Mary J. Plummer
Ethel May, d. 2/24/1928 at 0/0/5; Harold T. Hanson and Thelma A. Morse
Evelyn R., d. 7/28/1907 at 54/10/17; heart disease; Thomas Haniford and Evelyn Lord
Frank A., d. 1/13/1924 at 74/2/12 in Bethel, VT; chronic nephritis
Frank W., d. 9/20/1897 at 40; Bright disease; b. Dover; PH
Frank W., d. 1/16/1918 at 52/5 in Boston, MA; John J. Hanson and Sarah Smith
Fred E., d. 3/1/1903 at 30; alcoholism; PH

G. Herbert, d. 9/28/1898 at 17; valvular disease of heart; b. Dover; PH
George, d. 3/4/1932 at 74 in Concord; cancer of ear
George H., d. 9/26/1887 at 46/5/3; farmer; b. Dover; Stephen H. Hanson
 (Dover) and Martha A. Varney (Milton)
George H., d. 11/17/1894 at 43; typhoid fever; b. Dover; PH
Grace L., d. 4/24/1914 at 33/9/12; chronic nephritis; William H. Lindsey
 and Emma A. Albro
Grover L., Jr., d. 6/25/1937 at –; premature
Hans T., d. 6/5/1923 at 71/5/12; angina pectoris
Harrison, d. 10/2/1924 at 84/6/20 in Tilton; arterio sclerosis
Horatio G., d. 4/7/1896 at 62; organic dis. of heart; b. Dover; PH
Ida B., d. 4/10/1937 at 76/1/26; chr. myocarditis
Israel, d. 5/1/1927 at 80/5/15 in Tilton; organic heart disease
James L., d. 11/1/1891 at 42/5; single; Samuel H. Hanson (Dover) and
 Maria Deland (Wolfeboro)
James V., d. 5/5/1898 at 69; anaemia; b. Dover; PH
James W., d. 12/20/1887 at 48/8; painter; married; b. Dover; (Dover;
 Dover)
Jennie F., d. 8/24/1889 at 1/1/10; b. Dover; George W. Hanson (Dover)
 and Ellen Jordan (Boston, MA)
Jennie L., d. 5/19/1912 at 59/6/24; fatty degeneration of heart; Samuel
 Hanson and Melinda J. Hurd
John C., d. 9/14/1904 at 77/9/25 in Madbury; obstruction to right
 hypercond'm; PH
John D., d. 1/30/1926 at 75; arterio sclerosis; Moses Hanson and Olive P.
 Dearborn
John J., d. 7/2/1894 at 68; heart disease; b. NH; PH
John P., d. 12/4/1894 at 81; heart disease; PH
John P., d. 4/24/1901 at 39; pulmonary oedema; PH
John Q. A., d. 10/23/1910 at 76/3/24 in Chelsea, MA; chronic nephritis
John T., d. 7/8/1907 at 34/3/10; unknown; Enoch T. Hanson and Lydia ----
John T., d. 2/2/1919 at 46/4/20 in Cambridge, MA; fracture of skull
Joseph B., d. 8/7/1891 at 67/9/18; married; Jonathan Hanson (Waterboro,
 ME) and Mary Bean (Alfred)
Joseph H., d. 2/19/1917 at 86/11/24; senility; Joseph Hanson and Abigail
 Varney
Joseph W., d. 4/26/1930 at 50/8/14; carcinoma; George W. Hanson and
 Ellen A. Jordan
Kate Emily, d. 1/9/1911 at 32/7/28; acute nephritis; Alfred R. Sayer and
 Eliza L. Cook
Leander H., d. 10/13/1922 at 86/9/14; arterio sclerosis; Joseph Hanson
 and Abigail Varney
Lenora A., d. 11/5/1890 at 53; widow; John and Phoebe
Lydia, d. 10/4/1889 at 70 in Lewiston, ME

Lydia A., d. 12/21/1889 at 48/8/21; housewife; married; b. Dover; J. Austin (Dover) and Nancy Perkins (ME)

Malinda J., d. 1/2/1901 at 83/2/28; nephritis; PH

Margaret, d. 4/23/1907 at 71/1/4; senility; Jeremiah Caverno and Dorothy K. Balch

Margaret A., d. 11/29/1912 at 73/0/25; uraemia; John Simmons and Margaret Smith

Margaret Christina, d. 2/24/1937 at 82/5/3*

Maria, d. 10/11/1887 at 76/4; widow; b. Wolfeboro; ----- Deland and ----- Neal

Marion S., d. 9/6/1921 at 39/5/22 in Haverhill, MA; ch. inters. nephritis

Martha A., d. 11/16/1890 at 78/7/7; widow; Hopley Varney (Dover) and Lydia Varney (Dover)

Martha A., d. 8/20/1923 at 83/4/2; carcinoma of breast; Stack H. Locke and Mary E. Beal

Martha E., d. 1/22/1912 at 93/0/15; old age; Ephraim Hanson and Abigail Leighton

Mary, d. 1/2/1898 at 79; heart disease; b. Dover; PH

Mary E., d. 2/14/1936 at 84/6/15 in Rochester; apoplexy

Mary J., d. 10/19/1908 at 27/4/9; tuberculosis of lungs; John Haughey and Margaret Murray

Mary O., d. 3/2/1935 at 87/1/28 in Chelsea, MA; chronic valvular disease of heart

Mattie A., d. 8/23/1889 at 18/7/27; b. Dover; Enoch T. Hanson (Moultonboro) and Lydia Austin (Dover)

Mattie W., d. 7/28/1935 at 65/6/13; apoplexy

May A., d. 5/6/1921 at 84/5/1; senility; Alfred Demeritt and Mary E. Torr

Nathaniel E., d. 6/15/1901 at 64/4/10; uraemia; PH

Natt, d. 5/9/1928 at 49 in Brooklyn, NY; pneumonia

Olive, d. 4/14/1892 at 63; heart disease; b. Sanford, ME; (Sanford, ME; Sanford, ME)

Olive P., d. 12/7/1889 at 0/3/15

Philenia P., d. 2/28/1914 at 70/9/30; apoplexy; John L. Pickering and Marie J. Berry

Sarah R., d. 1/2/1914 at 83/0/16; pneumonia; Ebenezer Smith and Hannah Richardson

Stacy Locke, d. 1/1/1933 at 58/2/13; angina pectoris

Stella M., d. 8/17/1900 at <1; cholera infantum; PH

Susan, d. 11/21/1915 at 45/1/9; cerebral thrombosis; Thomas Lang and Katherine -----

William H., d. 10/27/1913 at 79/5/6 in Alton; syncope, dis. of heart

William J., d. 9/12/1905 at 0/1/17; ileo-colitis; buried in Austin Cem.

William J., d. 8/26/1925 at 64/10/9 in Dorchester, MA; myocarditis

HARDING,
Alice, d. 10/3/1906 at 95/10/29 in Woodstock, ME; old age; PH
Thomas P., d. 6/2/1889 at 78/4 in ME

HARDY,
Caroline E., d. 2/10/1903 at 98/0/9; old age; PH
Charles C., d. 2/10/1896 at 68; organic disease of heart; b. Exeter; PH
Elizabeth, d. 4/3/1908 at 66/0/27; heart disease; Alphonso Bickford and Mary J. Smith
Emeline, d. 6/24/1899 at 66; cancer; PH
Marcia S., d. 2/9/1908 at 80/5/30 in Malden, MA; insanity dementia
Margaret, d. 5/31/1895 at 0; senile gangrene; b. Dover; PH
Nettie, d. 3/8/1900 at 53 in Minneapolis, MN; epilepsy; PH
Peter J., d. 6/15/1931 at 51/11/14 in Yonkers, NY; mitral stenosis
Rebecca J., d. 9/2/1896 at --; marasmus; b. Dover; PH
Washington W., d. 4/9/1916 at 78/0/24; chron. val. heart dis.; Thomas Hardy and Sarah Rust

HARGRAVES,
Abbie M., d. 9/9/1912 at 65/5/25; chronic nephritis; Sampson B. Locke and Sarah Canney
Howard, d. 8/23/1915 at 74/9/27; senility
William F., d. 10/20/1922 at 64/1; intestinal carcinoma; John Hargraves and Mary McClaren

HARKINS,
James, d. 5/22/1917 at 11/4/17; uraemia; James Hawkins (sic) and Ann Flynn
James, d. 2/1/1925 at 67; chr. interstitial neph.; James Harkins and Margaret Dougherty
Margaret, d. 10/5/1887 at 64; widow; b. Ireland; Daniel Doherty (Ireland) and Bridget McLonghrin (Ireland)
Mary E., d. 3/12/1934 at 60 in Methuen, MA; chronic bronchitis
Michael L., d. 4/13/1935 at 67/6 in Methuen, MA; uremia

HARKNESS,
Laura A. O., d. 8/3/1890 at 63/0/9; married; Bradley Osgood (Raymond) and Mehitable Wood (Bradford, MA)

HARNETT,
Margaret V., d. 12/10/1928 at 27/4/20 in Medford, MA; septicemia; John Miniter and Catherine Lawless

HARRIGAN,
Anne, d. 11/21/1912 at 63; pneumonia
Catherine, d. 7/5/1888 at 3/3/9; b. Dover; John T. Harrigan (Ireland) and Joanne Lanorigan (Dover)
Hannah, d. 4/23/1907 at 47; cerebral hemorrhage; John Lannigan
John T., d. 5/6/1932 at 90/5/11; chr. intestinal nephritis

HARRIMAN,
child, d. 10/27/1926 at 3 hrs.; umbilical hemorrhage; Charles Harriman and Maud Blaisdell
Charles, d. 2/27/1930 at –; atelectasis; Charles Harriman and Maud E. Blaisdell
Ella M., d. 10/1/1903 at 33/1/15 in So. Berwick, ME; chronic gastritis; PH

HARRINGTON,
Almira T., d. 3/26/1890 at 63/2/6; widow; Frederick Shufeldt (Germany) and Mary Shufeldt (VT)
Franklin H., d. 4/26/1937 at 82/8/18 in Concord; arteriosclerosis heart
Jeremiah J., d. 12/31/1924 at 0/0/10; J. J. Harrington and Mary Crane
Mary E., d. 5/11/1908 at 48/6/12; embolism; Moses E. Clark and Mary W. Powers
Mary Jane, d. 2/27/1929 at 78/10/26 in Madbury; chronic valv. heart
Rebecca J., d. 8/1/1905 at 73/0/6; paralysis; PH

HARRIS,
Arthur, d. 1/3/1896 at –; inanision; b. Dover; SM
Bridget, d. 3/2/1897 at 34; chronic nephritis; b. Ireland; SM
Charles H., d. 11/22/1933 at 74/9/10; broncho pneumonia
Elizabeth, d. 8/4/1890 at 52; single; Thomas Harris (Ireland) and Sarah Brennan (Ireland)
Harriet W., d. 3/30/1903 at 79; nephritis
Isabella, d. 3/1/1907 at 66; heart disease; Thomas Harris and Sarah Brennan
Joseph, d. 2/24/1888 at 29/9/22; black; cook; married; b. St. Vincent, WI; Samuel Harris (St. Vincent) and Mary Walker (St. Vincent)
Thomas, d. 4/1/1908 at 29; malignant jaundice

HARRISON,
child, d. 10/14/1892 at –; stillborn; b. Dover; (Ireland; Ireland)
child, d. 7/13/1924 at –; stillborn; Fred F. Harrison and Edna French
Marion Lucille, d. 3/9/1920 at 0/0/14; premature birth; Fred F. Harrison and Edna French
Melbourne M., d. 11/10/1930 at 54/3/24 in Rollinsford; accidental
Mildred J., d. 5/28/1935 at 7/5/20; accidental drowning

HARRITTY,
[unnamed], d. 6/28/1901 at 48/0/0; sunstroke; SM

HART,
Ella L., d. 8/14/1920 at 63/7/3; cerebral hemorrhage; Allison Parker and Lillian Whitney
Gladys M., d. 11/21/1895 at 1; pneumonia and laryngitis; b. Strafford; buried in Strafford
Harriet F., d. 8/30/1913 at 59; acute gastritis; John Worster and Mary Woodbury
Henry, d. 7/20/1889 at 42; laborer; single; b. Ireland; (Ireland; Ireland)
Horace Greenleaf, d. 6/11/1912 at 63/6/17; valvular heart disease; William N. Hart and Olive Gowen
Iber Mabel, d. 10/19/1900 at 1; catarrhal pneumonia; buried in Strafford
Nellie A., d. 11/23/1901 at 26/9/6; Bright's disease; buried in Strafford

HARTFORD,
Anna D. L., d. 12/4/1912 at 59/5/17; sudden; Charles Harmon and Salome Manson
Annie S., d. 5/16/1928 at 59/0/17; hemorrhage; Robert Watts and Rachael Simonton
Charles, d. 7/22/1898 at 44; rheumatism; b. Rollinsford; buried in Rollinsford
Charles K., d. 3/15/1916 at 82/3/27; old age; Simon Hartford and Olive Goodwin
Elizabeth S., d. 10/28/1924 at 89/11/10; gen. arterio sclerosis; John C. Hayes and Lavina Danforth
Emma J., d. 2/1/1906 at 40/2/3; paris green, while insane; buried in Alton
George, d. 4/4/1935 at 67/1/2; chronic myocarditis
George T., d. 9/27/1930 at 74/1/20 in Boston, MA; cancer liver; Olive Hartford
Homer E., d. 8/8/1936 at 66/1*; b. Alton
James W., d. 3/11/1905 at 75/4; carcinoma of stomach; PH
Jennie B., d. 10/18/1892 at 58; complication of diseases; b. Tuftonboro; (Tuftonboro; Tuftonboro)
John H., d. 4/25/1890 at 58/7/20; married; Simon L. Hartford (Strafford) and Olive Goodwin (Berwick, ME)
Leon C., d. 3/22/1897 at 3 in Barrington; PH
Lyman, d. 1/22/1907 at 1/2/6 in Barrington; marasmus
Maud A., d. 5/30/1892 at 14; peritonitis; b. No. Berwick, ME; (Rochester; No. Berwick, ME)
Moses B., d. 6/19/1911 at 72; ac. dilitation of heart
Nellie G., d. 7/7/1922 at 60/8/28 in Chelsea, MA; cirrhosis of liver
Nellie M., d. 12/22/1919 at 76/5/25; heart disease; William Twombly, 3rd and Mary W. Caverly

Olive F., d. 4/6/1926 at 88/5/27; cerebral hemorrhage; Simon L. Hartford
Samuel B., d. 12/4/1924 at 71/7 in Berwick, ME; tubercular pneumonia
Seth T., d. 6/18/1892 at 61; heart disease; b. Rochester; (Lebanon, ME; Rochester)
Susan A., d. 11/22/1916 at 70/3/12; diabetic coma; David Wilson and Nancy Plummer

HARTIGAN,
John, d. 3/3/1929 at 77; chronic myocarditis; Patrick Hartigan and Mary Quark
Mary, d. 12/27/1922 at 74; abdominal tuberculosis; John Hartigan and Bridget Quark

HARTLEY,
Annie, d. 7/26/1892 at –; inflammation of bowels; b. Dover; (England; Scotland)
Willie, d. 4/1/1889 at 0/0/2; b. Dover; William Hartley (England) and Jessie Taylor (Scotland)

HARTON,
Anita, d. 11/16/1934 at 0/1/19; lobar pneumonia
Norman, d. 9/10/1935 at 7/9/25; fractured skull

HARTSHORN,
Annie M., d. 11/27/1903 at 78/3/8; valvular disease of heart; buried in Portsmouth

HARTSON,
Fred T., d. 1/25/1936 at 60/2/30 in Portsmouth; angina pectoris

HARVEY,
child, d. 12/11/1929 at –; prolapsus umb. cord; Ernest Harvey and Celia Desautels
Ellen M., d. 1/29/1933 at 81/7/14; cerebral hemorrhage
Fernando C., d. 10/23/1913 at 63/2/3; uraemia; William Harvey and Lucinda Hough
Frank B., d. 11/27/1922 at 77/4/9; cancer of bladder; Oren Harvey and Anna Mason
Hannah S. M., d. 8/26/1932 at 85/11/3; arterio sclerosis
James, d. 7/11/1911 at 66; heat stroke; Thomas Harvey and Sarah McGlone
John, d. 4/7/1913 at 66; exposure and neglect; Thomas Harvey and Sarah McGlone

Lewis V., d. 4/15/1911 at 42/2/1; accidental shooting; Alfred Harvey and
    Margaret Lake
Mary Ann, d. 1/30/1911 at 63; pulmonary tuberculosis; Peter Hughes and
    Alice Carragher
Patrick, d. 3/20/1902 at 27; phthisis pulmonalis; buried in Portsmouth
William, d. 6/9/1911 at 31 in Rochester, NY; accidental drowning

HARWOOD,
Anna, d. 8/5/1929 at 56 in New York, NY; cardiac

HASELTINE,
Clara Whyte, d. 9/26/1909 at 54 in Ipswich, MA; organic heart disease
Esther J., d. 9/23/1909 at 71/2/15 in Lee; marasmus; Benjamin Hoitt and
    Bethsheba Babb
Ira G., d. 2/15/1907 at 66 in Haverhill, MA; arteriosclerosis

HASH,
Joseph, d. 4/16/1922 at 55; angina pectoris; George Hash and Mary
    Dowaliby

HASHAM,
child, d. 9/2/1932 at –; stillborn
Mary, d. 9/12/1917 at –; miscarriage; Sarkes Hasham and Josephine
    Martin
Mary S., d. 12/28/1915 at 0/0/2; premature birth; Sarkis M. Hasham and
    Josephine Martin

HASHAN,
Michael, d. 1/12/1922 at 52 in Pembroke; pulmonary tuberculosis; Salib
    Hashan and Mary Peter

HASHEM,
Barbara M., d. 1/15/1927 at 0/7/4; tubercular meningitis; Sarkis M.
    Hashem and Josephine Martin
Doris, d. 3/6/1922 at 0/0/11; premature birth; Sarkis M. Hashem and
    Josephine Martin
Florence, d. 1/15/1921 at 0/0/9; premature birth; Sarkis M. Hashem and
    Josephine Martin
John, d. 8/13/1913 at –; debility; Cashem Hashem and Mary Halley
Joseph, d. 8/13/1913 at –; debility; Cashem Hashem and Mary Halley
Joseph, d. 10/9/1916 at –; premature birth; Sarkis Hashem and Josephine
    Martin
Joseph, d. 4/30/1923 at –; stillborn; Mosoud J. Hashem and Zephay
    Hashem

Joseph C., d. 2/26/1920 at 0/0/1; premature birth; Sarkis M. Hashem and Josephine Martin
Joseph E., d. 6/10/1923 at –; premature birth; Sarkis M. Hashem and Josephine Martin
Mansour, d. 4/1/1924 at 66; aortic insufficiency; Dyar Hashem
Peter M., d. 7/27/1919 at 88; paralysis of bladder; Mansur P. Hashem and Corna Joseph
Rachel M., d. 5/8/1933 at 53/11/30; carcinoma of intestine
Wilfred, d. 7/17/1913 at 0/9/4; acute pneumonia; Sarkis M. Hashem and Josephine Martin
William S., d. 3/16/1919 at 0/0/6; premature birth; Sarkis Hashem and Josephine Martin
Zelpha D., d. 9/2/1930 at 39 in Amesbury, MA; cancer of intestines

HASKELL,
Ezra, d. 6/23/1916 at 81/2/12 in Barrington; arterio sclerosis
Isabella R., d. 7/17/1888 at 56/5/18 in Portland, OR; married; b. Dover
William H., d. 7/23/1924 at 80; arterio sclerosis

HASKINS,
Albert E., d. 4/4/1919 at 18/6/14 in Newport, RI; pneumonia
Edward K., d. 9/21/1933 at 82/10/25 in W. Brookfield, MA; chronic gastritis

HASSAM,
Annie, d. 5/11/1916 at 2 in Rollinsford; not definitely determined

HASSAN,
Edward, d. 7/23/1933 at 0/1/8; premature birth
Michael J., d. 5/6/1933 at 26/2/2; lobar pneumonia
Raymond, d. 1/2/1928 at 9/4/0; accidental drowning; Massan Hassan and Zbee Hassan

HASSEN,
child, d. 9/23/1918 at –; stillborn; Joffer Hassen and Annie ——
Annie, d. 4/23/1913 at 1/4; pneumonia; Arsen Hassen
David, d. 1/3/1917 at 0/9; lobar pneumonia; Cassem Hassem (sic) and Mary Hashem
Dora, d. 6/20/1916 at 0/2/17; unknown; Cassen Hassen and May ——
Jennie, d. 2/5/1910 at 0/0/17; marasmus; Joseph Hassen and Ann Harje
Monsey, d. 8/16/1914 at 22 in Rollinsford; drowning

HASSETT,
James H., d. 8/26/1925 at 73; valv. heart disease; William Hassett and Mary McGraft

HASTINGS,
Florence, d. 6/2/1913 at 2/2/7 in Boston, MA; tuberculosis

HASTY,
Charles F., d. 1/31/1932 at 86 in Portsmouth; diabetes mellitus
Charles Linwood, d. 6/13/1890 at 0/0/1; Charles F. Hasty (NH) and Ruth E. Tibbetts (Dover)
Frank Warren, d. 1/8/1927 at 0/0/5; hemophilia; Harold C. Hasty and Jennie O. Sanborn
Lorette Edgerly, d. 7/8/1888 at 33/9/24; married; b. Durham; Joseph Edgerly (Dover) and Sarah Burleigh (Ossipee)
Ruth Ella, d. 3/27/1926 at 68/9/27; diabetes; Thomas L. Tibbetts and Ann Wyman
Thomas, d. 10/9/1932 at 74/4/15; chronic endocarditis
Walter E., d. 4/28/1916 at 25/11/10; suicide; Ervin E. Hasty and Carrie B. Boston

HATCH,
Alden S., d. 7/10/1934 at 78/3/4; arteriosclerosis
Annie E., d. 2/13/1907 at 74/9/20; osteo sarcoma of thigh; William H. Lockett and Hannah Collier
Christine, d. 10/5/1933 at 94/8/2; arteriosclerosis
Evelyn M., d. 2/25/1934 at 57/8/12; diabetes mellitus
Hannah N., d. 3/8/1907 at 71/6/1; chronic nephritis; Luther Nute and Susan Goodwin
Hartley E., d. 4/12/1910 at 34/0/23; pulmonary tuberculosis; Marshall Hatch
John K., d. 11/3/1924 at 47/6/10; cerebral hemorrhage; John Hatch and Alice C. Benton
Joshua C., d. 6/24/1912 at 86/3/14; senility; Berak Hatch and Mary Chick
Mary E., d. 9/30/1908 at 26/3; phthisis pulmonalis; Benton Nason and Rose Bunker
Olive J., d. 9/30/1919 at 66/3/17; acute nephritis; Joseph Bedell and Jane Ham
Sarah A., d. 3/11/1898 at 81; old age; b. Sanford, ME; PH
Sumner W., d. 12/26/1893 at –; pneumonia; b. Wells, ME; (Wells, ME; Wells, ME)
Thomas O., d. 7/10/1912 at 29/11/23; fracture of spinal column; Charles E. Hatch and Nellie Twombly

HATHAWAY,
son, d. 6/29/1888 at 0/0/1; b. Dover; James Hathaway (Fall River, MA) and Fannie Austin (Dover)
Charles A., d. 8/13/1934 at 56/2/8 in Rochester; carcinoma of liver
James H., d. 2/17/1935 at 72 in Chelsea, MA; cardio vascular disease

K. A., d. 5/10/1889 at 0/1; b. Dover; William Hathaway (MA) and Mary
    Cassilly (Ireland)
Mary, d. 7/22/1906 at 54; pulmonary tuberculosis
Mary, d. 7/1/1936 at 71; cor. artery disease
William, d. 5/9/1910 at 67; shock
William L., d. 10/9/1894 at –; anaemia; b. Dover; SM

HAUGHEY,
Alice, d. 2/5/1907 at 50; acute uraemia; John Haughey and Mary Haffey
Bridget, d. 7/10/1899 at 65; pulmonary phthisis; SM
Catherine, d. 6/2/1908 at 58; nephritis
Charles, d. 11/8/1904 at 0/3/21; gastro-enteritis; SM
Edward, d. 3/26/1891 at 85; single
Edward J., d. 10/28/1898 at 2; convulsions; b. Dover; SM
Eliza, d. 4/22/1888 at –; b. Dover; M. Haughey (Dover) and Ellen (Ireland)
Elizabeth, d. 6/12/1903 at 41 in Portsmouth; cancer
Ellen, d. 10/10/1894 at 36; phthisis; b. Ireland; SM
Ioline, d. 9/25/1907 at 0/1/12; Charles Haughey and Margaret Kidney
J., d. 5/16/1901 at 57/5; tuberculosis; SM
James, d. 5/17/1905 at 0/0/16; premature birth; SM
John, d. 3/4/1902 at 57; apoplexy; SM
John F., d. 4/5/1887 at 0/1/10; b. Dover; Michael Haughey (Dover) and
    Ellen McCoole (Ireland)
John F., d. 10/21/1907 at 4/28; acute nephritis; John Haughey and Phoebe
    Hughes
Margaret, d. 3/2-/1896 at 39; heart disease; b. Ireland; SM
Margaret, d. 4/24/1901 at 84/8; senile debility
Margaret, d. 11/7/1909 at 25/5/2; heart failure probable; William Kidney
    and Catherine Griffin
Mary, d. 11/20/1896 at 35; consumption; b. Ireland; SM
Mary W., d. 10/13/1918 at 54/0/27; arterio sclerosis; Thomas Keavener
    and Mary Kivel
Michael, d. 1/31/1902 at 50/10; apoplexy; SM
Stephen, d. 9/16/1892 at 3; gastritis - syncope; b. Dover; (Ireland; Ireland)
Thomas, d. 10/5/1890 at 29/11/25; single; John Haughey (Ireland) and
    Phebe Hughes (Ireland)
Thomas, d. 11/26/1905 at 39; tubercular enteritis; SM
Walter J., d. 4/29/1916 at 37 in Pembroke; pulmonary tuberculosis; John
    Haughey and Margaret Murray
Winnifred, d. 4/2/1901 at 38; cerebral hemorrhage; SM

HAULE,
son, d. 5/27/1888 at –; b. Dover; Rosa Haule (Canada)

HAWKES,
    Lowell H., d. 4/18/1909 at 50/0/9; exhaustion; James Hawkes and Sally Wentworth

HAWKINS,
    Andrew, d. 5/16/1919 at 63/9/15; fracture of spine; John Hawkins and Maria Foss
    Betsey M., d. 9/25/1920 at 76/5/22; cancer of rectum; Smith Hawkins and Sarah Foss
    Calestia A., d. 2/5/1907 at 57/5/6; pneumonia; Timothy Clarke and Patience Leighton
    Edward, d. 9/22/1905 at 44 in Concord; phthisis
    Hannah, d. 1/24/1891 at 56
    Herbert, d. 12/15/1912 at 0/0/2; premature birth; Edgar H. Hawkins and Mary E. York
    Mary, d. 9/10/1892 at 45; consumption
    Mary Ellen, d. 7/26/1914 at 2/10/15; burns; Edgar H. Hawkins and Mary E. York
    Sarah, d. 8/20/1896 at 77 in Strafford; gangrene of lung
    Sidney F., d. 2/14/1933 at 73/4/2; chronic myocarditis
    Smith, d. 6/11/1896 at 73 in Strafford; nephritis

HAWORTH,
    child, d. 1/29/1898 at 0; stillborn; b. Dover; PH
    Arthur A., d. 9/14/1904 at 36/11/6; pulmonary tuberculosis; PH
    Hattie B., d. 3/27/1935 at 71/9/12; pulmonary T. B.
    John E., d. 7/23/1901 at 2/0/29; cholera infantum; PH
    Mary, d. 8/12/1899 at 60; phthisis pulmonalis; PH

HAY,
    Cora B., d. 7/30/1927 at 61/1/11 in Auburn, ME; carcinoma of uterus
    John S., d. 5/18/1897 at 36 in Wolfeboro; consumption; b. Dover; PH

HAYDEN,
    Charles F., d. 12/22/1930 at 81/9/18; arterio sclerosis; William A. Hayden and Elizabeth P. Turner

HAYES,
    child, d. 4/13/1898 at 0; stillborn; b. Dover; PH
    child, d. 9/28/1922 at –; pro. of umbilical cord; William M. Hayes and Blanche E. Davis
    child, d. 4/5/1934 at –; prematurity
    Abbie M., d. 1/20/1913 at 66/10/29 in Boston; apoplexy
    Adelaide L., d. 2/19/1932 at 78/6/6; chronic enteritis

Alice M., d. 11/6/1908 at 35/6/5; rupture gall bladder; Thomas Dempsey and Mary Stewart
Almira E., d. 4/16/1928 at 73/3/26; cerebral hemorrhage; Moses Frost
Amanda S., d. 9/15/1900 at 72; disease of brain; PH
Annie I., d. 2/13/1932 at 71/4/10; chronic endocarditis
Annie W., d. 8/7/1922 at 71/9/11; carcinoma of uterus; Nahum Wentworth and Abagail A. Varney
Augusta E., d. 5/11/1899 at 34; haematemesis from stomach ulcer; PH
Augusta P., d. 6/3/1906 at 92/11; old age; PH
Auren W., d. 8/16/1924 at 72/0/9; cerebral hemorrhage; Mark D. Hayes and Mary J. Chase
Benjamin F., d. 1/16/1899 at 85 in Madbury; old age; PH
Brackett, d. 7/1/1901 at 72/5/6; Bright's disease; PH
Cedelia A., d. 1/18/1926 at 82/4/26; ptomaine poisoning; Peter Haynes and Betsy Hopkins
Charles, d. 11/24/1887 at 73/7/21; farmer; married; b. Dover; Jonathan Hayes (Madbury) and Mary Ham
Charles H., d. 12/10/1928 at 74/0/6; myocarditis; Samuel C. Hayes and Caroline Hooper
Charles S., d. 5/6/1922 at 37/5/16 in Haverhill, MA; tubercular meningitis
Charles W., d. 5/11/1904 at 44/10/3 in Wolfeboro; angiocarditis; PH
Charles W., d. 9/26/1915 at – in Madbury; arterio sclerosis
Chauncey E., d. 12/11/1920 at 73/4/18 in Durham; arterio sclerosis
Claraugusta L. S., d. 11/15/1897 at 74; old age; b. Alton; PH
Cora B., d. 11/13/1920 at 62/4/1; cancer of intestines; John Tibbetts and Clara Blaisdell
Cyrus F., d. 10/1/1900 at 81; cerebral apoplexy; PH
David, d. 2/5/1897 at 86 in East Rochester; pneumonia; PH
David B., d. 7/4/1910 at 66/7/13 in Madbury; valvular disease of heart
Dorothy, d. 8/10/1893 at –; congestion of lungs
Elijah, d. 1/6/1892 at 72; apoplexy; b. Lebanon
Eliza A., d. 3/25/1892 at 69; pneumonia; b. Dover; (Dover; Dover)
Eliza Ham, d. 3/25/1892 at 78; grippe; b. Dover; (Dover; Dover)
Elizabeth, d. 12/5/1906 at 61; chronic bronchitis
Elizabeth A., d. 11/16/1910 at 93/7/16 in Williamsburg, MA; cerebral hemorrhage
Elizabeth A., d. 2/15/1911 at 64/1/5; pneumonia; ----- Elwell
Elizabeth H., d. 10/29/1891 at 79/6/7; widow; John W. Hayes (Barrington) and Elizabeth H. Hayes (Barrington)
Elizabeth Kimball, d. 11/17/1936 at 91/3/16*
Ellen A., d. 2/6/1897 at 45; heart disease; b. Madbury; PH
Ellen M., d. 8/26/1933 at 90/3/27 in Boston, MA; carcinoma of colon
Eloise, d. 5/20/1924 at 0/0/2; unknown; William M. Hayes and Blanche E. Davis
Emily A., d. 9/4/1909 at 74/1/28 in Portsmouth; fracture cerebral vertebra

Emma, d. 9/3/1929 at 74/7/23; myocarditis; Alfred Hannaford
Emma F., d. 1/4/1927 at 65/7/19; pneumonia; Eleazer C. Hayes and Lizzie A. Cater
Enoch, d. 1/23/1905 at 78; angina pectoris; buried in Somersworth
Eunice M., d. 12/28/1910 at 73/2/25; apoplexy; Luther Dixon and Elizabeth Blaisdell
Ezra, d. 3/26/1899 at 67; anaemia of brain; PH
Francis, d. 3/23/1892 at –; pneumonia; b. Dover; (Ireland; Dover)
Frank L., d. 3/4/1927 at 60 in Ocala, FL; acute nephritis
Frank P., d. 7/23/1916 at 33/8/9; pulmonary tuberculosis; Auren W. Hayes and Adelaide L. Meserve
Fred Hooper, d. 4/29/1936 at 77/5/2; uremia
Fred S., d. 11/25/1929 at 72/7/8; gen. paresis; Paul W. Hayes and Amanda Hall
George A., d. 2/2/1932 at 65 in Brockton, MA; intestinal obstruction
George F., d. 2/26/1921 at 84 in Kittery, ME; chronic nephritis
Glendola Maud, d. 7/14/1892 at –; inanition; b. Dover; (Dover; Barnstead)
Golden, d. 4/1/1931 at 49/10; lobar pneumonia
Grace L., d. 1/14/1919 at 30/11 in Milford; influenza, pneumonia; Pearl P. Pike and Edith Willey
Harrison, d. 10/9/1900 at 7 in Lynn, MA; diphtheria; PH
Harry H., d. 11/14/1926 at 57/5/27; acute myocarditis; William Hayes and Sarah Dorcat
Henry G., d. 7/10/1930 at 70/2/14; angina pectoris; Reuben Hayes and Elizabeth Chadwick
Ida M., d. 2/4/1927 at 63 in Brookline, MA; cancer intestine
Ira W., d. 11/17/1928 at 78/6/17; herpes zoster; Thomas Hayes and Abigail V. Nute
Irving B., d. 1/3/1909 at 47 in Rosenfield, TX; accident
J. Chesley, d. 7/30/1916 at 65/0/18; chronic nephritis; James Y. Hayes and Alice A. Hayes
James, d. 1/2/1900 at 54; organic disease of heart; PH
James D., d. 1/27/1928 at 73/9/5; ch. valv. heart dis.; Oliver K. Hayes and Eliza Ham
James M., d. 11/24/1916 at 71/3/21; cerebral hemorrhage; Andrew Hayes and Elizabeth H. Hayes
James P., d. 1/18/1902 at 39/5/2 in Boston, MA; cerebral hemorrhage; PH
Johanna, d. 5/6/1914 at 51/1/19; cancer of uterus; ----- Foley and ----- McCabe
John F., d. 10/4/1909 at 81/0/21 in Lynn, MA; cerebral hemorrhage
John J., d. 5/14/1898 at 52; pneumonia; b. Ireland; SM
Jordan, d. 5/25/1924 at 60; accidental
Joseph, d. 11/2/1892 at 66; pneumonia; b. Farmington; (Rochester; -----)
Joshua, d. 11/8/1910 at 77/6; heart disease; Brackett Hayes and Rebecca Grant

Kate, d. 4/25/1906 at 42; bronchopneumonia; SM
Latilla, d. 1/12/1930 at 72/11/22; apoplexy; Dyer Hall and Maria F. Millard
Laura A., d. 11/14/1935 at 81/11/1; arteriosclerosis
Lillian A., d. 4/17/1919 at 53/8/7 in Medford, MA; tubercular peritonitis
Lizzie A., d. 9/6/1912 at 65/6/17; diabetes; James H. Moulton and Lizzie A. Cotton
Lydia S., d. 2/10/1904 at 75/11/14; PH
Malcom, d. 12/27/1900 at <1 in Rollinsford; bronchitis; PH
Margaret M., d. 1/30/1912 at 49/11/20; heart disease; Edward Duffy and Bridget McCooey
Marietta, d. 5/25/1927 at 75/6/3; senile dementia; Charles Hayes and Sarah A. Emery
Martha E., d. 5/11/1933 at 88/10/26; cerebral hemorrhage
Mary A., d. 9/14/1912 at 68; broncho pneumonia
Mary A., d. 7/27/1917 at 58/1/14 in Exeter; carcinoma of stomach
Mary Elizabeth, d. 1/2/1903 at 83/8/19; heart disease; PH
Mary J., d. 6/4/1897 at 74; nephritis; b. No. Berwick, ME; PH
Mary Y., d. 2/18/1919 at 76/2/12; lobar pneumonia; Oliver K. Hayes and Eliza Ham
Melissa, d. 6/23/1930 at 0/2/29 in Madbury; spina bifida
Olive C., d. 4/22/1918 at 79/9/16 in Lynn, MA; cerebral hemorrhage
Ora Belle, d. 3/9/1908 at 43/7/9; carcinoma of liver; Ivory Hatch and Martha H. Hobbs
Reuben G., d. 7/4/1925 at 71/9/14 in York Village, ME; cerebral hemorrhage
Robert H., d. 3/20/1921 at 0/8/12; broncho pneumonia; William M. Hayes and Blanche E. Davis
Samuel, d. 12/19/1893 at 71; organic disease of the heart; b. New Durham
Sarah A., d. 10/18/1906 at 81/6/17; catarrhal pneumonia; PH
Sarah A., d. 6/3/1923 at 86/8/21; la grippe; John S. Webster and Comfort B. Durgin
Susan B. M., d. 11/16/1926 at 79; arterio sclerosis; Joseph B. Morse and Margaret Boardman
Theresa H., d. 2/1/1936 at 71/0/24; cerebral hemorrhage
Victory F., d. 8/7/1919 at 0/7/12; diarrhea; William H. Hayes and Flora M. Shattuck
Washington M., d. 8/12/1896 at 00; cholera infantum; PH
William H., d. 10/12/1918 at 28/11; lobar pneumonia; John M. Hayes and Lenora -----
William W., d. 6/11/1921 at 74/0/5; cerebral hemorrhage; George W. Hayes and Mary E. Wood

HAYLER,
Mary A., d. 9/26/1911 at 55/6/21; phthisis; James Chandler

HAYNES,
Dorothy B., d. 3/30/1918 at 4/2/13 in Malden, MA; scarlet fever
Edward William, d. 3/8/1925 at 5/1/24 in Quincy, MA; broncho pneumonia
James Monroe, d. 8/9/1906 at 86/10/24; general paresis; PH
Louise H., d. 1/1/1908 at 47 in Philadelphia, PA; cancer in bladder
Nancy M., d. 12/11/1900 at 82; brain disease; PH

HAYWARD,
Harold, d. 8/20/1891 at 0/3/15; William E. Hayward (Salem, MA) and
 Phebe Warren (Limerick, ME)

HEAD,
Betsey L., d. 10/28/1889 at 74/9/25; housewife; widow; b. New Durham;
 William Cook (New Durham) and Nancy Cook (New Durham)
Mary Morgan, d. 9/27/1932 at 68/9/30; chronic endocarditis

HEALEY,
Albert E., d. 8/17/1935 at 60/5/25; gen. peritonitis
Ethel S., d. 12/11/1935 at 55/11/18; cerebral hemorrhage
Irving, d. 5/9/1924 at 28/11/14; diabetes; John Healey and Emma Davis
Nellie A., d. 2/1/1933 at 57/5/3; lobar pneumonia

HEALLEY,
Catherine, d. 11/20/1900 at 1; convulsions; SM

HEAP,
Robert S., d. 9/17/1905 at 30/8/3; heart failure; PH

HEARNE,
James J., d. 5/17/1909 at 50; chronic nephritis; John Hearne and Mary
 Bagnell

HEATH,
Anna P., d. 7/1/1930 at 53 in Emory Grove, MD; pulm. tuberculosis
Elizabeth E., d. 11/25/1934 at 61/5/27; broncho pneumonia
Fred E., d. 8/14/1937 at 76/0/4 in Exeter; cerebr. hemorrhage
Hattie, d. 5/27/1920 at 64/8/22; sclerosis of spinal cord; Charles Cox
Maude G., d. 7/18/1931 at 56/3/23; pernicious anaemia
Myra M., d. 11/26/1930 at 73; cremation; Alpheus Lyons

HEATON,
child, d. 12/1/1912 at –; stillborn; Anderson Heaton and Lillian E. White
Ada, d. 3/2/1937 at 62; coronary thrombosis
John William, d. 11/6/1918 at – in Rollinsford; stillborn

Sevena E., d. 11/7/1918 at 31/2/17 in Rollinsford; puerperal eclampsia

HEBERT,
child, d. 4/18/1891 at –; Jesse Hebert (Canada) and Marie Louise Dione (Detroit, MI)
child, d. 4/19/1891 at –; Jesse Hebert (Canada) and Marie Louise Dione (Detroit, MI)
child, d. 4/19/1891 at –; Jesse Hebert (Canada) and Marie Louise Dione (Detroit, MI)
child, d. 10/21/1925 at 0/0/½ hr.; miscarriage; Ernest Hebert and Laura Marion
Annie, d. 3/1/1917 at 39/11; tuberculosis of larynx; Francois Ouimette and Caroline -----
Arthur, d. 10/14/1905 at 23/4/19; aortic insufficiency
Beatrice A., d. 7/13/1926 at 2/9/9; tuberculous meningitis; Ernest Hebert and Laura Marion
Ernest, d. 5/18/1934 at 41/7/20; pulmonary tuberculosis
Joseph, d. 5/9/1918 at 0/0/2; premature birth; Joseph Hebert and Zephyrine -----
Leda, d. 7/10/1935 at 64; cerebral hemorrhage
Lorenzo, d. 8/28/1905 at 2/3/12; convulsions
Lorenzo L., d. 8/20/1907 at 0/5/7; gastritis; Ubald Hebert and Ann Oullette
M. B., d. 2/26/1901 at 0/2/11; unknown
Raymond, d. 7/14/1935 at 25/9/2; fractured skull
Theresa, d. 10/6/1929 at 3/11/26; pernicious anemia; Adalard Hebert and Aurore Couture
Thomas, d. 10/29/1916 at 64/4/3; phthisis pulmonalis; Peter Hebert and Esther Fontaine

HEENEY,
Elizabeth, d. 9/14/1935 at 68; cerebral hemorrhage
Hannah, d. 12/24/1925 at 79/4/16; apoplexy; Abraham Kay
Lawrence W., d. 11/7/1914 at 8/3; appendicitis; Joseph Heeney and Elizabeth Whitehead

HEFFERMAN,
Mary, d. 4/10/1907 at 67 in Somersworth; cancer of stomach

HEFFERON,
Mary, d. 5/14/1910 at 60; cancer; George Mitchell and Margaret Griffin

HEFFRON,
James, d. 7/20/1913 at 42; chronic myocarditis; Patrick Heffron and Mary Mitchell

Susan, d. 3/28/1915 at 76; acute pneumonia; Henry Cunningham and
   Rose Sloan

HEFTY,
Albert, d. 11/18/1911 at –; asphyxiation

HEGARTY,
Sarah A., d. 11/18/1894 at 56; fistula in uno; b. Ireland; SM

HEGGIE,
James, d. 5/1/1889 at 0/0/4; b. Dover; Oglevie Heggie (Scotland) and
   Mary Meikle (Scotland)

HEGLEY,
James, d. 9/5/1926 at 72; apoplexy

HELI,
Philip, d. 3/22/1936 at 38; cerebral hemorrhage

HELMS,
John E., d. 7/31/1898 at 0; cholera infantum; b. Dover; PH

HEMEON,
Henriette, d. 4/23/1908 at 58; cerebral hemorrhage; Oliver Charest and
   Henriette Paradis

HEMINGWAY,
Martha E., d. 10/24/1934 at 78/7/5; arteriosclerosis

HEMON,
Celina, d. 2/24/1912 at 39/6/22; pulmonary tuberculosis
Marie V., d. 1/1/1900 at 40; tuberculosis; SM
Theodore, d. 3/19/1911 at 41/11/17; pulmonary tuberculosis; Joseph
   Hemon and ----- Marion

HEMOND,
child, d. 12/10/1900 at <1; unknown
Aime, d. 2/22/1906 at 1/9/3; encephalitis
Alberic, d. 2/24/1905 at 0/9/10; capillary bronchitis
Angeline, d. 5/6/1907 at 14/9/1; acute pul. tuberculosis; Theodore Hemond
   and Elina Jackell
Blandine, d. 7/22/1910 at 0/2/29; cholera infantum; Theodore Hemond and
   Celina Jackell
J. Wilfred, d. 2/8/1900 at 4; pul. tuberculosis

Joseph, d. 12/27/1904 at 74/6/1; heart failure
Leonie, d. 6/29/1910 at 5/8/15; gastro-intest. indigestion; Israel Hemond
    and Celina Droulette
Lina, d. 3/14/1906 at 0/1/26; pneumonia
Marilda, d. 6/15/1896 at 2; broncho-pneumonia; b. Dover; SM
Philadelphe, d. 8/11/1901 at 1/0/20; cholera infantum
Valma, d. 4/23/1902 at 1/9; heart disease
Wilfred, d. 11/30/1914 at 12/9/5 in Manchester; perforation of intestines;
    Theodore Hemond and Celina -----

HENDERSON,
Alma A., d. 1/21/1930 at 70/4/2; cerebral hemorrhage; John A. Pickering
    and Sarah E. Mathes
Charles T., d. 4/9/1919 at 78/1/26; senile dementia; Samuel H. Henderson
    and Sarah A. Guppey
Cora M., d. 3/7/1922 at 51/11/12; cerebral hemorrhage; Charles
    Henderson and Elizabeth Chesley
Eliza J., d. 5/25/1906 at 72/5/5; cardiac asthenia; PH
Elizabeth C., d. 6/5/1913 at 73/3/2; pulmonary tuberculosis; Benjamin T.
    Bickford and Keziah Nason
Ellen E., d. 4/25/1909 at 65 in Chicago, IL; pneumonia
Flora E., d. 3/15/1930 at 69/3/29; cerebral hemorrhage; Howard
    Henderson and Elizabeth Bickford
George, d. 5/19/1919 at 75; softening of brain
George H., d. 4/3/1933 at 76/0/17; cerebral embolism
Grace B., d. 10/6/1937 at 65/10/9; carcinoma of uterus
Howard, d. 3/19/1904 at 90/5/1; old age; PH
James W., d. 3/15/1923 at 83/1/26; acute bronchitis; Howard Henderson
    and Maria Diman
John H., d. 10/13/1907 at 58/7/11; cerebral apoplexy; Thomas Henderson
    and Olive Bickford
Laura E., d. 1/27/1896 at 40; phthisis; b. New Bedford, MA; PH
Maria, d. 1/3/1935 at 80/7/4; cerebral hemorrhage
Mary E., d. 10/30/1921 at 45/1/20 in Concord; epilepsy; Samuel
    Henderson and Sarah E. Locke
Maud O., d. 3/31/1894 at 17; pulmonary consumption; PH
Olin, d. 2/24/1926 at 27/1/24; furuncle vest. of nose; L. C. Henderson and
    Alice Hodgdon
Olive, d. 4/3/1891 at 70/7/10; married; Joseph Bickford and Mary Frost
Sarah A., d. 10/10/1900 at 88; gastritis; PH
Susan, d. 9/11/1889 at 73; single; b. Rochester
Sylvanus, d. 11/20/1931 at 56/2/19; pulmonary tuberculosis
Thomas, d. 9/16/1894 at 84; disease of heart; b. Dover; buried at Dover
    Point

William C., d. 1/13/1925 at 70/3/16; probably nephritis; Samuel H. Henderson and Sarah A. Guppy
William M., d. 11/4/1891 at 86/6/4; widower; William Henderson (Dover) and Margaret Roberts

HENDRICKSON,
Lawrence, d. 2/21/1929 at 30 in Concord; general paralysis; Henry Hendrickson and Sophia Mason
Lorraine, d. 10/4/1926 at 0/4/22; uremia; Lawrence Hendrickson and Helen M. Wendell

HENDSBEE,
Woodrow, d. 2/22/1919 at 0/7/3; ac. lobar pneumonia; Lloyd J. Hendsbee and Jennie Knowlin

HENNAN,
Marie, ("E. de M"), d. 10/4/1890 at 21/9/22; single; John Hennon (England) and Mary Croghan (Ireland)

HENNELLY,
Joseph, d. 5/6/1924 at –; stillborn; William Hennelly and Madeline -----

HENNESSEY,
Alice, d. 4/10/1896 at 59; consumption; b. Ireland
Ann E., d. 4/28/1901 at 18 in Collinsville, MA; tuberculosis; SM
Ann J., d. 8/31/1887 at 5; b. Dover; (Ireland; Ireland)
Dennis, d. 9/14/1919 at 52 in Dracut, MA; cirrhosis of liver
Elizabeth J., d. 7/21/1931 at 71/10/13; carcinoma of stomach
Hannah, d. 2/6/1907 at 70; broncho-pneumonia
James H., d. 2/13/1919 at 60; valv. heart disease; John Hennessey and Ann Foley
John, d. 12/26/1896 at – in Dracut, MA; heart disease
John, d. 7/4/1926 at 4/8/4 in Somerville, MA; diphtheria
John V., d. 3/17/1894 at 52; b. Ireland; SM
Mary, d. 6/25/1901 at 59; herniplegia; SM
Thomas, d. 7/20/1887 at 45/6; shoemaker; married; b. Ireland; Patrick Hennessey (Ireland) and Margaret (Ireland)

HENNESSY,
Catherine, d. 3/9/1907 at –; heart disease

HENNESY,
Dennis, d. 7/22/1897 at 4 in Brockton, MA; internal aberitian; SM

Thomas J., d. 11/3/1922 at 50; cerebral apoplexy; Thomas Hennessey (sic) and Mary Clorisey

HENREUX,
Joseph, d. 3/26/1927 at 63/5/3 in Madbury; fracture of skull

HERBERT,
Edgar A. T., d. 7/20/1905 at 35; acute alcoholism; PH

HERLIHY,
Hannah, d. 2/16/1917 at 0/10/26; acute bronchitis; Patrick Herlihy and Rose Buckley
John L., d. 5/22/1932 at 23 in Pembroke; pulmonary tuberculosis
Nora, d. 11/4/1927 at 63/4/9 in Sanford, ME; dilatation of heart

HERNANDEZ,
Annah H., d. 11/15/1934 at 77/2/26 in Waltham, MA; diabetes mellitus

HERNENDY,
Melquides, d. 5/23/1929 at 76/5/23 in Strafford; angina pectoris

HERON,
Catherine, d. 8/17/1887 at 17/8/28; mill operative; single; b. Dover; John C. Heron (Ireland) and Ann McManus (Ireland)

HERRETT,
Margaret J., d. 2/26/1928 at 72; myocarditis; ----- Stewart

HERRICK,
Ira A., d. 5/30/1894 at 23; consumption; b. Hyde Park, VT; buried in Hyde Park, VT

HERRIN,
Anson L., d. 6/12/1922 at 37/5/1 in Bangor, ME; not determined
Lois A., d. 4/15/1932 at 66/2/1 in Boston, MA; coronary sclerosis

HERSEY,
Caroline A., d. 4/14/1930 at 87/2/19 in Portsmouth; pulmonary oedema
Edith Bell, d. 2/28/1911 at 41/8/17; brain tumor; Frederic B. Tibbetts and Caroline A. Lefavor
Elizabeth A., d. 12/18/1931 at 67/6/22; sarcoma (leg)
Frank A., d. 10/8/1893 at 17; tubercular meningitis; b. Kennebunkport, ME; (Hingham, MA; Newmarket)
Peter T., d. 11/2/1906 at 68/9/17; cerebro spinal meningitis; PH

William, d. 3/4/1934 at 63/0/17 in Brentwood; diabetes
William F., Jr., d. 1/9/1919 at 3/5/11; lobar pneumonia; William F. Hersey
and Grace M. Chellis

HESLIP,
George, d. 8/15/1890 at 35; Moses Heslip (Ireland) and E. Brown (Ireland)

HESSE,
Mary M., d. 12/7/1896 at 76; heart disease; b. Dover; SM

HESTER,
child, d. 5/26/1894 at –; stillborn; b. Dover; PH
Annie, d. 2/25/1923 at 63/6 in Lawrence, MA; renal calculus
Catherine L., d. 8/9/1898 at 0; cholera infantum; b. Dover; SM
Elizabeth, d. 5/29/1896 at 5; memb. croup; b. Dover; SM
Ellen F., d. 11/26/1895 at 0; convulsions; b. Dover; SM
John, d. 9/14/1909 at 76/2/15; continued syncope; Timothy Hester and
    Nancy Gowen
John, d. 9/23/1913 at 52/7/11; acute nephritis; John Hester and Sarah
    McGuire
Maria, d. 11/27/1888 at 3/6/23; b. Dover; John Hester (England) and Annie
    York (England)
Patrick, d. 6/27/1908 at 67; apoplexy
Sarah J., d. 11/27/1914 at 71/6/10; cerebral hemorrhage; Jeremiah
    McGuire and Sarah Shields
William, d. 10/2/1910 at 45; chronic endocarditis; John Hester and Sarah
    McGuinness

HEWITT,
George, d. 2/11/1930 at 60 in Lawrence, MA; angina pectoris

HIBBERT,
Dora, d. 3/30/1920 at 57 in Biddeford, ME; hemorrhage of brain; John
    Hibbert and Theda Phillips

HICKEY,
Charles, d. 8/13/1914 at 69; chronic intestinal nephritis; John Hickey and
    Sarah -----
Ellen T., d. 6/22/1889 at 22/9; housekeeper; single; b. Ireland; Jeremiah
    Hickey (Ireland) and Honora Costello (Ireland)

HICKS,
Adelaide S., d. 8/23/1937 at 77/5/9; fracture of skull

Hattie M., d. 3/23/1930 at 65/6/14; pneumonia; James B. Moulton and
   Hester A. Stevens

HIGGINBOTHAM,
Joseph, d. 5/14/1928 at 85/4/24; arterio sclerosis

HIGGINBOTTOM,
child, d. 5/30/1893 at –; premature birth; b. Dover; (England; England)
Samuel, d. 4/22/1888 at 41/10/3; mill operative; married; b. England; John
   Higginbottom (England) and Elizabeth Goodwin (England)

HIGGINS,
Addie, d. 8/22/1888 at 7/8/4; b. Dover; James Higgins (Salmon Falls) and
   Abbie Miller (Salmon Falls)
Bridget, d. 10/29/1915 at 72; diabetes mellitus; John Higgins and Mary ----
John H., d. 10/10/1901 at 40/6; phthisis pulmonalis; PH
Lillian A., d. 3/28/1888 at 27; single; b. ME; John Higgins (ME)
Lottie, d. 5/11/1887 at 11/6/26; b. Dover; James Higgins (Salmon Falls)
   and Abbie Miller (Salmon Falls)
Michael, d. 4/7/1907 at 72; shock; John Higgins and Mary Finnan
Mrs. Michael, d. 5/17/1903 at 68; tuberculosis and heart failure; SM

HIGGOTT,
J. C. Landers, d. 12/7/1911 at –; cerebral hemorrhage

HIGLEY,
Hannah B., d. 5/29/1908 at 61/6/4; cancer of intestine; Jonathan Morrison
   and Jane Boothby

HILL,
Abigail B., d. 9/25/1895 at 80; heart; b. Barrington; PH
Alice A. S., d. 5/11/1934 at 65/5/15; cerebral hemorrhage
Betsey R., d. 5/8/1893 at 72; pneumonia; b. Saco, ME; (Saco, ME; Saco,
   ME)
Carlton I., d. 10/25/1913 at 0/3/12; cholera infantum; Irving L. Hill and
   Emma M. Healey
Clara E., d. 1/8/1908 at 45/8/20 in Rochester; lobar pneumonia
Daniel M., d. 6/28/1888 at 28/10/14; merchant; single; b. Dover; Moses Hill
   (Newfield) and Mary (Durham)
Edith A., d. 12/11/1888 at 16/6/12; b. Pittsfield; John T. Hill (Northwood)
   and Sarah A. Locke (New Durham)
Eliza A., d. 5/14/1896 at 44 in Bradford, MA; phthisis pulmonalis
Elizabeth J., d. 1/6/1927 at 60; carcinoma of breast; Thomas Boyce and
   Mary Stain

Ellsworth O. C., d. 8/11/1934 at 45/10/29 in Andover, MA; cerebral
   apoplexy
Flora E., d. 7/31/1936 at 66/6/22*
Florence, d. 6/26/1906 at 48/9/24 in Roodhouse, IL; mitral incompetency;
   buried in Strafford
Frances A., d. 12/26/1929 at 82/11/18; senility; William Smith and Phoebe
   Faulkner
Frances R., d. 11/26/1923 at 81/4/4 in Durham; pulmonary emphysema
Frank, d. 11/2/1926 at 60/4/12; natural causes; Sylvanus B. Hill and
   Christie R. Rollinson
George, d. 3/2/1930 at 57/10/5; apoplexy; George O. Hill and Nettie
   Hammond
George E., d. 6/10/1936 at 74/7/25*; b. Lee
George W., d. 9/14/1919 at 70 in Boston, MA; hemorrhage
Georgianna S., d. 11/26/1936 at 82; coronary thrombosis
Grace Belle, d. 3/16/1902 at 11/9/15; pneumonia; PH
Grace D., d. 11/12/1935 at 79/4/2 in Northampton, MA; cerebral
   hemorrhage
Grace H. E., d. 12/4/1937 at 68/9/1; broncho pneumonia
Helen Louise, d. 2/1/1927 at 64/9/19 in Winchester, MA; cancer mesentric
   gland
Herbert C., d. 2/24/1924 at 71/5/23 in Boston, MA; carcinoma of bladder
Herman, d. 6/26/1927 at 70 in Concord; broncho pneumonia; Lebbeus Hill
Hollings, d. 12/20/1914 at 52/6/29; fatty degeneration of heart; John T. Hill
   and Mary Hollings
Ida B., d. 9/15/1924 at 79/6/5 in Durham; uraemia
John B., d. 8/24/1911 at 74/11/12; valvular heart disease; William Hill and
   Dorcas Rumery
John Tilton, d. 9/11/1922 at 83/1/4 in Pasadena, CA; chr. int. nephritis
Joseph E., d. 9/11/1922 at 59/5/8 in Concord; pericarditis; Plummer Hill
   and Lucy Holmes
Joseph G., d. 2/17/1918 at 80/7/15 in S. Berwick, ME; bronchial catarrh
Lebbeus, d. 8/22/1900 at 75; prostratis; PH
Levi G., d. 2/23/1898 at 85; exhaustion from pneumonia; b. Strafford; PH
Lydia A., d. 6/18/1891 at 68/5/2; single; William Hill (Saco, ME) and
   Dorcas Rummery (Saco, ME)
Martha L., d. 4/29/1895 at 80; old age; b. No. Andover, MA; buried in
   Chester
Mary E., d. 3/19/1927 at 70 in Boston, MA; cancer of breast
Moses Curtis, d. 1/2/1909 at 73/2; la grippe; Abraham Hill and Lydia C.
   Boston
Nathaniel E., d. 10/26/1907 at 79/11 in Malden, MA; arterio sclerosis
Newell, d. 6/24/1904 at 64 in Hathorne, MA; general paralysis; buried in
   Dover

Orrin, d. 2/15/1911 at 62/2/13; probably heart disease; Lewis Hill and Ann Proctor
Phebe A., d. 10/31/1895 at 63; uraemia; b. Tamworth; PH
Phoebe E., d. 10/11/1904 at 32/10/11 in Sanford, ME; chronic meningitis; PH
Walter H., d. 9/20/1893 at 20; opium poisoning; b. Dover; (Wells, ME; Alton)
Willie J., d. 5/6/1922 at 58/7/3; cerebral hemorrhage; John Hill and Mary Caldwell

HILLIARD,
Annie P., d. 4/7/1915 at 70; valvular dis. of heart; ----- Mason
Henry, d. 5/27/1891 at 77; widower
Samuel, d. 3/19/1900 at 54; heart disease; PH
Sarah E., d. 12/27/1932 at 75; cerebral hemorrhage
William P., d. 6/29/1901 at 57/9/21; apoplexy; PH

HILLS,
Arabella T., d. 7/14/1892 at 61; paralysis
Charles W., d. 9/14/1925 at 54 in Boston, MA; syncope; Charles D. Hills and Emma J. Martin
Charles Whitman, d. 5/16/1910 at –; asphyxia monatorum; Charles W. Hills and Gertrude N. Sullivan
Edwin A., d. 1/24/1905 at 75 in Washington, DC; cerebral hemorrhage; PH
Elizabeth C., d. 11/2/1920 at 53 in Lyndon, VT; nephritis; Edwin A. Hills and Arabella Smith
Ellen P., d. 1/15/1901 at 71/7/7; paralysis; PH
George E., d. 6/22/1901 at 56/0/23 in Georgetown, MA; phthisis pulmonalis; PH
Marilla M. H., d. 11/28/1901 at 94/8/8; la grippe; PH

HILTON,
Grace M., d. 12/29/1936 at 63/5/3; lobar pneumonia
Horace H., d. 1/3/1896 at 77; apoplexy; b. Wells, ME; buried in Rollinsford
Martha E., d. 4/17/1932 at 68/8/27; cardiac failure

HINES,
Arthur W., d. 10/16/1927 at 50/1/14 in Rochester; acute alcoholism
Edward, d. 8/23/1912 at 60/2/1; chronic endocarditis; Richard Hines and Mary Agnew
Ernest, d. 10/6/1935 at 52/5/21; heart disease
Lena M., d. 8/13/1898 at 0; disease of stomach; b. Dover; SM
Margaret, d. 11/16/1932 at 36/8/7; endocarditis
Margaret E., d. 2/15/1909 at 57/1/15; phthisis pulmonalis; James Vail and Eliza Drew

Mary C., d. 5/24/1920 at 39; phthisis; David Arling and Mary Doyle
William Joseph, d. 6/26/1919 at 5/5/6; accidental drowning; Arthur W. Hines and Christine Arling

HISLOP,
Jeremiah, d. 4/21/1890 at 0/0/16; George Hislop (Ireland) and Ellen Sullivan (Ireland)
Thomas, d. 4/29/1890 at 0/0/24; George Hislop (Ireland) and Helen Sullivan (Ireland)

HITCHCOCK,
Charles L., d. 4/3/1929 at 80/2/16 in Damariscotta, ME; valv. disease of heart; William Hitchcock and Emily Chapman
Malinda R., d. 3/15/1927 at 68/0/23 in Damariscotta, ME; cerebral thrombosis; Jehil S. Richards and Lenora Coggan

HOAR,
Hannah P., d. 4/–/1891 at 75

HOBART,
William H., d. 5/12/1912 at 31/11/20; acute nephritis

HOBBS,
child, d. 6/30/1918 at –; premature birth; Oscar Hobbs and Mary Sullivan
Emeline S., d. 2/26/1918 at 82/8/23; ulcer of stomach; Steven Smith and Sophia Chadbourne
Emma J. C., d. 8/20/1906 at 64/11/16; senile dementia; PH
George, d. 3/24/1895 at 77; Brights disease; b. Berwick, ME; buried in So. Berwick, ME
George L., d. 10/26/1904 at 58 in New York, NY; pneumonia; PH
George W., d. 3/19/1903 at 75/5/26; cerebral hemorrhage; PH
Nellie G., d. 11/29/1928 at 75; cerebral hemorrhage
Sarah A., d. 3/7/1904 at 73/0/12 in Alton; mitral regurgitation; PH
William H., d. 10/6/1928 at 69/10/9 in Brockton, MA; cerebral hemorrhage

HOBBY,
Louis H., d. 9/29/1924 at 61/3; angina pectoris; George P. Hobby and Clarissa Haight
Millie, d. 10/11/1926 at 54; diabetes mellitus

HODGDON,
Albert O., d. 6/27/1925 at 66/5/14; chr. intest. nephritis; Israel Hodgdon and Sarah Lang

Arthur C., d. 4/27/1928 at 67/11/7; cerebral hemorrhage; David W. Hodsdon (sic) and Elizabeth E. Clark

Caroline, d. 3/18/1891 at 85/10/16; widow; Edmund Curtis and Lydia Page

Caroline L., d. 10/4/1907 at 74/3/3; senility; Jonas Flint and Mary J. Spinney

Charles E., d. 12/22/1913 at 56/9/24; pulm. tuberculosis; Andrew J. Hodgdon and Hannah Tibbetts

Clarence M., d. 4/1/1923 at 46/5; acute indigestion; Frank P. Hodgdon and Georgianna Melcher

Daniel, d. 1/21/1902 at 77/2/2; abdominal cancer; PH

Edith M., d. 4/29/1919 at 49/2/21; chr. interstitial nephritis; George B. Johnson and Angie Parker

Elizabeth E., d. 1/22/1901 at 61/4/22 in Durham; PH

Ella, d. 1/27/1924 at 68/6 in Concord; septicemia; Jeremiah Leroy and Mary Carpenter

Emma F. W., d. 4/23/1917 at 48/4/15 in Somerville, MA; syphillis

Florence M., d. 12/23/1915 at 29/2; lobar pneumonia; James Boston and Lydia Thompson

Frank A., d. 3/23/1907 at 50 in Tewksbury, MA; acute enteritis

Frank P., d. 7/27/1916 at 62/5/5; chronic endocarditis; Andrew J. Hodgdon and Hannah Tibbetts

Harry E., d. 3/19/1918 at 51/2/4; acute oedema of lungs; Lyman Hodgdon and Harriet Delaney

Hervey U., d. 7/31/1910 at 46/5/4 in Walpole, MA; dilitation of heart

Joseph H., d. 11/3/1914 at 87/7/5; senility; Samuel Hodgdon

Lydia A., d. 9/13/1910 at 77/8/20; stran. umbilical hernia; Zebulon Dunn and Joanna Brooks

Malvina A., d. 6/17/1922 at 84/2/24; mitral regurgitation; Ephraim Bunker and Oliver Berry

Martha, d. 3/11/1892 at 87; la grippe - heart failure; b. Strafford; (Strafford; Strafford)

Mary E., d. 11/8/1927 at 64/9; lobar pneumonia; Edward E. Littlefield and Hannah E. Leighton

Nora J., d. 9/15/1934 at 74/10/1; lobar pneumonia

Susan A., d. 4/10/1911 at 62/9/18; nephritis; Charles H. Horton and Susan S. Lacoste

Susan E., d. 11/5/1930 at 69/8/26; cerebral embolism; Darius Stevens and Harriet A. Mathes

HODGE,
Arvilla A., d. 12/19/1896 at 33; phthisis pulmonalis; b. Lebanon, ME; PH

Charlotte R., d. 11/17/1933 at 70 in Somerville, MA; cerebral hemorrhage

Harry J., d. 3/23/1891 at 1/8/23 in Somerville, MA

James M., d. 4/13/1916 at 66 in Concord; myocardial insufficiency; David Hodge and Mary McKeteth

Joseph A., d. 12/19/1902 at 42/1/10; dropsy; PH
Mary E., d. 2/3/1894 at 37; heart disease; b. Dover; PH

HODGES,
Mary A., d. 12/7/1920 at 79/11/26; apoplexy; Henry Whitehouse and Abigail Welsh

HODGINS,
James, d. 5/9/1924 at 60/0/8; aneurysm

HODGKINS,
Barbara, d. 12/22/1918 at 0/0/2; purpura hemorrhagica; R. K. Hodgkins and Natalie Clarke

HODSDON,
A. Herman, d. 9/13/1928 at 66; cancer oesophagus; Andrew J. Hodsdon and Hannah -----
Abbie H., d. 8/8/1907 at 70; arteriosclerosis; Lemuel Hodsdon
George R., d. 4/23/1914 at 44/11/25; tuberculosis; Andrew J. Hodsdon and Hannah C. Tibbetts
George Sumner, d. 4/22/1912 at 57/5/9; pneumonia; Cyrus K. Hodsdon and Melinda Skinner
Georgianna B., d. 6/23/1928 at 76/8/1; cerebral hemorrhage; Daniel M. Melcher and Almira P. Randall
Hannah, d. 7/13/1912 at 84/8/1; angina pectoris; Samuel Tibbetts and Belinda Cross
Mary J., d. 6/4/1932 at 93/4/15; chronic nephritis

HODSON,
Ida B., d. 12/20/1934 at 78/9/15; aortic regurgitation

HOEY,
John, d. 7/2/1923 at 61; apoplexy; Patrick Hoey and Ann Martin

HOGAN,
Ann, d. 10/8/1919 at 77 in Concord; cerebral apoplexy
Charles, d. 1/26/1902 at 30 in Boston, MA; chronic intestinal nephritis; SM
Johanna, d. 9/20/1910 at 58; heart failure; Con. Sullivan
John, d. 12/29/1931 at 56 in Boston, MA; arterio sclerosis
John, d. 11/16/1933 at 64/1/25 in Concord; arteriosclerosis
Patrick, d. 8/5/1917 at 68; cerebral hemorrhage

HOGARTY,
William H., d. 11/5/1932 at 62/11/25; apoplexy

HOITT,
child, d. 3/1/1916 at –; stillborn; Edgar W. Hoitt and Vinnie Spencer
Abbie F., d. 12/28/1926 at 63/8/24; chronic nephritis; Warren D. Jones and Ruth S. Smith
Arthur H., d. 8/20/1927 at 73/0/19; arterio sclerosis; Levi Hoitt
Chesley W., d. 9/10/1915 at 19/1/5; chronic nephritis; George W. Hoyt (sic) and Sarah A. Place
Edgar W., d. 3/25/1896 at –; pneumonia; b. Dover; buried in Eliot, ME
Emeline, d. 3/12/1920 at 86/6 in Madbury; chronic bronchitis
Emma L., d. 3/11/1924 at 69/6/4; cerebral hemorrhage; George W. Jackson and Evangeline Hall
George W., d. 9/27/1897 at 70; nephritis; b. Deerfield; PH
Hatyville, d. 11/29/1915 at 86/10 in Madbury; cerebral softening; George B. Hoitt and Izannah Hall
Hiram B., d. 3/23/1887 at 0/9/23; b. Dover; Rodney B. Hoitt (Dover) and Abby F. Jones (Newmarket)
Martha J., d. 4/11/1922 at 77/6/25 in Durham; valvular heart disease
Mary, d. 5/26/1922 at 76; apoplexy; Luther Townsend and Mary Nichols
Mary A., d. 10/30/1901 at 67/6/17; cancer; buried in Newmarket
Mary A., d. 12/11/1918 at 78/3/1; sarcoma of lungs and throat; Edmund Boyce and Sabina Smith
Rodney B., d. 3/5/1924 at 61/2/7; ac. oedema of lungs; Hiram D. Hoitt and Clara L. Hadley

HOLDEN,
Annie S., d. 10/21/1908 at 80; old age; William Scallan and Anastasia Seniott
George C., d. 4/20/1918 at 66; epilepsy; Jonas F. Holden and Sarah L. Otis
Josiah B., d. 7/31/1918 at 83/2/28; arterio sclerosis; Nathan Holden

HOLLAND,
Alice, d. 2/28/1896 at 29; heart failure; b. Newmarket; buried in Newmarket
Emma A., d. 2/4/1934 at 79/6/7; uraemia
Fred, d. 9/22/1891 at 20/1/4 in Concord; single; Charles F. Holland (Great Falls) and Abby J. Curtis (Solon, ME)
George, d. 11/5/1906 at 79/7/5; chronic asthma; PH
Hannah, d. 3/12/1897 at 66; crystic hemorrhage; b. Taunton, MA; buried in Taunton, MA
John, d. 5/29/1900 at 69; apoplexy; buried in Taunton, MA
John J., d. 11/26/1916 at 49/8/14; starvation; George Holland and Margaret Woodcock
Margaret, d. 11/12/1906 at 78/5/10; cerebral hemorrhage; PH

Richard, d. 10/3/1887 at 30/6/3; loom fixer; married; b. England; George Holland (England) and Margaret ----- (England)
Richard G., d. 3/11/1900 at 13; accident; PH
Walter J., d. 10/25/1925 at 58; chronic myocarditis; William Holland and Catherine O'Brien

HOLLEY,
Gertrude A., d. 3/18/1937 at 53/4/24; arteriosclerosis
Laura E., d. 4/13/1911 at 53/0/8; diabetes; George W. Glines and Mary A. Varney
William L., d. 2/3/1914 at 72/2/12; chronic endocarditis

HOLLINGWORTH,
Benjamin F., d. 3/11/1900 at 66; heart disease; PH
Ida F., d. 9/20/1915 at 53/2/8; pyaemia; Benjamin F. Hollingworth and Sarah Perry
Sarah, d. 2/3/1902 at 66/9/22; inanition; PH

HOLLIS,
Alfred, d. 9/17/1905 at 1/10/11 in Madbury; dysentery

HOLLOM,
Wilmot W., d. 7/5/1910 at 87/7; senility; Charles F. Hollom and Lydia Crockett

HOLMAN,
Doris L., d. 3/21/1921 at 10/4/18; acute nephritis; Ansel Holman and Bertha E. Childs

HOLMES,
child, d. 10/30/1919 at –; stillborn; George E. Holmes and Marion L. Thompson
Abigail E., d. 11/21/1889 at 68/9/23; housewife; married; b. Barnstead; Moses Elliot (Barnstead) and Martha W. Tuttle (Dover)
Albert, d. 7/24/1923 at 72; softening of brain
Ellen, d. 4/2/1909 at 44 in Boston, MA; William Rafferty and Ellen -----
Hugh A., d. 7/2/1907 at 47/5/14; antotoxines, etc.; Hugh A. Holmes and Mary Kilty
Joel W., d. 5/29/1905 at 84/1/27; natural causes; PH
Marguerite E., d. 6/2/1909 at 9/10/2; ascetes; Hugh A. Holmes and Mary McLaughlin
Mary A., d. 5/2/1905 at 71/3/26; senility; PH
Mary J., d. 8/28/1888 at 69/0/19; b. Alton; William Colbath (Farmington) and Sarah Pinkham (New Durham)

Norman G. T., d. 12/28/1916 at 7/2/18; measles; George E. Holmes and Marion L. Thompson

HOLT,
Almira O., d. 12/5/1889 at 50; housewife; single; b. Dover
Curtis J., Jr., d. 8/21/1920 at 1/11/21 in Mystic, CT; cerebro spinal meningitis
Georgia F., d. 9/10/1932 at 54/11/13 in Woonsocket, RI; carcinoma gall bladder
Joseph N., d. 2/19/1913 at 78/1/15; brain disease; Asa Holt and Olive Rowe
Richard E., d. 8/10/1925 at 11/4/8; accidental drowning; Albert G. Holt and Ruth I. Edgerly

HOOD,
Fannie A., d. 1/28/1934 at 71 in Haverhill, MA; arteriosclerosis
William S., d. 11/15/1892 at –; malformation; b. Dover; (Turner, ME; Dover)

HOOK,
Arthur S., d. 3/21/1905 at 58/9/18 in Boston, MA; chronic spinal myetitis

HOOKE,
Dorothy E., d. 5/3/1936 at 25/6/4; cerebral embolism

HOOPER,
Alice B., d. 4/20/1932 at 61/7/17 in Salem, MA; carcinoma
Avery F., d. 10/18/1902 at 28/9/18; tubercular meningitis; PH
Charles, d. 6/4/1898 at 68; hypertrophy, dil. of heart; b. Dover; PH
Charles M., d. 6/28/1935 at 34/10/25 in Portland, ME; coronary occlusion
Dolly C., d. 2/27/1918 at 18/3/19; lobar pneumonia; Stephen Richard
Eleazer W., d. 7/13/1906 at 57/0/12; Brights disease; PH
Elizabeth, d. 10/23/1908 at 1/4/19 in Fitchburg, MA; diphtheria
Frank H., d. 3/13/1889 at 4/1/20; b. Dover; Frank W. Hooper (Dover) and Mary E. Hoitt (Dover)
George E., d. 3/7/1916 at 69/6/16; myocarditis; Eleazer W. Hooper and Olive C. Chute
Harry J., d. 5/25/1902 at 32/7/16; pneumonia; PH
James P., d. 2/24/1937 at 90/3/15; broncho pneumonia
Lizzie S., d. 10/6/1935 at 63/9/26 in Portsmouth; ac. pulmonary oedema
William, d. 4/9/1895 at 60; cerebral softening; b. Dover; PH
William P., d. 10/6/1928 at 57/7/24 in Fitchburg, MA; angina pectoris

HOORE,
James M., d. 1/27/1891 at 83 in Lawrence, MA

HOPE,
Cedona, d. 7/2/1905 at 0/8/26; pneumonia; SM

HOPEY,
child, d. 11/8/1919 at –; stillborn; Austin Hopey and Nora Driscoll
Margaret M., d. 9/22/1925 at 17/2/6 in Madbury; infantile paralysis

HOPKINS,
Frank E., d. 11/19/1907 at 61; cerebral hemorrhage; Elisha C. Hopkins
    and Julia Cochrane
George F., d. 6/16/1918 at 57; hemorrhage of stomach

HORLOR,
Abbie, d. 11/23/1906 at 67; pulmonary tuberculosis; PH
Arthur A., d. 7/.29/1895 at –; heart disease; b. Somersworth; buried in
    Somersworth
Charles W., d. 11/15/1904 at 68/8/24; carcinoma of liver; PH
George W., d. 7/17/1926 at 59/3; chr. pulm. tuberculosis; Charles W.
    Horlor and Abbie Jones
Harry E., d. 11/23/1929 at 53/0/18; chronic nephritis; Charles Horlor and
    Abbie Jones
Mary R., d. 4/18/1916 at 41/9; sarcoma of breast; William F. Milner and
    Mary Betton

HORN,
Christine B., d. 12/23/1893 at 43; chronic bronchitis; b. Dover; (Dover;
    Dover)
John W., d. 6/30/1921 at 72; gastro enteritis
Martha, d. 4/5/1916 at 87/0/7; endocarditis; David Wilson and Mercy
    Young
Nathaniel, d. 3/27/1914 at 78/7/27; uraemia; Oliver S. Horne (sic) and
    Sarah Estes
Sarah A., d. 12/21/1918 at 88/1/7 in Wilmington, MA; cardiac dropsy

HORNE,
child, d. 5/11/1908 at –; stillborn; Roscoe K. Horne and Florence E.
    Folsom
Alice E., d. 6/4/1904 at 28/3/13; pulmonary tuberculosis
Alonzo, d. 11/1/1910 at 83/6/21; cerebral apoplexy; Elijah Horne
Annie K., d. 7/26/1926 at 80 in Concord; senility; Charles Kingman and
    Mary E. Hanson

Betsey, d. 7/8/1887 at 79/8/25; widow; b. N. Berwick, ME; Thomas Chase (N. Berwick, ME) and Sarah Libbey (N. Berwick, ME)

Chrissie A., d. 12/10/1893 at 28; consumption; b. Dover; (Wolfeboro; Dover)

Edmund G., d. 4/24/1893 at 19; pulmonary phthisis; b. Dover; (NH; Dover)

Elizabeth, d. 1/18/1888 at 68/3/3; widow; b. Dover; William Hodgdon (Dover) and Susan Coffin (Dover)

Ellen H., d. 5/17/1895 at 60; diabetes; PH

Eunice H., d. 11/27/1888 at 67/7/ in Boston, MA

Evelyn A., d. 8/20/1905 at 62/8/20 in Stratham; valvular disease of heart; PH

Frank G., d. 11/27/1923 at 72/2/13 in Milton; cardiac dilatation

George E., d. 4/30/1896 at 58 in Boston, MA; cancer

George W., d. 1/16/1890 at 75/5/19; married; Jacob Horne (Rochester) and Abigail Twombly (Dover)

Hannah M., d. 5/4/1917 at 61; mitral regurgitation; Daniel Smith and Maria Hawkins

Harriet, d. 12/30/1905 at 78/0/29 in Malden, MA; nephritis; PH

Harry, d. 6/17/1924 at 55; acute endocarditis; Jethro E. Horne and Laura --

Helen Irene, d. 9/2-/1902 at 0/7/3; convulsions; PH

Ichabod, d. 12/13/1904 at 73/11; apoplexy; buried in family lot

Isabel D., d. 4/12/1937 at 85/9/1 in Exeter; cerebr. hemorrhage

Isabelle S., d. 12/31/1907 at 72 in Somerville, MA; cerebral hemorrhage

James A., d. 10/23/1923 at 78/4/19 in Beverly, MA; R. R. accident

James F., d. 7/28/1892 at 50; acute cerebritis; b. Dover; (NH; NH)

James M., d. 2/29/1908 at 74/11 in Boston, MA; arteriosclerosis

Janet, d. 6/13/1931 at 85/4/15; chronic nephritis

Jean, d. 3/20/1900 at 57; malnutrition; PH

Jeremiah, d. 4/12/1899 at 83 in Malden, MA; cystitis; PH

Lenora, d. 6/15/1920 at 76/7/6; chronic nephritis; George W. Varney and Mariam Hodgdon

Mary C., d. 7/8/1930 at 78/2/14; cerebral hemorrhage; Francis Sweet and Harriet Carter

Mary W., d. 7/1/1891 at 88/0/27 in Lawrence, MA

Mrs. John W., d. 8/24/1907 at 50; heart disease; Dennis Carroll

Nancy M., d. 6/26/1898 at 62; old age; b. Stratham; PH

Nathaniel, d. 2/11/1911 at 72/1/10; pneumonia; Nathan Horne and Sarah Roberts

Samuel R., d. 2/9/1896 at 79; old age; b. Dover; PH

Sarah, d. 6/21/1889 at 94/3/28; widow; b. Dover; S. Roberts and Mary Estes

Sarah J., d. 6/15/1910 at 73/3; senile dementia; Nathan Horne and Sarah Roberts

Wilbur F., d. 5/31/1908 at 62 in St. Louis, MO; suicide

William, d. 10/14/1887 at 72/0/23; married; b. Glasgow, Scotland; James Horne (Scotland) and Jane Perry (Scotland)

HORNEY,
Henry, d. 6/23/1904 at 37; tuberculosis pulmonalis

HORNIG,
child, d. 2/21/1901 at –; prolapse of cord during delivery; PH

HORR,
Lawrence H., d. 11/13/1929 at 16; accidental; Virgil L. Horr and Marion Newcomb

HORRIGAN,
son, d. 1/16/1890 at –; John Horrigan (Ireland) and Johanna Lanigan (Dover)

HORROCKS,
Jennie, d. 3/21/1904 at 33/1/29; uraemia; PH

HORSCH,
Abbie F., d. 8/29/1927 at 86/11/15; senility; James Littlefield and Sarah Bean
Carl Herman, d. 9/22/1891 at 69/2; married; (Saxony; Saxony)
Linna, d. 4/20/1920 at 61/5/23; cancer of lung; Carl H. Horsch and Abby Littlefield

HORSMAN,
Linnie S., d. 10/3/1918 at 15/1/8; lobar pneumonia; William S. Horsman and Melinda J. Randall

HORTON,
Annie, d. 6/5/1935 at 75/11/17 in Howard, RI; gen. arteriosclerosis
Charles H., d. 9/11/1898 at 81; herniaplegia; b. New York City; PH
Charles H., d. 5/8/1905 at 62 in Boston, MA; cardiac disease; PH
Elizabeth, d. 3/17/1897 at 66; pneumonia; b. Halifax, NS; PH
Ella E., d. 5/17/1924 at 73/10 in Boston, MA; pellagra
George E., d. 9/8/1916 at 69 in Danvers, MA; lobar pneumonia; Charles H. Horton and Susan Chase
Laura, d. 2/21/1936 at 68; rt. lobar pneumonia
Marshall C., d. 1/2/1899 at 26; typhoid fever; PH
Samuel B., d. 7/15/1916 at 91/0/13; senility; Stutley Horton and Lydia Babson

Susan S., d. 3/2/1890 at 72/7/6; married; John B. Lacoste (France) and Hannah Renaldi (Boston, MA)
Susie L., d. 6/29/1892 at 18; phthisis; b. Buckfield, ME; (Buckfield, ME; Columbia)

HOSMER,
Cyrus W., d. 9/5/1898 at 45; valvular disease of heart; b. Sweden, ME; PH

HOSSIPPIAN,
Nazareth, d. 4/13/1917 at 50; gangrene of mouth; Horsef Hossippian and Aghsig Markarian

HOUDE,
Aurore, d. 4/13/1908 at 2/6/28; cirrhosis of liver; Cesaire Houde and Cordelia Croteau
Aurore R., d. 5/19/1936 at 24/1/4*
Cornelia, d. 7/28/1933 at 50/2/28 in Eliot, ME; cerebral hemorrhage
Leo Norman, d. 12/18/1933 at 0/7/5; rickets

HOUGH,
Andrew Jackson, d. 4/23/1923 at 89; chronic endocarditis; Thomas Hough and Catherine Keniston
Carrie B., d. 3/19/1916 at 54/3/19 in Boston, MA; diabetes; ----- Morrill
Elizabeth R., d. 3/24/1912 at 64/11/11 in Brooklyn, NY; nephritis
George W., d. 3/10/1906 at 72/9/18 in Tilton; acute pneumonia; PH
Harry, d. 1/19/1917 at 62/11/12 in New York, NY; myocarditis; Ralph Hough
Julia A., d. 3/3/1913 at 73/0/26 in Sanford, ME; organic heart disease
Mary Ellen, d. 7/2/1924 at 89/6/7; atherona; Alonzo Roberts and Mary Torr
Morrill, d. 12/15/1917 at 28/2/5 in Denver, CO; tuberculosis; Harry Hough and Carrie B. Morrill
Philip, d. 4/27/1927 at 40 in Tampa, FL; septicaemia
Ralph, d. 3/6/1916 at 92/6/20; old age; Thomas Hough and Catherine Keniston
Sarah J., d. 5/15/1909 at 85/1/21; confinement, hip injury; John Delaney and Margaret Farrell
Thomas B., d. 5/18/1917 at 79/3/4 in Sanford, ME; hemiplegia

HOUGHTON,
Levina M., d. 1/27/1918 at 0/0/11; premature birth; William Houghton and Ann Turner
William, d. 9/24/1917 at 38/3/6 in Boston, MA; basilar meningitis; James Houghton and Elizabeth Booth

HOUGHY,
Patrick, d. 7/21/1907 at 64; cirrhosis of liver

HOULE,
Esther, d. 12/11/1922 at 7/7/29; tuberculosis meningitis; Alfred Houle and Anna Bourque
Lucie, d. 10/7/1898 at 45; heart disease; b. Canada; buried in Canada
Philip, d. 5/11/1898 at 0; gastro-enteritis; b. Dover; SM

HOURIHANE,
Thomas F., d. 6/13/1925 at 18/2/13; chr. valv. dis. of heart; Thomas F. Hourihane and Zita B. Sterling
Zeta B., d. 2/19/1935 at 53/5/12 in Somersworth; fractured skull, struck by auto

HOUSTON,
son, d. 2/2/1888 at –; b. Dover; James Houston (NY) and Lida Hamilton (VT)
son, d. 6/30/1890 at --; James G. Houston (NY) and E. J. Hamilton (Biddeford, ME)
Lida J., d. 5/12/1892 at 34; pneumonia; b. Biddeford, ME

HOVEY,
Fred G., d. 9/8/1917 at 0/4/4 in Whitman, MA; enlarged thymus
Naomi, d. 2/4/1916 at 95/7/30 in Whitman, MA; old age

HOWARD,
child, d. 4/25/1899 at –; stillborn; PH
child, d. 10/22/1921 at –; atelectasis; George A. Howard and Marion I. Clark
Almie F., d. 3/28/1936 at 63/7/15*
Almira, d. 11/15/1887 at 69; single; b. Rochester
Arthur, d. 9/5/1895 at 0; marasmus; b. Dover; PH
Carrie E., d. 5/14/1899 at 34; puerperal fever; PH
Clarence M., d. 10/2/1901 at 0/4/24; cholera infantum; PH
David M., d. 6/8/1929 at 85/11/16 in S. Berwick, ME; chr. valvular disease
Frank, d. 2/7/1897 at 59; pneumonia; b. Rochester; PH
Grover C., d. 12/13/1889 at 1/6 in Barrington; John Howard (US) and M. Davis (US)
Hattie M., d. 7/14/1913 at 36/3/12; Addison's disease; William H. Willey and Caroline M. Foss
Lamartine, d. 1/3/1922 at 65/11/28 in Antrim; capillary bronchitis
Lydia A., d. 12/2/1893 at 72; pneumonia; b. Berwick, ME; (New Bedford, MA; Berwick, ME)

Mary L., d. 7/13/1889 at 87/0/26; housewife; widow; b. Tuftonboro; Val.
    Sargent and Temperance ----
Mary M., d. 2/16/1919 at 42/3; anasarca
Nancy, d. 8/18/1889 at 81; married; b. Portsmouth
Phoebe M., d. 6/12/1926 at 85 in Rochester; chronic bronchitis
Rachael, d. 9/2/1894 at 72; debility of old age; b. Poughkeepsie, NY;
    buried in Woonsocket, RI
Susan May, d. 10/6/1893 at –; cholera infantum; b. Dover; (----; Dover)
William T., d. 11/28/1887 at 82/7/7; blacksmith; married; b. Dover;
    Stephen Howard (Dover) and Phoebe (Barrington)

HOWART,
John, d. 5/28/1895 at 28 in Salem, MA; pneumonia; b. Scotland; PH
William, d. 5/30/1906 at 1; cerebral meningitis; SM

HOWARTH,
child, d. 8/22/1903 at 0/0/1-4; convulsions; PH
Alice, d. 12/24/1927 at 64/6/21 in Lowell, MA; diabetes; Richard Howarth
    and Ann Runnell
Ann H., d. 7/30/1905 at 65/2/28; carcinoma of liver; PH
Catherine, d. 3/17/1906 at 44/8/21; cancer of stomach; PH
Dorothy E., d. 4/20/1903 at 1/1/16; cerebro spinal meningitis; PH
Leon F., d. 1/29/1916 at 20/5/8 in Exeter; pneumonia
Lily, d. 5/12/1912 at 25/11/26; pyaemia; Richard Howarth and Ann
    Rimmer
Margaret, d. 5/12/1908 at 42/0/21; typhoid fever; Daniel Holt and Mary ----
Richard, d. 5/1/1909 at 70; heart disease; Richard Howarth
Richard, d. 4/26/1921 at 60/3/14; heart syncope; Richard Howarth and
    Ann Rimmer

HOWAT,
Ellen, d. 12/23/1906 at 33/2; pulmonary tuberculosis
Ellen, d. 8/14/1921 at 78; myocarditis; Lawrence McGlone and Bridget
    McCabe
John A., d. 10/31/1908 at 37; pneumonia; James Howat and Ellen ----
John W., d. 4/7/1896 at 2; catarrhal pneumonia; b. Dover; PH
William J., d. 9/13/1905 at 2/8/13; meningitis; SM

HOWATT,
Mary C., d. 10/13/1918 at 12/5/29; tubercular meningitis; William Howatt
    and Ellen Harris
Mary G., d. 8/21/1926 at 64/5/21 in Providence, RI; myocarditis

HOWCROFT,
Adelaide S., d. 6/5/1909 at 76/4 in Exeter; valv. disease of heart

HOWE,
Bertha M., d. 9/16/1901 at 0/2/12; cholera infantum
Carol N., d. 11/22/1932 at 0/0/18 in Rollinsford; atelectasis
Elizabeth S., d. 7/11/1922 at 74/8/22; chr. inter. nephritis; Samuel Hussey and Susan Horne
Frank R., d. 12/3/1934 at 53 in Morristown, NJ; lobar pneumonia
Harry F., d. 10/2/1903 at 0/1/7; marasmus; buried in Somersworth
Ithamar S., d. 1/13/1898 at 43 in Rochester; diabetes, Brights disease; PH
John F., d. 5/24/1895 at 48 in So. Berwick, ME; apoplexy; b. Rochester; PH
John W., d. 7/12/1928 at 65 in Rochester; shock
Julia A., d. 10/18/1899 at 30; phthisis pulmonalis; buried in Dorchester, MA
Louisa, d. 5/17/1907 at 78; old age; Samuel Hall and Sallie Tuttle
Michael J., d. 3/2/1936 at 50*

HOWEROFT,
David, d. 2/25/1892 at 76; disease of heart; b. England

HOWLAND,
Ann, d. 5/3/1903 at 66; heart disease; SM
Anna D., d. 9/15/1901 at 51 in Boston, MA; arteriosclerosis
Elizabeth, d. 11/30/1919 at 75 in N. Andover, MA; chronic nephritis
Ellen, d. 12/1/1893 at 63; Bright's disease; b. Ireland; (Ireland; Ireland)
Fenton, d. 3/15/1905 at 63; shock; SM
Margaret, d. 1/9/1899 at 62; heart disease; SM
Margaret, d. 5/14/1904 at 30; heart disease; SM
Michael, d. 3/14/1907 at 40; Bright's disease; Fenton Howland and Ellen Cavanaugh
Minnie A., d. 9/1/1922 at 50/0/10 in Whitman, MA; chr. int. nephritis
Richard, d/ 5/3/1928 at 66; chronic endocarditis; Fenton Howland and Ellen Cavanaugh
William, d. 3/14/1906 at 64; Bright's disease
William, d. 1/30/1911 at 45; pericarditis; Michael Howland and Margaret Cash

HOWLEY,
Kate, d. 11/1/1893 at 55; chronic nephritis; b. Ireland; (Ireland; Ireland)
Michael, d. 9/20/1903 at 59; heart disease; buried in Portland, ME

HOYE,
Bennie, d. 12/23/1890 at 8/1; Patrick Hoye (Dover) and Rose E. Mason (Dover)
Elizabeth W., d. 4/20/1922 at 72/0/7 in Los Angeles, CA
James, d. 4/18/1904 at 50 in Lebanon, ME; apoplexy (see following entry)

James, d. 4/18/1905 at 50 in Lebanon, ME; heart failure (see preceding entry)
John, d. 7/2/1899 at 14; drowned; SM
John Andrew, d. 2/7/1922 at 76/11/28 in Los Angeles, CA
Rose, d. 12/9/1914 at 55 in Exeter; apoplexy; Michael Mason and Alice Brennan
Thomas, d. 5/19/1900 at 53 in Lebanon, ME; apoplexy; SM

HOYT,
Arthur D., d. 12/2/1898 at 0; capillary bronchitis; b. Dover; PH
Edgar W., d. 4/14/1932 at 71/5/5; chronic nephritis
George, d. 12/13/1897 at 57 in Boston, MA; chronic bronchitis
George A., d. 4/28/1911 at 49/8/10; cerebro hemorrhage; Richard P. Hoyt and Margaret M.
Hiram D., d. 12/14/1897 at 66; inflammation of the brain; b. Barrington; PH
Israel Monson, d. 11/9/1891 at 75/4/17; married; Israel Hoyt (Eastport, ME) and Margaret Crab
James, d. 2/10/1888 at 80; single; b. Milton
James T., d. 11/17/1922 at 64/3/6; myocarditis; Thomas Hoyt and Mariah Hull
John C., d. 2/13/1930 at 80/6/12 in Boston, MA; lobar pneumonia; John Hoyt and Louisa Decatur
Louisa, d. 1/19/1898 at 73 in Boston, MA; pneumonia; PH
Margaret, d. 2/13/1903 at 90/11/3; disease of heart and liver; buried in Berwick, ME
Mary A., d. 12/12/1930 at 45/0/26; arterio sclerosis; Albert McDaniel and Elizabeth -----
Mary Ann, d. 10/1/1927 at 76/4/7 in Boston, MA; cancer of uterus

HUARD,
Gideon, d. 5/20/1917 at 22; pulm. tuberculosis; George Huard and Zulea Foster

HUBBARD,
A. Franklyn, d. 5/4/1925 at 69/4/24; heart disease; George W. Hubbard and Maria A. Averill
Albert F., d. 10/1/1924 at 0/5/29; marasmus; Val. Hubbard and Elsie C. Capen
Francis G., d. 9/13/1907 at 68 in Wells, ME; abscess of liver
George S., d. 12/31/1933 at 54/4/20; broncho pneumonia
Herbert, d. 9/10/1917 at 43; smothered - burning house; Samuel Hubbard and Cynthia Daniels
John, d. 3/8/1937 at 73/1/8; chr. endocarditis
Laura A., d. 9/15/1936 at 66/3/7; cerebral hemorrhage

Samuel G., d. 10/20/1894 at 79; old age; b. Wells, ME; buried in Wells, ME
Sarah, d. 5/22/1887 at 48/5/23; mill operative; single; b. Somersworth; Joshua Hubbard (Berwick, ME) and Mary Tibbetts (Berwick, ME)
Zelva P., d. 3/6/1903 at 2/0/14; bronchitis; PH

HUCKINS,
William B., d. 12/17/1907 at 75/6/5; chronic nephritis; Nathan Huckins and Sophia Kelley

HUDON,
Albert, d. 10/26/1918 at 29/7; lobar pneumonia; Louis Houdon (sic) and Josephine Brown

HUDSON,
Elvira F., d. 3/4/1918 at 89/4/2; senility; William Lathrop and Elizabeth W. Drake

HUGHES,
daughter, d. 4/20/1890 at 0/0/1; John H. Hughes (Dover) and Adaline Stone (Canada)
child, d. 12/--/1892 at --; stillborn; b. Dover; (Ireland; Ireland)
child, d. 3/14/1894 at --; stillborn; b. Dover; SM
child, d. 7/30/1899 at 2; inanition; SM
child, d. 3/7/1900 at <1; premature birth; SM
child, d. 9/9/1903 at --; stillborn; SM
child, d. 3/22/1905 at 2; inanition; SM
child, d. 5/20/1905 at --; placentor previor; SM
child, d. 11/18/1908 at --; stillborn; Peter Hughes and Georgia Pool
child, d. 3/14/1910 at --; exc. uterine hemorrhage; Frank Hughes and Margaret Toner
child, d. 12/1/1932 at --; premature birth
Adeline, d. 6/21/1912 at 60/10/20; mitral regurgitation
Alfred, d. 6/20/1898 at 1; b. Dover; SM
Alice, d. 6/9/1891 at 54/4; married; Michael McNally (Ireland) and ----- (Ireland)
Allen, d. 10/8/1918 at 16; pneumonia; Hugh Holmes and Mary McLaughlin
Ann, d. 4/9/1892 at 78; old age; b. Ireland; (Ireland; Ireland)
Ann, d. 1/30/1904 at 42; cardiac dilation; SM
Annie, d. 4/27/1902 at 4; brain tumor; SM
B., d. 2/7/1906 at 37; pneumonia; SM
Barney, d. 5/7/1911 at 48 in Brentwood; pneumonia; Barney Hughes and Agnes McNally
Bernard, d. 9/22/1926 at 61; chronic Brights
Bessie, d. 5/30/1897 at 2; nephritis scarletinal; b. Dover; SM

Bridget, d. 9/27/1896 at 40; uterine tumor; b. Ireland; SM
Bridget, d. 12/3/1908 at 60; hemorrhage
Bridget, d. 1/17/1926 at –; stillborn; Peter Hughes
Bridget, d. 5/1/1926 at 79 in Manchester; terminal pneumonia
Catherine, d. 2/8/1901 at 77; la grippe; SM
Catherine, d. 1/11/1923 at 50; carcinoma of stomach; John Callahan
Catherine, d. 11/23/1924 at 61; interstitial nephritis
Catherine, d. 1/17/1930 at 70; lobar pneumonia; Felix Hughes and Nancy McKone
Catherine J., d. 1/28/1902 at 22; pulmonary tuberculosis; SM
Catherine T., d. 2/17/1900 at 32; tuberculosis; SM
Charles, d. 1/7/1889 at 5
Charles, d. 1/21/1890 at 71; married; James Hughes (Ireland) and Ann Hughes (Ireland)
Delia A., d. 9/4/1926 at 37; carcinoma of liver; Michael Bean and Ellen Malley
Edmond M. J., d. 5/12/1906 at 24/0/2 in Lawrence, MA; acute phthisis
Edward, d. 9/11/1910 at 43; acute nephritis; Peter Hughes and Katherine McCabe
Edward J., d. 4/27/1910 at 39/0/1; pulmonary tuberculosis; James Hughes and Sarah McKenna
Elinor, d. 11/26/1913 at 0/0/3; cong. atelectasis; Edward Hughes and Nellie V. -----
Eliza, d. 6/12/1891 at 34/10; single; John Hughes (Ireland) and Nancy A. Hughes (Ireland)
Elizabeth, d. 1/23/1892 at 1; meningitis, cerebral; b. Dover; (PEI; Dover)
Elizabeth, d. 2/23/1908 at --; stillborn; Frank Hughes and K. Callaghan
Elizabeth M., d. 12/20/1915 at 44; hyperaemia cerebral; Felix Hughes and Catherine McIntire
Ella, d. 12/7/1903 at 54; chronic nephritis
Ellen, d. 3/17/1887 at 34/7/13; housewife; married; b. Dover; Joseph H. Witham (NH) and Catherine Taylor (NH)
Ellen, d. 3/19/1892 at 34; typhoid pneumonia; b. Dover; (Ireland; Ireland)
Ellen, d. 11/7/1895 at 66; heart disease; b. Ireland; SM
Ellen, d. 1/20/1898 at 51; pneumonia; b. Dover; SM
Ellen T., d. 10/12/1917 at 70; pneumonia; Andrew Gleason and Mary Murray
Frances, d. 12/2/1912 at 52; phthisis; Thomas Hughes and Margaret Murray
Francis, d. 7/30/1899 at –; pneumonia; SM
Francis, d. 7/19/1900 at 40 in Rochester; falling down stairs; PH
Frank, d. 5/8/1926 at 46 in Concord; pulmonary tuberculosis
George T., Jr., d. 7/19/1915 at –; stillborn; George T. Hughes and Nellie Parle

Helena G., d. 5/28/1929 at 36; pernicious anemia; Michael I. Hayes and
Margaret Duffy
Hugh, d. 8/13/1917 at 55; pneumonia broncho; Patrick Hughes and Susan
Barrett
James, d. 8/5/1888 at 0/1; b. Dover; James Hughes (Ireland) and Mary
Evans (Ireland)
James, d. 1/10/1896 at 34; diabetes mellitus; b. Dover; SM
James, d. 2/14/1896 at 58; inflammation of bowels; b. Ireland; SM
James, d. 12/12/1899 at 3; diphtheria; SM
James, d. 2/2/1902 at 51; cancer of stomach; SM
James, d. 5/29/1902 at 70; pulmonary tuberculosis; SM
James, d. 4/8/1922 at 45/10 in Rochester; epilepsy; Edward Hughes and
Sarah Cotter
James A., d. 7/24/1896 at 21; peritonitis; b. Dover; SM
James C., d. 12/17/1907 at 27/10/24; empyema; John T. Hughes and
Bridget McCann
James E., d. 10/28/1898 at 25; phthisis; b. Ireland; SM
James Edward, d. 12/13/1931 at 0/0/3; intestinal hemorrhage
James Joseph, d. 12/1/1911 at 16/8/12; tuberculosis; Edward J. Hughes
and Margaret McCabe
James Joseph, d. 3/1/1920 at 45 in Providence, RI; broncho pneumonia
John, d. 4/3/1899 at 1; pulmonary phthisis; SM
John, d. 1/1/1901 at 35/3/6 in Rochester; consumption; PH
John, d. 5/26/1927 at 64; pulmonary tuberculosis; Arthur Hughes and
Rose -----
John D., d. 12/12/1932 at –; arterio sclerosis
John E., d. 7/24/1900 at 20; tuberculosis; SM
John H., d. 5/31/1918 at 65; carcinoma of prostate; Peter Hughes and
Bridget -----
John P., d. 8/20/1925 at 74; heart disease; Owen J. Hughes and Catherine
Mooney
Joseph, d. 7/6/1896 at 44; alcoholism; b. Ireland; SM
Joseph, d. 3/9/1906 at 27; curvature of spine; SM
Joseph, d. 2/7/1935 at 54; chronic nephritis
Joseph V., d. 1/4/1897 at 24 in Jersey City, NJ; phthisis pulmonalis
Kate, d. 3/29/1905 at 74; cerebral embolism
Katherine, d. 11/12/1908 at 52; pneumonia; Bernard Loughlin
Katherine N., d. 9/21/1922 at 22/0/1; miliary tuberculosis; John Hughes
and Catherine Hughes
Katie, d. 12/4/1897 at 5; Brights disease; b. Dover; SM
Lillian M. V., d. 8/29/1918 at 22/8/21; acute nephritis; Edward A. Keevan
and Teresa Grimes
Lizzie, d. 7/13/1892 at –; anaemia; b. Dover; (Ireland; Ireland)
Lizzie, d. 11/16/1894 at 35; b. Ireland; SM
Lizzie, d. 1/27/1908 at 43; endocarditis; Michael Hughes

M. A., d. 8/31/1889 at 0/3/7; b. Dover; Bernard Hughes (Ireland) and Lizzie Hughes (Ireland)
Madelaine, d. 8/7/1907 at 0/2/2; cholera infantum; Anne Hughes
Margaret, d. 6/18/1891 at 27; married; Frank Cassidy (Ireland) and Mary Hughes (Ireland)
Margaret, d. 12/2/1901 at 68; Bright's disease; SM
Margaret, d. 4/24/1907 at 75; old age
Margaret, d. 9/8/1910 at 90 in Manchester; broncho-pneumonia; John McClosky and Ellen Meehan
Margaret, d. 7/7/1915 at 44; valvular heart disease; Michael McCabe and Margaret Waters
Margaret, d. 2/12/1930 at 59; cancer of breast; William Higgins and Jane Smith
Margaret A., d. 8/26/1896 at 48; cerebral softening; SM
Margaret E., d. 4/14/1894 at –; cerebral meningitis; b. Dover; SM
Margaret E., d. 11/10/1928 at 74/8/19; chronic myocarditis; John Ryan and Maria Scully
Mary, d. 12/10/1887 at 68/8; widow; b. Ireland; Arthur Murray (Ireland) and Mary (Ireland)
Mary, d. 6/3/1897 at 45; dropsy; b. Ireland; SM
Mary, d. 7/29/1899 at –; cholera infantum; SM
Mary, d. 3/14/1900 at 33; consumption; SM
Mary, d. 11/5/1900 at 1; malnutrition; SM
Mary, d. 2/7/1902 at 54; carcinoma of stomach; SM
Mary, d. 10/3/1904 at 0/2; inanition; SM
Mary, d. 9/30/1915 at 78; broncho pneumonia
Mary, d. 7/25/1919 at 66 in Lawrence, MA; broncho pneumonia
Mary, d. 12/1/1926 at 70; diabetes mellitus
Mary A., d. 8/10/1891 at 0/3/15; James Hughes (Ireland) and Margaret Cassidy (Ireland)
Mary A., d. 10/31/1898 at 37; SM
Mary A., d. 8/6/1935 at 65; cancer of stomach
Mary B., d. 4/25/1900 at <1; inanition; SM
Mary E., d. 10/1/1905 at 0/9/15; athrepsia; SM
Michael, d. 9/12/1896 at 40; Brights disease; b. Ireland; SM
Michael, d. 12/31/1930 at 50 in Dayton, KY; lobar pneumonia
Michael C., d. 1/5/1890 at 2/6; James Hughes (Ireland) and Mary Lennon (Ireland)
Michael H., d. 3/17/1898 at 67 in Jersey City, NJ; phthisis pulmonalis
Michael H., d. 9/6/1899 at 10; peritonitis; SM
Minnie, d. 10/29/1888 at 3/5/18; b. Dover; Joseph Hughes (Ireland) and Mary Lemen (Ireland)
Mrs. P., d. 6/27/1901 at –; apoplexy; SM
Nancy A., d. 1/28/1899 at 61; old age; SM
Nellie, d. 10/9/1918 at 30/9/23; lobar pneumonia

Owen, d. 10/26/1897 at 72; asthma; b. Ireland; SM
P., d. 11/16/1900 at 41; paresis; SM
Patricia, d. 7/5/1934 at –; spina bifida
Patrick, d. 1/5/1894 at 60; paralysis; b. Ireland; SM
Patrick, d. 3/5/1905 at 74; old age; SM
Patrick, d. 1/12/1908 at 31; typhoid
Patrick, d. 8/26/1922 at 70; carcinoma of larynx; Frank Hughes and Ellen Carragher
Patrick, d. 12/26/1934 at 69 in Reading, MA; chronic myocarditis
Patrick F., d. 8/15/1930 at 48 in Middletown, CT; heart disease; John Hughes and Bridget McCann
Peter, d. 5/15/1898 at 24; phthisis; b. Dover; SM
Peter, d. 9/28/1923 at 82 in Togus, ME; gangrene
Peter, d. 12/11/1937 at 72/0/0; chr. endocarditis
Philip Edward, d. 3/5/1936 at 0/0/2; in. cran. hemorrhage
Phylis M., d. 1/4/1917 at 1/0/23 in Biddeford, ME; operated; Thomas J. Hughes and Mary Brennan
Rose, d. 12/6/1890 at 43; widow; Edward Mulligan (Ireland)
Rose, d. 7/25/1891 at 0/8/2; Bernard Hughes (Ireland) and Lizzie Hughes (Ireland)
Rose, d. 2/25/1897 at 35; typhoid pneumonia; b. Ireland; SM
Rose, d. 11/22/1897 at –; meningitis; b. Dover; SM
Rose, d. 3/5/1905 at 70; heart disease; SM
Rose, d. 11/27/1913 at 39/11/3; carcinoma of stomach; Patrick Hughes and Mary Rafferty
Rose, d. 11/21/1924 at 85/10/21; myocarditis; Patrick McCann and Sarah Hughes
Sadie E., d. 2/4/1911 at 4/3/1; pneumonia; Peter E. Hughes and Nellie E. Hughes
Sarah, d. 4/23/1894 at 33; pernicious anaemia; b. Ireland; SM
Sarah, d. 8/17/1898 at 0; brain disease; b. Dover; SM
Sarah, d. 3/9/1906 at 63; aortic incompetency
Sarah, d. 4/12/1914 at 41; Brights; disease; John Hughes and Ellen Moynihan
Sarah A., d. 10/28/1901 at 46/5/9 in Portsmouth; carcinoma of breast; PH
Sarah E., d. 7/16/1890 at 0/0/1; Edward Hughes (Ireland) and Margaret Burke (Ireland)
Susan, d. 10/5/1924 at 61 in Haverhill, MA; arterio sclerosis
Teresa, d. 4/23/1931 at 60; heart failure
Thomas, d. 2/18/1900 at 30; pul. phthisis; SM
Thomas, d. 8/18/1903 at 56; heart disease; SM
Thomas, d. 11/23/1905 at 82/8 in Portsmouth; old age; SM
Thomas, d. 12/11/1914 at –; acute nephritis; Peter Hughes
Thomas, d. 1/28/1916 at 54/1/16; chronic nephritis; Felix Hughes and Catherine McIntire

Thomas, d. 3/1/1936 at 68*
Thomas B., d. 1/22/1891 at 0/7; James Hughes (US) and K. Laughlin (Ireland)
Thomas F., d. 4/18/1903 at 56/1/16; heart disease
Walter, d. 12/13/1912 at 52/9/15; uraemia and accident; John C. Hughes and Margaret -----
William, d. 3/16/1919 at 0/5/10 in Boston, MA; bronchitis
William H., d. 11/5/1900 at 16; SM
William John, d. 8/3/1893 at 15; accidental drowning; b. Dover; (Ireland; Ireland)
Winnifred T., d. 11/15/1912 at 12; appendicitis; Thomas J. Hughes and Mary A. Brennan

HULL,
son, d. 10/16/1890 at 0/0/1; Charles H. Hull (Dover) and Nellie Drew (Durham)
son, d. 10/16/1890 at 0/0/1; Charles H. Hull (Dover) and Nellie Drew (Durham)
Blanche V., d. 9/28/1936 at 59/4/13; pyelonephritis
Catherine A., d. 3/9/1893 at 41; scrofulous disease; b. Belmont; (Canada; Alton)
Charles W., d. 5/15/1929 at 77/5/20; valv. heart disease; John B. Hull and Sarah Ham
Elizabeth H., d. 11/30/1918 at 65/5/17; chronic nephritis; Samuel R. Hanson and Elizabeth C. Furber
James H., d. 10/10/1920 at 79/6; acute cystitis
John B., d. 7/31/1888 at 68/5; blacksmith; widower; b. NH; ----- Hull (NH) and Patience Horne (NH)
Lawrence W., d. 9/5/1917 at 30/0/29; acute appendicitis; Charles W. Hull and Clara J. Towle
Samuel H., d. 6/15/1907 at 57/0/21; chronic nephritis; John B. Hull and Mary Horne

HULME,
Celia E., d. 12/27/1922 at 72/11/29 in Manchester; apoplexy
William E., d. 9/23/1898 at 48 in Manchester; disease of brain; PH

HUNEAU,
child, d. 2/19/1900 at <1; premature birth; SM
Joseph N., d. 9/5/1906 at 0/8/24; cholera infantum

HUNT,
Amelia L., d. 2/22/1918 at 37 in Boston, MA; aortic insufficiency; John Crowell
Blanche, d. 5/13/1916 at –; stillborn; John Hunt and Blanche F. Mayberry

Elizabeth E., d. 9/29/1893 at 52; typhoid fever
Lilla F., d. 3/5/1934 at 62/11/21; chronic nephritis
Mary B., d. 2/22/1923 at 70/7/3; senile dementia; John C. Bradley and
    Mary Emerson
Patrick, d. 3/17/1909 at 80 in Lawrence, MA; valvular dis. of heart

HUNTER,
Arthur W., d. 5/19/1924 at 0/2/1; entero colitis; Thomas J. Hunter and
    Florence Greenaway
Catherine, d. 11/7/1908 at 36; acute uraemia; John McHugh
Richard, d. 2/26/1893 at 19; typhoid pneumonia; b. Ulster Co., Ireland;
    (Ireland; Ireland)
Richard, d. 10/28/1936 at 70; chr. endocarditis
Thomas J., d. 3/23/1911 at 0/0/2; convulsions; Thomas J. Hunter and
    Florence Greenaway

HUNTINGTON,
Elisha S., d. 11/29/1927 at 82/6/12 in Janettsville, MD; broncho
    pneumonia
Helen L., d. 1/23/1928 at 26/0/30 in Belmont, MA; acute nephritis
Martha S., d. 11/10/1897 at 47 in Barrington; b. Lee; PH

HUNTLEY,
Lester W., d. 7/19/1916 at 0/1/27; athrep. from malnutrition; George E.
    Huntley and Margaret E. Holland

HUNTRESS,
Angelia S., d. 8/3/1917 at 84 in Boston, MA; diabetes mellitus
Elise M., d. 2/2/1929 at 70/0/4; angina pectoris
Hannah E., d. 6/5/1903 at 58/6/1 in Killingly, CT; Brights disease; PH
Leander S., d. 2/26/1895 at 69; heart disease; b. Portsmouth; PH

HURD,
Adelaide J., d. 3/2/1917 at 44 in Perry, MO; chronic nephritis
Albert E., d. 5/19/1934 at 85/9/28; senility
Almira J., d. 10/28/1902 at 63/11/19; disease of heart; PH
Annie E., d. 9/3/1906 at 75/2/7; cerebro spinal meningitis; buried in
    Somersworth
Caroline, d. 1/4/1911 at 84/5/11; obstruction of bile ducts; Benjamin Torr
    and Sarah Torr
Cena, d. 4/8/1929 at 73/0/16; fracture of hip; John B. Neal and Julia
    Goodwin
Charles M., d. 11/12/1918 at 46/8/6; typhoid fever; Henry E. Hurd and
    Frances E. Grant
Clara E., d. 2/5/1934 at 82/2/20; coronary thrombosis

Clark B., d. 10/3/1915 at 85/0/27; senility; Jonathan Hurd and Abigail Rand
Elizabeth C., d. 6/28/1893 at 81; paralysis; b. Roxbury, MA; (Westboro, MA; Westboro, MA)
Eva Gordon, d. 4/23/1915 at 62/7/12; influenza; John C. Gordon and Sally Robinson
Fannie, d. 8/6/1905 at 0/0/1; premature birth; buried in Somersworth
Frances E., d. 12/5/1895 at 61; heart disease; b. Stillwater, ME; buried in Somersworth
Frank H., d. 10/15/1937 at 69/4/8; coronary thrombosis
Frank S., d. 6/10/1934 at 81/9/10; chronic myocarditis
George A., d. 9/24/1905 at 46/0/22; acute endocarditis; buried in So. Berwick, ME
Guy Harold, d. 7/26/1918 at 32/11/2; general paresis; Frank S. Hurd and Clara E. Cameron
Harrison J., d. 3/24/1936 at 45/9/24; diabetes
Henry E., d. 9/15/1920 at 88/10/15; senility; Jacob Hurd and Eunice -----
Johanna H., d. 6/7/1901 at 70/4/15; diabetes mellitus; PH
John F., d. 3/6/1926 at 10/4/9; valvular heart disease; Arthur Hurd and Mildred Swain
John H., d. 4/20/1901 at 76/9/18; pneumonia; PH
John S., d. 12/12/1901 at 82/2/6; pneumonia; PH
Joshua, d. 4/14/1894 at 86; old age; b. Berwick, ME; buried in Somersworth
Lydia, d. 9/21/1910 at 87/4/20; had ascites; Samuel Hurd and Mary Brackett
Marie E., d. 10/25/1913 at 1/4/14; pneumonia; Charles M. Hurd and Mary Hughes
Mary R., d. 3/14/1899 at 59 in Chicago, IL; PH
Rolland B., d. 8/31/1920 at 24/11/29; septic endocarditis; Frank S. Hurd and Clara E. Cameron
Samuel F., d. 11/26/1897 at 58; cancer; b. Rochester; PH
Sarah A., d. 6/23/1905 at 26/1/26; exhaustion; buried in Berwick, ME
Thomas S., d. 2/12/1920 at 85/10/12; arterio sclerosis; Thomas Hurd and Mary Nason
William, d. 10/8/1889 at 58 in Boston, MA

HURLBURT,
Cornelia M., d. 4/24/1910 at 75/5/27; atony of the heart; Roswell Hurlburt and Wealthy S. Gleason

HUSSEY,
child, d. 9/24/1919 at –; stillborn; Ralph L. Hussey and Carrie F. Twombly
child, d. 2/9/1924 at –; stillborn; Ralph L. Hussey and Carrie F. Twombly
Abbie N., d. 3/19/1894 at 55; acute nephritis; b. Strafford; PH

Anjuvine H., d. 1/7/1892 at 47; meningitis; b. Dover; (Dover; Dover)
Benjamin R., d. 2/19/1894 at 61; heart disease; b. NH; PH
Charles, d. 8/23/1931 at 74 in Concord; chronic nephritis
Charles A., d. 2/20/1908 at 73/9/23; old age; John Hussey and Betsey Stevens
Charles H., d. 3/28/1893 at 49; apoplexy; b. Dover; (Rochester; Dover)
Charles M., d. 1/11/1898 at – in Rollinsford; PH
Cora Belle, d. 2/12/1923 at 67/5/10 in Weymouth, MA; influenza
Daniel B., d. 1/25/1906 at 0/6/22 in Somersworth; whooping cough; PH
Daniel K., d. 2/5/1910 at 62/9/21; left hemiplegia
Edwin G., d. 11/28/1907 at 60/8; bullet through head; Benjamin J. Hussey and Sabina Bunker
Elizabeth, d. 5/23/1897 at 83; old age; b. Rochester; buried in family lot
Ellen M., d. 3/15/1925 at 79/1/2 in Somersworth; angina pectoris
Emily, d. 5/3/1908 at 78/8/6; old age; Joseph Butler
Emma B., d. 12/3/1925 at 74/0/10; chronic myocarditis; Jeremiah Hackett and Mary Foss
Frank P., d. 11/2/1903 at 47/11/1; phthisis pulmonalis; PH
Fred W., d. 9/25/1913 at 50/6/9; pneumonia; Samuel Hussey and Susan Horne
Freeman, d. 12/5/1893 at 57; pneumonia; b. Rochester; (Rochester; Rochester)
G. Eugene, d. 10/7/1904 at 38/11/9; cerebral hemorrhage; PH
George A., d. 12/8/1930 at 71/9/15 in Milton, MA; cerebral hemorrhage
George T. H., d. 9/21/1915 at 78/4/19 in Somersworth; epithelioma of lip
Harold Francis, d. 8/9/1916 at 48; tubercular pleuritis; Stephen A. Hussey and Mary A. Lougee
Harry M., d. 4/23/1907 at 20/11/13; typhoid fever; Fred W. Hussey and Jennie Mitchell
Herman G., d. 5/28/1928 at 62/8/2; suicide by shooting; Paul Hussey and Phoebe J. Hayes
John S., d. 11/24/1898 at 73 in Strafford; consumption; PH
Leland M., d. 4/18/1920 at 28/3/29; intestinal obstruction; Herman M. Hussey and Vera H. Ellis
Lydia J., d. 4/8/1902 at 60/11/12; uterine cancer; PH
Mary A., d. 11/4/1916 at 63/2/12; mitral insufficiency; Samuel Hussey and Susan Horne
Mary E., d. 4/7/1905 at 62/4/6; myocarditis; buried in Rochester
Mary F., d. 10/31/1936 at 83/2/29; chr. myocarditis
Mary M., d. 1/3/1901 at 46/11/1; carcinoma; PH
Moses H., d. 3/18/1893 at –; debility; b. Dover; (Dover; Ipswich, MA)
Moses S., d. 8/4/1897 at 75; heart disease; b. Somersworth; PH
Nellie, d. 5/28/1912 at 68/11/8; valvular heart disease; Anthony Dana and Betsey Littlefield
Sally, d. 7/14/1895 at 68; uterine carcinoma; buried in homestead lot

Sarah O., d. 4/19/1906 at 57/11/25; general tuberculosis; PH
Susan, d. 3/21/1904 at 78/2/17; heart failure; PH
Susan Page, d. 4/19/1920 at 58/9/19 in Milton, MA; general carcinosis
Timothy, d. 2/1/1922 at 82/2/4; colitis; Timothy Hussey and Eliza Varney
Walter E., d. 8/23/1935 at 70/1/24; chronic myocarditis

HUTCHINGS,
Martin S., d. 10/15/1918 at 80/1/25; arterio sclerosis; Remington
    Hutchings and Mary Wherren

HUTCHINS,
Alice M., d. 1/3/1920 at 55/1/9; carcinoma of intestine; Peter T. Hersey
    and Carrie A. Pottle
Annie Belle, d. 1/19/1902 at 34; pulmonary tuberculosis; PH
Ardelia M., d. 9/8/1920 at 65 in Boston, MA; urticaria
Clara J., d. 1/21/1904 at 85/6/10; bronchitis; PH
Clarence L., d. 4/20/1916 at 15/2/7 in Kennebunkport, ME; peritonitis;
    Albert G. Hutchins and Mary H. Hammond
Curtis H., d. 9/2/1899 at –; cholera infantum; PH
Edith May, d. 5/20/1919 at 38/11/26 in Medford, MA; mitral obstruction
Effie C., d. 9/28/1899 at 36; carcinoma; PH
Florence A., d. 12/18/1911 at 22/1/24 in Kennebunkport, ME
Frank H., d. 8/21/1906 at 0/11/8; cholera infantum; PH
Glen, d. 2/5/1912 at 0/2/12; whooping cough; Henry Hutchins and
    Elizabeth Spencer
John Wesley, d. 1/15/1930 at 73/1/28 in Malden, MA; arterio sclerosis
Lewis C., d. 8/23/1912 at 33 in Meredith; suicide by shooting
Mary H., d. 2/28/1903 at 40/5/19; heart failure; PH
Olive A., d. 10/17/1909 at 68/3/9; chronic nephritis; John N. Champion
    and Eunice White
Roland, d. 8/22/1895 at 0; inanition; b. Dover; PH
Rolf G., d. 3/27/1893 at 1; acute meningitis; b. Dover; (Kennebunk, ME;
    Dover)
Sophia, d. 8/25/1900 at 54 in Concord; organic brain disease
Thatcher D., d. 8/16/1907 at 36/8/15 in Kennebunkport, ME

HUTCHINSON,
Emily A., d. 3/18/1898 at 62 in St. John, NB; phthisis; PH
Sarah F., d. 2/9/1893 at 40; died in Strafford Co. Asylum fire

HYDE,
Lena, d. 12/12/1914 at 29/3/19 in Rutland, MA; pulmonary tuberculosis;
    John Haughey and Margaret Murray
Walter, d. 3/7/1909 at 0/7/9; diarrhea; James E. Hyde and Lena Haughey

IGNATIUS,
Sister Mary, d. 1/8/1891 at 49/1/19; single; John Kelly (Ireland) and
    Margaret Partridge (Ireland)

ILLINGWORTH,
Olive E., d. 7/7/1937 at 29/1/3; acute nephritis
Virginia D., d. 3/2/1928 at 0/0/5; patent foramen ovale; George Illingworth
    and Mildred Gailey

INCOBA,
Armein, d. 12/1/1908 at 35; gen. tuberculosis

INGERSOLL,
Lovicey, d. 5/19/1922 at 69/11/25; chronic bronchitis; Leonard Farnsworth
    and Nancy Lyons

INGRAHAM,
Ermina M., d. 8/22/1911 at 65/5; abdominal tumor; Orimel C. Ingraham
    and Mary S. Hanson
Florence L., d. 2/4/1904 at 27/3/12; tuberculosis; PH
John H., d. 4/17/1893 at 40; Bright's disease
Mary S., d. 11/25/1904 at 83/10/12; pneumonia; PH
Orimal C., d. 10/9/1897 at 75; gastro enteritis; b. Canada; PH

IOVINE,
Emma, d. 8/21/1914 at 54/11/14; appendicitis; Charles Watson and
    Matilda M. Green
Gerald D., d. 8/20/1922 at 35/1/1; fracture of skull; Joseph D. Iovine and
    Mary C. Defreani
Joseph B., d. 9/17/1913 at 36/6/12 in Concord; gen. paralysis of insane;
    Joseph D. Iovine and Mary Deferan
Joseph D., d. 12/12/1912 at 63/8/7; pneumonia; Thomas Iovine

IRELAND,
Fred W., d. 1/11/1929 at 61/4/11; carcinoma of stomach; Nathaniel Ireland
    and Nancy Blake

IRVIN,
child, d. 11/7/1899 at –; stillborn; PH

IRVING,
David, d. 1/12/1909 at 54/9/2 in Brockton, MA; pneumonia
Mary, d. 12/7/1890 at 65/2/6 in Brockton
Mary, d. 1/9/1893 at 57; apoplexy - found dead in bed; b. Ireland

IRWIN,
Edmond, d. 1/25/1892 at –; asthenia; b. Dover; (Ireland; Dover)
Harry H., d. 6/8/1911 at 28/1/13; appendicitis; Joseph E. Irwin and Jennie M. Brownell
Jennie M., d. 2/15/1928 at 65/9/5; cerebral hemorrhage; Amaziah Brownell and Mary J. Burley
Joseph E., d. 2/26/1907 at 46/9/4; organic heart disease; James Irwin and Mary Hughes

ISAKSEN,
Gustav E., d. 11/20/1935 at 64/0/20; bronchitis

ISSA,
child, d. 7/14/1936 at –; premature birth
child, d. 4/11/1937 at –; premature
Fouard, d. 7/26/1926 at 9/4/12; intestinal obstruction; Murad Issa and Eva John

JABER,
Salem B., d. 6/15/1932 at 63 in Madbury; chronic myocarditis

JABRE,
George, d. 3/22/1928 at 36/4; miliary tuberculosis; Salem B. Jabre and Mary Rachele

JACKELL,
Arthur, d. 2/28/1914 at 44 in Eliot, ME; accidental; Frank Jackell

JACKMAN,
Sarah E., d. 10/27/1899 at 44 in Newburyport, MA; pulmonary tuberculosis; PH

JACKSON,
daughter, d. 6/14/1888 at –; b. Dover; Frederic Jackson (England) and Louise E. May (England)
child, d. 9/26/1901 at 5; diphtheria; SM
child, d. 3/31/1905 at –; stillborn; SM
child, d. 11/9/1930 at –; stillbirth; Frederick D. Jackson and Harriet Leadbetter
Alfred, d. 5/17/1929 at 44 in Concord; general paralysis; Frederick Jackson and Louise May
Anglina, d. 12/5/1901 at 77/9/28; pneumonia; PH
Bridget, d. 5/8/1890 at 50; married; Hugh Murney (Ireland) and Mary McKincine (Ireland)

Charles H., d. 1/3/1901 at 55/9/10; pneumonia; PH
Christopher W., d. 9/1/1921 at 66/8/5; angina pectoris; Christopher C. Jackson and Ann Webster
Elizabeth F., d. 10/31/1926 at 51; myocarditis; William J. Farley and Margaret Boyd
Emma F., d. 12/7/1926 at 69 in Waterville, ME; chronic myocarditis; Lemuel Perkins and Mahala Rogers
Estella K., d. 1/11/1919 at 47; lobar pneumonia; Mark Brown and Lucy Brown
Frances, d. 11/9/1898 at 46; shock - paralysis; b. England; PH
Frederick R., d. 2/6/1893 at 1; meningitis; b. Dover; (NS; Scotland)
George L., d. 2/12/1915 at 58/11/20 in Lynn, MA; gen. arterio sclerosis
Harold N., d. 8/26/1897 at 0; cholera infantum; b. Dover; PH
Henry G., d. 3/19/1895 at 75; heart disease; b. Madbury; PH
James A., d. 8/9/1917 at 7/8; secondary anemia; James Jackson and Florence Henderson
John, d. 5/17/1937 at 63/4; heart disease
Joseph, d. 2/5/1911 at 70; chronic nephritis; Thomas Jackson
Joseph, d. 1/10/1936 at 68; chronic endocarditis
Margaret, d. 12/12/1889 at 7/5; b. England; Joseph Jackson (Ireland) and Bridget Murney (Ireland)
Margaret J., d. 1/4/1913 at 15/10/13; tuberculosis; John Jackson and Elizabeth Farley
Martha A., d. 2/18/1901 at 51/0/29; exhaustion from la grippe; PH
Martha J., d. 7/17/1907 at 51/5/13; exhaustion; John Locke and Sarah Howe
Mary, d. 11/7/1921 at 50; fractured skull; Peter Mallen and Alice McKerran
Mary F., d. 4/22/1935 at 80/2/3; cerebral embolism
Mary S., d. 10/15/1908 at 57/1/6 in Salisbury, MA; pneumonia
Mathew, d. 4/2/1889 at 22; compositor; single; b. Ireland; Joseph Jackson (Ireland) and Bridget Murray (Ireland)
Pearley, d. 12/11/1899 at 1; pneumonia; PH
Rachel, d. 7/28/1917 at 13/4/1; septic pharyngitis; James Jackson and Florence J. Henderson
Robert, d. 5/20/1910 at 55/11/12 in Waterville, ME; tubercular pleurisy; Joseph Jackson and Mary
Rufus N., d. 3/19/1901 at 43/7/20 in Rollinsford; pneumonia; PH
Thomas, d. 11/30/1924 at 59 in Providence, RI; cancer
William E., d. 12/20/1934 at 0/10/29; tuberculosis meningitis

JACOB,
Annie, d. 11/16/1902 at 0/4/8; gastro-enteritis

JACOBS,
Amanda, d. 7/26/1916 at 60; nephritis

Margaret A., d. 8/13/1907 at 58/3 in Lawrence, MA; gall stones, liver dis.
Wolf, d. 7/28/1912 at 0/0/18; premature birth; Peter Jacobs and Sarah Katz

JACOBSMEYER,
John W., d. 7/4/1929 at 0/0/1 in Portsmouth; asphyxia monatorum

JACQUES,
Francois, d. 11/5/1913 at 56; cong. kidneys, sup.
Yvonne, d. 9/14/1905 at 0/5/21; cholera infantum

JALBERT,
Joseph, d. 9/4/1937 at 59/9/12; suicide by "Paris Green"

JAMES,
Catherine, d. 1/11/1903 at 68 in Concord; exhaustion of senile mania; buried in Dover
Lilla A., d. 4/20/1901 at 83/11/14; catarrhal pneumonia; buried in Madbury
Mary F., d. 4/7/1910 at 61 in Concord; organic heart disease; Andrew James and Lellis Bunker
Walter A., d. 9/12/1934 at 42; heart disease

JAMESON,
Mary S., d. 11/23/1932 at 74/6/6 in Durham; cancer
Robert A., d. 3/21/1905 at 4/2/26; acute tuberculosis; PH

JAMIESON,
Nancy, d. 11/28/1912 at 42/9/25; phthisis; ----- Austin and Sarah -----
Thomas, d. 12/22/1910 at 46/4/4; endocarditis

JANETOS.
child, d. 10/23/1930 at 0/0/½; atelectasis; Antony Janetos and Stella Theofelopoulos
Angeline, d. 9/9/1925 at 0/4/5 in Boston, MA; natural causes

JAQUES,
Elizabeth H., d. 4/2/1895 at 53 in New York City; rheumatism; buried in Dover

JARIE,
Charles, d. 6/29/1930 at 82/1/27; chr. gastro enteritis; Louis Jarie and Sophie -----

JARRY,
Mary, d. 4/13/1916 at 56; George Lessard

JAURRIN,
James, d. 10/21/1887 at 13; b. Somersworth

JEAN,
George, d. 9/12/1920 at 24/0/29; hemorrhage, etc.; Stanislaus Jean and Evelyn Beaulieu

JEFFERSON,
Mary, d. 7/31/1888 at 81/3/17; widow

JEFTS,
Anna M., d. 10/12/1889 at 22/7/23; housewife; married; b. NB; Jabob Perry (NS) and Alice R. Harris (NS)

JENDRAULT,
Henry A., d. 7/11/1904 at 57; unknown; PH

JENKINS,
child, d. 11/13/1891 at 0/0/1; Charles W. Jenkins (Madbury) and Maggie Casson (Lewiston, ME)
Abby T., d. 1/20/1899 at 70 in Durham; chronic asthma; PH
Annie D., d. 10/18/1928 at 73/8/19 in Epping; sclerosis of brain
Charlotte, d. 7/15/1920 at 70/9; progressive dementia; Cyrus Hatfield
Chester E., d. 3/11/1905 at 21/2/3 in Madbury; pneumonia
Edwin L., d. 4/30/1915 at 69/8/26; strangulated hernia; Stephen Jenkins and Sarah A. K. Hill
Ellen F., d. 1/25/1895 at 45 in Madbury; spinal; b. Rochester; buried in Rochester
Emma L., d. 6/15/1927 at 81 in Malden, MA; arterio sclerosis
Emma M., d. 3/12/1892 at –; pneumonia
Evelyn, d. 2/27/1937 at 86/9/27; cerebr. hemorrhage
Fred E., d. 8/8/1932 at 69/8/18 in Durham; cerebral hemorrhage
Horace W., d. 2/1/1924 at 59/11/24; shock - hemorrhage; Jonathan Jenkins and Martha Emery
Laura B., d. 6/24/1912 at 44/0/25 in Exeter; tuberculosis
Lydia E., d. 12/28/1919 at 85/11/23 in Amesbury, MA; mitral dis. of heart
Martha E., d. 3/18/1914 at 56/1/27 in Madbury; abdominal tumor; William H. Twombly and Malvina Nutter
Mary A., d. 8/26/1898 at 75; heart disease; b. So. Berwick, ME; buried in Newmarket

Mary C., d. 4/26/1896 at 91; pneumonia; b. Boston, MA; buried in No. Berwick, ME
Mary Elizabeth, d. 3/7/1910 at 70/6/11; marasmus; Elijah Jenkins and Mary Curtis Stevens
Reginald E., d. 6/23/1908 at 46/6/5; acute nephritis; S. S. Jenkins and Mary D. Duryer
Robert H., d. 4/3/1931 at 0/2/20; enteritis
Sarah A., d. 4/26/1895 at 78 in Madbury; pneumonia; b. Durham; PH
Sarah F., d. 3/22/1919 at 62/3/24; cancer of breast; Joseph Jenkins and Mehitable Bunker
Simeon S., d. 12/17/1907 at 75/2/5; heart disease; Elijah Jenkins and Mary Curtis

JENKINSON,
Albert, d. 12/4/1914 at 58; pessenchymotous nephritis; Isaac Jenkinson and Mary Connell
Dennis E., d. 10/12/1914 at 55/3/14 in Boston, MA; peritonitis
Isaac, d. 2/14/1903 at 84/0/3; senility; PH

JENKS,
John L., d. 2/5/1891 at 73/9/20 in Eliot, ME; married; ----- (Dover) and Deborah Leighton (Great Falls)

JENNEAU,
Jennie, d. 6/29/1936 at 75; cerebral embolism

JENNESS,
child, d. 7/31/1895 at 0; convulsions; b. Dover; buried in homestead lot
child, d. 5/6/1925 at –; stillborn; Lindley I. Jenness and Carrie B. Stackpole
child, d. 8/2/1933 at –; stillborn
Abbie J., d. 2/7/1918 at 74/5/8; apoplexy; Oliver H. Jenness and Eliza Plummer
Alice Dudley, d. 11/9/1929 at 63/0/10; chr. myocarditis; Frederick Dudley and Elizabeth Tarbox
Beatrice L., d. 9/22/1918 at 23/8 in Newport, RI; lobar pneumonia
Caroline M., d. 2/24/1893 at 24; phthisis; b. E. Saginaw, MI; (Madbury; Madbury)
Chesley R., d. 9/16/1894 at 60; phthisis; b. Wakefield; PH
Cyrus L., d. 10/29/1929 at 81 in Orlando, FL; angina pectoris
Eliza A., d. 3/28/1899 at 82; pneumonia; PH
Emily C., d. 3/19/1922 at 87/6/22; cerebral hemorrhage; William H. Smith and Clarinda Arnold
Emma F., d. 11/18/1930 at 70/9/28; carcinoma colon; George D. Watson and Hannah -----

Emma P., d. 8/7/1919 at 82/4/29; angina pectoris; William P. Leighton and Phoebe -----
Etta E., d. 11/6/1932 at 68/11/33; pulmonary embolism
Frances E., d. 7/25/1916 at 77/2/26; heart disease; Albert Wentworth and Rhoda Cook
Frank O., d. 8/1/1918 at 63/1/21; chronic Brights disease; Ebenezer Jenness and Susan Horn
George H., d. 1/2/1927 at 58/16/29; tuberculosis of larynx; George H. Jenness and Ellen F. Wentworth
George I., d. 4/2/1901 at 41/3/20; rheumatism; buried in Rochester
George T., d. 8/16/1904 at 60/8/13; nephritis; buried in Wolfeboro
Hannah D., d. 3/14/1921 at 81/2/1; chr. int'st'l nephritis; William Hill and Dorcas Rumney
Hannah J., d. 10/22/1921 at 77/5; fatty degen. heart; Eli York and Sarah Horne
Harry Edgar, d. 11/13/1894 at 22; consumption; b. Wakefield; PH
Henry A., d. 3/16/1932 at 71/8/2; arterio sclerosis
Ida F., d. 3/22/1891 at 19/7/25; single; John Jenness (Dover) and Harriet S. Brown (Berwick, ME)
John, d. 1/26/1909 at 73; apoplexy; Chesley Jenness and Martha Moulton
John H., d. 11/28/1891 at 54/2/1; married; Daniel Jenness and Mehitable Watson
John H., d. 12/28/1936 at 58/8/9; coronary thrombosis
Joseph, d. 1/5/1892 at 68; consumption; b. Rochester
Lydia E., d. 1/23/1912 at 72/9; pneumonia capillary
Lydia V., d. 10/5/1888 at 79/6/10; widow; b. Dover; Reuben Varney (Dover) and Elizabeth Jenkins (Eliot, ME)
Maria, d. 11/13/1888 at 64/8/29; single; b. Rochester; William Jenness (Rochester) and Anna Seavey (Rye)
Mary, d. 4/2/1898 at 76; cerebral apoplexy; b. Rochester; buried in Rochester
Mary O., d. 11/12/1900 at 36; heart disease; PH
May E., d. 4/3/1911 at 84/7/19; diabetes; Daniel Pinkham and ----- Edgerly
Nellie G., d. 3/19/1902 at 37/7/10; inanition from gastric catarrh; PH
Roland A., d. 2/25/1903 at 0/0/4; intestinal obstruction; PH
Sarah E., d. 4/16/1921 at 77/9/22; broncho pneumonia; Horace Holmes and Mary J. Colbath
Susan Ann, d. 11/23/1907 at 75; heart failure; Abraham Hill and Lydia C. Boston
Susan W., d. 8/5/1899 at 70 in Danville, NJ; organic disease of heart; PH

JENNINGS,
William, d. 7/17/1911 at –; miscarriage; Walter Jennings and Josephine Rowe

JEROME,
Youbelle Y., d. 12/16/1926 at 20/1/16; endocarditis; Edward Jerome and Mary Burt

JERRY,
John P., d. 9/24/1905 at –; accident or suicide; buried in Claremont

JEWELL,
child, d. 9/27/1906 at –; stillborn; buried in York, ME
Abbie S., d. 9/29/1898 at 42; typhoid fever; b. Strafford; PH
Charles H., d. 5/21/1929 at 6/5/24 in Rollinsford; burning, etc.; Walter H. Jewell and Gladys C. Saville
Frederick R., d. 5/21/1929 at 3/11/14 in Rollinsford; burning, etc.; Walter H. Jewell and Gladys C. Saville
J. Herbert, d. 5/26/1893 at 33; pulmonalis phthisis; b. NH; (NH; NH)
John W., d. 12/22/1920 at 89/4/28; old age; John M. Jewell and Nancy Colley
Narcissa, d. 11/29/1928 at 81; ac. intest. obstruction; Silas Goodwin
Olive A., d. 9/29/1906 at 29/8/14; uraemic poisoning; buried in York, ME
Sarah F., d. 12/25/1915 at 82/0/19; valv. disease of heart; Bartholomew Gale and Abigail Morrison

JOHNSON,
Abigail B., d. 3/2/1888 at 78/1/9; widow; b. Wakefield; John Sanborn (Wakefield) and Deborah (Wakefield)
Alberthana G., d. 3/21/1927 at 86/6/17 in Reading, MA; carcinoma small int.
Alice, d. 6/6/1921 at 64/1/27; apoplexy; Benjamin F. Magoon and Elizabeth Pollard
Almira C., d. 8/21/1895 at 55 in Rochester; valvular disease of heart; buried in Dover
Barbara H., d. 3/8/1919 at 0/0/13; unknown; Peter A. Johnson and Helen I. Bickford
Bradford H., d. 3/4/1909 at 80/6/4; nephritis; John T. Johnson and Betsey Thompson
Clara A., d. 3/29/1898 at 70 in Portland, ME; chronic nephritis; PH
Clara A., d. 9/12/1929 at 64/6/24; chr. myocarditis; Thomas B. Lord and Harriet Burbank
Della M., d. 5/5/1888 at 2/7; b. Norway, ME; Herbert A. Johnson (Broomfield) and Ellen Wood (Quebec, Canada)
Dennis, d. 9/9/1888 at 84/8/16; farmer; married; b. Barrington; Andrew Johnson (Barrington) and Hannah Twombly (Barrington)
Dennis A., d. 11/12/1919 at 82/11; chronic endocarditis; Dennis Johnson and Sarah Weeks
Edward, d. 4/13/1911 at 52; convulsions

Ellen, d. 7/15/1929 at 66/9/14; diabetes mellitus; William Woods and Marguerite McKee

Elzira, d. 4/21/1927 at 77/1/29; gen. arterio sclerosis; Dennis Johnson and Sarah Weeks

Emily, d. 7/14/1890 at 64/0/17 in Conway; married; Osgood Dolloff (Conway) and Olive Shackford (Conway)

Emily, d. 9/21/1894 at 67; heart disease; b. Brownfield, ME; buried in So. Paris, ME

Ernest E., d. 9/14/1930 at 5/11/2; fracture of skull; Peter A. Johnson and Helen G. Bickford

Ernest F., d. 8/11/1893 at –; cholera infantum; b. Dover; (Beverly, MA; Dover)

George F., d. 6/1/1890 at 26/8/29 in Nottingham; single; George Johnson (England) and Hasa Stevenson (England)

George Frank, d. 6/23/1924 at 68/6/23; dilatation of heart; George W. Johnson and Lydia Wilson

Harold J., d. 3/6/1891 at 0/10/6; Herbert A. Johnson (Brownfield, ME) and Ellen Woods (Canada)

Helen A., d. 12/3/1926 at 85/4/24 in Somerville, MA; cerebral hemorrhage

Henry, d. 6/14/1896 at 68; marasmus; b. Brookfield; PH

Herbert A., d. 1/24/1930 at 66/9/25; cerebral hemorrhage; William F. Johnson and Emily Huntress

Isaiah, d. 5/20/1920 at 72/4/2; epilepsy; Dennis Johnson and Sarah C. Weeks

J. Frank, d. 5/8/1907 at 40/8/20 in Concord; ex. in general paralysis; Robert Johnson

John Henry, d. 8/30/1899 at 57 in Reading, MA; gastric catarrh; PH

Lavina, d. 7/31/1912 at 83/11/6; senility following frac. thigh; Samuel Bottomley and Hannah Livermore

Mary Ann, d. 11/23/1926 at 92/5/14; fracture of hip

Melissa A., d. 6/18/1897 at 58 in Somersworth; asphyxia; b. Brookfield; PH

Orissa E., d. 12/22/1933 at 79/2/21; cerebral hemorrhage

Samuel F., d. 12/20/1910 at 77/1/22; apoplexy; John Johnson and Betsey Thompson

Sarah C., d. 6/15/1898 at 87; senility; b. Kittery, ME; buried in family lot

William, d. 4/22/1916 at 55 in Lowell, MA; accident

William C., d. 6/22/1937 at 74/9/22*

William H., d. 10/16/1924 at 82; gen. arterio sclerosis; Dennis Johnson and Sarah C. Weeks

Winston N., d. 4/12/1907 at 0/3/7; pneumonia; Albert L. Johnson and Lillian A. Proctor

JOHNSTON,
Oliver, d. 1/6/1890 at 70; widower

JOLIN,
Marie, d. 3/21/1927 at 72/10/12; ac. lobar pneumonia; Louis Pare and Domitule Roy
Theophile, d. 12/11/1920 at 78; chronic endocarditis; Charles Jolin and Marie Parent

JONES,
child, d. 9/25/1908 at 0/3; malnutrition; ----- Jones and Maggie Quinlan
Adelia A., d. 12/12/1901 at 74/3/13; mitral regurgitation; PH
Almira, d. 9/4/1915 at 79; apoplexy
Alphonse, d. 8/8/1932 at 85/11/2; arterio sclerosis
Annie H., d. 5/21/1929 at 60/9/10 in Wells, ME; chronic myocarditis
Carrie B., d. 12/3/1891 at 11; Thomas Jones (Ireland) and Mary E. Cummings (Thompson, CT)
Charles H., d. 5/27/1917 at 81/1/19; uraemia; Elijah Hussey and Caroline Hartford
Charles M., d. 12/31/1913 at 77/4/29; senile dementia; David Jones and Olivia Hughes
Clara D., d. 8/24/1908 at – in Boston, MA; apoplexy
E. F., d. 5/9/1893 at 57; pneumonia; b. Boston, MA
Eliza A., d. 10/17/1918 at 78/8/29 in Durham; influenza
Elizabeth J., d. 5/29/1900 at 26; pul. phthisis; PH
Emma, d. 12/4/1901 at 35/3/24; typhoid fever; PH
Ephraim M., d. 1/5/1905 at 77/4/22; fracture of hip; PH
Frank M., d. 12/21/1923 at 72/11/16; probably heart disease
George, d. 9/10/1905 at 50; accidental drowning; SM
George A., d. 2/21/1924 at 75; chronic endocarditis
Georgie E., d. 10/25/1918 at 23/7/3 in Concord; ac. dilat. of heart; George Danforth and Julia A. Lutolf
Grace L., d. 6/10/1919 at 38/7/1; chr. interst. nephritis; Winfield W. Brown and Emma M. Daniels
Hannah M., d. 11/30/1935 at 76/4/2; myocarditis
Harriet, d. 9/6/1892 at 57; epileptic fits; b. Rochester
Henry, d. 9/28/1934 at 74/3/30; cancer of stomach
Ida May, d. 1/12/1916 at 58/10/18 in Lynn, MA; lobar pneumonia
J. Woodbury, d. 7/4/1920 at 57; apoplexy; Woodbury Jones and Harriet Cross
Jennie May, d. 8/17/1888 at 0/4/10; b. Dover; Clara E. M. Jones (Dover)
Joseph, d. 5/6/1895 at 76; carcinoma; buried in Lee
Laura A., d. 3/20/1915 at 72; carcinoma of liver; ----- Jones
Louise A., d. 11/4/1933 at 73/1/1; cerebral hemorrhage
Lovie A., d. 3/4/1936 at 73/4/19*
Lyda E., d. 2/11/1936 at 51/11/27; pulmonary embolism
Lydia E., d. 1/12/1917 at 75; lobar pneumonia; Richard Blaisdell
Marie Henrietta, d. 1/10/1937 at 88; cerebr. hemorrhage

Mary E., d. 6/3/1930 at 79/8/22; cancer of bowel; William Cummings
Mary W., d. 3/4/1915 at 45 in Lawrence, MA; carcinoma of uterus
Rachel, d. 12/13/1902 at 52/5/24; heart disease; PH
Ralph W., d. 6/14/1929 at 50/8/8; pneumonia; Thomas Jones and Mary E. Cummings
Rhoda J., d. 1/5/1919 at 86/1/13; senility; Nathaniel Nowell and Rhoda Allen
Richard, d. 7/9/1891 at 72/1/12; widower; William Jones (Ireland)
Richard, d. 12/28/1915 at 65; acute dil. of heart; Richard Jones and Alice Cox
Robert, d. 2/23/1920 at 68/3/28; cancer of rectum; Richard Jones and Alice Cox
Robert T. J., d. 3/29/1910 at 30/0/21 in Lawrence, MA; lobar pneumonia; Richard Jones and Sarah Dermit
Samuel J., d. 4/28/1921 at 84/11/30 in Durham; cystitis
Sarah, d. 7/10/1912 at 61/4/4; cancer of stomach; John Dermit and Sarah Cox
Stephen A., d. 5/27/1911 at 46/11/28; pneumonia; Nathaniel D. Jones and Mary O. Hayes
Thomas, d. 6/30/1891 at 45/8/4; married; Richard Jones (Scotland) and Alvi Cox (Scotland)
Ulysses, d. 2/9/1893 at 25; died in Strafford Co. Asylum fire
Vashti B., d. 4/8/1894 at 67; gastritis; b. Danville; buried in Milton
Warren D., d. 5/8/1896 at 68; pneumonia; b. Strafford
Warren D., d. 1/25/1897 at 31; acute pneumonic phthisis; b. Newmarket; PH
William, d. 1/13/1921 at 73 in Wilkinsburg, PA; fracture of skull
William, d. 10/12/1923 at 76; apoplexy
William E., d. 10/23/1934 at 52/3/3 in Los Angeles, CA; valvular endocarditis
William H., d. 3/13/1898 at 59; phthisis; b. No. Berwick, ME; PH

JORDAN,
child, d. 11/6/1903 at –; stillborn; PH
Amelia Bell, d. 1/23/1914 at 89/2/8; arterio sclerosis; William Bell
George T., d. 3/20/1900 at 76; influenza; buried in Biddeford, ME
Elizabeth A., d. 12/24/1913 at 81/2 in Lynn, MA; senility
John, d. 11/25/1898 at 45; cerebral apoplexy; b. Dover; SM
John Sylvester, d. 1/17/1887 at 75; designer; married; b. Dublin, Ireland; Robert Jordan (Ireland)
John W., d. 10/11/1904 at 37/4/12; tuberculosis; PH
Lewis S., d. 5/7/1936 at 65/0/10; ac. myocarditis
Mary Anne, d. 1/4/1917 at 77/11/6; bronchitis; Patrick Jordan and Deborah Berry

Mary E., d. 11/6/1888 at 60/8/2; married; b. Saco, ME; Mark Haley (Saco, ME) and Lydia A. Hill (Saco, ME)
Mary J., d. 2/11/1930 at 76/0/12; cerebral apoplexy; Elijah Horne and Mary Stackpole
Mary J., d. 3/29/1930 at 78/1/8 in Concord; lobar pneumonia; John Littlefield and Polly Williams
Peter H., d. 4/9/1929 at 67/0/4; cerebral hemorrhage; John S. Jordan and Amelia Bell
Robert, d. 5/19/1912 at 61; cancer of the mouth; John S. Jordan and Amelia Bell
Robert Earle, d. 4/26/1893 at –; pneumonia; b. Dover; (Portsmouth; Dover)
Samuel, d. 6/20/1892 at –; heart defect; b. Dover; (Dover; Ireland)
Samuel T., d. 3/22/1908 at 50/2/21; gen. tuberculosis; John Jordan and Elizabeth A. Neill
Walter, d. 11/30/1931 at –; lobar pneumonia
William H., d. 5/30/1936 at 59/1/16 in Waterville, ME; can. stom. & metastasis

JORDE,
Marcus, d. 8/6/1905 at 75/4/14; carcinoma; PH
Martha O., d. 8/29/1905 at 75/9/26; cerebral apoplexy; PH
Ole T., d. 12/13/1910 at 57/11/7 in Lowell, MA; suicide

JORDON,
Robert L., d. 10/7/1933 at 29/8/3 in Barrington; auto accident
Samuel, d. 7/21/1887 at 32/6/16; shoemaker; married; b. Dover; John S. Jordon (Ireland) and Amelia Bell (England)

JOSEPH,
James, d. 4/6/1934 at 45; hemorrhage of brain

JOSEPHSON,
child, d. 2/25/1937 at –; stillborn

JOY,
Charles E., d. 4/15/1925 at 70/1/29 in New Haven, CT; senile gangrene of leg
Edward H., d. 10/25/1936 at 64/10/19; fractured skull
Effie B., d. 8/3/1903 at 46/5/28; typhoid fever; buried in Dover
Geneva M., d. 5/12/1891 at 0/0/12; Lincoln M. Joy (ME) and Lucy M. Welch (ME)
Harry, d. 8/14/1892 at –; marasmus; b. Dover; (St. Anthony, MN; Shapleigh, ME)
Ida E., d. 8/30/1918 at 9/3/11; burns; Frank D. Joy and Alice P. Kimball

Lucy M., d. 8/15/1905 at 43/11; pyaemia; buried in So. Berwick, ME
Naomi C., d. 4/7/1893 at 56; bronchitis and heart disease; b. Hartland, ME
Oliver A., d. 3/16/1920 at 83/11/3; gastro enteritis; Sewell Williams and
    Joanna Savage

JOYCE,
Asbury J., d. 4/10/1926 at 69/3/18; apoplexy
John, d. 3/26/1903 at 72; septicaemia

JUDD,
Justin, d. 9/8/1934 at 79/1/3; chronic myocarditis

JUDSON [see Locke],
Locke E., d. 3/5/1925 at 73/3/25; chr. gastro enteritis; Elisha Locke and
    Lavina French

JULIEN,
Louis, d. 5/2/1898 at 74; general debility; b. Canada; SM

JUST,
Alice A., d. 12/26/1922 at 70/10/16 in Pine Bluff, NC; acute bronchitis
Frank R., d. 2/28/1887 at 4/11/8; b. New Britain, CT; William Just (NY)
    and Alice A. Hackett (Dover)
William H., d. 10/31/1932 at 78/2/15; angina pectoris

KAFAFIAN,
child, d. 8/27/1906 at 0/0/1; inanition; PH
child, d. 1/13/1908 at --; stillborn; Jacob Kafafian and Lucy Kashaishia

KAFFEAN,
Antonio, d. 4/12/1915 at 0/4/29; broncho pneumonia; Christos Kaffean and
    Ellen Christopoulos

KAIME,
James, d. 2/28/1926 at 83/10; myocarditis; Dodavah Kaime and Lavinia
    Foye

KALIL,
Joseph, d. 6/19/1912 at --; prolapse of umbilical cord; Peter Kalil and Mary
    Peter

KALOGEROPOULOS,
Vas'l's, d. 1/20/1911 at 32; shock from accident; K. Kalogeropoulos

KAMARES,
child, d. 11/4/1920 at –; stillborn; James Kamares and Carrie Labrakos

KANELOPOULOS,
Eva, d. 2/14/1912 at 19/9/28; poisoning by bichlo. mercury; Charles Witham and Marietta Miller

KARABELAS,
Charles, d. 11/20/1914 at 0/3/20; broncho pneumonia; Lampros Karabelas and Vassilo Vaselopoulos
Peter, d. 7/11/1923 at 0/6/13; cerebral meningitis; John Karabelas and Mary Costopoulos

KARABELOS,
Lampros, d. 3/31/1934 at 69 in New York, NY; chronic myocarditis

KARALES,
James, d. 4/27/1919 at 0/2; intestinal interssusseption; Skareles Karales
Nickolas, d. 10/11/1918 at 1/0/3; pneumonia; Haralambos Karales and Helene Samarge

KARALIS,
Mary, d. 2/14/1923 at 0/4; pneumonia; Haralampos Karalis

KARAMBATSOS,
K'st'd'nos, d. 6/25/1921 at 1/4/12; laryngeal diphtheria; John Karambatsos and Stavroula Germanson

KARAMPOULOS,
Constant, d. 6/5/1911 at 20/1; tuberculosis; A. Karampoulos and Paraskere Flouri

KARANICOPOULOS,
James, d. 1/19/1920 at 0/11; septic peritonitis; Frank ----- and Panagiota Spilioti

KAREMOPOULOS,
Nestoras, d. 4/20/1911 at 0/8/11; fracture base of skull; L. Karemopoulos and V. Versolopoulos

KARGAS,
Dionysius, d. 8/11/1916 at 25 in Rollinsford; ac. pulm. tuberculosis; James Kargas and Fortula Kamugi
Kost, d. 3/29/1926 at 0/5; broncho pneumonia; G. Kargas

KARIS,
child, d. 8/4/1915 at –; stillborn; John Karis and Helen ----

KARKARVELAS,
Panagiotis, d. 8/5/1915 at 0/5/27; cholera infantum; George Karkarvelas and Taroula Jouvalis

KARKAVELOS,
Alfredette, d. 3/20/1920 at 4/7/2; influenza; George Karkavelos and Tasian Chevelin
Nicholas, d. 8/6/1931 at 9/3/15; accidental drowning

KARLINSKI,
Margaret M., d. 11/28/1918 at 24/10/10; tubercular meningitis; John Breen and Elizabeth Brownlee

KARRAS,
child, d. 2/24/1918 at –; premature birth; Costas Karras and Anna Wilde

KASS,
Saul, d. 3/17/1919 at 22/9; ac. gas. poisoning; Barnette Kass and Bessie Aronson

KATSECIPINO,
Militci, d. 1/9/1920 at 0/9/10; scrofula; Theodosies Katsecipino

KAVERNO,
Sarah, d. 5/30/1900 at –; stillborn

KAY,
son, d. 8/31/1889 at 0/0/1-6; b. Dover; John Kay (Dover) and Nora Maloney (Ireland)
child, d. 3/25/1911 at 0/0/2; hemophilia neonatorum; Clarence E. Kay and ----- Whitehouse
child, d. 3/3/1913 at –; stillborn; Clarence Kay and Alice M. Whitehouse
child, d. 4/8/1918 at –; premature birth; Clarence Kay and Alice Whitehouse
child, d. 1/26/1921 at 0/0/16; congenital debility; Clarence E. Kay and Alice M. Whitehouse
Alice May, d. 7/29/1930 at 47/6/15; cerebral embolus; Jasper Whitehouse and Alta ----
Ann W., d. 1/29/1888 at 57/3/18; married; b. England; J. Wright (England) and Margaret Carter (England)

Carrie Bell, d. 3/–/1893 at 35; consumption; b. Cincinnati, OH; (Wells, ME; Barrington)
Clarence E., d. 8/29/1925 at 48/10/23; acute appendicitis; Edward Kay and Martha S. Young
Edward, d. 1/30/1923 at 81/8/28; senility; Joseph Kay and Elizabeth Ham
Elizabeth, d. 2/11/1903 at 85/3/0; pneumonia; PH
George Fox, d. 2/15/1895 at 45; cancer; b. Dover; PH
George R., d. 7/12/1914 at –; premature birth; George R. Kay and Carrie Hall
Jno. M., d. 7/29/1892 at 28; heart disease - brnch. catarrh; b. US
Joseph, d. 7/10/1899 at 82; rheumatic fever; PH
Martha Young, d. 4/12/1917 at 63/4/21; valv. heart disease; Jonathan T. Young and Elizabeth Demeritt
Mary E., d. 4/14/1888 at 19/4/8; married; b. Dover; George Jordan (ME) and Mary Haley (ME)
Mary E., d. 2/18/1900 at 65 in Pawtucket, RI; grip and pneumonia; PH
Patrick, d. 12/28/1896 at 73; pneumonia; b. Ireland; SM
Richard H., d. 2/24/1900 at 64 in Pawtucket, RI; pneumonia; PH
Susan M., d. 4/15/1927 at 88/7/23; pneumonia; Joseph Kay and Elizabeth Ham

KEARNEY,
Alice M., d. 10/2/1935 at 86/5/27; cerebral hemorrhage

KEARNS,
John, d. 3/25/1905 at 79; sudden; buried in Manchester
Walter, d. 8/2/1892 at 5; croup; b. Great Falls; (Great Falls; Dover)

KEATING,
Sarah A., d. 4/21/1918 at 64/7/9; cancer of uterus; Daniel Grover and Sarah Crockett
William A., d. 8/21/1922 at 71; arterio sclerosis

KEATON,
Alvin G., d. 9/19/1915 at 13/2/13; accidental drowning; Alvin E. Keaton and Katherine Murphy

KEAVENEY,
Margaret A., d. 8/3/1931 at 57; chronic bronchitis
Mary, d. 3/19/1920 at 77; myocarditis; Patrick Kivel and Mary Welch

KEAY,
child, d. 10/10/1919 at 0/0/1; premature birth; Walter J. Keay and Elizabeth Sunderland

Aaron, d. 10/4/1904 at 73; valvular heart disease; PH
Albert D., d. 7/17/1901 at 24/7/1; hemorrhage of bowels; buried in Kittery, ME
Albert J., d. 1/11/1907 at 3; ascites; William E. Keay and M. S. Tatro
Ann M., d. 11/16/1905 at 65; acute rheumatism; buried in Kittery, ME
Beatrice M., d. 4/8/1922 at 0/3/27; marasmus; Charles E. Keay and Wavy N. Brackett
Catherine A., d. 8/19/1928 at 25/6/28; drowning; William C. Keay and Mary S. Tatro
Delson A., d. 8/5/1900 at <1; congenital disease of heart; PH
Emma A., d. 11/3/1908 at 1/9/21; tuberculosis; William Keay and Mary Tatro
Frank J., d. 10/10/1894 at 15; pulmonary phthisis; b. Dover; buried in Kittery, ME
John, d. 6/1/1911 at 0/2/5; acute indigestion; William Keay and Mary Tatro
Mary S., d. 12/21/1934 at 64/7/29 in Concord; cerebral hemorrhage
Olive J., d. 12/22/1903 at 74/3/1 in Milton; senility
William H., d. 5/28/1900 at 21; stomach trouble; buried in Haverhill, MA
William I., d. 10/25/1920 at –; premature birth; Walter H. Key (sic) and Annie M. Ferns

KEEFE,
James Joseph, d. 3/9/1921 at 0/0/2; prematurity; F. Clyde Keefe and Katherine F. Hanratty
John, d. 7/12/1921 at 67/11/17; chronic nephritis; Patrick Keefe and Jane Hughes
Mary E., d. 7/22/1929 at 74 in Hampton; myocarditis chronic; Thomas Jay and Annie Kelley

KEELEY,
Arthur, Jr., d. 7/7/1930 at 6; laryngeal diphtheria; Arthur E. Keeley and Mary C. Fagin

KEELTY,
Bridget, d. 2/26/1908 at 46; chronic nephritis
Clarinda, d. 12/26/1922 at 27/5/16; phthisis pulmonalis; Thomas Hebert and Celina Jendreau
Edmund, d. 9/2/1917 at 0/3/19; gastro enteritis; James Keelty and Lucia Grenier
Gertrude, d. 2/26/1900 at <1; bronchial pneumonia; SM
James J., d. 7/22/1914 at 45; valvular heart disease
James J., d. 9/3/1934 at 35/6/8; subacute bac. endo'tis
John J., d. 1/17/1930 at 58 in Portsmouth; embolism

KEENAN,
child, d. 10/7/1900 at <1; premature birth
child, d. 8/–/1905 at 0/8/23; cholera infantum
Albert H., Jr., d. 8/3/1930 at 1/10/4; accidental drowning; Albert H. Keenan and Blanche A. Merchant
Ann, d. 5/9/1900 at 62; grippe; SM
Bridget C., d. 8/6/1899 at –; cholera infantum
Catherine, d. 3/3/1904 at 0/6; meningitis; SM
Catherine, d. 5/17/1934 at 70/3; chronic myocarditis
Edward, d. 6/14/1904 at 40; ch. parenchyneatous nephritis
Ellen, d. 2/22/1897 at –; bronchitis; b. Ireland; SM
F., d. 4/6/1900 at 65; pneumonia; SM
Felix, d. 7/17/1889 at 0/2/12; b. Dover; Francis Keenan (Ireland) and Bridget Hughes (Ireland)
Felix, d. 7/12/1935 at 70; cerebral hemorrhage
Frances, d. 3/20/1915 at 26; tuberculosis of lungs; Patrick Keenan and Margaret Hughes
Frank, d. 1/25/1935 at 70; uremia
Frank H., d. 5/31/1917 at 55/11; paresis; Frank Keenan and Ann Kelly
James, d. 10/15/1909 at 48/11/1; diabetes; John Keenan and Kate McElroy
John J., d. 5/19/1906 at 42; contact with live wires; SM
Joseph, d. 12/21/1920 at 0/4/28; broncho pneumonia; Joseph Keenan and Teresa O'Neil
Mary, d. 7/31/1905 at 0/9; cholera infantum; SM
Mary, d. 9/20/1929 at 64 in Boston, MA; carcinoma
Mary, d. 9/18/1936 at 60/2 in Manchester; coronary occlusion
Mary A., d. 4/30/1919 at 54; Brights disease; Patrick Donnelly and Mary Carragher
Mary Ann, d. 2/7/1893 at –; laryngitis; b. Dover; (Ireland; Ireland)
Nellie, d. 5/20/1922 at 49; carcinoma of uterus; Frank Keenan and Ann Kelley
Nellie, d. 8/12/1924 at 51 in Andover, MA; Addison's disease
Thomas, d. 9/10/1905 at –; accidental drowning; SM

KEITH,
Hiram R., d. 5/25/1924 at 48/5/19; gastric ulcer; John Keith and Mary ―――

KELLEGHER,
Tim., d. 3/14/1889 at 17; b. Dover; (Ireland; Ireland)

KELLEHER,
Ellen, d. 5/15/1893 at 44; result of injuries on railroad; b. Ireland; (Ireland; Ireland)

KELLETT,
Alta A., d. 10/2/1918 at 31/7/15 in Amesbury, MA; accidental burns

KELLEY,
child, d. 5/14/1898 at 0; lack of development; b. Dover
child, d. 4/27/1907 at –; premature birth; Thomas Kelley and Mary
    Whitehill
Abbie E., d. 5/24/1908 at 75/5/26 in Madbury; disease of liver
Alice, d. 5/3/1927 at 72; chronic myocarditis
Ann, d. 11/11/1920 at 66; interstitial nephritis; Thomas Hughes and
    Bridget Hanratty
Annie L., d. 7/30/1894 at 48; heart disease; b. Rollinsford; PH
Bernard J., d. 1/13/1935 at 83 in Lowell, MA; cardiovascular
Bernice M., d. 8/22/1891 at 0/5/2; Frank Kelley (So. Berwick, ME) and
    Mary Maloney (Ireland)
Blanch C., d. 8/8/1891 at 0/4/19; Frank Kelley (So. Berwick, ME) and Mary
    Maloney (Ireland)
Bridget, d. 3/3/1924 at 72; chronic endocarditis; John Kelley and Alice
    Moan
Catherine M., d. 7/28/1910 at 2/0/23 in Portsmouth; convulsions
Christopher, d. 11/2/1892 at –; marasmus; b. Dover; (MA; Dover)
Elizabeth B., d. 10/6/1917 at 70/4/5 in Haverhill, MA; arterio sclerosis
Ellen, d. 9/6/1906 at 39; Bright's disease
Emma B., d. 3/14/1928 at 85/7/11; cerebral hemorrhage; Washington
    Leavitt and Susan Hanscom
Ethel E., d. 6/11/1892 at –; meningitis; b. Dover; (Falmouth, ME; New
    Sharon, ME)
Etta M., d. 6/12/1913 at 57/2/9; diabetes mellitus; Andrew Neal and
    Hariette Johnson
Francis E., d. 6/9/1910 at 12/8/13; drowning; Joseph Kelley and Mary
    Morissette
Frank, d. 3/17/1928 at 77; endocarditis
Frederick W., d. 11/11/1934 at 78/1/22 in Somersworth; coronary
    thrombosis
Harriet P., d. 9/20/1933 at 70 in Andover, MA; chronic myocarditis
Harry N., d. 6/19/1897 at 8; la grippe; b. Dover; PH
Hilda E., d. 8/20/1911 at 0/7/14 in Portsmouth; gastro enteritis
Ivory H., d. 6/8/1920 at 82/1/22 in Madbury; cancer of intestines
James, d. 5/17/1887 at 19; laborer; single; b. Ireland; John Kelley (Ireland)
    and Bridget (Ireland)
James A., d. 3/11/1923 at 77/3/20 in Farmington; influenza
James E., d. 1/14/1924 at 78; peritonitis; John H. Kelley and Emma B.
    Leavitt
James J., d. 5/30/1928 at 61/2/15 in Lawrence, MA; angina pectoris
James R., d. 12/14/1931 at 80 in N. Andover, MA; chronic nephritis

Joanna, d. 9/17/1917 at 74; valv. dis. of heart; Michael Dillon and Mary Hill
John, d. 7/8/1906 at 39/9; pulmonary phthisis; SM
John H., d. 2/20/1903 at 75/9/24; Brights disease; buried in family lot
Joseph, d. 9/25/1918 at 65; arterio sclerosis
Julia, d. 8/6/1912 at 68; heart failure; Michael Kelley and Margaret Leary
Kate, d. 12/11/1898 at 40; phthisis; b. Ireland; SM
Kate McIntire, d. 3/26/1892 at 6; membranous laryngitis; (Scotland; Scotland)
Katherine, d. 7/23/1924 at 70/1; chronic endocarditis; Martin Carney and Mary Wentworth
Lydia C., d. 5/28/1903 at 55/3/6 in Farmington; epilepsy; PH
Lydia L., d. 8/24/1898 at –; old age; b. Falmouth, ME; PH
Mabel E., d. 2/26/1907 at 19/5/17; influenza; Frank Kelley and Mary Maloney
Margaret, d. 9/3/1893 at 59; cholera morbus; b. Ireland; (Ireland; Ireland)
Margaret H., d. 10/11/1897 at 28; consumption; b. So. Newmarket; buried in Newmarket
Martha A., d. 5/31/1937 at 94/3/22*
Mary, d. 9/7/1914 at 57; pulmonary tuberculosis; Patrick McCabe and Betsy Morgan
Mary A., d. 3/13/1897 at 38; peritonitis; b. Sandown; buried in Sandown
Mary A., d. 5/11/1906 at 49/5/24; carcinoma of liver; SM
Mary A., d. 7/28/1916 at 60 in Lowell, MA; gall stones
Mary C., d. 10/25/1920 at 53/5/14 in Chelsea, MA; cerebral hemorrhage
Michael J., d. 6/22/1905 at 10/8/17; pneumonia; SM
Neal, d. 5/29/1907 at 63 in Lowell, MA; chronic nephritis
Peter, d. 2/5/1903 at 43; phthisis
Peter, d. 6/24/1914 at 82; old age; ----- Kelley and Bridget -----
Peter, d. 8/14/1915 at 62 in Tewksbury, MA; diabetes mellitus; Michael Kelley and Margaret O'Leary
Rose, d. 9/7/1887 at 0/3/19; b. Dover; Peter Kelley (Ireland) and Kate Connor (Ireland)
Susan, d. 10/4/1887 at 0/4/26; b. Dover; Peter Kelley (Ireland) and Kate ----- (Ireland)
William, d. 4/26/1900 at 28; consumption

KELLY,
Archibald, d. 4/3/1926 at 40/7/1 in Lowell, MA; gen. paralysis of insane
Bridget, d. 3/22/1891 at 55; ----- Hughes (Ireland) and ----- (Ireland)
Hugh, d. 9/18/1896 at 49; cirrhosis of liver; b. Ireland; SM
Michael J., d. 2/20/1933 at 71; stricture of oesophagus
Nellie E., d. 6/18/1890 at 28/9/18; married; Patrick Couhig (Ireland) and Mary Ryan (Ireland)
Rose A., d. 10/25/1888 at 0/1; b. Dover; Peter Kelly (Ireland) and Kate Connors (Ireland)

KELSEY,
Abbie A., d. 1/7/1898 at 73; heart disease; b. Nottingham; PH
Almie J., d. 1/16/1937 at 75/8/27; cerebr. hemorrhage

KELT,
John, d. 2/9/1890 at 0/8/18; Agnes Kelt (Scotland)

KEMPTON,
Harry D., d. 8/4/1937 at 37/2/25; tetanus

KENDALL,
Emogene, d. 10/5/1935 at 86/0/6; chronic nephritis
Stephen, d. 3/21/1892 at 85; old age

KENDRICK,
Annie K., d. 11/12/1932 at 71/5/8 in Pawtucket, RI; thrmbosis
Katie D., d. 6/11/1923 at 46/6/1; cancer of uteri; William A. Crook and Sarah A. Jones
William, d. 7/22/1896 at 41 in Somerville, MA; pulmonary tuberculosis; PH

KENDRICKS,
Flora S., d. 10/24/1898 at 8; typhoid fever; b. E. Somerville, MA; PH
Jennie B., d. 9/22/1898 at 13; tuberculosis; b. Pawtucket, RI; PH

KENERSON,
Leland D., d. 6/20/1936 at 69/1/7; heart disease
Susie A., d. 4/10/1923 at 65/2/25; apoplexy; Ezra Kenerson and Sarah French

KENISTON,
Caleb T., d. 7/1/1887 at 55/0/15; shoemaker; married; b. Holderness; Ezra H. Keniston and Jemima Thurston
Charles W., d. 11/3/1921 at 70/9/18; carcinoma of liver; Newell Keniston and Martha Sargent
Edward A., d. 5/9/1934 at 0/10/12; acute nephritis
Emma H., d. 4/20/1915 at 69; heart disease; John Hooper and ----- Guptill
Everett J., d. 2/7/1907 at 0/3/18; heart failure; E. E. M. Keniston and Ella B. Nealley
Ezra H., d. 7/31/1927 at 83/1/28; myocarditis; Ezra Keniston and Jemima Plaisted
Ida Belle, d. 9/19/1924 at 45/2/28; ac. dilatation of heart; Daniel D. Nealley and Mary Wagoner
Leonard F., d. 8/22/1925 at 59/8/25; abscess left abdomen; Ezra Keniston and Emma Hooper

KENNARD,
Benjamin F., d. 11/15/1914 at 80/3/16; pericarditis; John Kennard and Lydia Merrow
Benjamin R., d. 4/29/1906 at 1/1; acute nephritis; PH
Dorcas, d. 4/15/1907 at 66/4/17; pneumonia; James Rush and Dorcas Barnett
Edward P., d. 2/27/1921 at 72/3/17; carcinoma of throat; Martin P. Kennard and Caroline A. Smith
Elmer Rush, d. 7/1/1924 at 17/3/4; acute appendicitis; A. Ray Kennard and Mary W. King
Isaac D., d. 9/30/1915 at 79/6/15; senility; John Kennard and Lydia Morrow
Sarah A., d. 4/21/1901 at 64/9/18; valvular disease of heart; PH

KENNEDY,
daughter, d. 11/7/1887 at –; b. Dover; James H. Kennedy (Danville, MA) and Mary E. Richmond (Shirley, MA)
Ann, d. 4/10/1923 at 90; arterio sclerosis
Annie, d. 3/3/1904 at 47; inanition; SM
Annie, d. 12/14/1906 at 71; convulsions; SM
Arthur, d. 10/29/1917 at 21; traumatic shock; John H. Kennedy and Cynthia Babcock
Catherine, d. 4/2/1914 at 78; broncho pneumonia; Michael Maloney and Ellen Foley
Dennis A., d. 4/17/1895 at 37; consumption of bowels; b. Canada; SM
Francis P., d. 2/17/1934 at 43 in Methuen, MA; carcinoma of rectum
Francis T., d. 11/22/1923 at 32 in Billerica, MA; capillary bronchitis
Harold J., d. 12/12/1901 at 4; dysentery
Harry M., d. 12/17/1925 at 53/5; apoplexy; William Kennedy and Helen Gerrish
Helen M., d. 10/6/1907 at 64/10/26; apoplexy; Charles W. Gerrish and Eliza Knowles
J. Edwin, d. 5/7/1935 at 84/2/5; arteriosclerosis
James H., d. 10/19/1914 at 64/9/27; chr. intestinal nephritis
Johanna, d. 6/17/1896 at 78; old age; b. Ireland; SM
John E., d. 10/25/1916 at 69/6/8; chronic gastritis; Michael Kennedy and Johanna -----
Margaret, d. 7/7/1889 at 70; housewife; widow; b. Ireland; ----- McNamee (Ireland) and ----- Sheridan (Ireland)
Margaret, d. 4/19/1912 at 77 in Boston, MA; carcinoma of intestines
Margaret, d. 10/22/1924 at 65 in Concord; broncho pneumonia; John Lwick
Mary Ann, d. 5/26/1916 at 55 in Concord; cancer of stomach
Mary E., d. 5/4/1937 at 79*

Matilda A., d. 7/24/1925 at 36/8/8; introabdom. hemorrhage; William F. Milner and Mary E. Bowers
Michael R., d. 12/21/1894 at 41; pneumonia; b. Canada; SM
Minnie E., d. 1/1/1905 at 36/0/15; tuberculosis of lungs
Robert, d. 6/28/1908 at 65/2/14; cancer
Thomas, d. 10/28/1898 at 49; phthisis; b. Ireland; SM
W., d. 2/7/1890 at 0/2; James Kennedy (US) and ----- (US)

KENNELLEY,
Hugh, d. 5/18/1892 at 50; phthisis; b. Ireland; (Ireland; Ireland)

KENNEY,
Caroline T., d. 2/10/1936 at 28/0/6; paralytic ileus
Martha, d. 2/9/1893 at 56; died in Strafford Co. Asylum fire
Nora, d. 9/19/1900 at <1; cholera infantum; SM
Samuel, d. 11/1/1889 at 84/9/14; farmer; b. Barrington
Sarah A., d. 5/22/1906 at 91/0/20 in Peabody, MA; phlegmonous tonsilitis; PH
Thomas, d. 12/18/1924 at 42; chronic nephritis

KENNIE,
James H., d. 2/12/1914 at 70/5/29; gangrene; James Kennie

KENNISTON,
Jemmima, d. 3/11/1895 at 91; senility; b. Gilford; buried in Wolfeboro
John, d. 4/14/1900 at 73; pneumonia; PH

KENYON,
James, d. 3/21/1903 at 31/4/8; SM
James E., d. 3/21/1903 at 31; phthisis
Peter, d. 9/14/1898 at 0; cyanosis (congenital); b. Dover; SM
Thomas E., d. 6/1/1903 at 2; marasmus; SM

KEPPEL,
Georgianna, d. 6/18/1914 at 64/8; enlargement of heart; ----- Welch and Mary A. Horne
John F., d. 4/9/1903 at 69/7/27; endocarditis; PH

KERE,
Nellie M., d. 4/5/1934 at 69/9/26 in Durham; lobar pneumonia

KEREAZES,
child, d. 2/17/1929 at –; premature birth; George Kereazes and Annie Betsoulou

child, d. 2/17/1929 at –; premature birth; George Kereazes and Annie Betsoulou

KERR,
Daniel, d. 12/21/1926 at 76/8/26; arterio sclerosis

KERRY,
William F., d. 12/19/1913 at 55; hemiplegia

KERSHAW,
Ann, d. 1/10/1892 at 90; la grippe; b. England; (England; England)
Stephen, d. 10/23/1923 at –; asphyxia of labor; Benjamin S. Kershaw and Susie Meadowcroft

KEYES,
Bradley A., d. 2/10/1917 at 60; endocarditis
Ella C., d. 11/4/1920 at 62/5/15; cardiac asthma; Robert Whyte and Mary -

KICKLINE,
child, d. 11/20/1933 at –; prematurity

KIDDER,
Lanson F., d. 3/27/1900 at 56; progressive paralysis; PH

KIDNEY,
John, d. 2/27/1908 at 32; pul. tuberculosis; Maurice Kidney and Mary Corcoran
John L., d. 9/8/1907 at 0/2; gastro enteritis; Michael Kidney and Jane Redden
Lizzie A., d. 8/12/1917 at 65 in Portsmouth; cerebral hemorrhage
Maggie, d. 10/8/1900 at 6; pneumonia; SM
Marguerite, d. 6/29/1906 at 0/6/6; acute gastro enteritis
Mary, d. 10/12/1921 at 75; gen. arterio sclerosis; William Corcoran and Margaret Scannell
Maurice, d. 4/12/1890 at 49; married; William Kidney (Ireland) and Johanna Hearn (Ireland)
Michael J., d. 7/6/1928 at 60; cirrhosis of liver; Maurice Kidney and Mary Corcoran
William, d. 6/4/1903 at 0/4/21; convulsions

KIES,
William, d. 7/9/1898 at 1; cholera infantum; b. Dover; SM

KILBORN,
Katherine, d. 9/7/1906 at 74 in Boston, MA; cerebral hemorrhage; PH

KILCULLEN,
Bridget, d. 9/20/1905 at 3; anaemia; SM

KILE,
child, d. 1/18/1899 at –; stillborn

KILGORE,
Myrtle H., d. 8/8/1934 at 49/10/11 in Chicago, IL; inquest pending

KILLIAN,
Mary A., d. 2/14/1913 at 48 in Portsmouth; pneumonia; Francis McNally and Rose Cullen

KILLOREN,
Andrew, d. 2/19/1920 at 66/6/2; valvular heart disease; James Killoren
Bridget, d. 12/30/1900 at 77/11/30; old age; SM
Catherine, d. 5/1/1930 at 75/11 in Brookline, MA; carcinoma of stomach
Herbert L., d. 10/24/1897 at 6; pneumonia; b. Dover; SM
James, d. 10/8/1887 at 7/5/21; b. Dover; James Killoren (Ireland) and Susan O. Donald (Boston, MA)
James, d. 2/6/1912 at 65; heart disease; John Killoren and Bridget Scanlon
John, d. 10/12/1900 at 48 in Somersworth; heart trouble; SM
John J., d. 12/23/1898 at 10; congestion of brain; b. Dover; SM
Mary A., d. 7/3/1926 at – in Somersworth; chr. valv. heart disease; Bernard Fox and Ellen Qualey
Michael, d. 3/16/1897 at 47; heart disease; b. Ireland; SM
Susan A., d. 11/11/1913 at 65/0/5; gastric carcinoma; Charles A. Donnell and Annie Mullen
Thomas M., d. 5/21/1919 at 35/0/15; septicemia; James Killoren and Susan O'Donnell

KILTON,
Rebecca S., d. 4/26/1897 at 63; cerebral hemorrhage; b. Sheffield, VT; buried in Grafton

KIMBALL,
child, d. 11/2/1913 at –; stillborn; Harold H. Kimball and Eva D. Hobby
child, d. 8/18/1928 at –; stillborn; Richard W. Kimball and Helen B. Chase
Abbie, d. 3/28/1916 at 66 in Hartford, CT; broncho pneumonia

Abby Jane, d. 8/19/1891 at 73; widow; James Hanson (Rochester) and Hannah Place (Rochester)
Annie, d. 8/6/1903 at 74/2/17; heart disease; PH
Annie M., d. 7/29/1933 at 81/10/11; carcinoma of stomach
Ardena, d. 8/11/1911 at 2/5/21; tuberculosis; Alphonse E. Kimball and Myrtie E. Glidden
Azabah S., d. 2/24/1926 at 98/0/14 in Springfield, MA; ac. broncho pneumonia
Beatrice A., d. 12/10/1935 at 26/1/5; pulmonary tuberculosis
Charles H., d. 7/28/1923 at 51/0/5; intestinal obstruction; Jonathan Kimball and Abby Bennett
Doris B., d. 12/19/1907 at 0/6/3; chronic gastroenteritis; Alphonso E. Kimball and Myrtie E. Glidden
Eldredge, d. 5/9/1909 at 0/2/2; marasmus; Leslie J. Kimball and Mary R. Getchell
Elizabeth L., d. 2/16/1912 at 67/11/23; cerebral hemorrhage; William Lake and Betsey Green
Elizabeth P., d. 12/1/1904 at 78/2/8; heart disease; PH
Ellen J., d. 2/27/1919 at 80/7/11; mitral insufficiency; Richard Kimball and Margaret J. Pendexter
Henry, d. 2/9/1893 at 31; died in Strafford Co. Asylum fire
Herbert L., d. 1/31/1933 at 80/4/21; arteriosclerosis
Horace, d. 4/30/1899 at 83; old age and heart disease; buried in family lot
Howard D., d. 3/6/1893 at 79; rheumatic fever; b. Meredith; (Meredith; Gilmanton)
Ida F., d. 1/22/1930 at 76/4/28; angina pectoris; William Ham and Tamson Davis
John H., d. 1/24/1911 at 85/2/22; chronic endocarditis; George Kimball and Eleanor -----
John L., d. 11/8/1922 at 73/2/3; lobar pneumonia; Z. T. Kimball and Mary A. Mason
Joseph E., d. 6/26/1891 at 64/5; married; John D. Kimball (Kennebunk, ME) and Eliza Evans (Kennebunk, ME)
Joseph E., d. 3/20/1901 at 41 in Concord; paresis; PH
Laura A., d. 5/11/1898 at 47; consumption; b. Atkinson; PH
Leonora D., d. 4/12/1929 at 78/7/28 in Medford, MA; arterio sclerosis
Lillian E., d. 5/23/1927 at 20/0/13; heart disease; Irving W. Kimball and Ella D. Tufts
Lloyd W., d. 9/4/1915 at 49/8/3; strangulated hernia; John Kimball
Lydia Ann, d. 1/18/1929 at 85/3/5; lobar pneumonia; Eben Plaisted and Lydia -----
Martha W., d. 6/14/1913 at 46; ptomaine poisoning; Ebenezer Worster and Mary E. Keay
Mary Ann, d. 1/19/1890 at 82; single; Jonathan Kimball (Dover) and Polly Kimball (Dover)

Mary E., d. 4/20/1896 at 67; apoplexy; b. Rochester; buried at homestead
Moses Paul, d. 7/2/1888 at 24/11/20; com. traveler; single; b. Dover; John F. Kimball
Myrtie E., d. 1/1/1911 at 25/6/22; tuberculosis; George E. Glidden and Lemina Ricker
Orrin S., d. 5/11/1931 at 74/10/20; lobar pneumonia
Oscar F., d. 1/28/1929 at 75 in Winthrop, MA; ch. intes. nephritis; Moses L. Kimball and Hannah Eastman
Philip Hobby, d. 3/19/1916 at 1/4/15; malnutrition; Harold H. Kimball and Eva D. Hobby
Richard D., d. 11/11/1920 at 74/1/28 in Alton Bay; hardening of arteries; Richard Kimball and Elizabeth Hale
Robert H., d. 5/23/1916 at 1/6/18; oedematous laryngitis; Harold H. Kimball and Eva D. Hobby
Sallie, d. 1/22/1887 at 83/2/27; single; b. Dover; James Kimball and Nancy Horne (Dover)
William A., d. 1/25/1934 at 75/1/15; uraemia

KINCAID,
James, d. 3/9/1893 at 27; typhoid fever; b. Scotland; (Scotland; Scotland)
Lelia E., d. 1/23/1926 at 65/5/1; Isaiah Shaw and Hannah Small

KING,
child, d. 10/30/1922 at –; stillborn; Harry W. King and K. M. McLaughlin
Aaron B., d. 12/17/1887 at 39/8/26 in Lawrence, MA
Abbie B., d. 11/24/1908 at 27; cerebral apoplexy; John J. King and Catherine Murphy
Almira J., d. 12/25/1922 at 72 in Lawrence, MA; chronic myocarditis
Ann Barbara, d. 8/16/1929 at 0/0/1; premature birth; Leon A. King and Elsie C. Card
Archie C., d. 8/14/1910 at –; premature birth; Millard O. King and Effie M. Canney
Carrie Ada, d. 11/1/1922 at 44 in Portland, ME; lobar pneumonia
Charles, d. 11/3/1892 at –; disease of brain; b. Dover; (Kennebunkport; Durham)
Effie May, d. 9/28/1918 at 30/2/13; pneumonia; Isaac B. Canney and Sarah A. Woodus
Elizabeth, d. 4/24/1890 at 53 in Tewksbury, MA
Ella F., d. 11/14/1920 at 65/2/11; lobar pneumonia; James W. Ferguson and Emily A. Shaw
Elsie, d. 7/22/1925 at 80; arterio sclerosis
Gero, d. 9/7/1887 at –; b. Dover; Jerome King (Canada) and Addie Stone (Canada)
Hamilton E., d. 4/8/1908 at 0/7/16; marasmus; Harry M. King and Mabel B. Mathews

Helen Ada, d. 8/15/1929 at –; premature birth; Leon A. King and Elsie C. Card
Henry, d. 11/12/1927 at 57 in Boston, MA; cancer of colon; Charles W. King and Addie A. Scott
Lena, d. 8/12/1921 at 28/0/5; intestinal obstruction; James King and Catherine Reston
Louise M., d. 10/15/1933 at 76/2/14; carcinoma of stomach
Lulu B., d. 1/17/1913 at 52/1/3 in Somerville, MA; ch. Brights disease
Mary E., d. 3/4/1932 at 71; chronic endocarditis
Maud R., d. 6/18/1902 at 19/7/28; burning accident; PH
Nora M., d. 12/15/1933 at 22/4/11; chronic appendicitis
Patrick, d. 10/22/1919 at 45/9/8; cancer of stomach; Patrick King and Margaret Kildea
Samuel, d. 3/13/1916 at 70/5/26 in Thornton's Ferry; angina pectoris
Sarah, d. 8/8/1899 at –; cholera morbus; SM
Theo., d. 4/12/1900 at 54; pneumonia; buried in Raynham, MA
Theodore H., d. 8/31/1909 at 0/0/1; cardiac weakness; Millard O. King and Effie May Kenney
Thomas, d. 3/5/1892 at 88; pneumonia; b. England; (England; England)
Thomas, d. 7/27/1913 at 56/10/21; degeneration of brain; James King and Julia George
Thomas L., d. 5/8/1937a t 27/9/27; acute nephritis
W. Wallace, d. 3/1/1920 at 64/0/27 in Lawrence, MA; probably heart disease

KINGMAN,
John W., d. 12/–/1903 at – in Cedar Falls, IA; heart failure
Mary E., d. 1/27/1914 at 85/9/29; senility; Sargent Ham and Lou Jenkins

KINGSBURY,
Charles A., d. 5/31/1895 at 75; heart disease; b. Boston, MA; PH

KINNIE,
Etta M., d. 1/26/1913 at 40/1/2 in Portsmouth; pulmonary tuberculosis
Hattie I., d. 1/24/1913 at 1/1/17 in Portsmouth; meningitis tubercular

KINSMAN,
Ethel M., d. 5/28/1922 at 6/8; peritonitis; Frank S. Kinsman and Florence B. Morrison

KIRK,
Gertrude Emma, d. 7/20/1930 at 36 in Providence, RI; broncho pneumonia

KIRKMAN,
James, d. 3/31/1890 at 50/4/26; married; Peter Kirkman (England) and
 Ellen Kirkman (England)
Mary A., d. 9/25/1913 at 71 in York, ME; cancer of liver

KISTERMAN,
Anna S., d. 12/17/1891 at 69/6; widow; Sylvanus Wing (No. Falmouth,
 MA) and Hannah Swift (W. Falmouth, MA)
Carl V., d. 1/31/1898 at 37; pneumonia; b. Dover; PH
Elmira, d. 2/1/1888 at 64/9/14 in Stoneham, MA
Gustavus, d. 11/5/1888 at 69/9; book keeper; married; b. Germany; John
 P. Kisterman (Germany) and Julia Lemen (Germany)
Gustavus E., Jr., d. 1/12/1916 at 52/1/23 in Concord; general paresis; G.
 E. Kisterman and Anna Wing
Robert, d. 10/5/1895 at 64 in Stoneham, MA; chronic bronchitis

KITCHENS,
Norma J., d. 5/25/1932 at 0/0/11 in Portsmouth; hemorrhage

KITTREDGE,
Harriet N., d. 11/22/1906 at 67/11/7; acute uraemia; PH
John, d. 6/10/1906 at 69/10; heart hypertrophy; PH

KIVEL,
Catherine, d. 7/30/1890 at 82; widow; Dennis Donogher (Ireland) and -----
 Donogher (Ireland)
Eva G., d. 1/18/1919 at 61/11/5; general debility; Albert Ennis and
 Amanda A. Horn
Frank, d. 12/23/1922 at 42 in Tucson, AZ; pulmonary tuberculosis; John
 Kivel
John, d. 4/1/1924 at 69 in Newport; lobar pneumonia
Katherine, d. 10/28/1892 at –; gastric and intestinal catarrh; b. Dover;
 (Dover; Dover)
Maurice E., d. 9/18/1927 at 42/8/12 in Los Angeles, CA; pulmonary
 tuberculosis; John Kivel and Eva Ennis

KLEIN,
Wilhelminna, d. 11/13/1933 at 74/0/29; chronic myocarditis

KLEMKE,
Henry Paul, d. 6/24/1933 at 56/8/11; carcinoma of prostate

KLUSENER,
Alice B., d. 10/14/1900 at 18; typhoid fever; PH

KNIBS,
Henry, d. 3/8/1897 at 42; pneumonia; b. Newmarket

KNIGHT,
child, d. 8/14/1910 at –; stillborn; Frank G. Knight and Flossie Nowell
Edwin L., d. 3/25/1917 at 9/2/21; pulm. tuberculosis; Herbert L. Knight and Eva Wentworth
James Mendol, d. 12/31/1909 at 70/6/22; uraemia; Edmond Knight and Ann Smith
John, Jr., d. 7/2/1928 at 0/0/½; premature birth; John B. Knight and Florence J. -----
Joseph A., d. 11/30/1916 at 84/4/8; softening of brain; Joseph Knight and Tamson Caswell
Mary J., d. 7/16/1899 at 66; cancer; buried in Portland, ME
Rebecca A., d. 5/26/1923 at 85/5/12; gen. arterio sclerosis; Thomas Rogers and Olive Close
Sadie Helen, d. 2/16/1937 at 80/3/22; diabetes mellitus
Sarah E., d. 8/24/1896 at 35; phthisis pulmonalis; b. Rockport; PH

KNOTT,
Annie, d. 10/10/1916 at 59/5; acute nephritis; Patrick McManus and Catherine McGuinness
Catherine, d. 7/16/1909 at 64; diabetes; John Cassidy and Margaret McCarragher
Frank, d. 3/25/1900 at 44; mitral regurgitation; SM
Herbert L., d. 5/8/1890 at 0/0/27; Thomas Knott (Dover) and Mary Ryan (Portland)
Margaret, d. 11/28/1931 at 69; lobar pneumonia
Raymond W., d. 11/22/1888 at 0/1/7; b. Dover; Thomas Knott (Dover) and Mary A. Ryan (Portland, ME)
Richard, d. 1/14/1893 at 61; Bright's disease; b. Ireland; (Ireland; Ireland)
Richard, d. 3/8/1930 at 75; pulmonary oedema; Richard Knott and Ellen Hughes
Thomas, d. 8/17/1923 at 70; myocarditis; Robert Knott and Ellen Hughes
Thomas, d. 6/13/1934 at 19; frac. skull (accident)
Thomas H., d. 8/12/1889 at 4/4; b. Dover; Thomas H. Knott (Dover) and Mary Ryan (ME)

KNOWLES,
child, d. 9/9/1931 at –; stillborn
Jessie, d. 1/19/1926 at 80; septic hand and arm; Jesse Knowles and Eliza Pillsbury

KNOWLTON,
Blanche D., d. 11/25/1936 at 45/2/28; cerebral hemorrhage

KNOX,
Elizabeth J. B., d. 6/18/1912 at 88/11/27; hemiplegia; Andrew Pierce and Abigail Osborne
Jennie M., d. 9/15/1895 at 58; peritonitis; b. Effingham; buried in Effingham
William H., d. 1/3/1936 at 68/2/28; chronic nephritis
William O., d. 3/5/1897 at 33; pneumonia; b. Ossipee; buried in West Ossipee

KOKINOS,
Nicholas, d. 2/20/1922 at 45; angina pectoris; Elias Kokinos and Patria ----

KORN,
Otto J., d. 11/27/1936 at –; anencephaly

KOUMOUCHOS,
Mary, d. 8/2/1922 at 1/7/0; meningitis; Stephen Koumouchos

KOUTSOUNS,
Paraskeva, d. 10/6/1910 at 0/5; cholera infantum; George Koutsouns and Anastasia

KREKORIAN,
Lucia, d. 4/15/1905 at 0/7/28; convulsions; PH

KURTZ,
Barbara, d. 2/5/1933 at 6/9/13; acute mastoiditis

KYATT,
Afel, d. 10/31/1903 at 0/4/15; congestion of brain

LABBE,
child, d. 12/17/1926 at –; stillborn; Adelard Labbe and Florida Desharnais
child, d. 8/9/1929 at –; stillborn; Adelarde Labbe and Florida Desharnais
Gracia, d. 8/2/1913 at 0/5/15; cholera infantum; Joseph Labbe and Sophronia Bernard
Wilfrid, d. 5/17/1928 at –; atelectasis; Adelard Labbe and Florida Detremais

LABEL,
Blanche, d. 2/6/1930 at 17/1/17; toxic goitre; Rene LeBel (sic) and Valeda Vallei

LABONTE,
Adeline, d. 4/22/1936 at 86; myocarditis
Alice, d. 6/19/1927 at 43 in Biddeford, ME; cerebral hemorrhage; David
    Boulanger and Alphonsine Morin
Elmira F., d. 8/1/1915 at 7/7; post-diph. paralysis; Charles H. LaBonte and
    Alice Boulanger
France, d. 7/15/1920 at 75/11; shock; Xavia Labonte and Angelina Daigle
Irene H., d. 1/26/1917 at 1/4/2; convulsions; George A. Labonte and Lillian
    E. Morin
Mary C., d. 11/29/1936 at 53/8/5 in Somersworth; cancer of uterus
Paul, d. 1/10/1920 at 71/11/23; enlarged prostate; Francois X. Lebonte
    (sic) and Angelicis Daigle
Veronique, d. 11/10/1909 at 4/3/6; gastro-indigestion chronic; Pierre
    Labonte and Victoria Demers

LABOR,
infant, d. 1/21/1935 at 0/0/3; premature birth

LABRANCHE,
child, d. 1/8/1930 at –; stillborn; Philemon Labranch and Mary Elwell

LABRECK,
child, d. 11/21/1902 at 2; meningitis; SM

LABRECQUE,
Anna, d. 3/7/1928 at 60/3/20; goiter; Thomas Labrecque and Angeline
    Brochu
Delia, d. 3/21/1926 at 37/1/16; chronic myocarditis; Peter Dionne and
    Melvina Clouture

LABRETON,
Albert, d. 9/16/1918 at 7/4/27; acute lobar pneumonia; Andrew LaBreton
    and Malinda Rosineau

LABRICQUE,
Amedee, d. 10/4/1915 at 0/3; gastro enteritis; Joseph LaBricque and Eva
    Dionne

LABRIE,
Antoinette, d. 10/2/1918 at 5/7/29; acute lobar pneumonia; Joseph L.
    Labrie and Rose Arnold
Cedulie, d. 7/2/1925 at 74/6/7 in Concord; chronic myocarditis; Mathews
    Gauthier and Felicite Gagnon

Gregoire, d. 2/20/1892 at 2; phthisis pulmonalis; b. Fall River, MA; (Canada; Canada)
Irene, d. 4/20/1929 at 13/11/17; tuberculous meningitis; Exear Labrie and Marie Carrier
Joseph L., d. 5/2/1932 at 55/1/27 in Portland, ME; duodenal ulcer
Mary, d. 3/24/1925 at 41/7/3; cerebral hemorrhage; John Carrier

LACACOS,
Peter, d. 10/1/1908 at 17; chronic cerebral meningitis

LACHANCE,
Joseph, d. 12/15/1935 at 45/7/19; accidental drowning

LADUE,
Laurenda, d. 5/17/1893 at 17; phthisis; b. Altoona, NY; (NY; NY)

LAFLAM,
Cora, d. 2/29/1892 at 13; phthisis; b. Canada; (Canada; Canada)

LAFLAMME,
Annie, d. 7/14/1891 at 0/3/15; Nercise Laflamme (Canada) and Louise Laflamme (Canada)

LAFLECHE,
Nettie, d. 8/13/1891 at 0/2/27; Isaac Lafleche (Canada) and Delvina Cote (Canada)

LAFOND,
Joseph, d. 5/24/1891 at 53/11; Francois Lafond (Canada) and Judic Janelle (Canada)
Joseph F. X., d. 10/27/1892 at –; cholera infantum; b. Dover; (Canada; Canada)

LAFONTAINE,
Olive, d. 2/11/1891 at 0/11; Felix LaFontaine (Canada) and Orianne Fournier (Canada)

LAFORCE,
Leon, d. 5/13/1918 at 69/5/4; hemiplegia; Louis LaForce and Mary Boisvert
Mary, d. 3/11/1914 at 75/7/22; old age; E. Noury

LAFORTUNE,
Joseph, d. 7/8/1908 at 31; acute nephritis; Joseph Lafortune and Selina Parent

LAFOUNTAINE,
Mary, d. 2/9/1893 at 45; died in Strafford Co. Asylum fire

LAGACE,
Henrietta, d. 10/28/1891 at 3/10/18; Alphonse Lagace (Canada) and Vitaline Leveille (Canada)

LAGACY,
Joseph, d. 1/3/1936 at 90/9/1; coronary thrombosis

LAHEY,
Frank, d. 8/7/1925 at 70; cerebral hemorrhage; Isaie Labbee (sic) and Mary Proux

LAJENNESS,
Alice, d. 7/15/1897 at 0; diarrhea infantile; b. Dover; SM

LAJEUNNESSE,
Alexina L., d. 8/30/1936 at 55/11/21; ac. non-hem. s. lar.

LAMAR,
Hudson, d. 12/–/1902 at 28; acute nephritis; PH

LAMB,
child, d. 5/19/1917 at 0/0/1; premature birth; Robert H. Lamb and Mabel F. Foss
child, d. 5/19/1917 at 0/0/1; premature birth; Robert H. Lamb and Mabel F. Foss
child, d. 9/28/1924 at –; stillborn; John M. Lamb and Elizabeth E. Riley

LAMBERT,
Agnes, d. 8/31/1907 at 64 in Boston, MA; endocarditis
Jean M., d. 12/25/1937 at 58/4/17; lobar pneumonia
Philomene, d. 11/4/1934 at 90/6/6; bronchial pneumonia
Wilfred, d. 10/14/1896 at –; diarrhea infantile; b. Dover; SM

LAMOND,
Marion, d. 10/8/1905 at 0/7/21; cholera infantum; SM

LAMOREAUX,
Matilda B., d. 2/26/1937 at 78/8/19; cerebr. hemorrhage

LAMPESES,
Vasilo, d. 2/3/1920 at 2/6/6 in Rollinsford; broncho pneumonia; F. T. Lampesis and M. Kali Ganetos

LAMPESIS,
Stella, d. 9/2/1932 at 5/4/20 in Rollinsford; anaemia

LAMPREY,
Mary J., d. 3/18/1931 at 61 in Berwick, ME; apoplexy (see following entry)
Mary J., d. 5/18/1931 at 61 in Berwick, ME; apoplexy (see preceding entry)

LAMSON,
Hannah J., d. 5/8/1931 at 61/7/10; lobar pneumonia

LANAGAN,
Mary, d. 2/8/1919 at 58/7; cerebral apoplexy; John Lanagan and Catherine Grady

LANCASTER,
Johanna M., d. 10/26/1934 at 91/8/11 in Saugus, MA; arteriosclerosis
John, d. 1/17/1914 at 71/7/10 in Saugus, MA; cancer of stomach
John T., d. 4/2/1920 at 66/7; acute lobar pneumonia; John Lancaster and Mary Bibbey

LANDECKER,
Henry, d. 11/7/1900 at 60 in Detroit, MI; paralysis; buried in Somersworth

LANDER,
Freedom H., d. 9/10/1890 at 60/1/1; married; Lot Lander and Betsy Moody

LANDREY,
James, d. 6/18/1894 at – in Canada; cholera infantum; b. Canada; SM

LANE,
Abbie F., d. 7/27/1925 at 78/11/18 in Stratham; la grippe
Ann M., d. 3/6/1894 at 75 in Lee; influenza; PH
Edmund B., d. 12/5/1924 at 86/11/13; angina pectoris; Edmund J. Lane and Elizabeth Barker
Edward S., d. 12/9/1928 at 53/8/2; empyemia; Edmund J. Lane and Melinda Jenkins

Elizabeth G., d. 4/8/1890 at 43/9/2; widow; John Milne (Scotland) and
    Jane Trotter (Scotland)
Julia, d. 3/22/1925 at 93; gen. arterio sclerosis; John W. Healey and Nora
    Clancy
Lillie H., d. 7/1/1917 at 48/10/27; cerebral hemorrhage; John Hill and Mary
    Caldwell
Major A., d. 2/2/1899 at 77 in Lynn, MA; old age; PH
Mary, d. 4/9/1913 at 78; senility
Mary J., d. 10/4/1906 at 75/1/14; spinal sclerosis; PH
Mary J., d. 7/11/1913 at 88/4/1 in Lynn, MA; chronic bronchitis
Ralph F., d. 10/25/1937 at 57/8/11; asphyxiation by illuminating gas
William H., d. 11/27/1907 at 67/1/19; suicide by hanging; Levi Lane and
    Clarissa Thompson

LANG,
Catherine M., d. 10/12/1908 at 72/6; heart disease; Patrick McManus and
    Mary McCabe
John, d. 6/16/1897 at 1; scarlet fever; b. Dover; SM
Katherine T., d. 6/14/1897 at 3; scarlet fever; b. Dover; SM
Mary, d. 6/17/1930 at –; natural causes; Thomas Lang and Catherine
    McManus
Thomas, d. 3/4/1909 at –; old age
Thomas, d. 12/29/1932 at 64; chronic myocarditis

LANGDON,
Helen F., d. 2/23/1929 at 69/7/16; broncho pneumonia; John Towle and
    Kathleen West
Henry F., d. 6/21/1913 at 60; anaemia
Horace W., d. 2/8/1934 at 56/2/18; peritonitis
Olive Jane, d. 10/8/1917 at 70/9/19; anaemia; Ivory H. Foss

LANGEVIN,
Louis, d. 1/20/1936 at 52; ac. yel. at'phy liver

LANGFORD,
Susanna, d. 1/31/1908 at 62/9/19 in Madbury; paralysis

LANGLEY,
child, d. 3/9/1910 at 0/0/1; premature birth; Abraham L. Langley and Annie
    E. Bolo
child, d. 9/18/1930 at – in York, ME; difficult birth
Alice L., d. 1/5/1925 at 71/6/21; carcinoma rectum; Benjamin Jenness and
    Louisa Durgin
Claire E., d. 8/27/1937 at 31/4/12; car. cervix uterus

Currier W., d. 4/30/1928 at 79/8/29; cerebral hemorrhage; William C. Langley
Mary, d. 3/21/1887 at 87/2/21; single; b. NH; Thomas Langley (NH) and Deborah Randall (NH)
Mary E., d. 1/25/1927 at 56/9/25; Brights disease; Joseph M. R. Adams and Olive E. Libby
William C., d. 2/21/1896 at 22; phthisis pulmonalis; b. Dover; PH

LANGLOIS,
George E., d. 8/23/1905 at 0/7/14; cholera infantum
George P., d. 3/23/1925 at 50; pulmonary tuberculosis; John Langlois and Malvina -----
Joseph, d. 7/16/1905 at 24; accidental drowning; SM
Joseph, d. 6/21/1920 at 38/4/4; pulmonary tuberculosis; John Langloise (sic) and Malvina Sturgeon
Rudolf, d. 8/6/1909 at 5/11/22; tubercular meningitis; George Langlois

LANGMAID,
Alonzo E., d. 11/11/1925 at 83/10/13; gangrene; Samuel Langmaid and Elizabeth Woodman
Annie L., d. 10/21/1898 at 28; surgical shock; b. Nottingham; PH
Izetta W., d. 3/7/1937 at 89/1/13; arteriosclerosis
Jacob H., d. 4/11/1907 at 70/5; cerebral apoplexy; Minot Langmaid and Louis Willand
Joseph G., d. 4/24/1910 at 76/0/29; endocarditis; Samuel Langmaid and Elizabeth D. Woodman
Linville F., d. 10/28/1927 at 63/10/21 in Portland, ME; uraemia

LANONETTE,
child, d. 5/25/1896 at –; stillborn; b. Dover; SM
child, d. 3/19/1898 at 0; stillborn; b. Dover; SM
Mary D., d. 5/11/1898 at 0; premature birth; b. Dover; SM

LANOUETTE,
Delia, d. 2/15/1925 at 60/9/22; acute lobar pneumonia; Conzaque Morrissette and Margaret Empont
Raymond, d. 11/23/1915 at 0/0/10; premature birth; Henry Lanouette and Rosanna Fortin
Victor F., d. 4/13/1934 at 82/0/13; cerebral hemorrhage
William, d. 8/31/1927 at 60/3/1 in Ossipee; brain tumor; John Lanouette and Agnes Rogers

LAPHAM,
child, d. 3/16/1918 at –; stillborn; Andrew Lapham and Liva L'Esperance

Andrew G., d. 10/5/1918 at 40/5/20; acute lobar pneumonia; George Lapham and Addie Grover

LAPIERRE,
James, d. 6/6/1907 at –; drowned

LAPOINTE,
Albert, d. 10/17/1916 at 0/3/15; gastro enteritis; Napoleon Lapointe and Alice Jalbert
Leo, d. 12/9/1918 at 0/6/12; acute lobar pneumonia; Charles Lapointe and Catherine Kelliher
Mary, d. 9/2/1921 at 63/9/8; typhoid fever; Vital Gagne and Apoline Lessard
Roland, d. 7/20/1905 at 0/11/12; cholera infantum

LAPPAN,
Elizabeth E., d. 4/4/1890 at 0/6; Ed. Lappan (Ireland) and Elizabeth Mullen (Ireland)

LAPPEN,
Florence, d. 12/15/1929 at 39/4/5 in Concord; cerebral embolism; John F. Lappen and Caroline Stevens
Frances E., d. 5/21/1914 at 1 hr.; asphyxia during labor; Patrick Lappen and Florence Pray
Patrick E., d. 4/4/1923 at 34 in Lawrence, MA; pulmonary tuberculosis

LAROCHE,
Christine, d. 1/25/1892 at 16; typhoid fever; b. Canada; (Canada; Canada)
Gideon, d. 8/25/1895 at 0; diarrhea infantile; b. Dover; SM
Ludger, d. 11/26/1927 at 63/4/6; cancer of intestines; Joseph LaRoche and Mary Shevnell
Napoleon, d. 11/12/1908 at 0/5; entero colitis; Fraser Laroche and Adeline Gingras
Virginie, d. 9/25/1900 at 12; osteo-sarcoma
Wilfrid, d. 9/12/1906 at 0/4/25; cholera infantum

LAROCHELLE,
Ada Janet, d. 3/23/1937 at 67/3/19; cerebr. hemorrhage
Elizabeth M., d. 1/30/1933 at 30/2; abdominal hemorrhage
Osilda, d. 8/26/1890 at 0/7/13; Telesphore Larochelle (Canada) and Osilda Garselin (Canada)

LAROSE,
Joseph, d. 5/13/1898 at 1; pneumonia; b. Dover; SM

LARRETTE,
William H., d. 9/24/1915 at 0/3/15; malnutrition; Alfred Larrette and Lillian Keato

LARSEN,
Catherine V., d. 9/16/1928 at 25/1/25; pulm. tuberculosis; James Healey and Ellen Carroll

LARVIN [see Lavin],
Dominick E., d. 6/29/1897 at 9; accidental drowning; b. Dover; SM
Thomas W., d. 7/26/1920 at 62; carcinoma of stomach; Dominick Lavin (sic) and Bridget Brennan

LASKEY,
child, d. 4/27/1898 at 0; b. Dover; SM
Alfred D., d. 1/1/1913 at 9/4/1; accidental drowning; Edward Laskey and Mary Hughes
Edward J., d. 7/4/1911 at 44/4/3; heart dilitation; John P. Laskey
Ellen M., d. 1/8/1925 at 78/9/2; apoplexy; Hiram Rogers and Lucinda Wentworth
Frank S., d. 3/15/1918 at 43/7/18 in Somerville, MA; "see card"
Lewis B., d. 8/10/1902 at 55/11/16; angina pectoris; PH
Lewis E., d. 5/24/1899 at 29; tuberculosis; PH
Mary Ellen, d. 10/21/1923 at 56 in Manchester; cerebral hemorrhage; Charles Hughes
Mary J., d. 8/3/1914 at 78/8 in Rochester; cardiac weakness; Thomas Sharpe

LATHROP,
Moses Craft, d. 9/28/1911 at 81/4/7; heart disease; William Lathrop and Elizabeth W. Drake

LATOUR,
Sophie, d. 6/5/1936 at 54/1/1; acute gastritis

LATTIS,
John H., d. 3/29/1898 at 27; tuberculosis; b. Windsor, NB; PH

LAUGHLIN,
Bernard, d. 10/9/1889 at 2/5/18; b. Dover; Patrick Laughlin (Ireland) and Annie Grimes (Dover)
Margaret A., d. 7/25/1894 at 1; oedema of lungs; SM
Mary, d. 11/13/1889 at 1/4/6; b. Dover; Patrick Laughlin (Ireland) and Annie Grimes (Dover)

Mary, d. 1/12/1900 at 68; pleuro-pneumonia; SM
Thomas, d. 8/27/1900 at 47; nephritis; SM

LAUNI,
Achille, d. 6/24/1928 at 38/2/22 in Concord; gen. paral. of insane; Joseph Launi and Antonia Demanbro

LAUZON,
Louis, d. 8/23/1922 at 70/0/7; prim. lateral sclerosis

LAVALLEY,
Alexander, d. 7/2/1922 at 68/11/27; chr. paren. nephritis; Paul Lavalley and Mary -----
Annie, d. 1/14/1915 at 60/1/14; pulmonary tuberculoss; William Johnson and Katie Betie
Philip A., d. 5/21/1918 at 35/10/15 in Boston, MA; typhoid fever

LAVASSEUR,
Alfred R., d. 6/2/1910 at 0/0/24; broncho-pneumonia acute; Eugene Lavasseur and Laura Leblanc
Yvonne, d. 9/3/1911 at 0/2/5; athrepsia; Eugene Lavasseur and Laura Leblanc

LAVIN [see Larvin],
child, d. 11/11/1898 at 0; stillborn; b. Dover; SM
child, d. 2/13/1915 at –; stillborn; Margaret Lavin
Dominick, d. 6/20/1917 at 66; tetanus, etc.; Dominick Lavin and Bridget Cauley
Mary, d. 8/28/1893 at 2; cholera morbus; b. Dover; (Ireland; Ireland)
Mary E., d. 5/12/1895 at 27; quick consumption; b. PEI; SM
Thomas W., d. 5/12/1890 at 4/3/27; Thomas W. Lavin (Ireland) and Ellen Comnesky (PEI)

LAVINE,
child, d. 1/4/1900 at –; stillborn; SM
Mrs. D., d. 1/4/1900 at 32; child-birth; SM
James, d. 9/28/1915 at 83; old age
Lizzie, d. 2/9/1893 at 63; died in Strafford Co. Asylum fire

LAVINGE,
Catherine, d. 12/15/1907 at 65 in Beverly, MA; chronic nephritis

LAVOIE,
Anelle, d. 2/13/1913 at 0/8/2; acute pneumonia; Joseph Lavoie and Caroline Lizotte
Charles, d. 10/6/1925 at 70; cancer of stomach; Augustus Lavoie and Leocardie -----
John, d. 4/3/1931 at 76/3/1; erysipelas of face
Marie U., d. 5/18/1931 at 74/6/8; sarcoma of arm
Marie Y., d. 7/30/1913 at 7/7/12; accident, run over; Joseph Lavoie and Caroline Lizotte

LAW,
Emily, d. 12/15/1890 at 19/2/19; single; Joseph Law (England) and Mary Ridley (England)
Isaac, d. 2/10/1937 at 78/4/9; grippe
Thomas, d. 3/23/1891 at 52; single; John Law (England) and ----- (England)

LAWLESS,
Alice, d. 9/3/1936 at 40/7; pulmonary embolism
Edward, d. 8/12/1924 at 25/6/9 in Wells, ME; accidental drowning
James H., d. 11/25/1910 at 39/9; cirrhosis of liver; William Lawless and Katherine Fahey
Nora, d. 4/24/1932 at 72; carcinoma of rectum
Patrick, d. 6/22/1919 at 57/5; unknown; William Lawless and Catherine Fahey
Willie J., d. 10/23/1903 at 10; railroad accident; SM

LAWLOR,
Alice F., d. 5/7/1925 at 70 in Lowell, MA; cerebral hemorrhage
Bridget, d. 7/17/1912 at 80/6/22 in Somersworth; acute uremia
John C., d. 12/8/1930 at 42/4/18; lobar pneumonia; Edward Lawlor
Kate, d. 7/30/1914 at 60; pulmonary tuberculosis

LAWRENCE,
David, d. 1/5/1889 at 71/8; expressman; married; b. Meredith; Noah Lawrence (Meredith) and Priscilla Marston (Meredith)
Jane A., d. 4/14/1909 at 89/2/25 in Malden, MA; apoplexy

LAWSON,
Charles J. F., d. 4/22/1936 at 50/7*
Mary Drew, d. 7/4/1925 at 28/2 in Boston, MA; asphyxiation by compres.

LAYMOUR,
Mabel A., d. 4/24/1888 at 1/11; b. Dover; P. LayMour (Canada) and Minnie Arvaldy (Canada)

LAYN,
Susan M., d. 6/16/1930 at 94/10/2; arterio sclerosis; Samuel Layn and Elizabeth Hill

LEACH,
child, d. 4/13/1935 at –; stillborn
Charles A., Jr., d. 3/8/1937 at 41/8/12*
John E., d. 5/7/1908 at 78; old age; Dr. J. B. Leach and Rebecca Harrell
Mary A., d. 4/24/1932 at 74; carcinoma of stomach

LEANEY,
John, d. 3/20/1902 at – in Madbury; killed by train

LEAR,
Abbie E., d. 8/26/1892 at 36; chronic intestial nephriti; b. Effingham; (Porter, ME; Stillwater, ME)

LEARY,
Angie May, d. 9/29/1892 at 1; inanition; b. Dover; (Boston, MA; Barrington)
Annie J., d. 9/28/1919 at 48/8/18; chr. intestitial nephritis; Christopher Marley and Margaret Leonard
Benajah H., Jr., d. 7/31/1908 at 0/5/31; cholera infantum; B. H. Leary and Grace V. Smith
James, d. 6/9/1917 at 69; apoplexy
John, d. 11/20/1931 at 73/4/5 in Concord; arterio sclerosis
Joseph H., d. 11/17/1913 at 0/0/27; whooping cough; Benajah Leary and Grace V. Smith
Margaret, d. 8/23/1913 at 73; chr. endocarditis; John Quinn and Bridget ---
Octavia R., d. 5/11/1909 at 59/7/3; cancer; Benajah Howard
Ralph H., d. 6/7/1902 at 21/4/5; valvular disease of heart; buried in Rochester

LEATHERS,
Alphonse D., d. 9/28/1928 at 87/5/11; carcinoma skin; Oliver Leathers and Lucinda Boody
Hulda, d. 12/17/1923 at 78; angina pectoris; Robert Leathers and Elizabeth A. Arlin
Jennie E., d. 7/8/1888 at 38/3; b. Durham
John G., d. 6/20/1902 at 69/2/3; apoplexy; buried in Somersworth

LEAVITT,
child, d. 2/15/1921 at –; stillborn; Lester W. Leavitt and Margaret E. Morris
child, d. 8/2/1924 at –; stillborn; Harold Leavitt and Mary Connelly
Abbie M., d. 11/17/1934 at 64; heart disease
Austin E., d. 9/8/1902 at 50/7/14 in Goffstown; PH
Charles H., d. 9/17/1918 at 65/10/12; cancer of bladder; John C. Leavitt and Hannah Clark
Charles M., d. 11/27/1896 at 48 in Effingham; cerebral apoplexy; b. Effingham; PH
Clara A., d. 5/25/1900 at 52 in San Francisco, CA; tumor of the brain; PH
Clara Augusta, d. 3/14/1923 at 72/11/30; angina pectoris; John Wiggin and Mary Batchelder
Ellen, d. 1/25/1908 at 35; heart disease; Patrick Duffy
Fred E., d. 5/–/1893 at 16; parenchymatous nephrites; b. MA; (NH; MA)
Grace M., d. 3/2/1925 at 39/4/20; chr. parenchymat. neph.; Alexander Shaw and Eunice Littlefield
Jno. H., d. 12/13/1905 at 64; hiccough; buried in Newmarket
Mary, d. 7/30/1927 at 37/6/19; endocarditis; Thomas Leavitt and Helen Duffy
Nancy W., d. 11/2/1891 at 80/5/9; widow; Oliver Johnson and ----- Quimby
Rose, d. 6/27/1908 at 2; heart disease; Thomas Leavitt and Helen Duffey
Sarah R., d. 4/10/1910 at 88/2/28; chronic nephritis; Eliphalet Curry and Hannah Porter
Thomas H., d. 8/21/1931 at 70; myocarditis
William Chester, d. 12/13/1891 at 7/0/19; William C. Leavitt (Swampscott, MA) and Abba M. Berry (Barnstead)

LEBLANC,
Alphonsine, d. 10/4/1906 at 38/10/25; typhoid fever
Donat A., d. 8/19/1916 at 0/6/20; cholera infantum; Joseph Leblanc and Emilda Simoneau
Eugene, d. 11/1/1906 at 22/4/11; typhoid fever
Eugenia, d. 4/11/1905 at 17/7/19; tuberculosis of lungs
Gerard, d. 8/21/1935 at 23/9/1; septicemia
Irene, d. 3/26/1921 at 0/4/4; ac. lobar pneumonia; Joseph LeBlanc and Minnie Simoneau
Joseph F., d. 12/8/1891 at 52; widower; Joseph Leblanc (Canada) and Pauline Laflamme (Canada)
Joseph Henry, d. 9/25/1891 at 0/0/19; Ferdinand Leblanc (Canada) and Eloise Labiussouniere (Canada)
Theophile, d. 4/17/1905 at 51/0/25; heart failure

LEBOSQUE,
Fanny G., d. 7/26/1932 at 83/5/22; angina pectoris

LECLEIR,
Fred, d. 8/29/1888 at 1/1/1; b. Hooksett; Alf. LeCleir (Montreal) and Annie Terreault (Danville, Canada)

LECLERC,
Francois, d. 4/2/1900 at 58; pneumonia
Louis, d. 3/4/1934 at 2/4/8; intestinal obstruction
Sara, d. 6/2/1905 at 48/9/17; Bright's disease; PH

LEDGER,
Benjamin F., d. 4/13/1913 at 54; chronic endocarditis
William, d. 2/25/1931 at 21 in Montreal; bullet wound
William A., d. 11/4/1919 at 41/8/16 in Concord; septicemia; Anthony Ledger and Catherine Vannasen

LEDUE,
Annie, d. 5/3/1891 at 16/10; single; Michael Ladue (NY) and Matilda LaJoy (NY)

LEE,
Arabelle, d. 7/6/1929 at 65/10/15; natural causes; Joseph Witham and Catherine Taylor
Elizabeth, d. 10/6/1903 at 69/0/7 in Lee; cancer; SM
Michael, d. 6/3/1904 at 64/6/3 in Lee; general debility; SM

LEECH,
Frances, d. 8/20/1921 at 71; apoplexy; ----- Newsome

LEFEBVRE,
Alphonse F., d. 4/7/1926 at 0/0/3; premature birth; Alphonse Lefebvre and Catherine Tarney
Clara, d. 6/4/1914 at 16/4/12; typhoid fever; Wilfred Lefebvre and Mary Legasse
Georgianna, d. 1/8/1910 at 64/8; cerebral hemorrhage; Olivier Douville and Adelaide Vallee
Germaine P., d. 1/17/1933 at 89/10/9; carcinoma of throat
Gracia, d. 9/30/1906 at 0/1; marasmus
Joseph A., d. 9/21/1903 at 0/0/3; purpura hemorrhagica
Robert A., d. 7/20/1911 at 0/10/16; acute entero-colitis; Wilfred Lefebvre and Mary Legasse

LEGACE,
Albert, d. 4/7/1919 at 17/7/23; tuberculosis of kidneys; Pierre Legace and Albina Bachaud

Alfred, d. 1/12/1899 at 2; diphtheria; PH
Alphonso, d. 9/12/1903 at 58/7/17; cerebral hemorrhage
Godefroy H., d. 1/16/1905 at 1/3/5; pneumonia

LEGASE,
Albina, d. 3/24/1932 at 68/10/23; chronic myocarditis

LEGASSE,
Francis, d. 5/9/1892 at 6; diphtheria; b. Canada; (Canada; Canada)
Vitalene, d. 12/12/1920 at 72/11/12; cerebral hemorrhage; Francois
    Levelle and Teresa -----

LEGER,
Blesse, d. 9/25/1905 at 52/2/11; cerebral hemorrhage
Domitile, d. 8/25/1907 at 52/11; cancer of breast; Ambroise Dupries and
    Nathalie Landry
Joseph Eric, d. 9/9/1892 at 1; entero-colitis; b. MA; (NB; NB)
William, d. 1/7/1909 at –; stillborn; William J. Leger and Margaret Hughes

LEGG,
Abiah M., d. 12/25/1925 at 87/11/12; bronchial pneumonia
Lucien B., d. 4/19/1896 at 85; congestion of lungs; b. Dover; PH
Pricilla A., d. 2/10/1917 at 76/0/16 in Cambridge, MA; myocarditis

LEGIRE,
Marie Blanche, d. 8/7/1891 at 7/7/1; Bliss Legire (NB) and Blumatele
    Duppee (NB)

LEGRO,
Elmira M., d. 3/6/1918 at 78/0/11; broncho pneumonia; William Langley
    and Sarah Dearborn

LEHAY,
Joseph, d. 11/8/1907 at 38; concussion of brain

LEIGH,
Ann, d. 5/15/1905 at 72/11/1; pneumonia; PH
Charles E., d. 10/11/1898 at 50 in Somersworth; heart failure; PH
Fred W., d. 2/2/1896 at 36; disease of brain; b. Biddeford, ME; PH
George J., d. 1/9/1924 at 60/9/16 in Rochester; pneumonia
John, d. 8/18/1887 at 61/9/6; mill operative; married; b. England; Peter
    Leigh (England)
Sabra, d. 3/20/1889 at 93/11/26; housewife; widow; b. Rollinsford; T.
    Stackpole (Rollinsford) and Eunice Roberts (Rollinsford)

LEIGHEY,
William, d. 9/20/1887 at 28/10/13 in Farmington

LEIGHTON,
Amasa R., d. 1/18/1899 at 63 in Farmington; pneumonia; PH
Byron, d. 9/23/1926 at 86/11/26; chr. parench. nephritis; Adam Leighton and Julia A. -----
Charles W., d. 9/17/1929 at 77/3/6 in Chelsea, MA; carcinoma; Nahala Leighton and Sarah A. -----
Clarinda C., d. 12/20/1893 at 76; rheumatism; b. Middleton
Daniel M., d. 1/27/1897 at 74; shock; b. VT; PH
Drusilla D., d. 5/8/1895 at 69; cancer; b. Frankfort, ME; PH
Etta R., d. 5/21/1921 at 77/10/23 in N. Berwick, ME; lobar pneumonia
Forrest L., d. 11/28/1923 at 61 in S. Berwick, ME; angina pectoris
Freddie, d. 4/23/1891 at 0/2; Charles W. Leighton (Alton) and Lulu L. Blethen (CA)
H. H., d. 5/1/1904 at 73/3/20 in York, ME; pneumonia; PH
Hannah E., d. 1/29/1911 at 69/10/15; cardiac dilitation; George Leighton and Emily Roberts
Hiram K., d. 6/17/1932 at 74/1/22; cerebral hemorrhage
James B., d. 11/3/1922 at 0/3/9; acute indigestion; James B. Leighton and Edith Beaulieu
James W., d. 10/6/1917 at 67/1/1; acute alcoholism; Joseph L. Leighton and Clarinda Varney
John, d. 5/15/1889 at 91/2/4; farmer; married; b. Strafford; Isaac Leighton and ----- Twombly (Madbury)
John H., d. 6/6/1902 at 79/5 in Searsport, ME; cancer of bladder and prostate; PH
Lavinia S., d. 10/29/1892 at 81; consumption
Lewis L., d. 2/1/1891 at 60/5/12; married; Jedediah Leighton (Farmington) and Sally Murray (Farmington)
Mary, d. 12/5/1910 at 73/6/5; old age; H. K. Gould and Mary Ingalls
Mary Emma, d. 1/21/1926 at 73/1/15 in N. Berwick, ME; broncho pneumonia
Mary S., d. 2/21/1928 at 71/11/13 in Portsmouth; ptomaine poisoning
Ralph L., d. 4/2/1932 at 44/8/20 in Concord; paresis
Ruth A., d. 4/14/1933 at 73; general degeneration
Samuel H., d. 2/7/1901 at 58/4; pneumonia; PH
Susan B., d. 6/8/1900 at 66 in Deerfield; chr. pul. tuberculosis; PH
Susie E., d. 1/9/1926 at 65/7/16; chronic endocarditis; Thomas Tabbutt and Thankful McCaslin

LEITH,
Luther W., d. 2/27/1907 at 0/8/19; heart failure; Henry C. Leith and Lodo R. Perkins

LEIZER,
Alice J., d. 10/11/1929 at 80/5/28; carcinoma of cheek; Thadius C. Bowers and Hannah Willey
Grace A. B., d. 5/14/1920 at 36/2/27; sarcoma; John E. Leizer and Alice J. Bowers
John E., d. 5/30/1914 at 66/0/29; cystitis; Jacob Leizer

LEMAY,
Gerald, d. 1/16/1929 at 8/5/1; cere. spinal meningitis; Leven Lemay and Eva Renault
Jeremiah, d. 8/5/1891 at 0/4/12; Philip Lemay (Canada) and Alphonsine Dube (Canada)

LEMIEUX,
Ramona, d. 11/13/1933 at –; stillborn

LEMPKE,
Corinne, d. 4/27/1935 at 32/0/13; tuberculosis pulmonary

LENAGH,
Bridget, d. 11/27/1904 at 41/11; Bright's disease; SM
Peter, d. 8/10/1918 at 56 in Lawrence, MA; cancer of stomach

LENNON,
Elizabeth, d. 1/26/1912 at 0/2/17; acute indigestion; Frank Lennon and Mary Gologhy
Evelyn, d. 4/13/1912 at 0/5/5; malnutrition; Frank Lennon and Mary Gologhy
Frank, d. 10/12/1933 at 62/4/8 in Washington; cerebral hemorrhage
James R., d. 12/24/1926 at 0/0/3; hemorrhage disease; Francis Lennon and Ellen Clark
Mary, d. 12/13/1915 at 69/5/11; apoplexy; Samuel Stevenson and Ann Smith
Robert J., d. 1/2/1906 at 17/5; cerebro spinal meningitis; PH
Robert J., d. 5/21/1915 at 0/2/11; athrepsia; Frank Lennon and Mary Gallagher
Samuel J., d. 2/16/1935 at 50/7/13; cerebral hemorrhage

LEONARD,
Ella B., d. 3/1/1907 at 55/2 in Hyde Park, MA; tubercular ostitis

LEPENCER,
Lea, d. 11/24/1889 at 2/8/22; b. Canada; Philip Lepencer (Canada) and Lena Langloin (Canada)

LEPONSE,
Lea, d. 11/26/1889 at 3; b. Canada; Bernard Leponse (Canada) and Lena Blanchard (Canada)

LEROY,
Mary A., d. 12/17/1891 at 64/7/23; widow; John Christie (NB) and Mary E. Gates (Gardner, MA)

LESCO,
Napoleon, d. 10/26/1935 at 65; gastric hemorrhage

LESLEY,
Mabel, d. 12/29/1891 at 2/0/21; Frank Lesley (Newmarket) and Grace Meserve (Newington)

LESLIE,
David H., d. 2/21/1893 at 32; phthisis pulmonalis; b. Newmarket; (England; England)
Eliza J., d. 4/22/1900 at –; pneumonia; PH

LESPERANCE,
Richard, d. 1/7/1934 at 0/6/12; accidental asphyxia

LESSARD,
Paul, d. 9/24/1920 at 74/9/17; rupture blood vessel; Jacques Lessard and Modeste Gilbert

LESTER,
Thomas G., d. 2/21/1906 at 39/9/5 in Boston, MA; septicemia; PH

LETENDRE,
Celina, d. 5/16/1933 at 43/8/17; empyema

LETOURNEAU,
child, d. 10/22/1917 at –; stillborn; Narcisse Letourneau and Rose Fallon
George, d. 3/31/1918 at 1/9/29; acute gastric enteritis; Nelson Letourneau and Rose Talon
Nelson, d. 4/13/1934 at 52/11/26; coronary thrombosis
Wilfred A., d. 6/4/1921 at 12/0/28; endocarditis; Narcisse Letourneau and Rose Talon

LEVAILLE,
Bruno, d. 6/20/1915 at 28; internal hemorrhage; Joseph Levaille and Mathilde Salvas

LEVEILLEE,
Fidele, d. 2/20/1907 at 67; cerebral hemorrhage; Francois Leveillee and Therese Boileau

LEVEQUE,
Delmine, d. 10/7/1918 at 21/1/13; pulmonary tuberculosis; Maurice Leveque and Delmire St. Lawrence

LEVESQUE,
Arthur J., d. 4/13/1934 at 50/9/11; carcinoma of bladder
Joseph, d. 12/15/1935 at 65/2/3; accidental drowning
Robert C., d. 2/28/1920 at 1; lobar pneumonia; Arthur J. Levesque and Louise St. Jean

LEVVIE,
child, d. 11/9/1923 at 0/0/9 in Somersworth; gastro enteritis

LEWIS,
child, d. 7/8/1925 at –; premature birth; Frank W. Lewis and Annie A. Sagar
Belinda, d. 1/18/1905 at 56/0/16; consumption; PH
Cora G., d. 7/7/1936 at 55/5/11 in Portland, ME; chr. myocar. hyper.
Emma E., d. 4/9/1924 at 57; arterio sclerosis
Emma M., d. 1/20/1931 at 56/10; lobar pneumonia
George W., d. 2/24/1931 at 66/8/6; lobar pneumonia
Harry, d. 8/10/1929 at 74/2; cerebral hemorrhage; Jonathan Jenness and Mary Smith
Ida Ella, d. 12/27/1913 at 58 in Medford, MA; lobar pneumonia; John W. Pray and Harriet Long
Joseph, d. 4/19/1897 at 88 in Kennebunk, ME; la grippe
Joseph B., d. 8/19/1910 at 48/9/19; diffuse myelitis; Joseph S. Lewis and Sophronia Lear

LIBBEY,
Abby W., d. 4/26/1893 at 69; pneumonia; b. Farmington; (-----; Rochester)
Adeline, d. 3/9/1898 at 67; disease of heart; b. Strafford; PH
Annie W., d. 3/8/1923 at 68/2/12; cerebral hemorrhage; Edward Wing and Ann Fuller
Charles L., d. 2/9/1893 at 33; died in Strafford Co. Asylum fire
Dora B., d. 3/2/1904 at 48/10/12; nephritis; buried in So. Portland, ME
Elizabeth H., d. 9/13/1897 at 66; diarrhea; b. Dover; PH
Ella E., d. 2/9/1915 at 64/3/9 in Barrington; tuberculosis of lungs
George F., d. 4/23/1898 at 64; Bright's disease; PH

Ida B., d. 8/15/1930 at 68/7/10; cerebral hemorrhage; James D. Hall and Sarah E. Bunker
Joseph, d. 6/6/1908 at --; natural causes
Joseph T. S., d. 3/18/1907 at 83/4/18; senility; Paul Libbey and Elizabeth Sherbourn
Lydia J., d. 1/25/1911 at 87/6/9 in Auburn; old age
Mary, d. 6/11/1891 at 72/1/14 in So. Berwick, ME; widow; Solomon Neil (So. Berwick, ME) and Abigail Lord (So. Berwick, ME)
Mary L., d. 5/18/1888 at 0/11; b. Cape Elizabeth, ME; Frank M. Libbey (Gorham, ME) and Isadore Libbey (Cape Elizabeth, ME)
Morris, d. 7/8/1888 at 0/0/18; b. Dover; Robert Libbey (Dover) and Bridget McCarty (NY)

LIBBY,
Adin, d. 12/19/1932 at 77/10/9; coronary embolism
Clara L., d. 11/6/1926 at 81/0/20; cancer of uterus; Abel Whitney and Sarah Cole
E. Belle, d. 10/7/1925 at 53/3/29; chronic nephritis; Henry L. Wilkins and Nellie S. Howells
Fernald, d. 3/11/1917 at 79/1/19; senility; William Libby and Hannah Gould
Frank M., d. 3/27/1927 at 76/11/16; nephritis; Benjamin F. Libby and Lavina P. Whitney
Harriet D., d. 11/29/1913 at 65 in Boston, MA; carcinoma
Irving, d. 6/30/1910 at 33/10/14; acute pulm. tuberculosis; John Libby and Sabina Dillingham
Joshua, d. 9/23/1935 at 55/2/8; tuberculosis of rectum
Lucy E., d. 3/29/1915 at 73/2/3; pneumonia; Thomas L. Skillin and Eliza A. Libby
Mary A., d. 2/2/1932 at 85/11/24; arterio sclerosis
Nancy M., d. 7/25/1917 at 84/1/6; senility; ----- Miles
Virginia R., d. 11/20/1929 at 67 in Boston, MA; uremia, etc.
William R., d. 8/6/1924 at 60/4; valvular heart disease; Rufus Libby and Johanna Lord

LIGHT,
Joseph A., d. 7/12/1892 at --; spina bifida; b. Dover; (NB; NB)

LIGUETE,
Adolph, d. 9/20/1935 at 69/9/6; angina pectoris

LILLEY,
Kate, d. 8/11/1900 at <1; cholera infantum
Margaret V., d. 12/5/1905 at 14; general tuberculosis; SM

LILLIE,
Richard, d. 7/27/1929 at –; cancer of larynx

LILLY,
Annie, d. 1/21/1891 at 22/11/3; single; Charles Lilly (Ireland) and Mary McGerry (Ireland)
Bridget A., d. 6/20/1911 at 58/4/10; gastric ulcer; Maurice McCarthy and Margaret Sinnott
David, d. 3/18/1910 at 45/2/15; fibroid phthisis; Charles Lilly and Mary McGarry
Robert, d. 9/21/1898 at 40; consumption; b. Ireland; SM
Robert M., d. 11/27/1918 a 28 in Lawrence, MA; influenza

LIMBERIS,
Nicholas, d. 7/26/1912 at 33; suicide by shooting; George Limberis and Vasilo -----

LINDBORN,
Ingride, d. 4/15/1934 at 0/11/27; meningitis

LINDQUEST,
Felix, d. 1/10/1917 at –; accidental

LINDSAY,
Arthur R., d. 2/10/1917 at 35/0/28 in S. Berwick, ME; struck by R.R. train
Frank W., d. 12/28/1920 at –; cardiac asthma
Georgiana, d. 2/4/1896 at 21; eclampsy; b. Canada; buried in Canada
Inez Houston, d. 9/26/1910 at 79/8/11; cancer of liver; ----- Houston
Mathilda, d. 1/27/1896 at 35; anaemia pernicious; b. Canada; SM

LINDSEY,
LeRoy H., d. 7/5/1937 at 53/10/12; broncho pneumonia

LINNEHAN,
Sarah L., d. 3/11/1931 at 68; acute nephritis
Thomas E., d. 9/11/1923 at 78; R. R. accident; Jeremiah Linnehan and Bridget -----

LINSCOTT,
Albert W., d. 7/7/1930 at 51/10/20; carcinoma bladder; Albert F. Linscott and Josephine -----
Samuel J., d. 1/2/1934 at 51/0/11; monoxide gas poisoning

LISABELLE,
Rosalie, d. 3/30/1903 at 76/6; cerebral embolism

LIST,
Annie F., d. 9/6/1901 at 19/5/1 in Barrington; pulmonary tuberculosis; PH
Caroline B., d. 5/27/1892 at 7; scarlatina; b. Dover; (Saxony, Germany; Dover)
Charles H., d. 4/13/1901 at 57/11/28; heart disease; PH
Lizzie J., d. 11/22/1897 at 42; dilatation of heart; b. Dover; PH
Sarah F., d. 5/31/1902 at 14/10/4 in Pittsfield; consumption; PH

LITTLE,
son, d. 3/12/1888 at –; b. Dover; Frank Little (Pembroke, ME) and Jennie C. Baker (Dover)
son, d. 9/12/1889 at 0/0/8; b. Dover; Frank E. Little (Pembroke, ME) and Jennie C. Baker (Dover)

LITTLEFIELD,
A. L., d. 2/4/1898 at 58; heart disease; b. Lebanon, ME; PH
Aaron R., d. 5/19/1908 at 69/11/22; cancer of liver; John Littlefield and Polly Williams
Abbott L., d. 7/31/1890 at 36/5/15; married; James Littlefield (Wells, ME) and Sarah C. Brown (Gilmanton)
Adoniram, d. 4/9/1901 at 66/1/16; disease of heart and kidneys; PH
Albert H., d. 4/22/1890 at 68/0/13; married; Ralph Littlefield (Wells, ME) and Olive Edes (Wells, ME)
Alpheus, d. 9/8/1930 at 84/7/6; chronic nephritis; John Littlefield and Polly Williams
Alphonso E., d. 2/13/1912 at 61/10/12; pneumonia; John Littlefield and Polly Williams
Asa H., d. 9/12/1903 at 83/4/16; nephritis; PH
Betsey E., d. 2/9/1912 at 73/1/18; apoplexy; James Gray and Joanna ----
Caroline, d. 9/16/1894 at 68; cancerous tumor; b. Sanford, ME; buried in Kennebunk, ME
Cyrus, d. 4/1/1914 at 77/2/5; enlarged prostate; James Littlefield and Sarah Bean
Daniel, d. 1/10/1892 at 72; inanition from gastric catarrh; b. Strafford; (Strafford; Strafford)
David F., d. 7/21/1896 at 72; pneumonia; b. Strafford; PH
Edward A., d. 11/19/1923 at 68/3/21 in Somerville, MA; chronic myocarditis
Edward E., d. 11/17/1905 at 76/0/23; cerebral thrombosis; PH
Eleanor K., d. 2/22/1901 at 58/2/6; ptomaine poisoning; buried in Kennebunk, ME

Ellen T., d. 10/26/1923 at 59/7/27; carcinoma of pancreas; Samuel B. Horton and Elizabeth Tully

Emma A., d. 11/17/1933 at 78/5/29; arteriosclerosis

Erwin M., d. 8/16/1931 at 48/9/5 in Providence, RI; pneumonia empyema

Frank O., d. 10/13/1931 at 80/1/26 in Everett, MA; chronic nephritis

Fred I., d. 2/1/1896 at – in Helena, MT

George A., d. 10/17/1919 at 64/11; cancer; Joseph B. Littlefield and Elizabeth Jellison

George W., d. 8/26/1890 at 19/6/13; single; Jonathan Littlefield (Wells, ME) and Mary Smith (Wells, ME)

Gladys M., d. 4/3/1899 at –; malnutrition; PH

Hannah L., d. 8/20/1930 at 97/2/5 in Highland Park, MI; chronic myocarditis

Harriet B., d. 7/18/1904 at 84/6/15 in Boston, MA; senility; PH

Harriet J., d. 5/4/1910 at 66/4/3; nephritis; William G. Webster and Hannah Foss

Hartley, d. 1/26/1917 at 69/3/12; cancer of intestines; Ithamar Littlefield and Lucinda -----

Henry, d. 5/6/1917 at 58; chr. Bright's disease

Horace, d. 8/25/1898 at 80; b. Wells, ME; PH

Jean O., d. 5/9/1916 at 0/4/20 in Rochester; convulsions; William Littlefield and Ruth Pollard

John L., d. 9/11/1937 at 69/4/3; leukemia

John M., d. 11/14/1899 at 74; old age with heart disease; PH

Josiah A., d. 6/26/1919 at 64/2/28 in Rochester; carcinoma of stomach; John Littlefield and Polly Williams

Julia F., d. 4/30/1914 at 54/7/29; internal cancer; Ivory Cheney and Sophia -----

Louisa A., d. 6/19/1905 at 80 in So. Berwick, ME; uraemia; PH

Lucie C., d. 3/31/1921 at 72 in Boston, MA; chronic cholelithiasis

Lydia, d. 8/2/1913 at 68/7/3; senile dementia; Stephen Hanson and Martha A. Varney

Mabelle E., d. 4/17/1923 at 45/11/4; chr. inter. nephritis; Edward J. Littlefield and Vevia Hubbard

Martin J., d. 8/5/1905 at 0/6/2; cholera infantum; PH

Mary D., d. 1/29/1892 at 73; pneumonia; b. Farmington; (Farmington; Rochester)

Mary D., d. 11/25/1897 at 73 in Madbury; organic disease of heart; b. Dover; PH

Mary E., d. 11/12/1892 at 64; phthisis pulmonalis; b. Dover; (York, ME; New Durham)

Mary L., d. 11/23/1932 at 79 in Framingham, MA; hemiplegia

Mary M., d. 2/20/1931 at 79/8/2; chr. valv. heart dis.

Maurice C., d. 7/21/1917 at 65/10/16 in Nobscot, MA; cancer of prostate gland

Mercy, d. 7/30/1899 at 83; old age with scrofula; PH
Nellie, d. 9/29/1895 at 35; brain lesion; b. Lebanon, ME; PH
Rose M., d. 10/17/1925 at 63/8/13 in Somerville, MA; fracture of skull
Sarah H., d. 12/28/1893 at 71; pneumonia; b. Barrington; (Barrington; Barrington)
Sarah P., d. 2/13/1905 at 74/9/27; senile gangrene; PH
Solomon C., d. 4/5/1922 at 63/6/13; pericarditis; Moses R. Littlefield and Dolly A. Cummins
Susan E., d. 3/2/1902 at 82/0/15; apoplexy; PH
Susan M., d. 9/10/1907 at 76/2/6; senile meningitis; Theodore Littlefield and Betsy Saltmarsh
William C., d. 9/14/1913 at 29/2/4; accidental electrocution; Charles W. Littlefield and Sarah Cousins
William E., d. 3/20/19210 at 32/5/19; angina pectoris
William J., d. 4/6/1909 at 44/11; shock; Josiah Littlefield and Mary A. Hanson
William P., d. 12/28/1893 at 71; cancer; b. Farmington
Zelpha R., d. 8/2/1904 at 51/3/14 in Boston, MA; phthisis pulmonalis; PH

LIVERMORE,
Charles F., d. 3/25/1889 at 65 in New York, NY
Walter H., d. 8/10/1925 at 63/0/16 in N. Acton, MA; cerebral hemorrhage

LIVINGSTON,
Margaret, d. 1/23/1908 at 78/3/8; old age; Adam Cochrane and Margaret McGregor

LIVINGSTONE,
James, d. 6/20/1888 at 54; weaver; b. England; James Livingstone (England) and Catherine

LIVSEY,
Charles H., d. 4/20/1904 at 50/1/8; liver disease; PH

LOCHRAN,
John L., d. 10/6/1898 at 2; broncho-pneumonia; b. Dover; SM

LOCK,
J. S., Jr., d. 4/19/1888 at 28/8 in Amesbury, MA

LOCKE [see Judson],
child, d. 6/22/1914 at –; stillborn; Stanley Locke and Isabelle Chesley
child, d. 10/19/1930 at –; stillborn; S. E. Locke and Hazel L. Stimpson

Albert W., d. 5/16/1913 at 41/9/7; tuberculosis; Samuel Locke and Lydia Savery
Annie, d. 8/9/1919 at 53/1/11; pelvic carcinoma; Andrew Nute and Elizabeth McKone
Arthur L., d. 12/30/1931 at 63/8/9; fracture of skull
Charles, d. 9/10/1918 at 59/8/10; colitis; Howard Locke and Emma A. Wentworth
Darius W., d. 3/14/1920 at 70/10/11; cerebral hemorrhage; S. B. Locke and Sarah Canney
Elizabeth, d. 3/20/1893 at 35; congestion of brain; b. Canada; (Ireland; Ireland)
Elizabeth Nute, d. 4/18/1921 at 77/9/22; broncho pneumonia; Andrew Nute and Elizabeth McKone
Frank, d. 7/24/1926 at 59/2/12; cancer of lower jaw
Harriet N., d. 2/19/1907 at 79/9/9 in Amesbury, MA; pneumonia
Hattie J., d. 10/25/1893 at 33; shock
Lucy C., d. 9/26/1895 at 53; pulmonary consumption; b. Barrington; buried in Barrington
Martha A., d. 7/28/1902 at 63/5/14; diabetes; buried in Barrington
Mary A., d. 4/22/1892 at 15; choloratic anaemia; b. Dover; (NH; NH)
Mary E., d. 4/29/1891 at 79/4/12; widow; Zachari Beals (Portsmouth) and Hannah Taulton (So. Newmarket)
Mary F., d. 2/28/1917 at 69/7/21 in Somersworth; lobar pneumonia
Oliver B., d. 4/11/1911 at 76/1/11 in Haverhill, MA; angina pectoris
Samuel S., d. 11/27/1913 at 78/11/2 in Barrington; acute bronchitis
Thomas D., d. 6/27/1893 at 62; paralysis; b. US; (US; US)
Walter E., d. 1/3/1887 at 27/7/13; harness maker; single; b. Rochester; Samuel Locke (Rochester) and Lydia A. Seavey (Rochester)
William H., d. 5/20/1896 at 61 in Amesbury, MA; heart disease

LOCKETT,
daughter, d. 5/26/1888 at 0/0/1; b. Dover; William C. Lockett
Francis M., d. 7/4/1889 at 20/9/19; housewife; married; b. England; John Watson (England) and Mary Goodwin (England)
Sophia, d. 4/13/1888 at 62; widow; b. England; S. Halden (England)
William Calvin, d. 8/11/1891 at 25 in Passaic, NJ
Willie C., d. 5/28/1893 at 1; meningitis

LOCKWOOD,
Frank H., d. 9/19/1903 at 25/0/1; typhoid fever; PH
Hannah S., d. 8/5/1934 at 86/5/15; apoplexy
J. Henry, d. 1/10/1934 at 57/1/3; lobar pneumonia
John, d. 12/21/1904 at 63/7/7; uraemia; PH
Selina, d. 4/19/1896 at 62; senile gangrene; b. England; PH

LOHNAS,
Walter H., d. 7/3/1904 at 39; typhoid fever; SM

LOMBARD,
Albert L., d. 10/7/1907 at 33/11/4; probably heart disease; Ferdinand Lombard and Mary E. Wildes
Elmer H., d. 8/9/1937 at 67/4/16; cerebr. hemorrhage
Ferdinand, d. 9/13/1916 at 66 in Concord; myocardial insufficiency; John Lombard
Mary E., d. 3/28/1929 at 77/9/11; bronchial pneumonia; Ephraim Wiles
Sarah E., d. 10/11/1916 at 47/0/3; acute appendicitis; Henry Hallworth and Harriet Cowan

LONDREAU,
Paul, d. 6/5/1890 at 0/20/3; Joseph Londreau (Canada) and Leontine King (Canada)

LONG,
child, d. 5/16/1906 at – in Newmarket; stillborn; SM
Ann M., d. 4/17/1927 at 66/11/11 in Newmarket; acute nephritis
Annie, d. 11/19/1896 at 25; phthisis pulmonalis; b. Durham; SM
Catherine, d. 3/8/1911 at 65; diabetes mellitus; Patrick McMullen and Nancy Grimes
Catherine, d. 10/4/1918 at 94; old age; Dennis Canning
Clarence, d. 1/14/1897 at 3; meningitis; b. Dover; SM
Frank J., d. 3/14/1911 at 34/0/20; acute pneumonia; John Long and Catherine McMullen
John D., d. 11/23/1926 at 60; acute pancreatitis; James Long and Catherine Carnon
Lydia, d. 11/1/1906 at 13/4/17 in Rollinsford; septo meningitis; PH
Matthew, d. 7/21/1930 at 58; cancer of intestine; John Long and Catherine McMullen

LONGLEY,
Lawrence O., d. 3/21/1918 at 22; illuminating gas poison

LONGVEIN,
Lavina, d. 6/10/1893 at –; cholera infantum; b. Dover; (Canada; Canada)

LOOMIS,
Oliver S., d. 8/1/1904 at 66/4/15; heart disease; PH

LOONEY,
Annie, d. 9/13/1888 at 17/6/6; student; b. St. Johns; John Looney (St. Johns) and Eliza Eustace (S. Johns, NB)
Elizabeth, d. 2/27/1911 at 50; tuberculosis
Frank E., d. 6/1/1909 at 27; tuberculosis; John Looney and Elizabeth Eustas
Hannah, d. 1/21/1908 at 29/2/3; pulmonary tuberculosis; John Looney and Elizabeth Eustis
John, d. 2/28/1928 at –; arterio sclerosis
Timothy, d. 4/21/1892 at 55; phthisis; b. St. John, NB; (Ireland; Ireland)

LORD,
child, d. 11/21/1904 at –; stillborn; buried in Somersworth
Abbie F., d. 9/10/1890 at 42/11/5; married; Otis Baker (Rochester) and Lavina Hayes (Dover)
Alphonso G., d. 2/28/1900 at 53; pneumonia; PH
Alvin, d. 4/9/1903 at 59/11; progressive heart failure; SM
Anna A., d. 9/7/1928 at 65/0/24; chr. endocarditis; J. T. Young and Elizabeth L. -----
Annie M., d. 1/26/1903 at –; pulmonary phthisis; buried in No. Berwick, ME
Betsey A., d. 1/30/1893 at 56; heart failure; b. Dover
Charles, d. 2/22/1934 at 74/11/2; cerebral hemorrhage
Charles E., d. 11/17/1896 at 66; chron. disease of heart; b. Rollinsford; PH
Charles F., d. 4/19/1891 at – in Washington, DC; widower; John Lord (NH) and Susan Palmer (Milton)
Charles F., d. 6/17/1927 at 71/4/27 in Rochester; angina pectoris; Martin L. Lord and Lavina Varney
Eliza A., d. 11/29/1912 at 83/7/3; general debility; Josiah Calef and Eliza Nichols
Ella A., d. 8/13/1930 at 73/10/17; asthma; Luther Horne and Abbie Downing
Frank E., d. 1/9/1900 at 25; pneumonia; buried in Rochester
Frank H., d. 1/15/1932 at 66/2; septicemia
Fred, d. 7/16/1933 at 67; acute gastritis
George B., d. 4/19/1910 at 80; senility
George B., d. 12/1/1937 at 67/2/29; tuberculosis
Hannah, d. 6/6/1904 at 59 in Cambridge, MA; cancer of uterus; buried in Watertown, MA
Hattie, d. 1/29/1892 at 24; inflammation of bowels; b. Dover; (Alton; Farmington)
Hattie A., d. 3/17/1904 at 33; pneumonia; buried in East Rochester
Helena J., d. 8/14/1911 at 32/8/27; pulmonary tuberculosis; Thomas McClintock and Helen G. Fife
Kate, d. 8/19/1895 at 29; heart disease; b. Dover; SM
Leola R., d. 9/25/1900 at 21; tuberculosis; buried in Somersworth

Lillian E., d. 9/25/1918 at 0/1/20; acute lobar pneumonia; Arthur W. Lord and Ruth Jorgeson
Martin L., d. 10/12/1902 at 69/0/20; angina pectoris; buried in Somersworth
Moses C., d. 9/9/1890 at 63/11/16; married; Nathan Lord (ME) and Mary Chapman (ME)
Parker W., d. 4/26/1903 at 53/10/26 in Boston, MA; phthisis pulmonalis; PH
Rose Louise, d. 1/7/1912 at 42/6/21; surgical shock; Adolph Laplante and Matilda Mayo
Ruth A., d. 1/27/1919 at 6/7/1; lobar pneumonia; Ernest C. Lord and Nettie W. Jones
Susan E., d. 4/3/1918 at 76/1/20 in Concord; hemiplegia left; George W. Varney and Mariam Hodgdon

LORING,
Harriet A., d. 12/21/1930 at 89/3/21; arterio sclerosis; John W. Loring and Harriet Leach

LOTHROP,
child, d. 3/29/1909 at –; congenital heart malformation; Thomas W. Lothrop and M. Gertrude Colbath
child, d. 10/11/1914 at 0/0/1; premature birth; Thomas W. Lothrop and M. Gertrude Colbath
Carrie A., d. 5/11/1922 at 42/8/1; chronic endocarditis; Charles P. Andrews and Mary L. Drew
Elizabeth S. B., d. 12/6/1905 at 87/11/27; angina pectoris; PH
Harold, d. 3/29/1908 at 0/0/9; premature birth (6 m.); Thomas W. Lothrop and M. Gertrude Colbath
James E., d. 3/6/1907 at 80/3/6; heart disease; Daniel Lothrop and Sophia Horne
Llewellyn D., d. 9/21/1922 at 36/3/21 in Boston, MA; broncho pneumonia
Mary E., d. 4/24/1896 at 72; herniplegia; PH
Mary E., d. 10/2/1916 at 84/6/27; pneumonia; Joseph Morrill and Nancy Quimby
Mathew Henry, d. 6/7/1922 at 71/0/5 in Madbury; endocarditis
Olive M., d. 6/21/1923 at 67/8/19 in Melrose, MA; carcinoma - dementia
Thomas W., d. 3/29/1937 at 60/3/10*; b. Dover
William D., Jr., d. 6/5/1917 at 0/1/16; malnutrition; William D. Lothrop and Bertha G. Davis

LOUGEE,
child, d. 6/23/1920 at –; stillborn; Harold F. Lougee and Dulcie M. Hayes
Clara, d. 3/28/1918 at 71/10/16; dilatation of heart; John Twombly and Eliza -----

Frank B., d. 10/23/1914 at 57/7/15; pellagra; George W. Lougee and Mary J. Cannon
Lyman, d. 6/24/1911 at 92/11/18; old age; John Lougee and Nancy ----
Lyman B., d. 11/12/1895 at 66; abdominal cancer; b. Gilmanton; PH
Mary A., d. 2/1/1914 at 57/5/23; valvular disease of heart; John Akin and Mary A. ----
Mary A., d. 5/15/1923 at 90/0/11 in Rochester; cerebral hemorrhage
Nancy, d. 1/31/1907 at 83/6/7; old age; Benjamin Durgin and Comfort Caswell
William H., d. 1/7/1924 at 83/10/13 in Pasadena, CA; carcinoma of prostate gland; William Lougee and Drusilla Stevens

LOUGH,
Ida Frances, d. 3/18/1920 at 39/1/18; acidosis; James Morralley and Mary Moran

LOUGHLIN,
child, d. 6/11/1901 at --; stillborn; SM
Annie, d. 7/1/1925 at 65; arterio sclerosis
Annie M., d. 6/13/1935 at 43/5/8; accidental electrocution
Bernard J., d. 6/1/1915 at 29; tuberculosis; Peter Loughlin and Bridget Parle
Catherine, d. 1/13/1926 at 67; chronic myocarditis; Patrick Loughlin and Catherine Grimes
Edward G., d. 8/11/1915 at 0/6/12; gastro enteritis; James E. Loughlin and Ethel V. Graham
Ellen G., d. 8/12/1934 at 37/8/11; puerperal septicemia
Hannah, d. 11/4/1887 at 61; married; b. Ireland; (Ireland; Ireland)
Helen Ann, d. 3/24/1927 at 8; broncho pneumonia; James Loughlin and Ethel Graham
James, d. 2/11/1933 at 57/6/26; angina pectoris
Margaret A., d. 12/21/1937 at --; undulant fever
Michael, d. 7/18/1915 at 58; valv. heart disease; James Loughlin and Katherine N. Bennett
Patrick, d. 1/9/1914 at 52; septic arthritis; Bernard Loughlin and Mary McShane
Peter, d. 7/4/1910 at 55/0/8; apoplexy; Mary McShane
Peter, d. 10/27/1929 at 17 in Boston, MA; rheumatic heart dis.; James Loughlin and Ethel Graham

LOUGHRIN,
Daniel, d. 6/12/1898 at 46; cirrhosis of liver; b. Ireland; SM
Margaret, d. 3/24/1893 at 52; chronic inflammation of spine; (Ireland; Ireland)

LOUKAREA,
Frosa, d. 7/17/1909 at 0/2/22; cholera infantum; George Loukarea and Sofia Feras

LOVEJOY,
Etta, d. 6/20/1919 at 60/1; apoplexy; James A. Cornwell and Maria Buckman
George A., d. 8/11/1890 at 6/7/3; George W. Lovejoy (US) and Etta Walker (US)
Ruth M., d. 8/15/1898 at 0; cholera infantum; b. Dover; buried in Berwick, ME
Willis A., Jr., d. 6/1/1915 at 0/2/26; bronchitis; Willis A. Lovejoy and Lura S. Johnson

LOVERING,
Annie, d. 5/3/1922 at 83 in Berwick, ME; chronic endocarditis

LOW,
Mary, d. 8/20/1928 at 76/7/25 in Marlboro, MA; broncho pneumonia
Nathaniel, d. 5/1/1890 at 50/8/3 in New Hampton; Nathaniel Low (Berwick, ME) and Mary A. Hale (Dover)
Sarah, d. 12/14/1913 at 83/10/12 in Andover, MA; old age
Sarah R., d. 2/5/1909 at 79/10/3 in New York, NY; nephritis
William Hale, d. 2/24/1903 at 83/7 in Chicago, IL; pneumonia; PH

LOWD,
William H., d. 12/27/1932 at 74/5/23; cancer of tongue

LOWELL,
George G., d. 6/7/1893 at 68; heart failure; b. Hallowell, ME; (Hallowell, ME; Hallowell, ME)
George K., d. 2/23/1925 at 68/11/4 in Newton, MA; oedema of glottis
Phoebe H., d. 12/8/1894 at 72 in St. Louis, MO; acute pneumonia; b. US; PH

LOWNEY,
Patrick J., d. 1/29/1934 at 54/2 in Melrose, MA; blow on head, accident

LUCAS,
Alice A., d. 9/1/1909 at 0/1/25; cholera infantum; Albert H. Lucas and Harriet A. Wentworth
Azalea C., d. 4/17/1912 at 64 in Salem, MA; progressive arthritis
Ellen A., d. 4/29/1922 at 78/7/29; valvular heart disease; Stephen Jenkins and Sarah A. K. Hill

Fannie, d. 2/25/1902 at 26/8; suicide by drowning; PH
George H., d. 8/30/1902 at 58/0/5; heart disease; PH
Isaac Lee, d. 3/29/1927 at 90/0/18; senility; James Lucas and Nancy Lee
John, d. 4/3/1915 at 69/11; pneumonia; James Lucas and Nancy Lee
Louisa F., d. 2/7/1932 at 85/2/12; chronic endocarditis
Mary D., d. 8/29/1893 at 77; peloire tumor; b. Alton; (Gilmanton; Gilmanton)
Minerva E., d. 10/17/1896 at 66 in Portsmouth; diabetes; PH
William T., d. 7/10/1912 at 70/2/13 in Portsmouth; locomotor ataxia

LUCE,
Benjamin F., d. 8/21/1887 at 1/2/27; b. Farmington; Eben N. Luce (ME) and Lizzie A. (ME)
Ernest L., d. 7/7/1911 at 26/10/3; hemorrhage - stab wound; Eben Luce and Lizzie Harvey

LUCEY,
Bernadette, d. 5/24/1934 at 25/9/24 in Jersey City, NJ; agramillcytic angina
Mary F., d. 11/17/1933 at 22/3/15; bronchial asthma

LUCY,
James, d. 12/13/1934 at 87/2/12; bronchial pneumonia
Margaret, d. 10/28/1937 at 70; chr. myocarditis

LUDBERG,
Andrew P., d. 4/11/1934 at 46/9/13; frac. of skull (acc.)

LUDDY,
James, d. 3/31/1913 at 51/8; pulm. tuberculosis; ----- Luddy and ----- Flanigan

LUDGER,
Joseph E., d. 1/7/1917 at 0/0/3; congenital atelectasis; Jacques Ludger and Sophie Drapeau

LUENS,
child, d. 12/11/1905 at 0/0/18; inanition

LUNARD,
Emile, d. 2/8/1915 at 31; ac. fracture of skull; George Lunard and Mary Tremblay

LUNNEY,
Bridget, d. 7/7/1897 at 43; uraemia; b. Ireland; SM
John, d. 11/12/1912 at 64; diabetes mellitus; Patrick Lunney

LUNO,
Mathilda O., d. 10/31/1918 at 44/0/11; broncho pneumonia; Michael
    Overson and Mary -----

LUNT,
Albert N., d. 10/3/1923 at 72/4/3; angina pectoris; Albert Lunt and Sophia
    Hill
Augusta L., d. 2/9/1925 at 56/5/11; tubercular enteritis; Daniel G. Ricker
Edith F., d. 6/19/1926 at 29/9/26; peritonitis; William L. Holley and Laura
    E. Glines
Emma O., d. 2/26/1920 at 62/10/15; nephritis; Washington Oliver and
    Mary Hinckley
Frank A., d. 3/4/1924 at 72/10/26; chronic nephritis; Andrew F. Lunt and
    Amanda Clark
John M., d. 1/3/1919 at 86/7/26; senility; ----- Young

LUSCOMB,
William W., d. 9/7/1892 at 31; railroad accident; (Lawrence, MA;
    Lawrence, MA)

LUTOFF,
Mary J., d. 1/25/1929 at 86/5/1; senility

LUTOLF,
John, d. 4/30/1912 at 86/1/16; ulcer of stomach; Xavier Lutolf and Maria J.
    Kitchmann
Theresa F., d. 6/24/1903 at 68/1/17; plural effusion; PH
Xaver, d. 4/16/1899 at 83; cancer of stomach; PH

LUZION,
Peter, d. 10/3/1918 at 23 in Ayer, MA; pneumonia; Peter Luzion and Esma
    Hashan

LYMAN,
Edward B., d. 9/12/1925 at 64/7/5 in Worcester, MA; cerebral hemorrhage
Lydia, d. 3/1/1890 at 76; widow; John Jones (Portsmouth) and Betsey
    Henderson (Dover)

LYNCH,
Alice, d. 11/24/1896 at 1; laryngitis; b. Dover; SM

Andrew J., d. 10/11/1934 at 55/0/13; multiple sclerosis
Edward, d. 11/23/1909 at 0/3/15; pneumonia; Andrew J. Lynch and Cecilia Clouther
John H., d. 9/21/1932 at 66/4/18; chronic endocarditis
Thomas F., d. 3/1/1914 at 42; rupture of aneurism, aorta

LYNES,
Daniel William, d. 2/2/1915 at 21/6/14; Dennis J. Lynes and Johanna Lucey

LYON,
Helen Adams, d. 2/21/1920 at 30/5/2 in Providence, RI; pneumonia
Mary, d. 4/8/1900 at 63; coma; SM

LYONS,
child, d. 4/16/1905 at –; inanition; SM
Catherine, d. 5/28/1904 at –; carcinoma of breast; SM
Daniel, d. 7/29/1889 at 70; laborer; married; b. Ireland; David Lyons (Ireland) and Mary Welch (Ireland)
Elizabeth V., d. 8/3/1898 at 24; phthisis; b. Dover; SM
James, d. 11/16/1912 at 79; dilitation of heart
John, d. 10/7/1900 at 82 in So. Berwick, ME; chronic diarrhea; SM
John Joseph, d. 1/12/1910 at 43 in Warwick, RI; chr. valv. heart disease
John L., d. 6/29/1927 at 57/3/4; ulcer of stomach; Stephen Lyons and Johanna Dowd
Julia, d. 10/14/1906 at 37 in Lynn, MA; alcoholism; SM
Margaret, d. 12/19/1929 at 17 in Wareham, MA; acute gastritis; Margaret Hughes
Mary A., d. 11/22/1890 at 13/9; Thomas Lyons (Canada) and M. Gibbins (US)
Patrick, d. 10/1/1889 at 34/8 in Newmarket
Thomas, d. 7/2/1906 at 49 in Rockland, ME; probably heart disease; SM
William G., d. 2/10/1930 at 19/10/17 in Wareham, MA; asphyxia by drowning; James P. Lyons and Margaret Hughes

MABURIN,
Osmond, d. 7/15/1925 at 42/4/3 in York, ME; cerebral hemorrhage

MACAULEY,
Susan, d. 10/1/1932 at 52 in Boston, MA; ruptured aneurysm

MACDONALD,
George C., d. 6/12/1921 at 71; biliary calculi; George Macdonald
Neal, d. 8/26/1931 at 62/1/7; chronic Brights dis.

Wallace H., d. 5/16/1916 at 5/3/13; rheumatic fever; Hugh McDonald (sic) and Vivian Cahill

William D., d. 7/16/1916 at 50; acute pulm. oedema; Valentine M'Donald and Elizabeth Dillon

MACFAUN,
child, d. 9/22/1917 at –; atelectasis; Alden I. MacFaun and Estelle Green

MACGOWAN,
Ida M., d. 10/22/1934 at 48/10/15; chronic myocarditis

MACGOWEN,
Mary E., d. 9/21/1926 at 66/10; chr. valvular heart disease; David Conrad and ----- Cook

MACINTYRE,
Finlay, d. 9/16/1935 at 81/3/20 in Tuxedo, NY; carcinoma of spleen, colon

MACISAAC,
Christina, d. 12/16/1917 at 69/9/16; clen. inter. nephritis; John Morrison and Annie -----

MACK,
Albert F., d. 9/29/1919 at 69/5/13 in Taunton, MA; arterio sclerosis
Jeanette, d. 8/7/1896 at 68; gastric catarrh; b. Scotland; PH
John, d. 4/24/1890 at 72/8/27; James Mack (Scotland) and Isabella McFarlane (Scotland)
Victoria, d. 3/30/1889 at 29; married; b. Canada

MACKENNEY,
child, d. 8/4/1908 at –; stillborn; H. L. MacKenney and E. M. Wentworth
Elizabeth, d. 8/4/1908 at –; eclampsia; Andrew E. Wentworth and Ella A. Harrington

MACKLIN,
child, d. 5/22/1917 at –; stillborn; Patrick Macklin and Katherine Gorman
Mary, d. 6/11/1891 at 80; widow; Michael Mone (Ireland) and Rose McConville (Ireland)

MACLIN,
Walter, d. 4/11/1919 at 41/9/26 in Goffstown; pulm. tuberculosis; Patrick Maclin and Bridget -----

MACOMBER,
Fred B., d. 11/15/1936 at 66/9/5; gastric hemorrhage

MACPHIE,
Catherine, d. 7/8/1906 at 1/2/24; chronic meningitis
Catherine, d. 10/24/1907 at 31/3/13; pleuro-pneumonia; James McArdle and Margaret Tonan
John, d. 10/6/1907 at --; premature birth; John MacPhie and Katherine McArdle

MACROSSIE,
George A., d. 6/17/1913 at 39/3/9 in New York, NY; appendicitis; Alexander D. MacRossie and Mary Downey

MADAM,
Michael, d. 7/5/1888 at 87; widower; b. Ireland

MADDEN,
Catherine, d. 12/14/1932 at 89; apoplexy
Rose, d. 6/10/1928 at 68; broncho pneumonia; James Madden

MADDOX,
Annie, d. 11/23/1925 at 66 in Portsmouth; cancer of pelvis
Ivory, d. 6/8/1903 at 61/0/1; rheumatic endocarditis; buried in Berwick, ME
Susan, d. 1/31/1922 at 84/11/2; senility; Gilman Upham and Abigail Twombly

MAGEE,
Vincent F., d. 12/12/1888 at 0/4/13; b. Dover; James Magee (Ireland) and Lizzie Cassily (Ireland)

MAGUIRE,
Donald Lord, d. 9/10/1912 at 0/0/-1/8; premature birth; Leo McGuire (sic) and Addie E. Lord
Joseph H., d. 8/11/1887 at 0/8/24; b. Dover; George Maguire and Jennie Cooley (NH)
Mary J., d. 4/26/1903 at 38/8/26; tubercular peritonitis
Stanley, d. 12/21/1908 at 0/3/24 in Boston, MA; gastro enteritis; James A. McGuire (sic) and Bessie Symes

MAHAFFEY,
James, d. 6/7/1909 at 75; heart disease; Robert Mahaffey and Anne Lyons

MAHAFFY,
James, d. 1/6/1909 at 35 in Franklin; drowned

MAHER,
child, d. 12/13/1894 at –; inanition; b. Dover; SM
John, d. 11/–/1903 at 51; railroad accident; SM

MAHON,
Patrick H., d. 4/17/1915 at 42; cancer of liver

MAHONEY,
child, d. 4/27/1899 at –; stillborn; SM
Annie T., d. 10/6/1918 at 21/0/18; pneumonia; Patrick Mahoney and Ellen Sullivan
Cornelius, d. 9/12/1889 at 33/3/12; engineer; married; b. Ireland; David Mahoney (Ireland) and Ellen Drew (Ireland)
Daniel D., d. 5/6/1931 at 85/3/11; chronic endocarditis
David F., d. 12/12/1897 at 26; phthisis; b. Dover; SM
Elizabeth, d. 4/27/1898 at 51; apoplexy; b. Ireland; SM
Ellan, d. 6/5/1899 at 88; chronic heart disease; SM
Ellen, d. 8/20/1937 at 79; chr. endocarditis
Hannah, d. 5/18/1929 at 74 in Berwick, ME; cerebral hemorrhage
Honora, d. 12/28/1889 at 30/4/28; mill operative; single; b. Ireland; Jeremiah Mahoney (Ireland) and M. Leary (Ireland)
James, d. 6/5/1905 at 68; cardiac dilation; SM
Jeremiah, d. 11/9/1891 at 32/9/23; single; James Mahoney (Ireland) and Mary Goggin (Ireland)
Johanna, d. 12/28/1930 at 67; heart disease; Jere. L. Mahoney and Margaret O'Leary
Julia, d. 1/8/1925 at 68 in Melrose, MA; chronic endocarditis
Kate, d. 6/1/1902 at –; valvular heart disease; SM
Katherine, d. 12/4/1932 at 71/2/17; cancer of stomach
Kathryn D., d. 2/24/1932 at 82; chronic int. nephritis
Lawrence, d. 12/9/1927 at 47/9/11; pulmonary tuberculosis
Margaret, d. 3/12/1888 at 52; widow; b. Ireland; D. O'Leary (Ireland) and Hannah Sullivan
Margaret, d. 328/1897 at 64; dementia paralytica; b. Ireland; SM
Mary, d. 12/20/1894 at 52; chron. nephritis; b. Ireland; SM
Mary, d. 3/5/1906 at 78; old age; SM
Mary, d. 5/16/1908 at 76/6; shock
Mary, d. 8/1/1929 at 68; cancer of rectum; Daniel Mahoney and Mary Castlow
William, d. 9/3/1890 at 0/6; Michael Mahoney (Ireland) and Hannah Mulcahey (Ireland)
William, d. 1/9/1937 at 69/10/24; chr. endocarditis

MAHURIAN,
Ethel G., d. 11/25/1926 at 42/3/11; carcinoma of uterus; Thomas A. Prior and Sarah A. Nichols

MAILHOT,
child, d. 5/21/1900 at –; stillborn
child, d. 12/19/1902 at –; stillborn
Armine, d. 5/28/1930 at 62; ac. lobar pneumonia; Philas Lavielle and Philomene Lauriese
Edouard, d. 7/11/1900 at <1; cholera infantum
Ida, d. 3/1/1897 at 1; athrepsia; b. Dover; SM
Joseph, d. 3/8/1897 at 0; stillborn; b. Dover; SM
Maximilian, d. 8/1/1932 at 65/5/26; cancer of stomach
Ovila, d. 9/2/1905 at 0/11/23; entero colitis
Rosilia, d. 7/2/1895 at 0; jaundice; b. Dover; SM
Yvonne, d. 2/8/1910 at 0/0/20; broncho-pneumonia; Emile Mailhot and Maximillienne Cormier

MAIN,
Clara J., d. 7/17/1890 at 56/3/27; married; John Main (Rochester) and Susan Corson (Lebanon, ME)
Eliza A. H., d. 5/19/1928 at 84/9/24 in York, ME; pernicious anemia
John, d. 9/26/1924 at –; stillborn; John Main and Katherine Durnin
Josiah, d. 3/5/1915 at 74/10/15 in Boston, MA; arterio sclerosis; Mayhew Main and Irene Norwood

MALAPAGUES,
child, d. 6/13/1913 at 0/0/1; atelectasis; George Malapagues and Vassila Cochebon

MALAPANES,
James, d. 10/15/1918 at 34; pneumonia
Stavios, d. 9/27/1918 at 22; lobar pneumonia

MALCOLM,
Douglas, d. 11/10/1921 at 67/11/5 in Baltimore, MD; chronic nephritis

MALING,
Lucia, d. 10/9/1920 at 86/6/26 in York Beach, ME; carcinoma of uterus

MALLEN,
Ernest O., d. 11/2/1918 at 0/5; athrepsia; Francis J. Mallen and Laura Paul
John, d. 4/11/1928 at 81; chronic myocarditis; James Mallen and Rose McNally

John M., d. 2/2/1932 at 29/5/25; fracture of skull
John T., d. 12/14/1923 at 68; gen. arterio sclerosis
Maggie, d. 6/17/1892 at 35; pneumonia
Maggie Ann, d. 7/25/1893 at –; dysentery; b. Dover; (Ireland; Ireland)
Maggie C., d. 7/25/1893 at –; dysentery; b. Dover; (Ireland; Ireland)
Mary, d. 11/11/1915 at 67/0/4; cancer of stomach; Charles O'Donnell and Ann Mullen
Mary Frances, d. 10/29/1926 at 56/5/13; carcinoma of breast; John Kelley and Joanna Dillon
Patrick E., d. 7/3/1911 at 58; cardiac dilitation; James Mallen and Rose McNally

MALLEY,
Owen J., d. 2/9/1893 at 26; died in Strafford Co. Asylum fire

MALLON,
child, d. 9/12/1895 at 0; stillborn; b. Dover; SM
child, d. 9/12/1895 at 0; stillborn; b. Dover; SM
Alexander, d. 3/25/1900 at 33 in Concord; uncertain, brain or heart
Frank, d. 3/14/1913 at 64; primary dementia; John Mallon and Ellen McGuinness
James, d. 7/29/1899 at –; cholera infantum; SM
Mary, d. 9/6/1900 at –; marasmus; SM
Rose, d. 12/9/1890 at 68; (Ireland; Ireland)
Sarah, d. 9/26/1895 at 32; burns; b. Ireland; SM

MALLOY,
Mary, d. 9/16/1900 at –; overdose of saltpetre; SM

MALONE,
James, d. 2/15/1926 at 63; lobar pneumonia; Patrick Malone and Mary ----
John, d. 10/24/1907 at --; typhoid fever; James Malone and Sarah Gallagher
John, d. 5/2/1922 at 2/11/10 in Methuen, MA; diphtheria
Sadie, d. 5/22/1918 at 0/10 in Methuen, MA; measles; Patrick J. Malone and Rose P. Lawlor
Sarah, d. 2/18/1932 at 68/10/29; lobar pneumonia

MALONEY,
child, d. 11/23/1909 at –; stillborn; Michael Maloney and Lizzie Sunderland
Donald, d. 11/11/1921 at 10/7/14; accidentally shot; Michael Maloney and Elizabeth Sunderland
Elizabeth V., d. 9/25/1913 at 31/3/7; tuberculosis; Theodore Young and Annie Macklin

Elizabeth V., d. 10/13/1918 at 22/3/9; pneumonia; Thomas Mannix and Julia Fitzgerald
Florence E., d. 2/19/1909 at 0/8/14; pneumonia; Michael J. Maloney and Elizabeth Sunderland
John H., d. 4/26/1902 at 61/0/6; cancer of liver; SM
Martin, d. 8/24/1923 at 43; chronic nephritis; John H. Maloney and Mary Banks
Mary, d. 2/9/1893 at 50; died in Strafford Co. Asylum fire
Mary, d. 7/17/1917 at 71; apoplexy; John Banks and Ellen Cullinan
Michael J., d. 5/29/1921 at 49/10/15; cerebral hemorrhage; Patrick Maloney and Mary O'Kane
Mildred B., d. 10/2/1918 at 18/3/28; lobar pneumonia; Patrick D. Maloney and Georgia Evans

MALONZO,
Lilla, d. 10/22/1914 at 38/8/19; pulmonary tuberculosis; Daniel P. York and Susan M. Smart

MANETT,
Josephine B., d. 10/4/1918 at – in Providence, RI; nephritis

MANETTE,
Joseph, d. 12/13/1908 at 33; typhoid fever

MANGANE,
Mary, d. 7/30/1893 at 57; heart disease; b. Ireland; (Ireland; Ireland)

MANLEY,
Frances J., d. 1/1/1891 at 62/0/5 in Portsmouth; married; Jonathan Foster (Reading, MA) and Margaret R. Munsey (Barnstead)

MANN,
Joseph, d. 4/27/1901 at 84/9/16; old age; PH
Lucy, d. 6/11/1920 at 86/9 in Lynn, MA; arterio sclerosis
Mary A., d. 1/6/1914 at 80/0/17; unknown; Thomas J. Canney and Sarah Waldron
Mercy M., d. 3/13/1909 at 82/7/12; old age; James B. Varney and Sarah B. Riley

MANNING,
Catherine, d. 5/24/1912 at 74; old age; Andrew Scanlon and Honor Lavin
George S., d. 11/7/1906 at 67/8/12 in Manchester; progressive anemia; PH

Lydia A., d. 3/29/1912 at 71/3/8 in Manchester; pneumonia; Benjamin
    Hoitt and Sally Demeritt
Ruth, d. 12/4/1897 at 27; cardiac rheumatism; b. England; buried in
    Lowell, MA

MANNIX,
Catherine P., d. 5/15/1912 at 0/2; infantile atrophy; Thomas Mannix and
    Julia Fitzgerald
James A., d. 8/13/1896 at 1; cholera infantum; b. Dover; SM
Julia, d. 4/10/1910 at 2; tubercular meningitis; Thomas Mannix and Julia
    Fitzgerald
Margaret S., d. 5/18/1912 at 0/2; infantile atrophy; Thomas Mannix and
    Julia Fitzgerald
Richard B., d. 3/5/1919 at 8/2/21; ac. broncho pneumonia; Thomas
    Mannix and Julia Fitzgerald

MANNOCK,
Lizzie, d. 9/16/1889 at 23 in Winooski, VT; A. Bradwick (NY) and -----
    Henderson (Dover)

MANNOURES,
Ellen, d. 12/18/1930 at –; premature birth; Edward Mannoures

MANOCK,
Charles E., d. 6/13/1932 at 81/5/12 in Biddeford, ME; acute myocarditis
David, d. 6/15/1897 at 76; old age; b. England; buried in No. Andover
Ellen J., d. 9/22/1925 at 37 in Kearney, NJ; peritonitis
Frank, d. 12/23/1933 at 71/5/22 in Lawrence, MA; carcinoma of stomach
Mary, d. 5/2/1910 at 82/0/9; senility; Samuel Kershaw and Ann -----
Mary A. L., d. 9/27/1932 at 79/0/22 in Chevy Chase, MD; angina pectoris

MANSFIELD,
Chester C., d. 8/11/1910 at 0/4/17 in Alton; ileo colitis

MANSON,
Eliza Jane, d. 8/2/1907 at 76/1; heart disease; Samuel Manson and Eliza
    Sawyer
Eliza R., d. 3/28/1889 at 85/0/20; housewife; widow; John Sawyer and
    Eliza R. Sawyer
Letitia, d. 2/25/1920 at 69; arterio sclerosis
Norman, d. 12/18/1890 at 0/9/18; Charles Manson
Zahehie, d. 1/28/1930 at 66; fracture of hip; J. M. Borik and Basta
    Abraham

Zerviah, d. 11/27/1889 at 84/1/2; housewife; widow; b. Barrington; G. Sherborne (Barrington) and Eleanor Sherborne (Barrington)

MANSOUR,
Harold, d. 8/11/1931 at –; premature birth

MANSUR,
Joseph, d. 5/22/1922 at 76; cancer of prostate; Joseph Mansur and Margaret E. -----
Nancy W., d. 12/27/1900 at 72; heart disease; buried in Wakefield

MANUEL,
Ann Louise, d. 2/25/1930 at 2/6/10; membranous croup; Charles J. Manuel and Alice Wheaton

MANYON,
Daniel, d. 1/14/1898 at 76; rheumatism; b. Ireland; SM

MAPESINES,
James, d. 1/24/1913 at 27; pyoneplerosis, etc.

MARCHAND,
Blanche A., d. 1/29/1910 at 0/5/6; broncho-pneumonia; Alfred Marchand and Emma McNeil
Grace K., d. 4/13/1927 at 51/4/23 in Boston, MA; cancer uterus

MARCHAUD,
Eleanor, d. 1/25/1915 at 63; pulmonary tuberculosis; Francis Begin and Sophie -----

MARCOTTE,
child, d. 9/24/1921 at –; stillborn; Joseph Marcotte and Mary E. Commisky
child, d. 10/16/1921 at –; stillborn; Eugene J. Marcotte and Florence Mulligan
Adjutor, d. 2/2/1916 at 30/9/5; cirrhosis of liver; Hepolite Marcotte and Mayrance Pagger
Belle, d. 2/28/1904 at 0/2/17; athrepsia; buried in tomb
Irilla M., d. 3/10/1927 at 51/9/8 in Rochester; carcinoma of uterus; Alvah H. Foss and Vian Wentworth
J. William, d. 2/17/1901 at 0/0/½; premature birth
Louis, d. 1/3/1933 at 82/0/13; chronic nephritis
Olive C., d. 8/27/1932 at 0/6/3; suffocation
Phoebe, d. 7/14/1891 at 2/2/7; Joseph Marcotte (Canada) and Phoebe Nadeau (Canada)

Sarah, d. 11/7/1889 at 28/7/11; housewife; married; b. Canada; T. Bassett (Quebec) and Susanne Hamel (NH)
William F., d. 3/30/1909 at 0/0/15; pneumonia; Joseph Marcotte and Mary Cummisky

MARCOUX,
Joseph D., d. 8/27/1914 at 66/5/20; cerebral hemorrhage; Joseph Marcoux and Christine Lafond

MARDEN,
Augusta E., d. 10/26/1932 at 89/1/25; arterio sclerosis
Carrie, d. 6/23/1920 at 85/8/14 in Newark, NJ; asthenia incident to age; Abagail Marden
Charles C., d. 6/10/1914 at 0/2; athrepsia; Harry Marden and Fannie Welch
Charles N., d. 4/8/1893 at 50; unknown, sudden, no autopsy; b. Newburyport, MA
Frank, d. 6/27/1894 at 14; heart disease; b. Dover; SM
George F., d. 8/19/1888 at 0/0/22; b. Dover; Charles M. Marden (Newburyport, MA) and Margaret Ryan (Dover)
Hannah F., d. 11/24/1916 at 80/1/1; broncho pneumonia; David Harriman and Hannah F. Goodwin
John W., d. 5/22/1904 at 76/0/17; senile gangrene of foot; PH
Mary, d. 4/16/1906 at 6; heart disease; SM
Stephen J., d. 3/29/1891 at 63/4/7 in Brooklyn, NY; widower; Samuel Marden (Barrington) and Abbie Emerson (Lee)
William A., d. 6/18/1906 at 49/10/22; fracture of dorsal verterbra; PH
Woodrow J., d. 12/3/1914 at 1/9; lobar pneumonia; Harry Marden and Annie B. Welch

MARION,
Beatrice, d. 2/26/1919 at 0/1/23; athrepsia; Odilon Marion and Rose Larage
Delphise, d. 8/28/1889 at 0/11/5; b. Dover; John Marion (Canada) and Alponsine Bedard (Canada)
John, d. 11/24/1928 at 68/7; chronic myocarditis; Remick Marion and Marguerite Lambert
Leonora, d. 6/11/1928 at 36; sarcoma uterus; John Driscoll and Mary Hickey
Ludivine, d. 7/3/1911 at 2/1/16; acute nephritis; John Marion and Alphonsine Bedard
Rosanna, d. 9/18/1898 at 0; cholera infantum; b. Dover; SM

MARISON,
Mary T., d. 5/5/1907 at 3/10/19; tubercular meningitis; Theodore Marison and Mary Cox

MARKEY,
Alice, d. 9/29/1906 at 73; chronic endocarditis; SM
Alice J., d. 11/30/1933 at 63/1 in Laconia; cancer of uterus
Ann J., d. 10/3/1893 at 60; cirrhosis of liver; b. Ireland; (Ireland; Ireland)
Annie, d. 9/16/1916 at 40; cerebral hemorrhage; Michael E. Ring and Emma Colomy
Bridget, d. 9/19/1913 at 76; cerebral apoplexy; Frank Duffy and Mary McKearney
Bridget A., d. 3/28/1916 at 51 in Lawrence, MA; cancer of rectum
Edward J., d. 5/8/1928 at 60 in Lowell, MA; chr. valv. heart dis.
John, d. 8/7/1892 at 11; accidental drowning; b. Dover; (Ireland; Ireland)
John, d. 2/9/1920 at 73; chronic gastro enteritis
Josephine, d. 8/27/1903 at 15/5/5; appendicitis; SM
Mary, d. 1/19/1924 at 75; chronic myocarditis; Edward Martin and Alice Sheridan
Owen, d. 2/8/1900 at 21; tuberculosis; SM
Patrick, d. 11/11/1895 at 54; pulmonary gangrene; b. Ireland; SM
Patrick, d. 1/15/1897 at 30; pneumonia; b. Dover; SM
Rebecca, d. 4/12/1888 at 1/8/15; b. Dover; Owen Markey (Ireland) and Julia Bergan (Ireland)
Robert, d. 3/5/1906 at 28 in San Francisco, CA; phthisis pulmonalis; SM
Thomas, d. 12/11/1889 at 4/8; b. Dover; Owen Markey (Ireland) and Kate Smith (Ireland)
Thomas, d. 1/4/1912 at 65/6/10; heart disease; Edward Markey and Alice Printy

MARKOS,
Amartarios, d. 8/31/1926 at 67; uremia; John Markos
Apostolis, d. 4/25/1924 at 0/9; broncho pneumonia; Arthur Markos
Lamperas, d. 5/10/1921 at 7/3; accidental drowning; Arthur Markos and Chrisapo Yomdas

MARKS,
John, d. 4/28/1927 at 70; alcoholism

MARKUNIS,
Ignary, d. 2/23/1911 at – in Durham; suicide by hanging

MARNOCH,
Robert B., d. 3/30/1929 at 51/2/17; chronic myocarditis; William Marnoch and Jessie Brown
William S., d. 7/24/1932 at 29/8/16 in Beech Springs, SC; auto accident

MARNOCK,
Charles W., d. 2/18/1924 at 39/2/11 in Newark, NJ; lobar pneumonia

MAROIS,
child, d. 5/25/1902 at –; stillborn
Charles, d. 9/25/1901 at 3; ulceration of duodenum
Elizabeth J., d. 7/6/1905 at 0/9/9; pneumonia
Emma, d. 6/2/1902 at 12/7; burn
Exorie, d. 5/7/1931 at 69; cerebral embolism

MARROIS,
Louise, d. 4/19/1899 at 6; entero-colitis

MARS,
Ernest, d. 10/15/1935 at 75 in PA; compound fracture of left leg and shock

MARSDEN,
Emma F., d. 5/29/1903 at 41/3/12 in Saugus, MA; pneumonia; PH
M. E., d. 2/8/1902 at 4 in Saugus, MA; measles

MARSH,
child, d. 12/25/1893 at –; stillborn; b. Dover; (VT; VT)
Alice M., d. 6/24/1904 at 30 in Yonkers, NY; chronic nephritis; buried in Dover
Bessie A., d. 2/19/1935 at 55/5/22; carcinomatosis abdominal
Mary A., d. 12/29/1893 at 70; pneumonia; b. Burlington, VT; (VT; VT)
Oscar F., d. 12/13/1928 at 82; cerebral hemorrhage; John Marsh and Asenath Runnells

MARSHALL,
child, d. 8/16/1934 at –; stillborn
Alice, d. 3/21/1901 at 5/8/4; rheumatic fever; PH
Alice E., d. 3/19/1924 at 0/1/19; athrepsia; Otis E. Marshall and Alice ----
Anna A. G., d. 2/3/1924 at 47/10/22 in Rollinsford; tuberculosis of larynx
Annie A., d. 2/3/1890 at 23/3; married; Albert Marshall (US) and Arthusa Doty (US)
Bertha May, d. 4/30/1928 at 45/10/8; pulm. embolism; John Giddard and Ann Veese
Charles P., d. 2/11/1926 at 53/9/16 in Plymouth, MA; embolism

Clara B., d. 10/15/1899 at 11; cerebro spinal meningitis; PH
Esther, d. 10/14/1910 at 88 in Pittsfield; old age
Esther A., d. 12/28/1904 at 70/5/18; la grippe; PH
Fannie M., d. 3/18/1926 at 90; cerebral hemorrhage; Chase Flanders and Annie Lyman
Frank H., d. 12/20/1926 at 0/0/28; furonculosis; Clarence W. Marshall and Ida M. Miller
George E., d. 9/25/1889 at 5/4/23; b. NS; Timothy L. Marshall (NS) and Ina F. Filmore (NS)
Grace T., d. 4/1/1936 at 69/4/20; carcinomatosis abdominal
Helen L., d. 3/22/1928 at 0/1/12; congenital debility; Benjamin F. Marshall and Evelyn E. Tibbetts
Hollis Smith, d. 6/11/1913 at 0/2/20; convulsions, etc.; Melvin A. Marshall and Sophia I. Smith
James, d. 3/4/1906 at 68/0/9; nervous shock; PH
James, d. 9/16/1921 at 47/7/24; acute appendicitis; James Marshall and Jane Petrie
Jane Petrie, d. 4/3/1912 at 66/5/19; arterio sclerosis; Charles Petrie and Ann Parker
John M., d. 6/13/1928 at 63/11/13; chronic myocarditis; Joseph B. Marshall and Esther A. Smith
John O., d. 2/25/1896 at –; convulsions; b. Dover; PH
Joseph B., d. 9/18/1892 at 60; bilious colic; b. NS; (NS; NS)
Katherine R., d. 11/25/1930 at 25 in Rochester; intes. paralysis; Hugh Rodden
Luther B., d. 11/2/1897 at 3; accidentally burned; b. Dover; PH
Mabel, d. 4/19/1900 at 2; meningitis cerebral; PH
Myrtie B., d. 12/29/1932 at 53/3/14; cerebral hemorrhage
Ray John, d. 2/6/1927 at 2/1/3; purulent otitis; Ray J. Marshall and Marie Mulvihill
Robert F., d. 2/3/1929 at 2/1/28; broncho pneumonia; Benjamin F. Marshall and Evelyn Tibbetts
Robert St. C., d. 12/2/1920 at 61/7/29 in Rollinsford; cancer of stomach
Thomas D., d. 9/18/1899 at 82 in Pittsfield; cerebral apoplexy; PH

MARSTON,
Christina E., d. 3/7/1932 at 47/0/23 in Saugus, MA; carcinoma of breast
Earl L., d. 4/6/1904 at 1/2; spinal meningitis; PH
Emily F., d. 3/26/1932 at 71/0/20; carcinoma
Mary B., d. 10/29/1936 at 74/10/28*
Olive J., d. 7/26/1931 at 96/8/19; chronic myocarditis

MARTEL,
Eugenie, d. 11/17/1893 at 40; dysentery; b. Canada; (Canada; Canada)
Florida, d. 12/2/1897 at 7; brain disease; b. Canada; SM

Isaie, d. 8/22/1935 at 79/2/6; paralysis agitans
Marie A., d. 9/18/1908 at 16/0/5; typhoid fever; Isaie Martel and Philomene
    Beaulieu
Mary J., d. 8/22/1899 at 0; diarrhea infantile
Paul E., d. 4/10/1926 at 0/9/24; congenital enlargement; Wilfred J. Martel
    and Pauline Labrie
Philomene, d. 4/101/932 at 73/2/4; cerebral hemorrhage
Robert, d. 4/3/1931 at 0/3 in Madbury; membraneous
Virginia, d. 3/17/1911 at 1/6; pneumonia; Godfois Martel

MARTELL,
George R., d. 1/16/1893 at 2; croup; b. Pittsfield, MA; (Canada; Pittsfield, MA)

MARTIN,
child, d. 10/2/1918 at –; premature birth; Everard S. Martin and Anna G.
    Mitchell
Agnes, d. 8/20/1888 at 61/1/14; married; b. Scotland; G. Brown (Scotland)
Albert, d. 7/27/1914 at 6/4/21; accidental drowning; Etienne Martin and
    Clara Mercier
Albert Louis, d. 9/9/1912 at 15/2/19; cerebral abscess; Etienne Martin and
    Georgianna Breton
Albertine G., d. 8/11/1914 at 0/9/16; acute entero colitis; Etienne Martin
    and Clarice Mercier
Armand J., d. 5/18/1911 at 0/11/7; acute pneumonia; Etienne Martin, Jr.
    and Clarisse Mercier
Banzanna, d. 7/11/1910 at 1/0/19; cholera infantum; Etienne Martin and
    Clarisse Marchier
Caroline M., d. 8/21/1910 at 83/7; cerebral hemorrhage; Noah Martin and
    Jane Woodbury
Clara, d. 10/17/1917 at 18/5/11; broncho pneumonia; Etienne Martin and
    Georgianna Breton
Clara E., d. 2/17/1930 at 80/11/9; chronic endocarditis; James F. Bussiel
    and Laura J. Nason
Elizabeth A., d. 9/1/1889 at 63/1/5; single; b. Barrington; Noah Martin
    (Epsom) and Mary Woodbury (Barrington)
Emma, d. 8/24/1910 at 28/9/19 in Concord; paresis; Simon Martin and
    Georgiana Dube
Etienne, d. 7/21/1925 at 70 in Rochester; cancer of bladder; Louis Martin
Francois X., d. 6/17/1935 at 84/7/10; accidental fracture of right femur
Frederick B., d. 11/10/1922 at 0/2/7 in Boston, MA; pyloric stenosis; Fred
    L. Martin and Marion Banks
Frederick R., d. 12/24/1930 at 39/11/19 in Providence, RI; chr.
    endocarditis

Georgianna, d. 1/25/1930 at 69/6/26; carcinoma of colon; Zepherin Breton and Germaine St. Laurent
Georgie A., d. 7/6/1906 at 47; cancer of uterus; SM
Harold, d. 7/8/1911 at 0/7/24; cholera infantum; Harry Martin and Fannie Welch
Hassey T., d. 8/21/1928 at 54/4; carcinoma stomach - liver; Thomas Martin and Mary Doyle
Henry, d. 1/26/1915 at 62; acute nephritis
John, d. 4/1/1914 at 85/9/24; chronic nephritis; Samuel Martin and Marion ----

John, d. 5/23/1923 at 87; chronic myocarditis; John Martin
Lewis F., d. 9/1/1904 at 65/11/28; heart disease; buried in Manchester
Mary, d. 3/29/1900 at 84; sudden
Mary Laura, d. 6/13/1912 at 1/0/10; broncho pneumonia; Etienne Martin and Clarissa -----
Michael, d. 3/6/1930 at 71/3/8; chr. int. nephritis
Omee, d. 5/1/1934 at 19/11/22; subarachnoid hem.
Sarah, d. 11/30/1931 at --; cerebral hemorrhage
Theodore L., d. 6/5/1919 at 48/8/26; appendicitis; Adam Martin and Mary Schultz
William, d. 4/3/1924 at 72/8/23; chr. Brights disease
William W., d. 3/17/1934 at 81/1/29; coronary thrombosis

MARTINEAU,
William, d. 6/5/1929 at 22/5/1 in S. Berwick, ME; electrical burns; Arthur Martineau and Camille Cote

MARTINUS,
John, d. 11/13/1904 at 73 in Portsmouth; angina pectoris; PH

MARVIS,
Theresa, d. 8/6/1901 at 0/2/18; cholera infantum

MARX,
Marcus, d. 1/13/1896 at -- in New York City; apoplexy
Mary Susan, d. 9/23/1915 at 80/1/7 in E. Patchogue, LI; cancer of stomach

MASKOUSKI,
Adam, d. 7/17/1909 at --; intrauterine asphyxia; Stanislaus Maskouski and Mary Smoush

MASON,
child, d. 8/28/1922 at --; stillborn; Stephen R. Mason and Hortense Porter

Alice, d. 7/11/1900 at 60; jaundice and dropsy; SM
Frederick, d. 4/4/1890 at 1/1/11; Henry Mason (Dover) and Jennie Burns (PA)
Harry, d. 11/30/1908 at 43/5/8; cancer; John Mason and Susan W. Fowler
Jacob, d. 2/18/1917 at 67; broncho pneumonia
John W., d. 7/25/1887 at 0/1/11; b. Barrington
Julia A., d. 1/2/1916 at 90/6 in Lawrence, MA; broncho pneumonia
Katherine K., d. 5/8/1921 at 33 in New York, NY; ectopic gestation
Margaret, d. 2/1/1915 at 77; cirrhosis of liver
Martha A., d. 7/9/1915 at 82/1/27; fracture femur; William H. Whitehouse and Sophia Hartford
Mary, d. 4/27/1887 at 86/0/4; widow; b. NH; ----- Thompson (NH) and ----- Palmer (NH)
Mary Ann, d. 10/7/1896 at 86; senile debility; b. Stratham; buried in Wolfeboro
Nora, d. 8/29/1894 at 29 in Deerfield; heart disease; buried in Dover
Robert E., d. 9/15/1909 at 68 in Concord; senile dementia; George Mason and Elizabeth Rook
Thomas, d. 4/6/1921 at 75/10/14; gen. arterio sclerosis; John Mason and Elizabeth Bond
William, d. 12/25/1925 at 82/7/12; gastro enteritis

MASSE,
Rosanna, d. 11/30/1902 at 0/3/10; enteritis, acute

MASSINGHAM,
Alice M., d. 9/14/1916 at 36/5/28; unknown; John Slater and Annie Bayes

MASSON,
Joseph Arthur, d. 8/1/1890 at 0/6/6; Thomas Masson (Canada) and Lucie Gilbert (Canada)
Liza, d. 6/6/1904 at 23/10/27; tuberculosis of lungs; buried in Rollinsford

MATER,
Ferris, d. 5/26/1932 at 39 in Concord; paresis
Joseph, d. 11/26/1937 at 53; coronary embolism
Richard, d. 11/13/1931 at 51; uraemia
Tofie, d. 9/1/1915 at 8/11/18; accidental drowning; Richard Mater and Mary Boucaron

MATHERSON,
John W., d. 2/17/1899 at 53; phthisis; PH

MATHES,
child, d. 6/19/1918 at –; premature birth; M. Everett Mathes and Alice M. Varney
child, d. 6/19/1918 at –; premature birth; M. Everett Mathes and Alice M. Varney
Albert O., d. 7/20/1907 at 64/11/30; cerebral apoplexy; Robert Mathes and Mary F. Moulton
Barbara J., d. 12/27/1924 at 0/0/6; atelectasis; B. A. Mathes and Marion E. Pike
Betsey, d. 5/3/1889 at 90/2/23; housewife; widow; b. Lee; Levi Reynolds (Lee) and Mary Watson (Nottingham)
Burnham W., d. 2/13/1935 at 65 in Lynn, MA; heart disease probably
Charles A., d. 12/13/1919 at 65/0/5; angina pectoris; John Mathes and Parmelia Mathes
Elizabeth A., d. 2/9/1898 at 54; railway accident, shock
Fannie L., d. 11/25/1906 at 48/11/12; pneumonia; PH
John H., d. 9/26/1912 at 65/11/13; heart trouble; Samuel H. Mathes and Mary T. Perkins
John H., d. 2/9/1915 at 78/11/4 in Boston, MA; cerebral hemorrhage
Louisa F., d. 12/7/1901 at 83/10/23; senility; buried in Rochester
Mary E., d. 3/8/1934 at 82/5/24; cerebral hemorrhage
Mary J., d. 8/24/1922 at 74/10/3; cerebral hemorrhage; Stephen W. Drew and Mary Y. Chase
Mary T., d. 8/10/1899 at 79; old age; PH
Minnie M., d. 3/24/1889 at 13/7 in Eliot, ME; school girl; b. Eliot, ME; John H. Mathes (Durham) and Lizzie N. Young (Dover)
Samuel H., d. 2/21/1888 at 71/0/24; carpenter; married; b. Milton; William Mathes (Lee) and Sarah Varney (Milton)
Valentine, d. 11/27/1915 at 68/9/14; pneumonia (lobar); John Mathes and Pamelia -----

MATHESON,
Rebecca G., d. 8/24/1922 at 74/6/3; cerebral hemorrhage; John Parkman and Mary Audmore

MATHEWS,
Christiana, d. 10/13/1913 at 87/2/2; pneumonia; Francis Mathews and Nancy Page
Ellen, d. 7/20/1909 at 84/5/17; old age; John Clancy and Elizabeth Ahern
Forest C., d. 6/14/1936 at 54/9/17; car. of intestine

MATTER,
Mary, d. 6/17/1912 at 0/0/-1/3; premature birth; Simon Matter and Sarah George

MATTES,
Mary A. d. 2/3/1937 at 73/8/26; carcinoma liver

MATTHEWS,
Thomas E., Jr., d. 1/18/1917 at −in Newton, MA; broncho pneumonia

MATTICE,
Josiah L., d. 5/29/1892 at 59; hypostatic pneumonia

MATTOON,
Alice L., d. 2/20/1923 at 69/5/8; uraemia; Patrick Tobin and Ann Stevens
Junius T., d. 5/10/1925 at 70/10/7; lobar pneumonia; James Mattoon and Mary Alexander

MAURICE,
Angelbert, d. 1/21/1930 at 69/3/15; cerebral embolism; Paul Maurice and Marguerite Plamandon
Florentine B., d. 9/19/1937 at 70/10/5; chr. cholecystites
Maurice, d. 2/27/1897 at 0; acute enteritis; b. Dover; SM

MAURICETTE,
child, d. 5/26/1937 at −; stillborn

MAXCEY,
Almeda O., d. 11/6/1891 at 47/6/14; married; G. W. Bowley (So. Hope) and Ann Avery (Vinal Haven, ME) (see Maxcy)

MAXCY,
Almeda O., d. 3/6/1891 at 47/6/14; married; G. W. Barnly (South Hope) and Ann A. (Vinal Haven, ME) (see Maxcey)
Hattie F., d. 6/16/1892 at 21; kidney disease; b. So. Hope, ME; (So. Hope; So. Hope)
Joel B., d. 10/22/1896 at 59; Brights disease; b. Warren, ME; PH

MAXWELL,
Charlotte A., d. 7/28/1922 at 78/3/18; uraemia; Alpheus Littlefield and Charlotte Bowden
Hattie S., d. 4/19/1897 at 50; organic disease of heart; b. Barrington
John S., d. 5/3/1901 at 58/4/17 in Tilton; PH
Scott, d. 11/4/1916 at 61/3/27; cerebral hemorrhage; Arthur Maxwell and Elizabeth -----

MAY,
James, d. 5/15/1902 at 64; pneumonia; PH

MAYARD,
J. Lucien, d. 7/21/1896 at –; athrepsia; b. Dover; SM

MAYETTE,
Etta, d. 7/26/1931 at 67/1/26 in CA; chronic nephritis

MAYEWSKI,
Benjamin, d. 3/27/1935 at 60; chronic endocarditis

MAYNARD,
Hormisdas, d. 7/29/1904 at 39/1/21; cirrhosis of liver; buried in Biddeford, ME
Luzerne, d. 2/22/1927 at 72/2/7; acute gastro enteritis

MAYOTTE,
Dona, d. 7/20/1893 at –; cholera infantum; b. Quebec; (Quebec; Quebec)

MAYRAND,
child, d. 9/16/1905 at –; stillborn
Gertrude, d. 8/13/1902 at 1/2/15; ileo-colitis
Judith, d. 2/11/1905 at 1/4/4; meningitis
Julien, d. 1/7/1908 at 0/0/14; asphyxia; Phillipe Mayrand and Corinne Lebel
Leocardie R., d. 5/23/1936 at 78/2; car. ventri. & colon
Marie B., d. 11/22/1898 at 1; dysentery; b. Dover; SM
Onesime N., d. 7/30/1934 at 66/4/20; heart disease
William, d. 5/17/1908 at 20; acute appendicitis; Mose Mayrand and ----- Richard

McADAM,
child, d. 8/27/1933 at –; stillborn
Edward, d. 9/5/1935 at 42 in Springfield, MA; carcinoma stomach
Ellen, d. 2/25/1912 at 48; uremia; Thomas Hughes and Katherine Loughlin
James P., d. 5/4/1924 at 44/7/24; apoplexy; Peter McAdam and Ellen Hughes
Peter F., d. 5/8/1909 at 52; broncho pneumonia; Frank McAdam and Anne Durnin
Sarah J., d. 10/10/1904 at 10; hip joint disease; SM

McADAMS,
Annie G., d. 10/20/1894 at 22; phthisis pulmonalis; b. Ireland; PH

McALLISTER,
Abbie K., d. 2/17/1895 at 80 in Camden, NJ; exhaustion; buried in Dover

McALPINE,
Evelyn W., d. 1/5/1919 at 35/3/13 in Exeter; pneumonia
Shirley M., d. 2/27/1931 at 0/0/9 in Madbury; broncho pneumonia

McARDLE,
Alice, d. 8/28/1902 at 68; inflammation of liver; SM
Bridget, d. 8/11/1906 at –; heart disease; SM
Catherine, d. 5/21/1887 at 20/7; married; b. Scotland; Hugh McCabe
   (Ireland) and Catherine Welch (Ireland)
Catherine, d. 7/31/1887 at 0/4/3; b. Dover; James McArdle (Scotland) and
   Kate McCabe (Scotland)
Catherine, d. 5/13/1916 at 70; carcinoma; Patrick Haughey and Catherine
   -----
Elizabeth, d. 9/24/1920 at 88/1; acute enteritis; Patrick McCooey and
   Elizabeth Gormon
Ellen, d. 11/2/1891 at 59/0/2; widow; Patrick McShane (Ireland) and Ellen
   Reynolds (Ireland)
Frank, d. 8/9/1896 at 55; heart disease; b. Ireland; SM
Hugh J., d. 2/5/1908 at 24/6/7 in Manchester; tuberculosis of lungs
James, d. 5/11/1890 at 38; married; John McArdle (Ireland) and S. Dunlan
   (Ireland)
James, d. 6/20/1904 at 25; pulmonary tuberculosis
John, d. 5/13/1897 at 71; pneumonia; b. Ireland; PH
Lawrence, d. 9/4/1891 at 70; married; Patrick McArdle (Ireland) and Ellen
   Murray (Ireland)
Margaret, d. 11/15/1895 at 55; apoplexy; b. Ireland; SM
Margaret, d. 11/17/1934 at 35/8/16; arteriosclerosis
Martha, d. 5/29/1902 at 63/0/16; paralysis; SM
Mary, d. 12/8/1897 at 48; inflammation of stomach; b. Ireland; SM
Michael, d. 5/16/1924 at –; alcoholism
Rose Ann, d. 12/5/1912 at 45/3/21; endocarditis chronic; Peter McArdle
   and Ellen McShane
Sarah, d. 9/12/1891 at 97; widow; (Ireland; Ireland)
Sarah, d. 12/27/1927 at –; intestinal obstruction
Sarah A., d. 11/15/1927 at 102; chronic myocarditis

McARTHUR,
Louis G., d. 12/28/1907 at 58; heart disease; Caroline L. -----

McATARVEY,
child, d. 5/9/1918 at –; stillborn; James McAtarvey and Mabel Illingworth
James, d. 9/16/1920 at –; anencephalus; James McAtarvey and Mabel
   Illingsworth

McATAVEY,
M. A., d. 1/15/1896 at –; intersusception; b. Dover; SM
Michael, d. 5/22/1911 at 38/7; ac. artic. rheumatism; John McAtavey and Ellen Shea
Patrick, d. 1/16/1904 at 48; paralysis; SM
Rose Ann, d. 7/4/1912 at 13/9/9; tuberculous meningitis; Michael McAtavey and Mary Callaghan

McAULIFFE,
Patrick, d. 8/8/1923 at – in Scituate, RI; fracture of skull

McBENNETT,
A. J., d. 7/23/1888 at 14/5/7; b. Dover; Francis McBennett (Ireland) and Sarah Hughes (Ireland)
Bridget, d. 7/21/1890 at 63/2/21; married; Michael McKernan (Ireland) and Mary McKernan (Ireland)
Elizabeth, d. 5/4/1922 at 61/2/20; cerebral hemorrhage; Michael McBennett and Bridget McKernan
Margaret, d. 3/5/1903 at 37/7; pneumonia; SM
Mary A., d. 3/22/1936 at 77/11/9 in Concord; chronic myocarditis

McBRIDE,
Margaret, d. 2/1/1890 at 40; single; Patrick McBride (Ireland) and Annie Hughes (Ireland)
William, d. 10/30/1936 at 40/1/26; cancer of mouth

McCABE,
child, d. 11/25/1895 at 0; inanition; b. Dover; SM
child, d. 1/5/1906 at –; premature birth
child, d. 6/10/1908 at –; stillborn; Frank McCabe and Mary Kirkman
Alexander, d. 12/13/1923 at 0/3/5; ac. lobar pneumonia; Bernard J. McCabe and Catherine Cunningham
Alexander J., d. 7/21/1914 at 39/10 in St. Louis, MO; phthisis pulmonalis; Francis McCabe and Bridget McCaffrey
Annie, d. 3/21/1915 at 0/0/1; atelectasis of lungs; Bernard J. McCabe and Catherine A. -----
Bernard, d. 12/16/1894 at –; bronchitis; b. Dover; SM
Bernard J., d. 8/3/1928 at 43/8/16; "see card"; Francis McCabe and Bridget McCaffery
Bridget, d. 3/13/1887 at 49; housewife; married; b. Ireland; Arthur Murray (Ireland) and Mary Macklin (Ireland)
Bridget, d. 8/7/1895 at 48; cerebral meningitis; b. Ireland; SM
Bridget, d. 5/29/1927 at 46; carcinoma of stomach; Michael McCabe and Margaret Watters

Catherine, d. 4/12/1912 at 60/2/2; cardiac thrombosis; Daniel Davis and Polly Perkins
Catherine, d. 3/7/1927 at 83; arterio sclerosis
Catherine H., d. 2/27/1922 at 43/5/15; acute endocarditis; John McCabe and Catherine McCabe
Doris, d. 1/27/1913 at 0/1/22; tubercular meningitis; Frank J. McCabe and Mary Kirkman
Edward T., d. 4/17/1914 at 27/3/22; pulmonary tuberculosis; Thomas McCabe and Mary McGroty
Eliza, d. 7/26/1905 at 26/6/15; pulmonary consumption; SM
Ellen, d. 9/7/1922 at 69/4/23; apoplexy; Owen McCabe and Catherine Mallen
Ellen M., d. 3/15/1937 at 62; chr. endocarditis
Eva H., d. 3/15/1906 at 38/3/23; tuberculosis; PH
Frances H., d. 9/25/1893 at –; inanition; b. Dover; (Manchester; England)
Francis, d. 9/27/1889 at 3; James McCabe (Ireland) and C. McDonald (Ireland)
Francis J., d. 7/1/1914 at 27; valvular heart disease; Frank McCabe and Mary Murray
Frank, d. 9/10/1892 at 1; cholera infantum; b. Dover; (Ireland; Ireland)
Frank J., d. 1/9/1932 at 60/11/2; coronary thrombosis
Frank J., d. 11/13/1936 at 84; broncho-pneumonia
Frederick, d. 7/27/1899 at 20; ulcer of stomach; SM
James, d. 3/26/1898 at 2; auto infection; b. Dover; SM
James, d. 6/23/1929 at 64 in Durham; phthisis florida
James, d. 3/12/1936 at 69/0/29; natural causes
James J., d. 1/15/1897 at 6; cerebral meningitis; b. Dover; SM
John, d. 3/10/1889 at 0/0/1-6; b. Dover; Charles McCabe (Ireland)
John, d. 1/5/1907 at 32; tuberculosis; Patrick McCabe and Bridget Murray
John, d. 9/28/1914 at 71; found dead; John McCabe
John, d. 3/9/1926 at 95; chronic nephritis; Margaret Vallily
John F., d. 5/21/1898 at 0; pneumonia; b. Dover; SM
Josephine F., d. 6/22/1905 at 20/0/10; tuberculosis; SM
Kate, d. 11/28/1895 at 41; heart failure; b. Ireland; SM
Katherine, d. 12/14/1893 at 57; heart disease; b. Ireland; (Ireland; Ireland)
Margaret, d. 1/28/1920 at 80; cancer of uterus
Margaret, d. 6/21/1929 at 68; chr. endocarditis
Mary, d. 6/10/1888 at 48/9; widow
Mary, d. 5/9/1892 at –; hemorrhage; b. Dover; (Ireland; Ireland)
Mary, d. 12/9/1900 at 65; heart disease
Mary, d. 5/25/1917 at 38; eclampsia; James Kirkman and Sarah -----
Mary, d. 6/16/1926 at 62; angina pectoris; Michael McCabe and Margaret Waters
Mary Anne, d. 1/10/1922 at 1/2/24; acute lobar pneumonia; Bernard J. McCabe and Catherine Cunningham

Mary C., d. 1/3/1934 at –; myocarditis
Mary E., d. 8/8/1893 at –; marasmus; b. Dover; (Ireland; Ireland)
Mary E., d. 1/9/1897 at 2; cerebral meningitis; b. Dover; SM
Mary E., d. 5/20/1906 at 45; acute pulm. tuberculosis; SM
Mary E., d. 1/19/1914 at 42/5/4 in Boston, MA; natural causes; Edward Mulligan and Margaret Riley
Patrick, d. 9/22/1906 at –; heart disease; SM
Richard H., d. 9/18/1927 at 63/11 in Claremont; pernicious anaemia
Rose, d. 1/23/1937 at 82/5/8 in S. Berwick, ME; cancer of colon
Sarah, d. 11/8/1897 at 25; diabetes; b. Scotland; SM
Thomas, d. 12/22/1889 at 38; laborer; married; b. America; Owen McCabe (Ireland) and Catherine Mallen (Ireland)
Thomas, d. 11/16/1898 at 40; gastro-enteritis; b. Ireland; SM
Thomas J., d. 1/30/1915 at 24/2/17; lobar pneumonia; James J. McCabe
William, d. 3/9/1890 at 0/7/26; Thomas McCabe (Dover) and Mary McGroty (Salmon Falls)

McCAFFEREY,
Margaret, d. 6/8/1902 at 68; dilation of heart; SM

McCANN,
son, d. 4/19/1888 at –; b. Dover; James McCann (Ireland) and Bridget Riley (Ireland)
child, d. 3/29/1898 at 0; stillborn; b. Dover
child, d. 4/3/1905 at –; malnutrition; SM
child, d. 2/17/1908 at –; stillborn; John McCann and Mary E. Jackson
child, d. 11/23/1908 at –; stillborn; John McCann and Mary C. Jackson
Annie, d. 3/12/1935 at –; lobar pneumonia
Bernard, d. 11/24/1909 at 42; tuberculosis
Bridget, d. 3/10/1910 at 48; subacute rheumatism; John Carroll
James, d. 1/2/1913 at 56 in Concord; exhaustion in senile dem.; Ross McCann
James, d. 8/31/1915 at 59; chronic int. nephritis; William McCann
John, d. 5/17/1924 at 53/9; arterio sclerosis
John J., d. 7/12/1907 at 55; diabetes mellitus
John James, d. 10/1/1918 at 13/5/17; broncho pneumonia; James J. McCann and Minnie Connolly
Katherine, d. 9/1/1911 at 53; acute nephritis; Christopher Hughes and Mary McCaffrey
Mary, d. 2/9/1893 at 45; carcinoma of liver; b. Ireland; (Ireland; Ireland)
Mary, d. 12/21/1922 at 59/8/6; cancer of stomach; John Donnichear
Mary, d. 5/31/1929 at 68; carcinoma of breast

McCARNEY,
James, d. 4/4/1933 at 69; heart disease

McCARTEN,
child, d. 9/6/1903 at –; stillborn; SM
Annie, d. 3/12/1902 at –; premature birth; SM
Daniel, d. 9/24/1926 at 74 in Central Falls, RI; cerebral hemorrhage
Mary A., d. 8/27/1892 at –; bronchitis; b. Dover; (Ireland; Ireland)
Mrs. D., d. 1/23/1909 at 46; valvular heart disease; A. Mooney and Ann ---

McCARTHY,
Annie, d. 7/26/1904 at 30/6; convulsions; SM
Annie, d. 8/18/1904 at 0/0/1; inanition; SM
Christopher, d. 12/21/1899 at 0; pneumonia; SM
Dennis J., d. 5/6/1920 at 72; carcinoma of stomach
Edward J., d. 3/22/1924 at 60/1 in Manchester; cardiac syncope
Elizabeth T., d. 3/14/1915 at 0/4; scorbutus; Patrick McCarthy and Annie
    Green
Eugene O., d. 5/5/1908 at 61; paralysis; Eugene O. McCarthy and Joanna
    Regan
Jeremiah, d. 10/18/1911 at 43 in Somersworth; electrocution; Daniel
    McCarthy and Ellen McCarthy
John, d. 2/9/1903 at 49/7/8 in Portsmouth; cerebral lesion; SM
Julia, d. 6/26/1920 at –; cancer of liver; Jeremiah McCarthy and Mary
    Nagle
Margaret, d. 12/27/1922 at 65 in Manchester; angina pectoris
Mary, d. 4/5/1929 at 90 in Brockton, MA; "see card"; John O'Brien
Patrick, d. 12/14/1933 at 60/8/27 in Concord; cerebral hemorrhage
Patrick J., d. 10/13/1928 at 58/2/22; carcinoma; Daniel McCarthy and
    Margaret -----
Timothy, d. 2/11/1906 at 48; pneumonia; buried in Rochester
Timothy, d. 10/31/1912 at 27; convulsions; Thomas McCarthy and
    Margaret Daley

McCARTY,
Catherine, d. 10/8/1894 at 86; old age with heart failure; b. Ireland; SM
Catherine, d. 4/5/1897 at 74; old age; b. Ireland; SM
John, d. 12/1/1890 at 74/8/5; married; Patrick McCarty (Ireland) and Mary
    Dailey (Ireland)
John J., d. 5/19/1926 at 75/7/26; chronic myocarditis; John McCarty and
    Catherine Golden
John P., d. 10/26/1937 at 73; carcinoma stomach
Julia, d. 6/10/1911 at 24; measles; William McCarty and Julia Sullivan
Margaret M., d. 7/12/1894 at 23; chronic pneumonia; b. Ireland; SM
Michael, d. 4/1/1935 at 75; hypertrophy of prostate
Ross H., d. 11/12/1931 at 40/11/21; natural causes

McCAULEY,
E. L., d. 7/26/1900 at <1; cholera infantum
James W., d. 4/29/1901 at 3/0/5; diphtheria; SM

McCLELLEN,
Celia M., d. 12/9/1889 at 0/0/16; b. Dover; Celestine McClellen (PEI) and
    Eliza Riley (Ireland)

McCLINE,
Honora M., d. 9/23/1927 at 27/0/26; intestinal obstruction; Thomas Mannix
    and Julia Fitzgerald

McCLINTOCH,
Annie V., d. 7/3/1932 at 58/6/2; chronic myocarditis

McCLINTOCK,
Helen G., d. 5/16/1918 at 68/6/7 in Lawrence, MA; carcinoma of stomach
John, d. 10/9/1935 at 80 in S. Berwick, ME; chronic interstitial nephritis
Mary, d. 2/9/1893 at 38; died in Strafford Co. Asylum fire
Sarah, d. 2/9/1893 at 32; died in Strafford Co. Asylum fire
Thomas, d. 2/1/1937 at 87*
Walter T., d. 11/19/1898 at 5; diphtheretic laryngitis; b. Dover; PH

McCONE,
Alice, d. 4/5/1890 at 71; (Ireland; Ireland)
Edward, d. 5/29/1919 at 76; lobar pneumonia; Owen McCone and
    Catherine Nugent
Jennie, d. 9/27/1901 at 33/7/17; heart clot; SM
Katherine, d. 10/17/1929 at 68 in New York, NY; "see card"
Mary A., d. 10/28/1889 at 42; single; b. Dover
Mary E., d. 2/16/1923 at 67/2/26; lobar pneumonia; Patrick Gorman and
    Catherine McCooey
Michael, d. 2/24/1913 at 43/11/7; ch. intestitial nephritis; Bernard McCone
    and Rose A. Mulligan
Owen, d. 5/13/1894 at – in Chicago, IL; endocarditis; buried in Dover
Patrick, d. 3/6/1891 at 64; single

McCONNELL,
Charles H., d. 1/14/1896 at 8; typhoid pneumonia; b. Dover; SM
Elizabeth, d. 9/14/1888 at 23/6/1; married; b. Dover; James McCooey
    (Ireland) and Sarah A. Griffin (Ireland)
George W., d. 4/16/1919 at 0/0/½; premature birth; Joseph McConnell and
    Phylis Brooks

J. F., d. 7/21/1888 at 0/1/28; b. Dover; John W. McConnell (Ireland) and
  Elizabeth McC'y (Dover)
John, d. 6/24/1908 at 48 in Kalmar, Canada; pistol shot
Phyllis, d. 7/21/1930 at 30; anterior poliomyelitis
Raymond H., d. 8/8/1906 at 0/10/24; cholera infantum; SM

McCOOEY,
Bridget, d. 5/7/1924 at 88/3/5; chronic myocarditis; James Doran and
  Mary McNulty
Catherine, d. 5/13/1920 at 1/3/13; pneumonia; John J. McCooey and
  Elizabeth McCarthy
Daniel, d. 10/8/1888 at 42/3; wool sorter; married; b. Ireland; Patrick
  McCooey and Elizabeth Gorman (Ireland)
James, d. 1/17/1895 at 55; heart disease; b. Ireland; SM
John, d. 7/2/1911 at 73; ch. valv. heart disease; Patrick McCooey and
  Elizabeth Gorman
John J., d. 5/12/1906 at 30; pulmonary phthisis; SM
Mary, d. 3/12/1903 at 75; heart disease; SM
Mary A., d. 3/26/1909 at 64 in Concord; exhaustion in melancholia; Patrick
  McCooey and Elizabeth Gorman
Patrick, d. 10/22/1909 at 38/0/2 in Nashua; valvular dis. of heart; Daniel
  McCooey and Bridget Doran
Rose, d. 6/18/1898 at 53; phthisis; b. Ireland; SM

McCOOL,
John, d. 7/8/1932 at 72 in Salem, MA; chronic endocarditis
Margaret, d. 8/29/1906 at 0/8; entero colitis; SM
Mary, d. 6/13/1930 at 64 in Salem, MA; carcinoma of cervix
Patrick, d. 3/17/1909 at 28/2/5; broncho pneumonia; William McCool and
  Catherine Morris
Sarah, d. 3/26/1896 at 29; pul. tuberculosis; b. Dover; SM

McCOOLE,
Alice, d. 9/29/1897 at 59; acute pneumonia; SM
Catherine, d. 2/20/1912 at 33; pulmonary tuberculosis; Charles
  Cunningham and Margaret McGlaughlin
Charles M., d. 4/26/1926 at 0/0/1; prolonged labor; Charles McCoole and
  Gladys Hendrickson
Charles M., d. 6/1/1934 at 30; natural causes
Cornelius, d. 3/6/1910 at –; premature birth; John McCoole and Catherine
  Cunningham
Daniel P., d. 10/1/1918 at 10/1/23; acute lobar pneumonia; John P.
  McCoole and Kate Cunningham
Elizabeth, d. 12/21/1894 at 60; heart disease; b. Ireland; SM

Everett, d. 7/5/1887 at 0/6; b. Dover; John McCoole (Ireland) and Mary McQuillan (Ireland)
Frances Teresa, d. 12/2/1923 at 54/4/26; phthisis pulmonalis; John McCoole and Alice Mone
Herbert, d. 8/22/1891 at 0/3/4; John McCoole, Jr. (ME) and Margaret Hughes (Dover)
Hugh, d. 11/11/1930 at 78/2/20; arterio sclerosis; Dennis McCoole
John, d. 4/2/1902 at 57; fracture of skull; SM
John, d. 5/12/1902 at 25/9 in Manchester; SM
John, d. 4/1/1937 at 68; chr. myocarditis
Margaret, d. 12/16/1893 at 28; pulmonary tuberculosis; b. Dover; (Ireland; Ireland)
Margery E., d. 10/15/1906 at 0/3; whooping cough
Mary, d. 1/12/1898 at 63; bronchitis; b. Ireland; SM
Mary, d. 1/3/1910 at 21; tuberculosis; John -----
Rose Ann, d. 8/10/1906 at 0/0/26; whooping cough
William, d. 6/18/1891 at 40/7; widower; Dennis McCoole (Ireland) and Mary McLaughlin (Ireland)

McCRAREN,
Catherine, d. 5/30/1931 at 72; chronic endocarditis

McCREATH,
Lydia, d. 6/6/1899 at 50; paralysis agitans

McCRILLIS,
John, d. 3/12/1930 at 66; chronic endocarditis; John McCrillis and Mary ---

McCRISTAL,
Ann, d. 3/31/1897 at 36; heart disease; b. Ireland; SM

McCRYSTAL,
Catherine, d. 6/30/1931 at 36; chronic bronchitis
Mary, d. 7/28/1909 at 68 in Concord; exhaustion in senile dementia
Patrick, d. 1/15/1919 at 73/8/18; epithelioma - neck; James McCrystal and Ann McKenna

McCULLOUCH,
Samuel, d. 1/29/1927 at 65/5/15; chronic bronchitis

McCULLOUGH,
Louise E., d. 4/12/1910 at 16/9/16; tuberculosis; Robert McCullough and Jennie Lind Smith

Rachael J., d. 12/21/1929 at 70/7/23; cancer of breast; Robert McCullough and Rachael Hunter

McDANIEL,
Alvira C., d. 8/17/1898 at 80 in Everett, MA; fatty heart, valv. lesion; PH
Angie M., d. 3/3/1902 at 66/5/2; heart disease; PH
Frank, d. 7/27/1928 at 74/0/12; carcinoma of segmoid; True M. McDaniel and Rebecca Daniels
Hester S., d. 6/26/1914 at 87/11/8; pneumonia; John McDaniel and Sarah Chapman
Virgil H., d. 3/15/1897 at 60 in Everett, MA; disease of liver; PH

McDANIELS,
Elizabeth, d. 4/20/1917 at 61/2; strang. femoral hernia; True W. McDaniel (sic) and Rebecca Daniels

McDERMOTT,
Ann, d. 2/9/1893 at 43; died in Strafford Co. Asylum fire

McDONALD,
child, d. 9/8/1895 at 0; stillborn; b. Dover; SM
Ann, d. 4/13/1895 at 79; old age; b. Ireland; SM
Ann, d. 12/24/1925 at 63; softening of brain
Annie, d. 6/1/1898 at 63; inanition; b. Dover; SM
Annie, d. 11/26/1918 at 54 in Concord; influenza; Arthur Tammany and Ann Hughes
Bridget, d. 10/19/1900 at 32; acute nephritis; SM
Catherine, d. 11/11/1926 at 55 in Washington, DC; chronic myocarditis
Cornelius, d. 3/13/1895 at 87 in Barrington; bronchitis and old age; b. Barrington; SM
Cornelius, d. 1/18/1930 at 78/2 in Barrington; chronic myocarditis
Daniel, d. 6/30/1909 at 42 in Cocheco; pulmonary tuberculosis
Ellen F., d. 8/20/1927 at 65/0/4; cerebral apoplexy; Alfred Marden and Ellen McKenna
F. A., d. 1/26/1908 at 0/0/10; pneumonia; John McDonald and ----- McBennett
Frank, d. 9/5/1911 at 79; fibroid phthisis
Franklin H., d. 10/13/1936 at 91/8/13; arteriosclerosis
George F., d. 8/21/1890 at 17/2/21; single; Thomas McDonald (Dover) and Ida E. Kimball (Great Falls)
James, d. 6/7/1889 at –; b. Dover; James McDonald and Nellie Marden
James, d. 11/12/1896 at 53; chronic alcoholism; b. Ireland; SM
James, d. 8/7/1898 at 0; cholera infantum; b. Dover; SM
James, d. 10/7/1918 at 54/1/5; cerebral hemorrhage; Patrick McDonald and Mary Agnew

James, d. 9/16/1924 at 66; chr. Brights disease; Cornelius McDonald and Nora O'Brien
Jno. James, d. 1/23/1891 at 0/0/1; Fr. McDonald (Ireland) and Susan Mullan (Ireland)
John, d. 11/24/1934 at –; intestinal obstruction
John T., d. 10/19/1916 at 45/10/19; pulmonary tuberculosis; Patrick McDonald and Mary Agnew
Julia, d. 9/15/1912 at 68 in Lawrence, MA; hypertrophic cirrhosis
Kate, d. 5/5/1898 at 69; valvular disease of heart; b. Ireland; SM
Mary, d. 4/13/1903 at 0/0/2; premature birth; SM
Mary, d. 12/24/1912 at 42; burns; Patrick Riley and Bridget -----
Mary B., d. 8/21/1901 at 3/11/13; convulsions
Mary E., d. 11/26/1905 at 67; chronic interstitial nephritis; SM
Mollie E. N., d. 1/13/1902 at 18/8 in Rochester; nephritis; PH
Patrick, d. 12/22/1908 at 70; pneumonia; James McDonald and Annie Devlin
Sarah, d. 1/2/1933 at 78/7/8; arteriosclerosis
Sarah J., d. 4/28/1935 at 68; carcinoma of recto-sigmoid
Susan, d. 1/22/1899 at 36; phthisis pulmonalis; SM
Thomas, d. 11/29/1887 at 15/4/7; b. Dover; James McDonald (Ireland) and Mary Foye (Ireland)
Thomas, d. 1/28/1917 at 68 in Pembroke; pulm. tuberculosis; James McDonald and Ann Devlin
Walter A., d. 8/11/1904 at 54/4/6; probably heart affection; buried in Portland, ME

McDONNELL,
George, d. 8/23/1890 at 0/8/2; John McDonnell (Ireland) and Bridget Murray (Ireland)

McDONOUGH,
child, d. 4/9/1911 at –; stillborn; Thomas McDonough and Mary E. Brabson
child, d. 7/30/1929 at –; premature birth; Edward McDonough and Mary Lyons
child, d. 5/31/1934 at 0/0/1-8; dystocia
Bridget, d. 11/30/1926 at 83/0/23; cerebral hemorrhage; Patrick Fody and Mary Dyer
Bridget, d. 9/2/1933 at 74 in Brookline, MA; cancer of uterus
Catherine B., d. 7/8/1920 at 27/3/26; drowning accidental; Peter McDonough and Louise Murphy
Edward, d. 10/10/1934 at 68; coronary thrombosis
Esther A., d. 1/18/1914 at –; apoplexy; Michael Keough and Letitia Manning
Frederick T., d. 8/24/1933 at 21/0/23; punctured lung

Honor T., d. 10/11/1918 at 36/4/7; lobar pneumonia; Patrick McDonough and Bridget Fody
Honora, d. 6/1/1936 at 75*; b. Ireland
James F., d. 2/22/1927 at 0/5/5 in Washington, DC; meningitis
John, d. 7/31/1889 at 71/10; laborer; widower; b. Ireland; (Ireland; Ireland)
John, d. 6/12/1923 at 48/7/12; natural causes; Peter McDonough and Mary Clark
Louise, d. 11/9/1936 at 70; broncho-pneumonia
Maggie, d. 7/23/1898 at 2; summer complaint; SM
Mary, d. 11/30/1898 at 84; old age; b. Ireland; SM
Mary, d. 2/26/1908 at 84/0/24; shock
Mary, d. 8/17/1917 at 76; lobar pneumonia; Patrick -----
Mary, d. 2/25/1927 at –; premature birth; Edward F. McDonough and Mary Lyons
Mary E., d. 5/19/1915 at 35/4/18; Bright's disease; Peter McDonough and Mary Clark
Mary E., d. 1/4/1931 at 62; cerebral hemorrhage
Mary E., d. 9/17/1933 at –; chronic nephritis
Mary J., d. 1/14/1932 at 74 in Boston, MA; myocarditis
Michael, d. 5/23/1908 at 55; tuberculosis; James McDonough and ----- Kelley
Patrick, d. 1/1/1897 at 59; disease of liver; b. Ireland; SM
Patrick, d. 6/7/1905 at 66; senility; SM
Patrick, d. 12/20/1912 at 48; sarcoma of eye; Peter McDonough and Mary Clark
Patrick, d. 11/14/1917 at 60; lobar pneumonia; Patrick McDonough and Mary Hanghan
Patrick H., d. 10/6/1923 at 68/8/6; apoplexy; John McDonough and Catherine Manning
Peter, d. 11/18/1909 at 41/5; natural causes; Patrick ----- and Mary -----
Peter J., d. 1/16/1914 at 55; asthma, acute; John McDonough and Katherine Keelty
Sarah Ann, d. 11/8/1936 at 65; ar. heart-kid. trouble
Thomas, d. 2/18/1933 at 70/7/11; chronic myocarditis
Timothy, d. 3/8/1931 at 88 in Boston, MA; arterio sclerosis
William J., d. 7/17/1935 at 68 in Lawrence, MA; cancer of liver

McDUFFEE,
Dana, d. 1/24/1890 at 61/6/17; married; James McDuffee (Alton) and Joanna Wentworth (Somersworth)
Elizabeth J., d. 4/14/1890 at 69/9; married; Nathaniel Davis (Berwick, ME) and Susan Fernald
Ellen A., d. 2/15/1906 at 69/2/23 in York Beach, ME; exhaustion
Henry G., d. 5/11/1897 at 60; renal congestion; b. NH; PH

James, d. 5/20/1891 at 68/3/18; married; Seth McDuffee (Rochester) and Lucy Roberts (Rochester)

James H., d. 11/13/1893 at 25; phthisis pulmonalis; b. Dover; (Alton; Dover)

James Y., d. 7/10/1900 at 73; sudden, probably apop. syncope; buried in family lot

Louise W., d. 10/15/1914 at 61/1/16; cerebral hemorrhage; Lyman McDuffee and Mary A. Gilman

Lydia S., d. 4/21/1907 at 77/1/11; peritonitis; Moses Gilman and Abigail Hurd

Lyman, d. 5/4/1898 at 72; anaemia, heart disease; b. Alton; PH

Nellie M., d. 3/26/1937 at 73/6/4; cerebr. hemorrhage

McELHEARN,
Martha, d. 6/2/1922 at – in Goffstown; carcinoma of face

McELHERIN,
Patrick, d. 3/26/1911 at 55; hydrothorax; Peter McElherin and Mary Rafferty

McELHERN,
Catherine, d. 3/30/1921 at 60; endocarditis; Peter Fahan and Mary Murphy

McELHERON,
Mary, d. 3/25/1895 at 80; old age; b. Ireland; SM

McELROY,
Frank, d. 12/7/1928 at –; pernicious anemia

Hannah, d. 12/28/1890 at 33; widow; George Campbell (Ireland) and Mary (Ireland)

John, d. 6/22/1930 at 47 in Boston, MA; syncope

McENEANEY,
Annie M., d. 5/16/1914 at 0/0/20; spina bifida; Patrick McEneaney and Mary Casey

Mary, d. 10/16/1909 at 36; typhoid fever; John McCooey and Rose McShane

Patrick, d. 9/13/1931 at 60; coronary thrombosis

Teresa, d. 2/3/1920 at 58; obstruction of bowels; Frank Hughes and Bridget Rooney

McENERY,
Rose A., d. 10/27/1887 at 25/10/13; mill operative; married; b. Dover; George Moore (England) and Ann Cassidy (NS)

McEVOY,
Ellen, d. 7/1/1933 at 73/9; coronary thrombosis

McEWAN,
Frank W., d. 5/30/1912 at 39/8/27; anaemia; Joseph McEwan and Margaret Hough
Luke H., d. 5/17/1935 at 60/2/8 in Beverly, MA; cerebral hemorrhage
Margaret M., d. 8/16/1904 at 55/9/19; disease of brain; buried in Massena Cen., NY
Peter W., d. 4/8/1900 at <1; pneumonia; buried in E. Greenwich, RI

McFADDEN,
child, d. 11/7/1908 at --; heart disease; Hugh McFadden and Rose A. McMullen
Catherine, d. 2/9/1905 at 71; accidental burning; SM
David, d. 8/8/1916 at 48; acute parenchymatous; Patrick McFadden and Katherine Horan
Hugh E., d. 9/8/1899 at 8; gangrene; PH
James, d. 5/28/1911 at 45; natural causes; Patrick McFadden and Katherine Moran
James E., d. 12/1/1925 at 72; gangrene of foot; Hugh McFadden and Nancy Esdale
Mary A., d. 3/22/1903 at 36/6; peritonitis; buried in Biddeford, ME
Mary G., d. 12/31/1933 at 40/5/22; lobar pneumonia
Patrick, d. 3/28/1895 at 52; pneumonia; b. Ireland; SM
William, d. 11/19/1909 at 34; pneumonia
William H., d. 7/18/1896 at --; cholera infantum; b. Biddeford, ME; SM

McFARLAND,
George F., d. 4/13/1904 at 46/8/25; tubercular meningitis; PH
Idella F., d. 10/3/1928 at 72/5/24; cerebral hemorrhage; William B. Foss and Sarah J. Haines
Leonora, d. 11/12/1901 at 50/2/4; hemorrhage of stomach; buried in Farmington
Nahum, d. 5/15/1912 at 71/7/27; acute nephritis; Isaac McFarland
Ruth S., d. 9/20/1914 at 84/9/10; chronic bronchitis; John N. Clay and Hannah C. -----

McGAHAN,
James, d. 6/1/1918 at 47; phthisis pulmonalis; Edward McGahan and Susan -----

McGARRY,
Catherine, d. 6/15/1908 at 70; cancer of liver; Patrick Quinn

Ellen, d. 8/31/1913 at 60; chronic nephritis

McGAUGH,
Frances, d. 5/7/1898 at 1; meningitis; b. Dover; SM
Hugh, d. 2/12/1932 at 80; cancer of face
John, d. 8/1/1934 at 72; heart disease
Julia, d. 1/30/1923 at 80; cerebral hemorrhage; Bridget McLain
Margaret, d. 10/31/1897 at 5; pneumonia; b. Dover; SM
Michael, d. 12/6/1903 at 60 in Lynn, MA; enteritis
Susan, d. 4/5/1893 at 81; old age - effects of injury; b. Ireland; (Ireland; Ireland)
Susan, d. 5/31/1903 at 19; valvular disease of heart; SM

McGEE,
child, d. 9/11/1900 at <1; malnutrition; SM
Mary J., d. 5/13/1914 at 0/0/1; premature birth; Mary McGee
Rosilla, d. 2/25/1900 at 3; pneumonia

McGERRY,
John T., d. 3/18/1890 at 45/9 in Waltham, MA

McGILL,
Ann, d. 3/5/1930 at 87/10/5; arterio sclerosis; Michael Rossiter and Mary Kelley
Genevieve M., d. 2/24/1919 at 37/0/10; Bright's disease; Thomas Sherry and Maria A. Hughes
James, Rev., d. 4/9/1925 at 53/2/8 in Manchester; cerebral hemorrhage; Thomas McGill and Ann Rossiter

McGILLEN,
Patrick J., d. 4/--/1903 at 30; not determined; buried in Newburyport, MA

McGILLICUDDY,
Ella, d. 1/14/1927 at 61/0/20; lobar pneumonia; Jere McGillicuddy and Mary Sullivan

McGILLIVRAY,
Robert, d. 10/4/1936 at 61/2/8; coronary thrombosis

McGINN,
Ann, d. 4/5/1915 at 76; cerebral hemorrhage; Patrick Ackley and Mary McAdam
Lawrence, d. 12/26/1898 at 36; cirrhosis of liver; b. Ireland; SM
Mary, d. 5/17/1897 at 3; scarletinal nephritis; b. Dover; SM

McGLAUFLIN,
child, d. 2/17/1899 at –; stillborn; PH

McGLONE,
Ann, d. 6/18/1914 at –; apoplexy; Edward Markey and Bridget McAdam
Annie, d. 8/22/1912 at 68; cerebral apoplexy; Ferdinand Hughes and Ann Barker
Arthur B., d. 2/13/1902 at 1/5/3; diphtheria; SM
Didania, d. 9/4/1901 at 72/8/15; paralytic shock; buried in Pittsfield
James, d. 2/16/1907 at 44/4; typhoid fever; James McGlone and Mary -----
John, d. 5/20/1905 at 65/3/7; dilitation of heart; buried in Rollinsford
Mary, d. 5/3/1898 at 60; meningitis; b. Ireland; SM
Michael, d. 10/10/1889 at 70; laborer; married; b. Ireland; Michael McGlone (Ireland) and Kate Mullen (Ireland)
Michael, d. 12/12/1919 at 71; gen. arteriosclerosis; Lawrence McGlone and Bridget McCabe
Ronald R., d. 9/25/1937 at 0/4/12; acute l. pneumonia

McGONAGLE,
Grace, d. 11/12/1905 at 36; typhoid fever

McGONIGAL,
Daniel, d. 8/31/1898 at 0; cholera infantum; b. Dover; SM

McGOUGH,
Kate, d. 8/29/1889 at 3/1/11; b. Dover; M. McGough (Ireland) and S. Callaghan (Ireland)

McGOWAN,
Charles, d. 3/10/1928 at 74/12/9 (sic) in Concord; chronic myocarditis; John McGowan and Jane Smith
Frank, d. 12/7/1887 at 54; laborer; married; b. Ireland; Patrick McGowan (Ireland) and Bridget (Ireland)
John, d. 10/6/1930 at – in Providence, RI; myocarditis failure
Patrick, d. 4/21/1913 at 52; acute bronch. pneumonia; James McGowan and Bridget Mulligan

McGOWEN,
Dominick, d. 12/21/1925 at 63; acute myocarditis; Michael McGowan (sic) and Anna Sheren
Ellen, d. 2/12/1908 at 75; heart disease
John P., d. 5/13/1891 at 18/4; single; Frank McGowen (Ireland) and Ellen Laner (Ireland)

Mary, d. 3/5/1891 at 29/2; single; Bartley McGowen (Ireland) and Bridget Duny (Ireland)
Rita M., d. 9/25/1920 at 0/9/14; meningitis; Fred McGowan (sic) and Alice Hood
Thomas, d. 11/12/1891 at 26; single; Frank McGowen (Ireland) and Ellen Lane (Ireland)

McGRAIL,
Agnes C., d. 2/16/1920 at 45; uraemia; Daniel McDonald and ----- Cullen
John E., d. 4/8/1912 at 0/2/22; pneumonia; Thomas H. McGrail and Agnes C. McDonald

McGRATH,
Elizabeth, d. 3/20/1892 at 37; phthisis; b. Dover; (Ireland; Ireland)
Jane, d. 4/12/1921 at 73; infection of mastoid

McGRORY,
Patrick J., d. 7/15/1931 at 62; carcinoma of liver

McGROTY,
Alice, d. 3/7/1925 at 88; lobar pneumonia; John Quinlan and Margaret Lanigan
James, d. 11/5/1914 at 73/6; carcinoma of stomach; John McGroty and Catherine Brown

McGUIGAN,
son, d. 5/6/1888 at –; b. Dover; James McGuigan (Ireland) and Mary Macklin (Ireland)
Alice B., d. 10/14/1932 at 80/8/3; angina pectoris
Ann, d. 6/20/1894 at 43; chron. nephritis; b. Scotland; SM
Ellen, d. 12/7/1910 at 65; pneumonia; Patrick Hughes and ----- McGuigan
Frank, d. 6/15/1911 at –; stillborn; Patrick J. McGuigan and Nellie Morgan
James, d. 6/15/1911 at –; premature birth; Patrick J. McGuigan and Nellie Morgan
John, d. 4/1/1892 at 31; pulmonary phthisis; b. Ireland; (Ireland; Ireland)
Mark, d. 8/13/1893 at 19; rapid pulmonary phthisis; b. Scotland; (Ireland; Scotland)
Michael, d. 5/24/1916 at 75; broncho pneumonia; Patrick McGuigan and Mary Hughes
Owen, d. 5/2/1922 at 78 in Claremont; old age
Peter, d. 3/12/1921 at 78/2/15; myocarditis; Patrick McGuigan and Mary Carragher
Sarah, d. 2/13/1895 at 13; phthisis pulmonalis; b. Dover; SM

McGUINIS,
John C., d. 4/4/1891 at 40/4; married

McGUINNESS,
Catherine, d. 2/20/1902 at 76; apoplexy; SM
Catherine, d. 4/24/1904 at 60; ascetis; buried in Lawrence, MA
Edward J., d. 1/22/1922 at 42/7/11; chronic myocarditis; John McGuinness
    and Mary Grimes
Ellen, d. 6/1/1887 at 70; married; b. Ireland; Patrick Hughes (Ireland)
Ellen, d. 12/29/1888 at 70; widow; b. Ireland; L. Doran (Ireland) and
    Bridget McCone (Ireland)
Jno. A., d. 5/–/1891 at 38; P. McGuinness (Ireland) and S. Connolly
    (Ireland)
John, d. 9/16/1901 at 56; cancer of mouth; SM
Margaret, d. 8/5/1914 at 65; valvular disease of heart; Robert Armstrong
    and Margaret Morry
Mary, d. 2/25/1890 at 44; married; Henry Grimes (Ireland) and Sarah
    Barker (Ireland)
Mary, d. 5/16/1937 at –; cancer of liver
Mary Ann, d. 3/24/1926 at 70; angina pectoris
Michael, d. 5/31/1935 at 75; heart disease
Patrick, d. 11/23/1894 at 44; Bright's disease; b. Dover; SM
Patrick, d. 2/15/1900 at 75; shock; SM
Susan, d. 5/29/1892 at 71; phthisis; b. Ireland; (Ireland; Ireland)

McGUIRE,
child, d. 1/18/1926 at –; stillborn; Mary McGuire
Alice, d. 1/2/1932 at 62/9/27; arterio sclerosis
Bernard, d. 3/2/1924 at 50/0/18; carcinoma of stomach; Michael McGuire
    and Mary Hestler
Ellen, d. 12/10/1931 at 60; carcinoma of stomach
Patrick, d. 12/5/1911 at 63; sarcoma maxillary bone

McGUIRK,
John C., d. 10/9/1900 at 39 in Tewksbury, MA; ch. rheumatic arthritis; SM

McGUNNIGLE,
Sarah A., d. 10/24/1890 at 0/2/21; Daniel McGunnigle (Ireland) and Grace
    Kelley (Ireland)

McHUGH,
Michael, d. 4/29/1909 at 61/1/9 in Somersworth; chronic nephritis; Thomas
    McHugh and Margaret Mullen

McILROY,
James, d. 5/4/1897 at 0; premature birth; b. Dover

McINTIRE,
Charles E., d. 3/9/1890 at 3/4/0; Charles McIntire (Boston, MA) and Almeda M. Page (Great Falls)
Frances J. A., d. 3/30/1913 at 52/3/4; hydropericardium
John W., d. 5/10/1931 at 75/5/9; cerebral hemorrhage
Laura J., d. 8/7/1935 at 78/3/24; cerebral hemorrhage
Susan, d. 11/27/1892 at 23; pulmonary phthisis; b. Dover; (Ireland; Ireland)

McINTYRE,
child, d. 12/23/1892 at –; stillborn; b. Dover; (Scotland; NY)
child, d. 7/31/1916 at 0/0/1-4 in Kittery, ME; premature birth; D. S. McIntyre
Ann, d. 7/2/1894 at 62; liver and brain disease; b. Ireland; SM
Ann, d. 8/1/1902 at 70/3/18; old age; PH
Duncan, d. 2/6/1892 at 47; Bright's disease; b. Scotland; (Scotland; Scotland)
Duncan, d. 8/7/1934 at 77; arteriosclerosis
Ernest Leon, d. 6/30/1896 at 1; disease of brain with conv.; b. Dover; PH
Finlay, d. 1/4/1892 at 70; disease of the heart; b. Scotland; (Scotland; Scotland)
Hannah, d. 2/6/1907 at 77/8/10; chronic diarrhea; Thomas Garland
Henry, d. 11/15/1936 at 72; chr. myocarditis
John, d. 1/11/1912 at 64/3/14; acute indigestion; John McIntyre and Nancy Grimes
John D., d. 9/4/1918 at 68/1/28; cerebral hemorrhage; Finley McIntyre and Ann Donald
Margaret H., d. 8/31/1921 at 69/11/6; cerebral hemorrhage; William J. Horne and Jeanette Clark
Mary, d. 6/1/1892 at 63; dropsy; b. Ireland; (Ireland; Ireland)
Rose, d. 12/11/1896 at 50; Brights disease; b. Ireland; SM
Ruth E., d. 1/30/1901 at 35/9/21; consumption; PH
Samuel L., d. 12/17/1896 at 84 in Lebanon, ME; heart dropsy; b. Tuftonboro; PH
Susan B., d. 1/29/1919 at 65; carcinoma of uterus; William Lewis

McISAAC,
Mary, d. 12/1/1931 at 55; chronic myocarditis

McITHERIN,
Ann, d. 5/12/1913 at 70 in Concord; hemorrhage of bowels; Peter McItherin and Mary Rowerty

McKAN,
Annie, d. 4/9/1889 at 1/2; John McKan and Mary

McKARNON,
Mary, d. 10/30/1895 at 50; typhoid fever; b. Ireland; SM

McKAY,
Albert, d. 7/30/1928 at 20/11/20 in Benton; pulm. hemorrhage
Gordon D., d. 5/19/1934 at 60/7/26; chronic myocarditis
Hugh, Sr., d. 1/7/1934 at 69/2/26; arteriosclerosis
Isabella, d. 1/22/1931 at 69/10; lobar pneumonia

McKEARNEY,
Caroline, d. 4/6/1904 at 26/2/10; tuberculosis; SM

McKEE,
Catherine, d. 1/22/1891 at 51; married; William McNally (Ireland) and Mary McGuire (Ireland)
John Patrick, d. 8/5/1891 at 0/10; Patrick McKee (Ireland) and Mary Dobbins (Dover)
Mary, d. 1/7/1902 at 6/2/2; congestion of brain; SM
Mary, d. 6/9/1935 at 68; carcinoma of rectum
Mary E., d. 1/6/1902 at 6/2/21; typhoid fever
Rose A., d. 9/18/1889 at 0/10; b. Dover; Patrick McKee (Ireland) and Mary Dobbins (Dover)
Thomas, d. 10/29/1908 at – in East Kingston; killed by train

McKEEVER,
Ann, d. 8/10/1896 at 47; apoplexy; b. Ireland; SM
James, d. 2/2/1919 at 75/0/3; cerebral hemorrhage; Owen McKeever and Ann Rooney

McKENNA,
son, d. 5/6/1890 at –; George Reed and Maggie McKenna (Dover)
child, d. 12/26/1908 at --; stillborn; David McKenna and Lizzie Follett
child, d. 10/19/1919 at –; stillborn; John McKenna and Honor Axworthy
Ann, d. 5/9/1898 at 50; la grippe; b. Ireland; SM
Annie, d. 11/28/1893 at 3; croup; b. Dover; (Ireland; Ireland)
Catherine, d. 12/31/1898 at 83; paralysis; SM
Catherine, d. 1/12/1899 at 83; senility; SM
Catherine, d. 5/12/1909 at 52/6/12; pul. tuberculosis; Patrick McManus and Catherine McGuinness
Catherine, d. 4/13/1921 at 55/11/17; hypernephroma; Abram Cote and Mary Riley

Daniel, d. 12/7/1932 at 48/6/25 in Concord; general paresis
Edith, d. 3/28/1916 at 20/0/11; typhoid fever; James McKenna and Mary J. Cook
Elizabeth, d. 9/28/1933 at 46/9/8; fracture of skull
Flora Evelyn, d. 8/5/1890 at 2/0/26; James McKenna (PEI) and Katie Cady (US)
George, d. 7/1/1905 at 49; acute nephritis; SM
James, d. 2/14/1901 at 69; heart failure; SM
James A., d. 4/19/1889 at 2/10/19; b. Dover; James McKenna (PEI) and Catherine Cotil (NS)
John, d. 8/5/1904 at 35/0/8; heart disease; SM
Margaret S., d. 3/9/1925 at 57/5; typhoid fever; Hugh McKenna and Margaret O'Brien
Mary, d. 5/14/1904 at 57; cerebral thrombosis; SM
Mary E., d. 10/21/1910 at 18/5/10; phthisis; Thomas McKenna and Catherine McManus
Patrick, d. 1/8/1914 at 35/10/12; pulmonary tuberculosis; Hugh McKenna and Margaret O'Brien
Robert, d. 10/12/1929 at 0/2/3; inanition; John McKenna and Florence Conway
Sarah, d. 1/10/1907 at 50; acute nephritis; James Follett and Sarah Gillis
Thomas, d. 5/9/1927 at –; cerebral hemorrhage

McKENNEY,
Annie, d. 5/22/1921 at 59/0/24; angina pectoris; Frank Brennan and Bridget -----
Bernard, d. 12/3/1936 at 38/0/2; pulmonary tuberculosis
John, d. 12/1/1907 at 56; embolism; James McKenney and Ann Hughes
Mae Ellen, d. 5/6/1924 at 24; pulmonary tuberculosis; James Riley and Asse Ford

McKEON,
Daisy C., d. 6/19/1932 at 49/8/12; myocarditis
Patrick, d. 7/6/1900 at 33; myelitis; SM

McKEONE,
Mary A., d. 6/2/1932 at 69/2/1 in Biddeford, ME; chronic myocarditis

McKEOWN,
Catherine C., d. 1/13/1920 at 38; ectopic pregnancy; Michael Breen and Catherine Dillon

McKERNAN,
child, d. 12/17/1932 at –; prematurity
Catherine, d. 4/26/1901 at 64; heart failure; SM

James H., d. 1/20/1934 at –; arteriosclerosis
Katherine, d. 8/16/1933 at 62 in Boston, MA; cancer of pancreas
Margaret, d. 1/25/1900 at 36; organic disease of heart; SM
Margaret, d. 7/28/1906 at 42; chronic endocarditis; SM
Mary, d. 12/6/1901 at 4/2; congestion of lungs; SM
Patrick, d. 9/9/1918 at 86/4/3; falling down stairs; Patrick McKernan and Julia Carragher

McKERNON,
Bridget, d. 5/19/1893 at 80; old age; b. Ireland; (Ireland; Ireland)

McKINNEY,
John J., d. 7/2/1905 at 19/7/23; acute pulmonary tuberculosis
Katie, d. 5/20/1892 at 8; tubercular meningitis; b. Dover; (Ireland; Ireland)

McKLINE,
Mary, d. 8/15/1899 at 47; chronic gastritis; SM

McKNIGHT,
Ellen, d. –/–/1890 at –; Pat McKnight (Ireland) and E. McGruery (Ireland)
Ellen, d. 7/19/1892 at 32; enteritis; b. Ireland; (Ireland; Ireland)

McKONE,
Alice, d. 5/7/1918 at 58; chronic endocarditis; Patrick McKone and Isabel Moan
Annie, d. 2/16/1897 at 6; scarlet fever; b. Dover; SM
Bernard, d. 7/24/1899 at 57; Bright's disease; SM
Bridget, d. 12/28/1895 at 29; organic disease of heart; b. Ireland; SM
Daniel, d. 5/22/1929 at 65; arterio sclerosis; Felix McKone and Margaret McLin
Edward C., d. 10/10/1914 at 54/8/26; compression of brain; Peter McKone and Esther Colton
Fannie G., d. 2/25/1929 at 63/3/2 in Woburn, MA; gen. carcinomatosis
Grace L., d. 4/8/1927 at 65/2/4; cancer of liver; John Ham and Sarah Richards
John H., d. 11/10/1930 at 50/9/8; chronic nephritis; Felix McKone and Margaret McLin
John K., d. 3/27/1922 at 0/11/22 in Baldwin, NY; convulsions
Lizzie, d. 1/21/1900 at 45; Bright's disease
Margaret, d. 7/19/1889 at 42; housewife; married; b. Ireland; J. Macklin (Ireland) and Sarah (Ireland)
Raymond, d. 12/14/1928 at 42/0/1 in Ctr. Islip, NY; gen. paral. of insane
Rose A., d. 12/31/1913 at 70; apoplexy cerebral
Thomas, d. 10/22/1900 at 27; Bright's disease; SM
Thomas, d. 12/7/1918 at 63; natural causes; Patrick McKone

McKUSICK,
Bessie M., d. 1/25/1906 at 43/11/25 in Somerville, MA; chronic nephritis; PH

McLAIN,
Mary, d. 7/2/1901 at 65; hemorrhage from stomach; SM

McLANE,
Anna, d. 11/19/1932 at 62/11/28 in Stratham; abdominal cancer

McLATHLIN,
Charles H., d. 7/20/1890 at 52; married

McLAUGHLIN,
child, d. 6/15/1924 at –; stillborn; Daniel McLoughlin (sic) and Agnes S. Mallen
Bridget, d. 8/9/1892 at 53; pneumonia; b. Ireland; (Ireland; Ireland)
Catherine, d. 9/27/1930 at 65; cholecystitis; Thomas Hughes and Bridget Hanratty
Edward, d. 2/26/1894 at 31; phthisis acute; b. Ireland; SM
Ellen M., d. 10/14/1893 at 24; consumption (acute); b. Dover; (Ireland; Ireland)
John, d. 5/20/1898 at 14; accident; b. Amesbury, MA
John, d. 11/22/1922 at – in Manchester; fractured skull
John H., d. 11/14/1918 at 27/3/27; fracture of skull; Cornelius McLaughlin and Catherine Hughes
K. A., d. 1/16/1891 at 31; married; John Rafferty (Ireland) and Rose Rafferty (Ireland)
Margaret, d. 7/13/1891 at 38; married; Neal Kelley (Ireland)
Mary A., d. 3/22/1922 at 41; Brights disease; Edward McLaughlin and Margaret Kelley
Michael, d. 5/2/1898 at 62; influenza; b. Ireland; SM
Neil, d. 3/1/1920 at 53; septicemia; John McLaughlin and Catherine Kelley
Patrick, d. 2/20/1927 at 65/6/19; angina pectoris; Michael McLaughlin
William A., d. 3/26/1896 at –; influenza; b. Dover; PH

McLEAN,
George B., d. 7/8/1933 at 76/10/11; congestion of lungs

McLIN,
Catherine E., d. 1/16/1915 at 58; carcinoma uteri; Patrick McLin and Mary Mone
Patrick H., d. 6/15/1912 at 69/3; chronic bronchitis; Patrick H. McLin and Susan Cunningham

Raymond F., Jr., d. 7/28/1933 at 1/8; hemorrhage
Rose Marie, d. 4/10/1927 at 0/2/21; broncho pneumonia; Thomas J. McLin
    and Madeline H. Morgan

McLINN,
Bridget E., d. 8/8/1902 at 59/5/12; diabetes; SM
Edward J., d. 7/18/1889 at 0/3/18; b. Dover; Thomas J. McLinn (Dover)
    and Anna Tuttle (Newmarket)

McLOUGHLIN,
Margaret, d. 11/16/1912 at 56 in Lowell, MA; myocarditis

McMAHAN,
Eugenia E., d. 12/30/1918 at 62/9/10; cancer of stomach, etc.; Samuel J.
    Smith and Mary J. Doe

McMAHEN,
Mary E., d. 12/28/1889 at 30/9/24; housekeeper; b. US; Ed ------ (Ireland)
    and Isabelde Doherty (Ireland)

McMAHON,
James P., d. 1/17/1897 at 20; pulmonary phthisis; SM
John, d. 11/25/1910 at 33 in Sacramento, CA; frac. of vertebrae of neck;
    Patrick McMahon and Mary Lunney
John, d. 3/13/1911 at — in Barrington; natural causes
Mary, d. 5/25/1895 at 53; pulmonary tuberculosis; b. Ireland; SM
Patrick, d. 4/28/1896 at 50; b. Ireland; SM
Thomas, d. 2/11/1905 at 23/9/1 in Danvers, MA; consumption of lungs;
    buried in Lebanon, ME

McMANUS,
son, d. 11/14/1890 at —; Patrick McManus (Ireland) and Mary A. McArdle
    (Dover)
child, d. 11/16/1891 at —; Patrick McManus (Ireland) and Mary McArdle
    (Dover)
child, d. 11/16/1891 at —; Patrick McManus (Ireland) and Mary McArdle
    (Dover)
child, d. 2/2/1924 at —; atalectasis; Frank McManus and Bridget Murray
child, d. 7/19/1926 at —; stillborn; Frank J. McManus and Bridget Murray
Agnes, d. 8/5/1907 at 0/2/20; cholera infantum; Thomas McManus and
    Sarah Mulligan
Bridget, d. 7/21/1926 at 38/11; chronic nephritis; Thomas Murray
Catherine, d. 12/21/1920 at 76; arterio sclerosis; Bernard Rand and Ann
    Hughes

Cecilia, d. 5/16/1912 at 3/11/1; dysentery; Thomas McManus and Sarah Mulligan
Georgie, d. 11/5/1905 at 5; convulsions; SM
Gertrude, d. 9/22/1904 at 1/0/6; pneumonia
Mary, d. 2/18/1897 at 3; scarletinal nephritis; b. Dover; SM
Mary, d. 11/24/1902 at 31/6/4; SM
Mary D., d. 4/–/1893 at 52; carcinoma; b. Co. Clare, Ireland; (Co. Clare, Ireland; Co. Clare, Ireland)
Mary E., d. 11/9/1887 at 34/7/12; single; b. Dover; Patrick McManus (Ireland)
Michael, d. 10/21/1904 at 76; valvular heart disease; SM
Patrick, d. 5/10/1888 at 68/3; grocer; married; b. Ireland; Alexander McManus (Ireland) and Mary Crannan (Ireland)
Thomas J., d. 9/23/1932 at 60 in Boston, MA; pneumonia

McMILLAN,
Helen W., d. 1/14/1931 at 80 in Salem, MA; carcinoma of stomach

McMULLEN,
Adeline, d. 12/19/1902 at 46/9/15; acute enteritis
Bridget, d. 9/10/1903 at 45; peritonitis; SM
Mary, d. 4/15/1892 at 85; old age; b. Ireland; (Ireland; Ireland)
Samuel J., d. 8/12/1936 at 65/11/22; chr. myocarditis

McNALLY,
Agnes, d. 5/19/1889 at 33/0/4; house cook; single; b. Dover; Francis McNally (Ireland) and Nancy McNally (Ireland)
Alice, d. 3/8/1936 at 71/8/20; natural causes
Ann, d. 8/21/1894 at 64; paralysis; b. Ireland; SM
Ann, d. 8/21/1894 at 75; paralysis; b. Ireland
Bridget, d. 4/21/1899 at 42; phthisis; SM
Bridget, d. 2/11/1904 at 46; influenza; SM
Catherine, d. 11/21/1918 at 35 in Concord; influenza; John McNally and Elizabeth Duffy
Dennis, d. 8/22/1898 at 80; old age; b. Ireland; SM
Eliza, d. 11/14/1899 at 33; tuberculosis; SM
Francis, d. 1/9/1911 at 80 in Concord; broncho-pneumonia; Daniel McNally and Mary Cassidy
Harry, d. 5/29/1926 at 70; angina pectoris
James, d. 7/30/1909 at 60; endocarditis
James, d. 8/6/1910 at 56; intestinal obstruction
James, d. 12/6/1923 at 45/9/27; pulmonary tuberculosis; James McNally and Catherine Hanratty
John F., d. 7/4/1900 at 29; pistol shot; SM

Kate M., d. 1/25/1904 at 21/0/27; acute tuberculosis of lungs; buried in Dover
Katie, d. 7/12/1905 at 39; acute pulmonary tuberculosis
Margaret, d. 5/20/1917 at 59; myocardial insufficiency; Patrick Reynolds and Catherine McAtarvey
Margaret E., d. 6/4/1908 at 0/6/12; tubercular meningitis; James McNally and Mary York
Marie, d. 8/13/1929 at 49/2/19 in Glencliffe; pulmonary tuberculosis; George York and Mary Thompson
Mary, d. 4/8/1920 at 15/7/5 in Glencliffe; tuberculosis of lungs; James McNally and Marie York
Mary, d. 7/11/1926 at 68/10/27; angina pectoris; Bernard Markey and Margaret Connolly
Mary H., d. 12/15/1888 at 0/1/26; b. Dover; Henry McNally (Ireland) and Elizabeth Howells (Wales)
Mary Jane, d. 5/4/1896 at 34; ulcerative endocarditis; b. Dover
Mary L., d. 12/17/1910 at 26 in Waltham, MA; tuberculosis
Michael A., d. 9/17/1890 at 0/7/10; Michael McNally (Ireland) and Sarah McGuigan (PEI)
Nancy, d. 5/17/1908 at 75; organic heart disease
Patrick, d. 3/8/1888 at 70; widower; b. Ireland
Roland M., d. 2/19/1919 at 18/1/18; phthisis pulmonalis; W. F. McNally and Margaret Buzzell
Rose, d. 6/18/1889 at 40; mill operative; single; b. Ireland; George McNally (Ireland) and Margaret Murphy (Ireland)
Rose Helena, d. 1/14/1912 at 0/5/5; peritonitis; James McNally and Marie York
Susan, d. 5/18/1888 at 25; single; b. Ireland; Michael McNally (Ireland) and Mary McCann (Ireland)
William F., d. 9/7/1932 at 57; carcinoma of colon

McNEIL,
James, d. 7/9/1891 at 0/6/14; James McNeil (Ireland) and Rose M. Wilkinson (Ireland)
John L., d. 7/2/1920 at 12/3/8 in Concord; pylephlebitis; Michael McNeil and Katherine D. McIsaacs
Katherine A., d. 1/12/1920 at 42/0/19 in Concord; pulmonary tuberculosis; John McIsaacs and Anna McTherson
Margaret R., d. 10/16/1908 at 18/11/13; tuberculosis; James McNeil and Rose A. Wilkinson
Martha M., d. 12/7/1888 at 70/4/15; widow; b. Portsmouth; F. Wingate (Portsmouth) and Rebecca Dolloff (Portsmouth)
Mary, d. 2/11/1888 at 55; weaver; widow; b. Ireland; A. McAvery (Ireland) and Nancy Grimes (Ireland)
Rose A., d. 12/3/1933 at 66/0/0; lobar pneumonia

Sara Jane, d. 7/26/1920 at 26/6/1; pulmonary tuberculosis; James McNeil and Rose A. Wilkinson

McNEILL,
John, d. 1/18/1891 at 0/0/21; James McNeill (Ireland) and Rosanna Wilkinson (Ireland)
Mabel, d. 5/21/1923 at 42; typhoid fever; John Banks

McNISH,
Lavina J., d. 6/30/1923 at 83; fracture of hip

McNULTY,
William, d. 8/13/1907 at 68; heart disease

McNUTT,
John C., d. 10/13/1929 at 48/2/21; cholecystitis; Lindsay McNutt and Mary J. Brockelhurst

McOUGLE,
Rosanna, d. 12/12/1888 at 1/0/7; b. Salmon Falls; Michael McOugle (Ireland) and Susan Callahan (Ireland)

McPARTLAND,
Catherine, d. 5/6/1931 at 60/2/11 in Rockland, ME; apoplexy

McPHIE,
Annie, d. 10/6/1913 at 77; nephritis acute; John Hanratty and Rose O'Neil

McPHILLIPS,
Edward J., d. 12/12/1896 at 4; SM
James, d. 4/5/1902 at 45; pneumonia; SM
Katie, d. 8/7/1889 at 3/3/23; b. Dover; James McPhillips (Ireland) and Mary Mullen (Ireland)
Mary, d. 8/13/1922 at –; cancer of liver; Robert Mullen and Betty Brennan

McQUADE,
child, d. 12/21/1919 at –; stillborn; J. Francis McQuade and Catherine F. Connolly
child, d. 5/26/1923 at –; stillborn; J. Francis McQuade and Katherine Connelly
Frank, d. 4/1/1930 at 72; chr. int. nephritis
John, d. 4/1/1891 at 39/6/–; married; James McQuade (Ireland) and Mary Duffy (Ireland)
John, d. 1/31/1910 at 73 in Togus, ME; croupous pneumonia

Katherine F., d. 6/9/1923 at 39/1/23; embolism; Michael Connolly and
    Katherine Fox
Margaret, d. 8/27/1915 at 58/5/11; acute bronchitis; Patrick Sherry and
    Catherine Keating
Michael, d. 7/28/1892 at –; tubercular meningitis; b. Dover; (Ireland;
    Ireland)

McQUARRY,
Ronald, d. 1/28/1933 at 77/2/3; arteriosclerosis

McSHANE,
child, d. 5/–;1905 at –; stillborn; SM
Bridget, d. 2/8/1905 at 57; heart disease; SM
James, d. 12/20/1912 at 72; acute mania
Patrick, d. 12/1/1891 at 45/6; single; Peter McShane (Ireland) and Nancy
    Cosker (Ireland)
Peter, d. 4/25/1926 at 48; chr. parench. nephritis; James McShane and
    Bridget Sherry

McSHERA,
Michael J., d. 11/25/1933 at 61/9/21; carcinoma of parotoid gland

McSHERRA,
Michael, d. 9/6/1899 at –; cholera infantum; SM

McSORLEY,
Alice, d. 4/10/1889 at 0/0/1-6; b. Dover; Thomas McSorley (Dover) and
    Catherine Campbell (Scotland)
Alice, d. 2/17/1890 at 16; Pat McSorley (Ireland) and Catherine McKenney
    (Ireland)
Alice, d. 9/23/1892 at –; infantile disease; b. Dover; (Dover; Scotland)
Catherine, d. 8/15/1892 at 25; consumption; b. Ireland; (Ireland; Ireland)
Catherine, d. 4/8/1907 at 64; heart disease; James McSorley and Ann
    Hughes
James E., d. 10/5/1895 at 0; cholera infantum; b. Dover; SM
James T., d. 3/16/1923 at 0/1/26; marasmus; Thomas McSorley and
    Loretta Taylor
Jane, d. 10/27/1915 at 65; bed sores
John J., d. 7/20/1903 at 0/1/11; cholera infantum
Margaret, d. 8/4/1909 at 0/1/28; marasmus; Thomas McSorley and
    Catherine Kenneally
Pat, d. 10/26/1891 at 53; (Ireland; Ireland)
Thomas J., d. 1/13/1932 at 38/7/3 in Rutland, MA; tuberculosis of lungs

McTHY,
Ann, d. 8/29/1887 at 50; ring spinner; widow; b. Portland, ME; Matthew Sully (Ireland) and Mary E. Fitzpatrick (Ireland)

McVERRY,
Mary Ann, d. 1/11/1926 at 57; chronic myocarditis

MEADE,
Richard, d. 8/15/1903 at 70; cerebral thrombosis

MEADER,
child, d. 1/7/1899 at –; stillborn; PH
Albert C., d. 10/9/1906 at 28 in Boston, MA; empyema; PH
Arianna J., d. 3/15/1894 at 52 in Deering, ME; phthisis
Caroline, d. 4/10/1902 at 83/4/12; heart disease; buried in family lot
Eliza F., d. 2/1/1924 at 52/9/13 in Rochester; intestinal obstruction
Evelyn F., d. 5/27/1906 at 24/5 in Boston, MA; pulmonary embolism; PH
Florence M., d. 4/27/1891 at 35 in Camden, NJ
Fred York, d. 7/31/1901 at 18/3/28; spinal paralysis; PH
George S., d. 12/16/1889 at 39/10/8; farmer; single; b. Dover; Joseph Meader (Rochester) and Abigail Lamas
James J., d. 7/23/1909 at 69/0/27 in Portland, ME; consumption pulmonary
James V., d. 12/12/1926 at 81/0/5 in Madbury; cancer of colon
Julia E., d. 10/2/1925 at 77/1/10; arterio sclerosis; Levi Meader and Amanda Eastman
Margaret S., d. 8/27/1921 at 24/2/11; Hodgkins disease; Walter S. Meader and Lucy Hawkes
Martha A., d. 5/20/1904 at 65/1/20; shock; buried in Rochester
Mary Varney, d. 4/15/1892 at 67; disease of heart; b. Rochester; (Lee; Dover)
Moses, d. 5/20/1893 at 71; heart disease; b. Rochester; (Rochester; Dover)
Nancy, d. 2/17/1888 at 73/9; married; b. Barrington; Richard Berry and Abigail Evans
Sophia, d. 12/10/1887 at 69/11/9; single; b. Rochester; John F. Meader (Lee) and Deliverance Varney (Dover)

MEARS,
child, d. 8/8/1900 at <1; premature birth; PH

MEEDS,
Bridget, d. 6/16/1914 at 75; old age

MEEGAN,
Anna, d. 6/24/1904 at 29 in Boston, MA; valvular disease of heart; buried in Boston, MA

MEEHAN,
Catherine, d. 9/4/1909 at 86; senility
Edward, d. 1/14/1936 at 72/0/20; chronic myocarditis
Edward J., d. 5/31/1909 at 0/1/11; marasmus; Sadie Meehan
Frank, d. 7/19/1888 at 44/3/26; machinist; married; b. Ireland; John Meehan (Ireland) and Catherine McIntyre (Ireland)
John, d. 2/25/1888 at 28/6/20; farmer; b. Dover; John Meehan (Ireland) and C. McIntyre (Ireland)
Martha E., d. 9/11/1893 at 43; phthisis pulmonalis; b. Dover

MEHAFFEY,
Beatrice, d. 7/11/1932 at 79/6/27; endocarditis
William R., d. 8/18/1932 at 72/7/17; cerebral hemorrhage

MEHAN,
James, d. 7/7/1900 at 19; phthisis; SM

MEIGHAN,
James, d. 12/20/1889 at 31/10; teamster; b. Ireland; Owen Meighan (Ireland) and Martha Clark (Ireland)

MELANSON,
Joseph F., d. 8/31/1936 at 27/6/7 in Danvers, MA; frac. cer. vertebra
Paul K., d. 9/6/1915 at 0/0/29; cholera infantum; Annie G. Melanson

MELCHER,
Almira, d. 3/7/1891 at 85/0/25 in Seymour, CT; single; Daniel Melcher (Portsmouth) and Mary Flagg (Portsmouth)

MELLEN,
Dorothy C., d. 6/14/1901 at 61 in Middleboro, MA; apoplexy; PH
Fred E., d. 12/21/1923 at 42/2/5 in Worcester, MA; syphillis, cerebro spinal

MELLOORF,
George F., d. 7/6/1914 at 58/3/2; cerebral hemorrhage

MELNICK,
Abraham, d. 7/28/1936 at 87; arteriosclerosis

MELOONE,
Dorcas, d. 1/4/1899 at 73; heart disease; PH

MELVIN,
Emma A., d. 12/7/1898 at 48; cerebral paralysis; b. Dover; PH

MENDUM,
Susan, d. 1/11/1892 at 87; old age; b. Barrington

MENSEAU,
Melvina, d. 3/22/1892 at 33; phthisis pulmonalis; b. Canada; (Canada; Canada)

MERCHAND,
Henri, d. 1/17/1931 at 73/6/24 in Somersworth; heart failure

MERCHANT,
Arthur H., d. 11/19/1903 at –; suicide
Joseph, d. 7/2/1910 at 24; drowning; Frederick Merchant and Seda Belor

MERCIER,
child, d. 3/1/1932 at –; stillborn
Irene C. M., d. 7/2/1917 at 1/7/12; pneumonia lobar; Henry Mercier and Mamie Roe
Joseph, d. 6/4/1911 at 0/0/31 [sic]; premature birth; Joseph Mercier and Ludivine Frechette
Ludivine, d. 9/6/1912 at 29; septicemia; Isadore Frechette and Eleonard Goulette
Yvonne, d. 12/11/1918 at 16/1/15 in Everett, MA; broncho pneumonia; Joseph F. Mercier and Ludivine Pichette

MERRETT,
Billings B., d. 8/12/1913 at 75/9/6 in Lynn, MA; hypertrophy of prostate

MERRICK,
Nellie S., d. 2/13/1935 at 77/9/24; cerebral hemorrhage

MERRILL,
Abbie E., d. 1/24/1898 at 65; paralysis; b. York, ME; buried in So. Berwick, ME
Alby, d. 3/6/1920 at 74/5/3; carcinoma prostate gland; Abagail Morrill
Ann M., d. 7/14/1898 at 60 in Lawrence, MA; neurasthenia; PH
Anna L., d. 9/21/1937 at 66/5/5; augenia pectoris
Annie, d.10/29/1914 at 70; senile gangrene

Annie M., d. 1/12/1910 at 64/11/29; pneumonia; Samuel Stevens and
    Lydia M. Dennett
Betsy G., d. 4/25/1894 at 89; apoplexy; b. Pittsfield; buried in Chichester
Cerepta J., d. 4/19/1917 at 74/5/29; cerebral hemorrhage; Stephen D.
    Edmonds
Charles H., d. 5/26/1899 at 47; phthisis; PH
Charles W., d. 5/15/1900 at 57; abdominal tumor; PH
Edna Lillian, d. 1/14/1906 at 11/11/12; cerebro spinal meningitis; PH
Ellen A., d. 4/7/1935 at 88/8/23 in Concord; bronchial pneumonia
Esther F., d. 1/17/1894 at 21; phthisis pulmonalis; b. Dover; PH
Frank W., d. 11/25/1935 at 77/7; cancer of stomach
George A., d. 8/28/1917 at 70/6 in Harwich, MA; arterio sclerosis
George A., d. 2/6/1932 at 79/6/22 in Henniker; ac. myocardial failure
George W., d. 11/26/1920 at 51/5/13; parenchymatous nephritis; William
    G. Merrill and Crepta J. Edmonds
Georgianna, d. 11/27/1928 at 73/3 in N. Hampton; valv. heart disease
Jennie, d. 12/11/1913 at 52/3/17; cancer of uterus; Andrew Mitchell
Joseph F., d. 4/16/1923 at 81/8/25 in Concord; chronic myocarditis
Joseph W., d. 8/22/1929 at 15/4/25 in Richmond, ME; oedema of lungs;
    Leonard O. Merrill and Jessie Whitehouse
Justin B., d. 2/24/1903 at 78/3/17 in Berwick, ME; dropsy; PH
Leonard A., d. 5/13/1921 at 70/6/8; chronic p'r'n'y's nephritis; George
    Merrill and Elizabeth -----
Olive M., d. 12/5/1920 at 70/1/16; arterio sclerosis; Thomas D. Locke and
    Sophia S. -----
William G., d. 9/7/1902 at 70/4/14; Bright's disease; PH

MERRITT,
Ellen M., d. 2/25/1926 at 82/9/14 in Lynn, MA; mitral insufficiency

MERROW,
Elwyn S. W., d. 11/11/1911 at 48/0/10 in Portsmouth; Brights disease
Grace S., d. 3/17/1928 at 60/10/24 in Portsmouth; lobar pneumonia
John W., d. 8/7/1900 at 43 in York Beach, ME; apoplexy; buried in
    Tuftonboro
Joshua C., d. 1/18/1894 at 82; disease of brain; b. Farmington; buried in
    Lawrence, MA

MESERVE,
[female unnamed], d. 7/11/1888 at 26/19/23; married; b. Great Falls;
    William Thompson (Barrington) and Mary E. Whiton (Tamworth)
child, d. 4/6/1908 at --; hydrocephalus; Roswell Meserve and Georgianna
    Chamberlain
Amy E., d. 7/20/1893 at 29; peritonitis; b. Birmingham, England;
    (Gloucester, England; Gloucester, England)

Andrew, d. 10/4/1914 at 80; heart disease; Paul Meserve and Nancy Torr

Andrew E., d. 11/16/1911 at 47/0/7; acute abscess; Winthrop S. Meserve and Ann E. Tuttle

Caroline E., d. 2/23/1915 at 90/0/28; chronic endocarditis; Abram Miles and Eliza H. Joy

Clarence, d. 4/5/1898 at 72 in So. Berwick, ME; heart dis. and gangrene; PH

Edgar, d. 5/17/1916 at 60/4/24; chron. Bright's disease; James W. Meserve and Sarah J. Dow

Emily J., d. 11/12/1903 at 64/5/2; heart disease; buried in family lot

Emily J., d. 5/4/1920 at 70/2/26; chronic endocarditis; Edward Hiller

Frances, d. 5/7/1898 at 83; apoplexy; b. Madbury; PH

Frank E., d. 2/7/1920 at 53/1/10; cerebral hemorrhage; Albert F. Meserve and Frances A. Harty

Frank E., d. 7/5/1930 at 70/2/17; chr. endocarditis; Andrew Meserve and Emily J. Skillings

George H., d. 9/17/1910 at 65/11/18; valv. disease of heart; James Meserve and Sarah Dorr

Helen M., d. 2/17/1918 at 76/11; apoplexy; Ezra Stanton and Polly Otis

James K. P., d. 4/26/1896 at 46; pneumonia; b. Madbury; PH

James W., d. 7/1/1889 at 68/7; farmer; widower; b. Dover; Clement Meserve (NH) and M. Colman (NH)

John W., d. 4/7/1930 at 73/11/12; carc. esophagus; Seth Meserve and Mary Wentworth

Joseph A., d. 6/18/1932 at 27/4/6; fractured skull

Laura J., d. 3/31/1910 at 79/9/5; senility; Samuel Thompson and Betsey Seavey

Leon E., d. 9/4/1911 at 15/11/20; accidental drowning; Bert Meserve and M. E. Chamberlain

Lewis W., d. 8/22/1905 at 59 in Togus, ME; arteriosclerosis; PH

Lillian B., d. 10/26/1921 at 75/8/19; angina pectoris; Samuel H. Reed and Lucy J. Estes

Lizzie, d. 9/22/1895 at 40; phthisis; b. Groton Junction; PH

Marion, d. 4/12/1906 at 0/0/26; disease of liver; PH

Mary C., d. 9/9/1927 at 0/0/21; spina bifida; Charles R. Meserve and Mary C. Haley

Mary J., d. 10/16/1935 at 70/1/8; carcinoma of bladder

N. Gertrude, d. 3/26/1912 at 42/7/15 in Durham; valvular heart disease

Nicholas D., d. 6/4/1890 at 76/2/4; widower; Samuel Meserve (Madbury) and Sarah Pendergast (Durham)

Norman E., d. 5/21/1900 at <1; diptheria; PH

Oliver B., d. 8/20/1915 at 87/0/19; pneumonia; Stephen Meserve and Susan Henderson

Roswell, d. 1/12/1926 at 53/11/9; chr. parenchy. nephritis; George H. Meserve and Emily Hiller

Roy H. B., d. 10/19/1921 at 29/3/15; chronic dysentery; Charles R.
    Meserve and Amy Brown
Samuel, d. 11/17/1919 at 75/1/24; angina pectoris; James D. Meserve and
    Caroline E. Miles
Samuel E., d. 2/12/1937 at 61/0/14; carcinoma stomach
Sarah, d. 1/18/1899 at 65; paralytic shock; PH
Sarah J. W., d. 11/21/1904 at 72/11/16; valvular disease of heart; PH
Surmira L., d. 2/20/1890 at 50/10/18 in Haverhill, MA
Susie M., d. 8/17/1892 at –; meningitis; (Dover; Barnstead)

METOUSH,
Lilah, d. 2/14/1919 at 38; hemorrhage of lungs; Sallie Metoush and Dilke
    Begege

MICHAELOPOULOS,
A. A., d. 12/6/1921 at 54 in Portsmouth; peritonitis

MICHAELS,
Margaret V., d. 8/5/1921 at 42/9/21; cerebral hemorrhage; James Cavano
    and Catherine Hession

MICHAL,
Annie, d. 10/27/1888 at 17/1/26; single; b. Canada; Joseph Michel
    (Canada) and Lada Pichette (Canada)
Stamatis, d. 8/23/1923 at 70; diabetes; John Stenos

MICHALOPOULOS,
George, d. 3/25/1924 at 36; chronic nephritis

MICHAUD,
Adina, d. 4/20/1914 at 13/5/18; epilepsy; Francis Michaud and Maverline --
Basilis, d. 10/18/1892 at 41; hepatitis; b. Canada; (Canada; Canada)
Luminas B., d. 5/17/1891 at 30; married; Jean Baptiste Michaud (Canada)
    and Armen Meshode (Canada)
Philip, d. 6/11/1916 at 15/2/7; accidental drowning; Antoine Michaud and
    Mary Legace
Zenon, d. 10/9/1917 at 24/1/12; puss in plural cavity; Frances Michaud
    and Marceline -----

MICHEAUD,
Celina, d. 4/5/1892 at 41; phthisis; b. Canada; (Canada; Canada)

MICHEL,
Joseph, d. 1/26/1913 at 77; apoplexy; Francois Michel and Marguerite -----

Josephine, d. 12/6/1929 at 59/9/11; acute myocarditis; Joseph Michel and Leda Pichette
Leda, d. 11/10/1926 at 82/4/3; cerebral embolism; Pierre Pichette and Marie Gingras

MIELISH,
Charles, d. 3/13/1920 at 73/11/24; apoplexy

MIGUE,
Flora, d. 4/12/1913 at 25; typhoid fever; Norbert Joly and Esther Desrosier

MILBANK,
Charles A., d. 3/19/1912 at 73/6/25; pneumonia; Charles W. Milbank and Mary W. Ainsworth

MILCAHY,
Nora, d. 5/11/1909 at 65 in Newburyport, MA; angina pectoris

MILECHIS,
James, d. 7/14/1923 at 2/4/2; accident

MILES,
Alvin H., d. 7/22/1920 at 71/3/27; cerebral hemorrhage; Alfred Miles and Betsy P. Sinclair
Caroline F., d. 2/5/1899 at 72 in Sheffield, NH
Clara A., d. 5/30/1903 at 75/7/22 in Madbury; heart disease; PH
Florence P., d. 2/15/1931 at 48/8/1 in Madbury; carcinoma mediastinum
Jacob, d. 2/13/1908 at 81; gen. tuberculosis
Kezia M., d. 12/16/1891 at 62/8/17; widow; Francis O. Morrill (Gilmanton) and Kezia Bickford (Canada)
William B., d. 1/10/1901 at 75/11/14 in Manchester; diabetes; PH

MILLEN,
child, d. 8/6/1932 at –; asphyxia pallida
Gertrude, d. 1/20/1926 at 49/8/24 in Somerville, MA; broncho pneumonia
Mary F., d. 8/2/1907 at 59/8/3; cancer; Benjamin Hurd and Abiah Leonard
Nellie B., d. 5/18/1891 at 18/1/16; single; William H. Millen (Dover) and Mary F. Hurd (Great Falls)
William H., d. 4/6/1910 at 64/8/22; broncho-pneumonia; Henry Millen and Grace Marshall

MILLER,
child, d. 11/10/1908 at –; stillborn; Clifford Miller and Margaret Wesley

child, d. 1/14/1925 at 0/0/10; premature birth; Maynard W. Miller and Myrtle Judd
Alonzo G., d. 8/31/1916 at 29/4/4; chron. Bright's dis.; Augustus N. Miller and Margaret Hilton
Augustus N., d. 1/12/1912 at 72/10/1; chronic nephritis; Webster Miller and Louisa Roberts
Catherine M., d. 2/23/1918 at 25/10/17 in Milton; pulmonary tuberculosis; William Ham and Margaret Driscoll
Clifford, d. 6/30/1910 at 75/3; uraemic convulsions; Webster Miller
Daisy, d. 11/8/1898 at 2; pneumonia; b. Dover; PH
Gilbert, d. 9/14/1889 at 3; b. Dover; Augustus Miller (America) and M. Hilton (US)
Harriet, d. 9/20/1916 at 77 in New York, NY; cancer
Harry, d. 11/19/1903 at 0/0/7; convulsions; PH
Inez Abbie, d. 5/29/1910 at 44/9 in Boston, MA; uterine carcinoma
James W., d. 10/13/1918 at 25/5/1 in Rochester; pneumonia; Thomas Miller and Catherine McCabe
John B., d. 12/31/1933 at 68/7/4; diabetes
Margaret, d. 9/17/1911 at 52/3/6; tuberculosis; Morrill Hilton and Lydia Moody
Margaret, d. 2/4/1916 at 84 in Concord; pellagra
Mary C., d. 12/7/1932 at 42; angina pectoris
Minnie L., d. 3/1/1921 at 45/2/2 in Portland, ME; acute uraemia; Patrick Hogan and Johanna Sullivan
Richard E., d. 9/30/1923 at 1/8/18; ileo colitis; Maynard W. Miller and Myrtle Judd
Sarah A., d. 3/13/1905 at 74; bronchitis; PH
Thomas, d. 2/27/1915 at 85; senility

MILLETT,
child, d. 6/24/1918 at –; stillborn; James Millett and Hazel Pineo

MILLETTE,
Joseph M., d. 3/16/1915 at 0/1; pneumonia; Moses Millette and Mary Deutel

MILLIER,
Henry, d. 8/2/1914 at 34/9; trauma shock; Charles Millier and Denise Roux

MILLIKEN,
Mary A., d. 10/27/1916 at 71/6/15 in Newburyport, MA; cerebral hemorrhage

MILLMORE,
Arthur P., d. 2/17/1912 at 74/11 in Somerville, MA; arterio sclerosis

MILLS,
Annie G., d. 8/19/1919 at 68/8/26; carcinoma uterus; John O. Mealey and Margaret L. McCabe
Charles A., d. 3/3/1907 at 56; heart disease; Charles W. Mills and Clara A. Mathes
Edward B., d. 3/25/1907 at 67/1/11; acute pancreatitis
Ellen W., d. 11/8/1914 at 43/2/2 in Benton (Glencliff); pulmonary tuberculosis; Terrence Woods and Catherine Reynolds
Elva, d. 4/9/1894 at –; probably suffocation; b. Dover
Ethel May, d. 8/19/1900 at 1; cholera infantum; PH
Frank W., d. 12/29/1888 at 27/6/5; mechanic; married; b. NH; Joshua Mills (NH) and Mary E. Goodrich (ME)
George H., d. 1/29/1934 at 86/11/1; arteriosclerosis
Lucretia M., d. 9/30/1920 at 62/0/4; broncho pneumonia; John O. Malley and Margaret L. McCabe
Lucy M., d. 12/30/1926 at 69/11/11; apoplexy; Benjamin Moulton and Julia A. Trafton
Mary Ann, d. 7/28/1934 at 67/5/15; cerebral hemorrhage
Mary E., d. 6/26/1904 at 64/9/24; pulmonary tuberculosis; PH
Mary F., d. 11/28/1903 at 62/11/21; chronic nephritis; PH
Nellie M., d. 1/14/1887 at 22/8/23; married; b. Berwick, ME; Charles F. Coffin (Berwick, ME) and Sarah E. Knox (Berwick, ME)
Thomas A., d. 11/29/1898 at 2; diphtheretic laryngitis; b. Dover; PH

MILMORE,
E. A., d. 1/18/1888 at 18/8 in Boston, MA; telegraph op.; single; b. NB; A. P. Milmore (Scotland) and Mary F. Reed (NB)
M. Ella, d. 6/3/1922 at 45 in Boston, MA; lymphatic leuchaemia
Mary F., d. 11/6/1920 at 85/11/3 in Somerville, MA; exhaustion from old age

MILNE,
David E., d. 9/5/1914 at 0/11/24 in Rochester; meningitis
Theodore, d. 11/20/1904 at 0/0/1; premature birth

MILNER,
Henry, d. 5/30/1894 at 73; old age; b. Ireland
Mary E., d. 2/12/1933 at 79/2/26; arteriosclerosis
William Francis, d. 9/12/1930 at 78/0/26; chronic myocardititis; Henry Milner and Ann Crowley
William H., d. 5/2/1901 at 21; tuberculosis; SM

MILTON,
Sarah E., d. 6/16/1892 at 56; dropsy; b. ME

MINATER,
Michael, d. 10/2/1899 at 65; consumption; SM

MINEHAN,
Joseph P., d. 2/22/1916 at 33 in Boston, MA; chronic nephritis
Timothy, d. 9/2/1935 at 70; cerebral hemorrhage

MINITER,
John P., d. 6/6/1931 at 55/2/11 in Kittery, ME; arterio sclerosis
Michael, d. 3/26/1898 at 0; pneumonia; b. Dover; SM

MINITHER,
Andrew, d. 2/5/1895 at 52; phthisis pulmonalis; b. Ireland; SM

MINNEGHAN,
Timothy, d. 7/29/1901 at 0/10; cholera infantum; buried in Somersworth

MINNEHAN,
Elizabeth C., d. 1/9/1932 at 65/10/26; chronic arthritis
Florence, d. 6/3/1901 at 63/2/27; apoplexy; SM
Hannah, d. 7/17/1920 at 55/4/23; pulmonary oedema; Patrick McAtarvey
    [written in - Patrick McCarty and Margaret Sheehan]
Mary Ellen, d. 3/31/1926 at 68/7/4; cerebral hemorrhage; John F.
    Minnehan and Catherine Regan

MINSTER,
Thomas S., d. 3/14/1892 at 1; phthisis; b. Dover; (Ireland; Quebec)

MINTER,
Thomas, d. 12/6/1893 at 53; acute tuberculosis; b. Ireland; (Ireland;
    Ireland)

MITCHELL,
Alonzo, d. 12/26/1893 at 67; carcinoma; b. NH; (NH; NH)
Alvin, d. 8/17/1921 at 25/11/22; cerebral hemorrhage; Samuel Mitchell and
    Sally Drew
Amelia, d. 5/6/1911 at 41; cholecystitis with pleurisy
Andrew J., d. 2/16/1911 at 76/7/28; lobar pneumonia; Andrew Mitchell and
    Hannah York
Bridget, d. 1/8/1900 at 61; overwork and exhaustion; buried in Dover
Catherine, d. 1/5/1891 at 50/9/26; married; Peter Collins (Ireland) and -----
    (Ireland)
Charles, d. 1/6/1892 at 70; influenza; b. New Durham; (New Durham; New
    Durham)

Charles H., d. 6/5/1925 at 74/9/7; fracture base of skull; Charles Mitchell
and Susan Davis
Charles Louis, d. 4/13/1912 at 82/5/3 in Boston, MA; gastro enteritis;
Herbert McCabe and Teresa Ryan
Clara A., d. 7/23/1905 at 77/6/24; cancer; PH
Elizabeth, d. 1/29/1916 at 91/5/19 in Sanford, ME; senile debility; William
Mitchell and Lydia York
Ella, d. 1/27/1916 at 45/10/10; cancer of intestines; Daniel P. York and
Susan Smart
Frances J., d. 5/28/1919 at 79/11/29; lobar pneumonia; Benjamin H.
Twombly and Asenath Young
George W., d. 3/27/1894 at 72; fibroid phthisis; b. New Durham; PH
Hannah, d. 1/18/1899 at 68; catarrhal pneumonia from grippe; PH
Harry, d. 8/9/1931 at 64/2/1; articular rheumatism
Josiah King, d. 9/20/1916 at 80/4/8; gen. arterio sclerosis; Andrew Mitchell
and Hannah York
Lydia, d. 8/30/1911 at 86/2/20; old age; Paul Libbey and Elizabeth
Sherburne
Mary J., d. 6/12/1933 at 87/3/14; chronic myocarditis
Nellie B., d. 1/5/1924 at 77/5 in Boston, MA; cardiorenal sclerosis
Sarah L., d. 5/13/1907 at 80/7/6 in Milton; senility
Stella E., d. 8/2/1919 at 36/5/27; exoptihalnis goitre; Charles E. Mitchell
and Elizabeth B. Caton
Susan, d. –/–/1895 at – in Durham; buried in homestead cem.
Verna B., d. 1/6/1919 at 18/3/4; pneumonia; Henry G. Mitchell and Bessie
Morton

MITEAVERA,
Alick, d. 8/26/1888 at 3/0/14; b. Dover; Edward Miteavera (Canada) and
Georgie Miteavera (Lewiston, ME)

MITHAN,
Joanna, d. 9/19/1887 at 21/1; single; b. Ireland; Thomas Mithan (Ireland)
and Mary Pard (Ireland)
John J., d. 1/5/1904 at 0/1/14; strangulation from coughing; SM

MITHEN,
Clarence J., d. 1/13/1930 at 16/7/2 in Lawrence, MA; cerebro spinal men.;
James W. Mithen and Margaret Quinn
Evelyn, d. 7/29/1929 at 17/3/22; accidental drowning; James Mithen
Mary, d. 1/19/1898 at 44; b. Ireland; SM
Michael, d. 1/30/1916 at 68; broncho pneumonia

MOAN,
Arthur E., d. 1/14/1903 at 35 in Chicago, IL; pleurisy, with pneumonia; SM

Elizabeth J., d. 12/22/1926 at 49/10/22 in Georgetown, MA; acute alcoholism
Patrick H., d. 4/12/1894 at 22 in Georgetown, MA; phthisis pulmonalis; buried in Dover
Rose, d. 11/10/1908 at – in Georgetown, MA; paralysis
Thomas, d. 6/28/1893 at 24; pneumonia

MOHBAT,
Adelaide G., d. 8/24/1905 at 1/0/4; capillary bronchitis; SM

MOLLOY,
John A., d. 11/15/1925 at 64/5/10; cerebral embolism; Patrick Molloy and Marie McEvilly

MONAHAN,
Adele, d. 3/5/1934 at 46/1/19; carcinoma of uterus
Mildred, d. 5/11/1921 at 1/10/2 in transit; prolapse of rectum; George Monahan and Adelle Morin

MONDOR,
Julienne, d. 11/19/1916 at 62; diabetes; Augustin Mondor and Marine Goreau

MONE,
Patrick J., d. 12/11/1931 at 58/7/11; nephritis
Rose Ellen, d. 10/11/1915 at 6; ac. dilatation of heart; Patrick Mone and Elizabeth Tominey

MONGEAU,
Emma, d. 9/3/1924 at 80/6/23; cancer of liver; Felix Marcotte and Sophia Penain

MONNEGHAN,
child, d. 8/9/1903 at –; stillborn

MONOGHAN,
Margaret, d. 4/19/1926 at 69/5/19; la grippe; James Garvey and Mary Riley

MONROE,
Ellen E., d. 9/27/1933 at 65 in Milford, MA; chronic nephritis

MONTGOMERY,
E. M., d. 5/25/1894 at 58; Bright's disease; b. Strafford; buried in Northwood
Hattie, d. 1/8/1925 at 66/6/29 in Wells, ME; diabetes mellitus
Nathaniel, d. 10/30/1927 at 75/1/9 in Durham; cystitis
W. James, d. 8/20/1930 at 59/8/23; ruptured appendix; James Montgomery and Catherine -----

MONTMINEY,
Catherine, d. 12/13/1900 at 30; organic disease of heart; SM

MONTMINY,
Augustus, d. 9/24/1888 at 62; laborer; married; b. Canada; Gaymen Montminy (Canada) and Madel'da Pardin (Canada)
Delvina, d. 4/27/1897 at 5; scarlet fever; b. Dover; SM
Emma F., d. 5/3/1897 at 1; scarlet fever; b. Dover; SM
Isabella, d. 5/13/1897 at 3; scarlet fever; b. Dover; SM

MONTOUR,
Albert, d. 11/15/1931 at 87; arterio sclerosis

MOODY,
child, d. 10/24/1913 at –; premature birth; W. F. Moody and Edith Hussey
Charlotte A., d. 2/9/1930 at 89/11/4 in Arlington, MA; broncho pneumonia; George Chadbourne and Eunice Boston
Charlotte B., d. 7/14/1909 at 84/8/5; fracture of left hip; George Hemenway and Charlotte Brayshaw
Chester A., d. 9/10/1890 at 0/0/16; Harry E. Moody (Wells, ME) and Carrie F. Gibbs (Holyoke, MA)
Edwin, d. 9/11/1934 at 79/9/28 in Durham; arteriosclerosis
Edwin H., d. 12/16/1936 at 70/11/23; ac. lobar pneumonia
Flora F., d. 11/27/1920 at 82 in Wellesley, MA; heart disease
Frank, d. 3/4/1903 at 53/10/16; pneumonia; buried in Ossipee
George B., d. 11/22/1893 at 24; heart failure - typhoid fever; b. Tamworth; (Tamworth; Ossipee)
James H., d. 10/9/1912 at 72/5/21 in Durham; angina pectoris
Lydia L., d. 3/26/1909 at 84/2/25; pneumonia; Dearborn Davis and Lydia Leavitt
Mary Jane, d. 2/15/1891 at 79/11/8; widow; Francis Wingate (Portsmouth) and Rebekah Dolloff (Portsmouth)
Neana, d. 9/2/1887 at 80/9/10; widow; b. Dover; John Hobbs and ----- Lord
Stephen N., d. 12/21/1917 at 85/1/6 in Arlington, MA; arterio sclerosis
William E., d. 11/18/1918 at 51/1/13; strangulated hernia; Lorenzo D. Moody and Elvira Littlefield

MOONEY,
Agnes, d. 8/18/1909 at 0/4; acute enteritis; Michael Mooney and Elizabeth Mooney
Alice, d. 6/30/1899 at 87; old age
Alice, d. 6/24/1922 at 72 in Tewksbury, MA; arterio sclerosis
Alice M., d. 11/20/1892 at 1; scrofula; b. Dover; (Ireland; Dover)
Annie, d. 2/28/1895 at 29; pulmonary phthisis; b. Ireland; SM
Annie B., d. 11/30/1916 at 64; biliary calenli; Philip Mooney and Betsey McKone
Catherine, d. 6/30/1898 at 65; phthisis; b. Ireland; SM
Charles D., d. 3/19/1892 at –; anaemia; b. Dover; (----; Dover)
Coraline, d. 4/23/1890 at 80/4/3; widow; Enoch Sawyer (Alton) and Eleanor Horn (Alton)
Edward, d. 1/20/1900 at 34; Bright's disease; SM
Elizabeth, d. 12/6/1887 at 82/11; widow; b. Ireland; Owen McCone (Ireland) and Mary (Ireland)
Henry, d. 12/22/1916 at 53; broncho pneumonia; Patrick Mooney and Anne Mulligan
Ira, d. 10/5/1889 at 84/4/18 in Belmont
James, d. 2/8/1900 at 60; phthisis; SM
James E., d. 10/20/1927 at 24/2/4 in Portland, ME; abdominal carcinoma; Fred Mooney and Lillian Chase
Margaret, d. 9/13/1908 at 53; cerebral hemorrhage
Mary, d. 6/19/1898 at 31; phthisis; b. Ireland; SM
Michael, d. 4/11/1899 at 70; Bright's disease; SM
Michael, d. 3/15/1900 at 70; apoplexy; SM
Owen John, d. 6/6/1927 at 49/1/13 in Portsmouth; carcinoma of stomach; Owen Mooney and Kate Mulligan
Patrick, d. 11/19/1888 at 55/6/10; railroad; married; b. Ireland; (Ireland; Ireland)
Patrick, d. 5/30/1911 at 54 in Portsmouth; valv. disease of the heart; Michael Mooney and Mary Tatro
Patrick, d. 1/16/1913 at 43/10; cerebral meningitis; Michael Mooney and Margaret McEneaney
Rowena M., d. 5/15/1919 at 33/10/18; pulm. tuberculosis; Nelson U. Drew and Delia E. Maloney
Thomas P., d. 3/10/1906 at 0/0/1; premature birth

MOORE,
child, d. 3/17/1893 at –; heart failure; b. Dover; (Dover; Thompson, CT)
child, d. 6/12/1905 at –; debility - premature birth; PH
child, d. 5/9/1907 at –; stillborn; Frank J. Moore and Hattie Nichols
Alfred, d. 10/3/1887 at 45/7/27 in Lewiston, ME
Alfred E., d. 8/30/1922 at 19/5/14; typhoid fever; Moody M. Moore and Nellie F. Littlefield

Audrey Irene, d. 12/31/1922 at 2/11/22; ac. lobar pneumonia; J. Frank Moore and Hattie L. Nichols
Bertha, d. 10/30/1928 at 50/9/2; cerebral hemorrhage; Wesley Merrill and Annie Stillings
Charles, d. 1/22/1931 at 37/10/26; pulmonary tuberculosis
Charles A., d. 11/29/1890 at 25/9/26; single; Charles H. Moore (Parsonsfield) and Katie E. Lewis
Charles H., d. 8/9/1927 at 58/2/5; carcinoma of mouth; Moses H. Moore and Nancy J. Kendall
Clare E., d. 6/18/1911 at 53/10/23; anaemia; Noah S. Watson and Lucy M. Quimby
Donald H., d. 12/7/1928 at –; stillborn; George B. Moore and Venice Howard
Elizabeth H., d. 12/17/1921 at 80/2; atheroma; William Haigh and Hannah Brook
Elizabeth L., d. 3/3/1932 at 71/6/22 in Boston, MA; arterio sclerosis
Ethel B., d. 5/12/1887 at 1/6/4; b. Dover; George Moore (England) and Hannah (England)
Etta B., d. 6/21/1932 at 61/10/11; cancer of secum
Frank A., d. 7/4/1933 at 64/2/17; chronic nephritis
Frank P., d. 9/5/1913 at 60; cerebral hemorrhage; Moody M. Moore and Hannah S. Hayes
Fred A., d. 9/30/1916 at 45/1/17; osteomyelitis; John F. Moore and Louise C. Burley
Frederick E., d. 1/13/1899 at 2; acute bronchitis; PH
Hannah S., d. 9/14/1895 at 60 in East Wakefield; disease of liver; b. Strafford; PH
Henry, d. 4/19/1893 at 74; pneumonia; b. England; (England; England)
Herman C., d. 5/4/1931 at 45/1/7 in Rye; bullet wound
Jane, d. 8/–/1893 at 50; cholera morbus; b. England; (England; England)
John, d. 5/12/1894 at 62; angina pectoris; b. England; buried in Dedham, MA
John F., d. 5/3/1907 at 57/0/6; pneumonia; Joseph Moore and Hannah Hooper
John F., Jr., d. 12/20/1906 at 25/8/16; valvular heart disease; buried in Somersworth
Joseph, d. 3/3/1892 at 25; Bright's disease; b. England; (England; England)
Laura E., d. 12/14/1912 at 62/9/14; heart disease; Nathan Horne and Frances Straw
Lena, d. 5/17/1896 at 39; pulmonary phthisis; b. So. Berwick, ME; PH
Leon A., d. 2/8/1934 at 54/1/6; coronary thrombosis
Martha J., d. 12/11/1936 at 58/3/29 in Concord; cerebral hemorrhage
Mary, d. 1/10/1892 at 76; pneumonia; b. England; (England; England)

Michael, d. 12/26/1889 at 50; mill operative; married; John Moore
(England) and Mary (England)
Moody M., d. 7/3/1891 at 73/4/15 in Wakefield
Moses H., d. 3/30/1899 at 52; cancer of throat; PH
Nancy J., d. 12/9/1921 at 73/7/8; cerebral hemorrhage; Metpher Kendall
and Mary Chase
Nellie F., d. 10/30/1935 at 59/11/15; natural causes
Nora W., d. 3/13/1899 at 22; peritonitis; PH
Raymond A. M., d. 2/27/1920 at 18/8/26; influenza; Moody M. Moore and
Nellie F. Littlefield
Robert L., d. 11/23/1903 at 32; epileptic shock; SM
Thomas, d. 5/22/1911 at 76/2; pneumonia
William H., d. 7/4/1925 at 55/2; pernicious anemia; Alfred Moore and
Elizabeth Haigh
William H., d. 11/11/1930 at 79/4/6 in Manchester; acute bronchitis
Willis A., d. 6/3/1910 at 53/5/25 in Portland, ME; carcinoma of liver

MOOREHOUSE,
Adelaide M., d. 8/27/1918 at 75/2/27; acute bronchitis; Ivory Harmon and
Loretta M. -----

MOORHEAD,
Owen J., d. 8/30/1909 at 26 in Shady Side, NJ; drowning

MORAN,
Ann, d. 7/14/1890 at 75; widow; Jeremiah Murphy (Ireland) and Bridget
Cleary (Ireland)
Christopher A., d. 2/27/1913 at 26/2/2 in Concord; ex. in chronic insanity;
John Moran and Mary A. Fallon
Helen F., d. 8/7/1910 at 1/7/15 in Newtonville, MA; gastritis; James E.
Moran and Caroline M. Vaughn
John, d. 9/21/1888 at 84/3; laborer; married; b. Ireland; Thomas Moran
(Ireland) and Alice Quinlan (Ireland)
John, d. 8/14/1889 at 39/6/14; laborer; single; b. Dover; John Moran
(Ireland)
John, d. 10/23/1898 at 45; Bright's disease; b. Ireland; SM
Margaret, d. 11/21/1935 at 56/4/22 in Rochester; intestinal obstruction
Martin, d. 7/3/1890 at 63
Michael F., d. 9/20/1892 at 17; heart disease; b. Lewiston, ME; (NY;
Ireland)
Peter L., d. 9/16/1923 at 78/4; cancer of intestine; Patrick Moran and
Bridget Riley

MORANG,
Charles H., d. 2/14/1917 at 70/6/14; pneumonia; James Morang and Caroline Kelley
Sarah J., d. 1/15/1917 at 63/9/6; pneumonia; Horace Littlefield and Mary J. Kimball

MOREAU,
Gerard, d. 4/10/1916 at 0/2/8; athrepsia; Arcard Moreau and Gracien Noel
Madeline, d. 8/7/1922 at 10/1/12; epilepsy; Louis Moreau and Marion ——
Margaret L., d. 11/8/1925 at 11/5/25; Frederick's ataxia; Louis J. Moreau and Martha Therrien
Marie T., d. 5/11/1918 at 0/0/15; acute broncho pneumonia; Louis Moreau and Mary Therrien

MOREAULT,
Valeda, d. 7/29/1901 at 0/3/6; cholera infantum; buried in Newmarket

MOREHEAD,
John R., d. 7/27/1904 at 0/1/21; cholera infantum

MORELAND,
Fred W., d. 4/7/1917 at 35/7; uraemia; George B. Moreland and Margaret Leder

MORESET,
son, d. 8/19/1890 at –; Jules Moreset (Canada) and Odile Forest (Canada)

MORGAN,
child, d. 7/12/1895 at 0; premature birth; b. Dover; SM
child, d. 6/19/1898 at 0; stillborn; b. Dover; SM
child, d. 1/9/1906 at –; inanition; SM
Agnes, d. 6/25/1904 at 65; cardiac dilation; buried in Rollinsford
Alice, d. 4/1/1909 at –; premature birth; John J. Morgan and Annie McKenney
Ann, d. 11/2/1907 at 58; uraemic convulsions; Peter Hughes and Ellen McKenna
Ann, d. 5/16/1912 at 69; uraemia; William McNally and Mary McGuire
Ann, d. 1/23/1913 at 78; uraemia
Annie, d. 1/12/1887 at 17; single; b. Dover; James Morgan (Ireland) and Ann Haughey (Ireland)
Annie, d. 4/27/1904 at 0/0/1; convulsions; SM
Annie, d. 5/7/1934 at 60 in Lawrence, MA; chronic nephritis
Annie E., d. 8/8/1893 at 1; inanition; b. Dover; (Ireland; Ireland)
Annie E., d. 10/20/1906 at 0/11/27; cerebro spinal meningitis

Annie Jane, d. 7/30/1893 at 2; convulsions; b. Dover; (Dover; Dover)
Arthur, d. 4/4/1902 at –; unknown; SM
Catherine, d. 12/2/1905 at 23; uraemia; SM
Catherine, d. 2/10/1928 at 52/7; lobar pneumonia; John Bohan and Ellen -
Elisha E., d. 4/25/1896 at –; infancy; b. Dover; PH
Elizabeth B., d. 1/30/1929 at 51 in Lawrence, MA; aortic insufficiency
Fannie, d. 6/1/1933 at –; carcinoma of colon
George P., d. 11/8/1922 at 61/4/17; cerebral hemorrhage; Elisha M. Morgan and Rosilla Tucker
George William, Jr., d. 4/6/1917 at 0/6/15; marasmus; George Morgan and Mary F. Donovan
James, d. 6/13/1894 at 27; Bright's disease; b. Ireland; SM
James, d. 4/1/1903 at 50; chronic nephritis; SM
James, d. 11/25/1912 at 80/7; la grippe
James, d. 9/23/1921 at 40 in Lawrence, MA; prob. heart disease
James H., d. 10/4/1915 at 68; chron. prog. corea; Felix Morgan and Ellen Burns
James H., d. 3/10/1917 at 45; acute nephritis; Thomas N. Morgan and Sarah J. Alexander
Jennie B., d. 12/6/1937 at 63/0/0 in Manchester; cerebr. hemorrhage
John, d. 2/5/1908 at –; congenital disease of heart; John J. Morgan and Annie McKenney
John, d. 7/3/1932 at –; gastric ulcers
John A., d. 10/18/1902 at 40/0/27; SM
John A., d. 1/10/1913 at 32; endocarditis; Arthur Morgan and Ann McNally
Kate, d. 12/20/1887 at 11/6; b. Ireland; ----- (Ireland) and Mary (Ireland)
Katie, d. 10/3/1889 at 3/9; b. Dover; James Morgan (Ireland) and Mary Gammon (Ireland)
Maggie, d. 11/29/1893 at 25; acute tuberculosis; b. Dover; (Ireland; Ireland)
Margaret, d. 4/1/1909 at –; premature birth; John J. Morgan and Annie McKenney
Mary, d. 10/27/1887 at 18/7/10; mill operative; single; b. Dover; Peter Morgan (Ireland) and Mary McNally (Ireland)
Mary, d. 9/10/1889 at 48/7/11; mill operative; widow; b. Ireland; William McNally (Ireland) and Mary Maguire (Ireland)
Mary, d. 4/6/1927 at 50 in Pembroke; pulmonary tuberculosis
Mary A., d. 5/18/1920 at 66; hemiplegia; James Fallon and Katherine Mallory
Mary A., d. 2/10/1925 at 70; carcinoma of stomach; John ----- and Bridget Ash
Mary E., d. 12/29/1900 at 49; pneumonia; SM
Mary E., d. 1/31/1915 at 38/2; tuberculosis; Joseph Blanchette
Mary F., d. 11/15/1932 at 43/5; pulmonary tuberculosis
Michael L., d. 2/19/1928 at 60 in Lawrence, MA; carcinoma of bladder

Nellie, d. 2/27/1892 at 19; typhoid pneumonia; b. Ireland; (England; Ireland)
Patrick, d. 7/24/1910 at 64; chronic nephritis
Peter, d. 6/9/1928 at 62; pulm. tuberculosis; Patrick Morgan and Ann Hughes
Peter F., d. 5/29/1893 at 23; heart disease; b. Ireland; (Ireland; Ireland)
Rose Helen, d. 11/8/1923 at 34/6; endocarditis; Patrick H. Fenton and Mary Markey
Walter F., d. 11/11/1894 at –; croupous pneumonia; b. Dover; PH

MORIN,
John B., d. 2/26/1926 at 54/8/10; pyelitis; Joseph Morin and Emelie Couture
Joseph, d. 5/15/1912 at 0/0/1; premature birth; Jaffrey Morin and Octave Lemay
Pierre, d. 11/15/1926 at 67/9/5; arterio sclerosis; Jean Morin and Vitalene Provencher
Rita, d. 5/21/1928 at 4/4/21; nephritis; Elphege Morin and Marie Letendre
Theophile, d. 10/14/1908 at 57/7/16; intestinal obstruction; B. Morin and Charlotte Gobell
William C., d. 1/24/1907 at 46; pulmonary oedema; France Morin and Basilice Hebert

MORISETTE,
Mary Ida, d. 9/9/1896 at –; b. Dover; SM

MORISON,
George W., d. 2/19/1935 at 79/9/15 in Nottingham; coronary obstruction

MORISSETTE,
Jules, d. 6/2/1911 at 70/10/9; cancer of stomach; John Morissette and Julia Poirier

MORLEY,
John, d. 2/4/1916 at 57; pulmonary tuberculosis
Margaret, d. 2/24/1909 at 35; acute nephritis; John Quinlan and Maria Cassily
Mary Alice, d. 7/18/1891 at 0/2; John Morley (Lowell, MA) and Margaret Quinland (Dover).
William, d. 10/26/1914 at 54; lobar pneumonia

MORNEY,
Bridget, d. 4/11/1892 at 61; heart disease; b. Ireland; (Ireland; Ireland)

MORRELL,
Summer C., d. 11/4/1937 at 81/1/3; chronic nephritis

MORRICY,
Kate L., d. 6/29/1933 at 81/3/23; chronic myocarditis

MORRILL,
Almira J., d. 4/9/1908 at 80/5/30; pneumonia; Aaron Clark and Mercy Ham
Calista S., d. 3/12/1937 at 83/0/11; arteriosclerosis
Charles Joseph, d. 1/9/1920 at 69/3/24 in Los Angeles, CA; retention of urine; Joseph Morrill and Nancy Quimby
Edith, d. 1/30/1937 at 72/5/10 in Concord; broncho pneumonia
Edward, d. 4/4/1889 at 79; merchant; married; b. Salisbury; Samuel Morrill (Salisbury) and Annie Noyes (Seabrook)
Elmira, d. 2/–/1921 at –; myocarditis; Seth Mayo and Jemima Gifford
Ethel L., d. 2/28/1926 at 57/5/26; tubercular laryngitis; Charles H. Rines and Sarah Boston
Frances O., d. 5/13/1919 at 83/2/12; lobar pneumonia; Joshua Varney and Hannah Varney
George F., d. 12/13/1913 at 80/7/24; paralysis agitans; Abel Morrill and Ann M. Tucker
Helen B., d. 12/13/1935 at 46/1/24; carcinoma of breast
James E., d. 9/30/1895 at 68 in Davenport, IA; Brights disease
John F., d. 10/25/1918 at 78/4/1 in Concord; myocarditis; William Morrill and Abigail Seavey
Lucy A., d. 11/6/1891 at 62/3/13; single; William Morrill (Salisbury, MA) and Abigail Seavey (York, ME)
Maria, d. 4/18/1935 at 92/2/24 in Concord; chronic myocarditis
Mary F., d. 1/17/1905 at 71/10/2; pneumonia; PH
Rosennia A., d. 1/27/1920 at 77/3/13; arterio sclerosis; Joseph Morrill and Nancy Quimby
Sarah W., d. 4/23/1900 at 71 in Davenport, IA; grip, bronchitis; PH
William A., d. 9/6/1909 at 79/1/10; heart disease; Abel Morrill and Ann M. Tucker

MORRIS,
James I., d. 5/26/1891 at 27/1/27; married; Thomas Morris (England) and Mary Marshall (England)

MORRISETTE,
Achille, d. 8/8/1907 at 0/8/19; gastritis chronic; George Morrisette and Arabell Beauchemin
Bernadette, d. 6/4/1902 at 1/7/26; pneumonia
Pheby, d. 11/19/1909 at 35/4/21; acute pneumonia; Joseph Leblanc

MORRISON,
Andrew, d. 4/18/1915 at 72/10/28; dilatation of heart; Samuel Morrison and Hannah Tibbetts
Angie, d. 11/28/1934 at 69 in New York, NY; carcinoma of breast
Ansel H., d. 5/26/1906 at 48/2/17; unknown; buried in Danvers, MA
Arthur H., d. 3/28/1937 at 80/9/27; arteriosclerotic
Charles C., d. 10/28/1937 at 54/9; acute appendicitis
Daniel C., d. 7/7/1892 at 2; diphtheria; b. Dover; (Sanbornton; Great Falls)
Donald E., d. 12/18/1920 at 4/4/1; broncho pneumonia; John W. Morrison and Hally B. Elder
Ernest M., d. 3/23/1912 at 21
John Foster, d. 8/2/1912 at 3/0/20; diphtheria; John W. Morrison and Hally B. Elder
Margaret L., d. 6/9/1934 at 90/3/7; chronic nephritis
Marietta, d. 7/16/1918 at 60/6/22; chronic endocarditis; John W. Morrison and Abby A. Cate
Mary E., d. 6/24/1907 at 23/5/24; tuberculosis; Patrick Cox and Catherine -
Myrtle P., d. 11/6/1927 at 40/3/17; carcinoma cervix uteri; Charles Hodgdon and Delilah Foss
Naomi, d. 1/31/1905 at 84/2/11 in Durham; pneumonia; PH
Nellie M., d. 3/18/1921 at 57/9/18; acute nephritis; Joshua Atwood and Lucy Carter
Sarah, d. 3/16/1891 at 72; widow; Richard Morrison (Barrington) and Lydia Bodge (Barrington)
Susan A., d. 9/19/1909 at 68/1/8; cancer of uterus; Albra Morrison and Lucretia Butler

MORRISSETTE,
Albertine, d. 8/22/1900 at <1; cholera infantum
Flora, d. 1/29/1917 at 10/2/6; acute appendicitis; Louis Morrissette and Phoebe White
Honori, d. 8/2/1891 at 0/3/19; Thomas Morrissette (Bangor, ME) and Alice Paquette (Canada)
Napoleon, d. 6/5/1929 at 62 in Woodman; ac. dilatation of heart; C. Morrissette
Roland W., d. 1/27/1930 at 3/1/16; tonsilitis; Raymond Morrissette and Alice Labrie

MORRISSEY,
Bridget, d. 6/8/1887 at 77/6/10 in Springvale, ME; married; b. Berwick, ME; Thomas Grover (Berwick, ME) and Mary Shaw (Berwick, ME)

MORROW,
Margaret, d. 4/9/1899 at 67; cerebral paralysis; PH

MORSE,
Caroline F., d. 2/2/1933 at 94/7/26; arteriosclerosis
Charles E., d. 5/17/1919 at 12/4/14; appendicitis; Merce V. Morse and Susie Berry
Hannah M., d. 9/29/1917 at 70/1/8; mitral regurgitation; John R. Stevens and Matilda Barrett
Laura May, d. 1/5/1933 at 8/3/12; broncho pneumonia
Mary J., d. 8/10/1912 at 79/3/27; arterio sclerosis; Nathaniel Perry and Eliza Perkins
Susan A., d. 8/17/1918 at 83/5; carcinoma of arm; Joseph B. Boody and Abigail Nason
Walter, d. 12/16/1928 at 20/4/1; accidental; George Morse and Florence Allen

MORSS,
Mary C., d. 1/21/1911 at 49/11/13; Joseph B. Morss and Martha H. Boardman

MORTHAM,
Alice, d. 8/20/1902 at –; stillborn; PH

MORTON,
Ann E., d. 11/24/1914 at 81/8/3; pneumonia; William Clover and Elizabeth Duncan

MOSES,
Henry, d. 7/9/1897 at 53 in Rollinsford; insolation; b. Switzerland; SM
Leonard, d. 4/12/1891 at 81; married
Sarah, d. 9/23/1893 at 83; heart disease; b. Barrington

MOULTON,
A. Florence, d. 3/2/1924 at 68 in Haverhill, MA; chronic myocarditis
Allen Curtis, d. 4/13/1935 at 81/6/3; arteriosclerosis
Alvah, d. 8/16/1904 at 85/4/20; senility; PH
Alvah P., d. 9/15/1891 at 25/0/29; single; Alvah Moulton (Tamworth) and Susan Tapley (Dover)
Amy, d. 11/18/1924 at 56/4/3; arterio sclerosis; J. P. J. Moulton and Harriet N. Remick
Annie Caroline, d. 3/23/1928 at 76/11/23 in Dedham, MA; arterio sclerosis; Seth S. Moulton and Caroline Hanson
Annie M., d. 6/24/1931 at 77/2/20 in Durham; arterio sclerosis
Benjamin, d. 1/26/1891 at 76/7/12; Benjamin Moulton (York, ME) and Edith ----- (York, ME)
Catherine, d. 3/9/1907 at 89/9/14; la grippe; Joseph Malloy

Charles H., d. 2/27/1920 at 61; broncho pneumonia
Charles T., d. 9/11/1905 at 48/5/2; pneumonia; PH
Cynthia, d. 7/29/1906 at 74/0/12 in Danvers, MA; valvular heart disease
Daniel, d. 7/24/1892 at 78; heart disease; b. York, ME; (York, ME; York, ME)
Elizabeth D., d. 7/25/1901 at 84/10/13 in Malden, MA; aneurism
Frank L., d. 3/2/1909 at 24/4/10 in Somerville, MA; pul. tuberculosis; Fernando Moulton and Abbie M. Trask
George O., d. 5/20/1910 at 79/4 in Boxford, MA; gen. failure of old age
Helen I., d. 9/18/1929 at 72/5/8; cerebral hemorrhage; Ezra Twombly and Lucinda K. Hanson
John, d. 1/7/1891 at 34/10/9; married; Daniel Moulton (York, ME) and Elizabeth Drew (Dover)
Josiah S., d. 1/29/1918 at 74/4/5 in Cambridge, MA; intestinal statis
Mary E., d. 3/25/1925 at 80/8/26; la grippe; Samuel H. Mathes and Mary T. Perkins
Nellie S., d. 9/21/1932 at 71/1/28 in Exeter; acute pulmonary embolism
Sara Reade, d. 6/9/1901 at 38/10/1; phthisis pulmonalis; PH
Seth T., d. 3/16/1899 at 86 in Boston, MA; heart disease; PH
Susan A., d. 3/15/1901 at 63/3/2; diabetes mellitus; PH
Susan A., d. 9/22/1913 at 85/5/13; cerebral hemorrhage; John Tapley and Lydia Reade
William, d. 11/7/1937 at 68/7/13 in Ossipee; diabetes mellitus

MOURGINOS,
Andrew, d. 5/9/1932 at 4/4/29; hit by automobile

MOYNEHAN,
Ellen, d. 2/25/1906 at 63; chronic gastritis; buried in Portland, ME

MOYNIHAN,
Dana D., d. 2/8/1904 at 0/4/23; malnutrition; buried in Austin Cem.

MUDGETT,
Lizzie, d. 3/–/1905 at 66; neurasthenia; PH

MUGFORD,
Thomas, d. 5/5/1910 at 55; cerebral apoplexy

MULLEN,
Ann, d. 6/18/1902 at 60; nephritis; buried in Newmarket
Blanche R., d. 2/1/1897 at 1; scarlet fever; b. MA; SM
Bridget, d. 3/21/1890 at 75; married; (Ireland; Ireland)

Catherine J., d. 1/26/1892 at 30; pulmonary phthisis; b. MA; (Ireland; Ireland)
Elizabeth, d. 1/27/1923 at 53; pyelo nephritis; John McKerney and Bridget Mone
Ellen, d. 3/26/1887 at 0/8; b. Dover; Michael J. Mullen (Ireland) and Kate Duffy (Ireland)
George H., d. 11/10/1891 at 4; Bridget Mullen (Ireland)
John A., d. 7/30/1888 at 0/2/5; b. Dover; Patrick Mullen (Ireland) and Mary Morgan (Ireland)
Katie, d. 7/17/1893 at 39; dementia; b. Ireland; (Ireland; Ireland)
Mary, d. 5/4/1920 at 70/7/6; natural causes; Patrick Mullen and Elizabeth McKone
Mary A., d. 7/29/1892 at 23; heart disease; b. Ireland; (Ireland; Ireland)
Rose, d. 7/22/1889 at 7/11/4; b. Dover; Frank B. Mullen (Dover) and Mary Brenan (Ireland)
William J., d. 11/26/1902 at – in Manchester; acute pneumonia; SM

MULLER,
Elizabeth, d. 9/9/1902 at 0/10/15; cholera infantum; PH
James, d. 3/13/1897 at 1 in Manchester; valvular disease of heart

MULLIGAN,
child, d. 5/13/1909 at –; stillborn; Patrick Mulligan and Bridget -----
child, d. 12/11/1920 at –; stillborn; Clara F. Mulligan
child, d. 1/30/1937 at –*
Ann, d. 3/30/1910 at 78; bronchitis acute; James Haffey and Ellen Cassily
Frank, d. 10/9/1906 at 37/10/1; cerebral hemorrhage
Frank E., d. 9/27/1928 at 61; carcinoma pelvic bone
James, d. 11/12/1925 at 27/10/3; fracture of skull; Patrick J. Mulligan and Annie Cassidy
John Q., d. 3/20/1906 at 44/8/15; Bright's disease; SM
Margaret, d. 11/1/1924 at 75; acute myocarditis; Edward Gurry and Bridget Culley
Mary A., d. 9/8/1897 at 1; infantile disease; b. Dover; SM
Patrick J., d. 10/28/1905 at 0/3; malnutrition; SM
Patrick J., d. 3/28/1917 at 38; pulm. tuberculosis; Martin Mulligan and Margaret -----

MULLIN,
John, d. 4/25/1903 at 35; SM
John, d. 3/28/1934 at 2 hrs.; dystocia
Mary A., d. 10/4/1890 at 0/3; Michael Mullin (Ireland) and Kate Duffey (Ireland)

MULLINS,
Kathleen M., d. 2/24/1929 at 1/2/26; lobar pneumonia; Daniel J. Mullins and Annie M. Dobbins
Mary Jane, d. 8/24/1926 at 23/11/2; septicaemia; Joseph Gaudreau and Delina Ouellette

MULLOY,
child, d. 3/24/1894 at –; stillborn; b. Dover; SM

MULVEY,
Walter C., d. 4/23/1934 at 37/5/17; carcinoma of stomach

MUNDY,
Walter A., d. 11/27/1936 at 19/9/26; methanol poisoning

MUNROE,
child, d. 10/21/1902 at –; stillborn; SM
Richard, d. 5/10/1934 at 63/7/7; carcinoma of stomach

MUNSEY,
Annie M., d. 4/13/1893 at 54; cancer; b. Barnstead; (Barnstead; Barnstead)
J. Fred, d. 12/7/1911 at 47/7/2; tuberculosis intestinal; John Munsey and Mary Berry

MURCHIE,
Mary, d. 11/29/1932 at 44/2/13; pulmonary embolism

MURDOCH,
Francis B., d. 10/2/1929 at 79/7; apoplexy; Francis B. Murdoch and Mary Gaddis

MURPHY,
child, d. 5/31/1893 at –; debility - premature birth; b. Dover; (Farmington; Dover)
child, d. 7/27/1894 at –; premature birth; b. Dover; SM
Alice, d. 3/18/1920 at 70; lobar pneumonia
Ann, d. 3/27/1888 at 90/4; widow; b. Ireland; James Henratty (Ireland) and Mary Paul (Ireland)
Annie, d. 3/31/1893 at 49; acute gastralgia; b. Ireland; (Ireland; Ireland)
Anthony, d. 6/27/1916 at 28 in Lawrence, MA; acute pneumonia; Patrick Murphy and Mary Guimon
Bridget, d. 4/5/1923 at 65; cerebral apoplexy; Michael Hughes

Catherine F., d. 11/8/1924 at 0/1/7; marasmus; John Murphy and Margaret Haley
Charles M., d. 5/2/1888 at 52/2/27 in Boston, MA; married
Daniel, d. 3/16/1890 at 75; widower
Daniel W., Rev., d. 4/3/1911 at 72/4/9; old age; William Murphy and ----- Wigmore
Ellen, d. 2/7/1906 at –; nephritis; SM
Frances E., d. 10/7/1916 at 43/6/21 in Westbrook, ME; acute uraemia; Brigham Callahan and Julia -----
Frank, d. 5/4/1919 at 50; ulcer of stomach; John Murphy and Helen -----
Frank, d. 8/16/1935 at 67/3/27 in Providence, RI; organic heart disease
Frederick William, d. 1/22/1937 at 59/2/16*
Harry, d. 1/2/1933 at 38/8/7; angina pectoris
Helen J., d. 1/2/1926 at 72/11/29; lobar pneumonia; Moses Merrill and Mary Hilton
James, d. 9/1/1888 at 0/1; b. Dover; Michael Murphy (Ireland) and Margaret Philips (Ireland)
James, d. 12/30/1888 at 42; laborer; married; b. Ireland; John Murphy (Ireland) and Mary Murphy (Ireland)
James, d. 1/1/1935 at 58/10/27; natural causes
James H., d. 4/23/1889 at 18/5/1; clerk; single; b. Dover; John Murphy (Ireland) and Margaret McKearn (Ireland)
Jane, d. 9/1/1925 at 42; appendicitis; Frank C. Wright and Cecelia Edwards
Jno., d. 8/24/1889 at 47; laborer; single; b. Dover; Pat Murphy (Ireland) and K. Lyons (Ireland)
John, d. 1/10/1903 at 61; senility; SM
John, d. 10/28/1911 at 43 in Montville, CT; concussion of brain; Daniel Murphy and Hannah Duff
John W., d. 4/8/1927 at 74 in New York City; myocarditis
Julia A., d. 10/29/1893 at 77; old age; b. Ireland; (Ireland; Ireland)
Lizzie, d. 10/23/1899 at 19; typhoid pneumonia
Maggie, d. 5/13/1898 at 3; meningitis; b. Dover; SM
Margaret, d. 4/17/1887 at 46; married; b. Ireland; (Ireland; Ireland)
Margaret, d. 6/16/1907 at 64; R. R. collision; ----- Dempser
Margaret, d. 7/30/1912 at 63/17; entero colitis; James Largey and Catherine McGrory
Margaret, d. 7/16/1925 at 57 in Manchester; valv. heart disease
Mary, d. 6/23/1893 at –; premature birth; b. Dover; (Ireland; Ireland)
Mary, d. 7/5/1898 at 80; heart disease; b. Ireland; buried in Augusta, ME
Mary, d. 5/17/1926 at 64 in Concord; broncho pneumonia; Terrence Daley and Ella Rymes
Mary A., d. 2/8/1890 at 28; single; Daniel Murphy (Ireland) and Hannah Duffy (Ireland)
Mary C., d. 2/25/1937 at 26/8/18; chr. myocarditis

Mary R., d. 9/27/1913 at 13/9/25; change of life; Michael Regan
Matthew E., d. 12/7/1926 at 47/9/15; chronic myocarditis; Thomas Murphy
 and Annie Laughlin
Patrick, d. 12/2/1925 at 55/0/17; peritonitis; John Murphy and Rose Smith
Patrick E., d. 12/29/1902 at 36; angina pectoris
Patrick F., d. 4/12/1897 at 0; inanition; b. Dover; SM
Patrick J., d. 5/11/1907 at 34 in Boston, MA; oedema of brain
Peter, d. 1/21/1899 at 35; heart disease and influenza; SM
Peter, d. 3/21/1915 at 16/6/13; cerebral hemorrhage; Peter Murphy and
 Mary Loughlin
Peter, d. 3/8/1922 at 71 in Lawrence, MA; broncho pneumonia
Peter D., d. 9/14/1933 at 34; myocarditis
Peter J., d. 8/15/1932 at 51; cerebral hemorrhage
Robert A., d. 2/1/1919 at 0/2/14; gastro enteritis; John Murphy and Ethel
 Russ
Rose, d. 3/18/1893 at 1; meningitis cerebral; b. Dover; (Ireland; Ireland)
Sarah, d. 4/23/1935 at 65; diabetes mellitus
Thomas, d. 3/15/1890 at 63/2/23; married; Thomas Murphy (Ireland) and
 Anna Laughlam (Ireland)
William A., d. 1/27/1935 at 72 in Boston, MA; hypertrophy of prostate

MURRAY,
Bridget, d. 11/20/1927 at 78; chronic endocarditis
Daniel F., d. 9/11/1923 at 39/0/26 in Lowell, MA; carcinoma of stomach
Daniel W., d. 8/16/1893 at 46; fall, spinal injury, paralysis; b. Dover; (-----;
 Alton)
Daniel W., d. 12/8/1919 at 46/7/7; chr. nephritis; Patrick Murray and Sarah
 McKone
David, d. 9/17/1929 at 76 in Newton Ctr., MA; natural causes; George P.
 Murray and Martha Stackpole
F., d. 9/24/1904 at –; malnutrition; SM
Frank, d. 1/7/1890 at 45; married; Patrick Murray (Ireland) and Mary
 Murray (Ireland)
George A., d. 5/7/1928 at 71/3/13; cancer oesophagus; George A. Murray
 and Martha A. Stackpole
James, d. 8/4/1907 at 65; congestion of lungs
James M., d. 1/31/1933 at 83/10/6; arteriosclerosis
Joseph, d. 4/8/1892 at 2; marasmus; b. Dover; (Canada; Canada)
Joseph F., d. 7/25/1887 at 5/5/10; b. Dover; Frank Murray (Ireland) and
 Mary A. Quinn (England)
Martha Isabel, d. 12/19/1910 at 58/11/18; chr. brain disease; L. S. R. Gray
 and Mary A. Davis
Mary, d. 7/2/1889 at 26; mill operative; widow; b. Ireland; Peter McKone
 (Ireland) and Rose Hughes (Ireland)

Mary E., d. 8/13/1913 at 4/2/17; convulsions; Patrick Murray and Bridget McKernan
Owen, d. 12/6/1914 at 72; chronic myocarditis
Rosa, d. 3/2/1892 at 9; anaemia; b. Dover; (Canada; Canada)
Sarah, d. 2/1/1904 at –; ulcerative endocarditis; SM
Sarah A., d. 2/24/1936 at 79/11/7; lobar pneumonia
Sylvia M., d. 3/16/1896 at 72; cardiac asthma; b. ME; PH
Theresa, d. 3/31/1909 at 29; interssusception; Patrick Murray and Bridget -
William J., d. 8/7/1913 at 52/0/4; cerebral hemorrhage; Daniel J. Murray and Sylvia Damson

MURTAUGH,
James, d. 3/1/1925 at 84/10/24; cancer of larynx; Edward Murtaugh and Catherine Farrell
John E., d. 7/30/1891 at 29/3/30; married; Edward Murtaugh (Ireland) and Mary A. Mooney (Ireland)
Marie A., d. 1/10/1904 at 12/7/17; heart disease; buried in Dover
Martha J., d. 12/23/1893 at –; pneumonia; b. Dover; (Dover; Dover)
Mary G., d. 1/28/1934 at 45 in Boston, MA; myocarditis

MURTHA,
Elizabeth, d. 3/4/1917 at 80; chr. intestitial nephritis; Thomas Murtha and Mary Hanratty

MYERS,
Annie, d. 4/27/1901 at 5/0/3; diphtheria; SM
Annie, d. 11/17/1930 at 54/2/17; heart disease; Joseph Hughes and Mary Lennon
Beatrice D., d. 8/25/1915 at 0/2/3; infantile atrophy; John Myers and Annie Hughes
Catherine, d. 1/19/1897 at 3; brain disease; b. Dover; SM
Catherine, d. 3/25/1917 at 29/2/25; phthisis pulmonalis; Thomas Myers and Mary McAtavey
Catherine Ann, d. 3/18/1890 at 2/8/29; John Myers (Ireland) and Rose Goodwin (Ireland)
Francis, d. 11/14/1910 at 68; senility; John Myers and Mary McFadden
Frank, d. 1/20/1897 at 7; scarlet fever; b. Dover; SM
James, d. 9/23/1895 at 0; cholera infantum; b. Dover; SM
John, d. 1/24/1897 at 1; scarlet fever; b. Dover; SM
John F., d. 4/26/1936 at 68; chronic endocarditis
John Henry, d. 7/19/1895 at 0; cholera infantum; b. Dover; SM
Mabel, d. 2/26/1897 at 3; pneumonia; b. Dover; SM
Mary, d. 2/19/1920 at 54; uraemia; James McAtarvey
Mary A., d. 9/9/1935 at 63/9; chronic endocarditis
Minnie, d. 6/19/1907 at 2/8; meningitis; John F. Myers and Mary Flannelly

Rosanna, d. 7/4/1889 at 17/10/24; mill operative; b. Ireland; Francis Myers
 (Ireland) and S. Fitzpatrick (Ireland)
Roselind, d. 9/13/1901 at 35/0/29; tuberculosis; SM
Susan, d. 8/8/1926 at 76 in Boston, MA; valvular heart disease
Thomas F., d. 8/30/1935 at 73/8/27; fracture of skull and multiple fractures

MYHR,
Laurine, d. 2/26/1912 at 48/0/10; Brights disease; Lars Erickson and
 Agnete Hanson

MYLUS,
Joseph, d. 6/10/1905 at 25; concussion of brain; PH

NADEAU,
Albert J., d. 11/28/1929 at 25 in Rollinsford; accidental
Armand, d. 11/12/1936 at 9/9/4 in Rollinsford; fracture of skull
Joseph, d. 9/22/1921 at 44; septicemia; Vital Nadeau and Rose Peneault
Omer, d. 11/28/1929 at 17 in Rollinsford; accidental

NALLY,
Florence, d. 1/23/1901 at 17; phthisis
Mary, d. 10/18/1908 at 62; chronic nephritis; John Barron and Ellen
 Murray
Michael, d. 5/4/1907 at 64; chronic nephritis; Michael Nally

NASH,
Evart E., d. 4/23/1921 at 0/8/18; meningitis; Donald W. Nash and Alvina
 Cote
Georgiana V., d. 10/19/1930 at 77/7/16; chr. myocarditis; John Vaughn
 and Sarah B. Dorr
Goodwin E., d. 5/29/1921 at 55/11/9; cerebral hemorrhage; Roscoe S.
 Nash and Elizabeth R. Wiley
Philmore A., d. 9/1/1937 at 44; gas - accidental

NASON,
Addie, d. 3/14/1933 at 64/0/11; cerebral hemorrhage
Albert R., d. 2/27/1895 at 0; cerebro meningitis; b. Dover; PH
Charles E., d. 4/29/1887 at 6/2; b. Rollinsford; Samuel G. Nason (S.
 Berwick, ME) and Olive A. Staples (N. Berwick, ME)
Charles H., d. 8/31/1902 at 48/6/11; pneumonia; PH
Chester T., d. 8/21/1898 at 0; marasmus; b. Dover; PH
Frank, d. 11/30/1901 at 51/4/17; cerebral hemorrhage; PH
Frank, d. 1/25/1919 at 61; valv. heart disease

Frank E., d. 12/10/1930 at 64/3/2; arterio sclerosis; Reuben Nason and Vienna Davis
Hattie M., d. 9/5/1902 at 33/4/6; unknown; PH
Inez Ford, d. 1/15/1931 at 66/5/21 in Bradford, VT; angina pectoris
M. Etta, d. 9/22/1894 at 39; heart disease; b. NH; PH
Mark F., d. 2/3/1898 at 70; heart disease; b. So. Berwick, ME; PH
Martha A., d. 2/20/1895 at 43 in Boston, MA; chronic tuberculosis; buried in Dover
Mary W., d. 1/29/1893 at 65; dilation of heart
Moses B., d. 2/10/1914 at 46/3/1; sarcoma of intestines; John Nason and Armine Bennett
Orrin Edgar, d. 12/16/1926 at 77/3/3; heart failure; Elisha Nason and Julia A. Jenness
Raymond K., d. 12/19/1911 at 1/1/25; whooping cough; Harry P. Nason and Bertha M. Hoitt
Rebecca A., d. 3/10/1904 at 60/4/5; burned to death; PH
Reuben, d. 2/20/1906 at 69/5/11; diabetes; PH
Sara E., d. 5/23/1904 at 75/10/24; spinal paresis; PH
Vienna M., d. 11/16/1892 at 47; carcinoma; b. Farmington; (Farmington; Farmington)
William B., d. 10/8/1892 at 69; suicide by hanging; b. Dover; (Dover; Dover)
William D., d. 1/15/1930 at 58/11/15; valvular heart dis.; Daniel S. Nason and Olive A. Staples
William F., d. 9/6/1923 at 65/9/15; paralysis agitans; Joseph Nason and Susan Frost

NATHAN,
Chester B., d. 1/13/1923 at 16/8/21; pulmonary abscess; William Nathan and Rena E. Boutillier

NEAL,
Albert G., d. 5/13/1935 at 86/1/12; cerebral hemorrhage
Charles A., d. 3/18/1891 at 77/3/1; widower; Robert Neal (Portsmouth) and ----- (Portsmouth)
Clara G., d. 3/17/1915 at 77/10/11; senility; Gilman Hall and Eliza Tuttle
Delia A. H., d. 9/17/1914 at 71/3; fibroid tumor of uterus; Samuel H. Henderson and Sarah A. Guppy
Everett L., d. 1/27/1934 at 3/8/4; broncho pneumonia
Frank E., d. 5/31/1930 at 65/11/21; fracture skull; John Neal and Frances G. Butler
Fred H., d. 10/1/1925 at 66/1/7; prog. bulbar paralysis; William Neal and Clara G. Hall
James A., d. 9/26/1898 at 72; old age; b. Dover; PH
Lawrence S., d. 10/16/1935 at 49/10; rheumatic endocarditis

Nancy A., d. 11/17/1931 at 82/3/9; cerebral hemorrhage
Rupert W., d. 12/3/1893 at 20; Bright's disease; b. Kittery, ME; (Kittery, ME; Marblehead, MA)
Sarah J., d. 12/7/1898 at 74; old age; b. Effingham; PH
Terrence O., d. 5/7/1892 at 21; pneumonia; b. Ireland; (Ireland; Ireland)
William H., d. 7/3/1897 at 63; Bright's disease; b. Dover; PH

NEALAND,
John, d. 3/24/1929 at 68; chr. Brights disease; Patrick Nealand and Mary Cullen

NEALLEY,
Abbie P., d. 1/29/1895 at 77 in Saco, ME; fibrous cancer; PH
Benjamin F., d. 3/27/1911 at 71/5/3; gastric ulcer - hemorrhage; Benjamin M. Nealley and Abbie Pray
Benjamin M., d. 7/29/1888 at 76/9/26; married; b. Nottingham; Benjamin M. Nealley (Nottingham) and Sally Ford (Nottingham)
Donald, d. 12/21/1937 at 31*
Emma C., d. 8/25/1928 at 74/0/27; spinal sclerosis; Thomas H. Cushing and Caroline Torr
Grace Hanson, d. 1/10/1922 at 61/3/18 in Syracuse, NY; cancer of uterus
Harriet R., d. 10/12/1903 at 57/4/28; cardiac dilation; PH
Henry S., d. 9/24/1918 at 54 in Buffalo, NY; lobar pneumonia
John H., d. 12/6/1928 at 75/4/2; angina pectoris; Benjamin M. Nealley and Abigail Pray
Sarah A., d. 12/24/1906 at 71 in Syracuse, NY; cancer; PH

NEDEAU,
Annie, d. 11/16/1917 at 33; phthisis pulmonalis; Louis Reil and Matilda LaRose
Mary, d. 5/21/1916 at –; stillborn; Joseph Nedeau and Annie Rice

NEIMI,
Ellen Lea, d. 1/18/1931 at 13/0/10 en route; suddenly

NELSON,
Adelaide, d. 3/5/1928 at 74/0/22; chronic nephritis; Edward Nelson and Emily B. Marston
Annie P., d. 7/30/1935 at 74/3/11; angina pectoris
Chalmer, d. 12/30/1925 at 68/6/4 in Brockton, MA; broncho pneumonia
Emily A., d. 4/6/1892 at 5; paralysis of heart; b. Dover; (Great Falls; Kittery, ME)
Emily B., d. 9/22/1908 at 78/0/15; cerebral hemorrhage; Thomas Marston and Elmira Duncan

Frank B., d. 1/3/1919 at 62/6/12; apoplexy; John Nelson and Martha Conant
George W., d. 8/28/1905 at 43/7/22 in Haverhill, MA; carcinoma of intestines; PH
Halfden, d. 8/21/1900 at 22; tuberc. meningitis; PH
Harold, d. 7/7/1893 at –; premature birth; b. Dover; (Hebron; Grafton, MA)
Jesse M., d. 7/27/1908 at 25/10/29; pulmonary tuberculosis; Melvin E. Nelson and Annie P. Frisbee
John, d. 4/29/1924 at 75/7/14; spinal sclerosis
Louis, d. 2/7/1901 at 52/1/19; auto-infection; PH
Melvin F., d. 7/16/1916 at 60/5/14; heat exhaustion; Edward Nelson and Emily B. Marston
Thomas M., d. 2/15/1887 at 0/3/24; b. Dover; Chalmer Nelson (Great Falls) and Cora B. Hall (Barrington)

NEVENS,
James M., d. 3/7/1913 at 91/7/16; old age; James M. Nevins (sic) and Patience Goodwin

NEVILLE,
Bernard, d. 6/3/1925 at –; pulmonary tuberculosis; Edmund Neville and Margaret Mahone
Rose, d. 1/6/1936 at 69; bronchial asthma

NEVINS,
Mary M., d. 7/22/1908 at 80/3 in Bucksport, ME; arteriosclerosis

NEWCOMB,
Ellen, d. 10/15/1892 at 24; phthisis; b. Ireland; (Ireland; Ireland)

NEWELL,
Mrs. C. W., d. 5/26/1931 at 71; coronary thrombosis

NEWHALL,
Martha E., d. 1/14/1912 at 76; cerebral embolism; John Yelden and ----- Belknap

NEWLING,
Beatrice M., d. 12/21/1918 at 0/2/24 in Somerville, MA; simple meningitis
Charles H., d. 9/30/1929 at 62/8/17 in Rochester; endocarditis
Cynthia A., d. 2/13/1918 at 80/8/14; endocarditis; John G. Chick
Etta M., d. 12/26/1917 at 53/7/13; acute uraemia; Dennis Straw and Hannah Nutter
Lois, d. 10/3/1935 at –; stillborn

Robert A., d. 6/17/1916 at 0/2/18; acute indigestion; Earl H. Newling and
    Vera H. Bell
Wallace E., d. 9/29/1937 at 22/6/21; carcinomatous cirrhosis of liver -
    autopsy

NEWMAN,
Charles T., d. 10/14/1913 at 64/8/18; carcinoma; Benjamin F. Newman
    and Sybil C. Pishon
Vide H., d. 2/7/1906 at 55/8/5; insanity; buried in Bradford, MA

NEWSKY,
Louis, d. 10/9/1937 at 49*

NEWTON,
Alden C., d. 10/6/1918 at 13/9/27; influenza - pneumonia; Carlton A.
    Newton and Mary T. Chesley
Ann, d. 12/19/1911 at 86/4/4; senility; John Sylcock and Hannah Bramhall
Elizabeth H., d. 6/11/1907 at 50/7/27; carcinoma; James Newton and Ann
    Silcock
James, d. 3/26/1897 at 79 in Madbury; b. England; PH
Jesse, d. 3/3/1921 at 67/3/8 in Eliot, ME; chronic nephritis
Josephine A., d. 6/10/1901 at 42/9/15; phthisis pulmonalis; PH
Ruth E., d. 9/11/1906 at 0/2/9; cholera infantum; PH

NICHOLS,
Ella G., d. 6/8/1908 at 52/11/10; cancer; John W. Foote and Sarah E. Joy
Fred A., d. 10/29/1921 at 45/7/19 in Medford, MA; hemorrhage of
    pancreas
George, d. 3/14/1890 at 2/10/8; George Nichols (Biddeford, ME) and Nellie
    Hobbs (Dover)
Joanna, d. 2/14/1930 at 74; chronic nephritis; Michael Sullivan and
    Catherine Kenney
Mary F., d. 3/13/1900 at 65 in Boston, MA; pneumonia; PH
Walter S., d. 8/8/1933 at 84/1/6; cerebral hemorrhage

NICHOLSON,
Margaret, d. 11/1/1921 at 75/4/17 in Whitman, MA; myocarditis

NICKERSON,
Bertha E., d. 7/29/1931 at 38/4/20 in Newark, NJ; post operation shock
Lester E., d. 11/15/1913 at –; stillborn; E. B. Nickerson and Gertrude
    Spurling

NICKOLOPULOS,
John, d. 1/26/1907 at 17; destroyed by fire

NIEDZELSKI,
Nellie, d. 7/25/1911 at 0/11/23; cholera infantum; Ludvik Niadzelski and Mary Slemp

NIGHSWANDER,
Cost'a L., d. 6/17/1911 at 66/10/29; abdominal carcinoma; Charles H. Horton and Susan S. Lacosta

NILES,
Grace, d. 12/6/1935 at 70; chronic nephritis
Joseph W., d. 8/23/1926 at 70/3/1; carcinoma of stomach; Joseph Niles and ----- McGlort
Phoebe Damon, d. 5/26/1887 at 80/8; married; b. Reading, MA; (Reading, MA; Mont Vernon)

NISBET,
John W., d. 3/10/1893 at 14; cerebral meningitis; b. England; (England; England)

NISBIT,
Mary, d. 4/26/1892 at 3; sequelae of scarlet fever; b. Dover; (England; England)

NOBLE,
Ann C., d. 11/28/1887 at 47/11/17; married; b. Kennebunkport, ME; Samuel Anderson and Mary Bridge
Carrie Bell, d. 11/1/1892 at --; marasmus; b. Dover; (Dover; Dover)
Dolores, d. 2/28/1936 at 8/11/3 in Wrentham, MA; myasthenia gravis
Ellen T., d. 2/16/1919 at 65; apoplexy; Francis Alloisio and Lucy -----
Frank A., d. 1/29/1919 at 83/8/21; broncho pneumonia; Mehitable Thompson

NOEL,
Euphemie, d. 1/4/1931 at 81/12/2; chronic endocarditis
Eva M., d. 2/21/1936 at 52/8/14; cancer of rectum
Exelia, d. 1/26/1917 at 56/11/26 in Manchester; valvular dis. of heart; George Rocheleau and Delia Faucher
Henri F., d. 5/15/1920 at 10/3/13; septic endocarditis; John Noel and Rose Lefrebre
Henry, d. 12/21/1902 at 22; Bright's disease
Isreal, d. 11/30/1935 at 83/6/28; chronic myocarditis

John, d. 7/25/1918 at 35/0/26 in Portsmouth; accident; Alex Noel and Zelia Rocheleau
Joseph, Jr., d. 1/13/1917 at 0/0/1; congenital; Joseph Noel and Eva Aubin
Joseph Bertrand, d. 10/26/1921 at 0/2/3; gastro enteritis acute; Joseph E. Noel and Eva Soriel
Mary Jane, d. 11/16/1936 at 49/10/20 in Westbrook, ME; cerebral hemorrhage

NOFTALL,
Jessie, d. 2/12/1937 at 60/9/9 in Barrington; sudden heart failure

NOLCINE,
Charles A., d. 1/27/1895 at 65 in Salem, MA; pernicious anaemia; buried in Dover

NOLICINI,
Louisa F., d. 12/23/1896 at 64 in Swampscott, MA; cancer; PH

NORMAN,
Charles J., d. 2/2/1922 at 65/8/15 in Madbury; arterio sclerosis
Michael B., d. 11/10/1930 at 0/0/25; premature birth; Bernard Norman and Mary Bennett

NORRIS,
Charles W., d. 6/2/1892 at 65; found dead - apoplexy; b. Epping
Clara E., d. 12/17/1915 at 39/9/12; surgical shock; Nathaniel Foss and Ellen Drew
Elizabeth, d. 3/6/1895 at –; chronic asthma; buried in Lynn, MA
Ellen, d. 11/24/1908 at 57; chronic nephritis
Lucy A., d. 8/8/1890 at 42/0/24; married
Martha F., d. 3/6/1895 at 59; paralysis of heart; b. Wilmot; buried in Wilmot
Mary E. J., d. 12/23/1910 at –; organic heart disease

NORTON,
Alsada M., d. 7/6/1890 at 42/2/25; single; John H. Norton (Kittery, ME) and Anna S. Bragdon (York, ME)
Annie S., d. 7/29/1928 at 82/9/29; cerebral hemorrhage; Joel Bragdon and Sarah Goodwin
Charles C., d. 2/4/1918 at 61/10/17 in N. Berwick, ME; typhid fever; Charles C. Norton and Lucy Brock
Charles E., d. 12/31/1922 at 76/9/15; fatty degen. of heart; Simon Norton
Fred W., d. 12/30/1922 at 66/2/11; cancer of stomach; Thomas Norton and Harriet Hanson

George E., d. 8/3/1911 at 0/2/3; intestinal indigestion; Lyman F. Norton and Mattie E. Goings
John H., d. 12/3/1918 at 72/9/29; general arterio sclerosis; Samuel Norton and Caroline Haley
Mary E., d. 4/10/1928 at 68/4/29; diabetes mellitus; Thomas Coleman and Louisa A. Berry
Ralph F., d. 8/2/1921 at 0/2/15; acute indigestion; Clarence Norton and Mary Oates
Walter, d. 11/5/1924 at 37/10 in Concord; pneumonia; Fred Norton and Emma Young
Walter F., d. 11/10/1928 at 0/0/1; atelectasis; Michael Norton and Mary B. McDonough

NORWOOD,
Ephraim F., d. 6/10/1921 at 90/7/13 in Georgetown, MA; arterio sclerosis
Frank D., d. 1/20/1935 at 65/6/11 in Haverhill, MA; lobar pneumonia

NOSSIF,
Mary, d. 3/21/1904 at 0/8/3; pneumonia

NOSSIFF,
George, d. 2/20/1903 at 1; pneumonia; SM

NOURSE,
Ann E., d. 8/12/1911 at 87/7/15; cerebral hemorrhage; Zenas Slader and Melintha Wilson

NOYES,
Abbie M., d. 8/1/1900 at 53; abdominal cancer; buried in Somersworth
Charles E., d. 2/25/1918 at 80/6/6; senility; Arthur L. Noyes and Hannah Freethy
Charles E., Jr., d. 10/22/1899 at 26; pneumohydrothorax; buried in Somersworth

NUDD,
Benjamin L., d. 11/24/1903 at 75/4/6; heart disease; PH
Forest L., d. 3/19/1895 at – in Lowell, MA; pneumonia; buried in Dover
Mary A., d. 6/29/1900 at 73; heart disease; PH
Mary A., d. 4/25/1934 at 80/6/17; carcinoma of breast

NUGENT,
son, d. 3/1/1888 at –; b. Dover; Patrick Nugent (Ireland) and Mary A. Gorman (Ireland)

John G., d. 4/29/1908 at 2/10/6; drowned; Patrick Nugent and Veronica Joyce
Lizzie, d. 9/9/1889 at 5/1/8; b. Dover; Patrick Nugent (Ireland) and Mary A. Gorman (Ireland)
Patrick, d. 5/2/1888 at 65; R.R. builder; single; b. Ireland; Thomas Nugent (Ireland) and Allard McCilavay (Ireland)
Patrick, d. 11/10/1897 at 31; consumption; b. Ireland; SM
Peter, d. 12/13/1908 at 33; natural causes; John Nugent and Mary Dillon

NUTE,
Almira B., d. 4/15/1890 at 73/0/26; widow; Tobias Banfield (Portsmouth) and Elizabeth Whidden (Portsmouth)
Catherine L., d. 10/31/1888 at 64; married; b. Gilmanton; Enoch Moulton and Dolly Robinson
Clarence W., d. 11/8/1936 at 58; heart disease
Daniel A., d. 1/29/1910 at 72/5/22; peritonitis with perforation; Moses Nute and Betsey Avery
DeWitt C., d. 7/6/1920 at 72/10/6; cerebral hemorrhage; Sames Nute and Izette Keene
E. Jennie, d. 1/20/1903 at 57/3/6; Brights disease; buried in Somersworth
Elizabeth, d. 11/24/1906 at 79; old age; SM
Elizabeth A., d. 1/19/1900 at 62 in Farmington; inflammation of liver; buried in Dover
Ellen F., d. 11/10/1908 at 53/5/15 in Milton; cancer; Ivory H. Foss and Harriet Quimby
George E., d. 4/16/1905 at 62/4/14; chronic nephritis; buried in No. Wolfeboro
George F., d. 6/6/1904 at 76/0/30; senile debility
Greenleaf, d. 9/6/1900 at 76; apoplexy; buried in private
Hannah C., d. 10/1/1899 at 75; old age; PH
Harriet E., d. 5/15/1915 at 78/4/20; erysipelas; Simon Bradstreet and Elizabeth Odiorne
Ira W., d. 2/24/1896 at 64; marasmus; b. Milton; PH
Irena E., d. 12/11/1905 at 74/5/5; pneumonia; PH
Isaac, d. 8/5/1892 at 83; heart failure; b. Dover
Isabella H., d. 8/15/1889 at 54/6/11; married; b. Shapleigh, ME; R. P. Hutchings and M. J. Warren (Eliot, ME)
John A., d. 1/11/1927 at 77/1/11; chronic nephritis; Stephen Nute and Mary E. Abbott
John H., d. 6/18/1914 at 74/9/5; Stokes-Adams Disease; Isaac M. Nute and Mary A. Jenkins
Mary A., d. 1/6/1897 at 79; apoplexy; b. Madbury; PH
Matilda E., d. 4/18/1921 at 58/9/14 in Rochester; cancer of stomach; Moses Nute and Betsy Avery

Nellie M., d. 11/17/1921 at 64/9/9; angina pectoris; William I. Tibbetts and
  Sarah Varney
Oliver, d. 1/7/1894 at 75; shock; PH
Paul, d. 10/21/1903 at 91/3/17; old age; buried in family lot
Samuel, d. 1/19/1924 at 62/4/27; cancer of face; Stephen Nute and Mary
  E. Abbott
Sarah L., d. 10/15/1910 at 61/0/7; cancer of liver; Daniel Chesley and
  Margery Woodman
Senah M., d. 3/6/1919 at 83/11; chr. interstitial nephritis; John P. Cotton
  and Mary Towle
Susan, d. 4/4/1896 at 81; uraemia; b. Middleton; buried in Milton
Thomas, d. 11/9/1902 at 84/11/29; strangulated hernia; PH

NUTSEN,
Alice C., d. 5/4/1906 at 2/2/12; cretinism; PH

NUTSON,
Karen, d. 3/1/1936 at 69/6/18; cerebral hemorrhage

NUTTER,
Abigail R., d. 4/7/1893 at –; cerebral apoplexy
Charles F., d. 3/8/1924 at 70/6/18; ac. gastro enteritis; John W. Nutter and
  Ruth C. Pike
Frank, d. 2/9/1893 at 36; died in Strafford Co. Asylum fire
Henry N., d. 10/26/1912 at 53/8/19; accident; Henry Nutter and Emeline
  Edgerly
Mary, d. 2/9/1893 at 39; died in Strafford Co. Asylum fire
Minnie L., d. 12/16/1926 at 87/4/28 in Waltham, MA; cerebral hemorrhage
Nathaniel C., d. 12/20/1887 at 63/10/7; farmer; married; b. Portsmouth;
  Nathaniel Nutter (Portsmouth) and Ann Jackson (Madbury)
Nathaniel P., d. 12/11/1899 at 59 in Boston, MA; Brights disease; PH
Sarah J., d. 12/27/1903 at 79/6/19; old age; PH
Sophia, d. 12/11/1900 at 96; old age; PH

O'BRIEN,
[no name given - male], d. 2/22/1889 at 28; laborer; single; (Ireland;
  Ireland)
Alice, d. 1/21/1924 at 72/0/26; chronic myocarditis; Sylvester McNally and
  Ann Mallen
Annie, d. 10/22/1906 at 36/4; acute dysentery; buried in Rollinsford
Dennis, d. 3/4/1901 at 31; railroad accident; buried in N. Brookfield, MA
Edward, d. 7/31/1901 at 31/3/28; congestion of brain; SM
Ellen, d. 6/10/1921 at 71; arterio sclerosis; Patrick Regan and Honora
  Driscoll
Herbert F., d. 1/6/1919 at 26/2/6 in Northampton, MA; broncho pneumonia

Jeremiah, d. 6/7/1928 at 75; fracture skull; John O'Brien and Mary
    McCarthy
John, d. 8/2/1888 at 25; laborer; single
John, d. 11/12/1905 at 50; suffocation; SM
John P., d. 1/22/1910 at 44/7; pneumonia; James O'Brien and Bridget
    Quinn
Kate, d. 6/14/1891 at 0/9/11; Jerry O'Brien (Ireland) and Alice McNally
    (Dover)
Margaret, d. 2/25/1892 at 36; congestion of lungs; b. England; (Ireland;
    Ireland)
Mary, d. 4/30/1908 at 52; pneumonia; Daniel McGlone
Mary, d. 1/18/1927 at –; carcinoma of stomach
Mary A. P., d. 8/3/1902 at 81/0/20 in Newport, RI; carcinoma of intestines;
    PH
Mary E., d. 2/9/1904 at 27/4; tuberculosis of lungs
Michael, d. 11/8/1914 at 44 in Marlboro, MA; fractured skull; Thomas
    O'Brien and Honora Riley
Owen, d. 1/31/1910 at 68; gastro intestinal ulcers; Patrick O'Brien and
    Mary Carlen
Owen, d. 4/1/1925 at 58 in Warwick, RI; lobar pneumonia
Patrick, d. 9/17/1910 at 29/8/17 in Newburyport, MA; accidental drowning;
    Patrick O'Brien and Rose McCabe
Patrick, d. 9/22/1914 at 63; cerebral hemorrhage; John O'Brien and Julia
    McCarty
Timothy, d. 2/15/1908 at 70; pneumonia

O'CLAIR,
James, d. 6/1/1914 at 40/8; pul. tuberculosis; Louis O'Clair

O'CONNELL,
Dennis, d. 11/1/1901 at 59; heart failure; SM
Margaret, d. 12/12/1899 at 50; pulmonary phthisis; SM
Margaret, d. 12/28/1910 at 68; prolapse of rectum
Mary A., d. 8/11/1937 at 72/3/4; cor. artery disease

O'CONNER,
Hannah, d. 5/22/1905 at 52/9/7; probably heart disease; SM
Timothy, d. 3/14/1890 at 36; married; Timothy O'Connor (Ireland) and
    Ellen O'Conner (Ireland)

O'CONNOR,
Ellen, d. 11/17/1901 at 70; heart disease; SM
Frank, d. 5/26/1937 at 50/5/8; cerebral embolism
Joseph, d. 1/12/1890 at 22; Patrick O'Connor (Ireland) and B. Boyle
    (Ireland)

Lizzie, d. 3/15/1900 at 70; organic disease of heart; SM
Thomas E., d. 2/12/1923 at 75; arterio sclerosis; Thomas O'Connor and Margaret Leard
Timothy V., d. 5/15/1906 at 19/10/16; pernicious anemia; SM
William T., d. 8/2/1908 at 41/10/19; rupture of gall bladder; James O'Connor and Mary Behan

O'DONNEL,
Ellen, d. 11/5/1920 at 71; senility

O'DONNELL,
Joseph, d. 2/7/1930 at 44/7/2 in Lawrence, MA; cerebral hemorrhage
Susie, d. 6/9/1905 at 23; tuberculosis; SM

O'DOWD,
Teressa, d. 1/15/1927 at 37; ac. lobar pneumonia; George E. O'Dowd and Teresa McCarty

O'FEE,
Charles, d. 2/21/1918 at 55; cardiac asthma; Archie O'Fee

O'GARA,
James, Jr., d. 1/30/1913 at 28 in Chicago, IL; suffocated; James O'Gara

O'HARA,
Thomas, d. 9/3/1890 at 0/2/3; Matthew O'Hara (Ireland) and Mary Boyd (Scotland)

O'HARE,
Alice, d. 3/13/1922 at 70; chr. inter. nephritis; Patrick Loy and Rose McAlduff
Edward, d. 9/27/1900 at 49; heart failure; SM

O'HEARN,
child, d. 5/13/1910 at –; stillborn; James O'Hearn and Katherine Crossman
Ann, d. 3/29/1906 at 48/11/9; pneumonia; SM
Denis, d. 5/6/1916 at 68; exposure
John, d. 4/11/1906 at 27; laryngeal phthisis; SM

O'HERN,
child, d. 1/28/1912 at –; stillborn; James O'Hern and Catherine Crossan
James, d. 10/1/1918 at 39/10/4; acute lobar pneumonia; John O'Hern and Ann McManus

O'KAINE,
James, d. 7/5/1903 at 28/1/23; pulmonary oedema; buried in Rollinsford

O'KANE,
Bernard H., d. 12/28/1916 at 76; gen. arterio sclerosis; Bernard O'Kane and Catherine -----
Catherine, d. 1/5/1919 at 70; arterio sclerosis; Dennis Donovan and Mary Shannahan
Eliza, d. 7/19/1919 at 78; cancer of rectum
Vincent P., d. 6/4/1911 at 25/4/9; pulmonary tuberculosis; Bernard H. O'Kane and Katherine Donovan

O'LAUGHLIN,
Patrick, d. 10/3/1889 at 42/6/19; spinner; married; b. Ireland; Patrick O'Laughlin (Ireland) and Mary Hughes (Ireland)

O'LEARY,
Ann M., d. 10/29/1902 at 79; pulmonary phthisis; SM
Dennis T., d. 2/22/1930 at 67; cerebral hemorrhage; Dennis T. O'Leary and Mary Looney
Michael, d. 10/22/1907 at 82; general debility; Thomas M. O'Leary and Bridget O'Brien

O'MALLEY,
Michael, d. 2/19/1923 at 78; broncho pneumonia; Martin O'Malley and Mary Case

O'MARA,
Michael, d. 2/7/1902 at 42 in Griswold, CT; cerebral hemorrhage; SM

O'NEIL,
child, d. 5/29/1898 at 0; convulsions; b. Dover; SM
child, d. 10/20/1902 at –; premature birth; SM
Anna L., d. 6/20/1936 at 72; pneumonia, lobar
Annie May, d. 1/14/1893 at –; croup; b. Dover; (Ireland; Ireland)
Betsy Ann, d. 9/14/1913 at 83/9/21; cerebral hemorrhage; Thomas Berry and Comfort Jenness
Catherine, d. 8/16/1930 at 62; cancer intestines; John O'Neil and Ellen Hennessey
Catherine, d. 11/9/1935 at 54/5 in Revere, MA; carcinoma of liver
Catherine C., d. 10/12/1913 at 50; tachycardia; John Boyd
Dora Marie, d. 8/27/1927 at 39; pancreatitis; Leon Drouin
Elizabeth, d. 9/20/1896 at –; peritonitis; b. Dover; SM
Elizabeth, d. 4/15/1919 at 53 in Methuen, MA; abdominal carcinoma

Ellen, d. 8/1/1926 at 82; chronic myocarditis; Patrick O'Neil and Ellen
    Splaine
Emma, d. 3/13/1927 at 71; cerebral hemorrhage
Felix, d. 5/5/1903 at 32; peritonitis; SM
Felix, d. 12/11/1931 at 70; chronic nephritis
Francis J., d. 2/8/1909 at 55/10/4; cancer of bowels; William F. O'Neil and
    Betsy Ann Berry
George, d. 10/25/1929 at 79 in Brentwood; cyst of prostate
Ida J., d. 10/10/1901 at 45/10/26; cancer; PH
James, d. 1/19/1897 at 5; scarlet fever; b. Dover; SM
James, d. 8/29/1905 at 38; peritonitis; SM
James, d. 2/25/1911 at 73; senility
Jennie, d. 3/10/1918 at 56; chr. intestitial nephritis; Alonzo Whitehouse
    and Ann McGaugh
John, d. 10/27/1900 at 49; pernicious anemia; SM
John, d. 12/9/1914 at 43; cancer of liver; Hector O'Neil and Mary McElroy
Kate, d. 2/13/1895 at 29; pulmonary phthisis; b. Ireland; SM
Lizzie, d. 8/29/1918 at 55; cancer of breast
Mary, d. 1/2/1914 at 52; valvular heart disease
Mary C., d. 10/2/1918 at 0/0/66 (sic); premature birth; Terrence O'Neil and
    Mary C. Rogers
Mary C., d. 10/20/1918 at 0/0/1-4; premature birth; Terrence O'Neil and
    Mary C. Rogers
Owen, d. 4/5/1929 at 68; chronic endocarditis; Robert O'Neil and Rose
    Ann Hanlon
Robert M., d. 2/2/1897 at 0; bronchitis; b. Dover; SM
Terrence, d. 5/12/1900 at 75; old age; SM
Thomas J., d. 12/24/1914 at 46/2/14 in Newark, NJ; uraemia; William
    O'Neil and Betsey Berry
Thomas J., d. 4/11/1932 at 61/5/13; chronic endocarditis
Timothy, d. 12/29/1889 at 0/10/22; b. Dover; John O'Neil (Ireland) and
    Ellen Hennessey (Ireland)
William, d. 11/20/1919 at 65; arteriosclerosis; James O'Neil and Mary -----
William F., d. 8/27/1888 at 61/7/20; farmer; married; b. Dover; Francis G.
    O'Neil (Ireland) and Maria Grimes (Ireland)
William P., d. 12/16/1895 at 14; endocarditis; b. Dover; SM

O'NEILL,
Agnes, d. 8/30/1900 at <1; cholera infantum; SM

O'RILEY,
Sarah, d. 3/15/1892 at 84; old age; b. Ireland; (Ireland; Ireland)

O'ROURKE,
Ann, d. 5/23/1909 at 72; old age; Michael Rourke and Bridget Kelley

O'ROWELL,
Elizabeth F., d. 3/25/1925 at 29/11/8 in Hudson; broncho pneumonia; Francis O. Tyler and Jennie -----

OAKES,
Abner, d. 10/9/1933 at 29/0/17; streptococcemia
Alice J., d. 8/4/1918 at 75/3/22; chronic endocarditis; James Foss and Betsy Clark
Catherine, d. 5/17/1932 at 53/2/4; heart disease
James M., d. 6/26/1928 at 83; cerebral hemorrhage
Mabel E., d. 11/10/1929 at 58/7/11; lobar pneumonia; Oscar French

OATES,
child, d. 11/28/1891 at –; William H. Oates (Dover) and Mary C. Hester (England)
child, d. 1/24/1921 at –; premature birth; Joseph A. Oates and Eva Mailhoit
child, d. 5/9/1924 at –; stillborn; Joseph Oates and Eva Mailhot
Charles, d. 10/28/1930 at –; growth in lungs; Bernard Oates
Charles H., d. 12/16/1908 at 0/1/25; convulsions; Charles T. Oates and Alice Cote
Eliza, d. 2/20/1923 at 82; gen. arterio sclerosis; James Fields and Eliza ---
Rita M. R., d. 2/6/1925 at 0/0/2; premature birth; Joseph A. Oates and Eva Mailhot
Thomas, d. 4/24/1891 at 25/3/25; Bernard Oates (US) and Eliza Fields (US)
Walter Bassett, d. 2/15/1920 at –; asphyxia; Catherine Oats (sic)
William, d. 9/24/1913 at –; tuberculosis; Bernard Oates and Eliza Fields

OATS,
Bernard, d. 9/1/1911 at 71/5/14 in Togus, ME; mitral insufficiency

OBARA,
Andrew, d. 3/14/1914 at 0/1/8; bronchial pneumonia; Paul Obara and Victoria Nezoroiz

OBER,
Lutheria F., d. 2/8/1929 at 70/2/11; lobar pneumonia; John Campbell and Zeruiah Hatch

OCTIGAN,
Minnie, d. 4/13/1904 at 29 in Hartford, CT; acute nephritis; SM

ODETTE,
Joseph, d. 4/7/1896 at 2; congestion of lungs; b. Canada; SM

ODILON,
Victor, d. 7/27/1892 at –; cholera infantum; b. Dover; (Canada; MI)

ODIORNE,
Caroline E., d. 2/23/1921 at 92/3/29 in Clinton, MA; apoplexy
Charles W., d. 9/8/1898 at 75 in Clinton, MA; apoplexy; PH

OGDEN,
Earl R., d. 8/18/1898 at 0; cholera infantum; b. Dover; PH
Elizabeth, d. 3/15/1895 at 76; pneumonia; b. England; PH
Emma Locke, d. 5/19/1923 at 84/6/21 in Providence, RI; cerebral
    hemorrhage
James, d. 8/12/1896 at 78 in Newmarket; diarrhea
Walter, d. 1/12/1931 at 54/5; suicide by hanging
William C., d. 10/12/1903 at 37/8/8; typhoid fever; buried in Bronton, NJ

OLDROYD,
Joseph, d. 2/2/1906 at 74/3/2; cerebral apoplexy; PH
Margaret, d. 2/27/1896 at 61; heart disease; b. England; PH

OLDSON,
Francis T., d. 12/4/1906 at 44/5/17; cancer of stomach; buried in Salem,
    MA

OLSON,
child, d. 3/28/1932 at –; stillborn
Clara E., d. 1/20/1912 at 82/8/19; cerebral apoplexy; Thomas Matson and
    Sarah -----
John E., d. 2/16/1912 at 73/1/18; senility

OPENSHAW,
Horatio, d. 12/28/1902 at 60; nervous shock; PH

ORR,
Earl Arthur, d. 12/6/1925 at 0/0/20 in Kittery, ME; erysipelas
Ethel L., d. 11/28/1925 at 36 in Portsmouth; embolism
James Arthur, d. 12/14/1925 at 0/0/28 in Kittery, ME; erysipelas

OSBORN,
Charles A., d. 4/6/1887 at 25/6/26; teamster; b. Dover; Charles B. Osborn
    (Pittsfield) and Lucy A. Quimby (Sandwich)

Robert, d. 7/25/1887 at 26/5/19 in Lowell, MA

OSBORNE,
Addie E., d. 12/29/1901 at 32/11/23; consumption; PH
Harriett E., d. 3/19/1930 at 88/5/25; fracture of hip; Gideon Wiggin and Elizabeth Bean
Hiram S., d. 1/14/1911 at 79/9/18 in Rochester; chronic nephritis
Lucy A., d. 7/11/1915 at 88/1/13 in Exeter; senile gangrene
Marietta M., d. 8/27/1930 at 24/3/2; pulm. tuberculosis; George Osborne and Mary Tower
Mary E., d. 7/11/1926 at 78/1/29; lobar pneumonia; Jonathan P. Ham and Mary Waldron
Mary R., d. 3/31/1918 at 85/5/29 in Newton Highland, MA; chronic myocarditis
Warren G., d. 1/25/1924 at 85/5/14; cerebral hemorrhage; Green Osborne and Mehitabel Barton

OSGOOD,
Lucy J., d. 1/23/1929 at 49/9/12 in Rochester; pneumonia, hypostatic; William H. Jackson
Martha A., d. 11/23/1918 at 89/2/9; chronic nephritis; Bradley Osgood and Mehitable Wood
Rebecca W., d. 9/1/1901 at 80/1/24; fibro-cystic tumor; PH

OTASH,
Joseph, d. 7/3/1925 at 0/0/2-3; premature birth; Alexander Otash and Vasela Abie
Julia, d. 7/3/1925 at 0/0/1-3; premature birth; Alexander Otash and Vasela Abie

OTIS,
Ada B., d. 12/26/1895 at 34; pneumonia; b. Rochester; PH
Addie, d. 2/9/1893 at 41; died in Strafford Co. Asylum fire
Addie, d. 2/19/1914 at –; diabetes
Augustus H., d. 6/14/1925 at 63/4/29; chronic myocarditis; Lawrence G Otis and Frances A. Horne
Avis J., d. 9/13/1899 at 63; heart disease; buried in Lee
Charles S., d. 7/21/1908 at 61/8/6; cerebral embolism; Thomas J. Otis and Olive Goodwin
Clara A., d. 7/10/1889 at 74/1/17; housewife; widow; b. Dover; Tobias Cole (NH) and Sarah Drew (NH)
Daniel, d. 1/28/1923 at 77; pneumonia; Walter Otis and Sally Spencer
Desda M., d. 2/8/1895 at 66 in Concord; broncho pneumonia; buried in Dover
Emily D., d. 12/21/1893 at 73; catarrhal pneumonia; b. ME; (ME; ME)

Flora B., d. 2/23/1927 at 73/3 in York, ME; exhaustion
Florence G., d. 2/23/1917 at 24/5; septicemia; Marshall P. Snow
Frank P., d. 2/14/1911 at 51/7/18 in Concord; pneumonia; Sylvester Otis and Desda Hall
George E., d. 1/16/1897 at 22; pneumonia; b. Lee; PH
Hannah, d. 7/16/1891 at 40; single
Harriet S., d. 1/11/1934 at 81/4/7 in Waterville, ME; senile gangrene
Herbert K., d. 1/31/1917 at 46/11/8; septicemia; Orrin K. Otis and Sarah Garland
John C., d. 8/2/1897 at 82; old age; b. Strafford; buried in Somersworth
John E., d. 6/25/1888 at 29/1/28 in Madbury; shoemaker; married; b. Strafford; Moses Otis (Strafford) and Eliza Laighton (Canaan)
John H., d. 1/22/1896 at 53; general paresis; b. Boston, MA; PH
Julia E., d. 12/25/1918 at 64/5/2 in Concord; pneumonia; Andrew J. Kinney and Sarah Reel
Lucy A., d. 1/24/1915 at 73/1/30; chr. gastro enteritis; Benjamin F. Cole and Betsey T. Murphy
Mary A., d. 10/9/1887 at 75/6; widow; b. NH; Stephen Horne (NH) and Abigail Lee (ME)
Mildred, d. 5/16/1906 at 0/6/28 in Lawrence, MA; broncho pneumonia; PH
Moses, d. 8/14/1896 at 73; chronic diarrhea; b. Strafford; buried in Strafford
Stella A., d. 5/21/1920 at 51/10/1; cancer of oesophagus; John P. Otis and Arvis J. Snell

OUCTEAU,
Wilfred, d. 7/19/1905 at 0/9/3; cholera infantum

OUELETT,
Joseph C., d. 3/3/1898 at 0; disease of lungs; b. Dover; SM

OUELETTE,
child, d. 3/3/1926 at –; stillborn; Albert Ouellette and Julia Blackburn
Benjamin, d. 9/6/1924 at 75; lobar pneumonia

OUELLETTE,
Charles, d. 12/16/1936 at 83/1/12; chr. myocarditis
George R., d. 9/30/1928 at 25/0/19; septic sore throat; Cyprien Ouellette and Belle Marcotte

OWEN,
Elizabeth F., d. 6/22/1894 at 34 in Portsmouth; typhoid fever; PH
Herbert W., d. 4/8/1927 at 55/3/25 in Lowell, MA; strangulation
Sophia, d. 6/17/1930 at 76/5/10; epilepsy; Edward M. Canney and Deborah Ham

PACITTO,
Mary, d. 4/20/1933 at 0/4/0; lobar pneumonia

PACKARD,
Hiram H., d. 12/17/1911 at 52; heart disease

PAGE,
child, d. 12/17/1894 at –; stillborn; b. Dover; SM
Alfred D., d. 1/21/1925 at 49/5/18 in Springfield, MA; carcinoma of colon
Annie B., d. 3/22/1925 at 79/5/13; diabetes mellitus; Thomas Morrison and
    Susan Welch
Charles J., d. 2/21/1921 at 50/5; cirrhosis of liver
Daniel A., d. 7/23/1932 at 92/9/6; myocarditis
Eleanor, d. 5/22/1893 at 97; old age; b. Rochester; (NH; NH)
Eli, d. 9/14/1898 at 72; cancer; b. Rochester; buried in Rochester
Enos H., d. 2/12/1907 at 76/1/8 in Boston, MA; broncho-pneumonia
Frank, d. 2/9/1893 at 27; died in Strafford Co. Asylum fire
George W., d. 11/22/1890 at 61/10; married; Taylor Page (Parsonsfield,
    ME) and Martha U. Goodwin (Newmarket)
Ida M., d. 5/21/1916 at 35/5; erysipelas; Charles Twombly and Sarah E.
    Briggs
Jerome B., d. 2/17/1923 at 69/5/16; lobar pneumonia; John C. Page and
    Sarah -----
Joseph L., d. 12/26/1890 at 63/7; widower; Taylor Page (Parsonsfield) and
    Martha Goodwin (Newmarket)
Julia A., d. 4/29/1905 at 75/3/10; carcinoma; PH
Maria, d. 7/5/1910 at 65; heart disease
Melissa E., d. 12/17/1915 at 74/9/13; cerebral hemorrhage; William Pierce
    and Sarah Hanson
Moses D., d. 1/9/1899 at 70; liver disease; PH
Nancy A., d. 3/9/1916 at 76/4/29; valvular heart disease; E. G. Flower
Nellie, d. 10/12/1934 at 65; carcinoma of breast
Sarah A., d. 4/5/1889 at 57 in Nashua
Sarah A., d. 4/19/1913 at 66/10; surgical shock; William Fuller
Sarah M., d. 3/28/1889 at 89/6/14; housewife; widow; b. Rochester; F.
    Meader and E. Whitehouse
Smith C., d. 11/25/1909 at –; heart disease; Jefferson Page and Abigail ---
William T., d. 6/8/1924 at 71/1/7; diabetes; George W. Page and Julia A.
    Riley

PAITHAS,
Kostas, d. 10/9/1912 at 27; accident; George Paithas and Anastasia -----

PAITROS,
Fernand, d. 6/23/1929 at 7/4/3; fracture of skull; Etienne Paitros and M. Louise Berube

PALMER,
child, d. 1/15/1913 at –; stillborn; Floyd L. Palmer and Rebecca Walker
child, d. 2/8/1924 at –; stillborn; George E. Palmer and Lydia B. Pratte
Aaron A., d. 10/26/1889 at 69/1/9; laborer; single; b. Dover; Aaron Palmer (Lee) and Mary Garland (Dover)
Addie M., d. 9/12/1925 at 38/11/3; meningitis; Herman E. Canney and Cynthia Young
Alfrieda M., d. 9/10/1905 at 44 in Passaic, NJ; uraemia; PH
Annie E., d. 11/11/1895 at 47; concussion of brain; b. Topsham, VT; PH
Annie L., d. 10/10/1906 at 0/4/15; gastro intestinal catarrh
Annie M., d. 12/24/1906 at 66/3/22; diabetes; buried in Concord
Benjamin W., d. 9/26/1900 at 56; general paralysis; buried in Lawrence, MA
Charlotte M., d. 8/20/1891 at 71/0/2; single; William Palmer (Loudon) and Maria Kimball (Dover)
Elihu Bennett, d. 11/25/1923 at 76/10/25 in Belmont, MA; diabetic coma
Elizabeth W., d. 10/19/1918 at 31/1/12; pulmonary tuberculosis; Eugene W. Palmer and Nellie F. Hayes
Ellen A., d. 1/22/1909 at 61/3/9; carcinoma of uterus; George W. Varney and Miriam Hodgdon
Ellen A., d. 9/17/1930 at 83/9/12; fracture of shoulder; William H. Gray and Clara Woodin
Emma, d. 1/2/1891 at 29; single; William Palmer (ME) and Emily R. Russell (NH)
Emma G., d. 4/18/1908 at 49/0/16 in Boston, MA; cerebella Tumor; Caleb Brown and Eliza J. Tibbetts
Ethel F., d. 4/14/1892 at 6; cerebro spinal meningitis; b. Topsham, VT; (Dover; Topsham, VT)
Eugene W., d. 11/28/1934 at 82/6/5; arteriosclerosis
Eveline L., d. 10/14/1902 at 75/5/24 in Fall River, MA; peritonitis; PH
Fannie M., d. 6/10/1919 at 48/10/1 in Boston, MA; tuberculosis
George B., d. 6/17/1903 at 54/9/8; Brights disease; PH
George W., d. 3/18/1905 at 74 in Durham; acute bronchitis; PH
Grace A., d. 1/28/1907 at 4/2/24; laryngitis; Osmer Palmer and Mary P. Frost
Hannah H., d. 8/14/1919 at 80/4; fracture of hip; Samuel Pease and Martha Moulton
Lewis F., d. 3/2/1930 at 69/4/17; apoplexy
Loring C., d. 7/20/1932 at 72/3/29; carcinoma of face
Lucy A., d. 1/22/1907 at 66/11/29 in Passaic, NJ
Lydia B., d. 2/8/1924 at 18/1/27; peritonitis; Elise Pratte

Martha J., d. 5/4/1927 at 52/3/19; mul. sclerosis of spine; Aaron F. Corson and Susan J. Rollins
Mary, d. 5/9/1894 at 41 in Boston, MA; pneumonia; buried in Dover
Mary E., d. 1/2/1908 at 79/2; uraemia; Stephen Palmer and Abigail Horne
Morris D., d. 10/7/1897 at 72 in Fall River, MA; apoplexy; PH
Orrin J., d. 9/26/1917 at 66/6/17; carcinoma of intestine; Luther S. Palmer and Mary D. Woodsum
Richard L., d. 9/13/1933 at 0/0/26; premature birth

PANAKAKAS,
Peter, d. 12/23/1922 at 1/0/19; pneumonia; William Panakakas and Vaso Malcko

PANE,
Dana A., d. 11/3/1887 at 75/4 in Concord

PAPAGEORGE,
Koula, d. 10/9/1922 at 1/7; lobar pneumonia; Louis Papageorge
Martha, d. 9/1/1936 at 97; uremia
Mary, d. 2/9/1926 at 58; angina pectoris; Patrick Culkin

PAPANOUSE,
Nedour, d. 9/26/1919 at 47; fractured skull

PAPPAGEORGE,
Mary, d. 3/18/1923 at 38; lobar pneumonia; A. Karageorge and Anestasia Thufilo

PAPPAS,
George, d. 5/24/1912 at 22; mitral insufficiency; Louis Pappas and Katherine -----

PAQUETTE,
Elmer J., d. 3/8/1930 at 1/4/19; lobar pneumonia; Elmer Paquette and Louise J. Dubois
Harold P., d. 1/29/1917 at 0/1; lobar pneumonia; Eugene Paquette and Eve Villeneau
Henry, d. 1/19/1929 at 93; arterio sclerosis
Philip J., d. 6/26/1914 at 7/7; suffocation; Eugene Paquette and Eva Villenne

PARADIS,
Amand L. J., d. 7/11/1899 at –; entero colitis; SM
Exiria, d. 9/9/1900 at <1; entero colitis; SM

Mary, d. 2/28/1900 at 22; pneumonia

PARCHER,
Katherine E., d. 12/8/1892 at 17; consumption; b. Boston, MA; (Waterborough; NS)

PARE,
William, d. 5/6/1925 at 69/11/13; acute lobar pneumonia

PARENT,
Alfred, d. 9/11/1904 at 1/6/21; gastro-enteritis, acute

PARINGTON,
Lizzie, d. 3/11/1890 at 50; married; ----- McGuigan (Ireland)

PARIS,
Angie M., d. 1/13/1926 at 33/0/26; salpingitis; Reuben A. Davis and Flora I. Willey

PARK,
Isaac, d. 6/9/1931 at 80; chronic endocarditis

PARKER,
Cynda A. W., d. 4/30/1921 at 44/1/17 in Lawrence, MA; peritonitis
Elizabeth, d. 6/12/1891 at 82/0/26; single; Thomas Parker (Portsmouth) and Betsey Fall (Alton)
George E., d. 12/20/1935 at 57/5; hypertensive heart and kidney disease
George W., d. 3/24/1916 at 68/11; chronic nephritis; Daniel P. Parker and Cynthia I. Huntington
Henry R., Jr., d. 12/27/1894 at 19; Bright's disease; b. Wolfeboro; PH
Henry Rust, d. 12/29/1909 at 73/11/5; pneumonia; John T. Parker and Sally Seavey
Mary P., d. 1/26/1904 at 58/0/10; Bright's disease; PH
Mrs. R. R., d. 10/18/1892 at 73; cancerous disease of bowels; b. Waterboro, ME; (Waterboro; Waterboro)
Robert, d. 8/24/1905 at 67; nephritis; buried in Hampton
William M., d. 2/7/1898 at 27; suicide with razor; b. Camden, ME; buried in Camden, ME

PARKINSON,
John W., d. 6/24/1914 at 70/3/16 in Tilton; old age

PARKS,
Anna E., d. 1/30/1929 at 52/2/7 in Everett, MA; influenza; Patrick Lydon
    and ----- Flaherty
Charles A., d. 2/11/1926 at 75 in Berwick, ME; apoplexy
Mary J., d. 1/20/1892 at 70; catarrhal pneumonia; b. Berwick, ME;
    (Berwick, ME; Berwick, ME)
Sarah F., d. 10/1/1920 at 74/0/4 in Everett, MA; diabetes
William T., d. 12/4/1912 at 74/0/4 in Stoneham, MA; aortic and mitral dis.

PARL,
Mary, d. 9/12/1899 at 73; Bright's disease; SM

PARLE,
Anna S., d. 9/25/1892 at 78; apoplexy; b. Ireland; (Ireland; Ireland)
Catherine, d. 12/31/1927 at 86/9; arterio sclerosis; James Parle and Ellen
    Roche
Catherine A., d. 11/20/1928 at 56/6/8; pyelo nephritis; Thomas Parle and
    Mary Howland
Eliza, d. 12/13/1908 at 81; chr. intest. nephritis; Thomas Parle
Elizabeth, d. 10/31/1918 at 44/4; pulmonary tuberculosis; John Parle and
    Mary A. Dumphy
James, d. 2/22/1896 at 20; phthisis pulmonalis; b. Ireland; SM
Katie, d. 4/2/1899 at 13; pulmonary phthisis; SM
Luke, d. 6/10/1929 at 72; pulmonary tuberculosis; James Parle and Ellen
    Roche
Margaret, d. 2/17/1925 at 65/11/25; chronic pancreatitis; Thomas Parle
    and Mary Howland
Mary E., d. 9/23/1927 at 68 in Boston, MA; arterio sclerosis
Thomas, d. 7/19/1904 at 82; cerebral hemorrhage; SM
Thomas, d. 4/23/1934 at 82/11; epithelioma of face

PARSHLEY,
Amanda A., d. 4/18/1934 at 68/10/28; myocarditis
Cora B., d. 5/28/1916 at 70/1/5; aortic regurgitation; Gideon Burnham and
    Almira Giles
Herman R., d. 12/28/1935 at 68/3/25; suicide by poisonous gas
Sarah J., d. 10/17/1921 at 77/9/1 in Haverhill, MA; apoplexy

PARSONS,
Beatrice V., d. 12/24/1915 at 21 in Newport; lobar pneumonia
Bessie, d. 9/6/1891 at 23/10/7; married; Andrew Nute (Dover) and
    Elizabeth McCone (Ireland)
Edna W., d. 12/17/1901 at 5/10/17 in Saco, ME; malnutrition; PH
Elizabeth, d. 2/12/1912 at 82/5/10; cerebral hemorrhage; William King and
    Mary Butler

Howard F., d. 11/30/1909 at 73/7; acute cystitis; Enoch Parsons and
  Louise L. Page
James F., d. 4/22/1934 at 76/4/27; erysipelas
John J., d. 4/29/1888 at 0/9/4; b. Dover; M. Parsons (Ireland) and Isabel
  McGuiness (Ireland)
Martin, d. 1/16/1891 at 40; married
Mary J., d. 8/11/1904 at 83; senility; buried in Newmarket
Mary R., d. 3/24/1892 at –; puerperal peritonitis
Sarah A., d. 12/21/1916 at 78/1/9; softening of brain; George M. Varney
  and Marion Hodgdon

PARTRIDGE,
Granville, d. 10/22/1912 at 56; severe burn

PATERSON,
Charles, d. 9/8/1935 at 74/9/26 in Manchester; hypertrophy of prostate

PATON,
Archibald B., d. 12/4/1929 at 69 in Clifton S., NY; broncho pneumonia

PATTEE,
Georgie E., d. 9/30/1911 at 43/11/20; phthisis pulmonalis; John O. Kimball
  and Eliza C. Hill
John R., d. 4/26/1920 at 59/4/4; cerebral hemorrhage; John W. Pattee and
  Charlotte Polly

PATTEN,
Annie R., d. 10/28/1908 at 49/0/18; pulmonary tuberculosis; Levi E. Towle
  and Rebecca C. Jones
Irving S., d. 1/11/1913 at 55/10/7; endocarditis; Robert A. Patten and Dora
  R. Poland
Stephen D., d. 2/8/1897 at 80; old age; b. So. Berwick, ME; PH

PATTERSON,
Dorothy, d. 2/21/1915 at 1/5/19; pneumonia; Frank W. Patterson and
  Evelyn Higgins
Evelyn, d. 11/25/1924 at 39; natural causes; Patrick Higgins and Margaret
  ____
George H., d. 1/25/1910 at 67/10/10; pneumonia; George W. Patterson
  and Elizabeth Hall
Hannah J., d. 3/27/1925 at 81/4/4; chronic myocarditis; Samuel James
  and Sophronia Ware
Lydia A., d. 3/30/1912 at 70/7/11; cancer; John T. Drew and Alice
  Waterhouse

Robert T., d. 9/26/1894 at 35; malaria; b. Frankford, PA; PH

PAUL,
child, d. 6/9/1901 at –; stillborn
Abbie H., d. 11/14/1916 at 79 in St. Peter, MN; gangrene of bowel
Abby E., d. 12/6/1896 at 74 in Hampton; heart disease; PH
Abiah G., d. 2/13/1898 at 68; pneumonia; b. Farmington; PH
Abner G., d. 4/5/1916 at 70 in Boston, MA; arteriosclerosis
Anna A., d. 7/22/1900 at 49; Bright's disease; PH
Annie M., d. 12/29/1916 at 59/3/13; lobar pneumonia; John F. Mathews
 and Mary E. Rogers
Annie Mary, d. 5/6/1933 at 45/0/24; embolism
B. F., d. 5/19/1906 at 73 in New York, NY; nephritis; PH
Catherine, d. 6/3/1937 at 73/5/8 in Concord; diabetes mellitus
Dorcas Ellen, d. 6/1/1921 at 73/5/7 in Lynn, MA; Hodgkins disease
Ellen, d. 8/5/1894 at 86; old age; b. Ireland; SM
Fannie T., d. 1/12/1920 at 54/5/28 in Madbury; lobar pneumonia
Frances E., d. 10/11/1893 at 63; paralysis
George B., d. 2/18/1918 at 26 in Waterville, ME; run over by R.R. train;
 Samuel F. Paul and Annie M. Mathews
George O., d. 2/22/1893 at 76; Bright's disease
Henry, d. 2/26/1904 at 81/10/4; catarrhal pneumonia; buried in Dover
James, d. 3/5/1887 at 73; laborer; married; b. Ireland; Richard Paul
 (Ireland) and Chatrine Cavanaugh (Ireland)
James L., d. 5/13/1919 at 71/2; necrosis of ulna; James Paul and Sarah
 Jenkins
Joseph A., Sr., d. 11/28/1933 at 75/8/6; chronic endocarditis
Joseph O., d. 4/17/1934 at 31/6/5; hemorrhage of lungs
Joseph R., d. 12/8/1927 at 0/0/1; atelectasis; Joseph O. Paul and Caroline

Judith S., d. 7/4/1899 at 89; old age; PH
Marie, d. 6/4/1924 at 52/5/10; chronic nephritis; Francois Lamontagne and
 Phoebe Laflamme
Mary A., d. 8/17/1896 at 73; disease of liver; b. Dover; PH
Mary Ann, d. 1/17/1888 at 59/1/17; married; b. Barrington; Jacob Hayes
 (Barrington) and Margaret Hayes (Madbury)
Matthew, d. 1/25/1894 at –; cerebral meningitis; b. Dover; PH
Moses A., d. 12/26/1891 at 65/3/22; Moses Paul (Alfred, ME) and Susan
 M. Hodgdon (Dover)
Rosalie, d. 6/9/1893 at 8; pneumonia; b. Quebec; (St. Thomas; Hull,
 Ottawa)
Sarah, d. 12/28/1888 at 68/1/5; widow; b. Madbury; Ephraim Jenkins
 (Madbury) and Mary Varney (Rochester)
Sidney N., d. 2/5/1908 at 65 in Togus, ME; croupous pneumonia

Susan M., d. 3/29/1891 at 93/4/11; widow; Shadrach Hodgdon (Dover) and Elizabeth Gage (Dover)
William, d. 2/3/1888 at 62/10/12; farmer; married; b. Sanford, ME; John Paul (Sanford, ME) and Ruth Hutchins (Alfred, ME)

PAULET,
Eva, d. 10/27/1887 at 0/6/21; b. Dover; Napoleon Paulet (Canada) and Elizabeth (Canada)

PAULIOT,
Henry, d. 5/10/1892 at 7; drowned; b. Dover; (Canada; Canada)

PAYNE,
Alice Eva, d. 5/6/1922 at 0/0/21; premature birth; James Payne and Flora Paquette
Alice S., d. 6/20/1934 at 80/11; cerebral hemorrhage
Mary A., d. 7/1/1901 at 65/9/9 in Westboro, MA; secondary dementia, exhaustion; PH

PEABODY,
Desdemona, d. 3/21/1909 at 86/6/6; cancer of breast; Elias Watson and Nancy Grag
Emily A., d. 11/20/1904 at 70/6/30; nephritis; buried in Newbury, MA
George A., d. 9/1/1922 at 67/11/4; mitral regurgitation; David C. Peabody and Emily Hill
George A., Jr., d. 6/14/1936 at 54/10/14; chr. endocarditis

PEARL,
Joseph W., d. 5/24/1912 at 73; chronic myocarditis
Martha J., d. 9/3/1930 at 85/3/14; rheumatism; Frederick Waldron and Sarah Smith

PEARONTSOKON,
Katina, d. 10/5/1918 at 3/0/29; acute lobar pneumonia; Louis Pearontsokon

PEARSE,
Lucretia P., d. 5/26/1902 at 79/4/24; old age; PH

PEARSON,
Harry, d. 3/30/1912 at 47; cirrhosis of liver

PEASLEE,
Elsie O., d. 10/15/1894 at 87; heart disease; b. Dover; PH

John T., d. 8/15/1925 at 73/10/17 in Pittsfield; pulmonary tuberculosis
Joseph E., d. 11/14/1913 at 71/8/20; heart failure; Joseph T. Peaslee and Elsie O. Drew
Joseph T., d. 5/2/1888 at 77/7/18; farmer; married; b. Dover; Nicholas Peaslee (NH) and Hannah Titcomb (ME)
Martha A., d. 2/25/1914 at 67/6/15; pneumonia, catarrhal; Joseph T. Peaslee and Elsie O. Drew

PEAVEY,
Aidana, d. 3/12/1920 at 61; broncho pneumonia; Moses V. Peavey and Abigail -----
Anna O., d. 2/7/1891 at 4/5/17; William C. Peavey (Alton) and Nellie E. Rogers (Dover)
Annah, d. 2/3/1893 at 83; old age; b. Farmington; (Madbury; Farmington)
Ellen, d. 5/29/1899 at 62; apoplexy; SM
Levi, d. 8/26/1909 at 82; endocarditis

PEBEAU,
Olive, d. 5/24/1887 at 3/5/14; b. Nashua; (Canada; Canada)

PECK,
Eleanor R., d. 4/19/1932 at 20/7/22; pulmonary tuberculosis
Etta S., d. 12/25/1930 at 55/2/14; pulm. tuberculosis; Wellington Foster and Annie Heith
Herbert, d. 9/18/1927 at 20 in Pembroke; pulmonary tuberculosis

PEIRCE,
Andrew O., d. 4/9/1900 at 55 in Lowell, MA; pleuro pneumonia; PH
Annie Marilla, d. 4/29/1921 at 82/8/20; broncho pneumonia; Thomas J. Willey and Elizabeth Ricker
Charles C., d. 9/19/1893 at 23; suicide by hydrosynic acid; b. Dover; (N. Yarmouth, ME; N. Gloucester, ME)
Daniel M., d. 4/30/1899 at 69; Bright's disease; PH
Elizabeth A. V., d. 1/1/1921 at 91/7/9 in Boston, MA; chr. int'st'l myocarditis
Emma, d. 1/27/1919 at 64/9/17 in Newton, MA; probably heart disease; Stephen Jenkins and Sarah A. Hill
Fannie M., d. 4/11/1898 at 64 in Concord; ex. from acute diarrhoea; PH
Harriet W., d. 7/19/1895 at 75 in Lowell, MA; sarcoma; buried in Dover
J. Kittredge, d. 11/17/1923 at 96/5/19; disease of prostate; Andrew Peirce and Abigail Osborn
John D., d. 8/5/1903 at 34; traumatic shock; buried in Truro, NS
Joseph A., d. 2/28/1903 at 84/2/10; old age; PH
Joseph W., d. 8/25/1919 at 58/1/18; acute heart disease; Joseph A. Peirce and Lucy Waldron

Lucy, d. 2/4/1907 at 70/9/29; paresis; Wells Waldron and Lucy Peirce
Mary P., d. 1/9/1907 at 78/6/7; cardiac dilation; Cyrus Perkins and Martha
    Childs
William H., d. 5/25/1936 at 84/6/19; chr. myocarditis

PELKEY,
Gladys, d. 12/29/1916 at 17/7/25; goitre; Malcolm Pelkey and Nancy
    Hughes

PELLETIER,
child, d. 8/26/1899 at 3; pneumonia
Dorothy L., d. 4/1/1923 at 4/10; burns, accidental; Charles Pelletier and
    Lillian -----
Fannie, d. 1/21/1913 at 32/5/4 in S. Berwick, ME; ch. nephritis
Joseph L., d. 10/27/1902 at 0/0/2; premature birth

PEMBERTON,
Harry L., d. 12/14/1921 at 49/5/7; peritonitis; Charles H. Pemberton and
    Lucy E. Lee
Lucy E., d. 12/1/1915 at 72/11/14; cancer of liver, etc.; Simon P. Lee and
    Harriet Donald

PENDERGAST,
James M., d. 3/24/1916 at 57; suicide, cutting throat; Michael Pendergast
    and Bridget Haughey

PENDEXTER,
Edward, d. 1/13/1916 at 72/0/1 in Madbury; cancer of stomach
Eliza L., d. 4/1/1909 at 78 in Catskill, NY; pernicious anemia
Emma, d. 12/11/1931 at 69; lobar pneumonia
Helen, d. 7/22/1920 at 71/3/27; softening of brain; Fred Owen Pendexter
    and Eliza Lawrence
James E., d. 2/10/1935 at 79/0/26; arteriosclerosis
Martha C., d. 1/10/1892 at 73; pneumonia; b. Haverhill, MA; (Concord;
    Haverhill, MA)

PENEAU,
Mary J., d. 9/24/1904 at 93; senility; buried in Rochester

PENETTE,
Sarah E., d. 1/30/1930 at 71/9/29; arterio sclerosis; James D. Meserve
    and Caroline E. Miles

PENHALLOW,
Ellen M., d. 1/25/1905 at 73 in Portsmouth; influenza; PH

PENNELL,
Anna K., d. 5/25/1907 at 24/4; Bright's disease; James H. Kennedy and
    Mary E. Redmond

PENNEY,
Charles M., d. 7/3/1922 at – in Lawrence, MA; accidental drowning

PENNY,
Annie E., d. 6/20/1926 at 32/5/9 in Lawrence, MA; pulmonary tuberculosis
Edward F., d. 8/14/1929 at 35/1/22 in Rutland, ME; tuberculosis of lungs;
    Edward Penney (sic) and Hattie Connors
Emma J., d. 5/4/1921 at 53/0/22 in Lawrence, MA; gen. carcinomatosis
Isaac W., d. 12/19/1900 at 2; diptheria; PH

PEPIN,
child, d. 10/20/1907 at –; O. J. Pepin and Jennie E. Morris
child, d. 3/26/1917 at –; stillborn; Albert E. Pepin and Dulcona Gastonguay
Gabriel Lea, d. 4/1/1917 at 0/0/6; premature birth; Albert E. Pepin and Lea
    Brunelle
Octave J., d. 4/26/1933 at 62/3; cerebral tumor

PERCIVAL,
Daniel E., d. 4/2/1934 at 0/0/1; prematurity
Wilber L., d. 8/12/1889 at --; b. Laconia; Davis Percival

PERKEY,
son, d. 3/15/1888 at –; b. Dover; Mary Perkey

PERKINS,
daughter, d. 6/28/1888 at –; James F. Perkins (Dover) and Mattie Getchell
    (Newmarket)
child, d. 10/24/1894 at –; stillborn; b. Dover; PH
Abigail A., d. 3/30/1891 at 69/3; widow; Ephraim Plummer (Dover) and
    Judith Perkins (Dover)
Adam, d. 5/19/1893 at 80; heart disease; b. Rochester
Alberta A., d. 3/18/1900 at – in York Beach, ME; diabetes; PH
Amassa S., d. 8/7/1908 at 72/2/16; heart disease
Ana L., d. 2/11/1934 at 89/9/3; endocarditis
Anna, d. 9/28/1917 at 41/5/14 in Boston, MA; tumor of brain
Arthur, d. 9/6/1937 at 74/5 in Lawrence, MA; car. prostate gland

Augustus, d. 10/31/1890 at 71/1/19; married; Eri Perkins (Dover) and Mary Hodgdon (Dover)
Augustus T., d. 9/2/1888 at 30/1/20; baggage master; single; b. Dover; Winslow T. Perkins and Carrie Gray (Dover)
Carrie I., d. 2/11/1931 at 69/7/26; lobar pneumonia
Charles A., d. 10/13/1918 at 33/6/5; influenza - pneumonia; John P. Perkins and Eliza Watson
Charles D., d. 7/10/1917 at 62 in Manchester; organic heart disease; Martin Perkins and Olive Hartford
Charles E., d. 12/9/1920 at 84 in Palatka, FL; cerebral hemorrhage
Charles H., d. 2/17/1918 at 43/11/8 in Rochester; chronic alcoholism
Charles L., d. 8/18/1932 at 69 in Quincy, MA; general peritonitis
Charles N., d. 1/20/1909 at 14/3/3; valvular dis. of heart; Charles L. Perkins and Isabelle McDonald
Charles R., d. 11/15/1915 at 62/5; paralysis agitans; John Perkins and Nancy ----
Clarence M., d. 5/3/1893 at 11; rheumatic fever; b. Dover; (Dover; Canada)
Daniel T., d. 11/27/1912 at 53/8/1; intestinal obstruction; John Perkins and Eliza ----
Dudley C., d. 1/31/1888 at 59/3/26; nurse; married; S. Perkins (Middleton) and Mary Horne (Middleton)
Edward, d. 12/15/1894 at 10; drowned by accident; b. Dover; PH
Edward A., d. 1/19/1900 at 47 in Boston, MA; septo meningitis; PH
Edwin F., d. 10/29/1916 at 58/6/30; cerebral hemorrhage; Nathan Perkins and Cyrene Martin
Eliza, d. 7/12/1894 at 69; uremic convulsions; PH
Eliza J., d. 6/2/1893 at 65; sudden death - heart disease; b. York, ME; (York, ME; York, ME)
Emma A., d. 5/6/1920 at 63/1/3; carcinoma of rectum
Eri, d. 3/13/1888 at 57/6/20; engineer; married; b. Dover; Eri Perkins (Dover) and Mary Hodsdon (Dover)
Eva A., d. 1/1/1899 at -- in Rochester; marasmus; PH
Forrest E., d. 6/23/1918 at 61/2/17 in Amesbury, MA; cancer of stomach
Frank E., d. 9/15/1904 at 49 in Boston, MA; suicide, hanging; PH
Fred M., d. 7/29/1898 at 31 in Lawrence, MA; tuberculosis; PH
George F., d. 4/28/1902 at 54/10; probably continued syncope; buried in Rochester
George H., d. 4/15/1912 at 82/8/7 in Lynn, MA; locomotor ataxia
Hamilton C., d. 3/3/1929 at 41 in Boston, MA; lobar pneumonia
Hannah, d. 12/22/1899 at 70 in Lawrence, MA; valvular disease of heart; PH
Hattie E., d. 2/24/1897 at 7; b. Dover; PH
Hayes, d. 2/17/1900 at 74; apoplexy; PH
Helen A., d. 3/3/1897 at 34; Bright's disease; b. Lynn, MA; PH

Helena, d. 7/1/1911 at 74/0/22; ch. intestinal nephritis; Eri Perkins and Mary A. Hodgdon
Hiram M., d. 4/8/1911 at 72/1/19; cancer of rectum; Hiram Perkins and Mary S. Horne
Isabelle, d. 3/18/1918 at 54/6/13 in Auburn, ME; cancer of rectum; Patrick McDonnell and Mary Agnew
J. Frank, d. 6/25/1904 at 47/4/2; alcoholism chronic; PH
James, d. 3/12/1909 at 46 in Manchester; accident, fractured ribs
James F., d. 7/10/1931 at 65/11/14; acute nephritis
John A., d. 12/7/1894 at 38; gastro enteritis; b. Dover; PH
John H., d. 9/28/1893 at 28; phthisis pulmonalis; b. Dover; (Middleton; Ellsworth, ME)
Joseph, d. 1/27/1897 at 4; diphtheria; b. Dover; PH
Joseph, d. 1/6/1909 at 75/2/23 in York, ME; valvular dis. of heart
Julia A., d. 12/9/1930 at 79/6/13; myocarditis; Joseph King
Laura, d. 3/6/1925 at 32 in Boston, MA; toxemia
Laura A., d. 6/28/1894 at 64; inanition; b. Dover; PH
Lemuel, d. 10/4/1896 at 77; old age; b. Jackson; PH
Lydia A., d. 9/10/1906 at 78/11; senile dementia; PH
Lydia A., d. 1/1/1912 at 81/1; old age; Jeremy Perkins and Lydia A. Watson
Mabel A., d. 12/9/1901 at 0/3/25; erysipelas; PH
Mahala, d. 1/26/1906 at 84/8/29; valvular heart disease; PH
Martin V. B., d. 1/31/1899 at 63; paralysis; PH
Mary, d. 3/11/1922 at 50/9/11 in Ipswich, MA; cerebral hemorrhage
Mary A., d. 2/15/1898 at 68; cancer of liver; b. New York City; PH
Mary A., d. 12/24/1907 at 70/5/11 in Farmington; influenza
Mary S., d. 4/13/1897 at 88 in York, ME; shock; PH
Mattie L., d. 10/17/1890 at 20/11/25; married; Abraham Gatchell (Lisbon, ME) and Hattie Elizabeth Jones (Newmarket)
Michael R., d. 1/9/1911 at 90/9/5 in Concord; old age
Mildram, d. 12/30/1930 at 81/1/12; chr. myocarditis; Hollis Perkins
Moses P., d. 6/14/1904 at 75 in Chelsea, MA; apoplexy; PH
Nelson G., d. 7/6/1919 at 53/6/6; suicide by shooting; Jacob C. Perkins and Sarah S. Trott
Samuel H., d. 4/22/1888 at 0/6/20; b. Dover; Samuel Perkins (Dover) and Julia King (Montreal, Canada)
Sarah E., d. 8/14/1895 at 59; paralysis; b. Durham; PH
Susan B., d. 9/8/1902 at 78; drowned; PH
Thomas Allen, d. 9/18/1932 at 69/9/17; carcinoma of liver
Walter, d. 10/12/1921 at 47/0/25; frac. base of skull; Daniel W. Perkins
Walter T., d. 10/17/1907 at 56/1/3 in Lynn, MA; uremia
Winslow T., d. 1/15/1920 at 83/0/11 in Malden, MA; pyonephrosis

PERRAULT,
Edward, d. 6/14/1915 at 43; locomotor ataxia; Edward Perrault

PERREAULT,
Minnie, d. 2/5/1932 at 42/3/22 in Somersworth; influenza

PERRY,
Blanche, d. 5/9/1894 at 80 in Brooklyn, NY; erysipelas; buried in Dover
Camelia M., d. 1/1/1929 at 79/6/20; cerebral hemorrhage; William E.
    Gilson and Melissa Clay
George W., d. 5/7/1900 at 69 in Everett, MA; hypertrophy and dil. of heart;
    PH
Henry E., d. 9/5/1931 at 81/10/10; arterio sclerosis
Jean, d. 12/10/1935 at 2/4/1; tuberculosis meningitis
Lydia A., d. 10/16/1898 at 70 in Pittsfield; probably internal cancer; PH

PERSON,
Celina, d. 2/1/1930 at 73/5/27; cancer of liver; Frederick Demers and
    Rosie Pepin

PETER,
John, d. 5/21/1914 at 41/4; blood poisoning; Jasper Peter and Maria
    Gloria
Mary G., d. 6/25/1907 at 1/1/11; chronic pneumonia; John Peter and Mary
    Ferry

PETERS,
Catherine, d. 7/14/1934 at 28/0/10 in Providence, RI; septicemia
Catherine M., d. 2/22/1937 at 27; pyonephrosis
Kate, d. 5/17/1928 at 71/9; natural causes; Timothy Peters
Philip Said, d. 4/2/1922 at 0/7/16; measles; Said Peters and Shabbie Riely
Ruth, d. 6/5/1921 at 0/0/2; atelectasis of lungs; Bolus Peter (sic) and
    Emma Martin
Santo, d. 7/5/1932 at 18 in Haverhill, MA; auto accident

PETTICE,
William, d. 9/7/1891 at 0/1; James C. Pettice (Cambridge, VT) and Jane
    Annis (Albany)

PETTIGREW,
Ralph W., d. 8/15/1905 at 1/4/27; pneumonia; PH

PETTINGELL,
Henry J., d. 12/27/1930 at 65/7/21; cerebral hemorrhage; James Pettingill (sic)

PETTINGILL,
Etta M., d. 12/10/1923 at 63 in Madbury; cancer of uterus; Seth W. Rowe and Margaret Boston
Mildred F., d. 7/9/1927 at 82; chronic nephritis

PETTIS,
Abbie F., d. 3/3/1932 at 71/4/3; lobar pneumonia
Ethel R., d. 12/29/1919 at 0/3/12; athrepsia; James G. Pettis and Georgia H. Poole
Frank H., d. 11/14/1918 at 0/0/18; lobar pneumonia; James G. Pettis and Georgianna H. Poole
Fred E., d. 3/12/1932 at 6/2/15; toxemia
Hattie E., d. 8/5/1887 at 0/5/15; b. Dover
James C., d. 11/28/1923 at 76/7/8; cerebral hemorrhage; Jacob L. Pettis and Hannah W. Chase
James G., d. 12/3/1916 at 2/0/29; broncho pneumonia; James G. Pettis and Georgie Poole
Joseph William, d. 1/5/1917 at 1/1/18; membranous croup; James G. Pettis and Georgie Poole
Maggie, d. 3/28/1909 at 247/2; pul. tuberculosis; John Folland and Mary Hanna
Mary H., d. 6/1/1924 at –; stillborn; George J. Pettis and Georgie H. Poole
Prince Albert, d. 6/21/1905 at 17/4/8; Bright's disease; PH
Willetta J., d. 5/1/1913 at 54/7/23; cirrhosis of liver; Mark Annis and Betsy W. Burbank
Willetta J., d. 10/20/1918 at 9/7/24 in Rochester; pneumonia; James C. Pettis and Willetta J. Annis

PEVEAR,
Glenn, d. 7/3/1934 at 0/0/19 in Boston, MA; general septicemia

PEVERLY,
Peter, d. 5/23/1894 at 51; cancer of throat; b. Canada; PH

PEW,
Edwin B., d. 7/20/1936 at 81/8/21; con. heart failure

PEYON,
child, d. 7/6/1923 at –; stillborn; Marvondis Peyon and Annie Morley

John, d. 7/12/1920 at –; asphyxia of labor; Mavroodis Peyon and Annie Morley

PHAIR,
William T., d. 8/12/1932 at 37/11/28; peritonitis

PHANEUF,
Napoleon, d. 5/14/1935 at 65/10/8; cerebral embolism

PHILBRICK,
Charles E., d. 6/20/1913 at 77/2/1; ulcer of the stomach; Ithiel Philbrick and Miranda Blake
Ellen T., d. 11/15/1917 at 75/6/12; cerebral hemorrhage; Andrew Tuttle and Susan Demeritt
Ivory E., d. 9/21/1918 at 78/3/21; cancer of the pancreas; Ithel Philbrick and Amanda Blake
Jennie F., d. 1/17/1935 at 66/9/20; lobar pneumonia
Lurinza J., d. 6/19/1930 at 71/1/22 in Somerville, MA; diabetic gangrene
Mary A., d. 10/12/1917 at 80/0/2; arthritis deformans; Parkman Burleigh and Martha Ham

PHILBROOK,
George W., d. 3/27/1936 at 77/3/25*

PHILEORUM,
Foran, d. 8/29/1889 at 0/0/1; b. Dover; Foran Phileorum (Canada)

PHILLIPS,
LeRoy H., d. 8/18/1934 at 47/7/19; acute appendicitis
Lola F., d. 9/15/1900 at <1 in Norway, ME; cholera infantum; PH
Mary S., d. 11/14/1895 at 48 in Alton; paralysis; PH

PHILPOTT,
Annie, d. 4/29/1916 at 56; carcinoma of uterus; James Dolan and Alice Cairn
George Henry, d. 4/19/1923 at 37/1/15 in Lynn, MA; burns
Hattie V., d. 1/11/1928 at 28/9/2; pulm. & int. tuberculosis; Charles Philpott and Annie Doolin

PICARD,
child, d. 10/16/1917 at –; stillborn; Joseph Picard and Elizabeth Pomerleau
Clarinda M., d. 8/29/1926 at 42/8/13 in Madbury; carcinoma of pancreas; Napoleon Goudreau and Victoria Beaulieu

Isabelle, d. 3/2/1926 at 70/11/8; chronic myocarditis; Henry Demers and
 Mary Lambert
Joseph, d. 10/21/1911 at –; premature birth; Joseph Picard and Elizabeth
 Pomerleau
Julius, d. 2/10/1931 at 69/7/25; lobar pneumonia
Leo, d. 10/25/1921 at 15/10; emypemia; Henry Picard and Phoebe Brochu

PICHETTE,
son, d. 5/30/1888 at –; b. Dover; Napoleon Pichette (Canada) and Flora
 Cormier (ME)
George, d. 10/20/1899 at 4; after effect diphtheria; SM
Henry, d. 1/27/1896 at 2; diarrhea infantile; b. Dover; SM
Louis H., d. 2/22/1931 at 74/7/4; cerebral hemorrhage
Raymond E., d. 6/5/1909 at 0/5/10; congenital marasmus; Felix H.
 Pichette and Ruth M. Chase
Ruth E., d. 1/25/1909 at 0/1; marasmus; Felix Pichette and Ruth M. Chase

PICKERING,
Elizabeth, d. 2/9/1893 at 69; died in Strafford Co. Asylum fire
Lydia E., d. 10/2/1896 at 57 in Rochester; typhoid fever; PH
Mary J., d. 11/13/1908 at 90/2/18; old age; William Berry and Olive S.
 Locke
Phoebe, d. 8/5/1913 at 89/10/4 in Barnstead; pneumonia

PICKETT,
Nora, d. 10/18/1911 at 43 in Exeter; nephritis; ----- Pickett and -----
 Mulcahey

PICKUP,
Elizabeth A., d. 9/8/1928 at 65/8 in Manchester; heart failure; Joseph
 Wrigley and Mary Kenworthy
Ida, d. 10/30/1899 at 5; entero-colitis; PH

PIDGIN,
Charles W., d. 11/19/1912 at 34; acute pul. tuberculosis; William C. Pidgin
 and Eunice A. Applebee
Eunice A., d. 12/28/1898 at 59; cancer of uterus; b. Milton; PH
Lorvey, d. 6/7/1888 at 76/8/24; widow; D. Huntress and Abigail
William C., d. 4/27/1895 at 59; heart disease; b. Dover; PH

PIEDIELNICK,
Walter, d. 5/8/1926 at 8/0/9; accidental drowning; Andrew Piedielnick and
 Stifaxi Pielicki

PIERCE,
Abbie M., d. 3/3/1916 at 79/3/28; fracture of hip; James Pierce and Maria White
Adams True, d. 7/6/1910 at 76/1/26; heart disease; William Pierce and Sarah J. True
Alvina A., d. 4/22/1889 at 57; housewife; married; b. Lee; Alfred Hoitt (Northwood) and Susan Demeritt (Northwood)
Amy B., d. 12/14/1935 at 64/11/10 in Reading, MA; coronary thrombosis
Amy W., d. 4/3/1931 at 64/6/18; lobar pneumonia
Beniah, d. 6/1/1889 at 69/5/21; engineer; married; b. Rehoboth, MA; Israel Pierce (Rehoboth, MA) and Hannah Cole (Rehoboth, MA)
Benjamin Parker, d. 3/22/1912 at 86/6/13; old age; Andrew Pierce and Abigail Osborne
Clarence A., d. 11/24/1930 at 71/8/15; myocarditis, etc.; William B. Pierce and Deborah Whitehouse
Edwin, d. 1/4/1914 at 53/0/10 in Concord; exhaustion psychosis; Joseph Pierce and Lucy Waldron
Elona G., d. 2/6/1899 at 35; acute nephritis; PH
Frank B., d. 9/7/1894 at 37; suicide; b. Vassalboro, ME; PH
Hannah M., d. 4/6/1915 at 82/8; senility; James P. Hanson and Hannah Place
Hattie F., d. 1/14/1936 at 75/4/2; suicide by hanging
Jennie E., d. 11/28/1931 at 72/7/10 in Methuen, MA; cerebral hemorrhage
Martha A., d. 11/30/1918 at 52/5/2 in Laconia; cancer rectum, etc.
Martha E., d. 3/18/1924 at 66/7/20; pneumonia; John L. Pierce and Phoebe Ham
Mary, d. 3/23/1910 at 69; cerebral hemorrhage; ----- Corson and ----- Roach
Rachael N., d. 3/22/1921 at 83/3/20; nephritis; Joseph F. Cushman and Olive Sturdevant
Susan M., d. 11/26/1930 at 62/9/16; carcinoma left breast; William McDonald and Alice Newton
Thomas W., d. 10/7/1926 at 73 in Beverly, MA; prostatism obstruction
Willis B., d. 2/8/1923 at 38/6/2; lobar pneumonia; Frank B. Pierce and Laura E. Burnham

PIERONTSAKOS,
Georgia, d. 10/30/1919 at 30; suicide by shooting; Peter Pierontsakos and Stavicoula Economacon
John, d. 12/17/1919 at 1/3/11; convulsions; Louis Pierontsakos and Themtela Golkas
Peter, d. 6/5/1932 at 18/10/18; endocarditis

PIGOTT,
Josephine C., d. 10/25/1937 at 64/1/25; carcinoma breasts

PIKE,
Abby A., d. 1/2/1901 at 72/0/11 in Hanover; cancer of liver; PH
Albert A., d. 1/18/1899 at 69; paralysis; PH
Alice W., d. 10/16/1893 at 68; neuralgia of the heart; b. Farmington; (Farmington; ——)
Charles A., d. 4/6/1909 at 43/6/3 in Boston, MA; mitral regurgitation
Eliza A., d. 2/26/1913 at 72/11/8; cirrhosis of liver; Alexander Witham and Mehitable Moody
Emily S., d. 2/3/1890 at 65/3; married; Joseph Ayers (Greenland) and Ruth Nudd
John G., d. 7/31/1905 at 87/11/14; old age; buried in Rollinsford
John G., d. 5/18/1906 at 69/2 in Boston, MA; heart disease
Karl H., d. 4/1/1932 at 42/3 in Somerville, MA; lobar pneumonia
Lydia J., d. 8/7/1931 at 74/9/22; ulcerative colitis
Martha A., d. 5/7/1907 at 66/6/19 in Newton, MA; pneumonia
Mrs. Charles M., d. 3/30/1916 at 80; frozen feet
Robert Gordon, d. 1/9/1917 at 65/5/12; angina pectoris; Amos W. Pike and E. M. Chadbourne
William A., d. 2/27/1914 at 58/4/1 in Providence, RI; chronic endocarditis
William H., d. 11/18/1890 at 65/6; widower; John Pike

PILCHER,
Dennis, d. 12/18/1890 at 0/0/2; Aleck Pilcher (Canada) and Rosa Bergeron (Canada)

PILGRIM,
Jane, d. 12/26/1928 at –; cong. hydrocephalus; Mark J. Pilgrim and Ruth M. Burnham

PILOT,
Lionel, d. 5/23/1914 at 1/3/15; broncho pneumonia; Arthur Pilot and Mariam Martel

PINCINSSE,
Leonide, d. 12/18/1903 at 0/8/9; pnumonia

PINEO,
child, d. 12/14/1924 at –; stillborn; Charles Pineo and Eliza Tyler
Alice May, d. 10/3/1925 at 3/2/20; tubercular meningitis; Charles H. Pineo and Elizabeth Tyler
Annie D., d. 11/3/1900 at 45; suicide by drowning; buried in Contoocook
Annie S., d. 6/21/1901 at 65/11/27 in Madbury; cancer; PH
Edmund Paul, d. 6/22/1936 at –; stillborn
Eliza T., d. 2/13/1931 at 40/10/28; acute myocarditis

Ethel J., d. 11/20/1898 at 1; pneumonia; b. Dover; PH
George E., d. 4/20/1891 at 28/5/11 in Madbury; married; Isaac B. Pineo (NS) and Annie S. Tupper (NS)
Harmon G., d. 2/22/1937 at 81/11/28; cerebral embolism
Henrietta, d. 3/1/1927 at 68/2/9; lobar pneumonia; Adam Perkins and Eliza J. Abbott
Henry C., d. 8/27/1897 at 0; sudden - unknown; b. Dover; PH
Isaac B., d. 7/18/1911 at 72/9; arterio sclerosis; Stephen Pineo and Mary Huntley
Marjorie D., d. 7/21/1926 at 0/0/3; malnutrition; Charles H. Pineo and Eliza Tyler

PINGREE,
Charles W., d. 9/1/1910 at 13/4/13 in Lynn, MA; acute endocarditis
Elmer H., d. 7/20/1935 at 68/11/20 in Newburyport, MA; heart disease

PINKHAM,
child, d. 11/2/1932 at –; stillborn
child, d. 3/1/1935 at –; stillborn
Aaron, d. 3/14/1900 at 74; paralysis; buried at Dover Point
Alonzo, d. 3/20/1900 at 70; heart disease; buried at Dover Point
Alonzo T., d. 8/22/1906 at 58/11/6; Stokes-Adams disease of heart; PH
Amanda A., d. 10/16/1894 at 51; paralysis; b. Barrington; buried at Dover Point
Anna D., d. 5/1/1926 at 59/2/22; carcinoma; Joshua Pinkham and Emma Jaquith
Arthur B., d. 12/24/1915 at 24/7/22; acute dil. of heart; Henry M. Pinkham and Carrie M. Brewster
Belle M., d. 2/2/1925 at 62/9/11 in Madbury; valvular heart disease
Benjamin W., d. 2/6/1908 at 63/7/15; anaemia; W. B. Pinkham and Martha P. Gray
Bennie A., d. 10/20/1916 at 29/7/10; pneumonia; William T. Pinkham and Elizabeth A. Ricker
Betsy S., d. 9/22/1902 at 82/11/3; senile exhaustion; PH
Caroline L., d. 9/5/1907 at 64/2/12 in Chelsea, MA; carcinoma of stomach
Carrie M., d. 1/25/1914 at 0/0/1; premature birth; Arthur B. Pinkham and Mildred A. Beaupre
Carrie M., d. 4/23/1927 at 65/8/22; angina pectoris; Horatio H. Brewster and Mary A. Stevens
Charles E., d. 10/22/1929 at 81/7/5; myocarditis; John H. Pinkham and Nancy S. Emery
Charles W., d. 11/3/1888 at 32/2/6 in Merrimac, MA; painter; married; b. Dover; Janvrin Pinkham (Milton) and Desire York (Standish, ME)
Clara A., d. 2/24/1920 at 70/9/17 in Milton; embolism

D'Orville L., d. 7/17/1919 at 52/1/5; angina pectoris; John E. Pinkham and
    Emily J. Whitney
Desire L., d. 9/30/1905 at 84/6/12; old age; PH
Dorothy, d. 9/11/1905 at 91/2/9 in Amesbury, MA; entero colitis; PH
Edward H., d. 11/2/1930 at 52/8/15 in Boston, MA; brain tumor
Elizabeth A., d. 2/13/1923 at 71/0/14; broncho pneumonia; Leonard S.
    Ricker
Elizabeth A., d. 9/9/1928 at –; arterio sclerosis
Emily J., d. 11/13/1915 at 80/4/14; senility; Abel Whitney and Sarah Cole
Frances J., d. 2/20/1908 at 65/4/12; heart disease; Joseph Richardson and
    Ruth Colby
Friend M., d. 9/9/1925 at 73/5/25; valv. heart disease; Alfred Pinkham and
    Harriet Burnham
George H., d. 11/12/1888 at 46/4/9 in Concord; mechanic; married; b. New
    Durham; Luther H. Pinkham and Mary C. Wallace
George M., d. 4/5/1928 at 75 in Salisbury, MA; chronic endocarditis
George R., d. 10/28/1910 at 68/6/13; dilitation of heart; Daniel Pinkham
    and Sophia Drew
Grace G., d. 4/11/1927 at 55 in Concord; lobar pneumonia; Richard
    Pinkham and Mary Hart
Hannah J., d. 12/27/1902 at 78/1/2; gastric hemorrhage; PH
Harold F., d. 9/15/1915 at 3/2/26; acute gast. intest. indig.; Clarence W.
    Pinkham and Nellie M. Dow
Hattie E., d. 11/1/1907 at 26/11/15; septicemia; Joseph M. Ellis and Hattie
    C. French
Henry M., d. 8/28/1898 at 53; cancer; b. Dover; buried at Dover Point
Ira Francis, d. 2/14/1907 at 73/8/27; paralysis agitans; Enoch Pinkham
    and Hannah Pinkham
J. Burley, d. 8/14/1895 at 69; paralysis; b. Tuftonboro; PH
John E., d. 5/19/1906 at 71/2/3; rupture of heart; buried in family lot
Joseph, d. 2/19/1907 at 80/5/15; brain disease; J. G. Pinkham and Louise
    Blanchard
Lena, d. 10/6/1919 at 75/5/14; softening of brain; ----- Labounty
Lizzie S., d. 5/24/1890 at 36/5/22; married; Thomas Tuttle (Dover) and
    Hope Twombly (Dover)
Lydia N., d. 11/11/1906 at 88/4/17; apoplexy; PH
Madeline M., d. 10/24/1908 at 3/9/11; convulsions; C. W. Pinkham and
    Willie M. Drew
Maria E., d. 12/28/1916 at 55; gastro enteritis; Nathel Horne and Fannie ---
Marjorie, d. 4/16/1916 at 0/1/4; broncho pneumonia; Ernest H. Pinkham
    and Grace Brooks
Mary A., d. 8/4/1887 at 44/2/23; b. Farmington; Joseph Wentworth (Milton)
    and Mary Amazeen (Farmington)
Mary A., d. 5/10/1896 at 45; phthisis pulmonalis; b. Dover; PH

Mary A., d. 7/7/1897 at 57; chronic ulcer of stomach; b. Boston, MA; buried at Dover Point
Mary E., d. 11/29/1903 at 23/1/10; tuberculosis; PH
Mary E., d. 5/3/1919 at 72; arterio sclerosis; James Frye and Elizabeth ----
Mary L., d. 8/4/1903 at 67/8/4 in East Bridgewater, MA; hemiplegia; PH
Mary M., d. 9/14/1919 at 74/11/24; general arterio sclerosis; David Murray and Margaret Dore
Maud M., d. 10/12/1919 at 49/9/22; carcinoma of uterus; Albion Nason and Clara Whitney
May, d. 11/1/1919 at 70/5/13; acute nephritis; John L. Pickering and Mary J. Berry
Mildred M., d. 1/24/1914 at --; premature birth; Arthur B. Pinkham and Mildred A. Beaupre
Nancy S., d. 2/20/1903 at 83/11/22; senile gangrene; PH
Nellie E., d. 1/6/1935 at 60/0/29; cancer of pancreas and liver
Nettie I., d. 2/16/1889 at 1/9/12; b. Dover; George H. Pinkham (New Durham) and Olive A. Hurd (Dover)
Olive A., d. 5/13/1934 at 83/10/23 in Winchester, MA; myocarditis
Richard A.., d. 6/3/1888 at 57/7/5; brick mfr.; married; b. Dover; Enoch Pinkham (Tuftonboro) and Hannah Pinkham (Tuftonboro)
Sarah F., d. 9/19/1905 at 0/5/17; cholera infantum; buried in Newington
Syrena C., d. 1/21/1907 at 74/7/19; pneumonia; Amos Cousens and Matilda -----
Thomas H., d. 11/7/1929 at 64/6/12; apoplexy; Daniel Pinkham and Mary Penny
W. Leslie, d. 3/31/1892 at 18; phthisis pulmonalis
Warren F., d. 10/25/1924 at 82/3/7 in Haverhill, MA; myocarditis
Wilder, d. 8/31/1896 at --; stillborn; b. Dover
William, d. 12/3/1901 at 82/10/14; paralytic dementia; PH
William T., d. 11/20/1933 at 82/3; carcinoma of mouth

PIPER,
Alice M., d. 9/17/1905 at --; stillborn; PH
Charles E., d. 6/7/1921 at 54 in Boston, MA; brain tumor
Ellen F., d. 9/17/1919 at 82/8/21; fall; Thomas Young and Ann Furbush
Frank, d. 8/17/1891 at 0/2/5; James A. Piper (Tuftonboro) and Minnie L. Evans (Mt. Hope, WI)
George F., d. 3/21/1934 at 32/6/23 in Bedford, MA; general paralysis
George Fisher, d. 4/2/1926 at 84/10/30; lobar pneumonia; George Piper and Sally F. Smith
George Patrick, d. 1/31/1929 at 1/1/28; croupous pneumonia; George F. Piper and Margaret Spellman
Gilbert W., d. 5/26/1921 at 0/3/7; erysipelas; William A. Piper and Andianna Gilbert

James A., d. 6/2/1909 at 49/7/7; cancer of stomach; William F. Piper and
   Ellen F. Young
Mary L., d. 4/8/1908 at 73/10/6; acute bronchitis; Edmund Buchanan
Mary Smith, d. 11/6/1932 at 94/2/28; lobar pneumonia
Sarah B., d. 1/21/1897 at 73; gen. capillary bronchitis; b. Dover; PH
William F., d. 12/28/1929 at 92/2; arterio sclerosis; George W. Piper and
   Arvilla Copp

PITMAN,
Ann, d. 7/9/1929 at 76/3; apoplexy; David Bumford and Dorcas -----
Grace, d. 5/13/1892 at 42; phthisis pulmonalis; b. So. Boston, MA;
   (Ireland; Ireland)
John, d. 5/28/1893 at 16; phthisis pulmonalis; b. Dover; (Great Falls;
   Great Falls)
Mary, d. 2/4/1892 at 90; old age; b. Deerfield
Sarah J., d. 6/21/1923 at 83; valv. disease of heart; John Bodwell
Susan, d. 3/7/1893 at 73; pneumonia; b. Great Falls; (Rochester;
   Rochester)

PLACE,
Alonzo R., d. 11/23/1900 at 68; spinal trouble; PH
Alvan P., d. 4/9/1928 at 67/9/5; angina pectoris; James G. K. Place and
   Lavinia A. Kaime
Charles, d. 4/9/1913 at 69; acute dil. of heart
Charles H., d. 7/28/1932 at 76/2/11; arterio sclerosis
Comfort L., d. 6/5/1901 at 86 in Concord; exhaustion from senile
   dementia; PH
Hannah M., d. 6/14/1911 at 80/7/14; cerebral thrombosis; Smith Perry and
   Betsey Canney
Ira S., d. 7/26/1888 at 46/2/17; merchant; married; b. Sandwich; Ira Place
   and Nancy Robinson
James D., d. 1/5/1906 at 79/5/12; old age; buried in Farmington
John S., d. 2/14/1937 at 81/5/9*; b. NH
John W., d. 5/30/1912 at 74/4/27; mitral incompetency
Joseph M., d. 8/28/1895 at 33; epileptic convulsions; b. Dover; PH
Lavinia A., d. 2/26/1915 at 83/10/9; old age; Dodovah Kaime and Lavinia
   Foye
Melvina A., d. 11/12/1931 at 82/1/16 in Medford, MA; cardio renal disease
Sarah E., d. 6/11/1913 at 78; valvular heart disease

PLAISTED,
Laura Ruth, d. 9/2/1932 at 2/5/2; fracture of skull
Norman H., d. 10/20/1921 at 0/6/10; diarrhea - enteritis; Harry Plaisted
   and Nancy Pines

PLANT,
child, d. 6/9/1906 at –; stillborn; PH
Ida M., d. 6/18/1907 at 27/2/21; phthisis; H. M. Tuttle and Mary A. Stevens

PLANTE,
Cecelia A., d. 5/13/1925 at 0/1/13; acute lobar pneumonia; Victor Plante and Rosanne Dumas
Gerard Frances, d. 3/9/1936 at 0/5; broncho-pneumonia
Victor, d. 5/13/1910 at 2/0/12; acute cerebral meningitis; Victor Plante and Rosanna Dumais

PLATTS,
Bertha Grinnell, d. 7/26/1891 at 16/4/4; John L. Platts (Georgetown, MA) and Elizabeth Champion (Dover)
Elizabeth A., d. 5/31/1919 at 82/7/14; senility; Alvah Champion and Alphia Jones
John L., d. 5/10/1887 at 78/11/20; shoemaker; married; b. MA; John Platts (MA) and Mary Palmer (MA)
Simeon F., d. 8/24/1892 at 79; apoplexia; b. Georgetown, MA; (Groveland, MA; Georgetown, MA)

PLINO,
Henry, d. 1/16/1894 at 19; phthisis pulmonalis; SM

PLOUFFE,
Beatrice, d. 7/14/1937 at 0/1/17 in Exeter; hemorrhagic disease of newborn
Florence M., d. 12/24/1934 at 0/0/13; lobar pneumonia
Richard J., d. 3/27/1936 at – in Exeter; stillborn

PLOURDE,
Pierre, d. 10/22/1922 at 30/11; typhoid fever; Joseph Plourde and Aurelie Lebel

PLUMMER,
Frank H., d. 5/15/1934 at 74/5/29; chronic nephritis
Lizzie A., d. 10/9/1916 at 54/2/20; myocarditis; Moses Furbush and Abbie A. Hilton
Mary A., d. 9/13/1922 at 43/10/1 in Portsmouth; chr. int. nephritis
Moses, d. 4/26/1920 at 84/1/9; arterio sclerosis; Moses Plummer and Rhoda Potter

PLYMPTON,
Grace M., d. 10/25/1927 at 44; abdominal carcinoma; Joseph Lapoint and Justine Styork

POCKET,
Rosalee, d. 1/16/1901 at 44; heart disease; SM

PODVIN,
Fred F., d. 1/15/1919 at 34/3/23; hemoptysis; Daniel Podvin and Georgianna Laplante

POIRIER,
Mary, d. 9/20/1926 at 48/7/14; intestinal contraction; Joseph Poirier and Marie Gerard

POISSON,
Donat, d. 9/24/1917 at 17/4/19; accidental gas poisoning; Ludger Poisson and Clara Brunelle

POITRAS,
Alphiche, d. 2/21/1913 at 1/4; lobar pneumonia; Joseph Poitras and Annie Dupres
Irene, d. 1/16/1917 at 2/9/24; laryngitis oedema; Joseph Poitras and Emelie Dupries
Joseph J., d. 7/12/1908 at 0/9/2; abscess of temporal bone; Joseph Poitras and Armelina Dupries

POLAQUIN,
Joseph Lucien, d. 11/30/1919 at 0/1/28; premature birth; Lebune Polaquin and Olwine Chevalier

POLDOC,
Annie, d. 2/5/1910 at 40; pulmonary tuberculosis

POLLARD,
Ann, d. 7/23/1932 at 80/2/26 in Exeter; arterio sclerosis
Ann A., d. 1/15/1911 at 78; lobar pneumonia
Anne, d. 12/8/1932 at 1/3/2; angina pectoris
James, d. 7/14/1909 at 73/0/15; mitral regurgitation; John Pollard
Orrin, d. 5/21/1924 at 42/4/14; traumatic amputation; Melvin Pollard and Melissa Ward
Richard, d. 3/9/1907 at 55; cardiac dilation; John Pollard and Ruth Olget

POLOPOULOS,
James, d. 2/15/1924 at 47; cholecystitis

POMERLEAU,
Anastasie, d. 11/25/1914 at 66/6; chronic endocarditis; John Walsh and Marcelline Page
Mary R., d. 10/3/1913 at 2/6/7; membraneous croup; A. J. Pomerleau and Rose Allard
Philias, d. 6/25/1920 at 77/1/14; senility; Henri Pomerleau and Marie Grenier

POOLE,
Emma A., d. 12/19/1922 at 49/9/12; apoplexy; J. C. Atkinson and Emily Smith
Viola, d. 6/30/1922 at –; stillborn; George Poole and Katherine Oates

POPE,
Theodosia E., d. 3/21/1908 at 60/0/1; septicemia; John Pope and Mary Eaton

POPPLE,
Hannah, d. 11/24/1903 at 39/7/24; burning accident; PH

PORTER,
Alfred, d. 8/19/1889 at 20/2 in Wolfeboro; student; single; b. Dover; Charles A. Porter (Danvers, MA) and Sarah Applebee (Dover)
Andrew, d. 11/24/1932 at 72/2/19; myocard. insufficiency
Charles, d. 9/16/1895 at 57; machinery accident; b. Danvers, MA; PH
Harriet, d. 10/3/1904 at 77 in Brockton, MA; cancer of stomach; PH
Harriet M., d. 3/12/1897 at 80; apoplexy; b. Haverhill; PH
Isaac N., d. 7/24/1927 at 85/2/1 in New York City; endocarditis
Joseph E., d. 5/29/1920 at 71/11/10; cerebral hemorrhage; Timothy N. Porter and Harriet N. Ayer
Sarah E., d. 6/24/1924 at 79/10/17; intestinal tuberculosis; Simeon Applebee and Joan -----

POST,
Clarence O., d. 9/20/1918 at 27; influenza; Arthur H. Post and Ella Jadd

POSTLEWAIT,
Benjamin G., d. 11/28/1888 at 0/1/14; b. Dover; George Postlewait (England) and Winnifred McMullen (England)
Joseph, d. 11/25/1888 at 0/1/11; b. Dover; George Postlewait (England) and Winnifred McMullen (England)

POSTOLOPOULOS,
child, d. 12/3/1923 at –; stillborn; Charles Postolopoulos

POTOIA,
Ernstine, d. 7/8/1887 at 0/5/20; b. Dover; Arthur Potoia (Canada)

POTTER,
Maud K., d. 11/11/1920 at 48/5/11; cerebral hemorrhage; James B. Hussey and Eliza Twombly

POTTERTON,
Herbert S., d. 6/15/1924 at 0/4/24; cholera infantum; Clarence Potterton and Lilla M. Hodgdon
Roswell C., d. 4/12/1916 at 0/1/1; lobar pneumonia; C. S. Potterton and Zilla M. Hodgdon

POULOPOULOS,
child, d. 2/18/1918 at –; stillborn; Nickolas Poulopoulos and Paniota Semopoulos

POULOS,
Sophie, d. 7/21/1923 at 0/2; ac. lobar pneumonia; Nicholas Poulos and Pauline Dimopoulos

POUND,
Augusta L., d. 4/14/1907 at 46/8/26; fibroid tumor; Enos L. Welts and Julia A. Thompson
Mrs. Thos., d. 4/16/1889 at 70/11/29; housewife; married; b. England; John Boulton (England) and Mary Cary (England)
Thomas, d. 12/26/1894 at 79; heart disease; b. England; PH
Thomas H., d. 7/4/1933 at 80/7/27 in Rochester; nephritis

POWERS,
daughter, d. 9/3/1887 at 0/1/23; b. Dover; John S. Powers (Somerville, MA) and Sarah F. Barnard (Boston, MA)
Ellen, d. 2/9/1931 at 70; chronic endocarditis
Marilyn L., d. 3/22/1931 at 0/9/13; broncho pneumonia
Teresa, d. 7/25/1888 at 1/9/7; b. Dover; James F. Powers (Sterling, CT) and M. A. Murphy (Dover)
Teresa, d. 8/1/1892 at 4; pulmonary phthisis; b. Dover; (CT; Dover)

POWHATTAN,
child, d. 12/20/1930 at –; asphyxia pallida; Leslie Powhattan and Mabel Jenness

PRATT,
Fred, d. 7/27/1917 at 48; cerebral hemorrhage; Benjamin Pratt and Elizabeth T. Perkins
George I., d. 5/15/1935 at 81/6/19; diabetes mellitus
Harold W., d. 10/26/1918 at 31/3/19; pneumonia; Fred L. Pratt and Grace Watson

PRAY,
Andrew, d. 2/14/1904 at 79/1/13; valvular heart disease; buried in Rollinsford
Benjamin, d. 1/27/1900 at 92; senility; PH
Caroline E., d. 8/29/1907 at 74/7/12; herniplegia; Asa Ham and Sarah Marden
Carrie B., d. 5/7/1915 at 47/1/17; uraemia; James Stevens and Margaret Heath
Charles Albert, d. 12/8/1901 at 0/2/10; meningitis; buried in Newington
Charles F., d. 1/2/1930 at 78/3/16; cerebral hemorrhage; Humphrey Pray and Eunice Stackpole
Eliza M., d. 4/21/1905 at 86/9/17 in Melrose, MA; acute bronchitis; buried in Austin Cem.
Elmer E., d. 2/19/1909 at 43/10/12; acute nephritis; John W. Pray and Harriet T. Lang
Ernest, d. 1/14/1892 at –; stillborn; b. Dover; (US; US)
Frank, d. 9/27/1889 at 0/5/20; b. Dover; Frank Pray (US) and Catherine Fleming (England)
George E., d. 12/31/1888 at 32/7/14 in Madbury; milk dealer; married; b. Dover; John W. Pray (Lebanon, ME) and Harriet Lang (Wakefield)
Harriet T., d. 12/12/1904 at 78/0/14; congestion of lungs; PH
Jennie M., d. 3/4/1928 at 79/6 in Boston, MA; coronary thrombosis
John C., d. 4/9/1912 at 76/2/23 in Boston, MA; cystitis
John F., d. 1/31/1934 at 71/4/4 in Concord; valvular heart dis.
John L., d. 4/23/1935 at 73/4/20; third degree burn
John W., d. 10/15/1904 at 77/8/19; valvular disease of heart; PH
John W., d. 6/19/1909 at 57/10/11 in Northwood; chronic enteritis
Lillian V., d. 11/9/1897 at 28; acute tuberculosis; b. Lynn, MA; PH
Lizzie Martin, d. 1/13/1921 at 69/4 in Northwood; chronic endocarditis
Martha A., d. 11/5/1900 at 59; inanition; PH
Mary E., d. 6/7/1905 at 32/4/20; chronic nephritis; PH
Ruth A., d. 6/29/1916 at 83/6/18; peritonitis; David Gould and Susanna Beals
Samuel, d. 5/16/1901 at 71/8/2; organic heart disease; PH
Thomas J. W., d. 12/7/1888 at 69/3/7; physician; married; b. Lebanon, ME; Moses Pray (Lebanon, ME) and Lydia Worcester (Sanford, ME)
Thomas M., d. 9/8/1887 at 30/5/10; lawyer; single; b. Dover; Thomas J. W. Pray (Somersworth) and Sarah E. Wheeler (Dover)

PRECART,
Omer, d. 2/21/1900 at <1; strangulation

PRECOURT,
Ida M., d. 4/25/1907 at 13/0/10; acute meningitis; Louis L. Precourt and Mary S. Chagnon

PRENDALL,
Henry, d. 3/24/1909 at 83; pneumonia; Charles Prendall and Ada Pray
Sarah E., d. 10/12/1898 at 68; heart degeneration; b. Hiram, ME; PH

PRESCOTT,
daughter, d. 9/11/1889 at 0/0/3; b. Dover; F. W. Prescott (Deerfield) and Elizabeth Preston (NY)
daughter, d. 6/25/1890 at 0/0/1; Frank Prescott (Deerfield) and Elizabeth Preston (NY)
child, d. 8/20/1891 at 0/0/3; Frank W. Prescott (Deerfield) and Lizzie Preston (NY)
Elizabeth, d. 4/25/1900 at 34; uremic convulsions; PH
Ella Rhoda, d. 6/18/1923 at 71/5/27; myocarditis; Samuel Thompson and Rhoda Davis
Ezekiel, d. 4/4/1893 at 86; old age
Florence, d. 8/24/1919 at 75; chr. Brights disease
Frank W., d. 9/24/1901 at 0/7/10; cholera infantum; PH
George B., d. 6/12/1900 at 67; heart disease; PH
George M., d. 10/27/1931 at 68/5/10; lobar pneumonia
Hannah, d. 6/22/1920 at 81/2/22 in Rockport, MA; valvular heart disease
Ida B., d. 11/28/1936 at 68/9/14; cerebral hemorrhage
Joseph, d. 11/6/1909 at 78 in Madbury; delerium tremens
Laura A., d. 5/29/1922 at 81/6/25; endocarditis; Thomas Meservey and Caroline Johnson
Laura M., d. 6/16/1897 at 0; cholera infantum; b. Newburyport, MA; SM
Mary A., d. 2/3/1899 at 74; old age; PH
Melvina A., d. 10/28/1928 at 90/5; arterio sclerosis; Israel Swain and Susan Bennett
Myrtie N., d. 6/15/1927 at 46; septicemia; Horace A. Neal and Nellie A. Stacy
Sadie E., d. 3/14/1908 at 0/11/28 in Wakefield; acute bronchitis
Samuel, d. 5/23/1908 at 90/0/3; old age; Weave Prescott and ----- Locke
Sarah A., d. 10/21/1922 at 63/5/24; apoplexy; Benjamin French and Mary Jane Mone
True, d. 3/14/1901 at 83/7/28; old age; buried in Durant, IA
Walter L., d. 4/25/1898 at 0; overlaid by mother; b. Dover; PH
William H., d. 9/21/1925 at 70/9/21; arterio sclerosis; Jonathan Prescott and Deborah Giles

PRESTON,
child, d. 8/27/1904 at –; stillborn
Catherine, d. 10/4/1907 at 38; tuberculosis; B. Barkley
Ellen M., d. 6/26/1927 at 64/0/24; angina pectoris; John Butterworth and Ellen Booth
Fred, d. 8/28/1932 at 72/11/25; apoplexy
Frederick W., d. 12/24/1904 at 38/5/24; nephritis; PH
Isabelle C., d. 6/25/1906 at 48/10/3; neurasthenia; PH
James D., d. 1/25/1917 at 34/4/6; acute nephritis; James F. Preston and Oveline Ash
John, d. 5/12/1937 at 71; chr. myocarditis
Jonas, d. 8/21/1890 at 50/10/11 in Macon, GA; married; John Preston (England) and Rachael (England)
Olive H., d. 7/10/1892 at 76; paralysis
Rose A., d. 4/16/1898 at 0; pneumonia; b. Dover; SM
Velma B., d. 1/15/1910 at 4/7/19 in Somerville, MA; malignant endocarditis
William, d. 2/13/1901 at 23/8/13; consumption; PH

PRICE,
child, d. 9/16/1928 at 0/0/3-4; Arthur J. Price and Evelyn Varney
Olive Bell, d. 2/23/1927 at 29 in Washington, DC; pulmonary tuberculosis

PRIDHAM,
Samuel H., d. 8/11/1896 at 60; cerebral hemorrhage; b. England; buried in Manchester

PRIESTLEY,
daughter, d. 12/31/1890 at –; J. H. Priestley (US) and Agnes Wood (US)
Agnes, d. 12/31/1890 at 36/11/19; married; Daniel Wood (US) and Eleanor Brown (US)
Alice H., d. 8/24/1928 at 40/0/10; cerebral hemorrhage; Frank M. Hall and Annie Otis
James H., d. 10/10/1933 at 88/7/4; fracture of femur

PRIME,
Charles H., d. 7/7/1937 at 84/3/27*; b. Newmarket
Edna T., d. 5/1/1934 at 79/2/11 in Portsmouth; fracture of femur

PRINGLE,
Robert, d. 4/16/1923 at 65; hypernephroma; Robert Pringle and Jennie Locarbee

PRINTY,
child, d. 7/7/1922 at –; stillborn; John E. Printy and Charlotte Lovejoy
Alice, d. 12/25/1896 at 52; apoplexy; b. Dover; SM
Ann, d. 6/28/1922 at 75; acute arthritis; Patrick White and Ann Wilson
Annie, d. 10/28/1898 at 13; abscess from injury; b. Dover; SM
Annie, d. 8/30/1918 at 65/4/17; chronic int. nephritis; Cornelius Crowley and Mary A. Scanlon
Bridget, d. 8/13/1907 at 74; hernia; Richard Morgan and Catherine -----
John E., d. 11/18/1933 at 52/3/10; cerebral hemorrhage
Margaret, d. 5/12/1914 at –; general arterio sclerosis; Simon McKernan and Ann McElroy
Marguerite V., d. 2/4/1911 at 18; spastic cerebral paralysis; Owen Printy and Annie Crowley
Mary B., d. 4/15/1898 at 21; phthisis; b. Dover; SM
Michael, d. 1/20/1921 at 79/11/18; chronic endocarditis; James Printy and Margaret McKernan
Owen, d. 2/16/1914 at 62/10/12; heart failure - syncope; Michael Printy and Katherine McMahon
Thomas, d. 5/25/1900 at 68; heart disease; SM

PRIOR,
William W., d. 12/6/1893 at 45; la grippe with scrofula; b. Kittery, ME

PROCTOR,
Allen, d. 5/20/1891 at 0/4/14; Alvin Proctor (Biddeford, ME) and Margaret Leddin (Charleston, MA)
Ammer H., d. 12/23/1931 at 76/5/28 in Berwick, ME; carcinoma of rectum
Amy L., d. 8/7/1887 at 0/1/21; b. Dover; Tyler B. Proctor (Westfield, VT) and Clara B. Leighton (Farmington)
Deborah, d. 9/21/1895 at 82 in Salem, MA; cardiac disease; PH
Elsie M., d. 11/13/1896 at 13; scarlet fever; b. Dover; PH
Eva E., d. 10/22/1919 at 48/11/8; heart embolism; William Spinney and Ellen Spinney
Georgia E., d. 2/2/1922 at 69/0/7 in Madbury; pneumonia
Howard, d. 7/16/1892 at –; meningitis; b. Dover; (Biddeford, ME; Charlestown, MA)
Tyler B., d. 6/28/1887 at 39/5/5; shoemaker; married; b. Westford, VT; John Proctor and Eveline Bingham

PROULX,
Joseph, d. 2/7/1914 at 15/10/6 in Newmarket; cerebral hemorrhage; Joseph Proulx and Mary Petreu
Mary, d. 2/7/1914 at 57 in Concord; organic dementia

PROVENCAL,
Mary D., d. 1/11/1931 at 49; metastosis gall bladder

PROVOST,
Florida, d. 12/5/1917 at 59/8/25; acute nephritis; Isaac Labranche

PROYER,
Thomas A., d. 8/23/1916 at 72/0/10; broken cardiac comp.; Levi Proyer and Sarah Cushman

PRYOR,
child, d. 3/26/1910 at – in Rollinsford; surgical shock; Ralph A. Pryor and Annie Bedard
child, d. 6/19/1911 at –; prolapsed cord; Ralph A. Pryor and Annie H. Bedard
Sarah A., d. 6/27/1900 at 50; cancer; PH

PULSIFER,
Julia I., d. 7/7/1933 at 24/1/6 in York, ME; broncho pneumonia

PURBY,
Michael, d. 3/21/1913 at 40; gen. miliary tuberculosis

PURINTON,
Edward J., d. 4/25/1932 at 71/0/15; angina pectoris
G. M., d. 12/16/1894 at 72; apoplexy; b. Wolfeboro; PH
Maria, d. 7/8/1897 at 78; gastritis; b. Tamworth; PH

PURKEY,
Mary, d. 12/13/1934 at 66/3/11; cerebral embolism

PUTNAM,
Charles H., d. 12/24/1922 at 75/8/23; paralysis agitans
Jennie E., d. 8/26/1907 at 67/11/26; cancer of stomach; Samuel York and ----- Stafford
Katie, d. 12/16/1915 at 70/7/16 in Union, NY; org. valvular cardiac

QUADE,
Joseph B., d. 4/11/1888 at 30; reporter; married; b. Ireland; Dennis Quade (Ireland) and ----- Goodwin (Ireland)

QUAID,
Bridget, d. 1/24/1907 at 51/8; chronic endocarditis; Michael Morgan and Bridget -----

Joseph B., d. 9/9/1892 at 10; heart disease; b. Dover; (Ireland; Ireland)
Mary B., d. 12/21/1932 at 53/2/4 in Concord; pulmonary tuberculosis
Robert E., d. 6/26/1906 at 20/3/22; chronic endocarditis

QUAILEY,
Michael, d. 12/29/1898 at 61; cancer; b. Dover; SM

QUALEY,
Bernard W., d. 6/1/1899 at 26; Brights disease; SM
Edward, d. 3/13/1937 at 61/11/18*
Mary, d. 4/2/1912 at 50; epilepsy; Bernard Brady and Mary Calahan

QUILL,
Margaret, d. 4/2/1920 at 70; chronic endocarditis

QUIMBY,
Andrew L., d. 7/6/1892 at 55; cerebral softening
Charles M., d. 11/12/1904 at 57 in Rochester; alcoholism and exposure; PH
Elihu H., d. 10/20/1890 at 61/6/11; married
Ellery C., d. 12/2/1929 at 70/1/5 in Springfield, MA; ac. lobar pneumonia; Andrew Quimby
Eva, d. 5/4/1932 at 58/8/17; pulmonary tuberculosis
Frank K., d. 6/17/1923 at 63; cancer of liver
Frank W., d. 1/31/1928 at 71/1/29 in Rochester; septic peritonitis
Fred E., d. 10/13/1933 at 75/9/28; lobar pneumonia
Hannah E., d. 5/17/1891 at 79 in Rochester
Madeline L., d. 8/9/1924 at 0/0/10; nonclo. foramen ovale; Perly A. Quimby and Lilah G. Ellis
Marietta, d. 3/5/1931 at 69/7/18; carcinoma of breast
Mildred, d. 5/1/1935 at 47/5/18 in Boston, MA; hypertension
Susan Morse, d. 3/31/1912 at 75/7/25 in Providence, RI; acute lobar pneumonia
Walter S., d. 12/26/1917 at 54/3/26 in Haverhill, MA; apoplexy

QUINLAN,
daughter, d. 9/17/1889 at 0/0/1-6; b. Dover; M. Quinlan (Ireland) and Alice McKenna (Dover)
Alice Leone, d. 7/24/1929 at 45/1/24; ch. parench. nephritis; Edward Gouin and Celina Ruel
David, d. 4/18/1899 at 37 in Wakefield; railroad accident; SM
Ellen, d. 8/3/1915 at 75; fracture cerv. vertabrae; John Quinlan and Margaret -----
John, d. 4/17/1894 at 37; cancer; b. Dover; SM
John F., d. 9/17/1898 at 24; phthisis pulmonalis; b. Dover; SM

Margaret, d. 7/27/1902 at 58; burned to death
Mary, d. 11/27/1888 at 62/6; married; b. Ireland; John Bassett (Ireland) and Bess Ryan (Ireland)
Mary, d. 3/10/1897 at 70; pleuro pneumonia; b. Ireland; SM
Mary, d. 7/28/1899 at 2; convulsions; SM
Michael, d. 8/23/1910 at 68/3; chr. Brights disease; John Quinland and Margaret Landrigan
Michael William, d. 4/13/1936 at 52/8/28; typhoid fever
William, d. 11/30/1909 at 77/1/23; old age; John Quinlan and Margaret Sunigan
William H., d. 6/21/1924 at 39/4/7 in Rochester; cerebral thrombosis

QUINN,
child, d. 12/1/1904 at –; stillborn
Alice, d. 7/8/1890 at 23/11/8; single; Michael Quinn (Ireland) and Mary Brennan (Ireland)
Alice, d. 11/8/1897 at 68; heart disease; b. Ireland; SM
Alice, d. 11/14/1923 at 74/1; myocarditis; Thomas Loughran and Bridget Martin
Ann, d. 12/2/1915 at 63; lobar pneumonia; Laurence McGlone and Bridget McKone
Annie, d. 1/31/1897 at 5; scarlet fever; b. Dover; SM
Catherine E., d. 1/17/1913 at 52/8; shock; Felix Quinn and Nancy Keenan
Catherine T., d. 9/6/1926 at 50/9; pulmonary tuberculosis; John Quinn and Ann McGlone
Doris M., d. 10/15/1927 at 0/0/5 in Berwick, ME; malnutrition
Ellen, d. 8/21/1907 at --; cerebral apoplexy; Felix Quinn
Frank, d. 10/9/1923 at 60 in Boston, MA; cerebral hemorrhage; Frank Quinn and Susan McIntyre
James, d. 5/26/1897 at 70; old age; b. Ireland; SM
James, d. 4/6/1903 at 78; la grippe
James, d. 6/14/1907 at –; malnutrition; James Quinn and Emma Harris
James, d. 4/1/1908 at 53 in Rochester; interstitial nephritis
James M., d. 6/9/1913 at 38 in Boston, MA; septic leg, accidental fall; James Quinn and Sarah Cassily
John, d. 8/13/1889 at 35; laborer; married; b. Ireland; James Quinn (Ireland) and Alice Mallon (Ireland)
John, d. 2/16/1894 at 32; phthisis; b. Dover; SM
John, d. 12/29/1920 at 76/7/5; mitral regurgitation; James Quinn and Susan Hammer
John, d. 9/13/1927 at –; pulmonary tuberculosis; John Quinn and Ann McGlone
John H., d. 9/12/1921 at 72/5; cerebral apoplexy
Joseph, d. 5/1/1904 at 0/0/1; premature birth
Katherine M., d. 5/6/1893 at 47; carcinoma; b. Ireland; (Ireland; Ireland)

Maria A., d. 5/15/1914 at 22/3/3; pernicious anaemia; Cleophas Charest and Rosalie Deloge
Marie R., d. 8/8/1919 at 5/3/10; acute gastro enteritis; John P. Quinn and Amanda Charest
Mary, d. 7/13/1890 at 80; married; (Ireland; Ireland)
Mary, d. 4/25/1906 at 51; pneumonia; SM
Mary, d. 5/7/1906 at 70 in Concord; senile dementia
Mary, d. 9/29/1908 at 55; heart disease
Mary A., d. 4/22/1897 at 26; phthisis pulmonalis; b. Dover; SM
Mary K., d. 11/17/1902 at 32/1/10 in Boston, MA; chronic nephritis; SM
Nancy, d. 8/4/1916 at 60/5; cerebral hemorrhage; Felix Quinn and Nancy Keenan
Nellie E., d. 7/20/1907 at 48; heart disease; Felix Quinn and Nancy Keenan
Ralph, d. 1/18/1934 at 33 in New York, NY; chronic alcoholism
Sarah, d. 9/7/1903 at 49/3/27; prob. passive cong. of lungs; SM
Susan, d. 12/17/1893 at 70; pneumonia; b. Ireland; (Ireland; Ireland)
Susan, d. 3/13/1897 at 73 in Billerica, MA; senile diabetes
Susan, d. 2/9/1904 at 31; tuberculosis of lungs
Susan, d. 1/21/1915 at 55; chronic endocarditis; James Quinn and Mary --
Thomas, d. 1/16/1925 at 71/5/1; angina pectoris; John Quinn and Mary Tosney
William Peter, d. 7/17/1887 at 0/4/19; b. Dover; John Quinn (Ireland) and Ann McGlone (Ireland)

QUINT,
Alonzo H., d. 11/4/1896 at 68 in Boston, MA; angina pectoris; PH
Clara G., d. 4/--/1896 at 33 in Washington, DC; fibroid tumor; PH
Frances M., d. 8/18/1932 at 25/9/1; cerebral embolism (see following entry)
Frances M., d. 8/18/1933 at 25/9 in Rollinsford; peritonitis (see preceding entry)
Rebecca P., d. 1/3/1913 at 83/7/20 in Worcester, MA; pneumonia

RACKLEY,
Benjamin F., d. 4/26/1890 at 55/4/21; married; Jason Rackley (Greene, ME) and Nancy West Rackley (Greene, ME)
Eunice W., d. 4/4/1912 at 78/9; cerebral hemorrhage; William Hill and Dorcas Rumery
Matilda J., d. 1/4/1928 at 91/5/23; cerebral hemorrhage; James Frye and Elizabeth Burrows
Samuel, d. 1/14/1917 at 84; acute bronchitis; Jason Rackley and ----- West

RAFAELL,
Peter, d. 4/27/1908 at 15/2/6; appendicitis; Astfain Rafaell and Annie Solomon

RAFFERTY,
Ellen, d. 11/3/1902 at –; dropsy; SM
Mary Ann, d. 7/15/1907 at 45; general tuberculosis
Peter J., d. 5/31/1916 at 63/3/3; chron. Bright's dis.; William Rafferty and Ellen -----
William, d. 4/6/1908 at 77; pneumonia; William Rafferty and Nancy Agnew

RAINVILLE,
Emilie, d. 10/21/1929 at 80/8/26; carcinoma; Jean St. Hilaire and Marie ---

RAITE,
Caroline, d. 2/9/1893 at 41; died in Strafford Co. Asylum fire

RAITT,
Charles P., d. 2/2/1891 at 0/7
Edward, d. 8/8/1918 at 54/7/27; diabetes mellitus; James Raitt and Elizabeth Amazeen
John, d. 3/19/1929 at 75/1/11 in Eliot, ME; cerebral hemorrhage
John F., d. 1/7/1914 at 72/7/5; pneumonia; John Raitt and Betsy Ferguson
Susan A., d. 11/21/1926 at 88/2/22; apoplexy; Oliver Lord and Abigail Goodwin

RAMSAY,
Vienna S., d. 1/16/1905 at 88/0/8; senile decay; PH

RAMSBOTTOM,
Josie M., d. 12/15/1937 at 62/3/6*
Louise D., d. 2/7/1925 at 50/3/12; lobar pneumonia; Roscoe G. Green and Effie M. Hardy

RAMSDELL,
Alvah T., d. 5/28/1928 at 76/1/13; angina pectoris; William Ramsdell and Phoebe Boston
Arvilla T., d. 4/13/1913 at 82/3/29; cancer of bowels; Daniel Buck and Hannah Weston
Charles T., d. 5/31/1928 at 74/7/14; diabetes mellitus; Samuel Ramsdell and Arvilla Buck
Clifton H., d. 8/28/1889 at 9/10/4; b. Dover; Alvah T. Ramsdell (York, ME) and Ida F. Hurd (New Durham)

Samuel, d. 10/16/1911 at 26/7; pneumonia; Ira Ramsdell and Clarissa Robinson

RAND,
Albert, d. 9/15/1903 at 90/1/24; old age; PH
Dorothy M., d. 5/29/1891 at 75/5/7; widow; Elliott Fernald (Kittery) and Sallie Mudgett (Parsonsfield, ME)
Elizabeth H., d. 5/12/1892 at 77; old age - dropsy; b. Berwick, ME
Ethylin G., d. 5/18/1910 at 0/3/9; marasmus; George W. Rand and Laura J. Bennett
Eva L., d. 2/27/1900 at 26 in Boston, MA; phthisis pulmonalis; PH
Flora B., d. 4/9/1900 at 14; anaemia; PH
Frank P., d. 10/25/1925 at 71/11/28; carcinoma of stomach; David Rand and Nancy Edgerly
Fred Woodbury, d. 5/26/1891 at 0/10/11; James B. Rand (Durham) and Laura Wiggin (Dover)
James, d. 12/24/1888 at 73/3/19; clergyman; married; b. Parsonsfield, ME; John H. Rand (Buxton, ME) and Sarah Hancock (Buxton, ME)
James B., d. 10/24/1932 at 75/11/28; arterio sclerosis
James E., d. 5/7/1917 at 72 in Concord; Albert Rand and Nancy Pray
John E., d. 1/22/1890 at 48/9/2; married; James Rand (Parsonsfield) and Dorothy M. Fernald (Parsonsfield)
Linda L., d. 2/23/1901 at 51/7/16; cancer; PH
Nancy, d. 11/29/1891 at 79/4/1; married; Tobias Pray (Berwick, ME) and Mary Young (Wolfeboro)
Raymond, d. 4/1/1899 at –; inanition; buried at Dover Point
Roland, d. 2/21/1899 at –; pneumonia; buried at Dover Point
Sarah, d. 6/28/1922 at 76; arterio sclerosis; Bernard Rand and Ann Hughes
Sarah E., d. 5/25/1922 at 83/11/4; old age; Samuel Randall and Louisa Goodwin
Vienna, d. 2/4/1904 at 61/7/6; carcinoma of liver; PH
William E., d. 12/20/1909 at 62/9/16; heart disease; Jeremiah Rand and Cynthia Tuttle

RANDALL,
Amanda L., d. 3/20/1929 at 73/2/1; valv. heart disease; John Randall and Mary J. Demeritt
Charles E., d. 1/18/1922 at 69/8/12; uraemia; Benjamin Randall and Melinda Stillings
Elizabeth F., d. 12/1/1902 at 60/10/22; disease of heart; buried in Somersworth
Elmer G., d. 4/18/1889 at 1/10/17; b. Dover; Nehemiah Randall (Lee) and Annie Sherborne (Barrington)

Franklin B., d. 10/16/1891 at 25/3/15 in Rush City, MN; single; Sewell Randall (NH) and Mary B. Randall (NH)
George M., d. 6/12/1933 at 74/11/12; chronic nephritis
Helen M., d. 8/17/1903 at 71/9/21; septicaemia; PH
Hermon, d. 4/3/1923 at 54; carcinoma of liver; Ann Randall
Ira A., d. 8/13/1922 at 63/4/25; asthma; Richard Randall and Betsey Freeman
John A., d. 6/9/1895 at 67; tuberculosis; b. Somersworth; buried in Somersworth
John A., d. 12/24/1928 at 81/2/14 in Madbury; nephritis
Julia E., d. 8/11/1932 at 89/1 in S. Berwick, ME; chr. valv. heart dis.
Leonard O., d. 3/17/1909 at 61/0/28; heart disease; Nathaniel Randall and Mehitable Broton
Louisa, d. 7/27/1890 at 84/2/4; married; Joshua Goodwin (Lebanon, ME) and Sarah Copp (Lebanon, ME)
Martha J., d. 6/10/1930 at 72/2/8; heart disease; Andrew James and Lilla -
Nehemiah, d. 12/6/1905 at 58/7/19; apoplectic shock; PH
Susan, d. 3/7/1918 at 84/7 in Madbury; uraemia; Thomas Gerrish and Sarah Fox
Thelma E., d. 5/3/1925 at 3/6/27; accidental burns; Harry P. Randall and Hattie A. Clay
William C., d. 1/22/1892 at 77; la grippe - pneumonia; b. Canada; (Lee; Gilmanton)
Winfield S., d. 11/8/1921 at 60/0/26; enteritis; Jeremiah Randall and Lois J. Clark

RANDLETT,
Mary A., d. 3/29/1898 at 63; chronic nephritis; b. Northwood; buried in Northwood

RANKINS,
Fred W., d. 3/23/1910 at 51/1/8; acute nephritis; Isaac Rankins and Frances Buzzell

RANSOM,
Frank H., d. 1/25/1928 at 62/4/8; chronic nephritis; Reuben Ransom and Melissa Spiller
Melissa J., d. 7/27/1924 at 84/3/24 in Exeter; fracture of hip
Reuben, d. 5/2/1921 at 82/2 in Barrington; natural causes
Sophia B., d. 1/7/1894 at 86; old age; b. Durham; buried in Durham

RANVILLE,
Tresa Annie, d. 10/25/1911 at 0/4/16; hemorrhage of bowels; Leo Ranville and Delia T. Boler

RAPLEY,
Annie E., d. 8/29/1892 at 41; cancer; b. Calais, ME; (Pugwash, NS; St. David, NB)

RAY,
John, d. 2/26/1919 at 65 in Chatham; tuberculosis
John W., d. 12/18/1925 at 53; chronic endocarditis

REAGAN,
Ellen, d. 7/15/1917 at 63; cerebral hemorrhage; Timothy Reardon and Nora ----
Maggie, d. 9/26/1902 at 0/7; cholera infantum; SM
Michael, d. 4/17/1914 at 41; heart disease
Timothy J., d. 5/1/1919 at 22/5/24; pulmonary tuberculosis; William Regan (sic) and Ellen Carragher

REAL,
Aldeff M., d. 10/4/1900 at 1; tuberculosis; PH

REALL,
George W., d. 7/12/1888 at 1/2

REARDON,
Mary C., d. 11/15/1897 at 23; acute tuberculosis; b. Dover; SM

REDDEN,
child, d. 5/1/1898 at 0; inanition; b. Dover; SM
child, d. 9/26/1900 at <1; premature birth
child, d. 3/19/1906 at –; stillborn; SM
Catherine, d. 7/26/1937 at 70; diabetes mellitus
Daniel, d. 1/7/1896 at 18; pul. tuberculosis; b. Dover; SM
Daniel, d. 9/12/1901 at 2/3/3; cholera infantum; SM
Emma F., d. 7/28/1931 at 62/11/5; acute cardiac decom.
James, d. 4/7/1937 at 65; carcinoma oesophagus
James D., d. 4/24/1916 at 4/3/15; broncho pneumonia; William Redden and Emma F. Sterling
John, d. 8/24/1912 at 95; senile debility; Patrick Redden and Ellen Bray
John, d. 12/27/1918 at 3/4/8; acute lobar pneumonia; John Redden and Margaret O'Keefe
Marie B., d. 2/7/1902 at 2/4/25; cerebral hemorrhage; SM
Robert W., d. 4/16/1923 at 0/8; malnutrition; John J. Redden and Iona M. Dolan
William, d. 9/8/1904 at 0/9/5; athrepsia

William, d. 5/30/1925 at 60; myocarditis; John Redden and Katherine Roache

REDDON,
Kate, d. 2/6/1890 at 50; married; William Roach (Ireland) and Mary White (Ireland)

REDFIELD,
Henry A., d. 3/6/1917 at 77/2/4; carcinoma of stomach; Wyllys S. Redfield and Martha S. Woods
Kate M., d. 5/9/1901 at 28/8/21; phthisis pulmonalis; PH
Martha J., d. 6/1/1894 at 82; cerebral hemorrhage; b. Hollis; buried in Claremont
Mary H. F., d. 8/4/1913 at 69/3/5; senility; Henry S. Smith and Mary H. Hilliard
Wyllys H., d. 1/28/1893 at 16; phthisis pulmonalis; b. Dover; (Claremont; W. Claremont)

REDMOND,
Alice L., d. 1/15/1891 at 23/10/25; married; David E. D. Frost (Middleton) and Phoebe Ellis (Middleton)
J., d. 11/27/1904 at 36; tuberculosis; SM
John J., d. 11/28/1904 at 34; hiccough; SM
Mark, d. 3/31/1891 at 28; married; Owen Redmond (Ireland) and Margaret Kernan (Ireland)
Mark, d. 1/15/1919 at 27/9/23; broncho pneumonia; Mark Redmond and Margaret Parle

REDMYERE,
Joseph, d. 1/16/1906 at 71; chronic nephritis; PH

REED,
child, d. 8/20/1934 at –; premature birth
Catherine E., d. 3/9/1922 at 23/3/19; pulmonary tuberculosis; Stephen Reed and Rosanna O'Hearn
Charles H., d. 11/23/1925 at 76/4/21 in Winthrop, ME; cerebral thrombosis
Dolly, d. 5/29/1888 at 88/7 in Amesbury; married
Earl Charles, d. 12/9/1929 at 52/0/27 in Exeter; angina pectoris
Edward F., d. 4/10/1889 at 1/4/10; b. Dover; George F. Reed (Lowell, MA) and Annie Sayers (England)
Elizabeth R., d. 1/27/1925 at 77/8/8 in Winthrop, ME; cancer of breast; John Remick and Eliza Holmes
Hanson O., d. 1/25/1916 at 79/4/0; lobar pneumonia; Moses Reed and Nancy Odiorne
Helen, d. 12/8/1899 at 2; pneumonia; SM

Jacob, d. 3/30/1894 at 89; old age; b. Berwick, ME; PH
John J., d. 5/18/1903 at 1; cerebral meningitis; SM
Maggie, d. 3/20/1889 at 3/5/2; b. Boston, MA; George F. Reed (Lowell, MA) and Annie Sayers (England)
Mary, d. 8/25/1915 at 89/6/23; chronic int. nephritis; Michael Cavanaugh and Elizabeth Sennott
Mary H., d. 7/8/1921 at 82/6/20; chronic nephritis; Calvin Morrison and Mary Nason
Philip H., d. 12/24/1916 at 22/9/4; malignant endocarditis; William Reed and Carrie L. Neal
Stephen, d. 7/9/1931 at 72/8/27; chronic endocarditis
Thomas, d. 6/20/1895 at 70; pulmonary phthisis; b. Ireland; SM

REEL,
Sarah, d. 10/4/1906 at 8; typhoid fever; SM

REGAN,
child, d. 9/–/1902 at 0/0/5; inanition; SM
Annie, d. 9/9/1911 at 38; phthisis pulmonalis; ----- Burke
Dennis, d. 1/14/1895 at 23; acute pneumonia; b. Lawrence, MA; buried in Lawrence, MA
Elizabeth, d. 11/18/1919 at 32/1/21; cerebral hemorrhage; Daniel Collins and Grace Doherty
Michael, d. 11/23/1904 at 30; tubercular laryngitis; SM
Patrick William, d. 6/28/1901 at 16/4/6; accidental drowning; SM
Timothy, d. 4/21/1933 at 72/7/9; cerebral hemorrhage
William, d. 6/7/1925 at 65 in Boston, MA; cancer of stomach

REHILL,
James H., d. 12/17/1890 at 45/9; married; Bernard Rehill (Ireland) and Mary McGill (Ireland)

REID,
David, d. 3/14/1930 at 79/10; arterio sclerosis; James Reid and Sarah McGuire

REIL [see Riel],
Adolphe, d. 4/14/1916 at 44; phthisis pulmonalis; Louis Riel (sic) and Matilda LaRose
Julia, d. 2/9/1893 at 42; died in Strafford Co. Asylum fire
Louis, d. 9/10/1917 at 73; gen. arterio sclerosis; Francois Reil and Marie Fontaine

REILLY,
John, d. 1/4/1916 at 48; tuberculosis; John Reilly and Bridget McGrory
Thomas E., d. 3/29/1915 at 57/2/29 in Montreal, Can.; cerebral hemorrhage; Bernard Reilly and Mary Lynch

REINDEAU,
Mary D., d. 9/25/1918 at 32/10/25; influenza; James McKeever and Ann Connolly

REMICK,
Blanche M., d. 1/2/1926 at 28/4/2; septicemia; Thomas Bassett and Mabel B. Collins
Charles, d. 1/24/1914 at 0/6/17; acute cardiac dilitation; Charles Remick and Mary Bassett
Charles Edwin, d. 1/6/1926 at 49/3/28; double lobar pneumonia; Mark Remick and Eleanor E. Young
Charles F., d. 5/7/1914 at 57/8/19; tuberculosis of knee; William Remick and Elizabeth Brooks
Eliza, d. 6/12/1920 at 45/9/4; cancer of uterus; George Lucier and Aglee Vincent
Emma F., d. 9/30/1933 at 76/1/28; chronic nephritis
Herbert S., d. 11/20/1888 at 6/1/23; b. Dover; William Remick (Portsmouth) and Mary Irvin (Ireland)
James Albert, d. 11/17/1924 at 38; cerebral hemorrhage; William Remick and Mary Irwin
John, d. 3/11/1937 at 79/3/5; cerebral apoplexy
John H., d. 5/2/1917 at 41/10/25 in Boston, MA; pul. tuberculosis
Joseph, d. 12/2/1888 at 9/8/10; b. Dover; William Remick (Portsmouth) and Mary Irvin (Ireland)
Mary, d. 12/9/1907 at 50 in Lawrence, MA; pneumonia
William, d. 8/20/1897 at 45; heart disease; SM
William H., d. 7/26/1899 at 19; shock and heart disease; SM

RENAGHEN,
Mary M., d. 9/4/1892 at –; cholera infantum; b. Dover; (Ireland; Ireland)

RENAHAN,
Kate, d. 2/17/1893 at 34; puerperal peritonitis; b. Ireland; (Ireland; Ireland)

RENAUD,
Ethel, d. 3/16/1936 at 25/4/12; acute gastritis

RENE,
Eva, d. 3/18/1906 at 0/4; enteritis; buried in Somersworth

Joseph, d. 10/25/1935 at 57/7/29 in Concord; cerebral hemorrhage

RENSHAW,
Ann, d. 10/8/1894 at 87; old age; b. St. John's, NB; PH
Caroline A., d. 4/18/1917 at 79/0/19 in Dorchester, MA; chro. valv. heart dis.; Isaac Meader and Nancy Perry

REYNARD,
Arvilla, d. 10/28/1915 at 68/2/29; hemiplegia; William Andrews and Abigail Lord
James W., d. 3/4/1915 at 42/5/11; struck by R.R. engine; James Reynard and Mary Greenwood

REYNOLDS,
Benjamin O., d. 5/28/1923 at 86/5/25 in New York City; cerebral hemorrhage
Bernard, d. 5/29/1892 at 53; Bright's disease; b. Ireland; (Ireland; Ireland)
Bridget, d. 3/27/1914 at 77/1/25; old age; Bernard Conlen and Catherine Printy
Bridget, d. 3/3/1923 at 80 in Concord; aortic regurgitation; Michael Reynolds and Nancy O'Neil
Charles, d. 1/9/1919 at 53; pulmonary tuberculosis
Ellen, d. 3/12/1893 at 63; apoplexy - heart failure; b. Ireland; (Ireland; Ireland)
Frank, d. 9/25/1898 at 50; Bright's disease; b. Ireland; SM
George A., d. 3/13/1919 at 71/5/23 in Milford, MA; prog. cardiac asthenia
James A., d. 5/12/1919 at 64/10/27 in Barrington; chronic endocarditis; Stephen Reynolds and Sally Garland
John, d. 12/27/1926 at 64/8 in Sanford, ME; angina pectoris; Patrick Reynolds and Theresa Crumery
John F., d. 4/9/1911 at 47; probably apoplexy; Bernard Reynolds and Rose Mooney
John T., d. 2/9/1925 at 79/6/16; diabetes; Stephen Reynolds and Sally Garland
Juliette, d. 2/24/1895 at 61; phthisis; b. Dover; PH
Margaret, d. 5/16/1905 at 35; acute nephritis; buried in Newburyport, MA
Margaret, d. 7/16/1908 at 56/11/10; tuberculosis; John ----- and Ellen -----
Martha Dodge, d. 5/3/1891 at 49/0/25; married; John Hubbard White (Dover) and Rebecca E. W. Peirce (Dover)
Mary, d. 2/6/1899 at 33; uraemia; buried in Rochester
Mary, d. 2/1/1903 at 65; cerebral hemorrhage; SM
Mary, d. 5/16/1905 at 29; acute nephritis; buried in Newburyport, MA
Mary E., d. 11/5/1916 at 39/6/11; pulmonary tuberculosis; John Reynolds and Bridget Conlon
Mary F., d. 5/31/1931 at 24/9/3; natural causes

Michael, d. 5/12/1924 at 73; chronic endocarditis
Michael J., d. 8/25/1930 at 53; chronic nephritis; Francis Reynolds and Margaret McGuinness
Miriam S., d. 4/20/1903 at 70/4/11; heart disease; PH
Nellie A., d. 3/24/1926 at 50/7/17; lobar pneumonia; Daniel T. Caldwell and Mary S. Swain
Owen, d. 11/7/1896 at 36; chronic nephritis; b. Ireland; SM
Rose, d. 1/20/1908 at 69/0/14; exhaustion; John Mooney and Rose McQuaid
Rose, d. 4/1/1921 at 70; apoplexy; James Harkins and Margaret Doherty
Sarah, d. 3/6/1889 at 45/11/18; housewife; married; b. Dover; J. Austin (Dover) and Nancy Perkins (Bristol, ME)
Sarah H., d. 4/22/1898 at 87; old age; b. Dover; PH
Sarah M., d. 7/17/1915 at 73/7/5; unknown; Stephen Reynolds and Sally Garland
Sarah W., d. 11/3/1897 at 20; phthisis pulmonalis; b. Dover; PH
Teresa, d. 7/6/1900 at 65 in Rochester; malignant jaundice; PH
William S., d. 3/8/1929 at 63/11/2; natural causes; James A. Reynolds and Mairany Hanson

RHOADES,
Charles E., d. 4/29/1917 at –; premature birth; Frank Rhoades and Mildred Howe

RHODES,
Mildred H., d. 7/26/1929 at 39/6/22; valv. heart disease; Charles W. Howe and Abbie F. Horne
Mina E., d. 5/27/1935 at 67/10/19; carcinoma of breast
Victoria, d. 9/8/1927 at 69/6/21; cerebral hemorrhage

RICE,
Dorothy Althea, d. 2/3/1929 at 0/2/6; congen. malformation; Ernest P. Rice and Jane Durgin
Edward E., Jr., d. 1/28/1910 at 0/5/28; meningitis; Edward E. Rice and Leonor Turner

RICH,
Abram, d. 7/25/1891 at 60/0/20; married; Thomas Rich (MA) and Betsey D. Rich (MA)
Augusta, d. 9/24/1887 at 72/11/28; widow; b. ME; Joseph Bouchie (Canada) and Deborah McFarland (ME)
Marcia T., d. 2/27/1887 at 42/7; widow; b. Wellfleet, MA; George Baker (Wellfleet, MA) and Marcia Higgins (Wellfleet, MA)

RICHARD,
Georges, d. 10/20/1904 at 78/5; cerebral hemorrhage; SM
Jeannette, d. 10/28/1936 at 3/0/3; fractured skull
Margurite M., d. 5/7/1899 at –; unknown; SM
Zeila, d. 1/17/1895 at 45; bilious fever; b. Canada; SM

RICHARDS,
child, d. 3/23/1916 at –; premature birth; Alfred E. Richards and Catherine Barrows
George A., d. 10/24/1904 at 64/3/26; cancer; PH
John, d. 11/27/1898 at –; shock, blood poisoning; b. England; PH
Lillian H., d. 1/16/1926 at 38/4/12; carcinoma uterus; Matthew R. Johnson and Abigail D. McElman
Lucy A., d. 8/1/1916 at 69/2/22; cancer of stomach; Richard V. Piper

RICHARDSON,
child, d. 11/22/1894 at –; premature birth; b. Dover; PH
child, d. 6/14/1925 at –; stillborn; Fred H. Richardson and Lillian V. Spurling
Alice L., d. 10/1/1913 at 50/6/27; chronic nephritis; Augustus Richardson and Lydia Davis
Annie M., d. 10/29/1905 at 73/10/11 in Lynn, MA; carcinoma
Arthur E., d. 6/14/1919 at 61/4/19 in Portsmouth; angina pectoris
Arthur S., d. 5/9/1935 at 49/5/12 in Portchester, NY; lobar pneumonia
Augustus, d. 7/3/1894 at 83; bronchitis; b. Dover; PH
Caroline, d. 6/20/1928 at 84/3/26; arterio sclerosis; Augustus Richardson and Abigail Hanson
Elizabeth, d. 8/26/1937 at 67/11/20; arteriosclerosis
Everett G., d. 10/2/1918 at 12/7/22; lobar pneumonia; George Richardson and Marion Browning
Fred E., d. 2/11/1929 at 86/5/1; influenza
George, d. 2/15/1896 at –; lack of vitality; PH
George H., d. 2/4/1926 at 66/11/27; chronic myocarditis; George Richardson and Margaret Maitland
Harriett E., d. 8/4/1921 at 62/3/11; angina pectoris; George H. Curtis
Isabella F., d. 5/21/1921 at 74/8/5 in W. Newton, MA; arterio sclerosis
James H., d. 3/2/1901 at 46/10/13 in Manchester; neuralgia of heart; PH
John, d. 5/15/1910 at 60/3; pulmonary tuberculosis; George Richardson and Margaret Malcolm
John W., d. 8/9/1916 at 18; acute alcoholism
Maria L., d. 7/29/1905 at 64/10/27 in Madbury; peritonitis
Marion, d. 5/13/1913 at 30/3/21; pneumonia, lobar; Thomas Denning and Eliza Battle
Martha J., d. 12/16/1937 at 70; cerebr. hemorrhage
Mary E., d. 5/24/1893 at 13; diphtheria; b. Dover; (ME; NH)

Mary E., d. 5/12/1923 at 78/7/8; cerebral hemorrhage; Jacob Jackman and Betsey -----
Mertie E., d. 11/26/1911 at 42/7/8; acute diabetes; Augustus A. Davis and Eliza J. Woodus
Norman, d. 7/26/1909 at 0/11/23; diarrhea; George W. Richardson and Marion Denning
Phyllis, d. 4/20/1929 at 10/4/8; tuberculous meningitis; H. B. Richardson and Rose E. Doyle
Pierson, d. 2/19/1908 at 92/0/9; old age; Nathaniel Richardson and Eunice Sanders
Stephen H., d. 4/23/1924 at 81/8/25; chronic myocarditis
William Tufts, d. 9/18/1927 at 61/2/17; chronic endocarditis; James A. Richardson and Harriet Evans

RICHMOND,
Allen P., d. 9/14/1912 at 86/4/21; pneumonia; John Richmond and Mary P. -----
Benjamin R., d. 2/14/1904 at 68/10/27; Bright's disease; PH
Charles A., d. 1/29/1937 at 61*; b. Somerville, MA
Charles B., d. 1/14/1907 at 75/2/26; cardiac insufficiency; John Dorr and Mary P. Richmond
Hannah E., d. 9/25/1913 at 76/6/14 in Lawrence, MA; cerebral apoplexy
Leigh, d. 12/18/1893 at 45; pneumonia
Marcia V., d. 12/5/1933 at 72/11/24 in Hingham, MA; angina pectoris
Martha J., d. 9/22/1905 at 68/11/16; meningitis; PH
Matilda H., d. 9/18/1912 at 74/0/27; accident; Henry Crawford and Mary ---
Nellie B., d. 8/12/1917 at 63/9/22; uraemia; Daniel E. Emerson and Elizabeth Roberts
Robert N., d. 3/28/1931 at 80/0/27; myocarditis
Willard L., d. 8/26/1909 at 44/6/11; asphyxia by illuminating gas; Charles B. Richmond and Hannah E. Nason

RICKER,
Abbie V., d. 6/28/1912 at 84/5/2 in Strafford; senile debility
Annie S., d. 7/20/1937 at 68/10/14 in S. Berwick, ME; fracture of hip
Benjamin F., d. 11/16/1899 at 40; consumption; buried in Somersworth
Bertha B., d. 11/30/1888 at 2/3/6; b. Dover; Frank W. Ricker (Dover) and Susie L. Smith (Deerfield)
Charles A., d. 8/22/1918 at 63; acute Brights disease; William W. Ricker and Sarah A. Downs
Charles E., d. 2/24/1917 at 67/11/10; cerebral embolism; Leonard S. Ricker and Elmira Emery
Clara A., d. 6/5/1934 at 91/8/7 in Uxbridge, MA; arteriosclerosis
Daniel, d. 5/21/1890 at 74/1/11; single; Nicholas Ricker (Dover) and Elizabeth Randall (Dover)

Elizabeth B. H., d. 4/10/1909 at 3/6; anaemia; Christian Ricker and Annie Kunkel
Elizabeth L., d. 6/12/1897 at 50 in Salem, MA; cardiac hypertrophy
Ephraim W., d. 10/17/1922 at 80/7/6 in Old Orchard, ME; apoplexy
Eugene, d. 10/4/1909 at 51/7/20; heart disease; Albert R. Ricker and Sarah A. Hartford
Florence, d. 7/2/1937 at 48/8/16*; b. Dover
George A., d. 5/7/1924 at 73/6/26 in Lynn, MA; cancer of stomach
George W., d. 7/25/1899 at 48 in Rochester; suicide with knife; PH
Hannah, d. 5/8/1908 at --; fracture of hip joint; James Whitham
Harriet J., d. 2/15/1918 at 81/5/28; lobar pneumonia; Jedediah Felch and Mary Hill
Howard, d. 3/18/1919 at 87/3/17; pneumonia, catarrh; Thomas Ricker
James Elmer, d. 5/6/1892 at 16; acute peritonitis; b. Lebanon, ME; (Rochester; Lebanon, ME)
John, d. 7/4/1895 at 77; general decay; b. Rollinsford; PH
John W., d. 5/7/1922 at 78; apoplexy
Julia A., d. 1/10/1909 at 60/6/8 in Lynn, MA; pneumonia
Leonard S., d. 3/29/1888 at 71/3; card stripper; widower; b. Dover; Timothy Ricker (Dover) and Abigail Varney (Dover)
Lizzie A., d. 1/24/1915 at 27/1/10; pulmonary tuberculosis; Charles E. Ricker and Helen Campbell
Marilla M., d. 11/12/1920 at 80/7/28; cerebral hemorrhage; Jonathan B. Young and Hannah D. Stevens
Mary A., d. 10/10/1906 at 66/7/22; carcinoma; PH
Mary E., d. 5/6/1917 at 46/8/29; pulm. tuberculosis; John F. Bean and Amelia A. Lewis
Mary J., d. 12/7/1910 at 83/11/27 in Rochester; carcinoma of sigmoid flex
Mary L., d. 11/29/1897 at 68 in Everett, MA; hemorrhage from tumor; PH
Mollie A., d. 7/9/1906 at 22/9/27; pulmonary tuberculosis; PH
O. P., d. 2/7/1892 at 42; cerebro spinal fever
Parmelia, d. 11/16/1908 at 87/0/26; senile debility
Rhoda, d. 1/25/1898 at 87; old age; b. Greenland; buried in Somersworth
Sarah A., d. 10/8/1893 at 69; heart disease; b. Barrington; (Rochester; Rochester)
Sarah A., d. 4/11/1908 at 68/0/22 in Haverhill, MA; apoplexy
Sarah W., d. 1/30/1908 at 75/10/11; old age; Isaac Whittier and Abigail Patten
Susan A., d. 9/7/1912 at 69/1/1; probably heart disease; Leonard Corson and Maria Freeman
Susan L., d. 2/25/1888 at 22/9/3; married; b. Deerfield; Simeon Smith (MA) and Elizabeth Lovering (NH)
William C., d. 1/30/1932 at 58/3/27; cancer of face
William H., d. 4/30/1904 at 53/6/27 in Rollinsford; cardiac hypertrophy; PH
William L., d. 11/30/1897 at 71 in Everett, MA; suicide by hanging; PH

RIDLEY,
Jennie S., d. 10/10/1927 at 70/10/11; intestinal obstruction; Levi Bracy and Harriett Weymouth
William T., d. 7/23/1897 at 0; premature birth; b. Dover; PH

RIEL [see Reil],
Frederick, d. 11/30/1915 at 41; apoplexy; Peter Riel and Alice ------
Matilda, d. 5/22/1914 at 64; gangrene of the foot; Noel Riel and Julia Carignan

RILEY,
child, d. 9/18/1897 at 2; cholera infantum; b. Dover
child, d. 5/17/1899 at –; stillborn; SM
Agnes, d. 3/7/1892 at 42; phthisis pulmonalis; b. Ireland; (Ireland; Ireland)
Bridget, d. 2/3/1897 at 53; apoplexy; b. Ireland; SM
Bridget, d. 6/7/1903 at 33; heart disease; SM
Bridget, d. 3/17/1904 at 66; rupture of aneurism; SM
Catherine, d. 3/25/1920 at 77; gen. arterio sclerosis; John Riley and Catherine Murtaugh
Delia, d. 12/1/1895 at 1; bronchitis; b. NH; SM
George W., d. 8/5/1921 at 17/9/9 in Barrington; tetanus
John, d. 12/24/1916 at 0/0/4; spinal meningitis; Frank Riley and Angie N. Crosmore
John J., d. 4/28/1900 at 35; bronchitis; buried in Manchester
Margaret, d. 12/1/1898 at 4; membraneous croup; b. Dover; SM
Margaret T., d. 4/6/1930 at 69; entero colitis
Patrick, d. 1/22/1892 at 88; la grippe; b. Ireland; (Ireland; Ireland)
Patrick, d. 9/16/1910 at 45; debility; John Riley and Bridget McGrory
Patrick, d. 2/21/1924 at 76 in Concord; broncho pneumonia; Patrick Riley and Sara Grimes
Thomas, d. 10/21/1891 at 29/10; married; (Ireland; Scotland)
Thomas, d. 8/28/1896 at 56; heart failure in gastritis; b. Ireland
Thomas E., d. 8/31/1889 at 3/8/18; b. Dover; Thomas Riley (Scotland) and Margaret Tracey (Ireland)

RINALDI,
Eleiseo, d. 3/21/1932 at 46/9/17; lobar pneumonia

RINES,
Arthur, d. 3/26/1887 at 3/0/20; b. MA; Amos H. Rines (ME) and Mary A. (MA)
Ellen M., d. 3/7/1914 at 74/11/26; apoplectic shock; Hiram Goodwin and Draxey Gowell
Ellen M., d. 11/10/1917 at 68/8/19; cerebral hemorrhage; Bowen Russell and Mehitable M. Locke

Frank, d. 6/4/1910 at 51/11/9; intestinal nephritis; John W. Rines and
   Sevina T. Clark
Gertrude H., d. 12/13/1933 at 50/0/28 in Laconia; angina pectoris
James A., d. 10/25/1925 at 72/11/25; lobar pneumonia; John W. Rines
   and Sevina Clark
John W., d. 11/2/1911 at 82/5/3; arthritis deformus; Nathaniel Rines and
   Nancy Davis
Nellie M., d. 5/31/1933 at 73/10/25; arteriosclerosis
Roxanna, d. 10/14/1912 at 86/1/19; cancer sigmoid flexure; Thomas W.
   Tibbetts and Meribah Hartford
Serina, d. 2/27/1890 at 56/7/14; married; Nathaniel Clarke (Limerick, ME)
   and Lydia Grover (So. Berwick, ME)
Walter H., d. 11/17/1913 at 50/11/11 in Laconia; Brights disease
William E., d. 6/7/1921 at 74/11/17; chronic nephritis; William H. Rines
   and Roxanna Tibbetts

RING,
Clarence E., d. 2/2/1913 at 1/1/5; gastric enteritis; Clinton L. Ring and
   Sarah Margerison
Dennis J., d. 9/6/1890 at 8/1/29 in Farmington
Gerald D., d. 2/11/1923 at 18/1 in Somerville, MA; diabetes mellitus
Lawrence A., d. 8/13/1913 at 58 in Tewksbury, MA; acute bac. dysentery;
   Terrence Ring and Bridget Cannon

RINK,
Allie M., d. 5/7/1920 at 71 in Philadelphia, PA; carcinoma of stomach
John J., d. 1/28/1908 at 61/9/15 in Melrose, MA; carcinoma of liver

RIPLEY,
George H., d. 4/4/1904 at 76/9/1; erysipelas; PH
Nancy B., d. 3/15/1910 at 85/3 in Waltham, MA; broncho pneumonia

RITCHIE,
William C., d. 10/17/1926 at 50/8/1; cerebral hemorrhage; Lewis Ritchie

ROACH,
Ellen, d. 3/16/1888 at 41; widow; b. Ireland; D. Mulcahey (Ireland) and
   Norah Lane (Ireland)
Margaret, d. 7/5/1897 at 70; heart disease; b. Ireland; SM
Michael J., d. 5/31/1891 at 18/2; single; Dennis Roach (Ireland) and Ellen
   Mulcahey (Ireland)

ROBERGE,
child, d. 9/8/1927 at –; stillborn; Ernest Roberge and Aldea Brouchard

Alphonse, d. 3/18/1925 at 29/6/18; septicemia; Francois Roberge and Caroline Binette
Archie, d. 5/25/1926 at 49/10; frac. cervical vertebrae; John Roberge and Jane Pepin
Aurelie Gar'n, d. 11/16/1911 at 85; old age
Donat, d. 6/16/1911 at 2/2/27; diph. laryngitis; Ferdinand Roberge and Exilia Martel
Joseph D., d. 9/10/1901 at 0/1/15; diarrhea infantile; SM
Malvina, d. 12/14/1909 at 46; phthisis

ROBERT,
Georgianne, d. 9/29/1905 at 42/11; cerebral hemorrhage
Loring C., d. 12/14/1893 at 87; old age; b. New Durham; (New Durham; --)

ROBERTS,
Aaron, d. 1/2/1900 at 69; rheumatism; PH
Ada Maticha, d. 3/21/1923 at 67/0/13 in Cambridge, MA; abscess of liver
Andrew J., d. 1/12/1902 at 71/3/26; appendicitis; PH
Andrew T., d. 3/15/1909 at 81/1/13; old age; Alonzo Roberts and Mary Torr
Ann E., d. 4/3/1904 at 70/10/29; cerebral hemorrhage; PH
Ann E., d. 11/27/1912 at 74/4/27; Brights disease; Aaron Roberts and Mary Bennett
Arabelle, d. 1/13/1924 at 74/2/12; chr. gastroenteritis; Joseph Roberts and Sarah Barker
Cassius B., d. 8/3/1898 at 23 in Chickamauga, GA; enteric fever; PH
Charles A., d. 6/25/1928 at 70/7 in Woburn, MA; myocarditis
Charles S., d. 11/9/1920 at 63/1/6; apoplexy; John Roberts and Jane -----
Charles W., d. 10/1/1900 at 78; ch. interstitial nephritis; PH
Clara B., d. 1/15/1898 at 28; consumption; b. Newmarket; buried in Newburyport, MA
Clara J., d. 7/15/1918 at 37/3/3 in Cambridge, MA; uraemia
Clarence H., d. 4/17/1905 at 48/2/5; consumption; PH
Clarissa, d. 8/31/1889 at 72/4/5; housekeeper; married; b. Parsonsfield, ME; Joseph Cooper and Mary Glidden (Effingham)
Cyrus, d. 11/22/1910 at 82/0/4; erysipelas
Edgar A., d. 1/22/1906 at 63/9/8 in Effingham; gastric catarrh; PH
Edith L., d. 5/27/1904 at 0/7/10; meningitis; PH
Elijah Estes, d. 9/5/1921 at 84/7/1; senile changes, etc.; Elijah Roberts and Susan Taylor
Elmira, d. 3/5/1921 at 91/10/7; cancer of uterus; Stephen Roberts and Lovey C. Canney
Emeline, d. 5/8/1902 at 85/8/5; burned to death; PH
Emily C., d. 10/28/1888 at 66/8/14; widow; b. Cornish; Sam. Houston (ME) and Charity M. (ME)

Emma H., d. 3/17/1925 at 71/9/14 in Boston, MA; arterio sclerosis
Frank I., d. 7/30/1887 at 53/10/15; single; b. Gorham, ME; Isaac S. Roberts (Alfred) and Hannah H. Lord (Lyman, ME)
Fred H., d. 10/7/1928 at 69/7; natural causes; Howard M. Roberts and Sarah T. Roberts
George, d. 6/7/1893 at 25; peritonitis; b. Dover; (Dover Point; Providence, RI)
George C., d. 6/22/1889 at 1/3/4; b. Dover; Charles S. Roberts (Chelsea, MA) and Ida F. Gage (Dover)
Harriet B., d. 8/15/1902 at 48/9/24; carcinoma; PH
Helen A., d. 11/16/1916 at 61/11/1; post operative shock; George Perkins and Jane Poore
Henry, d. 8/23/1900 at 69; cancer; PH
Howard M., d. 7/27/1917 at 84/11/12; arterio sclerosis; Hanson Roberts and Lydia Roberts
James P., d. 6/20/1927 at 64/3/8 in Alton; apoplexy
Jane, d. 2/9/1893 at 68; died in Strafford Co. Asylum fire
John, d. 8/20/1891 at 72/6/8; widower; Hanson Roberts (Dover) and Lidia Henderson (Dover)
John, d. 7/24/1894 at 76 in Effingham; dropsy; buried in Dover
John F., d. 1/9/1930 at 77/7/28 in Somerville, MA; John Roberts and Clara Cooper
John Franklin, d. 10/27/1922 at 36/7/26; arterio sclerosis; Charles S. Roberts and Ida F. Gage
Juliette W., d. 2/8/1904 at 81/10/25; old age; PH
Lizzie, d. 12/25/1899 at 63; pneumonia; buried in Rochester
Marcia Anna, d. 1/2/1926 at 81; organic heart disease; Ichabod Roberts and Betsy Smith
Margaret, d. 9/24/1934 at 56/4/27 in Lawrence, MA; embolism
Maria, d. 5/30/1894 at 84; old age; b. Milton; PH
Mark L., d. 11/9/1891 at 33/1; married; Levi F. Roberts (Rochester) and Rachel M. (Conway)
Mary, d. 8/10/1892 at 85; age, hastened by diarrhea; b. Dover; (-----; Rochester)
Mary A., d. 7/19/1909 at 75; fatty degeneration of heart; ----- Fay
Mary C., d. 11/20/1921 at 0/0/3; intestinal obstruction; Oliver C. Roberts and Ruth S. Walker
Mary E., d. 4/9/1900 at 55; pneumonia; PH
Mary Jane, d. 8/16/1911 at 76/3/27 in Holbrook, MA; cerebral hemorrhage
Paul W., d. 9/5/1912 at 0/2/16 in Somerville, MA; ch. intest. indigestion
Preston F., d. 12/9/1936 at 80/1/7; arteriosclerosis
Rosetta M., d. 1/17/1935 at 89/1/5; arteriosclerosis
Sarah T., d. 5/29/1923 at 83/10/19; acute bronchitis; Alonzo Roberts and Mary Torr

Seth, d. 11/21/1889 at 54/5/29; butcher; widower; b. Dover; Aaron Roberts and Mary B. Roberts
Stephen, d. 6/17/1890 at 93/0/18; married; James Roberts (Dover) and Eunice Varney (Rochester)
Stephen W., d. 7/26/1930 at 58/5/19; chronic alcoholism; Howard M. Roberts and Sarah T. Roberts
Thomas H., d. 6/21/1900 at 75 in Boston, MA; bronchitis; PH
Walter H., d. 6/22/1921 at 63/7/21 in Boston, MA; chronic myocarditis
Warren E., d. 11/12/1920 at 0/0/8; premature birth; Charles E. Roberts and Daisy S. Bridges
William E., d. 3/29/1917 at 42/8/22; septicemia; Simeon B. Roberts and Lydia J. Shackford
William Hall, d. 3/21/1910 at 0/0/6; purpura hemorrhagica; William P. Roberts and Mary Diana Blanchard

ROBERTSON,
Andrew B., d. 2/12/1901 at 35/1/4; phthisis pulmonalis; PH
Rachel E., d. 1/27/1908 at 36/4/21; cancer of liver; William Sykes and Ellen Haigh

ROBINSON,
daughter, d. 7/12/1889 at 0/0/2; b. Dover; Fred Robinson (Newport, NS) and Lois Leathers (Great Falls)
daughter, d. 3/14/1890 at –; Edward Robinson (US) and Annie Robinson (US)
child, d. 1/18/1901 at –; stillborn
child, d. 3/16/1908 at –; stillborn; George A. Robinson and Jennie A. Willey
child, d. 12/9/1915 at –; congenital atelestasis; Ralph Robinson and Elin Roy
Abbie C., d. 7/16/1901 at 59/7/28 in Concord; PH
Albert A., d. 12/10/1912 at 68/10/23; brain disease; John Robinson and Ruth Sweet
Ann M., d. 8/8/1910 at 92/3/22 in Medford, MA; arterio sclerosis
Annie A., d. 3/5/1934 at 67/3/1; cerebral hemorrhage
Annie J., d. 7/18/1907 at 67/4/11; diabetes; Abraham Cousins
Barbara L., d. 7/23/1932 at 2/2/10; tuberculous meningitis
Bertha E., d. 7/23/1929 at 0/0/25; pyaemia; Edmund Robinson and Frances E. Babb
Blanche C., d. 6/28/1915 at 1/3/8; tubercular meningitis; Andrew Robinson and Catherine Gorman
Blanche G., d. 4/18/1909 at 20/11/4; tuberculosis; Thomas Robinson and Rose Morrisete
Charles H., d. 3/11/1901 at 0/11; pneumonia; PH

Clinton B., d. 4/4/1916 at 76/2/2 in Boston, MA; arterio sclerosis; Abra Robinson and Harriet Hutchins
Cornelius, d. 6/4/1900 at – in Lawrence, MA; cerebral hemorrhage; PH
Daniel, d. 10/30/1890 at 28 in Rollinsford
Donald R., d. 4/19/1918 at 0/8/4; acute lobar pneumonia; George J. Robinson and Elizabeth A. Virtue
Edmund H., d. 4/20/1936 at 27/11/16; typhoid fever
Edward H., d. 2/17/1914 at 76/7/4; cardiac sclerosis; William Robinson and Rebecca Hammon
Elizabeth, d. 6/12/1906 at 55 in Concord; cerebral hemorrhage
Ella, d. 7/20/1925 at 75/6/19; chronic endocarditis; Joseph Turnbull
Emma B., d. 7/19/1917 at 69/1/24 in Los Angeles, CA; atheroma; Jasper G. Wallace and Clarissa Hussey
Etta J., d. 9/29/1913 at 57/3/1; chronic int. nephritis; Jacob Emery and Harriet Wilds
Frederick A., d. 9/13/1922 at 59/10/13 in York, ME; apoplexy
George H., d. 3/12/1902 at 54/4/27 in New Durham; consumption; PH
Gertrude, d. 7/9/1912 at 36 in Concord; heat exhaustion
Grace, d. 3/30/1891 at 0/1/5; Edward S. Robinson (No. Berwick, ME) and Annie A. Robinson (US)
Harriet M., d. 6/8/1922 at 98/0/15 in Boston, MA; chronic nephritis
Harriet W., d. 2/18/1890 at 81/10/27; widow; Jonathan York (Candia) and Mary (Candia)
Helen P., d. 4/11/1915 at 75; myocarditis; Evans Hayes and Margaretta Emerson
Helena L., d. 6/3/1928 at 77/1/19; cerebral hemorrhage; Ansel Atkins and Margaret Walker
James W., d. 6/17/1908 at 55/4/12 in Alton Bay; falling under cars
Joseph A., d. 4/17/1933 at 73/0/14; cancer of rectum
Lena Maud, d. 7/10/1916 at 41/3/21; mitral regurgitation; Benjamin Robinson and Ella Tumbull
Lizzie, d. 4/17/1909 at 68/2/4; pneumonia; John Smith and Lucena Pindar
Lois L., d. 6/3/1922 at 63/9/18 in Portsmouth; pulmonary oedema
Lydia G., d. 9/5/1904 at 80 in Framingham, MA; valvular heart disease; PH
Margaret, d. 12/24/1913 at 73/10/11; broncho pneumonia; M. McGuinness and Ellen Hughes
Mary, d. 4/26/1905 at 68/5/3 in Haverhill, MA; osteo tuberculosis
Mary, d. 8/23/1912 at 73/7/29; progressive paralysis; William Robinson and Rebecca Hammond
Mary Ann, d. 7/29/1898 at 79; syncope; b. Durham; PH
Mary C., d. 12/12/1921 at 86/9/9 in Portsmouth; lobar pneumonia
Mary F., d. 2/6/1924 at 76/7/20; cerebral embolism; Charles Tracey and Olive Gooch

Melnot J., d. 7/31/1914 at 0/8/19; acute entero colitis; George S. Robinson and Alice G. Shuffleberg
Nancy, d. 7/30/1912 at 76; hypostatic pneumonia; Patrick McGlone and Margaret ----
Rose A., d. 9/21/1919 at 52/2/7; paralysis of intestines; Joseph Morrisette and Odel Fortier
Roy, d. 8/12/1893 at –; infancy; b. Dover; (NB; NS)
Samuel N., d. 4/–/1891 at 50/2/1 in Durham
William, d. 6/8/1894 at 85; heart disease; b. Dover; PH
William, d. 5/5/1913 at 69; acute gastro enteritis
William E., d. 3/14/1912 at 78/2/16 in Portsmouth; valvular disease of heart
Winnifred, d. 7/19/1898 at 0; cholera infantum; b. Ireland (sic); PH

ROBITAILLE,
Alice, d. 5/9/1899 at 18; tuberculosis of the lungs; SM

ROCHE,
Thomas, d. 11/8/1922 at 97; uraemia; Thomas Roche and Hannah Mahoney

ROCHELEAU,
Gerard, d. 2/16/1917 at 5/10/26; broncho pneumonia; Maurice Rocheleau and Josie Martineau

ROCHELIEU,
Adeline, d. 3/27/1910 at 77/2/26; broncho-pneumonia; Andre Fouche and Marie Dubois

ROCHELLE,
Jane Tyson, d. 6/18/1935 at 22 in Washington, DC; primary acute dilatation

ROCHETTE,
Hector, d. 8/20/1898 at 24; railroad accident; SM

ROCKWOOD,
child, d. 4/3/1906 at – in Keene; stillborn; PH
Bernice Elizabeth, d. 10/2/1937 at 58/3/21*

RODDEN,
Annie, d. 6/29/1894 at 29 in Somersworth; consumption; buried in Rollinsford
Bernard, d. 9/28/1905 at 45/10/16; cancer of stomach

Bernard Joseph, d. 11/18/1910 at 28/10/10; chronic nephritis; Daniel Rodden and Margaret Hughes
Daniel, d. 7/17/1898 at 67; valvular disease of heart; b. Ireland; SM
Hugh, d. 2/24/1899 at 61 in Tewksbury, MA; cardiac disease
James, d. 6/14/1929 at 70; arterio sclerosis; Daniel Rodden and Margaret Mallon
John, d. 4/8/1904 at 60; SM
John, d. 4/23/1922 at 89 in Boston, MA; intestinal obstruction
Margaret, d. 4/8/1904 at 47; apoplexy; SM
Marjory A., d. 6/16/1911 at 3/0/4; membraneous croup; Hugh Rodden and Annie Sullivan
Mary E., d. 7/9/1922 at 52; apoplexy; Alexander McPherson and Mary McDonald
Myah S., d. 11/28/1932 at 31/1/13 in Bangor, ME; gas poisoning
Sarah, d. 4/2/1914 at 86 in Boston, MA; ch. valvular endocarditis

RODGERS,
Mrs. S., d. 9/8/1890 at 75; J. Hoit (Ireland) and ----- (Ireland)

ROGERS,
Albert E., d. 2/20/1898 at 48; thrown from sleigh; b. Dover; PH
Alice, d. 10/29/1908 at 55; valv. disease of heart; Patrick McNally and Catherine -----
Amasa A., d. 1/5/1912 at 64/2/15 in Brockton, MA; valvular heart disease
Amasa S., d. 2/17/1902 at 75/7/25 in Somersworth; hypertrophy of heart; PH
Bridget, d. 4/20/1905 at 50; typhoid fever; SM
Charles L. R., d. 10/7/1918 at 23/11/17 in S. Berwick, ME; lobar pneumonia
Edward, d. 8/18/1889 at 6; b. Biddeford, ME; John Rogers (Biddeford, ME) and Delia Kearns (Ireland)
Emma H., d. 10/24/1900 at 81; old age; buried in Eliot, ME
Eva B., d. 10/29/1921 at 27/6/20; septicemia; John H. Ferrin and Emma F. Guppy
Everlyn L., d. 11/10/1890 at 33/11/10 in Lynn, MA; David E. Hoyes (Jackson) and Lenora Mudget (Tamworth)
Francis, d. 2/6/1905 at 57; sudden; SM
Hugh, d. 3/4/1892 at 100; old age; b. Ireland; (Ireland; Ireland)
James, d. 7/21/1922 at 65; chronic endocarditis; Hugh Rogers and Sarah Haughey
Jettie H., d. 4/1/1932 at 78/8/27 in S. Berwick, ME; chr. valv. heart dis.
John, d. 7/16/1916 at 58; arterio sclerosis; Patrick Rogers and Ann McIntyre
John, d. 2/24/1932 at 69/6/9; arterio sclerosis

Joseph W., d. 12/23/1892 at 40; Bright's disease; b. Dover; (Ireland; Ireland)
Maria, d. 8/31/1914 at 59; mitral stenosis; William York and Maria Dunn
Martha, d. 4/19/1906 at 60 in Exeter; cerebral hemorrhage; PH
Martha A., d. 4/29/1929 at 85/3/26; fracture of hip; Hiram Rogers and Lucinda Wentworth
Mary, d. 11/24/1888 at 60; widow; b. Ireland; Owen Printy (Ireland) and Bridget Mooney (Ireland)
Mary, d. 8/26/1889 at 4/5; b. Biddeford, ME; John Rogers (Biddeford, ME) and Delia Kearn (Ireland)
Mary A., d. 8/14/1928 at 68; chronic myocarditis
Mary A., d. 11/18/1933 at 78/6 in Somersworth; pernicious anemia
Nancy, d. 3/25/1906 at 94/1/19 in Hastings, MI; nervous prostration; PH
Nancy T., d. 4/17/1893 at 76; latent pneumonia; b. Seabrook; (Seabrook; Seabrook)
Ralph R., d. 5/16/1933 at 55/0/21; coronary thrombosis
Rose, d. 3/26/1924 at 65; acute bronchitis; Edward McNally
William, d. 8/21/1887 at 0/10; b. Biddeford, ME; John Rogers (Biddeford, ME) and Delia Kerns (Ireland)

ROLFE,
Sarah G., d. 1/1/1910 at 53; cancer of liver; Coleman Bickford and Mary --

ROLLINS,
child, d. 9/29/1903 at 0/0/22; marasmus
Abbie, d. 9/26/1906 at 62 in Alton; cancer; PH
Benjamin F., d. 5/15/1918 at 68/8/8; cancer of prostate
Betharlena, d. 1/1/1937 at 49/10/23; convulsions
Catherine W., d. 8/13/1913 at 52/7/1; carcinoma; Andrew Rollins and Mary E. Pease
Charles K., d. 7/20/1902 at 63/5/20; chronic nephritis; buried in Alton
Charles W., d. 6/13/1900 at 72; inanition; PH
Charles W., d. 8/19/1937 at 75/3/17; cerebr. hemorrhage
Clarence Ira, d. 1/21/1892 at --; meningitis, cerebral; b. Dover; (Alton; Kennebunk, ME)
Daniel, d. 1/24/1900 at 41 in Boston, MA; typhoid fever; PH
Edward W., d. 10/6/1929 at 78/10/11; broncho pneumonia; Edward H. Rollins and Ellen E. West
Elizabeth W., d. 3/27/1911 at 73/10/26; senility; Daniel Rollins and Mary Plummer
Ethel M., d. 2/14/1896 at 8; capillary bronchitis; b. Dover; PH
Frank O., d. 7/8/1887 at 13/3/4; b. Holyoke, MA; C. A. Rollins (Lee) and Mary A. Haley (England)
George A., d. 6/30/1896 at --; cerebral meningitis; b. Dover; SM
George M., d. 2/2/1921 at 31/3/16 in Deerfield; pulmonary phthisis

Gladys B., d. 7/19/1917 at 31/8/25; pneumonia bronchial; Seldon L. Brown and Nellie A. Hubbard

Goldie, d. 5/2/1888 at 0/1; b. Dover; True Rollins (Deerfield) and Hattie Stanton (Dover)

Hannah, d. 9/20/1893 at 30; cholera morbus; b. Dover; (Ireland; Ireland)

Harriet E., d. 1/5/1920 at 24/10/7; phthisis; William Rollins and Ellen O'Neil

Hattie M., d. 2/27/1892 at 27; la grippe and hemorrhage; b. Dover

Jane S., d. 5/13/1907 at 77/0/13; Bright's disease; Robert Patterson

John F., d. 7/18/1905 at 70/0/14; senile dementia; buried in Rollinsford

John L., d. 10/30/1935 at 65/9/14; cancer of stomach

John M., d. 1/8/1928 at 67/5; cerebral hemorrhage; John H. Rollins and Nancy McDuffee

John P., d. 6/22/1907 at 83; cerebral thrombosis

Lillian M., d. 11/28/1914 at 58/8/7; lymphadenoma; William Lamont and Mary Kittredge

Lydia H., d. 6/4/1926 at 85/3/10; intestinal obstruction; Augustus Rollins and Abiah Winkley

Mary, d. 11/9/1894 at 92; old age; b. Somersworth; buried in Rollinsford

Mary, d. 8/23/1908 at 74/9/23; sclerosis of nerve centers; Aug. Rollins and Abiah Winkley

Mary E., d. 11/5/1911 at 67/1/28; pneumonia; Eben Gilman and Caroline Whitehouse

Mary E., d. 8/21/1913 at 60/0/6; pulmonary oedema; ----- Owens

Mary E., d. 7/26/1914 at 50/0/14; cancer of liver; John J. Dunn and Elizabeth Cochrane

Mina V., d. 1/31/1900 at 33 in So. Berwick, ME; tumor; PH

Montgomery, d. 4/18/1918 at 50/7/24 in Newton, MA; lobar pneumonia; Edward H. Rollins and Ellen M. West

Nellie, d. 12/27/1926 at 61/8/4; nephritis; Edwin Varney and Rebecca Young

Olive E., d. 11/8/1902 at 76/1; valvular heart disease; buried in Rollinsford

Peter, d. 3/13/1916 at 64 in Barrington; acute bronchitis

Richard D., d. 5/4/1930 at 0/0/23; dermat. exfoliation; Louie E. Rollins and Leila Stokes

Richard T., d. 9/16/1917 at 63/9/4; cancer of colon; Hiram W. Rollins and Mary J. Roberts

Samuel P. K., d. 4/21/1896 at 59; phthisis pulmonalis; b. Alton; PH

Susan E., d. 11/18/1930 at 88/8/16; lobar pneumonia; Samuel Watson and Olivia Hayes

Susie Belle, d. 4/28/1890 at 0/8/4; Stephen E. Rollins (Alton) and Annie C. Noble (Kennebunkport)

Thomas, d. 12/2/1907 at 57; gangrene, albuminuria

ROONEY,
Blanche M., d. 7/22/1917 at 32/6/14; pulm. phthisis; Henry P. Rooney and Ellen Ward
Elizabeth M., d. 5/18/1909 at 27/11/23; tuberculosis; Henry P. Rooney and Ellen M. Ward
Ellen W., d. 9/26/1928 at 78 in Portland, ME; arterio sclerosis
Henry P., d. 11/20/1915 at 67/1/5; valv. heart disease; James Rooney and Mary Brien
Susan, d. 7/8/1918 at 79; cancer of colon; Frank Goodwin and Hannah Austin

ROPES,
Levina, d. 3/26/1894 at 78; heart failure; b. Dover; buried in homestead lot

ROSE,
Jessie I., d. 2/11/1923 at 72/5 in Farmington; cerebral apoplexy

ROSS,
child, d. 5/17/1923 at –; stillborn; William Ross and Sibell Morceau
Alice Norwood, d. 1/17/1925 at 56/7/21; chr. parenchymat. neph.; Caleb J. Norwood
Amasa L., d. 3/2/1925 at 80/10/23 in Madbury; valvular heart disease
Avesia W., d. 2/15/1930 at 75/0/11; cerebral hemorrhage; John Reycroft
Dorcas W., d. 9/10/1902 at 88/8/25; cerebral apoplexy; PH
George I., d. 1/26/1930 at 50/5/1; phthisis; Charles H. Ross and Lucy Tibbetts
Louise B., d. 2/24/1926 at 0/8/21 in Madbury; pneumonia
Mareana, d. 7/30/1889 at 0/5/6; Lemuel Ross (Ireland) and M. Rosecroft (Ireland)
Martha Ella, d. 4/4/1933 at 76/7/11; heart disease
Maurice E., d. 4/10/1911 at 5/5/7; broncho-pneumonia; Stella Ross
Richard N., d. 1/29/1897 at 79; senile dementia; b. Rochester; PH
Samuel B., d. 1/6/1903 at 54; tuberculosis; PH
William J., d. 1/1/1907 at 73/1/25; innutrition; James M. Ross

ROSSI,
Rosaline, d. 6/26/1914 at 6/2; suffocation; Batiste Rossi and Rose Suiaro

ROSSITER,
Ann, d. 5/12/1902 at 82; old age; buried in Lawrence, MA
Ellen E., d. 4/24/1894 at 19; abdominal tumor; b. Dover; SM
Joanna, d. 5/22/1906 at 70; cerebral embolism
Joseph, d. 3/14/1891 at –; Pat. Rossiter (Ireland) and Julia Sullivan (US)

Joseph, d. 6/27/1925 at 84/8/8; chronic endocarditis; Michael Rossiter and Mary Kelley
Joseph William, d. 7/23/1918 at 57/10/7; pernicious anemia; Patrick Rossiter and Mary A. Sullivan
Julia, d. 1/1/1893 at 41; Bright's disease - chronic; b. So. Boston, MA; (Ireland; Ireland)
Mary E., d. 1/20/1899 at 14; phthisis; SM
Michael W., d. 11/26/1903 at 15; tuberculosis; SM
Nellie, d. 1/25/1905 at 34/8/3; tuberculosis of lungs
Patrick, d. 12/29/1908 at 72; carcinoma of rectum; Joseph Rossiter and Annie Flynn
Patrick H., d. 6/11/1912 at 66/2/14 in Boston, MA; pernicious anemia; William Rossiter and Anne Cash
Walter I., d. 4/7/1918 at 22/11/20 in Brooklyn, NY; diphtheria
William A., d. 8/24/1898 at 21 in Chickamauga, GA; typhoid fever; PH

ROTHWELL,
Ann, d. 2/9/1893 at 44; died in Strafford Co. Asylum fire
Ellen, d. 5/5/1898 at 75; heart disease; b. England; PH
Jeremiah, d. 2/3/1908 at 69/11/24; cerebral apoplexy; Richard Rothwell and Alice Nuttal
Josephine E., d. 12/28/1898 at 60; heart disease; b. Portsmouth; PH
Lavinia Isabel, d. 2/10/1925 at 70/11/18 in Portsmouth; sclerosis of spinal cord
Matilda F., d. 12/15/1932 at 81/4; cerebral hemorrhage
Richard, d. 9/5/1895 at 79; old age; b. England; PH
Richard N., d. 10/4/1910 at 50/0/11; odema of lungs; Richard Rothwell and Alice Nuttal
William H., d. 9/4/1924 at 77/9/1 in Brockton, MA; organic heart disease

ROUILLARD,
Ernest, d. 12/3/1905 at 0/6/3; convulsions; SM

ROUKE,
Alphonse L., d. 4/27/1911 at 27/8/7; struck by moving train; Vincent Rouke and Mary Donovan

ROUNDS,
Holmes B., d. 8/23/1916 at 81/9/4; cystitis; Joseph Rounds and Elsie O. Drew

ROUNDTREE,
Anne, d. 3/13/1917 at 51; cirrhosis of liver
William R., d. 2/4/1889 at 0/8; b. Dover; Robert Roundtree (Ireland) and Annie Flaherty (Ireland)

ROUNDY,
Addie B., d. 2/16/1936 at 60/10/15*

ROURKE,
James E., d. 12/29/1931 at 51/7/22; acute myocarditis
Margaret, d. 3/28/1925 at 81/5/8; ulcers of stomach; James Parle and Ellen Roche

ROUSIANS,
Azelda, d. 9/16/1897 at 35; peritonitis; b. Canada; SM

ROUSSAN [see Rousseau, Roussin],
Elizabeth A., d. 7/27/1920 at –; premature birth; George Roussan and Barbara Corson

ROUSSEAU [see Roussan, Roussan],
child, d. 2/22/1913 at –; premature birth; Claudius Rousseau and Eva Moreau
child, d. 5/29/1924 at –; premature birth; George B. Roussin (sic) and Effie Corson
Alexena, d. 3/7/1913 at 22/9/29; pleurisy; Louis Rousseau and Leda Giroux
Alphonse, d. 8/27/1932 at 48; aneurysm
Eva, d. 2/22/1913 at 30; hemorrhage; Louis Moreau and Tracile Deharrais
Isaac, d. 4/24/1918 at 91; arterio sclerosis
Josephine, d. 7/26/1893 at –; cholera infantum; b. Gorham; (Canada; Canada)
Louis, d. 4/17/1927 at 73/10/1; gen. arterio sclerosis
Sarah, d. 1/6/1921 at 63; apoplexy; Peter Giroux and ----- Fournier

ROUSSIN [see Roussan, Rousseau],
George B., d. 9/22/1928 at 53/2/20 in Concord; general paresis; Basil Roussin and Christine Stebbins
Richard J., d. 1/1/1929 at 0/0/1; premature birth; George B. Rousseau (sic) and Effie B. Corson

ROUSSINE,
Malvina, d. 1/5/1893 at 28; pulmonary embolvin; b. Canada; (Canada; Canada)

ROUTH,
child, d. 11/14/1912 at –; stillborn; Henry Routh and Amelia Richard
Robert, d. 12/26/1908 at 0/2/20; arthrepsia; Henry Routh and Amelia Richard

ROUTHIER,
Olivine, d. 2/21/1924 at 46/11/9; carcinoma of uterus; Paul Lessard and Emily Gregoire
Stanilaus, d. 1/23/1937 at 55/9/22 in Portland, ME; carcinoma stomach
Theodore, d. 4/10/1936 at 60; drowning, accidental

ROUTLEY,
Mary E., d. 12/27/1926 at 0/0/4; injury at birth; Bertram E. Routley and Gertrude V. Tallis

ROUX,
Alice, d. 4/22/1911 at 2/9; diphtheria; Raoul Roux and Florida Marcotte
Cora, d. 10/7/1893 at 4; meningitis; b. Canada; (Canada; Canada)
Pierre, d. 4/1/1921 at 80/1/13 in Milford; cerebral hemorrhage; Prudent Roux and Pelazie Boucher
Raoul, d. 12/22/1920 at 44/6/25; burns; Pierre Roux and Cleopheo Savoie
Robert E., d. 8/28/1915 at 0/9/14; acute entero colitis; Raoul Roux and Florida Marcotte
Romeo, d. 8/27/1911 at 8/5/24; chronic nephritis; Raoul Roux and Florida Marcotte

ROWAN,
Alice, d. 11/15/1906 at –; chronic nephritis; buried in Lawrence, MA

ROWE,
Benjamin F., d. 2/21/1913 at 65/11/24; senile gangrene; John Rowe and Mary S. French
Della D., d. 1/6/1934 at 84/8/22; chronic myocarditis
Edgar T., d. 9/14/1931 at 48 in Chelsea, MA; accidental
Elizabeth, d. 8/11/1913 at 43 in Warren, MA; carcinoma of liver; Henry Forbes
Frank B., d. 2/9/1893 at 25; died in Strafford Co. Asylum fire
Hattie F., d. 7/19/1893 at 41; hemorrhage
Henry E., d. 5/9/1936 at 81/8/10; cerebral hemorrhage
James, d. 12/7/1888 at 60/11/13; shoemaker; single; b. Dover; John Rowe and Dorothy Evans
Jesse, d. 11/13/1887 at 46/6; single; b. Dover
Levi, d. 8/16/1906 at 62/8/14 in Salem, MA; malignant tumor; PH
Louisa E., d. 2/2/1924 at 71/2/2 in Madbury; uremia; Enos P. Wormell and Cynthia Kempton
Mabel, d. 1/25/1892 at 8; pneumonia; b. Dover; (Dover; Dover)
Margaret A., d. 12/23/1913 at 81/8; heart disease; Oliver Boston and Dorcas Davis
Nancy C., d. 5/16/1916 at 84/10/5 in Barrington; diabetes
Samuel C., d. 4/16/1923 at 83/3/6 in Madbury; lobar pneumonia

Seth W., d. 4/22/1909 at 78/2/6; senility; John Rowe and Dorothy Evans
Walter E., d. 1/8/1892 at 24; phthisis (see following entry)
Walter E., d. 1/8/1893 at 24; phthisis (see preceding entry)

ROWELL,
Frank H., d. 4/8/1933 at 86/4/10; chronic cystitis
Jennie I., d. 8/13/1936 at 42/6/4 in Rollinsford; carcinoma liver
Lilla M., d. 8/27/1900 at 25 in East Chester; hemorrhage of lungs; PH

ROWEN,
Patrick J., d. 12/22/1914 at 57; cancer of stomach; Michael Rowen and Bridget Riley

ROY,
Dorothy Mary, d. 10/10/1928 at 0/3/23; athrepsia; Wallace J. Roy and Rita McMooney
Edward J., d. 1/12/1919 at 34/4; influenza; Joseph Roy and Josephine Lecouline
Elizabeth, d. 1/12/1919 at 27/8/14; broncho pneumonia; Edward Mullen and Margaret Hughes
Flora B., d. 4/20/1922 at 44/0/22; cerebral hemorrhage; Warren G. Hagar and Abbie Littlefield
Joseph G., d. 5/26/1922 at 38/1/24; ac. lobar pneumonia; Jean B. Roy and Mary Pouliot
Louise G., d. 2/2/1931 at 0/0/4; premature birth
Marie, d. 11/2/1910 at —; premature birth; Joseph Roy and Anna Gingras
Mary, d. 12/12/1906 at 49/11/12; cancer of the womb

ROYCROFT,
John, d. 5/10/1930 at 63 in Haverhill, MA; carcinoma

ROYER,
child, d. 11/27/1931 at —; stillborn
Alphonse J., d. 9/20/1928 at 68/6/15; carcinoma of stomach; Alphonse Royer and Rosalie Turgeon
Theophile P., d. 2/5/1926 at 75/10/4; gen. arterio sclerosis; Prudent Royer and Emilie Poucis
Wilfred, d. 6/12/1933 at 32/5/8; intra cranial hem.

RUDDOCK,
Minnie, d. 6/30/1892 at 1; pneumonia; b. Boston, MA; (Charlestown, SC; Dover)

RUDOS,
George, d. 12/4/1911 at 20; fract. cervical vertebra; John Rudos and Loe Delifesis

RUEST,
Agnes, d. 7/20/1933 at 2/6/16; miliary tuberculosis

RUNDLETT,
James H., d. 10/17/1898 at 66; uremic coma, Bright's disease; b. Stratham; buried in Stratham
Margaret I., d. 10/27/1926 at 95/0/14; cerebral hemorrhage; John Brown and Margaret Parke
Samuel, d. 3/15/1906 at 91/11/4; old age; buried in Durham

RUNLETT,
Carrie E., d. 12/24/1931 at 88/7/3; cerebral hemorrhage
Ellen M., d. 5/31/1936 at 85/11/17*
Samuel, Jr., d. 3/4/1937 at 86/4/29*

RUSH,
Delia S., d. 2/24/1925 at 72; myocarditis; Patrick Feeney and Ellen Burns

RUSS,
Bernice Etta, d. 3/5/1888 at 0/3/9; b. Rochester; F. E. Russ (St. Johnsbury, VT) and Katie Downing (Concord)
Emily E. H., d. 11/7/1936 at 75/11/25; chr. myocarditis
Harry G., d. 3/19/1897 at 9 in Madbury; tuberculosis meningitis; b. Rochester; PH
Hattie M., d. 2/4/1894 at –; meningitis; b. Dover; PH
Orrin B., d. 5/2/1925 at 89/1/24 in Portsmouth; lobar pneumonia
Sarah, d. 4/6/1909 at 75; taxaemia

RUSSELL,
Abby O., d. 1/12/1901 at 35/1/8 in New York, NY; typhoid fever; PH
Adeline D., d. 11/27/1899 at 76 in Methuen, MA; mitral insufficiency; PH
Annie B., d. 10/5/1918 at 45/8/15 in Exeter; locomotor ataxia
Fannie M., d. 1/8/1916 at 35 in Lakeland, FL; dysentery
Florence D., d. 12/7/1888 at 1/5/4; b. So. Berwick, ME; George W. Russell (Andover, MA) and Lydia M. Grant (S. Berwick, ME)
George W., d. 2/7/1914 at 60/6/6; apoplexy cerebral; Joseph Russell and Martha Mears
Margaret, d. 6/6/1934 at 78/9/7; gangrene of leg
Mary E., d. 1/2/1900 at 61; heart disease; PH

Percy H., d. 7/8/1908 at 40/4/27; crushed chest and spine; Enoch G. Russell and Caroline V. Joll
Robert J., d. 7/4/1911 at 67/11/4 in Lynn, MA; locomotor ataxia

RUST,
Charles A., d. 11/14/1907 at 77/7/17 in Rochester; apoplexy
John R., d. 9/12/1899 at 71 in New York City; nephritis; PH
Mary A., d. 9/4/1901 at 73/7/23 in Rochester; phthisis pulmonalis; PH
Mary L., d. 3/3/1911 at 79/1/4; peritonitis; Andrew Pierce and Abigail S. Osborne

RUTLER,
George, d. 10/18/1935 at 73/1/9 in Lawrence, MA; cerebral hemorrhage

RUTTER,
Ann E., d. 5/20/1905 at 52/9/7 in Pleasant Twp., OH; apoplexy; PH
Emma, d. 2/18/1907 at 75/0/28; senility; John Silcock and Anna Bramhall
John W., d. 10/24/1925 at 70/11/24 in Lawrence, MA; lobar pneumonia
Thomas, d. 2/25/1887 at 58/2/4; farmer; single; b. England; George Rutter (England) and Ann Griffin (England)

RYAN,
Anastasia, d. 1/12/1919 at 81; cerebral apoplexy
Cornelius, d. 5/2/1903 at 82 in Somersworth; cystitis; PH
Dennis D., d. 1/31/1898 at 45 in Norwich, CT; intermittent fever; b. Ireland
Edward, d. 12/1/1921 at 70; carcinoma of stomach; James Ryan and Mary Whelen
Eliza, d. 7/14/1914 at 46/5/11; cancer of breast; James Ryan and Mary Pheland
Elizabeth, d. 5/7/1937 at 67/5/15*
Ellen, d. 11/15/1902 at 30; SM
Isabelle, d. 3/18/1889 at 23/6; mill operative; single; b. Portland, ME; Thomas Ryan (Ireland) and Mary Murphy (Ireland)
James, d. 10/9/1911 at 82/4/17; traumatism
James, Jr., d. 1/23/1898 at 37; scarlet fever; b. Dover; SM
John, d. 4/18/1889 at 71/10; laborer; married; b. Ireland; Peirce Ryan (Ireland) and Mary Durgin (Ireland)
Katherine, d. 8/23/1907 at 23/5/13; abortion; Michael J. Ryan and Capitola Sherman
Lucy O. C., d. 3/22/1899 at 28; pulmonary phthisis; PH
Maggie, d. 12/2/1902 at 35; SM
Margaret, d. 1/10/1899 at 70; old age; SM
Mary, d. 9/27/1889 at 59; housewife; widow; b. Ireland; H. Murphy (Ireland) and Ann Henetta (Ireland)
Mary, d. 1/31/1912 at 86; senility; Patrick Cronin and Catherine -----

Mary, d. 5/10/1915 at 86/4/20; atheroma; James Phelan and Mary -----
Mary A., d. 9/13/1908 at 41/9/13; pulmonary tuberculosis; M. McGuinness
 and Katherine Duffy
Mary J., d. 5/23/1931 at 75 in New York; chronic myocarditis
Patrick, d. 7/22/1899 at 80; strangulation with food; SM
Thomas, d. 7/29/1887 at 67 in Alton Bay; b. Ireland
Thomas, d. 2/3/1892 at 38; phthisis; b. Portland, ME; (Ireland; Ireland)

ST. CYR,
son, d. 7/2/1888 at 0/0/10; b. Dover; Olivia St. Cyr (Canada) and Georgie
 Dupee (Canada)
child, d. 4/14/1934 at –; stillborn
Dezilda, d. 6/19/1932 at 55/0/22; carcinoma
Mary, d. 3/14/1929 at 70/11/126; gen. arterio sclerosis; A. Grondin and
 Margaret Raiche
Thomas, d. 12/1/1923 at 0/0/2; icterus neonatorum; Joseph St. Cyr and
 Margaret McGinn

ST. HILAIRE,
Florentine, d. 4/25/1922 at 0/7/13; broncho pneumonia; William St. Hilaire
 and Laura Gilbert

ST. JEAN,
child, d. 11/26/1901 at –; stillborn
Alfred, d. 11/24/1902 at 0/0/13; gastro-enteritis
Arthemise, d. 3/1/1914 at 78; hemiplegia; Elaurie Tremblay and Marie
 Remond
Auguste, d. 9/15/1903 at 0/4/26; cholera infantum
Edmond, d. 9/7/1904 at 0/4/18; gastro-enteritis
Harold R., d. 2/24/1917 at 0/10/14; suppurative otitis media; Emma R. St.
 Jean
Harriett, d. 5/23/1934 at 63/2/2; acute myocarditis
Henry, d. 8/12/1891 at 0/4/15; Samuel St. Jean (Canada) and Hattie
 Lefebore (PA)
Henry, d. 5/3/1913 at 0/2/29; pneumonia; Louis St. Jean and Frances
 White
Joseph T., d. 3/20/1925 at 66/2/8; cerebral hemorrhage; Prudent St. Jean
 and Artemise Tremblay
Marie, d. 4/9/1925 at 70 in Concord; broncho pneumonia; Lewis Pencence
 and Angela Rockeford
Maud, d. 11/26/1909 at 34; gall stones; Placi Lefbher and Georgianna
 Docelle
Raymond, d. 4/6/1906 at 38; suicide by hanging; SM
Robert, d. 3/3/1914 at 0/1/5; marasmus; Samuel St. Jean and Hattie
 Lefebre

ST. JOHN,
Frank, d. 4/23/1901 at 1/8/28; pneumonia; SM
Harry, d. 8/31/1911 at 12/3; meningitis; Samuel St. John and Hattie
  Lefevre

ST. LAURENT,
Adelina, d. 9/29/1904 at 60/7/14; heart disease; buried in Newmarket
Albert, d. 1/29/1930 at 0/3/29; malformation; William St. Laurent and
  Faleda Grondin
Almena, d. 4/4/1906 at 3/9/25; pneumonia
Georgianna, d. 11/15/1901 at 46; cerebral paralysis; buried in
  Somersworth
Joseph, d. 7/25/1921 at 0/0/1-4; premature birth; William St. Laurent and
  Valida Grondin
Marie, d. 7/25/1921 at –; premature birth; William St. Laurent and Valida
  Grondin
Robert J., d. 10/1/1924 at 1/11/23; tubercular meningitis; Albert St.
  Laurent and Dora R. Lamothe

ST. LAWRENCE,
Arthur J., d. 9/14/1914 at 3/1/14; entero colitis; Emil St. Lawrence and
  Mary Croft

ST. MARIE,
Ludger, d. 5/3/1932 at 44; hit by automobile

ST. THOMPSON,
Elizabeth, d. 1/20/1906 at 71 in Newton, MA; amyotrophic lateral sclerosis;
  PH

SADLER,
Albert C., d. 12/26/1933 at 81/2; cerebral embolism

SAGA,
child, d. 7/7/1922 at –; stillborn; Mary Saga

SAGER,
John R. W., d. 6/16/1928 at 66/11/27; angina pectoris; Martin Sager and
  Alice -----
Mary Josephine, d. 3/4/1927 at 59/7/16; cerebral hemorrhage; Thomas
  Murphy and Ann Loughlan

SAKLERS,
Ellen, d. 9/14/1913 at 22 in Tewksbury, MA; tubercular peritonitis

SALINGER,
Carrie, d. 10/29/1927 at 83/0/5; cerebral hemorrhage; David Salinger and Rebecca Barstow
Julius, d. 5/28/1917 at 60/5/20 in Boston, MA; catarrhal jaundice

SAMPSON,
Edward, d. 4/19/1895 at 56 in Lynn, MA; acute pleurisy; buried in Dover
James, d. 10/24/1887 at 82/1/28 in RI
Mary, d. 10/23/1888 at – in RI

SANBORN,
Audrey, d. 1/28/1937 at 21/4/30; fracture of skull
Elizabeth T., d. 5/21/1934 at 63/9/1 in Birmingham, AL; carcinoma of cervix
Emily H., d. 4/30/1926 at 78/9/25 in Newbury, MA; cardiac insufficiency
Emma J., d. 11/16/1907 at 50/5/12; nephritis; John T. Manson and Mary J. Sawyer
Grover C., d. 7/28/1892 at –; diarrhea; (Great Falls; Madison)
Helen, d. 6/2/1893 at 47; consumption of the lungs
Hiram W., d. 9/14/1923 at 76/11/7; diabetes mellitus; Abram Sanborn
John G., d. 4/27/1924 at 41/4/22; Parkinson's disease; John J. Sanborn and Ella C. Grant
Leila A., d. 1/6/1903 at 56/3/6; apoplexy, cerebral; buried in Chichester
Mary P., d. 4/9/1910 at 24/5; pulmonary embolism; ----- Shelf and Mary Mallon
Mary R., d. 1/26/1925 at 82; arterio sclerosis; Abraham Sanborn and Mary Harriman
Moses, d. 8/2/1910 at 68/3/20; chronic nephritis; Benvolio Sanborn and Ann Lane
Willard T., d. 5/11/1911 at 51 in Birmingham, AL; cancer of pancreas

SANDER,
George J., d. 2/24/1919 at 0/0/2; hemorrhage of lungs; Henry F. Sander and Gesine E. Myer

SANDERS,
child, d. 4/26/1913 at –; stillborn; Mary Sanders
Anna, d. 4/22/1888 at 74/7/17; widow; b. Strafford; Jacob Drew (Strafford) and ----- Drew (Strafford)
Anna V., d. 7/28/1909 at 44/2; cerebral hemorrhage; Joseph A. Cate and Mary E. Leighton
Arthur K., d. 1/18/1918 at 61 in Middletown, CT; illuminating gas poison
Calvin, d. 1/16/1911 at 65 in Philadelphia, PA; cancer of stomach
Charles G., d. 6/19/1934 at 60/6/1; intestinal obstruction

Clara M., d. 12/17/1930 at 75/2/5; cerebral hemorrhage; Amos Cousins and Hannah Lord
Drusilla S., d. 11/4/1906 at 86/11/29 in Boston, MA; senility; PH
Ernest F., d. 3/21/1919 at 21/3/11 in Kittery, ME; lobar pneumonia
Etta E., d. 8/6/1898 at 50; suicide by hanging; b. Bucksport, ME; PH
Harriett A., d. 12/21/1899 at 0 in Madbury; malformation of heart; PH
John B., d. 7/12/1905 at 87/10/25; senility; PH
Levi G., d. 6/9/1909 at 64/9/5; chr. valvular dis. of heart; Levi Sanders and Anna Drew
Maribah B., d. 11/4/1912 at 87/2/6 in So. Haven, MI; senility
Orren S., d. 11/20/1898 at 78 in Boston, MA; uraemia; PH
Perley W., d. 1/6/1900 at 28 in Durham; acute Bright's disease; buried in Dover
Samuel, d. 9/11/1887 at 93/5/29 in Madbury; farmer; b. Strafford; William Sanders and Comfort Drew
Sarah V., d. 7/11/1931 at 30/10/5 in Exeter; miscarriage
Stanislaus S., d. 12/30/1929 at 80/7/22; angina pectoris; Dietritch Sanders and Anna -----

SANDIFORD,
Margaret E., d. 3/14/1931 at 61/0/14 in Lowell, MA; abdominal cancer
Richard H., d. 3/18/1907 at 0/1/25; bronchitis; William T. Sandiford and Margaret E. Howarth
William S., d. 2/13/1927 at 51/5 in Lowell, MA; acute peritonitis

SANDS,
Daniel, d. 3/24/1923 at 78/0/28 in Lewiston, ME; pneumonia
Frank H., d. 7/26/1890 at – in Lewiston, ME; single; Daniel Sands (England) and Lora Thatcher (VT)

SANFORD,
William H., d. 8/5/1923 at 56/3/25 in Wells, ME; cerebral hemorrhage

SANGER,
Dorcas M., d. 3/16/1913 at 0/2/27; acute pneumonia; George Sanger and Sarah E. Anthony

SARCHFIELD,
Catherine, d. 10/21/1899 at 71; pneumonia; buried in Rollinsford

SARGENT,
Alice O., d. 1/13/1930 at 72/9/12; chronic myocarditis; Nathan O. Mitchell and Nancy Pray

Annie M., d. 11/2/1910 at 77/10/15; old age; G. W. Wendell and Prudence
    Jenness
Benjamin, d. 3/6/1897 at 38 in Portsmouth; heart disease
Eben S., d. 10/17/1917 at 66/11; cancer of stomach; Caleb Sargent and
    Sarah J. Reed
James H., d. 7/21/1935 at 75/2/13; carcinoma sigmoid
James Kenneth, d. 6/23/1920 at 28/5/10; acute nephritis; James H.
    Sargeant (sic) and Alice O. Mitchell
Julia M., d. 2/8/1893 at 26; phthisis pulmonalis; b. Dover; (Sandwich;
    Brookfield)

SARKIAN,
Markon, d. 5/21/1915 at 50; acute oedema of lungs; Sarkos Sarkian and
    Miriam -----

SASAIN,
Peter, d. 1/2/1907 at 2/6; measles; George Sasain and B. Erabe

SAUNDERS,
Clara A., d. 10/17/1908 at 65/4/22; dropsy; Horace Taylor and Clara
    Perkins
Corinne, d. 8/6/1928 at 0/7/15; cong. malf. of heart; Myer Saunders and
    Goldie Kraft
Edward T., d. 2/6/1921 at 78/3/8; liver growth; Thomas Saunders and
    Betsey Flanders
Lena M., d. 8/13/1918 at 65/0/10; chronic Brights disease; Ira F. Pinkham
    and Syrena Cousins
Russell, d. 2/16/1911 at 63/4/30 in Barnstead; senile gangrene
W. H., d. 3/17/1891 at 62/3/19 in Chicago, IL; married; Job Sanders (Rye)
    and Polly McFarland (Derry)

SAVILLE,
Lizzie, d. 3/28/1921 at 66 in Brookline, MA; double lobar pneumonia

SAVOIE,
child, d. 8/2/1894 at –; lack of vitality; b. Dover; SM
Joseph, d. 7/9/1917 at 76/6; mitral regurgitation; Robert Savoie and
    Sophia Sylvester
Joseph W., d. 7/5/1911 at 38/4/13; acute meningitis; Joseph Savoie and
    Zoe Roy
Mary A., d. 8/19/1932 at 48/4/13; chronic nephritis
Raymond, d. 8/8/1915 at 0/4/10; acute entero colitis; Joseph Savoie and
    Caroline Lizotte
Zoe, d. 4/21/1927 at 83/5/4; chronic endocarditis; Laurent Roy and Emelie
    Blais

SAWTELLE,
Sarah D., d. 1/13/1894 at 46; phthisis pulmonalis; b. New York; SM

SAWYER,
Aaron, d. 2/15/1917 at 86; gastro enteritis
Abbie Martica, d. 5/7/1911 at 57/6/29; uraemia; W. C. Sturtevant and Nancy Hurd
Bradley M., d. 9/14/1921 at 16/8/15 in Washington, ME; poliomyelitis; Frederic R. Sawyer and Mabelle Molliet
Charles W., d. 1/18/1908 at 67/9/18; chronic cystitis; Jonathan Sawyer and Martha Perkins
Earle W., d. 10/24/1933 at 36/9; pulmonary tuberculosis
Edward, d. 1/22/1924 at 49/7 in Brunswick, GA; arterio sclerosis; Charles H. Sawyer and Susan Cowan
Elizabeth M., d. 9/11/1887 at 67/10/21; housewife; widow; b. Parsonsfield, ME; Daniel K. Moody (Parsonsfield, ME) and Eliza Sargent (ME)
Florence M., d. 3/8/1936 at 54/6/15; rt. lobar pneumonia
Frederick, d. 2/14/1929 at 74/1/7; arterio sclerosis; Thomas E. Sawyer and Elizabeth Moody
Frederick J., d. 11/28/1902 at 42/6 in New Bedford, MA; post diphthretic paralysis; PH
Gloria Mary, d. 4/30/1935 at 0/2/25 in Lee; asphyxia
Gorham H., d. 7/18/1923 at 57/1/3 in Lee; tabes dorsalis
Henry C., d. 6/3/1904 at 53 in Westboro, MA; general paralysis of insane; PH
Isabelle, d. 12/29/1896 at 37 in Boston, MA; cancer; PH
Jonathan, d. 6/20/1891 at 74/0/14; married; Phineas Sawyer (Harvard, MA) and Norma M. Whitney (Harvard, MA)
Joseph B., d. 7/18/1905 at 72/7/28; arteriosclerosis; PH
Lydia E., d. 3/10/1896 at 58; anaemia and heart disease; b. Dover; PH
Mabel, d. 5/16/1930 at 50/6 in Boston, MA; ac. lymph. leukemia
Martha P., d. 1/19/1896 at 79; nephritis; PH
Mary E., d. 2/26/1899 at 56; heart disease; PH
Susan E., d. 4/20/1899 at 59 in Boston, MA; cerebral effusion; PH
William, d. 5/17/1913 at 63/9/23; heart disease; Thomas E. Sawyer and Elizabeth Moody
William D., d. 11/12/1922 at – in New York, NY; cerebral hemorrhage

SAYER,
Alfred H., d. 8/30/1887 at 0/1/1; b. Dover; Alfred R. Sayer (England) and Elizabeth Cook (England)
Alfred R., d. 3/9/1934 at 82/1/9 in Conway; arteriosclerosis

SAYERS,
James A., d. 6/29/1919 at 59/5; pneumonia; James M. Sayers and Elvira Blakesley
Nellie A., d. 1/29/1903 at 20/2; typhoid pneumonia; PH

SAYLES,
Susan E., d. 1/19/1897 at 63; uraemia; b. Ossipee; PH

SAYLOR,
Franklin, d. 3/18/1927 at 74/1/17; cerebral hemorrhage; Jacob Saylor and Mary Bradley

SAYRE,
Eliza L., d. 2/12/1932 at 78/2/6 in Conway; myocarditis

SAYWARD,
Carol B., d. 11/28/1933 at 0/0/5; union of cranial bones
Edwin A., d. 12/6/1933 at 55/5/23 in Brookline, MA; cardiac embolism
Fred, d. 8/22/1926 at 70/5/27 in Seattle, WA; chronic myocarditis
George Henry, d. 11/20/1923 at 72/9/6 in Winchester, MA; chronic nephritis
Georgianna A., d. 3/31/1923 at 74/1/3 in Boston, MA; thrombosis
Henry, d. 2/11/1901 at 82/2/12; old age; PH

SCALA,
Innocenzo, d. 7/14/1935 at 54/11/14; pulmonary abscess

SCALES,
Burton T., d. 2/3/1922 at 48 in Philadelphia, PA; erysipelas; John Scales and Ellen T. -----
Catherine L., d. 4/28/1902 at 75/2/26 in Concord; organic heart disease; PH
Ellen T., d. 12/28/1920 at 77/6/28; broncho pneumonia; Alfred Tasker and Mary Hill
John, d. 7/7/1928 at 92/9; cerebral hemorrhage; Samuel Scales and Betsy True

SCAMMELL,
Margaret, d. 10/7/1928 at 78; gen. arteriosclerosis; William Corcoran and Mary Noonan
Sarah, d. 5/6/1895 at 70; apoplexy; b. Ireland; SM

SCAMMON,
Sarah F., d. 10/8/1920 at 89/11/17; cerebral hemorrhage; Joseph Stackpole and Lydia Wentworth

SCANLON,
child, d. 4/27/1899 at –; premature birth; SM
Andrew, d. 10/29/1893 at 53; peritonitis; b. Ireland; (Ireland; Ireland)
Bridget, d. 4/30/1900 at 35; exhaustion; SM
David, d. 6/5/1898 at 23; phthisis; b. Dover; SM
David, d. 3/9/1908 at 10; meningitis; William Scanlon and Bridget O'Neil
Elizabeth, d. 4/19/1920 at 21/1/17; pulmonary tuberculosis; James Scanlon and Sarah -----
Francis J., d. 7/2/1893 at 27; dropsy; b. Richmond, ME; (Ireland; Ireland)
Honora, d. 4/10/1896 at 55 in Ireland; Bright's disease; b. Ireland; SM
Joanna, d. 1/21/1917 at 64; gen. arterio sclerosis; William Corcoran and Mary Sullivan
John, d. 9/7/1898 at 2; meningitis; b. Dover; SM
John, d. 6/2/1920 at 0/2/20; athrepsia; Elizabeth Scanlon
John A., d. 9/18/1893 at 30; heart disease; b. Dover; (Ireland; Ireland)
Mary, d. 10/4/1893 at 72; old age; b. Ireland; (Ireland; Ireland)
Mary, d. 3/3/1897 at 19; pulmonary phthisis; b. Ireland; SM
Mary E., d. 7/26/1908 at 48; ascites; Andrew Scanlon and Honor -----
Mary E., d. 7/26/1908 at --; heart disease; John Scanlon and Mary -----
Mary S., d. 4/8/1920 at 58 in Haverhill, MA; metastatic car. of clav.
Nora, d. 4/28/1902 at 41/6/2; ulcerative stomatitis; SM
Patrick, d. 5/25/1892 at –; pneumonia; b. Dover; (Ireland; Ireland)
Patrick, d. 1/22/1899 at 46; heart disease; SM
Thomas F., d. 1/20/1894 at 29; pulmonary phthisis; b. ME; SM
William S., d. 7/8/1895 at 0; marasmus; b. Dover; SM
William S., d. 10/28/1932 at 62/8; influenza

SCANNEL,
Catherine, d. 7/19/1888 at 26/6/24; mill operative; single; b. Ireland; David Scannel (Ireland) and Ellen (Ireland)

SCANNELL,
Cornelius, d. 3/6/1919 at 77; apoplexy; Bartholomew Scannell and Julia Hanigan
Dennis, d. 5/7/1922 at 54; chronic endocarditis; Dennis Scannell and Ellen Leahy
Joseph, d. 12/19/1894 at 38; chronic pneumonia; b. Ireland; SM

SCARFF,
John W., d. 1/15/1902 at 39/0/22 in Rochester; pneumonia; PH

SCARPONI,
Donald, d. 12/27/1929 at 1/2; Amos Scarponi and Lona Potter

SCARR,
Alice M., d. 7/26/1926 at 59/5/25; chronic myocarditis; Sidney M. Towle and Lavonie Corson
Thomas, d. 7/12/1917 at 37 in Boston, MA; carcinoma, etc.

SCATES,
Eliza J., d. 3/2/1916 at 77/2/21; cerebral hemorrhage; Eri N. Scates and Mary W. Smith
George R., d. 10/29/1926 at 63/10/16 in Acton, ME; carcinoma of prostate; Theodore C. Scates and Eliza J. Drew
Theodore C., d. 9/29/1897 at 22 in Portland, ME; pulmonary tuberculosis; PH

SCHATZLE,
child, d. 11/5/1921 at –; asphyxia of labor; Max Schatzle and Emma Spillman

SCHOONMAKER,
Thomas W., d. 4/21/1928 at 63/8/2; angina pectoris; Thomas Schoonmaker and Elizabeth -----

SCHULTZ,
Annie G., d. 4/9/1928 at 60/9/7 in Concord; gen. para. of insane; Oliver W. Coleman and Emma L. Davis

SCHUYLER,
Augustus D., d. 4/11/1920 at 76/8 in Tilton; cerebral embolism
Catherine, d. 12/27/1913 at 68; epithelioma; M. McDonough and Mary Feeney
Mary E., d. 3/28/1916 at 43/1/5; catarrhal pneumonia; Augustus Schuyler and Johanna Goggin

SCHWARZ,
Ed. W., d. 3/25/1919 at 33; broncho pneumonia; Elsie -----

SCLERIS,
Elias, d. 3/14/1920 at 0/5/12; abscess of pharynx; George Scleris and Katherine Giftakis
Fortene, d. 5/10/1920 at 8/9/12; tubercular meningitis; George Scleris and Katherine Giftakos

SCLIRIS,
Pelagria, d. 10/21/1924 at 7/7/1 in Portsmouth; septic peritonitis

SCOTT,
child, d. 9/24/1920 at –; stillborn; John D. Scott and Alexina James
Carrie A., d. 10/31/1925 at 55/10/20 in Norwich, CT; chronic myocarditis
Clarence A., d. 12/20/1934 at –; stillborn
Daniel M., d. 11/3/1891 at 5; John Scott (Scotland) and Jane McIntire (Scotland)
David, d. 10/27/1891 at 10; John W. Scott (Scotland) and Jane McIntire (Scotland)
Jane McI., d. 3/2/1932 at 85/10/11 in N. Andover, MA; chronic myocarditis
Jessie, d. 4/27/1930 at 89/7/18 in S. Berwick, ME; chr. valv. heart dis.
John, d. 1/24/1918 at 82/0/24; chronic prostatitis; James Scott and Janet McCloud
John Anderson, d. 9/6/1892 at 24; phthisis
Nettie D., d. 11/13/1891 at 12; John W. Scott (Scotland) and Jane McIntire (Scotland)
Reuben, d. 2/3/1922 at 60; dilatation of heart
Robert L., d. 10/31/1891 at 7; John Scott (Scotland) and Jane McIntire (Scotland)
Susie A., d. 5/28/1920 at 83/11/10 in Concord; broncho pneumonia; John Main and Susan Corson

SCRIBNER,
Berton, d. 4/16/1903 at 0/1/6; inanition; PH
Flora I., d. 4/16/1933 at 77/11/14; chronic endocarditis
Maud H., d. 7/29/1889 at 14/2/20; student; b. Topsham, VT; B. Frank Scribner (Corinth, VT) and Maria N. Cilly (Topsham, VT)

SCRIGGINS,
Albert H., d. 5/27/1902 at 48/5/7; endo-carditis; PH
Alice C., d. 6/2/1887 at 83/11; single; b. Kingston
Frank, d. 2/9/1893 at 35; died in Strafford Co. Asylum fire
Mary M., d. 2/24/1914 at 99/9/2; old age; Daniel Quimby and Susan Murray
Mary S., d. 3/11/1892 at 72; valvular disease of the heart

SCRUTON,
Edward J., d. 6/27/1920 at 63/7/24; mitral regurgitation; Miles Scruton and Lydia A. Yeaton
Lewis A., d. 12/9/1932 at 64/2/12; natural causes
Lovey E., d. 1/1/1932 at 73/7/21; intestinal hemorrhage
Orrin A., d. 12/28/1933 at 68/3/2; coronary thrombosis

SCULLY,
Dennis, d. 10/21/1892 at 60; heart disease; b. Ireland; (Ireland; Ireland)

SEAMANS,
Annie A., d. 4/25/1916 at 46 in Taunton, MA; heart disease
Daniel C., d. 7/22/1915 at 21/5/17; diabetes mellitus; Henry C. Seamans and Rose A. Moreland

SEARS,
Deborah Ann, d. 11/17/1914 at 87/7/5; old age; Daniel York and Elizabeth Langley
Emily M., d. 7/31/1917 at 9/1/21; nephritis; Bernard Sears and Mary G. Rust
Lewis H., d. 10/3/1926 at 75/2/23; broncho pneumonia; Paul Sears and Eunice T. Crosby

SEAVER,
Dellow R., d. 6/27/1928 at 7/6/16; acute nephritis; Ralph K. Seaver and Agnes M. Leveille
Doris L., d. 8/9/1935 at 9/2/23; anterior poliomyelitis
George F., d. 1/9/1902 at 66/10/27; myetitis; buried in Somersworth
Hannah M., d. 1/19/1936 at 67/6/23*; b. Dover

SEAVEY,
Abbie S., d. 6/16/1900 at 59; cirrhosis of liver; buried in Rochester
Adelaide C., d. 11/12/1904 at 62/7; apoplexy; PH
Albert F., d. 12/16/1909 at 64 in Belmont, MA; cerebral thrombosis
Amy Thatcher, d. 8/28/1912 at 35/2/13; sarcoma of the pleura; George W. Thatcher and Harriet G. Steele
Andrew J., d. 12/12/1893 at 65; pneumonia - heart failure; b. NH; (NH; NH)
Arthur J., d. 6/28/1915 at 56/2/3; pneumonia; Jonathan T. Seavey and Abigail H. McDuffee
Aurelia J., d. 2/7/1909 at 85/0/18; pneumonia; James K. Jordan and Nancy Corson
Austin F., d. 7/7/1913 at 67/11/9; Brights disease; Warren Seavey and Mary Hussey
Caroline L., d. 1/2/1903 at 78/8/18; pneumonia; PH
Christianna M., d. 10/14/1918 at 72/5/13; influenza; Leonard Cheney and Christianna Haynes
Cynthia A., d. 10/5/1893 at 61; stricture of the bowels; b. Dover; (NH; Dover)
Frank W., d. 10/28/1921 at 63/11/29; myocarditis; Warren Seavey and Olive A. Staples

Harriet F., d. 12/4/1930 at 69/8/1; cerebral hemorrhage; Daniel Rokes and Laura Thompson
Helen Grace, d. 4/27/1902 at 19/6/5; typhoid pneumonia; PH
J. Herbert, d. 5/23/1916 at 68/4/25; cerebral hemorrhage; Jonathan Seavey and Abigail McDuffee
James Frank, d. 8/15/1920 at 82/0/1; cerebral degeneration; Samuel F. Seavey and Eliza Ham
John, d. 5/16/1897 at 83; old age; b. Barrington; buried in Rochester
Leonard R., d. 11/9/1933 at 27/10/4; chronic nephritis
Marietta Fogg, d. 11/24/1927 at 64/11/2; endocarditis; Charles F. Fogg and Rebecca Webster
Mary A., d. 11/11/1920 at 69/6/21; carcinoma of liver; John Yeaton and Susan F. Haley
Nellie A., d. 5/12/1927 at 62/1/12; myocarditis; Oliver Wentworth and Lucinda Willey
Reuben, d. 9/7/1896 at 84; old age; b. Alton; buried in Barrington
Sarah, d. 3/8/1887 at 88/0/4; widow; b. Pittsfield; ----- Sanborn
Sarah A., d. 7/11/1934 at 84/0/12; arteriosclerosis
Sarah F., d. 3/26/1900 at 61 in Pine Hurst, NC; hemorrhage tuberculosis; PH
Sarah Jane, d. 3/10/1902 at 70/9/10 in Westford, MA; cancer in breast; PH
Warren, d. 11/26/1887 at 76/3/15; farmer; married; b. Alton; Samuel Seavey (Barrington) and Abigail Davis (Barrington)
William H., d. 11/16/1898 at 76; fatty degeneration of heart; b. Dover; PG

SEAWARDS,
Cecil L., d. 9/24/1918 at 6/3/7; bronchial pneumonia; Cecil L. Seawards and Irene Allard
Harlan M., d. 10/2/1918 at 2/2/9; pneumonia; Cecil L. Seawards and Irene F. Allard
Horace M., d. 3/21/1929 at 87/3/3; arterio sclerosis; Richard Seawards and Sarah Patch
Maurice C., d. 6/27/1915 at 0/3; cong. heart malformation; Cecile L. Seawards and Irene F. Allard

SEEKINS,
Agnes S., d. 4/4/1893 at 49; chronic bronchitis; b. Cincinnati; (USA; USA)

SEGEE,
James S., d. 11/7/1914 at –; stillborn; Louis S. Segee and Hannah R. Bardsley
Marie A., d. 2/3/1919 at 0/11/10; entero colitis; Amedee Segee and Cordelia Royer
S. Russell, d. 11/6/1936 at 19/7/10*

SEIDEL,
Adolph, d. 11/18/1919 at 62/0/1 in Boston, MA; meningitis; Gotlieb and Bentia
Lena, d. 4/16/1902 at 40/2/9; nephritis; PH

SELLEA,
Annie E., d. 11/21/1924 at 79/3/18 in Grafton, MA; arterio sclerosis
John H., d. 3/24/1916 at 69/3/2; senile neurasthenia; Charles H. Sellea and Elizabeth Taylor

SELLECK,
Frances E., d. 7/25/1927 at 69/1/25; septicaemia; Zephaniah Eddy and Maria Morgan

SELLINGHAM,
Andrew J., d. 10/8/1930 at 75/6/7; lobar pneumonia
Elizabeth W., d. 2/27/1933 at 74/0/29; chronic nephritis

SENATE,
Howard E., d. 3/12/1937 at 64/6/11; chr. endocarditis

SENEY,
Frederick N., d. 5/26/1910 at 0/2/18; entero colitis acute; Napoleon Seney and Bessie May Shorey
Mabel E., d. 7/28/1909 at 0/4/12; gastroenteritis; Paul Seney and Bessie Shorey

SENNOTT,
Walter, d. 12/8/1918 at 55 in Boston, MA; chronic myocarditis

SENTNER,
William H., d. 2/17/1923 at 66/11; arterio sclerosis; George Sentner

SESIN,
Kasin, d. 8/26/1926 at 4/10/7; tubercular peritonitis; Bolus Sesin and Eva George

SEVERANCE,
Henry W., d. 2/12/1908 at 79/7; procitis; Luther Severance and Ann Hamlin
Joseph B., d. 8/14/1906 at 71/2/5; valvular disease of heart; buried in Biddeford, ME
Marion A., d. 3/15/1930 at 0/0/7 in Rochester; convulsions

SEVIGNY,
Alphonse, d. 4/24/1901 at 0/7; measles
Arthur, d. 2/2/1934 at 68/1/9; angina pectoris
Clarina M., d. 11/7/1913 at 0/1/1; pneumonia; Eugene Sevigny and
  Armenie Charest
M. Emilia, d. 7/22/1900 at <1; cholera infantum
Merina, d. 6/8/1931 at 24/4/1; tuberculosis of lungs
Philias, d. 7/19/1905 at 1/4/1; pneumonia

SEWELL,
Arthur, d. 9/14/1934 at 59/8/13; angina pectoris
Mary, d. 1/19/1937 at 52/2*; b. NB

SEYMOUR,
William T., d. 6/6/1901 at 32/4/25; phthisis; buried in Newmarket

SHABOT,
Joseph R., d. 9/17/1912 at 0/0/3; unknown; Lousa Shabot and Philomene
  Labonte

SHACKFORD,
Caroline C., d. 11/21/1897 at 50; pulmonary consumption; b. Ware; PH
Samuel B., d. 2/21/1934 at 62 in Boston, MA; cardiac val. disease

SHACKLEY,
Adelia F., d. 1/26/1929 at 74/1/11 in Framingham, MA; scarlet fever;
  Thomas Brown
Clara I., d. 2/13/1893 at 45; abdominal cancer; b. Sandwich; (Sandwich;
  Sandwich)
Cora A., d. 9/21/1914 at 49/8/11; chr. intestinal nephritis; Horace Shackley
  and Nancy Rounds
Frank W., d. 1/29/1912 at 58/5/18 in S. Framingham, MA; apoplexy
George D., d. 3/23/1935 at 69/4/15 in S. Portland, ME; myocardial
  insufficiency and pulmonary oedema
Marion E., d. 4/9/1896 at –; cerebral contusions; b. Dover; PH
Nathan, d. 6/5/1899 at 70 in Wolfeboro; atheroma of arteries; PH
Susan F., d. 7/4/1887 at 58/6/11 in Wolfeboro

SHAHEEN,
Avare, d. 5/19/1915 at 26; tuberculosis; Salem Gabers and Mary Resha
Robert C., d. 10/10/1926 at 7/4/8; unknown; Chickory Shaheen and Mary
  Frances

SHAIN,
Elizabeth J., d. 3/22/1931 at 83/10/6 in Effingham; bronchial pneumonia

SHANNAHAN,
John E., d. 9/5/1913 at 39; septicaemia; Michael Shannahan and Hannah McQuinn

SHANNON,
Francis E., d. 10/11/1924 at 2/3/2; pneumonia; S. W. Shannon and Isabel Beaulieu
Hugh, d. 8/10/1934 at 63/13/4; arteriosclerosis
John E., d. 12/7/1894 at 34; phthisis pulmonalis; b. England; buried in Somersworth

SHAPLEIGH,
Elizabeth J., d. 1/9/1899 at 81; old age; buried in Lebanon, ME
George E., d. 1/1/1900 at <1; pneumonia; PH
Julia, d. 3/18/1917 at 82/9/24; senility; John D. Dodge and Sophia Howard
Mary Ellen, d. 4/24/1891 at 46/4/2; married; John Lumbard (Saco, ME) and Olive A. Wilson (Biddeford, ME)
Percy C., d. 11/18/1918 at 33 in Brockton, MA; pulmonary tuberculosis

SHARP,
Marjorie C., d. 3/29/1931 at 56/8/11 in Norwood, RI; carcinoma of breast

SHARPE,
Ann James, d. 5/19/1918 at 87/5; chr. intestitial nephritis
William K., d. 8/4/1914 at –; angina pectoris

SHARPLEY,
George H., d. 1/12/1910 at 65 in Tilton; cancer liver and stomach

SHATSWELL,
Mary E., d. 4/7/1900 at 84; pneumonia; PH

SHATTUCK,
Annie M., d. 5/26/1923 at 68/9/27; diabetes; William Shepard and Demaris Tilton
Louise M., d. 8/15/1931 at 0/2/3; congenital heart dis.

SHAW,
child, d. 3/17/1891 at –; Newell H. Shaw (Freedom) and Emma A. Currier (Clinton, ME)

child, d. 9/16/1892 at –; debility - premature birth; b. Dover; (Freedom; Clinton, ME)
child, d. 8/6/1901 at 0/0/½ in Manchester, CT; no vitality; PH
child, d. 12/3/1919 at –; premature birth; Pliny G. Shaw and Alice M. May
Albert C., d. 12/16/1910 at 70; cancer of intestines
Albion K. P., d. 10/19/1897 at 68; heart disease; b. York, ME; PH
Alexander, d. 12/5/1916 at 70/5/23; acute indigestion; James Shaw and Jeannette Dickey
Annie, d. 4/30/1892 at 62; heart disease; b. Ireland; (Ireland; Ireland)
Christopher, d. 3/8/1918 at 75/11/12 in Strafford; arterio insufficiency
Clara A., d. 8/17/1922 at 75/1; carcinoma of intes.; H. A. Whitehouse and Clarissa D. Pierce
Clara J., d. 2/21/1935 at 51/4/24; cerebral hemorrhage
Henry A., d. 8/21/1899 at 38; meningitis; buried in Haverhill, MA
Jackson, d. 2/18/1907 at 78/2/18 in Effingham; consumption
Jennie H., d. 10/20/1919 at 68/8/10 in Manchester; cancer of lungs; Stephen Varney and Nancy -----
John A., d. 1/20/1907 at 59/5 in Camden, NJ; apoplexy
John L., d. 11/16/1904 at – in New York, NY; fatty heart; PH
Louise, d. 2/26/1935 at 82/11/6; chronic myocarditis
Martha, d. 8/5/1901 at 29/11/26 in Manchester, CT; child birth; PH
Mary A., d. 3/24/1900 at – in Brockton, MA; cancer; PH
Mary A., d. 5/6/1902 at 68/5/17 in No. Andover, MA; apoplexy and old age
Melvin A., d. 5/14/1889 at 1/6/6; b. Dover; Alexander Shaw (NS) and Louise Littlefield (Kennebunk, ME)
Nancy M., d. 4/5/1907 at 84/2/17 in Portsmouth; old age
Newell H., d. 4/14/1931 at 70/10/11; gen. arterio sclerosis
Richard G., d. 3/3/1931 at 58/2/18; nephritis
Robert J., d. 3/19/1908 at –; pneumonia; Robert Shaw and Margaret Johnston
Robert J., d. 12/14/1930 at – in Boston, MA; heart disease
Sarah E., d. 10/15/1933 at 90/3/9; chronic nephritis
William, d. 4/16/1910 at 77/11/10 in Lawrence, MA; myocarditis

SHEA,
Ed., d. 8/10/1891 at –; Ed. Shea (Ireland) and Bridget Shea (Ireland)
Ellen, d. 6/8/1907 at 74; old age; Dennis Sullivan and Mary Burke
John J., d. 12/23/1932 at 72 in Boston, MA; arterio sclerosis
John Morley, d. 6/27/1915 at 14/2/13; peritonitis; John Joseph Shea and Cecelia Fallon
Margaret E., d. 3/7/1919 at 73/8/24; cancer bowels and stomach; William N. Hart
Mary E., d. 1/9/1914 at 57; gangrene of leg; Jeremiah Shea and Ellen Sullivan

Mrs. Ed., d. 8/10/1891 at 26; married; Ed. Shea (Ireland) and Bridget McNally (Ireland)
Patrick J., d. 2/14/1932 at 73/10/4; arterio sclerosis
Rose, d. 8/19/1933 at 75; cerebral hemorrhage

SHEAFE,
Maria J., d. 1/26/1913 at 58/7/20; mitral regurgitation; Alexander Lane and Mary J. Snell
Rose E., d. 10/22/1935 at 79/7/4 in S. Berwick, ME; carcinoma uteri
William H., d. 3/1/1937 at 82/7/10 in Concord; valv. heart disease

SHEEHY,
child, d. 1/5/1911 at –; dystocia; Patrick Sheehy and Emma Rowe
Edward, d. 1/4/1923 at 65; gangrene (right leg); Patrick Sheehy
Hilda F., d. 10/19/1929 at 6/4/22; diphtheria; Patrick J. Sheehy and Maud A. Giroux
John F., d. 8/19/1896 at –; cholera infantum; b. Dover
Katherine, d. 12/1/1908 at 44; gastro intestinal indigestion; Owen Kelley and Katherine Markey

SHEGHAN,
Margaret R., d. 10/1/1932 at 13/1/1; meningitis

SHEHANE,
child, d. 9/3/1917 at 3 hrs.; premature birth; Shickory Shehane and Mary Francis

SHENTON,
child, d. 1/28/1927 at –; stillborn; Herbert Shenton and Rose Hassan

SHEPARD,
Charles P., d. 2/20/1897 at 71; prostration; b. Somersworth; PH
Charlotte E., d. 12/22/1919 at 69/4/2; probably apoplexy; John J. Nesmith and Lydia A. Richardson
Elizabeth A., d. 6/28/1894 at 68; paralysis; b. Somersworth; PH
Enoch F., d. 3/30/1904 at 84/2/27; senile dementia; buried in Strafford
Eugene G., d. 4/17/1935 at –; cerebral embolism
Hannah, d. 12/11/1894 at 83; vital exhaustion; b. Wolfeboro; buried in Wolfeboro
Susan, d. 9/17/1899 at 76; cerebral apoplexy; buried in Strafford

SHEPARDSON,
Ray, d. 1/3/1887 at 0/2/18; b. Dover; E. D. Shepardson (Shrewsbury, MA) and Mabel L. Jones (England)

SHERBURN,
Greenleaf R., d. 6/19/1901 at 55; PH

SHERLOCK,
Pauline, d. 11/12/1918 at 0/0/23; marasmus; John Sherlock and Margaret Mulligan

SHERMAN,
Ann S., d. 7/13/1900 at 60; aortic aneurism; PH
Ellen E., d. 5/5/1917 at 71/3/5 in Boston, MA; carcinomatosis
Susie I., d. 4/5/1900 at 29; val. disease of heart; buried in Somersworth

SHERRY,
child, d. 2/10/1896 at –; stillborn; SM
Ann, d. 9/9/1922 at 76/3/9; cerebral hemorrhage; Patrick McLin and Mary Mone
Bridget, d. 7/4/1911 at 68; hot weather; ----- Valley and Nancy Wood
Catherine, d. 11/16/1909 at 45/6/15; intestinal obstructions; John Lanigan and Catherine Grady
Frank J., d. 10/12/1905 at 42; accident or suicide; SM
James, d. 12/20/1923 at 82; cerebral hemorrhage; Patrick Sherry and Catherine Keating
John, d. 3/5/1917 at 73; post operative pneumonia; Patrick Sherry and Catherine Keating
Joseph J., d. 1/2/1912 at 15/10/28; acute dilitation of heart; Frank J. Sherry and Catherine Lanigan
Marie A., d. 12/23/1929 at 75/9/5; chr. endocarditis; John C. Hughes and Ellen McClosky
Marie G., d. 5/28/1928 at 30/3/7; typhoid fever; George H. Sherry and Jennie E. Early
Michael, d. 10/16/1924 at 78/6/15; angina pectoris; Patrick Sherry and Catherine Keating
Mildred V., d. 8/23/1913 at 12/6/26; miliary tuberculosis; George H. Sherry and Jennie C. Early
Patrick, d. 5/9/1896 at 60; accidental drowning; b. Ireland; SM
Thomas, d. 7/29/1923 at 72/3/26; chronic nephritis; Patrick Sherry and Catherine Keating
William James, d. 4/20/1893 at –; acute hydrocephalus; b. Dover; (Dover; Dover)

SHEVENELL,
Louis N., d. 5/26/1928 at 67/11/3 in Haverhill, MA; carcinoma rectum; Louis Shevenell and Philomene Ramillard

SHIBBEL,
child, d. 5/4/1928 at —; stillborn; Joseph Shibbel and Josephine Cyr

SHIBEL,
Calil, d. 4/15/1910 at 24; typhoid fever

SHIRLEY,
Harry B., d. 6/25/1890 at 35/2/13; single

SHOREY,
child, d. 1/19/1928 at —; stillborn; Clifton N. Shorey and Virginia Emerson
Annette, d. 12/20/1921 at 86; internal injuries; ––––– Farwell
Charles W., d. 1/4/1895 at 0; pneumonia; b. Dover; PH
Clara M., d. 1/13/1931 at 72/2/27; cancer of breast
Elbridge A., d. 2/26/1920 at 52/6/14; suicide by shooting; Simon Shorey
    and Adelaide Abbott
Francis A., d. 8/25/1907 at 79/0/28; nephritis; John Shorey and Mary A.
    Stanley
James F., d. 6/7/1896 at 1; pneumonia; b. Dover; buried in Somersworth
Lillie M., d. 12/10/1891 at 34/2; single; Henry Shorey (Great Falls) and
    Melissa Goodwin (So. Berwick, ME)
Norman A., d. 5/5/1936 at 60/1/7; pulmonary oedema

SHORTRIDGE,
John L., d. 12/6/1912 at 76/3/8; paresis; James Shortridge and Mary
    Nutter
Susan E., d. 8/25/1934 at 85/9/26; arteriosclerosis

SHRAMM,
Paul H., d. 8/4/1935 at 67/7/12; heart disease

SHUPE,
Glenwood W., d. 9/16/1915 at 4/2/14; acute dilat. of heart; Harry G. Shupe
    and Mildred E. Hanscom
Mildred E., d. 4/9/1922 at 32/0/7; lobar pneumonia; Frank C. Hanscom
    and Ella F. Dorrell
Richard C., d. 1/25/1935 at 0/0/3; congenital atelectosis

SHUTE,
Albert T., d. 2/10/1896 at 49; phthisis pulmonalis; b. Dover; PH
Josephine A., d. 9/25/1936 at 85/1; intes. obstruction

SIAS,
Charles, d. 6/6/1907 at —; drowned; a/k/a Charles Brown

Herbert, d. 9/27/1909 at 29/10/7; fract. skull by locomotive; Sylvester Sias and Sarah J. Philpot

SIBLEY,
Charles W., d. 2/25/1910 at 65; cerebral apoplexy

SIDEBOTHAM,
Edmund W., d. 2/9/1911 at 29/3/9; uraemia; John Sidebotham and Sarah H. Heeney

SIEGEL,
Max, d. 9/19/1915 at 38; appendicitis; Abraham Siegel and Florence -----

SIKISIS,
child, d. 2/5/1921 at –; stillborn; Niclis Sikisis and Helen Marko

SILCOCK,
Amelia, d. 12/22/1915 at 81/11; senility; John Silcock and Hannah Bramhall
Elizabeth, d. 11/24/1891 at 67/4/10; single; John Silcock (England) and Hannah Bramhall (England)

SILVA,
Manuel P., d. 7/30/1888 at 0/11/17; b. Dover; Manuel P. Silva (Portugal) and Mary E. McCone (Ireland)

SILVEY,
Adeline, d. 3/22/1923 at 83/5/26; la grippe; Calvin Hervey and Anna Lewis

SILVIA,
Mary E., d. 5/30/1935 at 74/5/30 in Lewiston, ME; cerebral embolism

SIMES,
Alice M., d. 8/21/1930 at 58 in Concord; acute dil. of heart; William Simes and Amanda Vickery
Amanda M., d. 3/11/1920 at 78/3/11; lobar pneumonia; John S. Vickery and Mary A. Cook
William, d. 12/17/1907 at 76/11/26; cerebral hemorrhage; Bray N. Simes and Martha Spinney

SIMMONDS,
Emeline B., d. 12/17/1928 at 81/1/10; fracture of skull; Benjamin F. Tyler and Joanna Fellows

SIMMONS,
Charles W., d. 8/20/1932 at 52/2/21; chronic myocarditis (see following entry)
Charles W., d. 8/23/1932 at 52; chronic myocarditis (see preceding entry)
Frank, d. 11/6/1887 at 61/7/12; laborer; married; b. Ireland; Peter Simmons (Ireland) and Mary (Ireland)

SIMON,
Simon E., d. 4/3/1917 at 1/7/6; convulsions; Elias Simon and Mary Coury

SIMONDS,
Georgia A., d. 7/29/1915 at 40/9/15 in Pittsfield; carcinoma; George Randall and Julia A. Burns
Rena R., d. 8/17/1895 at – in Worcester, MA; gastritis; buried in Dover

SIMONEAU,
child, d. 10/28/1914 at –; stillborn; Rose Simoneau
George E., d. 12/11/1907 at 0/0/3; acute hepatitis; George Simoneau and Isabelle Leary
Henry B., d. 8/15/1913 at 24/1/26; pneumonia; Joseph F. Simoneau and Celine M. Forrest

SIMPKINS,
Georgianna, d. 4/25/1907 at 61/10/3; burns; John Ricker and Parmelia Peavey
Luke, d. 3/23/1900 at 65; abdominal cancer; PH

SIMPSON,
child, d. 12/12/1917 at –; premature birth; John H. Simpson and Bertha G. Grant
Arthur, d. 6/4/1904 at 31 in Lebanon, NH; accident
Ellen, d. 7/2/1914 at 81/4/6 in Fitchburg, MA; old age
Harriet, d. 11/22/1912 at 75; senility
Ida G., d. 8/31/1917 at 51/9/9; secondary anemia; Samuel T. Dunn and Catherine T. Waldron
Inez, d. 9/14/1892 at 27; acute peritonitis; b. Dover
John, d. 5/16/1892 at 49; accident; b. England; (England; England)
Samuel L., d. 10/10/1907 at 75; valvular heart disease; William Simpson and Betty Firth
William P., d. 2/11/1913 at 53/10/4; pneumonia; Samuel Simpson and Ellen Pearson

SINCLAIR,
Harry H., d. 6/26/1937 at 67/10/5; coronary thrombosis

Willis, d. 3/25/1914 at 62/8/2; heart disease; Moses Sinclair and Lucarta Higgins

SINKERSON,
George A., d. 2/15/1901 at 31/6/24 in New York City; struck by locomotive; PH

SINKINSON,
Thomas, d. 5/5/1902 at 34/9/13; tuberculosis; PH

SINNOTT,
Margaret, d. 7/11/1930 at 81; natural causes; George Sinnott and Elizabeth Schall

SIRANIAN,
child, d. 6/20/1916 at –; knot in umbilical cord; John Siranian and Ruth Whitehouse
Nasaret, d. 2/19/1929 at 0/4/16; pneumonia; Siran Siranian

SISK,
E. J., d. 2/11/1892 at 41; paralysis and heart failure; b. NB; (Ireland; Ireland)
Martha A., d. 11/10/1915 at 64/4/2 in Waltham, MA; chronic myelitis

SKALTSIS,
child, d. 3/14/1919 at –; stillborn; James Skaltsis
child, d. 8/9/1921 at –; stillborn; George Skaltsis and Catherine Markos
Asenia, d. 1/18/1922 at 27; catarrhal pneumonia
Helen, d. 7/30/1931 at 38 in Boston, MA; pemphigus

SKELLY,
Edward J., d. 3/11/1911 at 63; phthisis pulmonalis (see following entry)
Edward J., d. 3/11/1912 at 60 (see preceding entry)
Herbert A. C., d. 1/24/1917 at 6/6/12; measles; Alexander Skelly and Mamie Cope
Thomas J. B., d. 12/13/1910 at 1/9/20; pneumonia; Alexander Skelly and Mamie Cope

SKILLING,
Adjutor, d. 2/28/1917 at 31/5/22; fracture 7th cerv. vert.; Ludger Skilling and Mary Jane -----

SKINNER,
Frank H., d. 9/16/1917 at 66; suicide by firearms; George G. Skinner

SLACK,
Francis A., d. 12/9/1898 at 3; spinal meningitis; b. Portsmouth

SLADE,
Caroline E., d. 10/18/1928 at 95/6/25 in Manchester; apoplexy

SLATER,
John, d. 1/23/1893 at 40; paralysis
Linwood L., d. 7/27/1916 at 48; septicaemia; John Slater and Nancy -----
Mary E., d. 1/8/1931 at 38/3/13; chronic endocarditis
Thomas, d. 1/25/1897 at 76; Bright's disease; b. Scotland
Thomas F., d. 6/4/1927 at 68/3/22; chronic cystitis; Thomas Slater and
   Mary Fleetwood

SLATTERY,
Fannie, d. 2/9/1893 at 67; died in Strafford Co. Asylum fire

SLEEPER,
Clara A., d. 4/22/1915 at 40/6/19 in Biddeford, ME; pneumonia
Evelyn M., d. 2/13/1924 at 15/1/13 in Biddeford, ME; peritonitis; John
   Sleeper and Clara A. Hanson

SLOAN,
Belle Varney, d. 6/28/1920 at 69/1/27 in Mansfield, MA; cancer of
   omentum
Charles, d. 1/18/1912 at 59/8/25 in Apponaug, RI; pneumonia

SLOANE,
Harry P., d. 4/1/1895 at 4; diphtheria; b. Dover; SM
Helen J., d. 2/11/1936 at 62/8/13*

SLOPER,
John F., d. 7/8/1937 at 92/1/8; heat exhaustion
Marilla J., d. 2/1/1901 at 54/2/28; carcinoma; PH

SLY,
Charles A., d. 7/7/1932 at 81/4/2; arterio sclerosis
Marian E., d. 10/1/1934 at 82/0/12; cerebral hemorrhage

SMALL,
Abbie M., d. 9/28/1913 at 79/3/29; angina pectoris; Daniel Davis and Abbie
   Campernell
Albina E., d. 8/18/1918 at 59/6 in Worcester, MA; carcinoma of stomach

Benjamin A., d. 3/25/1892 at 60; apoplexy; b. Newburyport; (Deer Island, ME; Newburyport)
Charles E., d. 8/3/1905 at 50/2/16; chronic nephritis; PH
Daniel M., d. 12/31/1906 at 73/2/1; cardiac dilation; buried in Cumberland, ME
Eliza R., d. 6/18/1933 at 82/1/3; cerebral hemorrhage
John F., d. 8/18/1930 at 74/2/8; chronic myocarditis; James E. Small and Hannah E. Caverno
Laura M., d. 2/28/1925 at 55/6/15 in Fairfield, ME; dropped dead; Alonzo Masters and Lauretta Stubbs
Louisa, d. 9/26/1901 at 66/7/1; carcinoma of breast; buried in Alfred, ME
Minnie E., d. 12/28/1909 at 24/1/9; marasmus; William H. Small and Ida M. Roach
Philip G., d. 9/25/1896 at 44 in Rochester; angina pectoris
William A., d. 4/2/1919 at 54; cancer of liver; Benjamin A. Small and Abbie M. Davis

SMALLEY,
Grace M., d. 3/28/1916 at 42/5/29; acute gastro enteritis; Lewis B. Hanson and Betsy Thurston

SMART,
Alice F., d. 3/11/1937 at 56/1/0 in Exeter; met. cancer in bone
Anna A., d. 11/4/1900 at 76 in Lawrence, MA; uterine cancer; PH
Annie (Frost), d. 10/12/1936 at 75/11/12*; b. Portland, ME
Caroline Bell, d. 11/29/1898 at 33; chronic nephritis; b. Newmarket; PH
Charles A., d. 1/14/1913 at 76/8/17; chronic nephritis; Eliphalet L. Smart and Eliza Tupper
Charles E., d. 7/29/1909 at 49/0/21; suicide; John M. Smart and Ellen M. Davis
Chester A., d. 11/11/1912 at 48/11/24 in Laconia; heart disease - nephritis
Dorothy E., d. 1/25/1929 at 23/0/6; puerperal septicaemia; Thomas McAvoy and Florence Brown
Earle Wyman, d. 6/14/1909 at 0/8/24; malnutrition; J. Guy Smart and Vella May Smith
Eda G., d. 11/16/1890 at 12/2/22; Charles A. Smart (Parkman, ME) and Lydia G. Manter (Anson, ME)
Elmer, d. 9/19/1915 at 19 in Portsmouth; accidental drowning
Eugene, d. 3/21/1925 at 78/6/7; gastro enteritis; John Smart and Betsey Bailey
Frank E., d. 12/7/1911 at 72 in Windham Junction; uraemia, nephritis, cystitis; Ezra W. Smart and Hannah Spaulding
Fred D., d. 6/30/1890 at 25/10/25; married; Frank E. Smart (Rumney) and Hannah S. Seavey (Hudson)
Fred M., d. 6/18/1900 at 41; septicaemia; PH

George H., d. 12/12/1893 at –; anaemia; b. Dover; (US; Ireland)
Grace B., d. 11/10/1924 at 54/8/13 in Durham; valvular heart disease
Hannah S., d. 2/25/1929 at 87/10/3 in Woburn, MA; angina pectoris; David
    Seavey and Sophronia Smith
J. Frank, d. 2/13/1892 at 31; organic disease of heart; b. Durham;
    (Durham; Boston, MA)
Jeremiah M., d. 8/13/1907 at 57/6/13 in Lawrence, MA; nephritis
Mabel, d. 9/7/1900 at 16 in Methuen, MA; diabetes; PH
Mary F., d. 9/24/1889 at 39/3/22; housewife; married; b. Effingham;
    George Beck (Farmington) and Huldah Meloon (Effingham)
Rose M., d. 6/4/1899 at 23; pneumonia; PH
Sophie A., d. 12/28/1933 at 60/5/21; apoplexy

SMELLIE,
Jessie, d. 8/23/1931 at 1/3/1 in Warren, NJ; arterio sclerosis
John, d. 2/13/1924 at 86/10/4 in Riverpoint, RI; chronic endocarditis
Martha N., d. 2/21/1917 at 86/7/4; chronic myocarditis

SMILEY,
Kenneth M., d. 4/6/1912 at 0/0/7 in Lowell, MA; congenital debility

SMITH,
child, d. 3/17/1900 at <1; premature birth; SM
child, d. 5/22/1913 at –; stillborn; Thomas J. Smith and Alice A. Drew
child, d. 2/20/1924 at 0/0/2; atelectasis; Edward V. Smith and Anna L.
    Murray
child, d. 10/29/1924 at –; premature birth; Frank W. Smith and Dorothy O.
    Welsh
child, d. 12/27/1925 at –; stillborn; Frank M. Smith and Dorothy O. Welch
Agnes M., d. 11/30/1935 at 33/6/13; G. C. peritonitis
Agnes S., d. 11/24/1902 at 50/1/28 in Franklin; cerebral hemorrhage; SM
Albion A., d. 2/27/1930 at 79/10/14; arterio sclerosis; Andrew Smith and
    Martha J. Hill
Alice, d. 3/14/1937 at 82/2/2; intestinal obstruction
Alice W., d. 4/10/1932 at 74/2/10 in Rollinsford; chronic nephritis
Alta May, d. 11/9/1896 at 6; diph. laryngitis; b. Belmont, MA; buried in
    Wolfeboro
Angeline H., d. 9/2/1903 at 75/4/10 in Cambridge, MA; nephritis; PH
Ann, d. 4/22/1909 at 71; senility; William Bingham and Jane McNally
Ann, d. 7/23/1929 at 69; chronic endocarditis; James McQuade and Ann
    McKee
Annie L., d. 12/20/1893 at 63; shock; b. Dover; (Effingham; Tuftonboro)
Annie R., d. 6/7/1935 at 85/2/29; chronic myocarditis
Arlene, d. 3/23/1935 at 5/11/12; lobar pneumonia
Arthur B., d. 10/29/1927 at 40/10/2; cerebral hemorrhage

Arthur Noel, d. 4/23/1925 at 73/9/23; myocarditis; Samuel W. Smith and Mary E. Nickerson
Asa C., d. 11/20/1896 at 71; shock; b. Dover; PH
Augustus F., d. 1/1/6/1906 at 70/4; Bright's disease; PH
Austin E., d. 9/18/1907 at 46/8; peritonitis; Mary A. Bunker
Bertha E., d. 8/20/1903 at 31/6/22 in Madbury; pulmonary tuberculosis; PH
Bertha T., d. 8/7/1932 at 55/1/10 in York, ME; angina pectoris
Blanch L., d. 7/5/1911 at 34/5/16 in Trenton, NJ; angina pectoris
Carrie E., d. 12/20/1934 at 83/10/30 in E. Rochester; general paresis
Charles F., d. 2/16/1937 at 69; intestinal obstruction
Charles L., d. 8/20/1890 at 69/6; married; Ezra Smith and Elizabeth Davis
Charles N., d. 2/3/1931 at 68; cancer rectum
Charles W., d. 10/8/1893 at 54; organic heart disease; b. Methuen, MA; (Dracut, MA; Allenstown)
Charles W., d. 1/7/1895 at 45; Brights disease; b. Parsonsfield, ME; PH
Charles W., d. 1/10/1899 at 36 in Colebrook; consumption; PH
Clara A., d. 10/24/1917 at 83/5/9; angina pectoris; Josiah Cooper and Sarah Baker
Clara Eliza, d. 9/17/1916 at 56 in Brockville, ON; ex. of mental dis.; Hiram A. Smith
Clara Lewis, d. 3/7/1925 at 60/6/24; chr. parenchymat. neph.; George Silvey and Adeline Hervey
Clifford N., d. 12/28/1932 at 29/4/11; cerebral hemorrhage
Cyrus, d. 11/10/1903 at 68 in Concord; exhaustion in senile dementia; PH
Delia, d. 7/31/1923 at 71; lateral sclerosis
Dora H., d. 9/29/1924 at 51/7/10; lobar pneumonia; Edwin H. Flint
Dorothy, d. 9/6/1908 at 0/5/5; cholera infantum; Charles W. Smith and Alice L. Rollins
Dorothy O., d. 1/1/1926 at 26/7/22; toxemia of pregnancy; Fred A. Welch and Maude G. Wheeler
Edward D., d. 1/15/1937 at 73/3/13; heart disease
Elbridge, d. 11/23/1895 at 62; pneumonia; b. Putney, VT; PH
Eliza J., d. 2/4/1909 at 72/7/14; paresis; Thomas Venner and Sophia Jackson
Elizabeth A., d. 12/17/1917 at 84/11/23; cerebral apoplexy; Josiah Emery and Nancy Sanborn
Elizabeth H., d. 5/7/1906 at 72/10/27 in Cambridge, MA; apoplexy; PH
Elizabeth J., d. 11/2/1914 at 74/5/3; pericarditis; Johnson Lovering and Caroline ----
Elizabeth R., d. 11/16/1915 at 82/10/12; cancer of stomach; Joseph H. Smith and Merribel Hanson
Ella F., d. 4/8/1916 at 60/0/3 in Portsmouth; cerebral hemorrhage
Ellen, d. 10/2/1907 at 69 in Tewksbury, MA; arterio sclerosis
Ellen J., d. 12/19/1907 at 72 in Boston, MA; artero sclerosis

Emma J., d. 11/1/1929 at 61/2/17; chr. endocarditis; William T. Berry and Lydia Foss

Eugene F., d. 3/4/1930 at 75/2/13; fracture base skull; Asa C. Smith and Eliza Venner

F. Gertrude, d. 10/6/1918 at 21; lobar pneumonia; Daniel Perkins and Carrie Corson

Florence M. B., d. 9/26/1892 at 30; phthisis; b. E. Montpelier, VT; (Marshfield, VT; Windham)

Forrest S., d. 3/14/1927 at 69/8/14 in Boston, MA; prostate hypertrophy

Frances J., d. 11/21/1934 at 70/3/25; endocarditis

Francis, d. 11/2/1936 at 17/11/25; shock & hemorrhage

Frank, d. 8/10/1907 at 19 in Chicago, IL; typhoid fever

Fred E., d. 9/9/1934 at 72 in Malden, MA; septic infection

Frederick R., d. 7/15/1899 at 40 in West Newton, MA; acute lobar pneumonia; PH

Genevieve, d. 4/21/1937 at 39/11/6; fibroid uterus

George D., d. 3/18/1920 at 60; broncho pneumonia

George E., d. 2/4/1908 at 37/6/11 in Boston, MA; injury to head

George E., d. 12/3/1910 at 58/4; hit by electric car; Daniel Smith and Maria Hawkins

George H., d. 4/27/1901 at 69/1; brain disease; PH

George R., d. 1/9/1927 at 67/6/2; acute endocarditis; Rufus B. Smith and Mary J. Copley

George S., d. 3/7/1914 at 67/7/16 in Peabody, MA; bronchitis

George W., d. 5/–/1896 at – in Sunapee; suicide

George W., d. 1/13/1911 at 67/11/5; gangrene of leg and foot; John Smith and Lydia Kimball

George W., d. 9/28/1912 at 55 in Portsmouth; cerebral hemorrhage

George W., d. 7/19/1924 at 69/11/24; cerebral hemorrhage; John P. Smith and Sarah Littlefield

Gilbert S., d. 12/25/1923 at 69/8/23 in San Francisco, CA; shock and hemorrhage

Hannah, d. 12/22/1933 at 70/3; coronary thrombosis

Hannah M., d. 3/20/1914 at 84 in Malden, MA; general arterio sclerosis

Hannah P., d. 9/23/1920 at 98/10/10; congestion of kidneys; Francis S. Maxwell and Susan Preston

Harley H., d. 3/29/1934 at 60/8/20; angina pectoris

Harriet S., d. 3/14/1896 at 70 in Lowell, MA; mal. dis. of stomach

Harriett E., d. 10/29/1927 at 47/8/2; carcinoma breast; George Rackham and Mary J. Smith

Harrison L., d. 11/5/1930 at 78/7/25; lobar pneumonia; Andrew Smith and Martha J. Hill

Harry, d. 1/2/1925 at 47/3/10 in Boston, MA; myocarditis

Harry A., d. 10/2/1918 at 30; pneumonia; Thomas Smith and Mary Donnelly

Herbert C., d. 2/18/1904 at 23/7/23; phthisis; PH
Hiram A., d. 1/5/1915 at 82 in Concord; myocardial insufficiency
Hugh, d. 1/14/1898 at 74; old age; b. Scotland; buried in Rochester
Hugh, d. 1/17/1898 at 67; old age; b. Rochester
Ida K., d. 6/20/1918 at 55; acute lobar pneumonia; Ephraim Mowe and Catherine McLeo
Izetta, d. 10/13/1936 at 76/0/4*; b. Stratham
James, d. 12/27/1923 at 74/3/5; gastro enteritis; James Smith and Ann Ricker
James, d. 2/8/1925 at –; fracture of skull; Daniel Smith and Ann Brigham
James, d. 1/14/1929 at 33/0/3 in Glencliff; pulmonary tuberculosis
James F., d. 6/11/1911 at 49/11/19 in Boxford, MA; accidental drowning
Jane, d. 5/24/1904 at 68; heart failure; PH
John, d. 5/22/1895 at 33; chronic alcoholism; b. Rochester; buried in Rochester
John, d. 12/4/1898 at 69; cancer of liver; b. Stark; PH
John A., d. 3/19/1892 at 63; neuralgia of heart
John D., d. 3/20/1918 at 67/0/5; chronic phthisis; William Smith and Bridget Fitzgerald
John W., d. 3/9/1893 at 24; phthisis pulmonalis; b. Ireland; (Ireland; Ireland)
John Wesley, d. 1/1/1925 at 83/8/22; mitral stenosis; Henry Smith and Betsy Boss
Julia Ann, d. 5/18/1915 at 78/3/2; lateral sclerosis; Oliver Dore and Frances Dore
Lizzie B., d. 4/26/1900 at 36 in Somersworth; chronic int. nephritis; PH
Louisa S., d. 7/10/1903 at 76/2/8 in Durham; cardiac dropsy; PH
Lucretia R., d. 2/20/1916 at 86/10/20 in W. Newton, MA; arterio sclerosis
Lydia A., d. 10/6/1918 at 68/3/25; valvular disease of heart; Enoch Bean and Anna Hilton
Lyman, d. 12/30/1904 at 89/11/6; valvular disease of heart
Mabel, d. 5/23/1897 at 33; pulmonary congestion; b. NS; PH
Margaret, d. 5/12/1887 at 24/2; single; b. Ireland; Patrick Smith (Ireland) and Jane (Ireland)
Margaret, d. 11/13/1896 at 80; heart disease; b. Dover; PH
Margaret A., d. 3/22/1922 at 48/10/4 in Rochester; ex. by abd. operation; William Smith and Mary Carberry
Marguerite L., d. 3/28/1907 at 9/3/2; meningitis; Melville J. Smith and Mary A. Lombard
Maria, d. 1/17/1893 at 75; heart disease; b. Brookfield; (NH; NH)
Marion H., d. 12/4/1899 at 4; cerebral hemorrhage; PH
Marion M., d. 9/10/1937 at 76/6/12; fracture of feveur
Martha G., d. 5/28/1907 at 61 in Somerville, MA; myocarditis; Daniel Smith and Martha Page

Martha M. L., d. 12/22/1920 at 83/8/29; old age; Charles O. Libby and Hannah McDougal
Martha N., d. 11/16/1901 at 75/8/14 in So. Berwick, ME; cerebral apoplexy; PH
Mary, d. 3/10/1895 at 50; pneumonia; b. Ireland; PH
Mary A., d. 12/17/1888 at 73/5/15 in Malden, MA; widow; Stephen Hardy (Portsmouth) and Mary B. Hill (Newmarket)
Mary A., d. 2/19/1906 at 72/4/10; tuberculosis; PH
Mary F., d. 12/28/1908 at 70/10/16 in Malden, MA; consumption
Mary H., d. 8/11/1900 at 61; dysentery; buried in Page's Cem.
Mary Lombard, d. 3/17/1922 at 60/5/24; appendicitis; Joseph H. Lombard and Sophronia Davis
Mary S., d. 12/18/1912 at 53/2/10; apoplexy; W. H. Merifield and Mary A. Mitchell
Mary S., d. 11/7/1913 at 74/5/26; cerebral hemorrhage; Rufus C. Varney and Sarah A. Foss
Mary V., d. 5/25/1929 at 36 in Lawrence, MA; diabetes
Melissa, d. 3/20/1915 at 77/10/8; nephritis; Moses Weston and Betsey Soule
Melissa M., d. 3/22/1922 at 86/3/23; gen. arterio sclerosis; John C. Hayes and Lavinia Danforth
Nellie J., d. 6/12/1903 at 46; phthisis pulmonalis; PH
Newton C., d. 7/21/1897 at 52; convulsions; b. Dover; PH
Nicholas E., d. 5/17/1936 at 70; carcin. of prostate
Perley R., d. 3/16/1926 at 52/5/11; cerebral hemorrhage; Marshall F. Smith and Ida M. Tebbetts
Plummer B., d. 2/24/1934 at 76 in Portsmouth; carcinoma of intestine
Robert, d. 2/13/1901 at 45; alcoholism; buried in Rochester
Robert J., d. 9/22/1931 at 25/2/20 in Ossipee; suicide
Roy C., d. 8/15/1928 at 54/5; suppurative nephritis; Charles W. Smith and Annie R. Adams
Rushton C., d. 4/29/1893 at 1; gastric tuberculosis; b. Dover; (VT; E. Montpelier, VT)
Russell, d. 10/8/1937 at 80/1/26; fracture of hip
Ruth Etta, d. 3/29/1899 at 67; pleurisy, pneumonia; PH
Samuel J., d. 10/1/1904 at 83/11/27; old age; PH
Sarah, d. 10/24/1909 at 59/4/25; heart failure; Caleb Smith and Susanna Hames
Sarah J., d. 9/6/1889 at 53/0/1; housewife; married; b. Buxton, ME; Josiah Emery (US) and Jane Flood (US)
Sarah Lizzie, d. 12/6/1937 at 82/8/6*
Sophronia, d. 8/23/1897 at 80; old age; b. MA; PH
Sophronia A., d. 4/14/1909 at 76/6/30 in Malden, MA; cerebral embolism
T. B., d. 7/13/1906 at 62; cancer of cervical glands

Thomas P., d. 7/17/1887 at 0/6; b. Dover; Thomas Smith (Ireland) and
    Mary Donnelly (Ireland)
Thomas P., d. 9/5/1937 at 21/7/30*; b. Dover
Virginia Evelyn, d. 12/4/1923 at 0/0/23; premature birth; Robert L. Smith
    and Cora F. Weeden
Vivian Elaine, d. 12/31/1923 at 0/1/10; premature birth; Robert L. Smith
    and Cora F. Weeden
William, d. 3/27/1935 at 92/7; chronic nephritis
William B., d. 7/24/1932 at 80/0/11; paralysis agitans
William H., d. 12/6/1894 at –; phthisis; b. Dover; PH
Winnie, d. 6/13/1890 at 35; married; Jonathan Clark (Ireland) and Mary
    Derrick (Ireland)
Winthrop, d. 7/5/1891 at 44/7/22; married; William Horatio Smith
    (Methuen, MA) and Sophronia Holt (Allenstown)

SNEIERSON,
child, d. 4/10/1903 at 0/0/1; hydrocephalic foetus

SNELL,
Amanda M., d. 6/28/1924 at 82/0/23 in Rollinsford; angina pectoris
Arthur L., d. 9/16/1921 at 56/5/9; angina pectoris; L. F. Snell and Ardelia
    Nichols
Arthur L., d. 3/3/1924 at 54/5/3 in Rollinsford; carcinoma of intestine
Donald, d. 4/22/1926 at 78/9/19; natural causes; Jerome Snell and
    Hannah Lord
Eliza C., d. 5/26/1927 at 68/11/25 in Barrington; chronic myocarditis
Frank T., d. 10/1/1918 at 60/4/20; acute nephritis; Timothy H. Snell and
    Mary A. Foss
George A., d. 3/8/1934 at 80/3/21; angina pectoris
Hannah, d. 3/18/1894 at 71; pneumonia; buried in Somersworth
Henry, d. 5/22/1925 at 25/11 in Rutland, VT; streptococcus haemol'sus;
    Frank Snell and Eliza Hill
Hiram L., d. 4/13/1900 at 46; pneumonia; buried in Somersworth
Hosea B., d. 2/18/1906 at 71/10/2 in Lee; PH
Lydia D., d. 9/22/1909 at 61/6/29 in Lee; cardiac dropsy
Martha A., d. 6/4/1920 at 84/1/17; cancer of bowels; Aaron Hanson and
    Deborah Hall
Mary E., d. 10/4/1887 at 77/9/12; widow; b. Dover; Timothy Hussey
    (Dover) and Elizabeth ----- (Rollinsford)
Mary E., d. 10/9/1925 at 77/4; chronic myocarditis; Ezekiel Perkins and
    Abigail Cate
Nancy, d. 6/25/1909 at 74/11/14 in Haverhill, MA; senile gangrene
Sarah H., d. 5/24/1919 at 72/10/1; cerebral hemorrhage; Walter Harmon
    and Laura B. Snell

Timothy H., d. 5/12/1888 at 0/8/10; b. Dover; Frank T. Snell (Dover) and Eliza C. Hill (Strafford)
Timothy H., d. 7/11/1900 at 69; fatty degen. of heart; PH
Walter S., d. 2/14/1898 at 21; typhoid fever; b. Dover; PH
William A., d. 7/13/1899 at 69 in Haverhill, MA; apoplexy; PH
William H., d. 7/3/1924 at 74/5/24; locomotor ataxia; Jerome Snell and Hannah Lord

SNOW,
Albert E., d. 6/29/1923 at 77/2/15; angina pectoris; Joseph Snow and Asenath Ladd
Alma M., d. 8/22/1932 at 77/7/7; apoplexy
Asenath T., d. 9/19/1888 at 79/11/10; married; b. Mt. Vernon, ME; James Ladd and Hannah Harriman
Charles Hiram, d. 9/17/1915 at 38/11/26 in Boston, MA; ulceration of larynx
Ethel M., d. 2/26/1892 at 6; heart disease and congestion; b. Dover; (Berwick, ME; Farmington)
Fannie C., d. 12/29/1897 at –; pneumonia; b. Farmington; PH
Frank C., d. 1/28/1925 at 71/7/23; myocarditis; Hiram F. Snow and Roxanna Gentleman
George W., d. 7/8/1919 at 61/11/7; acute indigestion; Hiram F. Snow and Roxanna D. Geuthman
Hiram F., d. 7/29/1899 at 73; ulcer of stomach; PH
Jennie H., d. 12/6/1899 at 38; cerebral apoplexy; PH
Nancy J. H., d. 6/18/1915 at 88/10/7; senile gangrene of leg; Thomas Hough and Catherine A. Keniston

SNOWMAN,
Burton C., d. 9/2/1931 at 54/10/3; cancer of colon

SNYDER,
Fred R., d. 8/20/1916 at 16/4/20; acute poliomyelitis; Fred S. Snyder and Mabel Robinson

SOLOMON,
Bessie May, d. 10/23/1905 at 0/5/3; tuberculosis; PH

SOMERS,
Ellen, d. 11/17/1918 at 81; general arterio sclerosis; Frank McCooey and Bridget Carragher
Harry W., d. 7/23/1899 at –; cholera infantum
James, d. 12/21/1924 at 57; heart disease probably
John H., d. 7/17/1894 at –; cholera infantum; b. Dover; SM
Mary, d. 3/18/1895 at 63; disease of brain; b. Ireland; SM

Morgan, d. 7/18/1898 at 73; endocarditis; b. Ireland; SM

SOMMERS,
Charlotte B. H., d. 12/25/1919 at 76/7/6 in Rochester; lobar pneumonia; John T. Drew and Alice Whitehouse
Lawrence, d. 4/8/1908 at 69/8 in Nashua; accidental burns; Lawrence Sommers and Mary Byrne
William, d. 3/1/1919 at 75/0/27 in Oconto, WI; carcinoma

SOPHER,
Sarah T., d. 3/20/1900 at 84; pneumonia; buried in Freeman, ME

SOUCY,
Francis, d. 2/9/1930 at 64/11/12; gastric ulcer; Francis Soucy and Adele Goyette
Jules, d. 6/7/1922 at 56/7; embolism; Hyacinthe Soucy and Tenpha Ouellette
Romeo, d. 3/22/1921 at 0/10/20; ac. lobar pneumonia; Isai Soucy and Rose Simoneau

SOUTHARD,
Ralph M., d. 8/6/1906 at 8/2/16; submersion; buried in Dexter, ME

SOUZA,
Amelia, d. 4/22/1930 at 0/0/2; premature birth; Manuel Souza and Sarah Sedlin

SOWERBY,
Deborah, d. 5/14/1901 at 64/4/12; gastric cancer; PH
John, d. 7/30/1930 at –; premature birth; John Y. Sowerby and Margaret E. Davis
John D., d. 7/17/1933 at 64; diabetes mellitus
Thomas, d. 2/8/1924 at 89/8/8; arterio sclerosis; Thomas Sowerby
Thomas J., d. 11/3/1918 at 48/4/9 in Boston, MA; cancer

SPALDING,
child, d. 7/23/1905 at –; stillborn; SM

SPANOR,
Theodore, d. 9/21/1911 at 0/3/24; cholera infantum; George Spanor and Annie Spanor

SPATHERMON,
Charles, d. 10/12/1918 at 0/11/7; broncho pneumonia; Stephen Spathermon

SPAULDING,
Annie, d. 4/30/1920 at 44/11/19 in Boston, MA; lobar pneumonia

SPEED,
child, d. 6/28/1915 at –; stillborn; Howard E. Speed and Della M. Maddox

SPEKE,
David, d. 6/6/1903 at 75/5/16 in Rochester; chronic nephritis; PH
Joseph, d. 8/20/1937 at 78/10/30*
Sarah A., d. 10/12/1897 at 69 in Rochester; insanity
Walter J., d. 11/5/1925 at 40/0/2 in Rochester; tabes dorsalis

SPELLMAN,
Edward, d. 8/24/1930 at 80; arterio sclerosis; John Spellman and Eliza Blackwell

SPENCER,
Bernice A., d. 3/18/1906 at 1/3; tubercular meningitis; buried in Berwick, ME
Charles A., d. 12/30/1899 at 24; accident; buried in Somersworth
Joshua E., d. 4/14/1924 at 86/10/15; stoppage of bowels
Lydia F., d. 9/26/1909 at 57/2/18; nephritis; Joseph Cooper and Eunice Smith
Mary B., d. 4/23/1902 at 44/11/23; fibroid of uterus; buried in Lawrence, MA
Mildred, d. 9/17/1895 at 2; membraneous croup; b. Dover; buried in Berwick, ME
William, d. 9/26/1895 at 0; diarrhea; b. Dover; SM

SPERTONAKON,
Stavroula, d. 1/15/1912 at 2/10; pneumonia; George Spertonakon and Maria Petrakon

SPILIOPOULOS,
Leonidas J., d. 10/5/1918 at 39; pneumonia

SPILLANE,
Charles M., d. 6/26/1917 at 42/10; accidental fall; Cornelius Spillane and Ellen Mahoney

SPILLER,
Frank D., d. 3/29/1930 at 82/10/28; cerebral hemorrhage; Joseph Spiller and Mary Dimond

SPINNEY,
Charles H., d. 4/5/1936 at 78/6/3; carcinoma of prostate
Chesley G., d. 2/10/1899 at 55; pulmonary phthisis; buried in Somersworth
Clara M., d. 2/25/1937 at 69/10/27; lobar pneumonia
Ella F., d. 10/23/1907 at 47/1/19; gall stones; Eri F. Pinkham
John Wallace, d. 6/1/1923 at 62/5/20; angina pectoris
Laura, d. 8/2/1935 at 62/7/4 in Concord; intestinal obstruction
Mary Frances, d. 6/29/1915 at 70/4/1; fracture femur; Andrew Whitehouse and Mary T. Wise
Wallace G., d. 4/11/1895 at 0; cerebral meningitis; b. Dover; PH

SPLINE,
Honora, d. 1/11/1900 at 83 in Chicopee, MA; chronic bronchitis; SM
Mary F., d. 7/7/1902 at 32 in Somersworth; tuberculosis meningitis; SM

SPRAGUE,
Ida May, d. 10/28/1893 at –; cholera infantum; b. Dover; (Calais, ME; Dover)
Maria B., d. 10/14/1905 at 94/8/5 in Boston, MA; endocarditis; PH
Rita D., d. 4/5/1919 at 0/0/28; premature birth; Winfield Sprague and Amanda Paul
Thomas F., d. 5/23/1893 at 23; accidental; b. Calais, ME; (Calais, ME; Calais, ME)

SPRING,
Arthur, d. 5/30/1906 at –; cerebral embolism; SM

SPRINGER,
Elvira E., d. 3/27/1927 at 90/3/5; senility; George W. Noyes and Mary Fairman
Viola J., d. 11/29/1892 at 24; cancer of liver; b. Colebrook; (Sheffield, VT; Columbia)

SPROUT,
Frank, d. 11/6/1922 at 69; carcinoma of rectum

SPURLIN,
Charles F., d. 10/19/1916 at 73/9/16; syncope of heart; Thomas T. Spurlin and Lucy Seavey

Lucy, d. 6/7/1887 at 63/10/25; married; b. Sandwich; John Brown (Sandwich) and Lizzie Blanchard (Sandwich)
Mary Eliza, d. 8/18/1917 at 66/6/8; mitral insufficiency; Robert Cook and Jane Taylor
Susan S., d. 5/30/1887 at 15/4/27; b. Wolfeboro; George A. Spurlin (Farmington) and Nellie A. Hall (Dover)
T. Franklin, d. 5/28/1905 at 34/7/9; cerebral hemorrhage; PH
Thomas, d. 9/12/1895 at 78; diarrhea; b. Tuftonboro; PH

SPURLING,
Albert H., d. 5/28/1891 at 17/2/20; George A. Spurling (East Kingston) and Nellie A. Hall (Dover)
Alice Josephine, d. 6/22/1907 at 50/5/19; nephritis; Thomas J. Spurling and Susan F. Goodwich
Ella M., d. 4/28/1927 at 79/3/10; cerebral hemorrhage; Thomas J. Spurling and Susan F. Goodrich
Emma S., d. 4/8/1908 at 55/7/28; cerebral hemorrhage; Clement Hayes and Lucinda Davis
George A., d. 9/28/1931 at 86/10/12; arterio sclerosis
Lydia H., d. 10/24/1890 at 78/9/27; widow; Elisha Goodrich (ME) and Temperance Hilton (ME)
Susan T., d. 5/11/1901 at 72/5/1; inanition; PH
Thomas J., d. 3/15/1888 at 64/8/2; farmer; married; b. Lebanon; Thomas Spurling (Lebanon, ME) and Betsey Lord (Lebanon)

SPURR,
Margaret C., d. 2/–/1901 at – in Exeter; phthisis pulmonalis

STACEY,
Arthur R., d. 5/8/1890 at 14/7/5; George W. Stacey (Eliot, ME) and Hattie A. Winkley (NH)
George H., d. 8/28/1888 at 1/4/12; b. Dover; George Stacey (Canada) and Abbie Miller (Salmon Falls)
Olla A., d. 9/27/1906 at 17/14/11 (sic); pulmonary tuberculosis

STACK,
Frank J., d. 9/15/1911 at 43; probably heart disease; Thomas Stack and Margaret -----
Nora, d. 7/22/1905 at 32/10; pulmonary phthisis; SM

STACKPOLE,
child, d. 4/11/1899 at –; stillborn; PH
child, d. 9/24/1915 at –; eclampsia; Arthur Stackpole and Ethel Titus
Albert F., d. 10/11/1923 at 74/10/9; cerebral hemorrhage; John Stackpole and Mary L. Gray

Benjamin F., d. 1/30/1927 at 78/9/10; chronic myocarditis; James
    Stackpole and Martha Hale
Carrie M., d. 5/29/1899 at 36; anaemia; PH
Charles E. N., d. 3/2/1937 at 84/3/27; chr. endocarditis
Dominicus, d. 12/16/1892 at 76; chronic eczema, hemorrhage
Edwin J., d. 3/21/1925 at 67/7/25; chronic myocarditis; Josiah Stackpole
    and Elizabeth Clay
Elizabeth, d. 2/17/1932 at 79/5/4 in Boston, MA; myocarditis
Elizabeth H., d. 8/19/1921 at 70/3/12; angina pectoris; King Emery and
    Hannah H. Emery
George A., d. 1/12/1934 at 77/7; chronic endocarditis
George I., d. 3/7/1937 at 83/3/10; cerebr. hemorrhage
James, d. 1/19/1893 at 67; Bright's disease; b. So. Berwick, ME; (So.
    Berwick, ME; York, ME)
John S., d. 4/17/1893 at 60; hernia; b. Lowell, MA; (So. Berwick, ME;
    Strafford)
Josiah, d. 6/24/1904 at 69/7/19; paralysis agitans; PH
Lowell B., d. 10/21/1903 at 58/6; cerebral hemorrhage; buried in So.
    Berwick, ME
Luetta G., d. 5/29/1928 at 62/5/6; chronic morphinism; Charles Whittier
    and Caroline Dale
Martha H., d. 3/31/1898 at 75; pneumonia; b. Barrington; PH
Mary, d. 5/25/1890 at 72/5/20; married; Thomas Young (Dover) and Annie
    Furbush (Lebanon)
Mary E., d. 2/5/1898 at 62 in Somersworth; paralysis and Bright's dis; PH
Mary E., d. 5/3/1917 at 80/9/2; atheroma; ----- Clay and Susan Brown
Nettie F., d. 5/4/1900 at 47 in Providence, RI; cancer; PH
Paul A., d. 3/28/1900 at 86; fell down stairs; PH
Walter H., d. 7/20/1899 at 38; cardiac fatty degeneration; PH

STACY,
George W., d. 12/29/1905 at 51/6 in Dighton, MA; pneumonia; PH
Hattie A., d. 11/23/1925 at 70/6/7; cerebral hemorrhage; Mark H. Winkley
    and ----- Leighton
Madeline, d. 5/14/1924 at 0/5/13; diarrhea and enteritis; Elmer G. Stacy
    and Mary Ellen Casey

STADIG,
Christine, d. 9/3/1918 at 74/7/29; arthritis deformans; Olaf Olson and
    Marret Nilsdotter
Lars, d. 7/15/1928 at 92/3/15; arterio sclerosis; Johan Stadig

STAFFORD,
Gertrude E., d. 1/22/1917 at 29 in Hurley, NM; tuberculosis
Thomas B., d. 4/27/1905 at 13/11/19; nephritis; PH

STAGE,
Beatrice L., d. 12/12/1932 at 35/11/12; carcinoma of colon

STAMATOURAS,
Mary, d. 4/4/1922 at 29/1/20; surgical shock; John Stamatouras and Mary Selery

STAMMOS,
Julia, d. 9/6/1911 at 0/8/3; whooping cough; William Stammos and Alice Lemay

STAMNAS,
Eleftheri, d. 8/16/1919 at –; asphyxia of labor; Chris. Stamnas

STANFORD,
child, d. 4/30/1913 at –; stillborn; Frank Stanford and Mable Goodwin
Bridget, d. 11/24/1888 at 86; married; b. Ireland
John J., d. 12/18/1894 at 27; pneumonia; b. Dover; SM
Mary A., d. 2/19/1903 at 58 in No. Attleboro, MA; pneumonia; SM

STANLEY,
Annie L., d. 5/25/1930 at 70; fracture femur
Dorothy May, d. 4/10/1910 at 1/2/19; catarrhal enteritis; Charles H. Stanley and Mary E. McDonough
Jeffrey, d. 3/29/1910 at 52 in Lowell, MA; alcoholism

STANTON,
Charles H., d. 6/30/1903 at 45 in Salem, MA; fracture of skull; PH
Emma A., d. 7/21/1930 at 72/10/16 in Lynn, MA; cerebral hemorrhage
Esther, d. 1/25/1904 at 81/11 in Salem, MA; paralysis from cereb. hemorrhage; buried in Dover
Nettie L., d. 6/11/1895 at 22; heart disease; PH
Sarah L., d. 11/9/1902 at 46/1 in Hyde Park, MA; cancer of uterus; PH

STAPLES,
Aaron C., d. 10/12/1896 at 45; intestinal tuberculosis; b. Eliot, ME; PH
Abbie S., d. 2/19/1922 at 87/6/20; senility; Granville Staples and Mary G. Roberts
Anna B., d. 11/28/1900 at 38; tuberculosis; buried in So. Eliot, ME
Annie M., d. 3/30/1924 at 72/9/7 in Union; mitral regurgitation
Charles, d. 12/21/1899 at 76; gradual decline; PH
Charles H., d. 8/11/1908 at 54; chronic nephritis
Chestina A. C., d. 5/9/1910 at 64/5/1; apoplexy; James Corliss and Maria Hamlet

Dorothea E., d. 4/9/1895 at 5; splenic tumor; b. Dover; PH
Ellen F., d. 9/11/1930 at 80; carcinoma of liver; Lemuel Berry and Olive Hoyt
Fannie A., d. 1/15/1927 at 75/5/12; chronic nephritis; James Hanscom and Lynthia Gerrish
Irma L., d. 10/20/1918 at 18/4/28; pneumonia; Leslie W. Glidden and Ozza Noble
Isabell, d. 8/4/1889 at 28/10/27; housewife; married; b. Dover; J. Gentleman (Effingham) and Isabella A. Cate (Eliot, ME)
Kate, d. 7/12/1891 at 26/7/14; married; James Golden (Ireland) and Ann Cawley (Ireland)
Lydia M., d. 12/30/1903 at 76/0/3; senile debility; PH
Simon, d. 1/10/1892 at 81; old age; b. No. Berwick, ME; (Kittery, ME; No. Berwick, ME)
Simon H., d. 4/18/1926 at 87/10/26; fractured hip; Simon Staples and Sarah Hanscom

STARK,
Ronald Lee, d. 5/18/1937 at 0/2/13; acute enteritis

STATHOPOULOS,
Georgea, d. 11/4/1920 at 1/3/15 in Boston, MA; pulmonary tuberculosis; Nicholas and Fatoula

STEAD,
Frank C., d. 7/25/1901 at 30 in Boston, MA; fracture of skull; PH
Willie, d. 5/24/1892 at 3; diptheria

STEADMAN,
Edwin K., d. 9/26/1930 at 79/10/28; cancer of stomach; William Steadman and Catherine Elherington

STEARNS,
Blanche S., d. 3/13/1927 at 35/7/13; chr. mitral valv. dis.; William J. Hartford and Annie S. Watts
Fred A., d. 1/20/1916 at 50/10/12; Brights disease; Albert Stearns
Hannah, d. 10/4/1910 at 82/11/10; diabetes; William Simons
Sadie Emma, d. 4/9/1926 at 50/4/7 in Portsmouth; pulmonary oedema

STEBBINS,
Harry E., d. 1/18/1935 at 63/11/5; diabetes

STEELE,
Caroline A., d. 3/28/1925 at 85/1/22; la grippe; Ephraim Leighton and Mary F. Edgerly
Thomas M., d. 7/1/1917 at 83/7/20; enlarged prostate; David Steele and Lydia Burnham

STEEVE,
Oliver, d. 5/31/1900 at 35; typhoid fever; buried in Gloucester, RI

STEEVES,
Frances Eliza, d. 3/15/1930 at 77/4/13; angina pectoris; Gilbert Chapman and Lelitia Cochrane
Hurd J., d. 11/16/1922 at 53/1/23; cancer of stomach; Joseph H. Steeves and Mary E. Bray
Lloyd A., d. 4/22/1929 at 46/8/13; angina pectoris; Mariner T. Steeves and Frances E. Chapman

STERLING,
child, d. 4/25/1916 at –; stillborn; James Sterling and Sarah Ellis
child, d. 1/28/1926 at –; stillborn; Harold D. Sterling and Helen Tibbetts
Abbie, d. 10/22/1906 at 68/11/6; heart failure; PH
Elizabeth A., d. 9/11/1926 at 78/8/21; chronic nephritis; Peter Chadwick and Nancy T. Jenkins
Ella Ianthia, d. 10/1/1937 at 83/1/25*
Ellen, d. 3/6/1903 at 56; pneumonia; SM
Ephraim A., d. 3/30/1888 at 76/4/20; timber dealer; married; b. ME; H. Sterling (ME)
Frank, d. 8/20/1904 at 0/3/4; cholera infantum; PH
Helen E., d. 9/26/1926 at 15/10/12; diabetic coma; Ernest Tibbetts and May Brady
Henry H., d. 2/10/1917 at 67/9/3 in W. Newton, MA; hemiplegia
James H., Jr., d. 10/14/1919 at 24/8/12; phthisis pulmonalis; James H. Sterling and Mary A. Downing
Jennie A., d. 11/7/1901 at 45/1; acute tuberculosis; buried in Effingham
Mary A., d. 2/4/1926 at 75/11/26; apoplexy; Miles R. Buzzell and Elmira Arlin
Maud L., d. 4/30/1899 at 19; heart failure; PH
Patrick, d. 10/10/1925 at 82 in Rochester; cerebral thrombosis
Sumner H., d. 6/9/1913 at 64/3/19; pyelonephritis; Ephraim Sterling and Susan Ham
Susan Ham, d. 5/19/1890 at 72/8/24; widow; Nathaniel Ham (Portsmouth) and Betsy Prime (Moultonboro)
Walter S., d. 8/23/1908 at 63/3/18; hemorrhage from bullet wound; James Sterling and Clara D. Amazeen

Wesley B., d. 1/13/1923 at 78/5/15 in Alton Bay; arterio sclerosis; Ephraim Sterling and Susan -----
William E., d. 1/17/1919 at 0/3/16; malnutrition; James H. Sterling, Jr. and Sarah Ellis

STERNS,
Moses W., d. 2/27/1897 at 41; dementia paralytica; b. New York, NY; buried in Somersworth
William, d. 4/13/1898 at 69; heart disease; b. Germany; buried in Somersworth

STETSON,
Carrie F., d. 7/15/1927 at 86 in Worcester, MA; broncho pneumonia
James B., d. 1/27/1913 at 79/8/7 in Arlington, MA; cerebral hemorrhage
Josiah W., d. 4/22/1898 at 73; paresis; b. Bath, ME; PH
Willis S., d. 8/21/1916 at 52/2/10; arthritis; Josiah W. Stetson and Jane D. Brown

STEUERWALD,
Fred W., d. 11/1/1913 at 34/9/3; hanging; Louis Steuerwald
Lewis, d. 1/10/1906 at 66/10/20; cerebral apoplexy; PH
Mary F., d. 11/15/1937 at 89/7/27; cerebr. hemorrhage
Ralph W., d. 1/31/1904 at 0/1/23; pneumonia, probably; PH
Sarah A., d. 9/14/1934 at 0/0/1; prematurity

STEVENS,
child, d. 1/7/1906 at –; stillborn; buried in private cemetery
child, d. 7/18/1925 at –; stillborn; Thomas J. Stevens and Catherine McKenney
Albert E., d. 5/27/1922 at 51/1/21; internal hemorrhage; Charles N. Stevens and Frances A. Loud
Alonzo, d. 9/17/1909 at 79/5/6; disease of spinal cord; Wheelwright Stevens
Benjamin F., d. 7/28/1918 at 0/2/22; broncho pneumonia; Frank B. Stevens and Alice G. Perkins
Betsey, d. 5/3/1888 at 92/6/20 in New Durham
Calvin L., d. 3/11/1937 at 79*
Caroline E., d. 4/22/1931 at 67/2/28; myocarditis
Carrie F. B., d. 5/2/1891 at 59 in Boston, MA
Charles A., d. 1/1/1909 at 11/8/25; phthisis; S. Walter Stevens and Mary P. Baker
Charles E., d. 11/25/1936 at 84/4/1 in Portsmouth; myocarditis
Doris A., d. 1/27/1934 at 0/0/2; intracranial hemorrhage
Durrell, d. 6/12/1891 at 92/8 in New Durham
Eliza, d. 3/28/1910 at 84/2/15; senility; Ira Libbey and Betsey Daniels

Elizabeth T., d. 10/5/1916 at 91/10/5 in Durham; senility
Elva A., d. 4/14/1914 at 48; oedema of lungs; Stillman Stevens and Emma
-----
Elvira J., d. 3/29/1900 at 42; cancer; PH
Emma B., d. 10/31/1934 at 80/3/17; fracture hip
Etta R., d. 4/8/1928 at 31/1/21; acute nephritis; Alonzo J. Stevens and Sarah E. Jellison
Ford E., d. 3/29/1934 at 28/9/1; frac. of skull (acc.)
Frank B., d. 3/18/1925 at 55/4/2; pulmonary oedema; Jonathan Stevens and Sarah Garland
Frank L., d. 11/15/1922 at 64/10/27; cerebral hemorrhage; Ludwick Stevens and Mary Brown
Frank P., d. 1/31/1926 at 73/5/26; acute bronchitis; George W. Stevens and Eliza Libby
Fred M., d. 12/29/1916 at 56/6/12 in Haverhill, MA; diabetes mellitus
George Frank, d. 3/12/1917 at 71 in Milwaukee, WI; broncho pneumonia
Gladys Caroline, d. 6/30/1924 at 25/3/8; septicemia; Thomas H. Pound and Augusta L. White
Harlem C., d. 4/23/1900 at 1; pneumonia; PH
Helen B., d. 4/8/1891 at 27/4/2; married; Moses B. Pettis (Topsham, VT) and Margaret M. Bacon (Bradford, VT)
Izette V., d. 7/28/1934 at 80/6/8 in S. Berwick, ME; fracture hip
Jabez H., d. 12/22/1928 at 71/4/23 in Durham; valv. heart disease
James M., d. 1/4/1917 at 69/4/10 in Brookfield; apoplexy; George Stevens
Jane Olive, d. 2/11/1923 at 81/5/22; acute indigestion; Augustus Woodbury and Sarah Bryant
Jennie S., d. 9/30/1918 at 66/1/25; cerebral hemorrhage; Moses Hanson and Eliza Hanson
Jennie S., d. 4/2/1933 at 78/4/9; congestive heart failure
John B., d. 11/19/1891 at 93/10/16; married; John Stevens and ----- Godfrey
John B., d. 3/1/1927 at 91/9/2; cerebral hemorrhage; John B. Stevens and Susan R. Smith
John Frank, d. 1/16/1902 at 39/8/13; pneumonia; PH
John Gilman, d. 10/14/1919 at 88/2/29; senility; John B. Stevens and Martha Buzzell
John P., d. 8/6/1918 at 0/3; pertussis; Frank B. Stevens and Alice G. Perkins
John Wallace, d. 5/9/1910 at 23/8/12; Brights disease; Frank L. Stevens and Carrie E. Smart
Lauretta, d. 3/14/1922 at 60/5/19; chr. inter. nephritis; Samuel S. Eaton and Mary E. Berry
Lilla M., d. 9/16/1906 at 32/10/4; pulmonary phthisis; PH
Lois J., d. 3/5/1931 at 83/8/15; chronic endocarditis
Lydia A., d. 6/25/1892 at 71; dropsy; (Litchfield; Litchfield)

Lydia A., d. 2/19/1927 at 87/3/3; cancer bowel; William Hammond and
    Mary D. Kimball
Marie A., d. 4/4/1935 at 41/4/26; cerebral hemorrhage
Mary, d. 11/3/1896 at 78; pneumonia; b. New Boston; buried in Amherst
Mary E., d. 11/24/1934 at 82/4/30 in Danvers, MA; aortic stenosis
Mary F., d. 10/22/1920 at 79/9/29; carcinoma of liver; Alfred Doe and
    Martha Ellison
Mary P., d. 1/10/1937 at 82/10/21*
Nancy H., d. 1/15/1917 at 83/11/19 in New Durham; arthritis deformans
Nathaniel, d. 7/16/1905 at 81/2/10 in Durham; valvular heart disease; PH
Nellie M., d. 2/11/1932 at 47/8/29; broncho pneumonia
Percy W., d. 3/20/1937 at 48/0/23 in Gonic; pulmonary embolism
Samuel, d. 2/27/1895 at 76; old age; b. Litchfield, ME; PH
Sarah E., d. 9/7/1890 at 86/11/7 in New Durham
Sarah F., d. 3/21/1888 at 48/7/2; married; b. Lebanon; R. Furbush
    (Lebanon, ME) and Phoebe Chase (N. Berwick)
Sidney F., Jr., d. 3/14/1912 at 0/0/6; puerp. hemorrhage; Sidney F.
    Stevens and Nancy E. Way
Susan, d. 8/23/1909 at 74/4/17; cancer of bowels; William Stevens and
    Rosannah Stevens
Susan R., d. 9/18/1893 at 91; old age; b. Alfred, ME
Thomasino R., d. 3/31/1934 at 1/2/16; broncho pneumonia
William S., d. 4/15/1897 at 80; cerebral hemorrhage; b. Canterbury; PH

STEVENSON,
Allan, d. 2/9/1931 at 81/4/3; apoplexy
James E., d. 8/15/1898 at 3; tubercular meningitis; b. Dover; PH
John C., d. 9/1/1888 at 0/9/23; b. Dover; Allen Stevenson (Scotland) and
    Aggie Leddin (Portsmouth)
Mary A., d. 6/17/1903 at 33/2/23; adeno carcinoma of uterus; PH
Thomas, d. 8/28/1887 at 78/10/17; farmer; widower; b. Wolfeboro;
    Thomas Stevenson (Dover) and Sarah (Brookfield)

STEWART,
child, d. 2/16/1912 at –; premature birth; Fred C. Stuart (sic) and Julia
    Ricker
Brooks D., d. 2/29/1916 at 72/8/5; acute delat. of heart; Isaac Stewart and
    Betsy Coburn
Charles, d. 8/31/1890 at 37/4/3 in St. Louis
George H., d. 5/24/1934 at 78; cerebral embolism
Isaac D., d. 6/7/1887 at 69/5/15; clergyman; married; b. Warner; John
    Stewart (Warner)
Laura A., d. 12/4/1896 at 31 in Danvers, MA; acute Brights disease; b.
    Cincinnati, OH; PH

Mary D., d. 5/9/1927 at 82/7/15; cerebral hemorrhage; Joseph Viles and Tamson Eldredge

STICKLES,
Patricia, d. 1/1/1934 at 0/0/13 in Boston, MA; prematurity

STILES,
child, d. 3/24/1900 at –; inanition; buried in Rollinsford
Franklin P., d. 12/6/1894 at 40; asphyxia from gas; b. So. Chatham; buried in So. Chatham
Mary, d. 8/14/1913 at 75/3/16; carcinoma of stomach; Charles Litchfield and Lucretia Hudson
Mary J., d. 7/17/1928 at 67/7/6; chronic myocarditis; William Price and Sarah Stout
Raymond H., d. 11/12/1922 at 39/11/20 in Quincy, MA; ac. dilatation of heart
Samuel B., d. 3/23/1891 at 37/9/23 in Brockton, MA

STILLINGS,
child, d. 10/18/1929 at 2 hrs.; premature birth; Maurice B. Stillings and Doris Allen
George E., d. 6/30/1898 at 21; injury; b. Dover; PH
Herbert, d. 5/7/1919 at 36/10/20 in Haverhill, MA; asphyxiation
Rufus I., d. 11/23/1919 at 69/11/29; arthritis deformans; Ivory Stillings and Lydia -----

STILLWAGON,
Thomas C., d. 8/25/1937 at 1/6; accidental drowning

STIMSON,
Edwin C., d. 9/17/1926 at 74/6/6; arterio sclerosis; Edward F. Stimson and Maria Davis

STIRLING,
child, d. 7/22/1919 at –; stillborn; Sumner D. Stirling and Maud V. Young
Alanson J., d. 11/19/1903 at 60/3/21; pneumonia; PH
John H., d. 9/13/1932 at 78/8/13; angina pectoris
Lizzie M., d. 4/28/1922 at 69/3/9; cerebral hemorrhage; Richard Foss and Lydia Durgin
Mabel Ray, d. 1/18/1905 at 22/9/6; diabetes mellitus; PH
Trueman, d. 6/6/1888 at 2/9/20; b. Dover; Sumner Stirling (Atkinson, ME) and Lizzie Chadwick (Holden, ME)

STOCKBRIDGE,
Emily A., d. 1/23/1923 at 80/2/20; cerebral hemorrhage
Horatio J., d. 10/25/1888 at 46 in Concord
Percy A., d. 7/30/1904 at 34/8/11; extreme inanition from insanity; PH

STOCKDON,
Mardel, d. 9/8/1897 at 1 in Somerville, MA; cholera infantum

STOCKER,
Joseph N., d. 5/1/1908 at 47/7/13; chronic nephritis; Harrison P. Stocker and Joanna Shost

STODDARD,
Arthur G., d. 10/30/1892 at 14; heart disease; b. Portsmouth; (Brookfield; Portsmouth)
Deering F., d. 5/14/1892 at 61; scrofulous disease of bowels; b. Brookfield; (Brookfield; -----)

STONE,
child, d. 1/26/1916 at –; premature birth; Delia Stone
child, d. 8/7/1926 at –; premature birth; George P. Stone and Mary M. Jones
Alfred, d. 9/13/1928 at 42/11/24; pulmonary oedema; Ludger Stone and Celina -----
Bertha May, d. 3/29/1933 at 54/4/21; perforated gastric ulcer
Betsey H., d. 9/7/1896 at 82; old age; b. Middleton; PH
Elizabeth, d. 10/6/1888 at 20/11 in NJ; single
Elizabeth S., d. 4/7/1911 at 86/9/10 in W. Newton, MA; carcinoma of liver
Fannie M. B., d. 12/28/1916 at 82/0/23; senility; William W. Burr and Frances McDonald
Frank A., d. 3/10/1937 at 82/8/2; chr. endocarditis
Frank C., d. 1/12/1933 at 42/7/26; cerebral hemorrhage
Frank C., d. 4/16/1937 at 65/1/7*
Frank E., d. 10/8/1899 at –; sudden - unknown; SM
Henry A., d. 4/15/1917 at 65/8/4; cancer of rectum; Asaph Stone and Susan Tarleton
Horace, d. 4/9/1926 at 89/5/1 in Montclair, NJ; chronic myocarditis
Jeannette, d. 10/14/1918 at 0/9/18; malnutrition; Olivene Stone
Jennie C., d. 3/12/1888 at 3/11/7; b. Swampscott, MA; George W. Stone (Lynn, MA) and Lydia A. Leavitt (Rochester)
Joseph, d. 2/8/1908 at –; polypus of larynx; Frazer Stone and Adeline -----
Lydia Alice, d. 5/27/1920 at 68/11/16 in Conway; cardiac insufficiency
Mary R., d. 12/1/1901 at 0/2/28; prob. acute tuberculosis; SM
Mary R., d. 6/24/1908 at 68/5 in Montclair, NJ; pneumonia

Nellie Susan, d. 5/27/1923 at 62/7/22 in Framingham, MA; chr. inter. nephritis
Oliver, d. 2/9/1902 at 85/7/2; catarrhal pneumonia; PH
Ralph E., d. 3/16/1917 at 19/10/8; chronic nephritis; Lauriston W. Stone and Clara E. Chick
Richard P., d. 3/1/1907 at 69/0/7 in Bangor, ME; la grippe
Sophia C., d. 1/15/1900 at 79; heart disease; buried in Rollinsford
Susan, d. 1/24/1914 at 88/7; uraemia; Mathew Tarleton and Elizabeth Colby
William Flint, d. 5/4/1890 at 21/7/21 in Pomona, CA; single; Richard P. Stone (Newburyport) and Fannie M. Burr (Dover)

STOOPP,
Rebecca, d. 8/24/1906 at 19/1; burns; buried in Somersworth

STORER,
Lavinia, d. 10/23/1915 at 78/0/14; brain disease; John B. York and Lavinia Wentworth

STOTT,
George T., d. 3/15/1918 at 79/11/14; uraemia; James Stott and Phoebe Knight

STOVER,
Helena M., d. 9/15/1887 at 47/2/13; married; b. Lovell, ME; Guy Howard (Phillips, ME) and Mahala Carlton
Mary L., d. 7/15/1937 at 89/9/3; cerebral embolism

STRACHAN,
child, d. 3/25/1928 at 0/0/1; prematurity; Raymond C. Strachan and Beatrice St. Laurent

STRACHEN,
Beatrice A., d. 4/7/1929 at 20/2/17; ulcerative tub. colitis; Alfred St. Laurent and Adelaide Demers

STRAINE,
Mary, d. 3/30/1900 at 65; heart failure; SM

STRATTON,
George D., d. 1/31/1922 at 68/8/8; chronic myocarditis; Jonathan Stratton and Nancy Tetherly
Jno. D., d. 8/18/1894 at 70; heart disease; b. NH; PH
Nancy B., d. 1/16/1892 at 70; old age – heart failure; b. ME; (ME; ME)

Sarah J., d. 1/27/1915 at 60/5/3; carcinoma of stomach; William Paul and
Abrah G. Ham

STRAW,
Fred E., d. 9/17/1918 at 28/1/15 in Kittery, ME; pneumonia
Isaac E., d. 6/11/1924 at 46/1/17; alcoholic poisoning; Joseph Straw and
Susan Kimball
Jennie, d. 10/11/1933 at 75/2/14; coronary thrombosis
Melvin R., d. 10/1/1933 at 68/11/10; angina pectoris

STREAMFIELD,
Nora B., d. 3/29/1917 at 43/9/7; epileptic convulsions; Nathaniel Clough
and Mary D. Pinkham

STREET,
Stanley E., d. 2/11/1921 at 7; accidental gunshot wound; William W.
Street and Jennie E. Daniels

STRITCH,
Catherine, d. 1/26/1908 at 79/5; haemoplytis

STROM,
John A., d. 3/7/1922 at 64/1/13; natural causes

STROTH,
child, d. 9/19/1932 at –; stillborn

STUART,
Isabella M., d. 5/13/1914 at 82/6/25 in Lowell, MA; old age
John C., d. 10/17/1906 at 82/10/11 in Lowell, MA; arteriosclerosis; PH
Mary A., d. 5/25/1914 at 89/6 in W. Brookfield, MA; senile dementia
Michael J., d. 12/11/1935 at 68; anemia
Sarah H., d. 1/24/1908 at 80/5/8; old age; Daniel Stuart and Sally Tibbetts

STUBBS,
child, d. 7/16/1907 at –; stillborn; William A. Stubbs and Mabel LeFavoure
Lauriet A., d. 2/16/1920 at 73/8/10 in Newport, ME; organic heart disease

STUDLEY,
Joseph, d. 8/8/1897 at 49; suicide by drowning; b. Rockland, ME

STURGEON,
Annie, d. 8/20/1918 at 48/9; cancer of rectum; John Sturgeon and
Elizabeth -----

STYLES,
Edward A., d. 3/24/1887 at 54/2/4; merchant; married; b. Dover
Jane E., d. 11/2/1935 at 88/9/5; chronic myocarditis

SULLIVAN,
child, d. 6/29/1894 at –; stillborn; b. Dover; SM
child, d. 3/5/1899 at –; inanition; SM
child, d. 10/6/1900 at <1; pneumonia; buried in Lewiston, ME
child, d. 6/17/1919 at –; stillborn; Cornelius Sullivan and Annie McCarthy
child, d. 1/3/1937 at –; stillborn
Abbie F., d. 7/10/1929 at 63/5/21; chr. interst. nephritis; Joseph Witham and Catherine Taylor
Adelaide J., d. 1/22/1932 at 50; chr. valv. heart dis.
Agnes, d. 11/1/1925 at 63; chronic nephritis; James McKone
Alice Gertrude, d. 1/3/1937 at 41/11/8; gang. appendicitis
Ann, d. 2/20/1904 at 62; ascites; SM
Anna, d. 2/19/1910 at 0/4; malnutrition; John Sullivan and Mary Loughlin
Annie, d. 8/21/1892 at 7; convulsions; b. Dover; (Portsmouth; London, England)
Bridget, d. 9/23/1892 at –; tubercular meningitis; b. Dover; (Portsmouth; England)
Catherine, d. 7/7/1890 at 70; widow; Daniel Brick (Ireland) and Johanna Dunleavy (Ireland)
Catherine, d. 6/28/1931 at 59; natural causes
Charles E., d. 1/28/1887 at 0/11/7; b. Dover; Patrick Sullivan (Ireland) and Julia Mahoney (Ireland)
Charles E., d. 2/23/1914 at 0/0/20; acute nephritis; Cornelius Sullivan
Cornelius J., d. 7/13/1933 at –; cancer of prostate
Daniel F., d. 1/10/1909 at 0/3; pneumonia; Cornelius Sullivan and Annie McCarthy
Daniel H., d. 11/21/1911 at 23/7/4 in Suncook; pul. tuberculosis; John Sullivan and Anne Riley
Delia G., d. 8/30/1908 at 17/7/12; phthisis pulmonalis; Jere Sullivan
Dennis, d. 3/25/1905 at 57; acute gastritis
Dennis, d. 4/6/1908 at 53; cerebral hemorrhage; Timothy Sullivan and Ellen Hurley
Edward E., d. 4/24/1912 at 46/10/15; heart disease; Daniel Sullivan and Mary Ellis
Elizabeth, d. 3/15/1933 at 59; coronary thrombosis
Ellen, d. 10/10/1887 at 35/10/14; married; b. Ireland; Daniel Lynch (Ireland) and Ellen Cotton (Ireland)
Ellen, d. 12/3/1926 at 83; chronic endocarditis
Ellen C., d. 8/12/1920 at 55; cancer of stomach; Michael Sullivan and Catherine Kenney
Eugene, d. 5/28/1892 at –; inflammatory laryngitis; (Ireland; Dover)

Honora, d. 7/6/1894 at 29; phthisis; b. Ireland; SM
Jere. D., d. 11/30/1892 at 28; typhoid fever; b. Ireland; (Ireland; Ireland)
Jeremiah, d. 4/9/1889 at 17; laborer; single; b. Ireland; Thomas Sullivan (Ireland) and Ellen Carroll (Ireland)
Jeremiah, d. 3/22/1922 at 54 in Concord; cerebral art. sclerosis; John Sullivan
Jeremiah D., d. 12/24/1903 at 0/2/22; pneumonia
John, d. 8/19/1893 at 47; pulmonary phthisis; b. Ireland; (Ireland; Ireland)
John, d. 3/14/1906 at –; heart disease; SM
John, d. 1/22/1907 at 39; erysipelas, alcoholism
John, d. 1/20/1911 at –; premature birth; John Sullivan and Mary Loughlin
John, d. 9/10/1937 at 69; cor. artery disease
John F., d. 9/8/1893 at 11; cerebral meningitis; b. Dover; (Boston, MA; Chicago, IL)
John J., d. 2/15/1906 at 39 in Portland, ME; pulmonary tuberculosis; SM
John J., d. 1/3/1933 at 63/10/11; cerebral hemorrhage
John L., d. 11/23/1929 at 0/1/22; marasmus; John L. Sullivan and Hazel Thompson
Joseph, d. 4/19/1910 at 25/4/8; asphyxia; John Sullivan and Mary Fleming
Julia, d. 2/9/1893 at 30; died in Strafford Co. Asylum fire
Julia, d. 12/2/1899 at 60; accidental; SM
Julia, d. 5/11/1926 at 54; oedema; Daniel Sullivan and Julia McCarthy
Kate, d. 2/15/1896 at 15; mitral insufficiency; b. Dover; SM
Mamie, d. 7/30/1896 at 14; b. Dover; SM
Mary, d. 4/11/1906 at 65; interstitial nephritis; SM
Mary, d. 5/4/1913 at 58; septic meningitis; Martin Fleming
Mary A., d. 9/21/1887 at 28; married; b. NY; Robert Bogle (Ireland) and Mary Murray (Ireland)
Mary E., d. 6/5/1906 at 23/5/23; acute pulm. tuberculosis
Mary F., d. 5/1/1933 at 62; cerebral apoplexy
Mary T., d. 4/19/1900 at 37; peritonitis - acute; SM
Miah B., d. 12/25/1916 at 59/6/26; cerebral hemorrhage; Jeremiah Sullivan and Rebecca Gilman
Michael, d. 5/14/1932 at 80/11/4; cancer of bladder
Michael J., d. 1/6/1922 at 51 in Lawrence, MA; pulmonary tuberculosis
Nora, d. 2/28/1923 at 46 in Tewksbury, MA; lobar pneumonia
Patrick, d. 3/9/1897 at 40; phthisis; b. Ireland; SM
Rebecca G., d. 1/23/1900 at 78; la grippe; buried in Lewiston, ME
Sabrah R., d. 8/18/1913 at 35/8/25; delirium tremens; George F. Clough and Hannah D. Bedell
Teressa, d. 11/6/1887 at 1/6/10; b. Dover; John Sullivan (Ireland) and Ann Riley (Ireland)
Theresa, d. 12/1/1923 at 46; myocarditis; Michael Brennan and ----- Carroll
Thomas, d. 10/15/1912 at 70/5/12; cancer; Ellen Linehan

Thomas H., d. 5/25/1931 at 62 in Lynn, MA; heart disease

SUMMERS,
Catherine E., d. 10/18/1926 at 62/3/14; cerebral hemorrhage; John Summers and Mary Stanford
James S., d. 11/12/1932 at 67/0/16 in Pembroke; acute asthma

SUNDERLAND,
Annie, d. 10/6/1898 at 2; bronchitis; b. Dover; SM
Catherine J., d. 6/22/1924 at 68; cancer of stomach; John Sunderland and Catherine McCooey
Ellen M., d. 12/30/1929 at 51; uterine fibroid; William F. Milner and Bridget Coffey
Frank, d. 2/24/1898 at 14; accident; b. Ireland; SM
John, d. 1/15/1933 at 74/6/20; lobar pneumonia

SUTHERLAND,
Harry W., d. 3/7/1931 at 66/4/27 in Detroit, MI; chronic myocarditis
Margaret F., d. 6/13/1926 at 68/11/17; chr. Brights disease; Patrick J. Desmond and Johanna Sweeney

SUZONI,
Peter, d. 10/2/1918 at 25 in Camp Devens, MA; lobar pneumonia

SWAIN,
child, d. 6/4/1912 at 0/0/1; premature birth; Roy V. Swain and Mattie E. Tucker
Abbie, d. 7/17/1937 at 80/11/26 in Rollinsford; angina pectoris
Anginette E., d. 10/12/1932 at 66/10/15; cerebral hemorrhage
Charles G., d. 12/10/1915 at 84/7/7; fracture arm and hip; Richard Swain and Sally Sherburn
Dudley, d. 6/27/1907 at 78; senility
Elizabeth Ellen, d. 8/13/1917 at 85/5 in Portsmouth; old age
Etta H., d. 4/5/1922 at 56; apoplexy; Edmund Layne and Malinda Jenkins
Fannie M., d. 6/10/1900 at 44; pneumonia; PH
Frank H., d. 8/18/1925 at 71/6/4 in Rollinsford; chr. valv. dis. heart
Harry W., d. 8/1/1888 at 0/9/21; b. Dover; Frank Swain (Boston, MA) and Belle Witham (Dover)
Irene F., d. 6/19/1921 at 59/4/8; cerebral apoplexy; Asa G. Ham and Julia A. Adams
John, d. 11/15/1936 at 52/11/17; cerebral embolism
John D., d. 6/3/1902 at 74/10/10 in Nashua; apoplexy; PH
Louisa M., d. 12/14/1894 at 85; abdominal aneurism; b. Dover; buried in Northwood
Mary, d. 11/26/1893 at 82; old age; b. MA

Sarah J., d. 12/4/1910 at 82/5/17; chronic nephritis; Israel Swain and
 Susan Bennett
Susan C., d. 2/17/1893 at 80; Bright's disease
Wilbur H., d. 6/18/1932 at 41/2/21; fractured skull
William C., d. 3/5/1916 at 56 in Washington, DC; carcinoma of stomach

SWAINE,
C. Jennie, d. 12/10/1910 at 75/5/23; chronic nephritis; Daniel Clough and
 Mehitable Watson
Emma F., d. 10/13/1930 at 72/1/28 in Madbury; coronary
George A., d. 11/29/1916 at 65/11/23; uraemic poisoning; George A.
 Swaine and Lydia Flanders
George A., d. 1/14/1930 at 75/1/21; chronic myocarditis; Daniel Swaine
 and ----- Ham
Georgia T., d. 6/7/1906 at 78/7/4; acute uraemia; PH

SWALLOW,
Beulah P., d. 8/22/1912 at 0/0/2; congenital malformation; Henry E.
 Swallow and Caroline Perley
Elizabeth J., d. 12/18/1929 at 74 in Danvers, MA; arterio sclerosis
Ellen R., d. 1/29/1914 at 74 in Berwick, ME; pneumonia (see following
 entry)
Ellen R., d. 2/1/1914 at 74 in Berwick, ME; pneumonia (see preceding
 entry)
Fred, d. 8/5/1923 at 66/10/30; phthisis pulmonalis; Harry Swallow and
 Sarah Horner
George P., d. 3/25/1894 at –; meningitis; b. Dover; PH
Henry, d. 10/17/1898 at 77 in Madbury; chron. bronchitis, old age; b.
 England; PH
Henry E., d. 11/18/1934 at 52/11; gastric hemorrhage
Herbert, d. 2/9/1894 at 38; phthisis pulmonalis; b. England; PH
John, d. 5/16/1913 at 63/0/3; heart disease; Henry Swallow and Sarah
 Horner
Sarah, d. 4/21/1898 at 73 in Madbury; old age; b. England; PH

SWAN,
Edmund, d. 11/18/1922 at 50/3/7 in Milford, MA; pulmonary tuberculosis
Edmund M., d. 2/28/1902 at 73/5/25; cysto-nephritis; PH
Everett E., d. 10/8/1898 at 18; phthisis pulmonalis; b. Dover; PH
Herbert H., d. 5/31/1893 at 4; inflammation of bowels; b. NY; (Woodstock,
 VT; -----)
Irving M., d. 5/16/1899 at 19; phthisis pulmonalis; PH
Jennie A., d. 6/27/1929 at 98/9/16 in Manchester; senile changes
Mary F., d. 10/18/1915 at 37/2/21; chronic Brights disease; Patrick J.
 Murphy and Mary Cragin

Susan F., d. 3/6/1910 at 72/11/2; paralysis of apoplexy; William H. Clark
and Mary E. Hoitt
William C., d. 4/15/1932 at 64/2/23; pulmonary tuberculosis

SWASEY,
Annie B., d. 2/14/1928 at 55; carcinoma of stomach; Zebelon Knight and
Sarah F. Norman
Frank A., d. 5/12/1930 at 78/7/5 in Somersworth; cancer prostate
Joseph P., d. 7/30/1915 at 90/7/20 in Rochester; valv. heart disease
Mary E., d. 4/3/1899 at 71 in Rochester; uraemic poisoning; PH
Mary E., d. 1/27/1935 at 85/5/11 in Newmarket; lobar pneumonia
Rena, d. 12/20/1931 at 38/1/7; embolism - heart

SWAZEY,
William H., d. 1/23/1891 at 28/6/23 in Portland, ME

SWEAT,
Samuel D., d. 12/23/1889 at 2; b. Dover; S. D. Burley (US) and S. E. Price
(US)

SWEENEY,
Allen, d. 2/11/1913 at 75 in Somersworth; probably heart disease
Catherine, d. 3/29/1910 at 84/3 in E. Kingston; ashthma
Edward, d. 1/28/1923 at 82 in New York, NY; arterio sclerosis
Ellen, d. 2/16/1890 at 2/1/23; Patrick Sweeney (Ireland) and Margaret
Mahoney (Ireland)
Honora, d. 12/2/1927 at 82; arterio sclerosis
James, d. 3/30/1900 at 40; phthisis; SM
Margaret, d. 9/14/1917 at 67; pulmonary oedema; Cornelius Mahoney and
Mary Connell
Patrick, d. 2/19/1920 at 73; uraemia; John Sweeney and Mary Harrigan

SWEET,
Alfred, d. 8/8/1916 at 50; osteomyelitis

SWEETSIR,
Ruth, d. 8/10/1936 at 2/3 in Portland, ME; surg. sh., ac. cir. col.

SWETT,
Sarah E., d. 2/9/1893 at 40; died in Strafford Co. Asylum fire

SWIFT,
Edward, d. 5/17/1915 at 52/1/20; acute dilat. of heart; Alfred Swift and
Mary A. O'Brien

John J., d. 8/4/1934 at 46; emphysema
Mary A., d. 11/15/1925 at 62; diabetes mellitus; Peter Nugent and Eliza Griffin
Michael, d. 6/17/1892 at 25; Bright's disease; b. Ireland; (Ireland; Ireland)
Michael, d. 12/14/1933 at 41 in Pembroke; pulmonary tuberculosis
R., d. 3/9/1906 ar 34; chronic interstitial nephritis; SM

SWINERTON,
Frank, d. 2/14/1926 at 58; acute gastro enteritis

SYKES,
Ellen, d. 12/18/1914 at 81/7/20 in Somersworth; old age
William, d. 11/15/1917 at 87; chronic prostatitis; Walter Sykes and Betty Taylor
William W., d. 7/20/1888 at 8/7/20; b. England; William Sykes (England) and Hellen Haigh (England)

SYLVAIN,
Caroline, d. 7/24/1932 at 99/4/7; acute bronchitis

SYLVESTER,
Delphine, d. 3/30/1934 at 90/5/5; chronic myocarditis
James, d. 9/28/1922 at 80/2/18; broncho pneumonia; Hinchman Sylvester and Mary Alexander

SYLVESTRE,
Annie, d. 5/16/1904 at 20/5; septic peritonitis; SM
Blanche E., d. 5/21/1904 at 0/5/15; acute endocarditis; SM

SYMES,
Chester F., d. 9/21/1892 at 4; croup; b. Dover; (Newfield, ME; Durham)
Frank E., d. 1/5/1917 at 54/11/21; nephritis; Eben Symes and Olive Goodwin

SZUFLAT,
Walter, d. 11/3/1926 at 12/5/3; abscess of brain; Joseph Szuflat and Rosie Dzika

TAGLE,
Mary Jane, d. 4/22/1930 at 42/4/16 in Portsmouth; ac. dil. of heart

TAILBY,
George, d. 7/23/1891 at 0/1/3; George Tailby (England) and Maggie Riley (Scotland)

Margaret E., d. 8/14/1896 at –; cholera infantum; b. Dover; SM

TALBOTT,
Peter, d. 4/27/1928 at 74; chronic endocarditis

TALON,
Angelina, d. 3/17/1933 at 70/4/8; carcinoma of uterus
James, d. 2/11/1928 at 78; acute gastro enteritis
John B., d. 11/2/1931 at 78/5/6; cerebral hemorrhage

TANGUAY,
Alexis, d. 12/21/1896 at 47; heart disease; b. Canada; SM
Antoine, d. 7/26/1892 at 14; accidental drowning; b. Canada; (Canada; Canada)
Mary, d. 6/10/1913 at 67/4/9; endocarditis; Patrick McCabe and Catherine Hughes

TANNER,
Hervey E., d. 12/25/1929 at 66/4/25; arthritis deformans; Martha Wiggin
Mary H., d. 2/7/1908 at 69/1/13; cerebral hemorrhage

TANTON,
William H., d. 8/9/1927 at 85/5/27; gen. arterio sclerosis; Thomas Tanton and Fannie Pengilly

TAPLEY,
Caroline R., d. 4/4/1932 at 75/5/12; chronic endocarditis
Clara H., d. 10/9/1893 at 59; Bright's disease; b. Portsmouth; (Portsmouth; Eliot, ME)
Elizabeth, d. 4/11/1932 at 62/3/5; angina pectoris
Gilbert C., d. 8/5/1903 at 71/11/25; Brights disease; PH
John S., d. 9/17/1896 at 72; angina pectoris; b. Dover; PH
William R., d. 9/3/1897 at 77; heart disease; b. Dover; PH

TARDIFF,
Frank, d. 5/1/1910 at 59; cerebral apoplexy
Frank, d. 12/31/1933 at 59/7/30 in Concord; broncho pneumonia

TARMELEY,
Hannah E., d. 7/31/1907 at 0/9; convulsions; Patrick Tarmeley and Kate McNulty

TARNEY,
James Joseph, d. 4/7/1935 at 33/6/10; empyema

James P., d. 4/3/1913 at 44; cerebral apoplexy; Thomas Tarney and Catherine -----

TARR,
Charles M., d. 6/21/1911 at 52/8/21 in Manchester; chronic bronchitis; Seth Tarr and Carrie Montgomery
Hattie B., d. 12/6/1916 at 53 in Manchester; surgical shock; Charles H. Twombly and Elizabeth Snell
Seth A., d. 4/15/1888 at 0/1/19; b. Dover; Charles M. Tarr (Iowa) and Hattie Twombly (Dover)

TASH,
Edwin S., d. 3/16/1895 at 57; suicide; b. New Durham; PH
Ellen M., d. 11/7/1917 at 66/10/15; deg. brain disease; Joseph A. James and Mary M. Fernald
Florence J., d. 12/17/1891 at 0/19/3; Edwin S. Tash (New Durham) and Ellen J. James (Lee)
Marianna W., d. 2/21/1887 at 36/4; widow; b. Dover; Daniel K. (Derry) and Elizabeth Downs (Milton)
Martha S., d. 8/24/1914 at 44 in Philadelphia, PA; after inquest

TASIKAS,
Christos, d. 9/2/1935 at 54; coronary thrombosis

TASKER,
Albert P., d. 8/28/1902 at 5/7/24 in Alton; accidental drowning; PH
Avilla, d. 2/23/1934 at 78 in Concord; val. heart disease
Charles A., d. 9/2/1922 at 65/10/18; diabetes mellitus; Lorenzo Tasker and Mary L. Allen
Charles H., d. 2/22/1926 at 67 in Newton, MA; arterio sclerosis
Charles W., d. 1/14/1923 at 77/3/28 in New Haven, CT; broncho pneumonia
Elizabeth M., d. 9/3/1899 at 71; diabetic coma; PH
Enoch O., d. 4/28/1918 at 71/1/2; internal hemorrhage; Thomas J. Tasker and Comfort Bickford
Henry, d. 1/7/1899 at 82; cerebral apoplexy; PH
Jennie E., d. 2/11/1898 at 40; apoplexy; b. Deerfield; PH
John C., d. 1/2/1919 at 75/4/16 in Saco, ME; exhaustion
John G., d. 7/1/1891 at 70; married; Elisha Tasker (Strafford) and Mary Buzzell (Barrington)
Maria B., d. 1/8/1926 at 82/4/23 in New Haven, CT; vascular venal disease
Mary C., d. 5/12/1917 at 85/1/5; atheroma; Jonathan Hall and Lydia Demeritt
Sarah McDuffy, d. 1/17/1936 at 83/9/19*
Ursula M., d. 3/9/1936 at 85/2/14; frac. of rt. femur

William A., d. 3/6/1920 at 73/6/7; lobar pneumonia; Jewett Tasker and
   Lydia Lefavour
William H., d. 8/14/1920 at 71/11/13 in Medford, MA; cerebral hemorrhage

TATE,
child, d. 7/24/1923 at –; premature birth; Walter P. Tate and Chrissie G.
   Carpenter
Elizabeth I., d. 10/13/1934 at 9/10/29; frac. of skull (acc.)
Hazel, d. 10/8/1918 at 30/5/9; lobar pneumonia; Charles H. Clark and
   Lillian Sanford
James Henry, d. 3/28/1933 at 67/9/18; arteriosclerosis
William A., d. 12/1/1924 at 75 in Boston, MA; arterio sclerosis

TATRO,
daughter, d. 6/10/1888 at –; Joseph Tatro (Dover) and Mary E. Knott
   (Dover)
Catherine, d. 1/24/1896 at 43; shock; b. Dover; SM
Mary H., d. 8/28/1936 at 66*
Mary Selina, d. 2/6/1892 at 4; cerebro spinal meningitis; b. Newmarket;
   (Dover; England)

TAUNTON,
Lavina, d. 4/30/1925 at 76/1/15; chr. arthritis deformans; James Stevens
   and Sarah -----
Thomas D., d. 5/14/1928 at 83/0/6; cerebral hemorrhage; Thomas
   Taunton and Fannie Pengilly

TAYLOR,
child, d. 8/29/1892 at –; asphyxia; b. Dover; (England; Ireland)
child, d. 1/20/1934 at 0/0/2 in Summit Union, NJ; prematurity
Alice, d. 7/21/1928 at 64/8/17; apoplexy
Annie B., d. 5/26/1889 at 4/1/19; b. England; William H. Taylor (England)
   and Lois Walton (England)
Beatrice G., d. 8/23/1888 at 0/6/1; b. Dover; Charles T. Taylor (Pembroke,
   MA) and Annie C. (Dover)
Catherine, d. 12/10/1909 at 75; heart failure
Catherine I., d. 8/6/1935 at 81; cerebral embolism
Charles F., d. 11/14/1931 at 70/7/21; carcinoma stomach
Clara E., d. 10/15/1926 at 79/8/11; cerebral hemorrhage; Andrew Tuttle
   and Susan Demeritt
David F., d. 6/20/1898 at 0; inanition; b. Dover; PH
Ella E. D. Towle, d. 4/7/1936 at 56/11/27*; b. NH
Ethel, d. 8/24/1887 at 0/1/20; b. Dover; Henry Taylor (England) and
   Jeanette Brown (Scotland)
Fannie C., d. 3/28/1909 at 46/9/28 in Somersworth; valvular dis. of heart

Haven, d. 8/4/1890 at 0/0/16; Charles F. Taylor (Pembroke) and Anna
  Pinkham (Dover)
Henrietta, d. 3/27/1900 at 46; acute nephritis; PH
Ida M., d. 4/3/1900 at 23; consumption; PH
James F., d. 11/20/1920 at 56 in Portland, ME; myocarditis; Prestly Taylor
  and Mary Renshaw
John J., d. 8/25/1902 at 43/0/8; heart disease
Lois, d. 2/2/1893 at 27; phthisis pulmonalis; b. England; (England;
  England)
Mary Ann, d. 1/24/1899 at 34; paralysis; PH
Mary F., d. 8/2/1905 at 74/1/26; convulsions; PH
Mary M., d. 9/20/1910 at 80/6/27 in Somersworth; enteritis
Maud V., d. 4/26/1901 at 0/1/18; marasmus; PH
Nathan L., d. 12/18/1904 at 69/8/8; pneumonia; PH
Norman F., d. 2/25/1923 at 30/2/5; tubercular enteritis; Charles F. Taylor
  and Ida M. Eastman
Ovid, Sr., d. 12/8/1933 at 66/1/15; chronic endocarditis
Peter, d. 6/4/1888 at 67/3/22; mac. printer; widower; b. England; James
  Taylor (England) and Margaret Kenyon (England)
Priestley, d. 9/23/1903 at 64/9/10; cerebral hemorrhage; PH
Roger E., d. 3/21/1934 at 9/11/14; lobar pneumonia
Sarah, d. 1/15/1888 at 69; married; b. Boston, MA
Sarah, d. 2/20/1896 at 80; paralysis; b. Greenfield; buried in Nashua
Sidney Edward, d. 12/17/1929 at 60/8/10; angina pectoris; Priestly Taylor
  and Mary Renshaw
William D., d. 1/2/1894 at 44; suicide by hanging; b. Amherst, NS; PH

TEBBETS,
Eva L., d. 12/27/1900 at 2; meningitis; PH

TEBBETTS,
Alma F., d. 8/28/1914 at 55/4/23; cancer of uterus; William M. Roach and
  Lavena C. Master
Clarence E., d. 1/23/1896 at 40 in So. Berwick, ME; heart disease
Emma E., d. 2/22/1935 at 73 in Plymouth, PA; pneumonia
Eva May, d. 11/17/1905 at 29/0/24; pulmonary tuberculosis; PH
Fairybelle S., d. 3/15/1936 at 57/2/15; carcinoma of rectum
Jasper M., d. 1/1/1906 at 34/9/26; septic infection; PH
Samuel A., d. 6/15/1919 at 82/1/1; gangrene foot and leg; Isaac Tebbetts
  and Maria Fuller
Walter R., d. 5/8/1935 at 62/11/17; fractured skull

TEBBITTS,
Deborah, d. 12/1/1888 at 84/2/23; widow; b. Meaderboro; M. Meader and
  Sarah Varney

TEEL,
Alonzo, d. 11/23/1907 at 70/11/22; broncho-pneumonia; James Teel and Malinda Johnnet

TEELE,
Margaret, d. 5/23/1924 at 79/10/19; cancer of neck; Matthew Scholey and Margaret Fitzgerald

TEELING,
Grace E., d. 1/27/1933 at 76/8/1; chronic nephritis

TEERI,
Esther M., d. 8/23/1898 at 48; cancer; b. Durham; buried in Durham

TEIKER,
Bernard, d. 3/21/1888 at 36/1/21; pedlar; married; b. Germany; Murace Teiker (Germany)

TERREAULT,
Clifford, d. 10/6/1924 at 63; broncho pneumonia

TERRY,
Mattie, d. 10/4/1902 at 33; chronic Bright's disease, etc.; buried in family lot

THATCHER,
Emily J., d. 9/12/1914 at 86; acute indigestion; George Cook and Jennie Crosby

THAYER,
Alice E., d. 5/13/1934 at 85/4/15; arteriosclerosis
Allen I., d. 5/17/1891 at 55/5/28; married; Otis Thayer (Randolph, MA) and Lavena Cleaveland (Brookfield, VT)
Hiram B., d. 12/12/1896 at 49; insanity; PH
Lucy M., d. 11/6/1903 at 67/7/24; softening of the brain; PH
Mary Jackson, d. 1/30/1928 at 39/7/23 in Somersworth; suicide by shooting
William E., d. 5/31/1935 at 0/2/28 in Auburn, ME; jaundice of new born

THEBEAULT,
John, d. 3/14/1927 at 49/6/6; acute alcoholism; Jean B. Thebeault and Cleophie Boucher

THEBERGE,
Delia, d. 12/27/1924 at 42; intestinal obstruction

THEOPHEL,
Aveania, d. 8/7/1920 at 36; myocarditis

THEORET,
Ludger, d. 10/17/1923 at 65; cancer of thigh; Louis Theoret and Adelaide Brunnel

THERRIAN,
Leo, d. 8/20/1900 at <1; cholera infantum

THERRIEN,
Achille, d. 4/11/1909 at 0/3/20; pneumonia; Philippi Therrien and Lila Beauchesnes
Delvina, d. 2/11/1937 at 76/7/18; chr. endocarditis
Eva, d. 1/27/1909 at 8; typhoid fever; Joseph Therrien and Philomene Chaines
Fred, d. 8/29/1901 at 0/4; cholera infantum
Joseph, d. 11/18/1935 at 44/10/12 in Boston, MA; fractured spine
Joseph H., d. 5/9/1908 at 0/3/19; marasmus; Philippe Therrien and Lily Beauchesnes
Julien E., d. 6/26/1911 at 0/4; ac. gastro-enteritis; Philip Therrien and Lilly Beauchesne
Lena, d. 10/6/1920 at 0/10; lobar pneumonia; Philip Therrien and Lily Beaushean
Lilly, d. 3/3/1921 at 37/4/4; tuberculosis of lungs; Ansel Beaushanes and Alvinean Gregoire
Marie Anna, d. 9/4/1914 at 0/1/18; acute pneumonia; Alfred Therrien and Clorida Demers
Philippe, d. 11/23/1937 at 58/6/22; myocarditis spandylitis
Phillips Napoleon, d. 10/5/1911 at 1/5/23; gastro enteritis; Napoleon Therrien and Adele Boissoneau
Rudolph L. J., d. 8/8/1915 at 0/3/5; marasmus; Napoleon Therrien and Adile Boissoneau
Telesphore, d. 2/27/1919 at 60/1; chronic bronchitis; Telesphore Therrien and Lucille Larocles
Wilfred J., d. 10/27/1925 at 42 in Lawrence, MA; natural causes
Zephtrin, d. 3/3/1919 at 38/3/1; tuberculosis of lungs; Telesphore Therrien and Delphine Boufort

THEVIERGE,
Leon M. A., d. 3/29/1922 at 0/0/2; intestinal hemorrhage; Frank Thivierge and Theodora Dion

THIBAULT,
Alphonsine, d. 6/29/1906 at 22; eclampsia
Eva, d. 7/16/1905 at 18; accidental drowning; buried in Gonic

THIBEAULT,
Francis, d. 5/13/1916 at 64; chron. Brights dis.; Francis Thibeault and Teressa Bouhan
George I., d. 5/27/1925 at 51/1/25; cancer of rectum; Camille Thibeault and Olive Duchame

THIBRAULT,
Emelie, d. 7/6/1927 at 76/5; gen. arterio sclerosis; Arsene Lassell and Emelie Beaulieu

THOMAS,
child, d. 6/27/1923 at 0/0/½; premature birth; Jennie Thomas
Abraham, d. 9/23/1916 at 75; broken cardiac com.
Ann, d. 6/23/1927 at 51; lateral sclerosis
Annie, d. 3/30/1900 at 52; apoplectic coma; PH
Jacob W., d. 5/31/1936 at 50/0/24*; b. PA
Mary J., d. 5/30/1908 at 48; cancer of the liver

THOMPSON,
Agnes, d. 12/12/1927 at 77/2/18 in Durham; paraplegia
Alice P., d. 12/10/1933 at 85/0/22 in Burlington, VT; arteriosclerosis
Augusta W., d. 11/5/1935 at 86/7/26; cerebral hemorrhage
Carrie B., d. 7/31/1919 at 48/2/24; acute indigestion; Charles Thompson and Mary J. Meader
Charles, d. 9/25/1895 at 75; heart disease; b. Farmington; buried at Dover Point
Charles, d. 3/19/1914 at 78 in Alton; pneumonia
Charles A., d. 8/2/1903 at 53/1/9; probably lead poisoning; PH
Charles A., d. 4/25/1919 at 64/3/29; natural causes; Isaac Thompson and Asenath Norman
Charles H., d. 2/12/1907 at 60 in Wakefield, MA; valvular heart disease
Clyde, d. 1/27/1930 at 38; empyemia; Eugene Thompson and Ida H. Goodwin
Edward F., d. 8/23/1890 at 45/11/22; married; Mark Thompson (Lebanon, ME) and Prudence Church (Barrington)
Edward J., d. 2/1/1904 at 0/3/5; convulsions; SM

Elizabeth, d. 6/5/1915 at 43; acute miliary tuberculosis
Ella J., d. 7/17/1925 at 68/6/12; carcinoma of intestines; Lyman Lougee and Nancy Durgin
Emeline B., d. 6/18/1909 at 68/6/19; cardiac dilation; Robert Thomson, M.D. and Isabella Spencer
Ernest C., d. 12/15/1933 at 56/3/24 in Lynn, MA; cerebral apoplexy
Ernest M., d. 12/21/1904 at 2/3/10 in Boston, MA; broncho-pneumonia; PH
Fannie R., d. 6/28/1920 at 40/2/8; diabetes; Stephen R. Freeman and Fannie R. Chamberlain
Frank E., d. 5/17/1930 at 76/8/19; apoplexy; John Thompson and Mary A. Marchant
George, d. 2/27/1901 at 61; paralysis; buried in Rochester
George A., d. 4/13/1907 at 76/8/22; pneumonia; Mark Thompson and Prudence Church
George A., d. 8/6/1914 at 45 in Hillsboro; acute alcoholism
Grace E., d. 10/8/1918 at 30/7/27 in Pittsfield; pneumonia - bronchitis; Joseph E. Hill and Flora E. Webber
Harold L., d. 10/7/1918 at – in Pittsfield; stillborn; Albert L. Thompson and Grace E. Hill
Harriet N., d. 11/15/1901 at 95/4/16; cardiac dilitation; PH
Henry F., d. 8/12/1937 at 80*
James, d. 10/16/1892 at 30; gastritis; b. Berwick, ME; (Ireland; Ireland)
James A., d. 1/1/1920 at 80/8/2; chronic nephritis; Mark Thompson and Prudence Church
Jedida M., d. 2/17/1896 at 66; paralysis; b. Union, ME; PH
John, d. 12/13/1898 at 88; old age; b. Lee; PH
John, d. 2/18/1904 at 48; acute tuberculosis; SM
John, d. 3/10/1907 at 42/6; myelitis; William Thompson and Barbara Retchoe
John A., d. 12/3/1936 at 83*
Louisa J., d. 5/31/1901 at 66/10/10; cerebral hemorrhage; PH
Leroy S., d. 11/9/1913 at 63; heart disease; Samuel Thompson and Louisa Scilley
Martha J., d. 2/29/1928 at 81/7/1 in Lynn, MA; arterio sclerosis
Mary A., d. 4/10/1907 at 72/7/24; pneumonia; Mark Thompson and Prudence Church
Mary E. L., d. 8/22/1921 at 68/9/22; lobar pneumonia; Charles H. Trickey and Martha S. Cater
Mary H., d. 4/21/1900 at 77; heart disease; PH
Mary J., d. 2/8/1905 at 57/0/18; pernicious anemia; PH
Mary J., d. 1/4/1910 at 84/4/25 in Durham; acute bronchitis
Mary J., d. 1/12/1911 at 73/9/12; heart disease; Joseph Meader and Abbie Nason
Mary L., d. 1/30/1915 at 65/4/24; cancer of stomach; John E. Thompson and Mary J. Pickering

Mary L., d. 2/21/1924 at 71/1/7; ac. lobar pneumonia; Clark Robinson and Annie Hall
Mary M., d. 5/26/1935 at 71/7/7 in Somersworth; angina pectoris
Max S., d. 6/11/1911 at 4/10/27; cerebral thrombosis; Alexander C. Thompson and Minnie B. Carl
Prudence, d. 3/4/1895 at 91; la grippe - heart disease; b. Barrington; PH
Raymond L., d. 9/17/1916 at 0/11/17 in Pittsfield; pneumonia
Rhoda, d. 4/22/1909 at 82/6/15; senility; Miles Davis and Betsey ----
Robert, d. 12/8/1898 at 0; pneumonia; b. Dover; PH
Rosanna, d. 3/26/1891 at 63/4/26; widow; James Calleghan (Ireland) and ---- (Ireland)
Rose, d. 4/16/1896 at 2; catarrhal pneumonia; SM
W. L., d. 9/30/1894 at 71 in Augusta, ME; cancer; buried in Dover
William, d. 1/26/1887 at 65/0/10; miner; widower; b. Scotland; John Thompson (Scotland) and Mary McVicker (Scotland)
William J., d. 5/11/1934 at 40/8/29; cardiac dilatation

THOMSON,
Isabel, d. 6/10/1888 at 78/4; widow; b. Scotland; Adam Spencer (Scotland) and Jessie Duncan (Scotland)
Isabella D., d. 1/14/1920 at 85; bronchitis; Robert Thomson and Isabella B. Spence
James D., d. 9/19/1903 at 72 in Boston, MA; heart disease

THORIN,
Likard S. E., d. 3/24/1925 at 0/0/14; diarrhea and enteritis; Gustav Thorin and Gerda Magnusen

THORNTON,
Mary J., d. 7/9/1922 at 50/5/13; tuberculosis of kidney; Joseph Pearson and Mary ----
Novello W., d. 3/22/1898 at 20; peritonitis; b. England; PH
Thomas W., d. 4/3/1923 at 61/9/5; secondary anemia; John Thornton and Elizabeth Kenyon

THOROUGHGOOD,
child, d. 9/17/1904 at 0/0/6; unknown; buried in Austin Cem.

THORPE,
Harry, d. 5/12/1924 at 31/8/28; scurvy; Ebenezer Thorp (sic) and Jane ----

THURSTON,
Charles W., d. 12/10/1901 at 73/3/25; burned to death; PH

Clara A., d. 3/29/1890 at 81/8/13; married; William Chase (Seabrook) and Ruth Lowell (Amesbury, MA)
Eugene B., d. 3/28/1916 at 76/5/4; paresis; Joshua Thurston and Clarissa A. Leach
James, d. 9/15/1899 at 83; catarrhal fever; PH
Lydia E., d. 1/1/1905 at 62/5/10; organic heart disease; buried in Lee
Sarah S., d. 10/4/1911 at 65/10 in Kennebunkport, ME; apoplexy
Susan Emily, d. 6/10/1903 at 75/0/10 in Exeter; chronic bronchitis; PH

TIBBETTS,
Annie B., d. 3/24/1923 at 53/9/25 in Boston, MA; syncope
Augusta L., d. 10/21/1908 at 83/6/14 in Durham; cancer
Beatrice E., d. 7/15/1918 at 17/11/22; coma; John J. Tibbetts and Frances M. Lane
Caroline A., d. 4/19/1920 at 86/3/12; lobar pneumonia; Robert Lefavour and Mary Peck
Charles E., d. 10/23/1903 at 79/4/24 in Madbury; heart disease; PH
Charles W., d. 4/11/1891 at 43/0/23; married; Elijah H. Tibbetts (Berwick, ME) and D. Meader (Farmington)
Clarence J., d. 11/22/1896 at 30; scarlet fever; b. Milton; PH
Dorothy M., d. 8/26/1932 at 20/2/6; pulmonary tuberculosis
Edna M., d. 1/30/1917 at 36/10/3 in Concord; suicide; Andrew Wormell and Roxanna Hanson
Ellen E., d. 3/22/1894 at 49; anaemia; b. Barrington; PH
Eri L., d. 8/22/1930 at 66/11/27; carcinoma intestines; R. B. Tibbetts and Nancy H. Buzzell
Fannie S., d. 3/14/1928 at 82/5/7; cerebral hemorrhage; John Noble and Eliza Kelsey
Frank E., d. 12/16/1931 at 65/11/29; pulmonary oedema
Fred N., d. 11/14/1888 at 20/11/14; heel cutter; married; b. Milton; James H. Tibbetts (Gardiner, ME) and Mary Wakeham (Milton)
Frederick A., d. 2/8/1919 at 54/3/8; natural causes; Frederick B. Tibbetts and Caroline A. LaFavour
Frederick B., d. 8/12/1910 at 82/2/15; pneumonia; Nathaniel Tibbetts and Ann W. Hodgdon
George B., d. 4/17/1917 at 70/9/11; carcinoma of face; Jeremiah Tibbetts and Mary Drew
Herbert C., d. 5/2/1916 at 8/2/27; Ernest C. Tibbetts and Mary Brady
Ichabod, d. 11/5/1903 at 85/5/9; shock; PH
Isabel C., d. 1/25/1913 at 68/10/10; progressive paralysis; Samuel Harrison and Melinda J. Hurd
James H., d. 11/11/1922 at 78/3/25 in Whitman, MA; arterio sclerosis
Jane H., d. 11/4/1909 at 65/2/4 in Saco, ME; chr. intest. nephritis
John K., d. 9/23/1899 at 69; old age; buried in East Rochester

Lillian May, d. 10/21/1909 at 0/6/12; marasmus; Ernest C. Tibbetts and Mary Brady
Lola E., d. 10/16/1934 at 75/1/8; uterine carcinoma
Lydia, d. 8/29/1900 at 80; old age; PH
Mary, d. 9/15/1932 at 48/0/15; asphyxiation
Mary E., d. 6/2/1916 at 67/10/29 in Whitman, MA; chronic nephritis
Mary E., d. 1/16/1934 at 78; heart failure
Mary W., d. 4/1/1911 at 81/11/24 in E. Bridgewater, MA; cerebral hemorrhage
Nancy H., d. 10/9/1918 at 87/10/24; general arterio sclerosis; Jonathan Buzzell and Polly Hill
Sarah A., d. 12/31/1905 at 75/11/13; PH
Sophronia, d. 6/22/1900 at 72 in So. Berwick, ME; Bright's disease; PH
Stephen, d. 4/23/1922 at 80/8/18 in Saco, ME; chronic nephritis
Wesley J., d. 9/3/1917 at 19 in Old Orchard, ME; drowned
William L., d. 5/29/1902 at 64/7/15; cerebral hemorrhage; PH

TIBEAULT,
Catherine, d. 1/10/1892 at 52; heart disease; b. Ireland; (Ireland; Ireland)

TIERNEY,
Joseph, d. 2/20/1912 at 28/5/5; epilepsy; Joseph Tierney and Jessie Fountain

TIGHE,
Alice, d. 5/13/1897 at 80 in Rollinsford; valvular disease of heart

TILTON,
Martin V. B., d. 11/19/1912 at 72/2/10; diabetes mellitus; Samuel Tilton and Sally Sinclair
Mary E., d. 6/9/1931 at 78; pernicious anaemia

TIMMINS,
child, d. 10/11/1905 at –; stillborn
Catherine, d. 2/15/1897 at 65; dysentery; b. Dover; SM
Edgar, d. 4/5/1930 at 56; shock, etc.; Melinda Phillips
Mildred, d. 9/6/1932 at 29 in Boston, MA; pelvic cellulitis

TIMMONS,
child, d. 1/18/1897 at 0; stillborn; b. Dover
Annie, d. 2/23/1896 at –; marasmus; b. Dover; SM
Mary, d. 6/10/1894 at 1; convulsions; b. Dover; SM
William F., d. 2/22/1905 at 41/3/13; pneumonia; buried in Kennebunk, ME

TIMSON,
Charles, d. 10/14/1924 at 75; broncho pneumonia

TINGUE,
Joseph, d. 3/22/1913 at 40/4; Joseph Tingue and Pamelia Mercier

TINKER,
Arthur C., d. 12/4/1928 at 47/9/16; tuberculosis of kidney; Irving C. Tinker and Martha Whitworth
Charles E., d. 10/4/1896 at 17; typhoid fever; b. Lawrence, MA; PH
Everett J., d. 2/2/1896 at –; pneumonia; b. Dover; PH
Irving C., d. 2/6/1930 at 74/0/11; cancer of bones; Hosea Tinker and Mary J. Billings
Martha E., d. 12/11/1933 at 74/7/14 in Portsmouth; cerebral hemorrhage
Mary E., d. 8/12/1933 at 52/10/12; suicide - drowning

TIRRELL,
Catherine E., d. 7/25/1932 at 47/3/20; broncho pneumonia

TITUS,
Lilla E., d. 9/18/1921 at 49/3/14; general debility; Charles W. Segee and Charlotte I. Worden

TOAS,
Eliza, d. 6/24/1913 at 60/8/8; abdominal carcinoma; John Brown and Ann Hewitt

TOBEY,
child, d. 12/2/1905 at –; stillborn; SM

TOBIN,
Charles, d. 11/24/1922 at 53; carcinoma of large intestine; Patrick Tobin and Ann Stevens
James, d. 11/8/1903 at 51; pneumonia; SM
Susan, d. 9/17/1916 at 68; intestinal obstruction; Patrick Donnelly and Margaret Burns
Susan V., d. 6/4/1930 at 54; cancer of uterus; James Tobin and Susan Donnelly

TOBY,
Eliza Jane, d. 6/4/1916 at 82/5/10 in Manchester; pneumonia; Thomas Dana and ----- Whitney
Hannah E., d. 7/25/1921 at 58/1/6; pneumonia; John H. Brackett and Olive A. Lang

Olive E., d. 9/5/1889 at 0/4/22; b. Dover; Charles H. Toby (Dover) and
   Ellen H. Brackett (Dover)
Willard R., d. 5/24/1902 at 60/10/20 in Oxford, MA; renal apoplexy; PH

TOLMAN,
Edmund, d. 1/31/1887 at 93; b. Dorchester, MA

TOLMAY,
Ellen, d. 5/3/1897 at 57; Brights disease; b. Hallowell, ME; SM
Nicholas, d. 4/4/1917 at 76/4; cerebral hemorrhage; Nicholas Tolmay and
   Anne King
Rose, d. 12/16/1897 at 43; shock; b. Hallowell, ME; SM
Thomas, d. 1/18/1924 at 80/10/10; gen. arterio sclerosis; Nicholas Tolmay
   and Ann King

TOMNEY,
Ann, d. 10/30/1897 at 55; apoplexy; SM

TOMONY,
Sarah, d. 3/6/1922 at 58; diabetic coma; Arthur Tomony and Ann Hughes

TOMPKINS,
Adrianna C., d. 6/27/1914 at 63/1/29; uraemia; David Tompkins and
   Hannah Stevenson
Frank S., d. 1/21/1916 at 62/5/10; abdominal carcinoma; David Tompkins
   and Hannah Stevenson
Hannah S., d. 12/23/1900 at 84; bronchitis; PH
Raymond J., d. 4/9/1910 at 8/1/28; appendicitis; Frank S. Tompkins and
   Sarah A. Jordan

TONER,
Owen, d. 2/23/1900 at 50 in Portsmouth; heart disease; PH

TOOF,
child, d. 12/29/1921 at –; undeveloped; Arthur S. Toof and Irene Robinson
Abbie J., d. 12/21/1926 at 83/1/8; la grippe; Mark Vitturin and Julia M.
   Mudgett
Beatrice E., d. 2/20/1915 at 16/0/3; diabetes mellitus; Mark J. Toof and
   Maud J. Crapeau
Herman L., d. 1/13/1922 at – in DeLand, FL; chronic nephritis

TOOLIN,
Mary A., d. 12/26/1918 at 38/7/11; pneumonia; Owen Toolin and Mary
   Hughes

TOOTHILL,
John, d. 5/21/1925 at 79/2/6 in N. Attleboro, MA; cerebral hemorrhage

TOOTIL,
John H., d. 5/12/1896 at 26; phthisis; b. Southbridge, MA; PH

TOOTILL,
Hester A., d. 4/25/1914 at 72/6/3 in Wakefield; pneumonia
Jane A., d. 12/1/1889 at 41/0/12; housewife; married; b. England; ----- Wilkinson (England) and Anna Cronshaw (England)
Lizzie P., d. 4/9/1908 at 63/4/2; disease of brain; Nathaniel Perry and Eliza Perkins
Mary A., d. 6/30/1889 at 0/3/26; b. Dover; John Tootill (England) and Jane Wilkinson (England)

TOPPAN,
Ida R., d. 1/18/1892 at 43; pneumonia; b. Dover; (Porter, ME; Brookfield)
John Q., d. 9/26/1913 at 74/7/25 in Rochester; uraemia
Stephen, d. 10/20/1891 at 41/4/15; married; Stephen Toppan (Newburyport, MA) and Emma Smith

TOREY,
child, d. 8/26/1906 at –; stillborn; PH

TORR,
Abel Stanley, d. 11/26/1909 at 0/0/3; hemorrhage from nose; Frank S. Torr and Maude S. Witham
Adelaide H., d. 8/21/1912 at 55/1/25 in Concord; diarrhea and enteritis; John S. Torr and Caroline Dudley
Andrew, d. 8/25/1918 at 70/3/22; arterio sclerosis; Simon J. Torr and Mary J. French
Charles Wesley, d. 6/7/1930 at 77 in Portsmouth; pernicious anaemia
Clara French, d. 6/10/1892 at –; malformation; b. Dover; (Dover; Peabody, MA)
Edith F., d. 11/15/1936 at – in Rochester; stillborn
Emma C., d. 4/14/1911 at 58/10/7; tuberculosis of the bowels; Jeremiah York and Evelyn Bennett
John Francis, d. 9/5/1926 at 70/3/11; arterio sclerosis; Simon J. Torr and Mary J. French
Keith H., d. 5/4/1932 at 0/1/16; malnutrition
Ralph D., d. 11/30/1893 at –; convulsions; b. Dover; (Dover; Peabody, MA)
Simon Jones, d. 7/21/1899 at 78; heart disease and old age; PH

TORSNEY,
Timothy, d. 12/17/1916 at 61; dilatation of heart; John Torsney and ----Winn

TOSTEN,
Harry, d. 4/3/1921 at 0/1/8; intestinal obstruction; Charles E. Tosten and Arvilla Welch

TOUPIN,
Albert, d. 10/30/1907 at 0/1/9; arthrepsia; Eugene Toupin and Edourdina Allard

TOUREGNY,
Fred, d. 10/8/1906 at 33; SM

TOWLE,
child, d. 6/29/1912 at –; stillborn; Irving W. Towle and Maud E. Otis
child, d. 1/14/1922 at 0/0/5; bronchial pneumonia; Everett L. Towle and Augusta Brown
Alamanzor R., d. 1/11/1910 at 78/5/26; acute intest. obstruction; John W. Towle and Mary Roberts
Alice I., d. 9/16/1930 at 57/7/29; carcinoma; Channing Folsom and Ruth F. Savage
Annie Marie, d. 6/21/1928 at 76/2/11; chronic myocarditis; John Dunn
Charles N., d. 11/25/1914 at 73/5/3 in Concord; diabetes; George W. Towle and Mary Roberts
Elsie Davis, d. 4/9/1910 at 17/9/27; epilepsy; Hiram G. Towle and Martha A. Davis
Emma F., d. 3/4/1890 at 53/11/9; married; Jeremiah York (New Durham) and Hannah Nason (Acton, ME)
Emma F., d. 8/13/1936 at 82; arteriosclerosis
F. A., d. 2/20/1889 at 51; widower; b. Thomaston, ME
Frank, d. 10/14/1935 at 73/0/19 in S. Berwick, ME; cerebral hemorrhage
George Farrar, d. 5/4/1920 at 81/7; cerebral hemorrhage; John W. Towle and Mary Roberts
Georgia E., d. 5/8/1917 at 57/10/18; cerebral apoplexy; George H. Prescott and Emily A. Taylor
Gilman D., d. 12/14/1917 at 90/10/18; senility; Levi Towle and Sally Dudley
Harry G., d. 3/1/1903 at 27/10/1; congestion of lungs; PH
Herbert E., d. 11/5/1936 at 67/3/24; lobar pneumonia
Ida Welts, d. 5/23/1936 at 77/8/26; diabetes mellitus
Jennie C., d. 10/7/1918 at 47/11/24; lobar pneumonia; Hiram Corson and Hannah Horne
Jeremy B., d. 5/28/1918 at 87/0/15; senility; Levi Towle and Sally Dudley

John W., d. 8/19/1887 at 76/11/12; farmer; married; b. Hanover; Jeremiah Towle (Raymond) and Deborah Bean (Alton)
Josephine, d. 6/25/1893 at 34; organic disease of the heart; b. Somersworth; (Somersworth; -----)
Lavinia C., d. 4/30/1900 at 59; cancer; PH
Levi E., d. 9/26/1908 at 79/6/12; pyaemia; Levi Towle and Sally Dudley
Levi W., d. 6/28/1918 at 63/5/14; nephritis; Jeremy B. Towle and Mary A. Nute
Martha A., d. 2/23/1915 at 55/0/4; pulmonary oedema; Charles H. Davis and Sarah Willey
Mary Ellen, d. 8/8/1929 at 67/7/11; cerebral hemorrhage; Levi E. Towle and Rebecca C. Jones
Mary F., d. 4/18/1930 at 84/6; arterio sclerosis; Hiram Wiggin and Mary Huntress
Maude E., d. 9/1/1930 at 47/7/26; natural causes; Roscoe S. Otis and Ida Locke
Patrick, d. 5/19/1890 at 42; married; Thomas Towle (Ireland) and Mary Cassidy (Ireland)
Rebecca C., d. 2/4/1887 at 68/9/9; b. Topsham, VT
Robert F., d. 8/27/1907 at 4/0/25 in Somerville, MA; lenkaernia
Sara Alice, d. 3/5/1929 at 46/4/5; pelvic abscess; Hiram G. Towle and Mattie A. Davis
Sarah J., d. 5/6/1899 at 60; apoplexy; PH
Sidney M., d. 10/25/1896 at 60; rheumatism; b. Wolfeboro; PH
Zulema K., d. 1/12/1919 at 85/11/22; senility; John W. Towle and Mary Roberts

TOWN,
William, d. 11/–/1930 at – in Somersworth; natural causes

TOWNE,
Josiah, d. 12/28/1930 at 71/9/22; ac. lobar pneumonia; James Towne and Susan Huff
Rollin, d. 7/18/1922 at 68/2/21 in Rochester; natural causes

TOWNES,
Walter E., d. 10/5/1929 at 38; cerebral thrombosis

TOWNSEND,
Annie B., d. 5/11/1929 at 67/0/21; cerebral hemorrhage; Jonas D. Townsend and Elizabeth M. Hayes
Charles, d. 10/3/1911 at 80/5/21; probably heart disease; Samuel Townsend and Esther Jackson
Elizabeth M., d. 3/20/1897 at 64; apoplexy; b. Alton; PH
Hattie E., d. 2/14/1925 at 70; diabetes mellitus

Jennie D., d. 9/1/1930 at 72/8/13; arterio sclerosis; Jonas D. Townsend
    and Elizabeth M. Hayes
John F., d. 5/23/1914 at 70 in Trenton, NJ; apoplexy
Jonas D., d. 3/29/1889 at 80/9/13; gas works; married; b. MA; David
    Townsend (MA) and Elizabeth Dix (MA)
Jonas D., d. 10/26/1906 at 42/5/18; cerebral apoplexy; PH
Margaret E., d. 1/23/1918 at 62/6/11; mitral regurgitation; Fred Feltmann
    and Margaret ----

TRACY,
Bridget, d. 4/28/1923 at -- in Concord; cerebral hemorrhage; Thomas
    Tracy and Winnifred Hefferman
Gordon E., d. 3/12/1917 at 17/2/4; pneumonia; John W. Tracy and Namie
    M. O'Neil

TRAFTON,
Abby G., d. 4/13/1908 at 90/11/25; senile gangrene; John Guppy and
    Hannah Dame
Hazel M., d. 9/13/1925 at 19/5/7; typhoid fever; Arthur S. Toof and Levinna
    Martin
Lydia L., d. 12/7/1931 at 70; cancer of bowels

TRAINOR,
child, d. 4/1/1929 at --; stillborn; Michael J. Trainor and Angelina Raymond
Catherine, d. 8/29/1915 at 56; gliomata of brain; Philip McNally and Alice
    Morgan
James E., d. 2/19/1891 at 4/8/20; Peter Trainor (New Durham) and Kate
    McKee (Ireland)
John, d. 6/8/1904 at 49/11/14; ch. catarrhal bronchitis; SM
John P., d. 4/15/1910 at 56; endocarditis; Peter Trainor and Catherine
    Moorhead
Kate, d. 9/28/1905 at 37 in Lowell, MA; alcoholic gastritis; SM
Katie, d. 8/15/1894 at 2; anaemia and convulsions; b. Dover; SM
Katie E., d. 11/11/1890 at 3; Peter Trainor (US) and K. McKee (Ireland)
Matthew, d. 3/12/1923 at 48/0/20; acute bronchitis; John Trainor
Michael, d. 6/21/1889 at 5/5/16; b. Dover; Peter Trainer (NH) and Mary
    McKee (Ireland)
Patrick, d. 5/25/1904 at 25; pulmonary phthisis; SM
Peter, d. 6/18/1895 at 80; old age; b. Ireland; SM
Stella May, d. 3/16/1891 at 0/1/14; Peter Trainor (Alton) and Kate McGee
    (Ireland)

TRAKAS,
John, d. 3/16/1925 at 38; valvular dis. of heart; Charles Trakas and Doris -

TRANK,
child, d. 7/26/1908 at --; stillborn; Joseph H. Trank and Alphonsine Legasse

TRASK,
child, d. 11/25/1920 at --; premature birth; Ralph C. Trask and Helen D. Yeaton
Albina, d. 2/19/1924 at 57/11/13; chronic endocarditis; Ansel Trask and Maria Otis
Elizabeth, d. 8/24/1890 at 46/2/7; married; Andrew Moore (England) and -- --- (Isle of Man)
George S., d. 9/25/1916 at 82/2/5; acute bronchitis; Timothy Trask and Lois Scott
Maria, d. 8/28/1919 at 85/11/17; senility; Lock Otis and Jemima -----
Mary G., d. 9/3/1921 at 79/3/4; cerebral hemorrhage; Reuben Chamberlain and Martha Sanborn

TRAVERS,
Albert B., d. 7/2/1906 at 58/11/5; paralysis agitans; buried in Manchester

TRAVERSY,
Ambrose, d. 6/20/1918 at 66/0/5; chr. intestitial nephritis; Charles Traversy and Margaret -----
Jessie, d. 3/10/1931 at 72/6/22; gastric ulcers

TRAXLER,
Elizabeth B., d. 8/15/1914 at 65/9/24 in Glen Cove, NY; carcinoma of breast
James A., d. 10/26/1933 at 85/11/18 in Manchester; arteriosclerosis

TRAYNOR,
Thomas, d. 11/17/1888 at 19/6; laborer; single; b. Ireland; John Traynor (Ireland) and Celia Murray (Ireland)

TREDICK,
Dorcas H., d. 5/13/1891 at 83/10/17 in Newburyport, MA; widow; George Frost (York, ME) and Sarah Bartlett (Eliot, ME)
Edward, d. 2/17/1914 at 58 in Philadelphia, PA; lobar pneumonia
Emma, d. 5/29/1925 at 78/1/2; pulmonary oedema; Henry Tredick and Dorothy Locke
Sarah A., d. 11/23/1910 at 70 in Philadelphia, PA; chronic myocarditis

TREFETHEN,
Charles, d. 2/3/1901 at 75/4/21 in Manchester; pneumonia; PH

E. Josephine, d. 7/31/1904 at 52 in Danvers, MA; general paralysis; PH
Elsie, d. 3/3/1895 at 83; bronchitis; b. Isles of Shoals; PH
Francena, d. 5/15/1927 at 75/4/11; carcinoma of breast; Alvah Runnells
 and Martha Wentworth
Hannah, d. 11/13/1890 at 75/0/25 in Kittery, ME; widow; Thomas Card
 (New Castle) and Phoebe Trefethen (New Castle)
Isabel M., d. 7/4/1909 at 81/9/11; senility; Thomas Curtis and Catherine
 Barri
Josiah S., d. 5/30/1909 at 84/9/4; suicide by hanging; William Trefethen
 and Mary Sterling
Martha E., d. 4/21/1901 at 77/6/27 in Manchester; gastro-enteritis; PH
Martha G., d. 4/28/1929 at 51/11/7; tuberculosis of kidney; James Stevens
 and Mary T. Doe
Thomas A., d. 12/28/1921 at 75/0/1 in Milton; broncho pneumonia;
 Archillus Trefethen and Mary S. Abrams

TREMBLAY,
Therese L., d. 12/19/1931 at 0/0/4; cerebral hemorrhage

TREMBLY,
Mary A., d. 2/6/1913 at 59 in Ossipee; gastro enteritis; Martin Carney and
 Mary McCabe

TRICKER,
Newell Cork, d. 2/11/1929 at 68/9/1 in Lynn, MA; chronic myocarditis

TRICKEY,
Addie E., d. 12/4/1893 at 58; pneumonia; b. Brookfield; (Brookfield; Acton,
 ME)
Betsey E., d. 8/5/1928 at 90/6/8 in Lynn, MA; chronic myocarditis
Charles H., d. 2/2/1896 at 62; laryngitis; b. Brookfield; PH
Charles H., d. 9/9/1899 at 51 in Bow; cirrhosis of liver; PH
Charles W., d. 6/21/1896 at 72 in Lee; general debility; PH
Eliza A., d. 2/7/1908 at 67 in Somerville, MA; paralysis
Florence M., d. 5/30/1890 at 2/11/14 in Somerville, MA
George K., d. 3/6/1905 at 77; pneumonia; PH
James E., d. 1/14/1916 at 66/5/30; chronic nephritis; Samuel Trickey and
 Sarah A. Johnson
Maria G., d. 3/6/1899 at 93; marasmus, senile; PH
Martha S., d. 1/2/1897 at 72 in Epping; organic disease of heart
Mary E., d. 2/15/1895 at 36 in Somerville, MA; phthisis pulmonalis; buried
 in Dover
Sarah, d. 12/5/1892 at 80; eczema, dropsy, general waste; b. Barnstead;
 (Belfast, ME; Newington)
Walter L., d. 10/2/1929 at 70/9/19 in Medford, MA; hemiplegia

William D., d. 12/19/1936 at 70/1/2; can. bron. rem. neck
William H., d. 2/27/1931 at 90/1/5; chronic nephritis
William M., d. 11/5/1901 at 74/2/17 in Somerville, MA; old age; PH

TRIPE,
George A., d. 9/22/1919 at 65/7/22; valvular heart disease; Robert H. Tripe and Alice D. Bridges
Mary E., d. 4/2/1906 at 80; old age; buried in Haverhill, MA
Robert H., d. 7/4/1901 at 87/4; old age; PH

TRIPP,
Fannie B., d. 4/4/1929 at 72/9/28; diabetes mellitus; Horace Littlefield and Sarah P. Locke

TROCHART,
Joseph, d. 7/27/1889 at 0/9; b. Canada; Joseph Trochart (Canada) and Marie Marchaux (Canada)

TRUDEAU,
Madeline, d. 4/3/1923 at 4/9/21; ac. lobar pneumonia; George Trudeau and Julia Haughey

TRUE,
Alice, d. 1/21/1914 at 73/8/14; paralysis agitans; Richard N. Rothwell and Alice Nuttle
Clara Belle, d. 5/14/1923 at 44/0/24; carcinoma cervix uteri; Jamesson Greeley
George S., d. 12/3/1925 at 57/2/10; probably heart disease; John S. True and Alice Rothwell
Harry R., d. 2/2/1898 at 22 in Rochester; typhoid fever; PH
John S., d. 2/1/1911 at 70/7/28; suicide by hanging

TRUMBULL,
James B., d. 2/5/1934 at 47/0/17; cerebral hemorrhage

TRUMPOLT,
Richard R., d. 7/23/1892 at 29; consumption; b. Germany; (Germany; Germany)

TSALTAS,
Vaselios, d. 4/9/1918 at 20; homicide by firearms; Christos Tsaltas and Stavoula Athena

TSEMEKLIS,
child, d. 2/14/1923 at –; stillborn; Mike Tsemeklis

TUCKER,
Charles A., d. 2/20/1890 at 20/3/26; single; Lucius W. Tucker (Keene, NY) and Amanda Langley (NY)
George H., d. 8/19/1910 at 73/1/14; senile debility; John Tucker and Eliza Hussey
Samuel P., d. 11/19/1910 at 56/0/28; sarcoma of femur; William N. Tucker and Sarah -----
Willard, d. 10/9/1918 at 24/6/29 in Portsmouth; influenza

TUFTS,
son, d. 11/17/1887 at –; b. Dover; George W. Tufts (Dover) and Addie S. Venner (Durham)
Annie B., d. 4/28/1907 at 80/0/12; uraemic coma; John Souther and Matilda Reed
Arthur G., d. 1/11/1911 at 59/7/5; heart disease; Charles A. Tufts and Annie B. Souther
Charles A., d. 2/12/1899 at 77; pyelo nephritis; PH
Charles Edwin, d. 4/3/1936 at 74/10/24 in Rochester; acute gastrocutulus
Charlotte M., d. 8/22/1910 at 67/3/1; diabetes; John M. Smith and Comfort York
Edith S., d. 1/24/1935 at 72/11/25 in Wellesley, MA; angina pectoris
Elias P., d. 9/6/1932 at 76/10/4; arterio sclerosis
Ellen F., d. 9/26/1889 at 61/7/7 in Reading, MA; single; b. Dover; Asa A. Tufts (Dover) and Hannah Gilman (Dover)
George W., d. 2/10/1901 at 42/0/28 in Middleboro, MA; typhoid fever with complications
Laurence T., d. 9/28/1935 at 26 in Syracuse, NY; carcinoma
Lily Fay C., d. 3/25/1933 at 78/9/1; cerebral hemorrhage
Mary J. F., d. 12/22/1902 at 6/11/29 in Rochester; pernicious anemia; PH
Ruth, d. 3/3/1914 at 85/11/23; arterio sclerosis; John Hussey and Betsey Stevens

TULLY,
Emma C., d. 3/23/1896 at 73; gastritis; b. Dover; PH
John, d. 3/3/1894 at 61; paralysis; b. Halifax; PH

TURBAVILLE,
Helen Marie, d. 4/22/1926 at –; stillborn; Thomas R. Turbaville and Isabelle C. Clough

TURCOTTE,
child, d. 12/24/1922 at –; miscarriage; Joseph S. Turcotte and Elizabeth T. Casey
child, d. 7/9/1935 at 0/0/1-½; premature
Albert, d. 1/21/1906 at 0/0/21; pulmonary congestion; SM
Leontine, d. 12/24/1936 at 50/3/28*
Lucy H. G., d. 6/20/1925 at 86/0/10; chr. intest. nephritis; Samuel Linscott and Hannah Gowen
Ludger, d. 6/19/1916 at 20/1/8; appendicits; Xavier Turcotte and Rose Perreault
Mary C., d. 7/31/1930 at 6/5/4; acute appendicitis; Joseph L. Turcotte and Elizabeth Casey

TURGEON,
Alfreda, d. 5/28/1918 at 11/10; Potts disease; Hector Turgeon and Annie Lapointe
Eugenie, d. 7/20/1889 at 1/5/8; b. Dover; Philias Turgeon (Canada) and H. Mabeux (VT)
Helen, d. 7/10/1932 at –; stillborn
J. Edward, d. 6/24/1934 at 44/7/8; suicide by gas
Joseph, d. 12/31/1912 at –; stillborn; Hector Turgeon and Annie Lapoint
Mary, d. 9/9/1913 at –; premature birth; Victor Turgeon and Annie Lapointe
May, d. 9/9/1913 at –; premature birth; Victor Turgeon and Annie Lapointe
Roland, d. 5/21/1932 at 2/5/24; accidental drowning

TURKSHAM,
Etta M., d. 1/14/1936 at 69/6/28; pulmonary embolism

TURNER,
daughter, d. 11/2/1888 at –; b. Dover; William Turner (England) and Catherine Ingham (England)
Albert, d. 8/25/1887 at 0/4/14; b. Dover; William Turner (England) and Kate Ingam (England)
Alice, d. 12/8/1905 at 24/0/12; uraemia; PH
Archie, d. 11/7/1929 at 57/11; carcinoma intest.; Thomas Turner and Elizabeth Ellis
Elizabeth, d. 10/29/1903 at 47/6/10; cancer of uterus; PH
Eunice C., d. 1/20/1925 at 63/1/29 in S. Berwick, ME; carcinoma of stomach
Florence H., d. 2/17/1906 at 26/2/22; heart disease; PH
Henry H., d. 8/29/1916 at 56/7/13 in Rollinsford; valv. disease of heart
Jane, d. 11/13/1921 at 67/4/1; acute bronchitis; William Gibson and Maria Stansfield
John, d. 9/11/1907 at --; suicide

Mary, d. 6/13/1895 at 84; old age
Mary Ann, d. 9/14/1892 at —; dysentery; b. Dover; (England; England)
William, d. 11/3/1930 at 75; apoplexy; William Turner

TUTEN,
Esther Pamelia, d. 4/14/1927 at 78/5/22; undetermined; Robert P. Tuten and Nancy Stevens

TUTTLE,
Abbie F., d. 11/13/1892 at 54; pneumonia
Albert C., d. 8/14/1926 at 57/4/14 in Pamillas, NY; cirrhosis of liver
Asa C., d. 11/13/1898 at 82; internal injury, accident; b. Dover; buried in Friends Cem.
Caroline H., d. 5/4/1902 at 7/9/10; pneumonia - peritonitis; PH
Charles, d. 11/13/1925 at 44 in Boston, MA; pulmonary tuberculosis
Charles M., d. 3/13/1926 at 43 in Pembroke; pulmonary tuberculosis; Horace Tuttle and Annie Carberry
Charles M., d. 1/31/1928 at 45/11/9 in Nottingham; tuberculosis of lungs; Hazen M. Tuttle and Mary M. Stevens
Charles W., d. 12/8/1900 at 53; bronchitis; PH
Charlotte D., d. 8/25/1889 at 73/10/26; housekeeper; single; b. Dover; Otis Tuttle (Dover) and Hannah Varney (Dover)
Charlotte E., d. 11/20/1900 at 88; old age; PH
Chester M., d. 7/1/1903 at 0/1/24; convulsions; buried in Austin Cem.
Clara, d. 11/15/1888 at 70/5/19; married; b. Strafford; Ephraim Caverly (Barrington) and Mary Holmes (Strafford)
Elijah V., d. 1/12/1891 at 70/7/17; single; Otis Tuttle (Dover) and Hannah Varney (Dover)
Elizabeth Ann, d. 4/25/1910 at 53/5/15; cancer of liver; Joseph Wilkinson and Mary Routledge
Emery L., d. 11/23/1920 at 63/1/12 in Lowell, MA; chronic heart disease
Emma B. Lord, d. 1/2/1937 at 64/0/4*
Evangeline, d. 5/1/1908 at 41/11/14; lobar pneumonia; James F. Heeney and Charlotte Yates
Forrest Arthur, d. 7/23/1929 at 0/0/6; blue baby; Effie Tuttle
Frank H., Jr., d. 2/25/1900 at <1; inanition; PH
Freeman H., d. 2/3/1909 at 68; heart disease; John L. Tuttle and Elizabeth Wormwood
George W., d. 2/22/1937 at 71/4; cerebr. hemorrhage
Hannah, d. 4/30/1923 at 87/9/12; chronic nephritis; Samuel Hall and Sally Tuttle
Hannah C., d. 11/26/1908 at 76/2/21; senility; Samuel Hanson and Clarissa Varney
Hanson H., d. 2/20/1911 at 58/6/5; pneumonia; John Tuttle and Sally Hill

Harry B., d. 1/4/1925 at 36/5/15; lobar pneumonia; Hanson H. Tuttle and
   Sadie E. Leighton
Harry H., d. 9/22/1914 at 45/4/4; traumatic shock; Hazen M. Tuttle and
   Mary A. Stevens
Hattie A., d. 10/5/1902 at 46/11/19; carcinoma; PH
Hope, d. 2/1/1897 at 77; chronic nephritis; b. Dover; PH
Ida May, d. 6/17/1936 at 59/10/10; cardiac insufficiency
James S., d. 3/31/1906 at 76 in Rollinsford; pneumonia; PH
John, d. 10/30/1914 at 57; tuberculosis pulmonalis
John T. G., d. 4/21/1923 at 81/10/20; arterio sclerosis; John W. Tuttle and
   Sarah A. Tuttle
Joseph R., d. 12/12/1921 at 21/6/11 in Boston, MA; tuberculosis
   meningitis
Lewis E., d. 6/23/1906 at 36/5; accidental shooting; PH
Lizzie B., d. 6/10/1936 at 81/10/20 in S. Berwick, ME; angina pectoris
Lydia M. C., d. 9/17/1896 at 64; abdominal cancer; b. Parsonsfield, ME;
   buried in family lot
Mary, d. 10/15/1925 at 52 in Boston, MA; organic heart disease
Mary A., d. 2/19/1906 at 62/3/14; pneumonia; buried in Newmarket
Mary J., d. 10/27/1897 at 54; cerebral hemorrhage; b. Dover; PH
Mary J., d. 2/9/1904 at 25/9/7; tuberculosis of lungs; buried in Austin Cem.
Nettie, d. 10/1/1899 at – in Rochester; lympho-sarcoma of neck; PH
Orrin, d. 4/24/1888 at 35; b. Lee
Ralph F., d. 6/10/1910 at 0/3/7in Somerville, MA; Charles W. Tuttle and
   Mary E. Toomey
Richard H., d. 7/19/1915 at 69 in Pittsburgh, PA; general paresis
Sarah A., d. 8/14/1895 at 89; old age; b. Dover; PH
Stephen A., d. 7/23/1928 at 73/10/15 in Lynn, MA; chronic int. nephritis
Susan, d. 9/6/1895 at 85; heart disease; b. Northwood; PH
Thomas W., d. 9/2/1929 at 70/6/24; arterio sclerosis; Thomas Tuttle and
   Lois Wingate
Viola C. T., d. 1/26/1934 at 46/0/11; lymphosarcoma
William Penn, d. 5/4/1911 at 87/10/8; senility; Joseph Tuttle and Sarah
   Pinkham
William R., d. 7/8/1907 at 58/2/27; nephritis; William Tuttle and Abigail
   Perkins

TWINDLE,
Nora, d. 2/9/1893 at 57; died in Strafford Co. Asylum fire

TWOMBLY,
Abbie S., d. 1/4/1908 at 85/11/28 in Madbury; la grippe
Albert H., d. 10/21/1936 at 79/9/11; coronary thrombosis
Alice S., d. 1/25/1898 at 34; uraemia; b. Dover; PH

Ann Janette, d. 9/12/1930 at 89/8/8; arterio sclerosis; Ira Libbey and Betsey Daniels

Ann M., d. 12/17/1916 at 77/10/18; valvular heart disease; Hiram Drew and Mary A. Robinson

Ann R., d. 9/21/1910 at 82/2/17 in Manchester; paralysis

Anna M., d. 3/4/1895 at 68; heart disease; b. Boston, MA; buried in Boston, MA

Carrie A., d. 6/3/1924 at 48/8/13; Brights disease; Herbert O. Perkins and Mary E. Wiggin

Charles, d. 7/26/1892 at 69; Bright's disease; b. Dover; (England; NH)

Charles H., d. 7/21/1891 at 54/1/16 in Madbury; married

Daniel, d. 12/13/1914 at 93/9/20 in Cambridge, MA; cholecystitis

Edgar H., d. 1/27/1920 at 74/6/5; broncho pneumonia; William Twombly, 3rd and Mary W. Caverly

Edwin A., d. 12/12/1913 at 53/7/29; acute endocarditis; Reuben Twombly and Susan Corson

Eliza C., d. 11/18/1894 at 60; heart disease; PH

Elizabeth N., d. 1/12/1896 at 69; paralysis of brain; b. Somersworth; PH

Frank A., d. 6/3/1936 at 41/11/24 in Portsmouth; pul. tuberculosis

Frank H., d. 6/11/1907 at 55 in Fall River, MA; haemoptysis and heart disease

Fred A., d. 8/13/1918 at 52/9/9 in Haverhill, MA; cerebral hemorrhage

George, d. 7/25/1904 at 58/8/25; general tuberculosis

George B., d. 11/17/1934 at 73/1/15; broncho pneumonia

George H., d. 4/29/1899 at 69 in Exeter; consumption

George Orrin, d. 3/12/1923 at 72/9/23; pericarditis; Ira Twombly and Sarah Snell

Georgia E., d. 1/30/1918 at 49/7/6 in Portsmouth; pubescent insanity

H., d. 4/27/1893 at 79; apoplexy; b. Farmington; (Madbury; Strafford)

Harry N., d. 5/11/1934 at 50/3/22; cerebral hemorrhage

Harry R., d. 11/24/1927 at 55/0/11; chronic endocarditis; Charles H. Twombly and Eliza C. Snell

Henry W., d. 6/2/1904 at 68/5/24; cholecytetis with peritonitis; PH

Herbert L., d. 12/27/1929 at 47/11/8; carcinoma rectum; Edwin E. Twombly and Abbie Nute

Hopeley, d. 10/12/1899 at 85 in Windham; shock - apoplexy; PH

Jacob H., d. 11/17/1905 at 52 in Concord; mitral regurgitation

Jacob K., d. 4/4/1899 at 75; Bright's disease; PH

Jacob K., d. 6/21/1915 at 39/8/26; acute dilatation of heart; John Twombly and Mary A. Loud

James F., d. 12/23/1901 at 31/2/9 in Boston, MA; pernicious anemia

James T., d. 7/26/1913 at 83/10/22; senility; Hurd Twombly and Lavinia Tuttle

James W., d. 12/15/1933 at 74/4/13; carcinoma of stomach

Jennie A., d. 2/1/1920 at 52/1/19; softening of the brain; Robert Austin

John E., d. 8/24/1888 at 52; watchman; married; b. Milton; James M. Twombly (Milton) and E. Burroughs (Lebanon, ME)
John G., d. 4/20/1914 at 54; acute oedema of lungs; Moses Twombly and Levicey Tripp
John H., d. 2/10/1908 at 56/6/11 in Cambridge, MA; diabetes mellitus
John H., d. 3/2/1927 at 78/4/13 in Manchester; lobar pneumonia
John R., d. 8/29/1893 at 49; cerebral meningitis; b. Newburyport, MA; (Dover; Durham)
Joseph B., d. 7/9/1914 at –; pneumonia
Juliet, d. 5/7/1925 at 64/1/17; arterio sclerosis; Charles Perkins and Susan E. Lufkunn
Lucinda K., d. 7/19/1910 at 82/6/20; cardiac myasthenia; Israel Hanson and Eunice -----
Lydia A., d. 3/17/1912 at 70/2/6; diabetes mellitus; Stephen Walker and Mary Mathes
Lydia Ann, d. 7/16/1916 at 73/6/12 in Boston, MA; carcinoma of stomach
Lydia M., d. 12/6/1906 at 86/10/12 in Lowell, MA; senility; PH
Malvina N., d. 11/3/1907 at 68/4/13; heart disease; Leonard F. Nutter and Lucy H. Whitten
Margaret, d. 6/7/1906 at 38; neurasthenia; PH
Marion, d. 11/1/1890 at 0/0/3; J. Walter Twombly (Dover) and J. Etta Perkins (Wells, ME)
Martha, d. 2/22/1890 at 90; old age; b. NH; buried at Simon Torr's
Martha A., d. 8/24/1897 at 73; nephritis; b. Dover; PH
Mary Bessie, d. 2/27/1915 at 50/9/24; cerebral hemorrhage; Henry W. Twombly and Ann J. Libby
Mary E., d. 4/21/1895 at 59 in Jamaica Plain, MA; pneumonia; b. Strafford; buried in Dover
Mary E., d. 5/9/1912 at 69/1/27 in Madbury; cerebral hemorrhage
Mary E., d. 6/2/1918 at 73/0/28; chronic rheumatism; Stephen Walker and Lydia Ham
Mary E., d. 2/22/1936 at 72/4/14*
Mary E., d. 3/4/1936 at 64/3/18; cerebral hemorrhage
Mary Ellen, d. 7/25/1927 at 82/5/24; lobar pneumonia; Wingate Twombly and Susan Chapman
Mary G., d. 10/26/1901 at 29 in Lynn, MA; diabetes; PH
Mary L., d. 5/17/1916 at 74/8/5; heart disease; John H. Nute and Abigail Tanner
Maud Emma, d. 12/18/1937 at 64/7/14*
Mehitable B., d. 1/24/1893 at 79; apoplexy; b. Dover; (Dover; Dover)
Nathaniel, d. 12/25/1909 at 90/9/18; nephritis; Hurd Twombly and Sarah Caverno
Nellie E., d. 7/30/1910 at 55 in Biddeford, ME; taxaemia with cong. of lungs; George Twombly and Caroline Dawley

Reuben, d. 1/4/1888 at 70/6/11; machinist; married; b. Dover; I. Twombly (Dover) and Susan Tuttle (Dover)
Reuben H., d. 1/21/1893 at 65; paralysis; b. Dover; (Durham; Lee)
Roger I., d. 5/29/1913 at 43/9/15; suicide; Chester A. Twombly and Marietta Varney
Sarah S., d. 5/29/1931 at 78/4/3; arterio sclerosis
Sophia G., d. 6/1/1901 at 78/1/14; paralytic shock; PH
Thomas, d. 11/8/1905 at 72/3/11; heart disease; PH
Thomas B., d. 8/5/1887 at 83/6/5; carpenter; married; b. Dover; William Twombly (Dover) and Mehitable Baker (Dover)
William, d. 5/5/1889 at 91/6/17; farmer; widower; b. Strafford; Joshua Twombly (Barrington) and Hannah Willey
William, d. 2/9/1893 at 65; died in Strafford Co. Asylum fire
William H., d. 4/10/1902 at 70/11/18; inanition; PH

TYLER,
child, d. 11/22/1926 at –; stillborn; Herbert Tyler and Bernice Freeman
Abbie, d. 1/1/1913 at 59; ch. intestitinal nephritis; John Arlin and Betsey Brown
Annie, d. 11/21/1929 at 46; alcoholism; John McGonigle and Katherine O'Brien
Capitola W., d. 10/10/1935 at 74 in Washington, DC; myocarditis
Francis O., d. 8/14/1928 at 75/0/16; chronic myocarditis; Daniel Tyler and Emeline Tyler
Howard, d. 5/9/1909 at 60 in Philadelphia, PA; acute indigestion
John B., d. 11/25/1924 at 38/5/4; mitral stenosis; George Tyler and Abbie Arlin
Judith F. O., d. 6/7/1925 at 0/0/27 in Lee; nephritis
Lawrence, Rev., d. 7/15/1925 at 40/1/22 in Watertown, NY; angina pectoris
Marion, d. 10/9/1924 at 34 in Concord; pulmonary tuberculosis; Herman Canney

UNIACK,
child, d. 11/7/1922 at 6 hrs.; premature birth; John Uniack and Margaret Ryan

UPHAM,
Frank, d. 2/18/1936 at 87/9/9; acute myocarditis
James, d. 4/6/1926 at 58; angina pectoris

UPTON,
John, d. 11/1/1915 at 56; cancer prostate gland; James Upton

VACHON,
August, d. 9/15/1919 at 51/7/26; locomotor ataxia; Paul Vachon and Julie Lachance
Ernest J., d. 7/2/1920 at 22/0/19 in Alton Bay; tuberculosis; Thomas Vachon and Demerise Sylvain
Etianna, d. 8/13/1899 at –; entero colitis; SM
George E., Jr., d. 9/5/1925 at 0/3/28; catarrhal enteritis; George E. Vachon and Elizabeth Jalbert
Georgianna M., d. 2/14/1925 at 53/2/14; pulmonary tuberculosis; Alexander Cantin and Marie Marcoux
Ronald, d. 5/15/1936 at 0/10/0; lobar pneumonia

VAILLANCOURT,
Demerise, d. 3/14/1921 at 60/9/14; pulmonary oedema; John Allaire and Cecil Ruel
Frank, d. 1/27/1929 at 73/6/6; pernicious anemia; Frank Vaillancourt and Annie -----

VALENTINE,
Emma Z., d. 12/30/1918 at 29/2/7 in Boston, MA; lobar pneumonia

VALLALY,
Catherine, d. 11/15/1893 at 61; old age; b. Ireland; (Ireland; Ireland)

VALLEE,
Annette, d. 1/13/1932 at 0/10/9 in Somersworth; natural causes

VALLELY,
Francis, d. 1/23/1923 at 80; gastro enteritis; John Vallely and Susan Mulligan
Nick, d. 11/11/1891 at 18; Mary Vallely (Ireland)

VALLEY,
Frank, d. 8/16/1888 at 42/5/23; shoemaker; married; b. Ireland; (Ireland; Ireland)
Julia A., d. 8/4/1893 at 47; poisoned; b. Dover; (Shapleigh, ME; Clinton, ME)

VALLIERE,
Philip, d. 10/1/1918 at 37/6; pneumonia; Theophile Valliere and ----- Boutin

VALLILY,
Alice, d. 4/30/1921 at 78/8/29; gen. arterio sclerosis; James Toner and Nancy Hagan

Nancy, d. 7/15/1900 at 20; tuberculosis; SM
Terrence, d. 5/25/1921 at –; gen. arterio sclerosis; John Vallily and Susan Mullen

VAN ALLEN,
Alice, d. 10/24/1924 at 72 in Manchester; dilatation of heart

VAN TASSEL,
John N., d. 5/31/1894 at 54; consumption; b. Tarrytown, NY; PH

VANASSE,
Adelard, d. 7/26/1913 at 33/4; acute nephritis; Adelard Vanasse and Malvina Roudeau

VARLEY,
child, d. 5/5/1925 at –; premature birth; David W. Varley and Sarah M. Farrill

VARNEY,
Abigail, d. 5/12/1892 at 70; meningitis; b. Dover; (-----; Somersworth)
Ada B., d. 1/30/1898 at 24 in Malden, MA; pneumonia; PH
Adeline A., d. 8/5/1931 at 80/10/22 in Rochester; chronic nephritis
Albert, d. 11/3/1920 at 82/2/26; cerebral hemorrhage; Amos Varney and Annie Locke
Alfred L., d. 9/18/1898 at 22 in York, ME; drowning accident; PH
Amanda, d. 12/14/1907 at 69/0/16 in Newburyport, MA; apoplexy
Annie A., d. 11/25/1927 at 59/6/3; anaemia; Albert Varney and Antoinette Crockett
Annie L., d. 3/22/1928 at 86/8/18; angina pectoris; John Mann and Lucretia Smith
Antoinette, d. 4/24/1912 at 64/10/18; cerebral hemorrhage; Daniel B. Crockett and Sarah H. Ricker
Arthur L., d. 1/17/1932 at 66/10; intestinal obstruction
Caroline M., d. 10/9/1909 at 98/10/7 in Rochester; failure of vital forces
Charles H., d. 3/18/1934 at 57/8/4; cerebral embolism
Daniel, d. 2/14/1927 at 80/1/15; apoplexy
Daniel W., d. 9/14/1891 at 54/7/14; single; George W. Varney (Barrington) and Mariam Hodsdon (Barrington)
Dorothy F., d. 6/8/1904 at 1/9/3 in Lawrence, MA; broncho-pneumonia; PH
Edwin H., d. 6/29/1903 at 61/10/29 in Hartford, CT; pleurisy; PH
Elias C., d. 9/10/1929 at 94/3/12; chr. int. nephritis; George W. Varney and Sarah Hanson
Eliza A., d. 3/8/1895 at 82 in Stoneham, MA; bronchitis; buried in Dover
Eliza A., d. 6/24/1904 at 77/9; pulmonary oedema; PH

Eliza J., d. 4/24/1920 at 74/0/1; chr. interstitial nephritis; William Hodgdon and Eliza T. Gray

Eliza P., d. 3/7/1904 at 88/6/1; fracture of hip; buried in Austin Cem.

Elizabeth U., d. 5/15/1920 at 65/9/21 in Boston, MA; nephritis

Ellen M., d. 5/5/1896 at 32; appendicitis; b. Moultonboro; PH

Emily A., d. 3/5/1897 at 62 in Chelsea, MA; la grippe

Emily W., d. 1/2/1908 at – in Hartford, CT; cardiac degeneration; Daniel Webster

Frank F., d. 2/15/1919 at 69/11 in Boston, MA; broncho pneumonia; Andrew Varney and Susan Footman

Fred Moulton, d. 12/3/1919 at 51/4/18 in Gardner, MA; cerebral hemorrhage

Frederick S., d. 11/27/1932 at 44/8/17 in Boston, MA; coronary sclerosis

George E., d. 3/13/1912 at 55/9/7; catarrh of stomach, etc.; George W. Varney and Lucinda A. Nevens

George E., d. 2/4/1920 at 65/9/5; arterio sclerosis; George Varney and Laura A. Work

George H., d. 7/22/1918 at 75/2; chronic Brights disease; Samuel Varney and Mary Archer

George H., d. 12/25/1930 at 60/3/14; acute myocarditis; George G. Varney and Jennie Gray

George W., d. 1/27/1917 at 95; arterio sclerosis

Harriet O'Brien, d. 6/16/1921 at 54/7/7; sarcoma intestines; John R. Varney and Isabella G. Kimball

Harry L., d. 8/19/1890 at 0/3/10; Harry L. Varney (NH) and Sarah E. Hallworth (MA)

Hester A., d. 6/25/1910 at 62/6/19; cerebral hemorrhage; Elias Varney and Eliza Foss

Isaac, d. 9/2/1912 at 86/7/11; hemiplegia; Joseph Varney and Margaret Horne

Isabel, d. 8/29/1910 at 71/0/20 in S. Berwick, ME; paresis from cereb. hem.

Isabella G., d. 12/6/1919 at 84/9/5; interstitial nephritis; Richard Kimball and Margaret Pendexter

Ivory, d. 6/6/1898 at 61; peritonitis; b. Dover; PH

James M., d. 11/17/1916 at 56/11/5 in Moultonboro; gangrene of foot

Joanna M., d. 6/2/1913 at 77/11/22 in Mansfield, MA; ch. intestitial nephritis

John A., d. 4/15/1911 at 74/0/19; Shubael Varney and Rebecca Paul

Joshua, d. 1/7/1890 at 75/9/5; widower; John Varney and Mary Varney

Laura A., d. 8/4/1887 at 56/8/11; married; b. Webster, MA; Ezra D. Nook (Woodstock, VT) and Paulina H. (Cambridge, MA)

Lorraine M., d. 5/7/1937 at 0/0/7; prenative

Luella A., d. 3/11/1904 at 47/10/8; gangrene of feet; PH

Mary, d. 3/8/1893 at 92; pneumonia; b. Milton; (Dover; Dover)

Mary E., d. 8/16/1919 at – in Chelsea, MA; chr. int. nephritis
Mary E., d. 1/25/1933 at 59/9/17; osteomyelitis
Mary H., d. 9/8/1925 at 89/6; bed sores; Benjamin Willey and Mary H. Davis
Minnie A. B., d. 10/29/1908 at 46/4/23; cerebral hemorrhage; Ira Banfield and Mary A. Tolman
Moses M. R., d. 8/11/1900 at 75; ascites; PH
Naomi W., d. 1/11/1888 at 80/8/25 in Wenham, MA
Robert M., d. 3/29/1889 at 65/11; farmer; widower; b. Dover; Robert Varney (Dover) and M. Stackpole (Somersworth)
Roxanna, d. 5/5/1902 at 67; nephritis; buried in Austin Cem.
Sarah, d. 3/13/1891 at 68; single; James B. Varney (Rochester) and Sarah B. Riley (Dover)
Sarah B., d. 9/24/1920 at 82/9 in Walpole, MA; cerebral hemorrhage
Sarah F., d. 6/13/1907 at –; pelvic sarcoma; Archeson Moody and Dolly Nickerson
Sarah M., d. 5/10/1925 at 26/3/4; nephritis of pregnancy; William H. Farnhill and M. Marg. Hutchinson
Seth W., d. 4/19/1893 at 74; protracted debauch; b. Milton; (Rochester; Milton)
Sophia R., d. 1/10/1920 at 63/7/29; apoplexy; William Scott and Esther Roberts
Thomas E., d. 3/8/1920 at 61/1/6; myocarditis; George Varney and Laura A. Work

VARRILL,
Robert W., d. 12/11/1934 at 68/5/17; heart disease

VASCILLIAN,
Lazarus, d. 1/24/1917 at 0/0/4; intestinal hemorrhage; Bagdasar Vascillian and Mary Alexander

VAUGHN,
Alice, d. 3/27/1924 at 72 in Newburyport, MA; pulmonary embolism
Austin, d. 9/10/1915 at 45/11/25; acute dilat. of heart
Fanny, d. 4/12/1896 at 51; strangulated hernia; b. VA; PH
Sarah B., d. 11/23/1915 at 99/0/7; old age; Benjamin Dorr and Mary Brackett

VEASEY,
James A., d. 6/15/1930 at 79/5/27 in Stamford, CT; myocarditis
Minnie E., d. 1/20/1922 at 57/5/22 in Stamford, CT; car. of rt. submaxillry

VENNARD,
child, d. 12/25/1928 at 0/0/2; atelectasis of lungs; Fred S. Vennard and Gertrude E. Kennard
Samuel J., d. 10/13/1932 at 65/6/10; chronic nephritis

VENNER,
Christine S., d. 8/3/1926 at 59/1/4; valvular heart disease; Louis Steuerwald
Clementine R., d. 1/8/1920 at 77/2/11; valvular disease of heart; Benjamin Randall and Matilda Stillings
James M., d. 3/6/1919 at 80/0/19; influenza; Thomas Venner and Sophia Connell
W. Irving, d. 5/29/1913 at 46/10/23; pneumonia lobar; James M. Venner and Clementine Randall

VENO,
Wilson J., d. 3/26/1919 at –; stillborn; Simon Veno and Zeline Martin

VERES,
Theodore, d. 7/9/1910 at 0/0/16; gastro-enteritis acute; Louis Veres and S. Panagrotopoulos

VERRET,
Aldian, d. 7/9/1891 at 0/1/18; Napoleon Verret (Canada) and Illa Greene (Canada)

VERRETT,
Mary A., d. 7/8/1903 at 1/4/18; pneumonia

VERRETTE,
Arthur, d. 9/27/1902 at 2/5/1; pneumonia
Rosie, d. 5/2/1904 at 0/11/26; phthisis

VETTERLINE,
Julia A., d. 5/21/1909 at 65/10/3; ascetes; ----- Moore and Joanna Salisbury

VEYETTE,
Emily, d. 2/27/1919 at 68; cerebral hemorrhage; Francis Vassar and Catherine Trudeau

VICKERY,
Abbie E., d. 6/11/1932 at 80 in Providence, RI; acute bronchitis

Amanda G., d. 9/14/1911 at 74/6/1; cerebral apoplexy; John Crockett and Elizabeth Ham
Annie B., d. 12/24/1937 at 75/1/9; abdominal carcinoma
Ellen H., d. 3/3/1930 at 84/3/18 in Portsmouth; myocarditis
Emily, d. 10/9/1889 at 67 in Haverhill, MA
Hattie A., d. 4/20/1908 at 74/5/15; senility; Winthrop Hayes and Hannah Clough
Mary F., d. 6/24/1932 at 82/7/20; cerebral hemorrhage
Oliver M., d. 8/31/1929 at 77/0/9; abdominal carcinoma; Joshua Vickery and Mary Green
Sarah A., d. 8/15/1896 at 77 in Lowell, MA; disease of heart
William H., d. 9/16/1889 at 68/0/23 in Rochester; farmer; married; b. Wakefield; Samuel Vickery (Newburyport) and Mary Allen (Stratham)
William H., d. 3/10/1916 at 77/0/23; mitral regurgitation; John S. Vickery and Mary A. Cook

VIENS,
Elmina, d. 2/9/1935 at 69/9/2; intestinal obstruction by a band

VIER,
Charlotte A. T., d. 7/10/1933 at 46/10/15; cardiac failure

VILES,
Ernest L., d. 9/23/1929 at 65/10/5 in Owasco, NY; myocarditis
Ida M., d. 6/27/1935 at 72/7/3; cerebral hemorrhage

VILLEAUCOUR,
John H., d. 5/14/1892 at 2; convulsions, cerebral; b. Dover; (Canada; Canada)

VINAL,
Edith P., d. 11/11/1928 at 62/11/18 in Boston, MA; broncho pneumonia; Ben. P. Pierce and Elizabeth A. Twombly
Edward E., d. 5/4/1909 at 43/6/11 in Boston, MA; pistol shot wound

VINCENT,
Joseph R., d. 11/19/1916 at 21/11/4; intestinal obstruction; Arthur Vincent and Angeline Manville

VIOLA,
Albert, d. 2/25/1925 at 0/3/9; inanition; Benedetto Viola and Philomene Placido

VITTUM,
Benjamin F., d. 6/5/1910 at 82/9; cerebral paralysis; David Vittum and Dolly Beede
Elizabeth J., d. 10/24/1892 at 65; nervous prostration; b. NH; (MA; NH)
Frank P., d. 5/29/1907 at 54/7/6; pulmonary phthisis; Benjamin F. Vittum and Elizabeth Pierce
George H., d. 10/29/1904 at 40/4; chronic nephritis; PH
Hattie M. Platts, d. 1/23/1891 at 43/3/2; married; John L. Platts (MA) and Harriet Mitchell (MA)

VOGE,
Andrew A., d. 7/9/1908 at 24/11/13 in Boston, MA; phthisis pulmonalis

VON HEIMBURG,
Ant'ne, d. 9/21/1932 at 66/5 in Rollinsford; cerebral embolism

VON HINBERG,
George, d. 2/24/1923 at 61 in Boston, MA; aortic aneurysm

VYTH,
Dora, d. 9/26/1923 at 77/1/6; enteritis; David Salinger and Rebecca Basstoff
Herman, d. 7/14/1917 at 76/10 in Concord; hypostatic pneumonia; Isaac Vyth

WADE,
Edith Martha, d. 4/3/1928 at 73/5/19 in Brockton, MA; apoplexy
Frank A., d. 7/7/1933 at –; premature birth
Maurice F., Jr., d. 10/9/1932 at 0/1/5; debility

WADLEIGH,
Clara E. R., d. 8/15/1921 at 78/2 in Lexington, NH (sic); chronic myocarditis
Eben R., d. 2/27/1931 at 92/3/12 in Worcester, MA; cardiac renal vascular
Elijah, d. 11/20/1892 at 80; disease of brain; (North Hampton; North Hampton)
Eliza A., d. 11/27/1897 at 52; ictemis gravis; b. So. Berwick, ME; PH
Francis F., d. 10/4/1936 at 86/9/14*
George H., d. 7/11/1927 at 84/9/14 in Lexington, MA; arterio sclerosis
Mary, d. 6/21/1895 at 95 in York, ME; old age; buried in Dover
Mary G., d. 6/30/1930 at 75/5/25 in Union; chr. val. heart dis.
Nathaniel, d. 10/2/1901 at 65/4/15; fracture of skull; PH
Olive J., d. 2/23/1927 at 81/5/26 in Wells, ME; pneumonia
Sarah H., d. 4/13/1906 at 91/3/23; shock; PH

Willis J., d. 8/28/1931 at 64/1/11 in Boston, MA; appendix abscess

WAITE,
William S., d. 3/22/1916 at 61/9/8 in Foxboro, MA; acute gastro enteritis

WAITT,
Norman H., d. 1/12/1902 at 3/1/22 in Brockton, MA; membraneous croup; PH

WAKEHAM,
Joseph B., d. 5/11/1897 at 73; heart disease; b. Milton; PH

WALCOTT,
Loren, d. 3/31/1893 at 69; disease of brain; b. Dudley, MA; (-----; Newark, CT)

WALDRON,
Catherine A., d. 8/31/1900 at 46; uraemia; PH
Charles G., d. 7/27/1928 at 49/0/28; peritonitis; Frank P. Waldron and Catherine -----
Clara A., d. 5/14/1894 at – in Chicopee, MA; valvular disease of heart; buried in Dover
Frances P., d. 4/21/1888 at 53/0/22; married; b. Waterboro, ME; ----- Payson (ME)
Frank P., d. 6/23/1927 at 70/11/14; pulmonary oedema; George Waldron and Hannah Hall
George, d. 6/8/1904 at 76/8/4 in Wolfeboro; apoplexy; buried in Dover
Gideon, d. 11/8/1896 at 85 in So. Berwick, ME; inflammation of bladder; PH
Juliette A., d. 11/4/1892 at 54; paralysis of heart; b. Dover; (Dixmont, ME; -----)
Margaret F., d. 5/9/1904 at 28/1/20; peritonitis; PH
Martha A., d. 1/31/1899 at 63 in So. Berwick, ME; pneumonia
Mary, d. 6/16/1891 at 86/5/22; widow; Ichabod Canney (Madbury) and Mary Waldron (Dover)
Mary E., d. 6/24/1888 at 59/3/29; widow; b. Strafford; Michael Berry (Strafford) and Eliza Kimball (Alton)
Richard, d. 8/2/1889 at 84/2/7; farmer; married; b. Dixmont, ME; Richard Waldron (Dover) and Elizabeth Kimball (Dover)
Richard A., d. 8/7/1900 at 68 in Nottingham, IN; PH

WALKER,
child, d. 8/11/1927 at –; compression of cord; Glenn W. Walker and Eva D. Willey

Albert D., d. 1/6/1922 at 85/6/25 in Sanbornton; cancer of prostate
Andrew J., d. 7/16/1894 at 70; heart disease; b. Sanford, ME; PH
Archibald I. C., d. 12/4/1909 at 63/11/6; apoplexy; James Walker and Marion Fergerson
Charles D., d. 2/26/1890 at 23/0/11; single; John C. Walker (Strafford) and Matilda Smith (Halifax, NS)
Charles F., d. 1/1/1896 at 36; peritonitis; b. Dover; PH
Charles G., d. 3/30/1889 at 83/0/26; gardener; married; b. England; Charles G. Walker (England) and T. Hepworth (England)
Charlotte, d. 1/10/1901 at 2/10/0; marasmus; SM
Charlotte, d. 8/9/1907 at 0/7; gastroenteritis; Albert T. Walker and Hattie M. Drew
Edward, d. 4/27/1890 at 4/11/3; Joseph H. Walker (Portsmouth) and Elizabeth Tibbetts (Gardner)
Elizabeth, d. 8/10/1894 at 77 in Merrimac, MA; herniplegia; PH
Elizabeth, d. 8/21/1936 at 61/1/10; cerebral hemorrhage
Elizabeth S., d. 12/14/1914 at 70/4/27; cerebral apoplexy; ----- Tibbetts
Ellen K., d. 3/13/1901 at 79/11/20; grippe; PH
Frederick W., d. 7/27/1892 at –; brain disease; b. Dover; (NS; Dover)
George, d. 4/27/1930 at 60 in Lebanon, ME; obstruction of bowels
George A., d. 8/17/1927 at 21/1; drowning; Herbert E. Walker and Addie Johnson
George H., d. 10/8/1909 at 85; pyaemia
Glenn W., d. 9/10/1936 at 23/2/9 in Rollinsford; shock, hem., frac.
Harold R., d. 12/2/1898 at 1; broncho-pneumonia; b. Dover; SM
Hiram J., d. 9/4/1914 at 56; pyelonephritis
Jennette, d. 9/24/1890 at 0/1; John Walker (NS) and Lillie E. (Dover)
John, d. 3/3/1913 at 60; cerebral hemorrhage; John Walker and Elizabeth Hilldrop
John C., d. 3/8/1917 at 55; pulm. tuberculosis
John Colby, d. 2/17/1902 at 30/6/8 in Revere, MA; heart failure; PH
John H., d. 8/1/1887 at 0/10/15; b. Dover; Hiram J. Walker (NS) and Margaret (Ireland)
Joseph E., d. 11/15/1897 at 0; umbilical hemorrhage; PH
Joseph H., d. 4/5/1899 at 59; herniaplegia; PH
Leona, d. 7/27/1908 at 41/5/21; anachroism of aorta
Lizzie, d. 11/6/1927 at 68/7/24 in Concord; arterio sclerosis
Lydia Ann, d. 6/11/1924 at 64/10/19; locomotor ataxia; Charles L. Chapman and Sarah Witham
Lydia J., d. 1/1/1891 at 74/0/2; widow; William Ham (Strafford) and Mary Roberts (Strafford)
Martha E., d. 9/10/1925 at 71/1/24; broncho pneumonia; Micajah Gilman and Lydia Libby
Mary, d. 12/25/1929 at 78/3/16; cereb. hemorrhage; Robert Davidson and Mary Patterson

Matilda S., d. 11/15/1911 at 85/7/20 in Salem, MA; cerebral hemorrhage
May, d. 5/5/1930 at 59/11/16; myocarditis; George Meserve
Nellie M., d. 5/23/1904 at 0/2/9; marasmus; buried in So. Berwick, ME
Paul Henry, d. 3/2/1917 at 0/3/2; whooping cough; Ralph S. Walker and
    Catherine A. Sullivan
Raymond, d. 7/20/1900 at <1; tuberculosis; SM
Raymond E., d. 2/13/1899 at − in So. Berwick, ME; accidental; PH
Samuel T., d. 4/29/1887 at 4/2/21; b. Dover; Joseph T. Walker (NH) and
    Sarah E. Tibbetts (ME)
Sarah E., d. 6/13/1902 at 60/9/6; abdominal cancer; buried in Barnstead
Stephen, d. 6/16/1890 at 72/11/3; married; Independence Walker
    (Strafford) and Annie Caswell (Strafford)
Tamer, d. 6/16/1899 at 65 in Everett, MA; acute Bright's disease; PH
William F., d. 3/22/1931 at 76/1/26; arterio sclerosis
William L., d. 4/30/1936 at 40/11/20; car., head of pancreas

WALKINS,
child, d. 3/8/1932 at −; stillborn

WALL,
Peter, d. 5/21/1914 at 55; tuberculosis, pulmonary

WALLACE,
Albert, d. 1/31/1905 at 0/0/5; malformation
Arthur L., Jr., d. 12/1/1928 at 0/0/5; atelectasis of lungs; Arthur L. Wallace
    and Yvonne Gagnon
Charles L., d. 7/15/1937 at 76 in Malden, MA; arteriosclerosis
Clara L., d. 3/7/1906 at 81/8/6; ulceration of bowels; PH
Edwin S., d. 6/10/1936 at 69/6/10; cancer of stomach
Frank R., d. 7/2/1925 at 45; hem. from varicose veins; Reuben Wallace
    and Emma J. Haniford
Grace S., d. 10/15/1931 at 75/2/19; chronic myocarditis
Harry S., d. 1/24/1900 at 42 in Boston, MA; probably cardiac disease; PH
Horace H., d. 5/4/1910 at 91/4 in Lawrence, MA; cerebral hemorrhage
Joan H., d. 7/7/1893 at 79; organic heart disease - dropsy; b. Barrington;
    (Barrington; Barrington)
John, d. 3/7/1917 at 72; chr. Brights disease
Lillian R., d. 2/15/1915 at 0/4; spinal meningitis; Arthur L. Wallace and
    Doris Demarais
Ralph B., d. 9/6/1934 at 8/11/18; rheumatic heart dis.
Sarah E., d. 10/23/1924 at 57/5/3; cerebral hemorrhage; W. H.
    Whitehouse and Emma York
Willie, d. 6/16/1896 at 12 in Wolfeboro; heart disease

WALLINGFORD,
Alta L. G., d. 3/5/1891 at 81/0/16; widow; Joseph Hilliard (Cambridge, MA) and Sarah Langton (York, ME)
Charles, d. 5/26/1914 at 47; chronic nephritis; Seth O. Wallingford and Betsy Ricker
Clara B., d. 2/13/1935 at 80/7/22; cerebral hemorrhage
Louisa F., d. 4/12/1908 at 26/10/11; phthisis pulmonalis; C. W. Wallingford and Clara B. Sterling
Nellie P., d. 5/24/1911 at 67/2/27 in Weston, MA; chronic bronchitis; Jedediah Cook and Lucinda Harris
T. C. N., d. 7/3/1918 at 69/11/10; general arterio sclerosis; Ira Wallingford and Delaney Thompson
Walter S., d. 3/27/1926 at 36/8/23 in N. Providence, NJ; lobar pneumonia

WALMSLEY,
Elizabeth, d. 4/2/1937 at 87/11/28 in Manchester; arteriosclerosis
William, d. 6/27/1927 at 49/7/12 in Lee, ME; angina pectoris

WALSH,
Catherine, d. 11/29/1907 at 70; apoplexy; Patrick Carragher and Catherine Flannigan
Donald A., d. 5/28/1937 at 22/9/18; accidental drowning
Edward, d. 1/4/1903 at 0/0/19; pneumonia; PH
Mabel Frances, d. 1/28/1928 at 18/3/2; suspected tuberculosis; John H. Walsh and Elizabeth Gooch
Thomas, d. 11/13/1908 at 7/2/11; pneumonia; Thomas Walsh and Mary Kane

WARD,
Alfred, d. 7/8/1903 at 0/6/26 in St. Louis, MO; entero-colitis; PH
Bertha E., d. 7/1/1892 at –; inanition; b. Dover; (Brockton, MA; Brockton, MA)
Charles A., d. 6/22/1917 at 58/5/8; chr. interstitial nephritis; Daniel S. Ward and Jane P. Eastman
Charlotte H., d. 1/14/1935 at 65 in Boston, MA; angina pectoris
Daniel S., d. 12/20/1898 at 67 in Rollinsford; pyletis; b. NH; PH
Edward H., d. 4/27/1937 at 78/5/4; chr. myocarditis
Henry E., d. 6/5/1923 at 60; chr. Brights disease
Jane P., d. 5/9/1909 at 79/8/11; spinal paralysis; Stephen R. Eastman and Nancy -----
John E., d. 6/13/1926 at 82/11/16; apoplexy
Lottie E., d. 1/5/1932 at 79/7/10; chronic endocarditis
Mary K., d. 9/6/1901 at 79/7/28; debility of old age; PH
Nathaniel B., d. 11/3/1907 at 52/7/4; carcinoma of stomach; John Ward and Mary A. Bright

WARDWELL,
Loella M., d. 7/22/1936 at 76/8/29; carcinoma uterus
Sarah S., d. 9/16/1905 at 48/3/22; Bright's disease; buried in Lowell, MA

WARNER,
Roy A., d. 1/19/1900 at 17; typhoid fever; PH

WARNICK,
Eliza, d. 4/10/1927 at 78; paralysis agitans

WARNOCK,
Mary, d. 9/17/1889 at 60; weaver; single; b. Ireland; Jno. Warnock
    (Ireland) and ----- (Ireland)

WARREN,
child, d. 10/5/1927 at 0/0/6; congenital constriction; Delma Y. Warren and
    Beatrice A. Crooker
Abbie E., d. 6/29/1929 at 69/3/25; carcinoma of uterus; Jerome Canney
    and Nancy Wentworth
Allena F., d. 7/3/1922 at 74/2/17 in Boston, MA; arterio sclerosis
Arabella E., d. 4/9/1922 at 70/2/21; chronic nephritis; Hayes Perkins and
    Lydia Ann Wiggin
Chadbourne H., d. 5/3/1909 at 84/9/8 in Auburn, ME; valv. disease of
    heart; Chadbourne Warren and Sally Swain
Delia A., d. 12/31/1900 at 58; cerebral apoplexy; buried in Rollinsford
Edward P., d. 5/9/1899 at 43 in York Beach, ME; valvular disease of heart;
    PH
Fred, d. 7/4/1928 at 71/6; arterio sclerosis
George H., d. 12/13/1894 at 41; pleuro-pneumonia; b. Willimantic, CT;
    buried in Stonington, CT
George M., d. 3/5/1894 at 40; brain fever; buried in Farmington
Georgia R., d. 4/17/1931 at 76/0/14 in Swampscott, MA; arterio sclerosis
Helen J., d. 8/14/1905 at 0/10/24; cholera infantum; SM
Jennie L., d. 4/16/1912 at 49/4/9 in Swampscott, MA; pneumonia
Martha A., d. 11/26/1919 at 86/4/5 in Stricklands, ME; senility and
    endocarditis; Ethan Allen
Matilda C., d. 1/27/1892 at 78; cancer of stomach
Moses P., d. 5/4/1896 at 74; suicide by hanging; b. Dover; PH
Myron H., d. 3/27/1892 at 1; hydrocephalus
Pamelia A., d. 8/29/1895 at 72; old age; b. Dover; PH
Sarah F., d. 9/22/1933 at 87/4/1 in Rollinsford; cancer of stomach
Sarah P., d. 5/26/1907 at 85/3/4; paralysis; Anthony Cook and Sally
    Langley
Susan M., d. 10/9/1917 at 81/6; apoplexy; David Smith and Mercy Lang

Susan W., d. 9/12/1914 at 89/6/5 in Swampscott, MA; general arterio sclerosis
Thomas, d. 8/6/1898 at 95; old age; b. Ireland; SM
William H., d. 2/16/1918 at 71 in Boston, MA; apoplexy

WARSOWITCH,
Wt'lystouvos, d. 9/5/1915 at 1/0/15; gastro enteritis; Joseph Warsowitch and Mary Yaros

WATERHOUSE,
Ella P., d. 11/30/1925 at 73/3/6; lobar pneumonia; Demeritt Place and Jane Foss

WATERS,
George, d. 12/24/1934 at 43/3/6 in Concord; tubercular meningitis
Patrick, d. 8/26/1888 at 45; laborer; married; b. Ireland; Peter Waters (Ireland)

WATSON,
child, d. 5/8/1895 at 0; stillbirth; b. Dover
child, d. 3/19/1918 at −; stillborn; Daniel W. Watson and Hazel M. Hansen
child, d. 12/18/1927 at −; stillborn; Harold E. Watson and Lillian A. Boyd
Abigail, d. 8/18/1899 at 84; old age; PH
Ann E., d. 7/22/1896 at 72; old age; b. Dover; PH
Ann E., d. 4/7/1909 at 65/1/8; cerebral apoplexy; John Mooney and Jane Roberts
Annie M., d. 3/15/1892 at 48; heart disease - dropsy; b. NH; (NH; NH)
Annie N., d. 5/29/1931 at 94/4/6; senile dementia
Arabella S., d. 10/10/1923 at 61/6/2; myocarditis; George P. Bennett and Abigail Straw
Arthur R., d. 5/8/1931 at 61/7/10; valv. heart disease
Bernard G., d. 9/20/1910 at 73 in Brockton, MA; bloody dysentery
Carrie Fogg, d. 9/6/1888 at 39/0/9; married; b. Solon, ME; James Tebbetts (Concord, ME) and L. June (N. Anson, ME)
Charles, d. 2/15/1905 at 86/4/28; heart disease; buried in Philadelphia, PA
Christianna, d. 10/22/1891 at 87; single; b. Dover; Nathaniel Watson (Dover) and ----- (Boston, MA)
David A., d. 12/2/1930 at 49/3/22; lobar pneumonia; David W. Watson and Harriet Soule
Edna Allison, d. 7/12/1930 at 47/1 in York, ME; brain fever
Ernest L., d. 9/15/1935 at 66/11/16; diabetes
Frank R., d. 5/1/1895 at 43; pneumonia; b. Biddeford, ME; buried in Biddeford, ME
Grace M., d. 7/17/1934 at 57/1/17; cerebral hemorrhage

Hannah H., d. 8/20/1898 at 77; diabetes; b. Hollis, ME; buried in Biddeford, ME
Hannah R., d. 12/22/1896 at 38; apoplexy; b. Madbury; PH
Henry A., d. 7/24/1905 at 55/11/22; heart disease; PH
Ida A., d. 4/7/1909 at 56/1/6; nervous shock; Martin H. Cannavan and Clarice Waldron
J. Sumner, d. 12/27/1936 at 77/6/8*
Jessie S., d. 2/25/1918 at 65/9/3; acute cardiac dilatation
John, d. 1/30/1894 at 68; congestion of kidneys; b. Barrington; buried in Newmarket
John H., d. 5/18/1936 at 81/11/14; gen. arteriosclerosis
John L., d. 10/10/1892 at 84; debility from age; b. Wakefield; (Wakefield; -----)
Jonathan S., d. 8/24/18888 at 68/6/2; married; b. Wolfeboro
Joshua, d. 9/21/1924 at 73/7/9; cerebral hemorrhage; Joshua Watson and Abigail -----
Katherine L., d. 5/5/1897 at 68; chronic nephritis; b. Bloomfield, ME; PH
Lucy M., d. 5/8/1911 at 89/8/10; senility; Johnson D. Quimby and Mary Collins
Lydia A., d. 8/4/1908 at 61/5/12; cancer; Ichabod Tibbetts and Lydia Watson
Lydia A., d. 10/17/1910 at 87/4/9; cancer in back; Nat Horne and Sarah Roberts
Mabel S., d. 11/15/1920 at 61/4/14 in Somerville, MA; sarcoma of intestines
Martha C., d. 5/12/1888 at 1/1/12; b. Dover; Thomas E. Watson (Dover) and Hannah R. Small (Madbury)
Mary G., d. 5/10/1920 at 69/3/12; dilation of heart
Mary H., d. 4/26/1900 at 60 in Concord; exhaustion; PH
Mary P., d. 2/19/1904 at 56/4/17; heart disease; PH
Matilda M., d. 7/11/1898 at 78; diabetes mellitus; b. England; buried in Philadelphia, PA
Nathaniel, d. 11/15/1887 at 59/10/17; painter; widower; b. Dover; Samuel H. Watson (Portsmouth) and Susan Haley (Dover)
Nathaniel H., d. 4/7/1896 at –; stillborn; b. Dover; PH
Nathaniel H., d. 3/3/1922 at 56/6/21 in Effingham; angina pectoris
Noah S., d. 2/9/1892 at 72; influenza; b. Tamworth; (Newmarket; Eliot, ME)
Perley B., d. 7/9/1902 at 70/5/10; general paresis; PH
Robert H., d. 8/18/1932 at 6 hrs.; atelectasis
Sarah M., d. 3/6/1895 at 79; disease of heart; b. Topsham, VT; PH
William T., d. 5/10/1937 at 78/0/21; paralysis agitans

WATTERS,
John F., d. 4/21/1935 at 46/5/30; lobar pneumonia

Nellie, d. 9/28/1920 at 57/4/14; cerebral apoplexy; John Mallen and Katherine Fox

WATTS,
Charles S., d. 4/21/1890 at 85/1/25 in Brookline
Sarah, d. 1/7/1891 at 77/1/25 in Brookline, MA

WAY,
Georgia A., d. 12/28/1914 at 59/4/16; cerebral hemorrhage; Walter Plaisted and Mary Cram
Ida M. Bosworth, d. 8/26/1937 at 72/6/22; cerebr. hemorrhage

WEATHERBEE,
Veronica E., d. 2/22/1918 at 3/7 in Boston, MA; stricture of oesophagus

WEATHERS,
Lalia, d. 5/26/1905 at 12/6/11 in Boston, MA; suppuration appendicitis; buried in Durham

WEAVER,
Annie E., d. 1/8/1903 at 55/0/13; heart disease; PH

WEBB,
William, d. 4/23/1928 at 74/2/17; chronic endocarditis

WEBBER,
Alvina, d. 11/30/1922 at 88/2/10; gen. arterio sclerosis; Abraham Witham and Sally Brooks
Elizabeth, d. 12/22/1919 at 64/5/27; chronic Brights disease; Daniel M. Webber
Hannah R., d. 9/9/1898 at 77 in Pittsfield; dysentery; PH
Herman, d. 5/–/1896 at 75 in Strafford; organic disease of heart
John P., d. 11/12/1914 at 72/2 in Strafford; myocarditis
Joyce Marie, d. 7/9/1927 at 0/2/8; malnutrition; Russell W. Webber and Sadie C. McManus
Julia E., d. 4/2/1916 at 72/10/25 in Pittsfield; pneumonia; Samuel Pierce and Martha White
Mary Ann, d. 7/20/1904 at 70; cancer of uterus
Mercy E., d. 8/31/1909 at 75; cerebral hemorrhage
Russell V., d. 5/25/1933 at 19/5/6; spinal meningitis

WEBSTER,
child, d. 3/7/1889 at 0/0/½ in Boston, MA
child, d. 12/29/1933 at –; stillborn

Annie E., d. 2/18/1918 at 73/0/11 in Newburyport, MA; mitral insufficiency
Charles E., d. 1/21/1904 at 65/11/1; senile debility; buried in tomb
Cora G., d. 2/28/1912 at 43/8/21; surgical shock; Jerry Webster and Lydia
    A. Bean
Edwin, d. 3/7/1889 at 0/0/½ in Boston, MA
Elizabeth P., d. 9/29/1900 at 84; catarrhal pneumonia; buried in private
George A., d. 3/13/1911 at 71/9/6; angina pectoris; John Webster and
    Sophia L. Wendell
George K., d. 10/27/1914 at 56/7/15; typhoid fever
Hannah H., d. 3/9/1895 at 63 in Brockton, MA; septicaemia; buried in
    Dover
John, d. 8/6/1887 at 81/8/18; mason; widower; b. Hartford, CT
Lydia A., d. 4/1/1916 at 72/8/25; angina pectoris; Daniel K. Webster and
    Hannah Ham
Roscoe, d. 11/22/1892 at 1; heart disease

WEDGEWOOD,
Charles, d. 11/5/1910 at 80; general paralysis
David, d. 2/1/1890 at 59/5/8; married; Jonathan Wedgewood (ME) and
    Charlotte Moore (ME)
Rose L., d. 2/19/1916 at 81/8/18; acute bronchitis; Moses Rumery and
    Martha Brackett

WEED,
Betsey S., d. 4/9/1897 at 89; fracture and cystitis; b. Alfred, ME; PH

WEEDEN,
Albert W., d. 4/29/1904 at 84/11/14; hepatitis; buried in Lebanon, ME
Blanche G., d. 10/5/1918 at 25/4/12; lobar pneumonia; Melnot B.
    Robinson and Nellie A. Clark
Daniel F., d. 2/21/1930 at 73/3/16; chronic myocarditis; Albert W. Weeden
    and Lydia J. Hersom
Dorothy E., d. 10/10/1918 at 7/0/23; pneumonia; Scott L. Weeden and
    Blanche G. Robinson
Myra W., d. 8/11/1928 at 66/0/25; encephalitis; Oliver Bickford and Elmira
    Canney
Oliver Scott, d. 10/2/1918 at 2/1/19; influenza; Scott L. Weeden and
    Blanche G. Robinson

WEEKS,
Annie F. H., d. 9/10/1904 at 42/4; surgical shock; PH
Eliza, d. 10/19/1902 at 92/10/10; paralysis; PH

WELCH,
child, d. 12/21/1921 at –; congenital atelectasis; Edward Welch and Catherine Casey
child, d. 2/6/1935 at –; intracranial hemorrhage
Alice, d. 10/31/1932 at 19; fracture of skull
Alice T., d. 1/31/1899 at 6; septicemia; SM
Azilla A., d. 9/12/1934 at 82/6/4; broncho pneumonia
Carrie I., d. 8/13/1905 at 31/11/25 in Haverhill, MA; carcinoma; PH
Charles W., d. 2/24/1920 at 49/8/9; lobar pneumonia; Samuel W. Welch and Dorothy O. Gray
Dorothy O., d. 8/31/1918 at 86/9/3; senility; Henry Gray and Dorothy Otis
Ellen E., d. 7/4/1898 at –; cancer; b. Dover; SM
Everett T., d. 9/2/1902 at 1/1/10; cholera infantum; PH
Frank N., d. 5/13/1937 at 65/5/3; peritonitis
Fred A., d. 4/16/1935 at 76/0/24; cerebral hemorrhage
George G., d. 10/20/1936 at 76/3/19; cerebral hemorrhage
George Gregg, d. 3/24/1915 at 29/6/6 in Brookline, MA; chronic infections arthritis; John T. Welch and Elizabeth McDonald
James, d. 1/2/1889 at 1; b. Dover; James H. Welch (Gloucester, MA) and Sarah J. Cassily (Dover)
John, d. 11/6/1890 at 23; single
John, d. 10/12/1897 at 60; suicide by drowning; b. Ireland; SM
John T., d. 9/22/1919 at 62/9; Brights disease; Joseph W. Welch and Mary E. Tapley
John W., d. 3/7/1931 at 81/8; arterio sclerosis
Kathryn, d. 1/18/1929 at 40; broncho pneumonia; Patrick Casey and Katherine Cronin
Madeline M., d. 9/26/1912 at 0/0/22; pneumonia; John P. Welsh (sic) and Elizabeth B. Grimshaw
Margaret A., d. 3/18/1893 at –; marasmus; b. Dover; (MA; Dover)
Mary, d. 10/14/1897 at 60; pneumonia; b. Ireland; SM
Mary A., d. 8/25/1889 at 1/8; b. Dover; James H. Welch (Lawrence, MA) and Sarah Cassily (Dover)
Mary E., d. 11/20/1904 at 82/10/2; cerebral apoplexy; PH
Mary Reade, d. 6/12/1915 at 66/0/16; paralysis; Joseph W. Welch and Mary E. Tapley
Rose A., d. 11/3/1918 at 62; apoplexy; Thomas Agnew and Bridget Haughey
Samuel E., d. 10/15/1927 at 70/3/12; chronic endocarditis; Samuel M. Welch and Dorothy Gray
Samuel M., d. 6/24/1903 at 76/1/16; endocarditis; PH
Sarah J., d. 6/10/1893 at 32; phthisis pulmonalis; b. Dover; (Ireland; Ireland)
Sarah Jane, d. 1/1/1889 at 0/0/1-6; b. Dover; James H. Welch (Gloucester, MA) and Sarah J. Cassily (Dover)

Thomas, d. 10/20/1904 at 57; acute alcoholism; SM
Thomas, d. 10/19/1937 at 47; enceph. lethargica
William F., d. 11/7/1895 at 36; phthisis pulmonalis; buried in Lawrence, MA

WELDRON,
Rosie, d. 10/27/1890 at 65; married; Dennis Kelligeer (Ireland)

WELLMAN,
Blanche W., d. 8/11/1936 at 60/7 in Concord; art. heart disease
Horace B., d. 3/22/1909 at 70 in New York, NY; carcinoma
W. B., d. 1/12/1892 at –; whooping cough

WELLS,
Carrie M., d. 4/18/1909 at 63/7/4; tetanus; Nathan Preston and Mary Smiley
Edwin B., d. 9/20/1901 at 63/7/18; angina pectoris; PH
Herbert E., d. 2/27/1935 at 52/5/20 in Los Angeles, CA; third degree burns over face, hands, parts of body
Holton E., d. 12/16/1931 at 83/11/16; chronic nephritis
James F., d. 8/17/1927 at 19/2/13; drowning; Arthur W. Wells and Nora Richardson
Orianna H., d. 6/30/1933 at 73/3/7; carcinoma of bladder
Sarah E. C., d. 9/7/1899 at 86; senile inanition; buried in Deerfield Center

WELSH,
child, d. 12/24/1919 at –; stillborn; Harland H. Welsh and Mabel W. Neal
John J., d. 10/11/1912 at 34; peritonitis; James Welsh and Anne Downey
Michael J., d. 9/7/1914 at 47 in Portsmouth; John Welsh and Mary Flaherty

WELTON,
Mabel F., d. 8/6/1926 at 48/7/22 in Eliot, ME; carcinoma of stomach

WELTS,
Enos Loren, d. 5/2/1917 at 84/2/21; myocardial insufficiency; Enos Welts and Cloe Howard

WENDELL,
Caroline R., d. 12/15/1930 at 83/0/16; lobar pneumonia; Daniel H. Wendell and Huldah Jenness
Charles E., d. 3/23/1933 at 79/2/6; cancer of prostate
Daniel H., d. 12/26/1895 at 81; pneumonia; b. Dover; PH
Edward, d. 8/28/1906 at 0/6/11; cholera infantum; PH

Edward W., d. 9/30/1929 at 59/6/9; cerebral embolism; George S. Wendell and Nellie Varney
Ellen A., d. 4/25/1933 at 73/1/22; acute myocarditis
Emily L., d. 10/4/1912 at 85/3/8; heart disease; David Sargent and Lydia H. Cushing
George, d. 4/29/1907 at 0/0/12; malnutrition; Edward Wendell and Catherine Murphy
George W., d. 5/6/1922 at 81/3/11; lobar pneumonia; George Wendell and Sally Ham
Isabell F., d. 6/5/1936 at 80/3/13 in Rochester; chr. endocarditis
Lydia J., d. 12/9/1908 at 42/10/7; pneumonia; John W. Cole and Lydia J. -
Oliver C., d. 11/5/1912 at 67/5/29 in Belmont; double pneumonia
Sarah Butler, d. 10/5/1910 at 64/11/10 in Cambridge, MA; left hemiplegia
Vienna, d. 3/20/1895 at 88; exhaustion; b. Strafford; PH

WENTWORTH,
child, d. 9/20/1905 at –; stillborn
Abbie F., d. 12/9/1923 at 75/7/13; accid. gas poisoning; John P. Gowen and Eleanor Perkins
Abigail A., d. 12/19/1906 at 93/8/27; old age; PH
Aldo P., Jr., d. 6/24/1915 at 2/8/16; rheumatic fever; Aldo P. Wentworth and Edna L. Davis
Alvara B., d. 10/4/1905 at 18/11 in Boston, MA; accidental fall; PH
Andrew P., d. 2/29/1916 at 67/2/13 in New Gloucester, ME; arterio sclerosis; James Wentworth and Mary A. Tuttle
Andrew W., d. 1/20/1888 at 48/4/5; painter; married; b. Moultonboro; C. Wentworth (Moultonboro) and Eliza Carity (Sanbornton)
Angeline L., d. 5/26/1904 at 66/9/25; cerebral paralysis; PH
Annie E., d. 6/29/1901 at 67/11/24 in Newton, MA; abscess of liver; PH
Annie J., d. 2/10/1920 at 52/11/17; chronic nephritis; Andrew W. Wentworth and Jeannette McFarland
Barton M., d. 11/8/1930 at 76/2/5; cerebral hemorrhage; Jacob Wentworth and Zilpha Roberts
Bessie E., d. 4/6/1919 at 35/1/14; hemorrhage; Henry F. Howe and Julia M. Hanscom
Charles B., d. 5/27/1926 at 64/4/22; natural causes; George B. Wentworth and Angeline Leavitt
Charles E., d. 8/17/1903 at 73/5/20; heart disease; PH
Charles H., d. 12/30/1905 at 74/4/28 in Rochester; tuberculosis pulmonalis; PH
Charles H., d. 11/26/1914 at 56/9/5; accidental drowning; Alvin H. Wentworth and Henriette Pickering
Delphine H., d. 8/13/1915 at 94/9/19 in Hartford, CT; arterio cap. fibrosis
Edward M., d. 2/25/1934 at 21/10/21 in Hanover; carbon mon. poisoning
Elizabeth A., d. 6/11/1894 at 87; pneumonia; b. Alton; PH

Elmer Marston, d. 4/13/1936 at 74*
Emily F., d. 11/17/1894 at 38 in Wolfeboro; pulmonary tuberculosis; PH
Emily F., d. 8/1/1895 at 54; Brights disease; b. Barrington; buried in family lot
Emma J., d. 10/28/1929 at 70/5/5; cerebral hemorrhage; William Wendell and Lydia E. Sargent
Ephraim, d. 3/11/1922 at 78/7/28; angina pectoris; Ivory Wentworth and Rebecca Bickford
Esther, d. 1/24/1932 at 29 in New York, NY; gas asphyxia
Esther A., d. 4/1/1936 at 90/9/20*; b. Newfield, ME
Fannie, d. 9/15/1914 at 65; carcinoma of uterus
Fannie, d. 4/15/1924 at 65; chr. Brights disease
Flavius J., d. 11/15/1929 at 91/6/12; arterio sclerosis; James J. Wentworth and Clarissa J. Hall
Florinda S., d. 1/21/1920 at 53/10/15 in Somerville, MA; lobar pneumonia
Frank H., d. 2/19/1901 at 33/11/18; nephritis; SM
Fred M., d. 2/1/1914 at 46/2; suffocation by smoke; George B. Wentworth and Angeline Leavitt
Frederick C., d. 2/26/1917 at 5/8/1; lobar pneumonia; Erving F. Wentworth and Florence M. Churbuck
George A., d. 5/24/1906 at 70/9/24; valvular disease of heart; buried in Exeter
George B., d. 1/13/1888 at 58/0/1 in Haverhill, MA; shoe manufr.; married; b. Rochester; B. Wentworth (Rochester) and Sarah Roberts (Rochester)
George G., d. 12/13/1937 at 71/5/15; uremia
George L., d. 4/1/1888 at 42/4/14 in Concord; b. Salmon Falls; J. B. Wentworth (Salmon Falls) and ----- (S. Berwick, ME)
George W., d. 6/2/1898 at 62; cancer; b. Dover; buried in family lot
Grace E., d. 6/19/1898 at 29; phthisis pulmonalis; b. Providence, RI; PH
Hannah, d. 3/13/1887 at 76/9/7; housewife; widow; b. Parsonsfield, ME; Marston Ames (Newmarket) and Mary Manning (Berwick, ME)
Harriett A., d. 5/25/1931 at 69/9/6 in Reading, MA; infection
Harry S., d. 4/10/1900 at 22; pneumonia; SM
Hattie J., d. 9/21/1917 at 71/10/21 in Haverhill, MA; mitral regurgitation
Helen, d. 3/14/1897 at 0; pneumonia; b. Dover; PH
Henry E., d. 7/16/1919 at 55; fracture of skull; Stephen Wentworth
Henry G., d. 1/26/1898 at 4; diphtheritic croup; b. Dover; buried in Rollinsford
Herbert, d. 9/6/1896 at 20; b. Dover; PH
Herbert E., d. 4/10/1909 at 56/2; broncho pneumonia; Charles Wentworth and Eliza -----
Herbert T., d. 3/17/1930 at 59/1/3; chronic endocarditis; John Wentworth and Mary Stackpole
Isaac E., d. 5/25/1908 at 25/10/0 in Haverhill, MA; pulmonary tuberculosis

Israel P., d. 12/25/1888 at 84/4/8 in Strafford; farmer; married; b. Madbury; F. Wentworth and Elizabeth Pierce
James F., d. 12/9/1903 at 0/0/1; inanition; PH
Jeannette F., d. 1/21/1907 at 66/2/2; pneumonia; ----- McFarland
John, d. 9/14/1891 at 73; single
John Norris, d. 5/17/1899 at 63; cancer of stomach; PH
John T., d. 5/11/1931 at 84/7/14 in Portland, ME; arterio sclerosis
Jonathan, d. 1/19/1892 at 54; phthisis; b. Hiram, ME; (Hiram, ME; Hiram, ME)
Julia A., d. 3/26/1897 at 61; chronic nephritis; b. Moultonboro; PH
Katherine S., d. 3/16/1920 at 23/9 in Boston, MA; peritonitis; Albert F. Seavey and Marietta Fogg
Lillian M., d. 12/18/1934 at 65/6/5 in Haverhill, MA; cerebral hemorrhage
Lucinda, d. 9/29/1924 at 82/2/19; cerebral hemorrhage; Aaron Willey and Susan Mills
Lucinda P., d. 7/5/1912 at 83/5/22; valvular disease of heart; F. S. McDonald and Susan A. -----
Lucretia W., d. 10/24/1908 at 71/0/11; fatty degeneration of heart; Samuel Woodes and Betsey Perkins
Lydia S., d. 7/26/1909 at 71/6/23; chronic interstitial nephritis; James Y. Hayes and Alice A. Hayes
Margaret E., d. 2/16/1891 at 35/8/26; married; Patrick Judge (Ireland) and Mary Lavine (Ireland)
Margaret E., d. 11/24/1896 at 1; inanition; b. Dover; buried in Rollinsford
Martha G., d. 9/23/1896 at 81 in Boston, MA; heart disease
Martin V. B., d. 8/4/1904 at 70/3/26; pyelo-nephritis; PH
Mary, d. 7/26/1906 at 50/4/22; phthisis pulmonalis; PH
Mary E., d. 12/16/1928 at 53/8/7; lobar pneumonia; William Ham and Margaret Driscoll
Minnie A., d. 7/3/1906 at 30/3/22; acute uraemia; PH
Nancy T., d. 4/14/1890 at 50/5/12; married; Titcomb Wentworth (Newfield, ME) and Hannah Ames (Parsonsfield, ME)
Nathaniel C., d. 7/22/1911 at 61/5/21; concussion of brain; John Wentworth and Elizabeth Pierce
Olive A., d. 1/3/1910 at 85/3/25; nephritis; G. S. Staples and Mary A. Roberts
Olive A., d. 12/26/1913 at 79/10/1 in Rollinsford
Oliver W., d. 3/12/1909 at 85/7/9; pneumonia; Charles Wentworth and Harriet Thompson
Raymond, d. 9/21/1937 at 46/10/26; chr. ercepelectis
Rebecca E. S., d. 4/5/1897 at 54; pneumonia; b. Rochester; PH
Reginald, d. 9/7/1931 at – in Bar Harbor, ME; uraemia
Richard W., d. 2/23/1926 at 0/1/3; chronic nephritis; Roland Wentworth and Regina Veil
Sally B., d. 7/2/1934 at 85/8/10; cerebral hemorrhage

Sarah A., d. 5/26/1902 at 75/5/24; pneumonia; buried in Newmarket
Sarah Ellen, d. 4/12/1921 at – in Strafford; cerebral hemorrhage; Joel
   Caverly and Mary -----
Sarah F., d. 5/15/1912 at 65/11/16; cancer of bladder; James J.
   Wentworth and Clarissa J. Hall
Sarah J., d. 5/9/1921 at 58 in Portland, ME; locomotor ataxia; Levi H. Foss
   and Julia A. Foss
Sarah N., d. 2/2/1888 at 56/0/20; married; b. Moultonboro; O. Wentworth
   (Moultonboro) and Betsey Caswell (Moultonboro)
Sarah O., d. 4/21/1909 at 76/7/16; valv. disease of heart; Walter N. Cotton
   and Ellen Robinson
Sophia R., d. 12/25/1932 at 80/9/19; lobar pneumonia
Susan, d. 11/10/1892 at 85; dropsy and old age
Thomas, d. 2/12/1893 at 69; cardiac disease
Thomas, d. 1/27/1899 at 62; pneumonia; PH
Thomas, d. 10/24/1925 at 63/11/2 in Boston, MA; natural causes
Wendell, d. 8/27/1889 at 0/3/9; b. Dover; George H. Wentworth (Dover)
   and E. J. Wendell (Dover)
William T., d. 1/21/1907 at 74/9/10; cerebral hemorrhage; Stephen
   Wentworth and Lois Trickey
William W., d. 9/30/1893 at 53; phthisis pulmonalis; b. Milton

WESENGER,
Willard D., d. 3/4/1923 at 25 in Malden, MA; pulmonary tuberculosis

WESLEY,
Alice C., d. 7/19/1913 at 1/9/7; congestion of brain; John H. Wesley and
   Kate J. Breen
Catherine, d. 1/11/1910 at 59/8; chronic nephritis; Michael McGaugh and
   Susan -----
Evelyn, d. 9/23/1907 at –; asphyxia; John H. Wesley and Katherine Breen
George, d. 12/23/1888 at 7; b. Dover; John Wesley
John H., d. 1/9/1919 at 46; diabetes; George Wesley and Kate McGaugh

WESSENGER,
John F., d. 7/26/1910 at 57/11/6; heart disease; John Wessenger and
   Mary Doyle

WEST,
Donald Lee, d. 2/13/1926 at 0/1/9; intestinal hemorrhage
Martha L., d. 1/16/1930 at 64/5/2; cerebral embolism; Hazen B. Tower and
   Sarah Snowdon
Mary Elizabeth, d. 11/19/1892 at 64; consumption

WESTERN,
John, d. 5/6/1902 at 34 in King's Park, NJ; general paresis; SM

WESTON,
Alonzo, d. 6/18/1908 at 70/5/13 in Berwick, ME; valvular disease of heart
Mary J., d. 1/27/1907 at 81/8; senility; Green Brown and Nancy Corrick
Ruth G., d. 12/10/1896 at – in Somersworth; inanition; PH

WESTRAN,
Everett M., d. 9/22/1904 at 0/3/4; malnutrition; PH
William, d. 2/13/1903 at 51/5/12 in Lowell, MA; general peritonitis; PH

WHALEN,
Joseph, d. 2/8/1907 at –; stillborn; Joseph Whalen and Lucy Sallinger

WHALLEY,
Timothy, d. 11/29/1907 at 80; senility

WHEATON,
Florence A., d. 8/22/1905 at 7/0/11; meningitis; PH

WHEELER,
Daniel, d. 5/6/1933 at –; congenital eventration
James H., d. 1/26/1893 at 61; cancer of bowels; b. Dover; (Dover; Dover)
John Henry, d. 4/5/1930 at 59/3 in Boston, MA; cardiovascular dis.
Priscilla C., d. 2/14/1902 at 79/4/25 in Boston, MA; senility; PH
William N., d. 4/26/1901 at 69; alcoholism; buried in Medford, MA

WHEISBORT,
Johanna, d. 8/12/1892 at 74; old age, fractured clavicle

WHELAN,
child, d. 7/16/1899 at –; stillborn; SM
Bridget, d. 8/12/1908 at 30; tuberculosis of hip; Patrick Calkin and Mary O'Neil
Ellie Frances, d. 7/30/1910 at 35/8/16; tuberculosis of lungs
James N., d. 10/5/1915 at 53; dilatation of heart
Mary, d. 4/20/1903 at 71/8/4; senile gangrene; buried in Biddeford, ME
Mary, d. 12/7/1913 at 41; mitral regurgitation; Henry Cox and Catherine Hughes

WHIDDEN,
Frances G., d. 1/12/1899 at 91; pneumonia; PH

WHIPP,
Bernice E., d. 3/21/1897 at 14; cancer; b. Dover; PH
Elizabeth T. B., d. 7/19/1924 at 66/8/19 in Newmarket; valv. disease of heart
Ella F., d. 6/7/1907 at 53/7/5; chronic bronchitis; Frederick L. Whipp and Mary C. Colby
Florence E., d. 1/15/1896 at 4; pneumonia; b. Dover; PH
George E., d. 6/9/1934 at 74/8 in Portland, ME; chronic myocarditis
Mary C., d. 3/31/1911 at – in Rollinsford

WHITCHER,
Herbert P., d. 8/4/1904 at 0/8/17 in Berlin; bassilar meningitis; buried in Dover

WHITCOMB,
Annie M., d. 6/19/1909 at 35; pulmonary tuberculosis; Terence Woods and Catherine Reynolds
Fred E., d. 4/26/1937 at 73/6/14 in Conway; lobar pneumonia

WHITE,
son, d. 5/26/1889 at 1/1; b. Dover; Mary White (Dover)
child, d. 10/23/1914 at –; stillborn; Roy S. White and Edith Haley
Abby, d. 11/6/18888 at 13/0/21; b. Great Falls; Frank White (Canada) and Mary Hall (Canada)
Angie, d. 11/10/1910 at 51/6/4; cerebral hemorrhage; George Beck and Hulda Meloon
Annie T., d. 11/10/1925 at 53/6/9; pulmonary tuberculosis; Michael Flanagan and Ann Welch
Belle, d. 12/7/1918 at 40; carcinoma of uterus
Caroline Z., d. 3/17/1932 at 97 in Philadelphia, PA; myocarditis
Clara E., d. 5/30/1908 at 38/3/12 in Portsmouth; appendicitis
Elizabeth M., d. 8/9/1888 at 60/11/22; married; b. Exeter; Ezekiel and Lucretia Hill
Elizabeth R., d. 1/28/1919 at 93/9/10; cerebral hemorrhage; Taylor Lougee and Jerusha Tibbetts
Emma, d. 8/18/1889 at 47/4/23; housekeeper; married; b. Dover; G. W. Wendell (Dover) and Prudence Jenness (Dover)
Fred H., d. 1/14/1919 at 55/10/12; chr. intestinal nephritis; John H. White and Sophia S. Hutchins
George E., d. 7/2/1931 at 74/10/23; endocarditis
Harry H., d. 10/18/1937 at 52/2/24; heart disease
Hattie R., d. 2/9/1901 at 47/4; gastritis; PH
Ida L., d. 5/3/1934 at 60/11/28; chronic nephritis
John, d. 10/18/1912 at 81/4/16 in Portsmouth; dis. of coronary arteries
John, d. 12/19/1928 at –; dead at birth; John White and Ellen E. Redden

John W., d. 1/28/1899 at 50; pulmonary gangrene; PH
Joseph F., d. 2/20/1936 at 81/1/6; chronic myocarditis
Madeline, d. 8/22/1912 at 0/3/8; chronic gastro enteritis; John White and
    Annie Flanagan
Maggie, d. 2/9/1893 at 69; died in Strafford Co. Asylum fire
Malissa L., d. 11/24/1920 at 71/8/5; valvular heart disease; John Carlton
    and Aseneth Upton
Margaret C., d. 3/11/1933 at 88/6/3; arteriosclerosis
Mary, d. 12/27/1909 at 73; cerebral hemorrhage; William O'Brien and Julia
    Canty
Mary Anne, d. 10/25/1935 at 74/2/15; cancer of liver
Mary F., d. 5/31/1936 at 53*
Natt. H., d. 9/14/1905 at 2/1/23; cholera infantum; PH
Robert M., d. 4/12/1899 at –; pneumonia; PH
Stephen M., d. 9/17/1930 at 80/6/26; paralysis agitans; John P. White and
    Frances Betts
Thatcher T., d. 12/9/1890 at 61/1/21; married; Thomas White (Alfred, ME)
    and Lydia Taylor (Exeter)
William, d. 12/25/1917 at 52; ac. gas poison; John White and Mary
    Morrison
William B., d. 7/28/1929 at 60 in Brooklyn, NY; cancer

WHITEHEAD,
Agnes I., d. 7/11/1893 at 30; phthisis pulmonalis; b. Woodstock, VT;
    (Scotland; Scotland)
Eliza, d. 6/9/1917 at 76/1/9 in Southbridge, MA; cerebral hemorrhage
Francis, d. 7/19/1911 at 81/6/23; intestial nephritis; Isabella Anderson
James F., d. 12/15/1932 at 77/8/21; uraemic coma
Jennie E., d. 9/20/1900 at 39; pul. tuberculosis; PH
Mary C., d. 10/20/1933 at 75 in Portsmouth; cerebral thrombosis
Mary L., d. 1/28/1900 at 32; sarcoma; PH
Maude C., d. 9/4/1924 at 61/4/28; uterine cancer; John L. Grant and Maria
    L. Chase

WHITEHOUSE,
child, d. 11/29/1916 at –; stillborn; Charles F. Whitehouse and Lulie A.
    Butler
child, d. 9/22/1924 at – in Portsmouth; stillborn
Alonzo F., d. 4/30/1917 at 74/9/12; mitral regurgitation; Jesse Whitehouse
    and Clara Pierce
Ann, d. 2/23/1931 at 94; acute bronchitis
Arthur P., d. 11/28/1894 at 21; Bright's disease; b. Dover; PH
Benjamin T., d. 4/21/1934 at 82/10/22; chronic myocarditis
Catherine, d. 11/25/1903 at 84/5/20 in Somerville, MA; marasmus; PH
Charles A., d. 1/30/1896 at 45; consumption; b. Dover; PH

Charles E., d. 3/12/1889 at 68 in Revere, MA
Charles F., d. 3/8/1925 at 62/4/15; multiple fracture; Enoch Whitehouse
 and Adeline Goodell
Charles S., d. 12/2/1919 at 68/10/4 in Manchester; cancer of bowels
Charles W., d. 10/14/1937 at 73/0/7; heart disease
Clarissa D., d. 10/15/1899 at 90; old age; PH
Daniel F., d. 1/19/1921 at 74/2/9 in Revere, MA; chronic endocarditis
Edward L., d. 11/4/1897 at 31; suicide with pistol; b. Dover; PH
Edwin, d. 2/6/1891 at 78/8/12; married; James Whitehouse (Great Falls)
 and Susanna Titcomb (Dover)
Eliza J., d. 2/7/1925 at 78/7/16; myocarditis
Elizabeth A., d. 11/27/1905 at 91/3/12; old age; PH
Ellen F., d. 9/18/1896 at –; diarrhea; b. Dover; PH
Ephraim H., d. 3/5/1922 at 90/0/5; senility; James S. Whitehouse and
 Abigail Bickford
Esther C., d. 6/14/1912 at 59/7/17; heart dilitation; Alfred Whitehouse and
 Lucy M. Twombly
Ethel S., d. 2/20/1915 at 20/7/20; puerp. eclamp. postpartum; William D.
 Kennard and Hattie J. Ellis
Fred K., d. 1/13/1897 at 5; oedema; b. Dover; PH
George, d. 6/25/1926 at 54; apoplexy; Alonzo Whitehouse and Ann
 McGaugh
George F., d. 5/5/1916 at 75/0/20; chronic endocarditis; Turner
 Whitehouse and Hannah Wallingford
Hannie F., d. 3/26/1903 at 39; entero-colitis; buried in Dover
Harriette, d. 1/30/1918 at 53/8/23; cirrhosis of liver; Elijah Bunker and
 Clara McCoy
Helen, d. 1/5/1914 at 58/0/12; mitral regurgitation; Charles A. Foster and
 Mary Libby
Henry Ford, d. 8/16/1916 at 4/1/17; acute entero colitis; C. J. Whitehouse
 and Martha Case
Hilda, d. 1/31/1919 at 0/11/11; burns - scalding; Charles Whitehouse and
 Martha Case
James, d. 8/28/1888 at 72; mason; married; b. Dover; James W.
 Whitehouse (Somersworth) and Susanna (Dover)
James E., d. 9/3/1921 at 67/8/19 in Joliet, IL; carcinoma of bladder
Jennie E., d. 11/12/1911 at 38/3/7; cancer of uterus; George W. Hutchins
 and Sarah E. Hill
Julia A., d. 5/31/1919 at 77/3/13; lobar pneumonia; James Y. Hayes and
 Alice A. Hayes
Lizzie M., d. 5/26/1889 at 28/4/1; housekeeper; married; b. Lebanon; -----
 Cummings (US)
Louise F., d. 9/14/1923 at 80/3/5; chronic nephritis; Philip F. Franklin and
 Maria Mowry
Loving L., d. 9/11/1915 at 29/4 in Dresden, ME; volvulus of intestines

Lucy M., d. 5/27/1897 at 84; apoplexy; b. Dover; PH
Lusebe, d. 5/20/1902 at 91/1/25; pneuminia; PH
Margaret M., d. 3/6/1911 at 83/9/28; cerebral hemorrhage; Ithiel Philbrick and Melinda M. Blake
Mark G., d. 3/27/1903 at 68/0/22; paralysis; buried in Somersworth
Martha A., d. 5/24/1935 at 58/6/9; acute endocarditis
Mary, d. 8/19/1887 at 72/4/17; housewife; married; b. MA; Joslyn Hilldran (CT) and Mary Samples (MA)
Mary E., d. 9/27/1910 at 61/11/23; cerebral hemorrhage; Alfred Whitehouse and Lucy M. Twombly
Mary F., d. 11/26/1892 at 53; heart disease; b. Dover; (Dover; NH)
Mary H., d. 9/7/1898 at 1; cholera infantum; b. Dover; PH
Nellie, d. 9/17/1896 at 3; cholera infantum; b. Dover; PH
Nellie, d. 11/17/1920 at 74; chronic bronchitis
Robert C., d. 4/23/1923 at 0/0/21 in Haverhill, MA; pyaemia
Robert M., d. 4/24/1905 at 81/7/3; cerebral hemorrhage; PH
Sarah J., d. 3/3/1925 at 71/10/2; diabetes mellitus; Miles R. Buzzell and Elmira Arlin
Tamsen, d. 9/17/1916 at 74/5/20 in Madbury; mitral regurgitation

WHITELEY,
Rachael W., d. 1/25/1914 at 79/9/25; amyotrophic lateral sclerosis; John Holland and Harriet Ruggles
Thomas F., d. 12/27/1896 at 63; heart disease; b. England; buried in Fall River, MA

WHITING,
Charles B., d. 2/6/1912 at 72/3/19; marasmus; John Whiting and Lorania Barnard
Charles H., d. 1/14/1916 at 58/7/26; apoplexy; Henry C. Whiting and Caroline B. Balcome
Minerva, d. 3/28/1936 at 88/1/6; arteriosclerosis

WHITMARSH,
James, d. 6/28/1890 at 53/6/33 (sic); married; ----- Whitmarsh

WHITMORE,
William H., d. 9/28/1915 at 80; hemorrhage from stomach

WHITNEY,
Annie E., d. 2/3/1928 at 75/8; angina pectoris; Abel Whitney and Sarah Cole
Edward H., d. 5/2/1906 at 62/1/25 in Cambridge, MA; disease of coronary arteries; PH
Fannie L., d. 4/11/1935 at 74/7/15 in Roxbury, MA; cerebral embolism

Jennie H., d. 11/29/1918 at 72/3/12 in Cambridge, MA; chr. mitral disease
Lillian B., d. 12/21/1935 at 56/5/17 in Brookline, MA; accidental
    traumatism of skull - epilepsy
Victoria H., d. 3/1/1912 at 56/5/10; pneumonia; James Gray and Joanna --

WHITTEMORE,
Arthur G., d. 10/13/1931 at 75/2/17; myocarditis
Caroline R., d. 5/25/1934 at 75/7/24 in Belmont, MA; carcinoma of breast

WHITTEN,
Fred, d. 9/18/1935 at 73/9/15; cerebral hemorrhage
Lydia K., d. 1/5/1918 at 94/10/14; senility; John Drew and Abigail Kent

WHITTIER,
Albert W., d. 10/16/1929 at 81/9/7; cerebral embolism; Albert T. Whittier
    and Martha Caldwell
Deborah, d. 12/28/1890 at 87/9/4; widow; Moses Burnham (Nottingham)
    and Zipporah Shaw (Newfield, ME)
Eliza J., d. 11/12/1922 at 87/0/3; arterio sclerosis; Josiah Whittier and
    Sally Whyte
Joseph F., d. 1/5/1907 at 59; la grippe; Moses Whittier
Osgood T., d. 1/7/1906 at 76/6/29; cancer of pancreas; PH
Rhoda J., d. 1/8/1892 at 89; heart disease; b. Boscawen; (Boscawen;
    Boscawen)
William, d. 7/3/1931 at 67/8/20 in Waltham, MA; intestinal cancer

WHORISKEY,
Richard, d. 2/22/1922 at 46/2/19 in Durham; acute nephritis

WHYTE,
Eleanor, d. 3/19/1897 at 76 in Haverhill, MA; phthisis, cardiac asthma; PH

WICKS,
Alice, d. 1/13/1897 at 4; scarlet fever; b. Dover; PH
Samuel N., d. 6/4/1937 at 85/10/17 in Somersworth; carcinoma of throat

WIGG,
Mary A., d. 11/30/1924 at 78/1/22; cancer of bowel; John Dorr and Mary
    Richmons

WIGGIN,
child, d. 4/17/1899 at --; inanition; PH
Abbie S., d. 8/5/1919 at 86/8/15; cancer of bowel; Aaron Hanson and
    Deborah Hall

Abbie S., d. 12/16/1919 at 82/4/6 in Lawrence, MA; acute nephritis
Almira B., d. 3/19/1919 at 84/10/26 in New Haven, CT; pneumonia
Carrie B., d. 1/17/1890 at 28/9/19; married; C. W. Tufts (MA) and Eliza A.
    Marshall (NH)
Catherine M., d. 12/25/1932 at 24; pulmonary tuberculosis
Charles E., d. 4/3/1904 at 1/5/27; catarrhal bronchitis; PH
Charles E., d. 12/30/1912 at 65/5/9; abdominal carcinoma; Woodbury W.
    Wiggin and Martha A. Achorn
Charles E., d. 5/17/1933 at 21; fracture of skull
Charles W., d. 5/8/1893 at 70; general paresis; b. NH; (NH; NH)
Daniel C., d. 10/24/1898 at 67; rheumatism; b. Tuftonboro; PH
Edward H., d. 3/26/1924 at 56/5/4 in Boston, MA; appendicitis
Ellen, d. 3/26/1890 at 34/9/15; married; William Simpson (England) and
    Betsey Firth (England)
Emma J., d. 3/19/1892 at 32; disease of stomach; b. Dover; (Wells, ME;
    New Durham)
Evelyn M., d. 9/6/1899 at –; cholera infantum; PH
George, d. 2/14/1904 at 88/10/25; pneumonia; buried in Barrington
George D., d. 8/20/1899 at 38; disease of heart; PH
Hannah I., d. 12/26/1893 at 88; old age and la grippe
Harry M., d. 10/2/1925 at 67/3/25; suppurative nephritis; Charles W.
    Wiggin and Mary A. Brooks
Harvey F., d. 10/27/1901 at 63 in Gardiner, ME; suicide by hanging; PH
Ida, d. 4/7/1923 at 67 in Philadelphia, PA; cardiac failure
James I., d. 4/12/1930 at 73/6/2; cong. heart failure; George Wiggin and
    Sophia Hayes
James M., d. 4/5/1935 at 92/2/24; chronic myocarditis
Jennie M., d. 10/12/1897 at 50; inanition; b. Dover; PH
John, d. 8/22/1890 at 74/2/16; widower; John Wiggin (Northwood) and
    Charlotte Batchelder (Northwood)
John E., d. 4/22/1910 at 54/11/22; suicide; George Wiggin and Sophia
    Hayes
Joseph A., d. 1/3/1895 at 61; phthisis pulmonalis; b. Tuftonboro; PH
Lottie A., d. 8/19/1904 at 0/7/1; marasmus; PH
Lucy J., d. 3/28/1918 at 54/3/1; acute pulmonary oedema; Levi A. Fuller
    and Elvira L. Bemis
Martha, d. 10/5/1900 at 58; pneumonia; PH
Martha Ann, d. 6/12/1926 at 88/6/7; arterio sclerosis; Ebenezer Faxon and
    Olive Thompson
Mary A., d. 9/17/1913 at 89/10; old age; Oliver Brooks and Susan Horn
Mary L., d. 8/30/1896 at 72; gastro-enteritis; b. New York; buried in No.
    Dana, MA
Orlando R., d. 10/16/1935 at 76/11/5; arteriosclerosis
Roy Everett, d. 1/13/1926 at 37/1/8; arthritis deformans; Orlando R.
    Wiggin and Mary L. Morrison

Ruth, d. 6/27/1901 at 79/10/28; pneumonia; PH
Susie E., d. 2/23/1932 at 73/9/13 in Farmington; influenza & pneumonia
Uriah, d. 10/5/1890 at 78/10/24; married; Nathan Wiggin (Stratham) and Mehitable Norris (Pembroke)
Warren E., d. 10/5/1918 at 26/4/12; lobar pneumonia; Orlando R. Wiggin and Mary L. Morrison
William, d. 2/19/1894 at 64; heart disease; b. Durham; buried in Newmarket
William E., d. 12/14/1932 at 74/8/29; arterio sclerosis
Woodbury, d. 4/1/1905 at 82/2/24; valvular heart disease; PH

WILBUR,
George Sayles, d. 3/27/1921 at 68/7/5; diabetes; John E. Wilbur and Eliza Young
Osman S., d. 4/20/1925 at 70; suicide by hanging; Warren W. Wilbur and Sarah Sanborn

WILDES,
child, d. 11/10/1917 at –; stillborn; Richard C. Wildes and Doris H. Blaisdell
Joseph H., d. 5/13/1926 at 41/9/13; pulmonary hemorrhage; Joseph Wildes and Della Brown
Minnie F., d. 4/26/1889 at 6/3/13; b. Saco, ME; B. D. Wildes (Kennebunkport) and Ella Fletcher (Biddeford, ME)

WILDS,
Roxanna M., d. 12/6/1889 at 6/4/24; b. Kennebunkport; George F. Wilds (Kennebunkport) and Emma F. Foss (Dover)

WILHELM,
Hannah J., d. 3/16/1915 at 38/3/14; chronic endocarditis; Francis Kerr and Hannah J. Short
Louis, d. 12/30/1926 at 59/6/27; epilepsy

WILKINS,
Mary E., d. 11/5/1904 at 40/5/7 in Hyde Park, MA; dropsy; PH
Nettie L., d. 1/7/1893 at –; bronchitis

WILKINSON,
Joseph, d. 12/19/1907 at 82/9; enlarged prostate; James Wilkinson and Mary Weighton
Mary, d. 2/9/1906 at 77/8/0; fall down stairs; PH
Rachel R., d. 7/10/1937 at 50/9/22; chr. myocarditis
Sarah G., d. 2/22/1931 at 72/2; arterio sclerosis

Thomas W., d. 6/25/1931 at 77/9/6; chronic myocarditis

WILLAND,
child, d. 3/10/1906 at –; stillborn; buried in Rollinsford
Albert W., d. 5/22/1921 at 59; arthritis deformans; George K. Willand and Ann E. Alloway
Amy A., d. 5/24/1888 at 0/2/21; b. Dover; Frank A. Willand (Dover) and Margaret Mansur (Concord)
Angie L., d. 3/4/1897 at 51; heart disease; b. Somersworth; PH
Ann E., d. 8/16/1912 at 79/11/5 in Bristol; hepatitis suppuration
Annie A., d. 7/13/1900 at 42; Bright's disease; PH
Calista A., d. 7/17/1915 at 66/1/18; hemorrhage from lungs; Samuel Chesley and Maria Scruton
Delia, d. 5/22/1907 at 38/1/10; organic heart disease; Edward McMahon and Mary Daley
Edward A., d. 7/8/1915 at 69/1/27; bullet wound; Nathaniel H. Willand and Anna F. Hubbard
Endicott E., d. 11/15/1914 at 62/11/10; chr. intestitial nephritis; Edward Willand and Betsey J. Brown
Frank A., d. 4/13/1908 at 52/7/28; osteosarcoma of sup. max.
George K., d. 3/5/1889 at 59; painter; b. Dover; Paul Willand (Dover) and Abigail Stiles (Dover)
George L., d. 2/2/1901 at 50/3/23; Bright's disease; PH
Grace M., d. 4/24/1930 at 56/9/21 in Boston, MA; malig. brain tumor; Nicholas ----- and Almira Clement
John, d. 5/4/1934 at 86/0/22 in Howard, RI; chronic myocarditis
Leroy G., d. 3/3/1927 at 0/0/8; hemorrhage; Walter G. Willand and Evelyn Smith
Lucy N., d. 9/10/1910 at 55/3/6; chronic endocarditis; Samuel Brown and Joanna -----
Mary A., d. 11/7/1928 at 75/7/18; intest. obstruction; James Wood and Mercy J. Tibbetts
S. M., d. 2/26/1890 at 5; Frank A. Willand (US) and M. A. Augusta Mansur (US)
William W., d. 11/19/1930 at 71/5/26; paralysis agitans; George K. Willand and Anne Alloway

WILLARD,
George W., d. 11/30/1933 at 79/6/25 in Concord; arteriosclerosis

WILLETT,
Susie, d. 10/5/1924 at 67; cancer of liver; Catherine -----

WILLEY,
child, d. 4/21/1934 at 0/0/1-4; prematurity

Cecelia, d. 7/24/1936 at 48/3/13 in S. Berwick, ME; sarcoma vertebrae
Charles F., d. 2/15/1919 at 74/3/16; epilepsy; Thomas J. Willey and
  Elizabeth Ricker
Charles L., d. 7/10/1909 at 57/10/9; nephritis; George W. Willey and Mary
  Berry
Charles W., d. 2/1/1915 at 56/3/3 in Lynn, MA; diabetes mellitus; Rachel
  Isabel
Charles W., d. 12/22/1921 at 67 in Concord; nephritis
Cyrus D., d. 1/17/1934 at 83/1/13; chronic endocarditis
Daniel H., d. 4/22/1919 at 73/9/15; accidental burns; Benjamin Willey and
  Maria Hutchins
Elijah, d. 10/24/1903 at 61/0/16; angina pectoris; PH
Elizabeth, d. 7/17/1888 at 78/11/16; widow; b. Dover; William Burnham
  (Dover) and Lydia Fogg (Dover)
Elizabeth E., d. 1/25/1930 at 70; cerebral embolism; James Ashton
Emily F., d. 11/27/1921 at 79/3/4; cerebral hemorrhage; John Bushy and
  Almira French
Emma, d. 3/6/1893 at 29; phthisis pulmonalis
Ethel B., d. 1/31/1909 at 20/2/6; lobar pneumonia; Wiliam A. Hines and
  Margaret Vail
Frank A., d. 12/19/1926 at 82/10/23; septicemia; Enoch Willey and Sarah
  Hodgdon
Frank B., d. 7/9/1913 at 39/2/9; pneumonia; Frank Willey and Annie
  Howard
George E., d. 12/14/1932 at 23/8/6 in Cambridge, MA; diabetes mellitus
George H., d. 3/18/1925 at 43/11 in Boston, MA; nephritis
George W., d. 6/20/1911 at 86/6/19; senility; John Willey and Nancy
  Whitehouse
Harold E., d. 5/10/1930 at 26/3/9; chronic nephritis; George H. Willey and
  Jeanette Ham
Harriet, d. 11/8/1923 at 85/3/28; chr. gastro enteritis; Lemuel Willey and
  Martha Stackpole
Jacob M., d. 12/1/1898 at 66; Bright's disease; b. No. Conway; buried in E.
  Sumner, ME
Josephine H., d. 11/20/1934 at 72/5/5; angina pectoris
Lillian M., d. 9/26/1914 at 0/6/13; cholera infantum; Frank B. Willey and
  May E. Bailey
Mary, d. 1/17/1898 at 38 in Durham; disease of brain; PH
Mary A., d. 2/16/1902 at 30/6/8; acute pulmonary tuberculosis; PH
Mary E., d. 1/12/1893 at 52; disease of liver; b. Dover; (Strafford; Dover)
Mattie A., d. 10/10/1921 at 55/3/24; cancer rectum; Charles R. Stevens
  and Laura A. Gove
Rachel M., d. 9/14/1890 at 92/10/9; widow; Jacob Mitchell (No. Yarmouth)
  and Phoebe Buxton

Robert, d. 2/18/1898 at 52; phthisis pulmonalis; b. New Durham; buried in Rochester
Sarah Elizabeth, d. 7/5/1924 at 69/8; erysipelas of face; Ira Willey and Mary A. Stevens
T. William, d. 2/7/1920 at 65/9/5; arterio sclerosis; George W. Willey and Mary I. Berry
Walter S., d. 8/2/1914 at 59 in Somersworth; fatty degeneration of heart; George W. Willey and Martha J. Clark

WILLIAMS,
son, d. 10/13/1890 at 0/0/12; W. C. Williams (Massena, NY) and Mary F. Ewer (Albion, ME)
Agnes, d. 10/17/1887 at 48/4/18; married; b. England; John McGowan (Ireland) and Catherine Connelly (Ireland)
Carrie L., d. 8/31/1933 at 81/5/9; cerebral hemorrhage
Chesley J., d. 11/29/1924 at 0/10/19; acute enteritis; H. H. Williams and Ethel G. Hoitt
Elizabeth, d. 11/16/1925 at 52; cancer of breast
Ellen, d. 2/12/1930 at 80; myocarditis
Frank B., d. 10/31/1920 at 70/2/9; prostatic carcinoma; Isaac B. Williams and Hannah Chamberlain
Frank G., d. 8/12/1911 at 68/11/13 in Melrose, MA; heart disease
George A., d. 1/14/1933 at 78/11/13; arteriosclerosis
Hannah C., d. 3/8/1917 at 92/6/10; old age; Eleazer D. Chamberlin and Hannah Hayes
Harriet A., d. 5/31/1900 at 60 in Melrose, MA; carcinoma; PH
Henry, d. 12/27/1895 at 53; alcoholism; b. England; PH
Ida M., d. 1/8/1902 at 18/2 in Somersworth; carbolic acid poisoning; PH
John, d. 7/6/1904 at 67/12/10 (sic); paresis; SM
John B., d. 8/27/1918 at 55/3/4 in Boston, MA; wound of neck
Lois A., d. 6/17/1922 at 48/3/21; surgical shock; Henry A. Spencer and Evelyn Abbott
Margaret, d. 11/14/1888 at 17/4/15; single; b. Portsmouth; Elias Williams (England) and Jane Holland (England)
Mary, d. 1/23/1937 at 24/8/8; pulmonary tuberculosis
Mary B., d. 3/4/1931 at 0/7/18; pneumonia
Richard L., d. 2/14/1930 at 96/5/11; arterio sclerosis; Douglas Williams and Sophronia Hokum
Sarah A., d. 9/17/1896 at 80 in Danvers, MA

WILLIAMSON,
John R., d. 6/10/1934 at 80/8/12; chronic myocarditis

WILLMAN,
Edouard, d. 6/27/1908 at 36/4/9; chronic alcoholism; Augustus Willman and Sara Trudel

WILLOUGHBY,
Abner L., d. 10/23/1926 at 64; chronic nephritis; Taylor Willoughby and Rosetta Sargent

WILLS,
Arabella E., d. 11/22/1907 at 60; heart disease
Bertha, d. 11/11/1893 at 17; pistol wound; b. Dover; (Phillips, ME; Dover)

WILSON,
child, d. 4/13/1931 at –; stillborn
Amos E., d. 3/1/1907 at 66/10/21; anaemia; Joseph Wilson and Ruth Thomas
Andrew J., d. 5/10/1917 at 66/4/3 in Durham; uraemia
Eleanor F., d. 11/8/1936 at 1 hr.; prematurity
Henry C., d. 6/18/1923 at 65; angina pectoris
John E., d. 7/5/1924 at 68/11/10 in Enfield; carcinoma of liver
John Gardner, d. 9/10/1916 at 82; apoplexy
Lafayette, d. 1/22/1892 at 40; influenza
Lina, d. 2/23/1930 at 78/4 in Haverhill; cerebral hemorrhage
Margaret, d. 3/7/1914 at 76; myocarditis
Marion H., d. 8/26/1905 at 37/3/9; acute nephritis; PH
Mary, d. 2/9/1893 at 40; died in Strafford Co. Asylum fire
Mary J., d. 1/10/1926 at 77/0/22 in Rochester; pneumonia
William F., d. 11/13/1936 at 50/9/3; heart disease

WINFREY,
Mildred, d. 9/4/1912 at 0/1/15; cholera infantum; Green Winfrey and Minnie Follett

WING,
Ann, d. 2/26/1894 at 73; pneumonia; b. England; PH
Frank, d. 8/11/1895 at 37; Brights disease; b. England; PH
Ida, d. 11/10/1897 at 36 in Boston, MA; dysentery; PH

WINGATE,
Anne E., d. 1/27/1908 at 80 in Bangor, ME; heart disease
Arvilla S., d. 3/22/1925 at 77/4/15; cerebral hemorrhage; John Clements and Abigail Drew
Daniel, d. 7/27/1917 at 91/4/19; carcinoma of prostate; Daniel Wingate and Sebina Tebbetts

Jeremiah Y., d. 4/12/1915 at 73/9/27; chronic nephritis; William P. Wingate and Lydia Chandler
John J., d. 5/3/1893 at 77; heart disease - congestion liver
Joseph W., d. 8/23/1905 at 78/1/8; uremic poisoning; PH
Mary E., d. 9/16/1908 at 73/7/22; heart disease; John Clough and Lucy Rust
Sarah E. H., d. 11/27/1893 at 49; pistol shot; b. Eliot, ME; (Eliot, ME; -----)
Sarah R., d. 9/19/1900 at 71; Bright's disease; PH
William I., d. 12/18/1906 at 40/5/13; typhoid fever; buried in Rochester

WINGREN,
John, d. 10/2/1912 at 51; struck by freight train; Magnus Wingren and Augusta Lindroth

WINKLEY,
Abbie V., d. 5/12/1909 at 64/5/24; phthisis; Samuel Winkley and Lydia Foye
Alta G., d. 9/17/1900 at 27; phthisis pulmonalis; PH
Arabelle, d. 9/13/1918 at 64 in Brattleboro, VT; nephritis; Aaron Pinkham and Vasta Roberts
George Edgar, d. 11/16/1891 at 0/0/9; Paul Edgar Wentworth (sic) (Strafford) and Ella F. Tyler (Dover)
Grace G., d. 2/24/1919 at 32/8/6 in Chicago, IL; influenza
Jeremiah S., d. 3/17/1906 at 89/4/9; old age; buried in Strafford
John F., d. 10/30/1908 at 62/8/25; tuberculosis; Joseph Winkley and Polly Cater
Joseph, d. 10/30/1890 at 76/4/24; widower; Francis Winkley (Kittery, ME) and Sarah Drew (Barnstead)
Sarah, d. 6/22/1891 at 72/5/26; widow; John McDuffee (Rochester) and Sally Hayes (Rochester)

WINN,
Eleanor I., d. 12/5/1917 at 0/0/17 in Eliot, ME; Winkel's disease

WINSLOW,
Deborah F., d. 4/26/1912 at 78/3/24; marasmus; George Saward and Eunice Dame
George H., d. 4/3/1921 at 45/1/13; chr. int'st'l nephritis; Jonathan H. Winslow and Deborah F. Seaward
Jonathan H., d. 2/10/1920 at 91/7; senility; Calcard Winslow
Mary, d. 5/4/1908 at 0/0/3; inanition

WISLOW,
Harold, d. 3/20/1899 at 3 in New York City; acute Bright's disease; PH

WISWALL,
Henry T., d. 10/2/1899 at 76 in Washington, DC; cerebral hemorrhage; PH

WITHAM,
Addie E., d. 4/18/1922 at 59; leuchaemia of spleen; George Knox and Hannah L. Cole
Charles, d. 9/16/1914 at 55/7/5; alcol. gastritis and cirrhosis; Samuel Witham and Hannah Welsh
Charles, d. 2/15/1916 at 38/10/4; Bright's disease; Charles Witham and Etta Miller
Charles C., d. 2/10/1923 at 72/8 in Farmington; cardiac dilatation
Cora, d. 2/20/1897 at 0; infantile tetanus; b. Dover; PH
Ellen D., d. 2/24/1919 at 68/7/7 in Farmington; myocarditis; Simon French and Hannah Varney
Eva M., d. 3/1/1907 at 0/2/24; acute gastroenteritis; Charles Witham, Jr. and Celina Larose
George, d. 7/2/1920 at 65/0/8; angina pectoris; Samuel Witham and Hannah Welch
Harry B., d. 12/16/1902 at 21/2/27; cirrhosis of liver; PH
Joseph, d. 8/17/1901 at 0/3/17; cholera infantum; PH
Josiah D., d. 8/2/1894 at 36; consumption; b. Milton; PH
Mary C., d. 11/1/1892 at 71; cardiac dropsy; b. Parsonsfield, ME; (ME; ME)
Mary E., d. 7/23/1905 at 0/2/1; unknown; PH
Nettie M., d. 2/16/1929 at 76/4/22; cerebral hemorrhage; Abel Baxter and Hannah Lougee

WITHRELL,
James, d. 10/30/1923 at 72/8/12 in Boston, MA; chronic nephritis

WIZA,
Grace B., d. 2/13/1937 at 41/10*; b. Portsmouth

WOJNAR,
Andrew M., d. 4/30/1929 at 27/7/4; acute pyelonephritis; Jacob Wojnar and Catherine Paradayaz

WOLCOTT,
Ada M., d. 8/14/1936 at 82/2/19; chr. myocarditis
Charles A., d. 3/3/1904 at 50/3/21; pneumonia; buried in Rochester, VT
Charles L., d. 6/4/1936 at 84/3/22; chr. intes. nephritis
Eliza, d. 9/27/1888 at 27/4/17; married; b. Springfield, VT; Ed. Walker (MA) and Rosetta (NH)

Mary Rachel, d. 6/24/1917 at 54/8/24; uterine fibrous cancer; Loren Wolcott and Mary B. W. -----

WOLFENDEN,
Hassa, d. 12/15/1911 at 65; asphyxia fumis
Richard L., d. 1/20/1924 at 49 in Concord; epilepsy
William H., d. 10/8/1914 at 38/11/26; apoplexy; Richard Wolfenden and Hassa -----

WONG,
Mary, d. 11/22/1923 at 0/4/25; cerebral meningitis; Wong Chong Quong and Lan She

WOOD,
child, d. 6/19/1918 at –; stillborn; Albert I. Wood and Celia F. Gunnison
Anna, d. 10/12/1918 at 1/6/8; pneumonia; Enoch Wood and Margaret Printy
Bertha, d. 7/1/1893 at –; inanition; b. Dover; (Brockton, MA; Brockton, MA)
Carrie G., d. 8/29/1887 at 40/3/7; shoe finisher; married; b. Newton, MA; Thomas (England) and Louisa (Wakefield)
Charles, d. 1/26/1909 at 68/11/23; Brights disease; John Wood and Mary Howarth
Charles A., d. 3/21/1893 at 33; consumption; b. Saco, ME; (Saco, ME; Alfred, ME)
Elizabeth, d. 10/3/1937 at 50/6/0; apoplexy
Ellen, d. 6/23/1912 at 73/11 in Lawrence, MA; malignant obstruction
James S., d. 9/3/1926 at 91/11/4; gen. arterio sclerosis
John S., d. 10/30/1912 at 55/0/20; septicemia; James S. Wood and Mercy J. Tibbetts
Josephine B., d. 4/29/1895 at 36; apoplexy; b. Milton; PH
Margaret, d. 11/3/1918 at 33; pulmonary tuberculosis; Michael Printy and Ann White
Margaret A., d. 8/20/1925 at 71/0/9 in Rochester; gastro enteritis; James Bentley and Annie Gurley
Mary A., d. 4/24/1907 at 86/9/22; pulmonary oedema; Elijah Hanson and Mary Ricker
Paula B., d. 8/18/1911 at 0/6/8; pneumonia; Alfred Wood and Alice McClintock
Samuel S., d. 6/7/1896 at 5 in Newmarket
Sarah Ann, d. 6/8/1891 at 51/2/20; married; Thomas Meehan (England) and Rebecca Hayfield (England)
William, d. 2/26/1891 at 53/3/9; married; James Wood (England) and Alice Rushton (England)
William, d. 12/21/1933 at 42/10/6; chronic endocarditis

WOODES [see Woods],
Ida J., d. 8/2/1911 at 49/11/3; accidentally burned; Wilson E. Tufts and Marcia E. Kelly
Jennie H., d. 8/11/1916 at 74; chronic nephritis; William Decatur and Caroline -----
John H. C., d. 3/20/1909 at 66/5; apoplexy; Samuel Woodes and Betsey Perkins
Nellie W., d. 4/6/1933 at 65/1/15; pulmonary embolism

WOODMAN,
child, d. 3/18/1908 at --; prematurity; H. C. Woodman and Helen M. Bragdon
Anne E., d. 1/7/1915 at 76/3/28; chronic nephritis; George W. Allen and Mary J. Brewster
Carrie, d. 7/1/1932 at 59/10/20 in Boston, MA; chronic cholecystitis
Charles W., d. 1/24/1888 at 78/1/17; lawyer; married; J. H. Woodman (Sanbornton) and Sarah Chase (Portsmouth)
Edwin L., d. 10/3/1888 at 35/6/3; cab. maker; single; b. Boston, MA; Jacob S. Woodman (Durham) and Lucy A. Stearns (Paris, ME)
Eliza A., d. 6/3/1925 at 74/0/5; abdominal carcinoma; Joseph Garland and Olive L. Buzzell
Elizabeth C., d. 10/26/1891 at 47/6 in Boston, MA
Frank F., d. 12/29/1930 at 69/3; chr. endocarditis; Thomas P. Woodman and Esther -----
George, d. 5/8/1915 at 60/1/17; carcinoma of rectum
Leroy W., d. 4/6/1935 at 81/7/22; chronic myocarditis
Maria C., d. 4/12/1905 at 81/1/2 in West Newton, MA; sclerosis of coronary arteries; PH
Marjorie, d. 5/5/1910 at 0/3/9; pneumonia; Monson B. Woodman and Flossy L. Hatch
Mary P., d. 11/10/1909 at 65/11/12; apoplexy; Charles W. Woodman and Charlotte Pearse
Sarah C., d. 4/6/1915 at 67/3/3 in Belmont, MA; cerebral hemorrhage; Charles Woodman and Sarah Coffin
Susan, d. 5/18/1932 at 82/6/3; angina pectoris
Theodore W., d. 10/11/1912 at 71/3/18; intestinal obstruction; Samuel Woodman and Lydia E. Rollins
William, d. 3/12/1894 at 43 in Templeton, MA; general paralysis; b. Dover; PH

WOODS [see Woodes],
child, d. 10/20/1924 at -; stillborn; Jacob Woods and Mary Levesque
Catherine, d. 10/12/1888 at 72; single; b. Ireland; Frank Woods (Ireland) and Margaret Hughes (Ireland)

Catherine, d. 11/2/1915 at 90; chronic int. nephritis; Michael Reynolds and
    Ellen McShane
Charles W., d. 4/14/1926 at 75/3/18; arterio sclerosis; Charles Woodes
    (sic)
Ed., d. 2/21/1901 at 28; acute Bright's, retention of urine; SM
Helen, d. 3/8/1907 at 28 in New York, NY; taxaemia
James, d. 1/12/1899 at 60; carcinoma of oesophagus; SM
Mary, d. 1/3/1906 at 68 in Concord; mitral regurgitation

WOODUS,
Albert F., d. 5/21/1923 at 19/4/28 in Schenectady, NY; lobar pneumonia
Amy M., d. 1/4/1890 at 16/11/29; George F. Woodus (Farmington) and
    Mary E. Chase (Albany)
Charles H., d. 11/21/1929 at 67/9/3; cancer of throat; John Woodus
Elizabeth W., d. 1/5/1897 at 71; apoplexy; b. Farmington; PH
George, d. 7/15/1895 at 61; heart disease and dropsy; b. Jackson; PH
George F., d. 1/24/1917 at 71/2/19; senility; Walker Woodus and Elizabeth
    Canney
Mary E., d. 5/28/1909 at 65/9/8; debility; Gilbert M. Chase and ----- Brown

WOODWORTH,
Frank G., d. 10/14/1930 at 76/10/9; chr. myocarditis; Walter Woodworth
    and Sarah Goodrich

WOOLEY,
David, d. 10/28/1910 at 75; chronic nephritis

WORCESTER,
child, d. 2/14/1916 at –; stillborn; Kirk Worcester and Harriet N. Perkins
Isabell, d. 8/23/1907 at 43/10/9; cancer; Davis Kenneson and Lucy Shedd
Loring H., d. 1/13/1932 at 74/10/20; cerebral hemorrhage
Richard L., d. 7/21/1935 at 19 in Natick, MA; compound fracture of skull

WORDEN,
Helen W., d. 11/9/1933 at 67 in Concord; arteriosclerosis

WORMELL,
Aubrey M., d. 9/18/1922 at 0/1/1; marasmus; William H. Wormell and
    Alice J. Brown
Frederick V., d. 6/10/1930 at 14/0/10; appendicitis; William H. Wormell
    and Alice J. Brown
Leo W., d. 9/1/1917 at 0/1/19; diarrhea and enteritis; William Wormell and
    Alice J. Brown

Phyllis E., d. 5/28/1930 at 0/2/7; catarrhal enteritis; William H. Wormell and Alice J. Brown
Roxanna, d. 1/8/1927 at 81/8 in Somersworth; lobar pneumonia

WORMWELL,
William E., d. 10/14/1909 at 0/1/1; malnutrition; William H. Wormwell and Alice J. Brown

WORSTER,
Asenath H., d. 5/9/1899 at 1; haematemesis; buried in Eliot, ME
John, d. 8/2/1911 at 87/7/1; arterio sclerosis; John Worster and Hannah Gowell
John R., d. 12/29/1927 at 72/3/9; chronic endocarditis; Jonathan Worster and Olivia Pike
Margaret B., d. 1/6/1935 at 68/10/17; carcinoma of liver
Mary M., d. 5/24/1912 at 84/4/23; sarcoma of heart and neck; John Woodbury and Betsey Quimby
Olin J., d. 1/28/1928 at 65/0/14; tumor of bladder; Moses Worster and Mary Wentworth

WORTHEN,
Ann M., d. 1/15/1918 at 78/9/9; angina pectoris; Isaac Page and Catherine Shapleigh
Charles O., d. 4/14/1910 at 76/1/11; cerebral hemorrhage; Joseph Worthen and Dorothy Morrill
Frank P., d. 5/26/1904 at 44/8/29; heart disease; PH
Henry A., d. 2/21/1912 at 72/7/27; heart disease; Joseph Worthen and Dorothy Morrill
Leola S., d. 3/31/1909 at 57; diabetic coma; Alphonso Severance

WRIGHT,
Albert T., d. 9/13/1900 at <1; indigestion; PH
John F., d. 11/22/1901 at 1/3/6; diphtheria; PH
Margaret H., d. 8/15/1912 at 0/5/1; meningitis, cerebral; Robert J. Wright
Margaret W., d. 7/19/1932 at 62/6/2; cerebral hemorrhage
Mary, d. 7/28/1905 at 52; carcinoma; PH
Mary, d. 12/24/1929 at 71/5/21; cholecystitis; Robert Greenaway and Mary Toten
Robert E., d. 4/11/1897 at 2; diphtheria; b. Dover; PH
Robert J., d. 4/7/1934 at 72/11/20; chronic myocarditis

WYATT,
Hannah E., d. 11/22/1914 at 71/11/20; acute Brights; Oliver Wyatt and Hannah Foss
Julia A., d. 6/10/1903 at – in Boston, MA; heart disease; PH

Mary E., d. 12/21/1893 at 49; carbuncle; b. Dover; (York, ME; Portsmouth)
Oliver, d. 7/16/1891 at 79/0/1; widower; Benjamin Wyatt (Exeter) and
    Theodosia Young (Wells, ME)
Sarah F., d. 10/2/1928 at 85/11/9; cerebral hemorrhage; Oliver Wyatt and
    Hannah Foss

WYLIE,
Gilbert, d. 1/6/1915 at 83/4/6 in Lynn, MA; arterio sclerosis
Lucy N., d. 10/5/1911 at 79/8/27 in Old Orchard, ME; senile decay

WYNOTT,
Selina, d. 1/9/1925 at 79/10 in Waltham, MA; cerebral hemorrhage

YEATON,
Henry D., d. 3/17/1936 at 74/11/28; senility
J. William, d. 2/1/1901 at 46/9/12 in Rochester; acute gastritis; PH
John H., d. 10/28/1887 at 0/9/3; b. Dover; Henry D. Yeaton (Strafford) and
    Abby E. Hanson (Dover)
Lela Anna, d. 10/6/1918 at 35/9/21; acute lobar pneumonia; William A.
    Yeaton and Lettie Palmer
Lillian, d. 8/1/1914 at 50; cerebral hemorrhage; Ira Rand and ----- Ham
Mary, d. 10/6/1936 at 81*
William A., d. 11/8/1923 at 61/7/8 in New Durham; probably heart disease;
    Joseph Yeaton and Anna G. Green

YELL,
Albert, d. 9/23/1905 at 0/3/2 in Durham; cholera infantum; SM
Mary, d. 6/27/1907 at 24/6/8; pulmonary tuberculosis; John Ayotte and
    Marie Pivin

YERKES,
child, d. 12/7/1923 at –; premature birth; James Yerkes and Violet Libby

YORK,
child, d. 1/20/1901 at –; stillborn; buried in Rochester
child, d. 8/7/1903 at 0/5/11; tubercular meningitis; SM
child, d. 4/6/1907 at –; stillborn; William York and Catherine Rothwell
child, d. 2/12/1924 at –; stillborn; Bessie York
Albert A., d. 6/3/1909 at 80/6/13; cardiac dilation; Daniel York and
    Elizabeth Langley
Alliah T., d. 4/1/1901 at 50/8/13; dilitation of heart; PH
Anna, d. 8/13/1900 at 24; acute gastric catarrh; SM
Austin E., d. 1/24/1933 at 0/8/14; lobar pneumonia

Charles A., d. 12/30/1919 at 54/9; mitral disease; George T. York and Martha Young
Clarrisa, d. 6/9/1888 at 83/10 in Newmarket
Daniel P., d. 7/28/1912 at 77/10/27; chronic gastro enteritis
Edward D., d. 6/21/1926 at 48/9/21; cancer of rectum; Simeon D. York and Mary E. Keith
Edwin M., d. 2/27/1905 at 0/9/26; pneumonia; PH
Elijah S., d. 3/6/1899 at 62; diabetes; PH
Elizabeth, d. 10/25/1907 at 62; cancer of stomach; William York and M. Rogers
Ellen Deborah, d. 5/5/1937 at 85/8/0*
Ellen F., d. 2/7/1905 at 53/7/29; uterine cancer; PH
Ellen T., d. 6/13/1913 at 43/9/16; acute gastro enteritis; ----- Heffron and Mary Mitchell
Emma F., d. 1/25/1905 at 48/6/20; heart failure; PH
Emma Hannah, d. 1/15/1912 at 0/2/18; marasmus; Herbert W. York and Hannah E. Hanscom
Evelyn M., d. 1/25/1927 at 95/7/29; arterio sclerosis; Benjamin Bennett and Lydia Morrison
Fred, d. 2/7/1931 at 57/8 in Wakefield, MA; chronic myocarditis
George, d. 3/22/1889 at 46/2/27; saloon keeper; married; b. Lowell, MA; William York (Ireland) and Mariah Drew (Ireland)
George H., d. 8/28/1899 at –; cholera infantum; PH
George T., d. 10/6/1903 at 70/0/9; cancer of stomach; PH
Hannah B., d. 3/28/1891 at 91; old age; PH
Hannah C., d. 2/13/1894 at 67; valvular disease of heart; b. New Durham; PH
Herbert, d. 4/13/1921 at 47/7/10; tuberculosis; George T. York and Martha W. Young
Ida May, d. 2/10/1925 at 40/10/19 in Hampton Falls; tuberculosis of lungs
James, d. 10/6/1889 at 19; clerk; b. Dover; George York (Lowell, MA) and Mary Thompson (US)
James G., d. 3/22/1899 at 58; pneumonia; PH
James H., d. 10/31/1928 at 57; angina pectoris; George T. York and Martha E. Young
James R., d. 3/10/1907 at 0/1/29; pneumonia; Herbert W. York and Hannah Hanscom
Jeremiah, d. 6/2/1888 at 85/9; watchman; married; b. Middleton; George York and Margaret Guppy
Jeremiah, d. 4/13/1903 at 76/3/9; pneumonia; PH
Joseph, d. 9/1/1921 at 0/8/23; septic diarrhea; William York and Katherine Rothwell
Lavina, d. 3/19/1897 at 91; senile gangrene; b. Rochester; buried in New Durham
Margaret, d. 8/12/1902 at 0/4/12; intestinal catarrh; SM

Martha E., d. 8/6/1912 at 65/6/11; old age; James T. Young and Mary A. Nute
Mary, d. 10/23/1889 at 36/5/8; housewife; widow; b. Lawrence, MA; James Thompson (Ireland) and Rosa O'Kallahan (Ireland)
Mary Elsie, d. 8/15/1915 at 73/7/15 in Sharon, MA; found dead
Mina M., d. 9/23/1926 at 48/9/29 in Concord; cancer of rectum; William Cole and Lucia Brown
Reuben J., d. 12/31/1930 at 83/1/20 in Lynn, MA; gen. arterio sclerosis
Rita, d. 9/21/1919 at 0/1/27; intestinal indigestion; William York and Catherine Rockwell
Rosanna, d. 4/19/1888 at 1/4/8; b. Dover; George York (Lowell, MA) and Mary Thompson (Lawrence, MA)
Simon D., d. 4/7/1927 at 85/2/16 in Tilton; arterio sclerosis
Thomas, d. 7/2/1913 at 0/9/19; acute intest. indigestion; William York and Catherine Rothwell

YOUNG,
daughter, d. 3/5/1887 at 0/0/3; b. Dover; Edwin Young (Great Falls) and Mary Hathaway (Fall River, MA)
child, d. 10/9/1902 at –; stillborn; buried in family lot
child, d. 9/5/1905 at 0/1/20; marasmus; buried in Strafford
Aaron, d. 12/23/1903 at 76/6/7 in Portsmouth; cerebral hemorrhage
Aaron C., d. 11/13/1901 at 46/2/6 in Brookfield, MA; apoplexy; PH
Addie, d. 8/10/1904 at 66/9/25; old age; PH
Alice A., d. 5/3/1917 at 76/10/12; acute ascending paralysis; Jonathan Young and Sophia M. Ricker
Alice R., d. 12/19/1904 at 46/8/18 in Portsmouth; tuberculosis of saorum; PH
Amanda S., d. 7/14/1921 at 80/10/16; Brights disease; William W. Wiggin and Sarah M. Hayes
Amy M., d. 9/20/1895 at 37; syphilis; b. Berwick, ME; buried in Berwick, ME
Andrew H., d. 12/10/1890 at 63/5/24; married; Aaron Young (Barrington) and Lydia Daniels (Barrington)
Angie M., d. 2/8/1931 at 63 in Augusta, ME; erysipelas
Anna, d. 1/30/1891 at 93/4; widow; Joseph Furbush (Kittery, ME) and Martha Lord (Lebanon, ME)
Annie F., d. 5/22/1906 at 57/9/22 in Haverhill, MA; pulmonary tuberculosis; PH
Annie W., d. 12/26/1935 at 82 in Boston, MA; pneumonia - myocarditis
Asa, d. 10/6/1912 at 75/2/20; angina pectoris; Eleazer Young and Keziah Rowe
Asa R., d. 4/20/1906 at 31/11/25; general tuberculosis; buried in Kittery, ME

Bessie E., d. 9/22/1894 at 48; cancer; b. Lebanon, ME; buried in Somersworth

Caroline, d. 2/22/1890 at 75; widow; Thomas Spurlin (Madbury) and Lydia Lamos (Dover)

Carrie M., d. 5/17/1890 at 28/5/23; married; Frank A. Noble (Kennebunk, ME) and Ann C. Anderson (Kennebunk, ME)

Charles H., d. 12/25/1902 at 0/0/21; marasmus; buried in Strafford

Charlotte M., d. 10/17/1900 at 59 in Strafford; heart disease; PH

Clara E., d. 12/23/1930 at 71/5/22; lobar pneumonia; Jonathan T. Young and Elizabeth L. Demeritt

Cora Etta, d. 2/29/1932 at 71/1/15; cerebral hemorrhage

Cynthia E., d. 10/11/1904 at 71/2/15 in Rochester; apoplexy; PH

E. Maud, d. 12/23/1905 at 21/2/12; natural causes; PH

Edward S., d. 10/9/1934 at 66/10/24; coronary thrombosis

Edwin A., d. 9/9/1922 at 59/3; cerebral hemorrhage; Simon D. Young and Joanna Ricker

Eleanor F., d. 9/10/1925 at 48/9/10; cancer of omentum; George F. Taylor and Emma Shaw

Elizabeth L., d. 2/27/1894 at 68; heart disease; b. NH; buried family lot

Ella M., d. 7/26/1928 at 67/11/14; chr. valv. heart dis.; Jonathan Hodgdon

Ella Margaret Bender, d. 5/2/1937 at 67/1*

Ellen A., d. 2/6/1914 at 76; cerebral hemorrhage; Charles Young and Mary Hanson

Ellen F., d. 9/19/1887 at 66/5/28; single; b. Dover; Jeremy Young (Madbury) and Anna Kimball

Frances E., d. 9/21/1929 at 65/8/3; arterio sclerosis; Charles Lord and Hannah Hubbard

Frank H., d. 1/27/1913 at 55/5/28; heart disease; Simon D. Young and Johanna Ricker

Frank H., d. 2/12/1914 at 64/0/20 in Madbury; renal dropsy

Frank Henry, d. 8/27/1932 at 58/8/17; chronic myocarditis

George A., d. 2/1/1887 at 29/2/4; farmer; single; b. Dover; Jonathan Young (Dover) and Elizabeth L. (Woodstock, VT)

George D., d. 5/23/1889 at 0/3/22 in Boston, MA

George H. A., d. 8/17/1910 at 0/3/23; marasmus; Harry C. Young and Rose M. Richards

George K., d. 4/13/1900 at 49; pneumonia; buried in family lot

George W., d. 12/3/1904 at 74/4/9 in Rochester; PH

George W., d. 7/4/1922 at 75/6/11; cerebral hemorrhage; James T. Young and Mary E. Nute

George W., d. 11/21/1935 at 92/1/17; broncho pneumonia

Haldiman P., d. 4/11/1934 at 70/4/28 in San Francisco, CA; coronary occlusion

Hannah A., d. 1/9/1936 at 79/9/6; chronic myocarditis

Harry N., d. 5/24/1920 at 50/11/24; mitral regurgitation; Jacob N. Young and Addie Murray
Henry E., d. 2/20/1913 at 60/2/16; locomotor ataxia; Simon D. Young and Johanna Ricker
Herman F., d. 6/17/1922 at 15/9/28; sarcoma of hip; Carl Young and Madeline Urles
Irving R., d. 12/15/1933 at 77/0/10; disease of prostate
Jacob D., d. 11/8/1901 at 77/10/10 in Madbury; neuralgia of heart; PH
Jacob D., d. 12/1/1927 at 75/10/17; cerebral hemorrhage; J. T. Young and Elizabeth L. Demeritt
Jacob N., d. 12/27/1912 at 73 in Portland, ME; septicemia
James T., d. 5/17/1914 at 58/6/15; heart disease; J. Thompson Young and Elizabeth L. Demeritt
Jane, d. 2/17/1913 at 92/1/3; general debility; Daniel Alley and Hannah Leavitt
Joanna, d. 6/21/1898 at 62; senile gangrene; b. Waterboro, ME; PH
John, d. 6/24/1905 at 80/4/15 in Milton; chronic nephritis; PH
John F., d. 1/29/1906 at 14; meningitis; SM
John L., d. 12/20/1914 at 49/8/16; heart disease; J. Thompson Young and Elizabeth L. Demeritt
Jonathan F., d. 6/24/1905 at 74/1/18 in York Beach, ME; cerebral hemorrhage; PH
Joseph J., d. 10/1/1889 at 0/1/3; b. Dover; Theodore L. Young (Dover) and Annie McLinn (NY)
Lilla M., d. 11/11/1900 at 33; pul. oedema; PH
Lucy Maria, d. 1/15/1890 at 53/9/5; married; ----- Witham (Stark, ME) and Lucy Maria Witham (Stark, ME)
Mabel G., d. 7/6/1902 at 42/0/6 in Merrimac, MA; tuberculosis kidney & bladder; PH
Margaret, d. 6/7/1892 at –; debility; b. Dover; (Ireland; Ireland)
Mary A., d. 4/18/1890 at 69/10; widow; Stephen A. Nute (Alton) and ----- (Alton)
Mary A., d. 7/17/1909 at 58/10; cancer of stomach
Mary Anna, d. 4/26/1916 at 76/10/12; senility; Joseph H. Joy and Jane Straw
Mary B., d. 9/7/1935 at 61/3 in S. Berwick, ME; arteriosclerosis
Mary D., d. 1/11/1905 at 80/8/29; valvular disease of heart; buried in So. Berwick, ME
Mary F., d. 3/8/1927 at 85; lobar pneumonia
Mary F., d. 4/10/1929 at 75/0/5; cancer of stomach; Oliver Stevens
Mary Frances, d. 3/8/1922 at 82/7/14 in Portsmouth; uraemia
Mary J., d. 8/17/1905 at 41/5/21; acute nephritis; PH
Mary Jane, d. 4/30/1930 at 88/2/22; chronic myocarditis; Rufus Bolo and Susan Young

Melvin J., d. 9/14/1891 at 32/5/10; single; Joseph Young (Ossipee) and Hannah Allen (Bartlett)
Moses C., d. 2/9/1890 at 80/10; widower; Joseph Young and Elizabeth
Nellie N., d. 2/1/1920 at –; umbilical hernia; Horace Foss and Betsey Berry
Newell H., d. 1/9/1933 at –; broncho pneumonia
Orlando, d. 8/27/1895 at 69; heart disease; b. Madbury; PH
Richard B., d. 4/12/1927 at 57/10/26 in New York City; carditis
Robert A., d. 3/10/1931 at 76/11/16; bowel stoppage
Rose Tuttle, d. 1/23/1891 at 82/11/23; widow; Elijah Pinkham (Dover) and Eunice Tuttle (Dover)
Roxana, d. 6/18/1929 at 82/7/14; fracture of femur; John Young and Rosa T. Pinkham
Sara C., d. 9/14/1918 at 87/7/23 in Madbury; carcinoma abdomen
Sarah E., d. 2/12/1913 at 80/6/13 in Rochester; cancer of stomach
Sarah M., d. 2/9/1892 at 60; cancer
Simon H., d. 11/28/1887 at 5; b. Dover; Edwin A. Young (Great Falls) and Mary J. Hathaway (Fall River, MA)
Simon P., d. 2/24/1929 at 70/10/2; cancer of stomach; Moses C. Young and Sarah W. Gallison
Susan E., d. 11/15/1915 at 83/2/18; cerebral hemorrhage; Tichenor Miles
Telesfore, d. 1/16/1908 at 62/5/19; cancer of ear
Theodore L., d. 5/14/1912 at 60; shock; Moses Young and Mary Varney
Thomas F., d. 8/7/1900 at 64; brain disease; PH
Tristram A., d. 1/18/1912 at 63/0/11; organic disease of heart; J. Thompson Young and Elizabeth L. Demeritt
Walter H., d. 11/20/1926 at 67/1/13 in Haverhill, MA; heart disease
William E., d. 1/11/1924 at 74/2/12; carcinoma of rectum; Hiram Young and Ann Howard

ZABERICK,
Antoine, d. 2/17/1932 at 58/2 in Somersworth; cerebral hemorrhage

ZABRICK,
Mary, d. 4/25/1931 at 20/8/13 in Baltimore, MD; cellulitis of neck

ZACKAROPOULOS,
Antonio, d. 2/22/1919 at 0/7/1; influenza; James Zackaropoulos and Sosit Fotino

ZERBINOPOULOS,
Canst't'e, d. 12/30/1927 at 62/8/6 in Concord; Peter Zerbinopoulos and Katherine Zanga

ZIS,
John, d. 1/11/1907 at 19; pneumonia; Nicholas Zis and Helen Arcope

ZULPA,
Charles, d. 1/7/1932 at 60; lobar pneumonia

UNKNOWN OR NO SURNAME GIVEN,
child, d. 9/30/1887 at –; b. Dover; Timothy E. (Ireland) and Sarah E. Sterling (Dover)
"an unknown tramp", d. 11/3/1890 at 40
child, d. 1/5/1892 at –; stillborn; b. Dover; (Canada; Canada)
child, d. 2/21/1892 at –; anaemia; b. Dover; (Ireland; England)
child, d. 5/4/1892 at –; unknown; b. Dover; (Dover; ME)
child, d. 6/14/1892 at –; stillborn; b. Dover; (So. Union, ME; So. Hope) (possibly Maxcy)
child, d. 8/11/1892 at –; premature birth; b. Dover; (Belfast, ME; Fitchburg, MA)
child, d. 8/29/1892 at –; premature birth; b. Dover; (Dover; Dover)
child, d. 7/27/1893 at –; b. Dover; (Ireland; Ireland)
child, d. 12/2/1893 at –; stillborn; b. Dover; (Canada; Canada)
child, d. 6/19/1896 at – in Nashua; stillborn; b. Nashua
child, d. 1/29/1898 at 0 in Malden, MA; exhaustion; PH
child, d. 8/11/1898 at – in Portsmouth; stillborn; SM
"unknown child", d. 7/–/1905 at –; unknown
"unknown man", d. 4/–/1909 at 45; drowning
"infant - unknown", d. 4/27/1911 at –; strangulation
"unknown male", d. 6/10/1914 at – in Rollinsford; probably neglect
person, d. 8/–/1915 at – in Cocheco River; probably drowning
"unknown male", d. 6/30/1916 at –; accidental drowning
"unknown", d. 5/27/1923 at –; probably hemorrhage, etc.
"unknown man", d. 10/–/1923 at –; fracture of skull
"unknown", d. 8/–/1928 at –; unknown
"unknown", d. 4/–/1930 at –; "found dead"
Sarah D., d. 2/2/1898 at 57; capillary bronchitis; SM

Other Heritage Books by Richard P. Roberts:

Alton, New Hampshire Vital Records, 1890-1997

Barnstead, New Hampshire Vital Records, 1887-2000

Barrington, New Hampshire Vital Records

Dover, New Hampshire Death Records, 1887-1937

Gilmanton, New Hampshire Vital Records, 1887-2001

Marriage Records of Dover, New Hampshire, 1835-1909

Marriage Records of Dover, New Hampshire, 1910-1937

Milton, New Hampshire Vital Records, 1888-1999

Moultonborough, New Hampshire Vital Records

New Castle, New Hampshire Vital Records, 1891-1997

New Hampshire Name Changes, 1768-1923

New Hampshire Name Changes, 1923-1947

Ossipee, New Hampshire Vital Records, 1887-2001

Rochester, New Hampshire Death Records, 1887-1951

Vital Records of Durham, New Hampshire, 1887-2002

Vital Records of Effingham and Freedom, New Hampshire, 1888-2001

Vital Records of Farmington, New Hampshire, 1887-1938

Vital Records of Lyme and Dorchester, New Hampshire, 1887-2004

Vital Records of New Durham and Middleton, New Hampshire, 1887-1998

Vital Records of North Berwick, Maine, 1892-2002

Vital Records of Orford and Piermont, New Hampshire, 1887-2004

Vital Records of Tamworth and Albany, New Hampshire, 1887-2003

Vital Records of Tuftonboro and Brookfield, New Hampshire, 1888-2005

Vital Records of Wakefield, New Hampshire, 1887-1998

Vital Records of Warren, New Hampshire, 1887-2005

Wolfeboro, New Hampshire Vital Records, 1887-1999

www.ingramcontent.com/pod-product-compliance
Lightning Source LLC
Chambersburg PA
CBHW070904300426
44113CB00008B/930